FOURTH EDITION

ANTHOLOGY OF WORLD SCRIPTURES

Robert E. Van Voorst

Western Theological Seminary

WADSWORTH

THOMSON LEARNING ™

Australia • Canada • Mexico • Singapore • Spain • United Kingdom • United States

WADSWORTH

THOMSON LEARNING ™

Publisher: Holly J. Allen
Religion Editor: Steve Wainwright
Assistant Editor: Kara Kindstrom
Editorial Assistant: Anna Lustig
Technology Project Manager: Susan DeVanna
Marketing Manager: Worth Hawes
Marketing Assistant: Justine Ferguson
Project Manager, Editorial Production: Mary Noel
Print/Media Buyer: Rebecca Cross
Permissions Editor: Robert Kauser
Production Service: Matrix Productions, Inc.
Text Designer: Cynthia Bassett

Photo Researcher: Terri Wright
Copy Editor: Vicki Nelson
Cover Designer: Gopa and Ted2
Cover Image: KUPKA, Frantisek. *The First Step.* (1910–13?; dated on painting 1909) Oil on canvas, 32¾ × 51″ (83.2 × 129.6 cm). The Museum of Modern Art, New York. Hillman Periodicals Fund. Photograph © 2000 The Museum of Modern Art, New York.
Cover Printer: Webcom, Ltd.
Compositor: TBH Typecast, Inc.
Printer: Webcom, Ltd.

Printed in Canada
2 3 4 5 6 7 06 05 04 03 02

For more information about our products,
contact us at:
Thomson Learning
Academic Resource Center
1-800-423-0563
For permission to use material from this text,
contact us by:
Phone: 1-800-730-2214
Fax: 1-800-730-2215
Web: http://www.thomsonrights.com

Wadsworth/Thomson Learning
10 Davis Drive
Belmont, CA 94002-3098
USA

Asia
Thomson Learning
60 Albert Street, #15-01
Albert Complex
Singapore 189969

Australia
Nelson Thomson Learning
102 Dodds Street
South Melbourne, Victoria 3205
Australia

Canada
Nelson Thomson Learning
1120 Birchmount Road
Toronto, Ontario M1K 5G4
Canada

Europe/Middle East/Africa
Thomson Learning
Berkshire House
168-173 High Holborn
London WC1V 7AA
United Kingdom

Library of Congress Cataloging-in-Publication Data

Van Voorst, Robert E.
    Anthology of world scriptures / Robert E. Van Voorst.—4th ed.
      p. cm.
    Includes bibliographical references and index.
    ISBN 0-534-60201-0
    1. Sacred books.   I. Title.
BL70.V36 2002
291.8′2—dc21
                                  2001055916

THIS BOOK PRINTED ON ACID-FREE RECYCLED PAPER

To James and Genevieve Bos
My parents-in-law
In gratitude for your friendship

Contents

CHAPTER FOUR

Jainism   109

CHAPTER SEVEN

Taoism   163

CHAPTER ELEVEN

Christianity   245

CHAPTER TWELVE

Islam   285

Preface

The major living religions of the world have all expressed their teachings and practices in writing. Over the course of time, some of these writings gained unique standing in their traditions and became scriptures. As scriptures, they continue to influence the course of their religions. To read the scriptures of the world, therefore, is to encounter world religions in a direct and meaningful way.

This book is designed to facilitate this encounter for the general reader and especially for the student of religion. Its pages contain the most notable and instructive scriptures of Hinduism, Buddhism, Jainism, Sikhism, Confucianism, Taoism, Shinto, Zoroastrianism, Judaism, Christianity, and Islam. This anthology not only presents scripture readings, but also sets them in the context of their application in the traditions themselves, taking into account recent scholarship on the role of scriptures in religion. Moreover, it does this in one volume and in one format. Designed to be used as a secondary textbook, the anthology has an organization that is easily adaptable to a range of primary textbooks and most of the current methods of teaching comparative religion. New to this edition is a chapter treating the scriptures of five leading "new religious movements": Baha'i, Christian Science, the Church of Jesus Christ of Latter-day Saints, the Unification Church, and Scientology.

Anthology of World Scriptures is organized as follows: The first chapter examines the general phenomenon of scripture in the world's religions—its nature, use, and place in modern scholarship. Chapter 1 also introduces the reader to the art of reading scripture with practical suggestions, a pronunciation guide for foreign words, and other aids.

Chapters 2–12 present the scripture of a single religion and are organized as follows: Three or four vignettes about scripture and its usage draw the reader's interest and imagination. Then an introduction sets the context by explaining the overall structure, origin, development, and use of the scripture in its religion. (If the name of the scripture poses a problem for students, this is given a brief treatment before overall structure.) The first grouping of scripture passages concerns the history of the religion, especially the founder (if any) and early history of the tradition. The second grouping covers main doctrinal teachings, including divine or ultimate reality, creation and the environment, human nature, and human fulfillment. The third grouping deals with ethical systems, both personal and social; topics such as war and peace, justice, and the role of women will be anthologized as fully as possible here. The fourth grouping focuses on organization, both the ways that religion orders itself and seeks to order its wider culture. The fifth grouping includes worship, devotion, ritual, and meditation. Chapter 13 has a different organization, one that keeps the scriptures of each new religious movement together. Each chapter has full pedagogical aids, including introductions to each passage, tables listing scripture canons, full annotations to explain difficult items in the readings (placed at the bottom of the page for easy access), questions for study and discussion, a glossary with pronunciations, and suggestions for further reading.

The translations used here have been selected for their accuracy and readability. I have been fortunate to receive permission to reprint many of the finest and most current English translations of many world scriptures. Where it has not been possible to get permission, or where recent English translations are incomplete or too technical for undergraduate students, I have relied on a few older translations that have proven their worth over time and are now in the public domain. I have edited these to update vocabulary, spelling, and occasionally syntax, removing the peculiarities of the Victorian English in which these translations were done. But I have endeavored to let the "voice" of both text and translator come through.

The scriptures presented here come from the religions commonly understood to be the major living world religions, both old and new. By "world religion," scholars generally mean those religions that have had an impact on the world's leading cultures, not necessarily religions that are spread throughout the world. But why not include here the writings of other important contemporary religions, such as those of Africa or North America, or the ancient religions of Egypt, Greece, or Central America? The main reason is that *these religions do not have scriptures as this term is defined today.* Ancient religions had comparatively little writing, and this writing was not used in religious practice in a way that qualifies it as scriptural. The tribal/primal religions of Africa and North America rely on oral traditions, which, though powerful and important, are not written, scriptural traditions. Those that are written down have been compiled and used as texts mainly by anthropologists, not by the believers themselves. That these religions are nonscriptural does not, of course, imply that they are any the less religious. It does mean that they cannot be included here.

This fourth edition incorporates, in addition to dozens of smaller changes, the following significant revisions:

❖ Chapter 1 incorporates the latest discussion of comparative world scripture, especially on women's reception and use of scripture.

❖ Many vignettes that open each chapter have been revised and updated to keep them fully contemporary.

❖ A new chapter has been added to treat the scriptures of five leading new religious movements: Baha'i, the Church of Jesus Christ of Latter-day Saints, Christian Science, the Unification Church, and the Church of Scientology.

❖ The Internet site available to assist students in their encounter with world scriptures is augmented with links to the scriptures of the new religious movements.

❖ Three new readings have been added on *jihad* ("struggle/holy war") in Islamic tradition.

❖ All scholarship is updated throughout.

I am very grateful for the strong reception this book has received. I trust that this edition will continue to stimulate its readers to explore the world of religion more deeply.

ACKNOWLEDGMENTS

I would like to thank here the many people who have helped me in the writing of this book. The library staff of Lycoming College, where I formerly taught, and of Western Theological Seminary helped me in the large task of gathering materials for this book. Some research for the fourth edition was carried out at the Bodleian Library of the University of Oxford, England, while I was on sabbatical leave there. My capable secretaries at Western Seminary, Rayetta Perez and Beth Smith, and student assistant Arika Theule-Van Dam gave excellent assistance in completing this edition. Not least in importance, my students in Lycoming College and Western Seminary used earlier drafts and editions of this book and contributed many helpful suggestions that found their way into it.

The editorial and production staff at Wadsworth have been fine partners in developing and producing the fourth edition of this book. While they all have done excellent work for me, I especially want to thank religion editor Peter Adams (now an editor in economics) and assistant editor Kara Kindstrom, Merrill Peterson of Matrix Productions, and my copyeditor Vicki Nelson.

Scholars at other institutions offered detailed, insightful critiques at many points along the way. For reviewing this book in of the first three editions, I thank Vivodh Z. J. Anand, Montclair State University; Paul Bernadicou, University of San Francisco; James Cook, Oakland Community College, Orchard Ridge; Marianne Ferguson, Buffalo State College; Etta Hesselink, University of Michigan; Roger Keller, Brigham Young University; William K. Mahony, Davidson College; Michael McKale, Saint Francis College; Vivian-Lee Nyitray, University of California, Riverside; Christopher Queen, Harvard University; Stephen J. Reno, Southern Oregon State College; Philip Riley, Santa Clara University; Roger L. Schmidt, San Bernardino Valley College; Philip Schmitz, Eastern Michigan University; Daniel Sheridan, Loyola University of New Orleans; Robert Smith, Trenton State College; Donald Swearer, Swarthmore College; James Whitehill, Stephens College; Boyd Wilson, Hope College; and Glenn Yocum, Whittier College. For the fourth edition, I thank the professors, all of whom adopted the third edition of this book, who responded to the publisher's survey and offered their suggestions for this revision. I must thank them as a group, because their names are too numerous to list here. However, I should thank Roger Keller of Brigham Young University for reviewing Chapter 13 in such a helpful way.

Though all these people made this a better book, any errors that remain are mine alone. I would be most grateful if those of you who use this book and my website on scripture would send me your comments and suggestions for improving them. You can reach me by my postal address (Western Theological Seminary, 101 East 13th Street, Holland, MI 49423-3622) or my e-mail address (bob.vanvoorst@westernsem.org).

Finally, this fourth edition gives me the happy opportunity to renew my deep expression of gratitude especially to my wife, Mary, and also to our children, Richard and Nicholas, for all their love and support. "Her sons rise up and call her blessed; her husband also, and he praises her: 'Many women have done excellently, but you surpass them all'" (*Proverbs* 31:28–29).

CHAPTER ONE

Scripture among the World's Religions

- ❖ In Great Britain, Salman Rushdie tentatively comes out of hiding from would-be killers. Rushdie's controversial novel, *The Satanic Verses,* allegedly committed blasphemy against the *Quran*. In 1989, Iranian officials put a $2 million price on his head. In 1997, the reward was increased by a half million dollars, which Rushdie mocked as "just a cost-of-living increase." In 1998, the official death threat was lifted, and Rushdie has since gone about openly for the first time in almost ten years, but he is still in some danger from those who would do him harm.

- ❖ In New York City, the government of Taiwan takes out a large, expensive advertisement on the op-ed page of the *New York Times*. It argues that Taiwan is an orderly, virtuous, and industrious society because it is founded on the principles of Confucius' *Analects* and *Great Learning,* the key texts of Confucian scripture. Therefore, the advertisement says, Taiwan is an excellent partner in international trade.

- ❖ Near the federal prison in Terre Haute, Indiana, demonstrators gather at the execution of Timothy McVeigh for the bombing of the federal office building in Oklahoma City in which 169 people died. Some protest his execution by carrying signs with words from the *Bible:* "You shall not kill." Some counterprotesters also carry signs with biblical words: "You shall not allow a murderer to live."

- ❖ In an Indian city, Hindu priests and Sanskrit-language scholars call a news conference to criticize a song, "Shanti," in an album by the American pop singer Madonna. Unlike most religious critiques of rock music, which focus on a supposed lack of moral values, the Hindus' criticisms focus on Madonna's pronunciation of that ancient divine name. Reflecting Hindu spoken use of scripture, the priests and scholars state that the spiritual power of this name is not effective unless it is pronounced correctly.

The influence of scripture is felt throughout the world in ways both extraordinary and commonplace. Not all contemporary examples of scripture usage are as dramatic or controversial as these sketches suggest. They do indicate, though, that the scriptures of the world's religions have a continuing profound impact on life and culture. This anthology introduces the reader to these scriptures and encourages a deep encounter with them in all their variety. Scriptures of the world are so vast in number

—Max Müller's *Sacred Books of the East*[1] series had fifty volumes when it was finished in 1910, and its coverage of Asian scripture was still far from complete—that some sort of sampling is necessary for all but the most expert specialist. An anthology is by its very nature a selection; it includes some key passages, but unhappily many more must be left out. The best that can be hoped for is that the anthology selects excerpts from each tradition that faithfully reflect the history and continuing life of the tradition. These selections offer the reader the possibility of a meaningful insight into the religions of the world.

This introductory chapter is organized into several sections. "A Brief History of Scripture Scholarship" outlines the main periods of the study of world scriptures. "The Nature and Definition of Scripture" discusses the term *scripture* as a comprehensive generic label suitable to religious scholarship, followed by a consideration of the varied functions of scripture in "The Uses of Scripture." "Advantages and Disadvantages" deals with the important question of the strengths and weaknesses of this approach. "World Scriptures and Modern Scholarship" discusses the impact of Western academic study on how we understand world scriptures. "Scriptures on the World Wide Web" examines how students can best use the growing number of world scriptures on the Internet. "The Plan of This Book" explains how the scripture selections are organized, and "A Guide to Pronunciation" provides some general rules for saying aloud the proper nouns in the readings. Finally, "Suggestions on How to Read Scriptures" gives helpful hints on the process of reading scripture for the fullest possible comprehension.

A BRIEF HISTORY OF SCRIPTURE SCHOLARSHIP

The scholarly study of world scripture[2] in the last hundred years has passed through three distinct stages that have strongly influenced how we read scriptures.[3] Near the middle of the nineteenth century, European scholars began a vast enterprise of making critically reliable translations of the world's scriptures, with a special focus on the little-translated sacred literature of Asia. Their concern was to translate individual texts, an important and necessary first step, not to examine the general religious phenomenon of scripture. They treated scripture as a mine out of which to dig the history and doctrine of religions, with little regard for the ways scripture functioned in

---

[1]F. Max Müller, gen. ed., *The Sacred Books of the East,* 50 vols. (Oxford: Oxford University Press, 1879–1910; reprinted in 1969 in India, with some volumes still in print).

[2]By "world scriptures" I mean scriptures of the major religions of the world, not necessarily scriptures that are spread *throughout* the world.

[3]For an excellent comprehensive discussion of the history of the academic study of world religions, with some detailed comments on scripture study, see E. Sharpe, *Comparative Religion: A History,* 2d ed. (LaSalle, IL: Open Court Press, 1987). Perhaps the best succinct presentation of this topic is by S. Cain, "History of the Study of Religion," in M. Eliade, ed., *Encyclopedia of Religion* (New York: Macmillan, 1987), vol. 14, pp. 64–83.

religious communities. Müller's *Sacred Books of the East* is the most prominent result of this movement.[4]

The academic movement customarily known by its German name, *Religionswissenschaft,* dominated the second stage in the study of scriptures. Usually translated as "history of religion," this name means more accurately "science of religion." This school, which continues to exert a strong influence today, analyzes the historical development of each religion. Perhaps in reaction to the earlier methodological reliance on world scriptures, scholars like Joachim Wach and Mircea Eliade relied on the study of other, nontextual elements of religion, such as ritual, myth, symbols, and the like. Scripture was largely neglected at this stage. Such a magisterial treatment of comparative religion as Gerardus van der Leeuw's *Religion in Essence and Manifestation*[5] contains only a spare discussion of scripture as a universal religious phenomenon. Moreover, as social-scientific methods increasingly entered the field of religious scholarship, researchers turned away from literary sources from the past in favor of the study of present-day living communities of faith.[6]

Although this second stage is still very influential, a third stage is emerging in which religious studies are rediscovering the value of scripture. The overreliance on scripture characteristic of the first stage and the neglect of scripture in the second stage are being balanced as scholars increasingly view scripture as an important phenomenon among the religions of the world. One new element here is that scripture is correctly seen as one religious phenomenon among many and therefore not to be isolated from the others. Another new element is an emphasis on the actual ways in which scripture is viewed and used in world religions. To understand scripture, according to this view, we must know not just the text, but also how it comes alive in the total life of the religion.

Recent research in comparative religion gives evidence of this emerging third stage. Large-scale studies of comparative religion such as Geo Widengren's *Religionsphänomenologie* ("Phenomenology of Religion")[7] and Friedrich Heiler's *Erscheinungsformen und Wesen der Religion* ("Manifestations and Essence of Religion")[8]

---

[4]A continuing manifestation of this first stage are the popular anthologies of world scriptures that have been published almost continually for many years. To cite only a few examples, Robert Ballou's *The Bible of the World* (New York: Viking, 1939) and its abridgment in *World Bible* (Viking Portable Library; New York: Viking, 1944) have remained in print continually, although not revised. The Unification Church has published *World Scripture: A Comparative Anthology of Sacred Texts,* ed. Andrew Wilson (New York: Paragon House, 1991). And Philip Novak has edited *The World's Wisdom: Sacred Texts of the World's Religions* (San Francisco: HarperSanFrancisco, 1994). Popular anthologies, like the first scholarly stage of study, use world scriptures as a mine for enlightenment with little attention to how scripture functions in world religious communities.

[5]Gerardus van der Leeuw, *Religion in Essence and Manifestation* (London: Allen & Unwin, 1938); German original, 1933. One short chapter, 64, deals almost exclusively with Western scripture.

[6]For example, the widely used *Reader in Comparative Religion: An Anthropological Approach,* ed. W. A. Lessa and E. Z. Vogt, 4th ed. (New York: Harper & Row, 1979), has excellent readings in all the basic topics in the cultural-anthropological study of religion—symbol, myth, ritual, shamanism, magic—but not one essay on scripture and its uses.

[7]Geo Widengren, *Religionsphänomenologie* (Berlin: de Gruyter, 1969).

[8]Friedrich Heiler, *Erscheinungsformen und Wesen der Religion,* 2d ed. (Stuttgart: Kohlhammer, 1979).

both deal extensively with the nature and use of scripture among the world's religions. Ninian Smart's recent *Sacred Texts of the World*[9] uses scripture to approach several different religious phenomena in each world religion. Five recent books deal with scripture and its role in religion: *The Holy Book in Comparative Perspective,* by Frederick Denny and Roderick Taylor[10]; *Sacred Word and Sacred Text,* by Harold Coward[11]; *Rethinking Scripture: Essays from a Comparative Perspective,* by Miriam Levering[12]; *Sacred Texts and Authority,* by Jacob Neusner[13]; and, most important, *What Is Scripture? A Comparative Approach,* by Wilfred Cantwell Smith.[14] As a result of this research, the comparative study of scripture is today one of the leading features in the study of world religions.

Smith, of Harvard University, and some of his former doctoral students have had a strong influence on current scripture study. They argue for scripture study centered on the actual reception and use of scriptures. The work of William Graham on the oral dimensions of scripture has been especially influential.[15] A measure of the strength of this stage is that it is now appearing in textbooks, where several works are notable: T. W. Hall, R. B. Pilgrim, and R. R. Cavanagh, *Religion: An Introduction*[16]; Kenneth Kramer, *World Scriptures: An Introduction to Comparative Religion*[17]; Roger Schmidt, *Exploring Religion*[18]; Jean Holm and John Bowker, *Sacred Writings*[19]; Richard Viladesau and Mark Massa, *World Religions: A Sourcebook for Students of Christian Theology*[20]; and most recently, Ian Markham, *A World Religions Reader.*[21] As a representative of this third stage of scripture study, the present work offers a wide range of scripture selections from the religions of the world, with introductions and annotations to set the readings in the context of their actual usage.

---

[9]Ninian Smart, *Sacred Texts of the World* (London: Macmillan, 1982).

[10]F. M. Denny and R. L. Taylor, eds., *The Holy Book in Comparative Perspective* (Charleston: University of South Carolina Press, 1985).

[11]Harold Coward, *Sacred Word and Sacred Text* (Maryknoll, NY: Orbis, 1988).

[12]Miriam Levering, ed., *Rethinking Scripture: Essays from a Comparative Perspective* (Albany: State University of New York Press, 1989); contains two programmatic essays by Wilfred Cantwell Smith, an essay on the oral character of world scriptures by William Graham, and chapter-length treatments by others of Buddhism, Hinduism, Jainism, and Judaism.

[13]Jacob Neusner, ed., *Sacred Texts and Authority* (Cleveland: Pilgrim, 1998).

[14]Wilfred Cantwell Smith, *What Is Scripture? A Comparative Approach* (Philadelphia: Augsburg Fortress, 1993).

[15]See especially William Graham's *Beyond the Written Word: Oral Aspects of Scripture in the History of Religion* (Cambridge: Cambridge University Press, 1983).

[16]T. W. Hall, R. B. Pilgrim, and R. R. Cavanagh, *Religion: An Introduction* (San Francisco: Harper & Row, 1985). This book contains a finely nuanced chapter on scripture as one of the varieties of religious expression on pp. 108–124.

[17]Kenneth Kramer, *World Scriptures: An Introduction to Comparative Religion* (New York: Paulist, 1986). Kramer approaches scripture by means of narrative.

[18]Roger Schmidt, *Exploring Religion*, 2d ed. (Belmont, CA: Wadsworth, 1988). Schmidt has a chapter-length treatment of world scripture.

[19]Jean Holm and John Bower, *Sacred Writings,* Themes in Religious Studies Series (London: Pinter, 1994).

[20]Richard Viladesau and Mark Massa, *World Religions: A Sourcebook for the Student of Christian Theology* (New York: Paulist, 1994). As its subtitle indicates, this book intended for those who study world religions from within a Christian perspective.

[21]Ian S. Markham, ed., *A World Religions Reader* (Oxford: Blackwell, 1996).

THE NATURE AND DEFINITION OF SCRIPTURE

At first glance, defining our term seems easy enough. Scripture is the holy writing, the sacred text of a religion. All religions seem to have scriptures, and all appear to use them in the same way. As a phenomenon among religions, scripture seems on the surface to be a constant. On closer examination, however, these simple notions vanish. Books of world religions that are traditionally regarded as scriptures vary in several important aspects. The content of this anthology will bear out this variety, but it would be well to sketch in some of it here.

The first variation among scriptures is in *literary form*. Scripture as a general category implies that all scriptures look alike in literary form and content. Persons who come from religious traditions with scriptures naturally tend to assume that the sacred texts of others look and function exactly like theirs. Scripture, however, has a literary variety as numerous as the religions and cultures from which it comes. Some scriptures, especially those of the three main Western religions (Judaism, Christianity, and to a lesser degree Islam), prominently feature historical **narratives,** the telling of an event in story form, in which God's self-disclosure comes in history. Scriptures from other religions, especially those Asian faiths that consider salvation a release from historical existence, have few narratives or none at all. Some scriptures have their vision of a moral life enshrined in law codes, some feature more loosely bound moral precepts, and still others do not seem concerned about ethics. Poetry is the leading literary form of some scriptures; others feature prose. Some scriptural books (the Hindu *Upanishads*) have metaphysical philosophy, others (the Confucian *Analects,* the wisdom literature of the *Bible*) moral philosophy, but many have no explicit philosophy at all. Some scriptures (the Hindu *Vedas*) contain directions and songs for sacrifice, whereas others (the *Analects*) have no prescriptions for rites and ceremonies. We also find myth, legend, prophecy, sermons, love poems, divination, and magic, among many other such **genres,** or types of literary forms, in the scriptures of the world.

Even this cursory overview of the world's sacred literature shows that scriptures do not entail a fixed literary form, because almost every type of form can be found in them. Therefore, we cannot open a book, browse though its contents, and pronounce it scriptural. Scripture is primarily a relational, not a literary, phenomenon. As William Graham has written, "The sacrality or holiness of a book is not an *a priori* attribute but one that is realized historically in the life of communities who respond to it as something sacred or holy."[22] Communities shape and receive scripture, and scripture shapes the life of faith. The relation between scripture and religion is reciprocal and dynamic.

The second variation among world scriptures has to do with their *number* within any one religion, which can range from one book to an entire library. Like the *Quran,* scriptures can be one unified book of moderate size under two covers. Like the Jewish and Christian scriptures, they can be many different short books collected into one scripture corpus, usually of a larger size. In Asian religions, they can be different books ranging in number from the many Hindu texts, to the dozen or so Confucian texts (depending on how the Classics are numbered), and to the more than 1,000 texts found in Taoism and in some forms of Mahayana Buddhism.

---

[22]W. A. Graham, "Scripture," *Encyclopedia of Religion,* vol. 13, p. 134.

The third variation in scripture lies in *function*. In some religions, scripture is so central—or so it may look to the outsider—that the life of the believer seems virtually dictated by scripture. Zoroastrianism, Judaism, Christianity, and Islam are all properly called "religions of the book" because of the high place and powerful function their scriptures have. Islam is often said to be most fully a "religion of the book" because of the all-pervasive influence of the *Quran* in Muslim life. Asian religions often have a more informal relationship to their scripture, which devotees consult mainly for general guidance and inspiration.

The varying oral and textual dimensions of scripture also lead to differences in function. Some religions—as, for example, Hinduism—view the spoken word of scripture as primary. Hindus regard the *Vedas* essentially as speech rather than as printed word and see the written text as inferior to the "oral text." In other religions, the power and function of the book seem to depend upon its written, textual nature. Muslims, for example, believe that the *Quran* is a transcription of a book already written in heaven. A later section of this chapter will deal more fully with the topic of the uses of scripture, but enough has been said here to suggest that they function in different ways.

Given all this variety, is it possible to define scripture in a way that can take variety into account and yet serve as a valid conceptual category for all world religions? Although some scholars of world religions answer in the negative,[23] most would argue that a comprehensive definition of scripture is possible and necessary. Despite its inherent ambiguities and difficulties, scholars commonly accept and use this term generically. The definition we will use here is this: **Scripture** is *the writing accepted by and used in a religious community as especially sacred and authoritative.* We can follow up on this definition by looking more closely at its key words and its implications. In what follows we will discuss both the formal and functional aspects of scriptures— what they are and how they are used.

First, all scripture is a *writing*. Scripture exercises much of its authority as a book, and we encounter it as such. Some scholars argue that **oral tradition,** the passing down of material by word of mouth only, is "scriptural."[24] Although oral and written traditions do have some similar characteristics and functions, strictly speaking "oral scripture" is a contradiction in terms—all scripture is by definition written. The scripture of every religion, however, does have continuing, significant oral and aural dimensions.[25] Speaking and hearing the scriptural words are essential to the meaning and function of scripture. Most scriptures originated in oral tradition and stayed in oral tradition for several generations before being put down in writing. Although the

[23]In *Rethinking Scripture,* for example, the essays by Coburn and Folkert reject the term *scripture* for *the Word* and *canon,* respectively. But the other authors keep scripture as a conceptual category, and it is the dominant category in the volume as a whole, as the title implies.

[24]See, e.g., Schmidt, *Exploring Religion,* p. 208: "Broadly conceived, *scripture* refers to oral as well as written traditions that a people regard as sacred. Each religious community has a scripture, a body of sacred oral or written traditions."

[25]We will consider this topic more fully later in this chapter, but it is important enough to merit a preliminary statement here. See especially Graham, *Beyond the Written Word.* For a general treatment of orality, see W. Ong, *Orality and Literacy* (New York: Routledge, Chapman and Hall, 1982), and J. Goody, *The Interface between the Written and the Oral* (Cambridge: Cambridge University Press, 1982).

writing down of scripture obscures its oral dimensions, the orality of the text is still embedded in the writing, waiting to be drawn out by faithful vocalizing of the words. Scripture comes most fully alive when believers read it aloud and hear it in worship. Most believers, even those in highly literate cultures, hear scripture in worship more often and more meaningfully than they read it privately. In this book, as in any book, we encounter scriptures as texts. The reader must always remember that these texts are also meant to be spoken and heard.

The second element of our definition is that scriptures are *especially sacred*. They have special religious significance in pointing to ultimate reality and truth. Sacredness should not be seen simply as of divine origin, or even as the "wholly other," Rudolf Otto's influential conception of sacredness that suits Western religions but not many Eastern faiths. For example, the sacred *Tao* ("Way") witnessed by the *Tao Te Ching* is not wholly other but is hidden in the universe and the self, waiting to be discovered and "tuned into." Moreover, only a few books among world scriptures explicitly claim sacrality for themselves, with the *Quran* and the *Adi Granth* of Sikhism the most notable examples. Most scriptures receive their sacred status only after they have been written, circulated, and widely accepted as reflecting the faith in some special sense. Again, the relational aspect of all scripture comes to the fore. Writings become scripture as they are recognized, received, and used as authoritative in a religious community.

Notice that scriptures are books held to be *especially* sacred. Most religions have a secondary religious literature that is also viewed as holy, instructive, or authoritative. For example, Jews believe that their *Talmud* (the law code of Judaism written down in the fifth century C.E.) is the "oral Torah," the fully inspired and holy counterpart of the *Bible*. Until recent times many Jews have spent as much effort to understand the *Talmud* as the *Bible*.[26] In Islam, the *Hadith* are collected traditions about Muhammad that supplement the *Quran* and are often used to explain its difficulties. Some new religious movements place their especially sacred books alongside other sacred literature. For example, the *Book of Mormon* is called "Another Testament of Jesus Christ" in reference to the Christian New Testament. This may seem to complicate the matter of defining the idea of scripture. On what basis can one say that a certain holy book in a religious tradition (e.g., the *Quran*) is scripture but another (the *Hadith*) is not? The answer lies in the special reception and usage given to works seen as especially sacred. Most religions explicitly or implicitly hold other works to be secondary to scripture. The *Talmud* may be "oral Torah," but it is still not the *Bible;* the *Hadith* is not the *Quran*. Almost every religion has commentarial, devotional, or legal literature that follows up on scripture, but it makes a distinction between scripture and these works with some care.

Another mark of special holiness is use in ritual. When believers read books aloud in worship, when they speak their words to carry out sacrifice, and especially when they venerate books during worship, we have a sure indication that these books are especially sacred. (Secondary religious literature as described earlier rarely makes its

---

[26]The essay by J. Rosenbaum, "Judaism: Torah and Tradition," in F. M. Denny and R. L. Taylor, eds., *The Holy Book in Comparative Perspective* (Columbia, SC: University of South Carolina Press, 1985), gives a good treatment of the holiness of the *Talmud* as compared to that of the *Bible*.

way into worship.) Different types of veneration are practiced in Judaism, Christianity, Islam, Zoroastrianism, and Sikhism. Even in everyday life, scripture enjoys special respect: The Christian *Bible* is the only book in the West still often bound in leather; Muslims wrap the *Quran* in silk and store it in a special place; Buddhist scriptures for monastic use are still handwritten on palm leaves. In the new religious movements, the key writings of their founders that function as scripture are often printed and bound to resemble more traditional holy books.

The third element of our definition is the authority of scripture. Just as sacredness is an aspect of all scripture, scripture is also *especially authoritative* for its communities. Among all written texts, scripture is always the most authoritative and is often the court of final appeal in religious matters. The range of this authority and the way it is exercised vary depending on the nature of the religion and the content of its scriptures. In the Western "religions of the book," scripture is comprehensive in content and regulates much of life. In the Eastern religions, scripture is often not authoritative in the same way as scripture in the Abrahamic traditions. Yet Asian scriptures often express the heart of their faith, the way of salvation. The *Lotus Sutra* in Japanese Nichiren Buddhism is a prominent example of a book with a limited theme and purpose that has great standing in the sect because it addresses what is perceived as the heart of the religion. Moreover, "at least four of the six South Asian or Far Eastern fundamentalist-like movements . . . do in fact privilege a sacred text and presume to draw certain fundamentals—beliefs and behaviors—from it."[27] The authority of scripture for most followers of a given religion is paradoxically acknowledged even when some occasionally reject it. For example, some Hindu Brahmins burn their *Veda* books when they become ascetics. For the sake of greater enlightenment, some Zen Buddhist monks make disparaging comments about the Buddha (e.g., "That old degenerate!") and his scriptural teachings.

Scriptures are generally authoritative for their communities alone, who accept them as expressing the heart of the religion. One prominent exception to this rule is Christianity's acceptance of the Jewish scriptures, which it has renamed the *Old Testament*.[28] Another exception is in Chinese religion, where some older Classics like the *I Ching* are used to some degree as scripture by both Confucians and Taoists. More typically among the world's religions, to receive one's texts as scripture is automatically to exclude the texts of others. For example, most Muslims do not read the Jewish or Christian scriptures because the *Quran* fulfills and corrects the *Bibles* of the Jews and Christians. Confucian scriptures like the *Analects* are generally not given scriptural authority by Taoists, even though Confucian texts form the basis of education for all Chinese, including Taoists. As the *Tao Te Ching* cuttingly remarks against two Confucian virtues in the *Analects*, "When the great way [*Tao*] falls into disuse, there are benevolence and rectitude."[29]

The authority of scripture comes with a special class of scholars who are the guardians of scripture and recognized experts in its interpretation. In Islam, certain scholars become masters of *tafsir*, the science of Quranic interpretation that forms an

---

[27]M. E. Marty and R. S. Appleby, eds., *Fundamentalisms Observed* (Chicago: University of Chicago Press, 1991), p. 820.

[28]Religion scholars prefer the term *Hebrew Scriptures* over the more partisan *Old Testament*.

[29]*Tao Te Ching* 18:1.

entire branch of religious scholarship. In Buddhism, monks with special training and ability teach the sacred writings to other monks and inquiring laypeople. The Confucian scholar is the master of the Classics and teaches them to others. In virtually every faith, including new religious movements, therefore, the authority of its scripture is mediated largely by those recognized as its official interpreters. **Commentary** has a large role in the history of many religions and regulates how scriptures are received and used, especially at the official level. As John Henderson states, "commentaries and commentarial modes of thinking dominated the intellectual history of most premodern civilizations. . . . Until the seventeenth century in Europe, and even later in China, India, and the Near East, thought, especially within high intellectual traditions, was primarily exegetical in character and expression."[30] Moreover, only quite recently in the sweep of human history have books appeared and mass literacy become possible. This is another reason for having a special class to read, comment on, and relate sacred books to a religious community. Of course, the uses of scriptures at the level of the ordinary follower of a religion will at times be quite different from this official interpretation.

Two other features of scripture not directly related to our definition should be stated here. First, scriptures of each religion are often heterogeneous but are nonetheless *seen as a unity* by their communities. This is obvious for scriptures, such as the Jewish and Christian, that comprise different documents—many books bound as a single book, diverse yet one. Some religions recognize different levels of authority and originality in their scriptures, as Judaism does for the first five books of the *Bible*, the Torah. Still, Jews considered their *Bible* to be one book. This is also the case with Asian religions, as in Hinduism's distinction between Vedic scripture, which is called *Shruti* ("what is heard" from the beginning) and the post-Vedic *Smirti* ("what is remembered"). All of it is the scripture of Hinduism, and believers see it as speaking essentially the same message. In China, the principle holds even in reverse: The secondary scriptures are the earlier Classics, and Confucians see the later *Analects* and Taoists the *Tao Te Ching* as one with earlier tradition. Modern scholarship has shown that the *Quran* has passed through different phases of development during and after the life of Muhammad. But neither the researches of scholars nor the acknowledged inconsistencies and difficulties of the *Quran* calls its unity into question for a Muslim.

A second main feature of scripture is that it has *a degree of closure*. This closure is often called a **canon,** a list or collection of books recognized as scriptural.[31] This canon is absolutely fixed in Zoroastrianism, Judaism, Christianity, Islam, and Sikhism. All the scriptures of these religions have long ago been officially identified, and nothing can now be added or subtracted from their canons. With Hinduism, Buddhism, Jainism, Confucianism, and Taoism, however, the situation is quite different. First, their sacred literature is vast, and the problems in defining a canon for a religion like Taoism, which has 1,200 sacred texts, are enormous. Second, the process of producing scripture has not officially ended. Where new books can be added, as Taoists added one at the beginning of the twentieth century, a closed canon cannot exist.

---

[30]J. B. Henderson, *Scripture, Canon, Commentary: A Comparison of Confucian and Western Exegesis* (Princeton: Princeton University Press, 1991), p. 3.
[31]For a general discussion of the idea of canon, see the article under that heading by G. T. Sheppard in *Encyclopedia of Religion*, vol. 3, pp. 62–68.

How can a religion relate to its scriptures when they are so vast that no one person or group can know them all, let alone be expert in them all? In traditions with large canons, certain books, such as the *Tao Te Ching*, are basic for almost everyone. Also, different groups in a religion attach themselves to a few select scriptures that reflect their particular interests. In Taoism, as L. G. Thompson explains, "the practitioner or priest would usually be an adherent to one of the several major 'schools' or traditions of Taoism, and would specialize in those texts relevant to his school's interests."[32]

This tendency to choose one's own books from among the total corpus of scripture results in a "canon within the canon." Most commonly it occurs in religions with very large numbers of books, but it also can be found in religions with smaller canons. For example, although all Christians accept the whole *New Testament* as the capstone of their scripture, each of the three main branches seems especially attracted to one part of the *New Testament.* Eastern Orthodox Christians have a special affinity to the gospel and letters of John, Roman Catholics have an affinity to the gospel of Matthew and the later letters, and Protestants have historically fastened on the letters of Paul. In sum, scripture canons can be either completely closed or open to development and change. No matter how readily they can be altered, canonical texts are still viewed and treated as scripture.

THE USES OF SCRIPTURE

When scripture is set in the full context of the everyday life of its religion, its uses become plain. How believers use scripture shows its status and role in a religion. The following chapters of this book will outline the varied uses of scripture in each religion. In this section, we will discuss some basic dimensions of the comparative study of scripture usage.

First, scripture is a source for establishing and defending key doctrines. Scriptures can be used doctrinally because they typically contain the key teachings of the faith and because believers usually see them as continuing the voice of the founders. They have primary importance as statements of the deep truths of the universe and the right way to live in it. These teachings can assume different forms: God(s) and humanity; human imperfections and salvation; beginnings and ends of the individual and the cosmos; the moral life and how to achieve it. When scripture is used to establish doctrine, this is most often done by its official interpreters—monks, priests, scholars, and the like. Sometimes it is done by formal debate in councils or assemblies, sometimes within the confines of a monastery or temple. Defending doctrine occurs less often at the popular level, but even here scripture can function authoritatively. An appeal to a passage of holy writ is often the final word in any argument about religion.

Second, scripture is also prominently used in public worship. Worshippers often display and read it aloud. Although this is characteristic especially of the so-called "religions of the book," it is also significant in religions such as Hinduism and Buddhism that are not so book oriented. The worship that goes on in a Buddhist

---

[32]"Taoism: Classic and Canon," in Denny and Taylor, *Holy Book*, p. 205.

monastery, for example, prominently features the scriptures. Monks read them, chant them, meditate on them, and walk around them in solemn procession. Even when the book is not prominent in worship, its content often permeates the ceremonies of most scripturalizing religions. Prayers, sacrifices, and hymns come from and echo the language of scripture. Many lyrics of the music of worship are drawn from the scriptural text. Hymns and chants, with their emotional power, are significant vehicles for use of scripture in most religious traditions in the East and West.

Perhaps the place and function of scripture are never so prominent as when worshippers formally venerate it. Almost every religion in the world with scripture pays it ritual respect in some way. Hindus speak the words of a *Veda* with great care. These words are the center of holiness in worship, though the *Veda* book is usually not to be seen. In certain Taoist and Confucian temples, the location of the scripture collection is itself holy. In Judaism, the scrolls are removed from their ark at the front center of the synagogue with great solemnity and on certain festival days are paraded around the synagogue. In many Christian churches, everyone stands for the gospel reading. **Bibliolatry** [bib-lee-AHL-ah-tree] results when believers give excessive veneration to their scriptures or become absolutely dependent on them.

A third typical use of scripture is in meditation and devotion. This is usually private and individual, but it can also occur in group settings, as when Buddhist monks meditate in session on sutra passages or on mantras drawn from scripture. Sometimes they meditate on the words and other times "look through" the words to find the truth "behind" them. The conclusions of many Hindu scriptures specify a blessing on those who listen or read faithfully. In Western religions, the scripture books are often marked into sections for devotional reading; it is the duty of believers to read, ponder, and often memorize the words. In meditation and devotion, the scriptures teach the truth of the religion and promote the growth of the reader into the fullness of the faith.

All these uses of scripture can be described as primarily *cognitive,* understanding and thinking in some way about the words and their meaning. Another important dimension of the usage of scripture, one often overlooked, is *noncognitive* usage. Here the words are used in a variety of ways without any attempt to understand their meaning rationally.

A first noncognitive type of usage occurs when scriptures are used in a language that cannot be understood by the follower of the faith. This is especially the case when a religion like Hinduism or Islam holds that its scriptures are so essentially bound to their original language that they cannot be translated and retain their sacred nature. Arabic is a foreign tongue for most Muslims, yet Muslims in Turkey, Africa, Indonesia, and America can be found memorizing passages from the *Quran* and then using them in life and worship with very little notion of what their Arabic words mean. The *Quran* has power to transform the life of believers whether they understand the words or not.

A second noncognitive use of scripture is decorative and **iconic,** or revered as a holy object. Many Hindus cannot read their sacred literature, but images and pictures of the gods and their stories are all around them. One cannot live in any Muslim area without encountering Quranic verses everywhere. They are displayed on private houses and public buildings, often in a stylized calligraphy that is a mainstay of art in

Muslim lands. These word decorations are not meant to be read so much as to be felt, thereby exercising their holy presence for the blessing of the community. In these and other iconic usages of scripture, the appeal is more to the imagination and emotion than to the mind.

A third noncognitive application mixes religion and magic. The power of scripture is such that it can bring blessing and keep away evil; it has an objective supernatural power quite by itself. We have already spoken of scripture as used in charms or talismans, a manifestation of the magical power of scripture. Perhaps this was the function of the oldest surviving archeological fragment of the scripture of a modern religion, a tiny Israelite silver scroll from the seventh century B.C.E. with a priestly blessing written on the inside, probably worn on a necklace. The mere possession of a holy book also has power to bless and ward off evil. For example, putting a certain Taoist text in the hands of a woman undergoing a perilous childbirth is said to cause the immediate safe birth of her child. In many religions, those who can afford it will often buy a holy book for possession in the home. Often family genealogical records will be written into the front of this scripture in the home; this practice is especially common in Christianity and Islam.

Perhaps the most striking popular use of scripture is **bibliomancy** [BIB-lee-oh-man-see], the use of holy books to foresee the future and guide one's response to it. Many religions feature the informal practice of opening a scripture book at random and reading the first passage that meets the eye. This passage, it is thought, has special power to direct the believer through an uncertain or difficult situation in life or just through the difficulties of the new day. One of the most famous ancient conversions to Christianity, that of St. Augustine, featured such bibliomancy. Some printed editions of the *Quran* have symbols at the top of the page by which a reader opening the book at random can discern whether a planned action is advisable, inadvisable, or neutral. Sikhism has formalized bibliomancy in its "taking the word" ceremony. Some Taoists read the *I Ching* philosophically, but more use it in divination. Its many hexagrams and their fortunetelling interpretations are selected by a special procedure with sticks. All these forms of bibliomancy assume that a supernatural guidance is exercised in and through the book for the blessing of the believer.

The usages described here have been categorized in other ways (beyond cognitive and noncognitive) by scholars of religion. Perhaps the most helpful is that of Sam D. Gill, who proposed that uses of scripture are informative and performative. *Informative* means imparting information in various ways, such as in doctrine and history. *Performative*, in contrast, *does* something, as for example when scripture is used to make sacrifice, to make the laws of a religious or civil community, or to bless and curse.[33] In both its informative and performative aspects, scripture is also used for transformation. This transformative power is a result of its sacrality and authority. Scriptures come from a sacred source and are themselves sacred. This sacred quality generally entails some power to make holy those who read or listen to them.

The transformative power of scripture occurs in both an individual and communal way—for example, to gain insight on personal or group problems and find the

---

[33]Gill, "Nonliterate Traditions and Holy Books: Toward a New Model," in Denny and Taylor, *Holy Book,* p. 234.

resources to solve them. Not all religions consider their scriptures to be divinely inspired, but all hold them to be inspiring and transformative in some way. This transformative power can be based on cognition, in which believers directly encounter the scriptures and experience their life-changing meaning. It can also happen just as often in noncognitive ways, as described earlier.

ADVANTAGES AND DISADVANTAGES

The study of the world's religions through their sacred scriptures has both advantages and disadvantages. We need to be aware of the limitations of this method and work from strengths to ameliorate the weaknesses as much as possible.

The first disadvantage is that scriptures are *not universal*. Some religions do not have them—if a culture has no writing, it obviously can have no scripture. This is the case with most of the traditional indigenous religions of Africa and North America. Of course, not having a scripture does not invalidate a religion. The religions and cultures of nonliterate peoples do have oral traditions that function prominently in storytelling and in rituals that enact myths. A religion based on oral traditions is every bit as living and real for its followers as a religion that produces and uses scripture.

Second, as we saw earlier, the reception and use of scripture is *not uniform* across religions. Religions regard their scriptures in different ways, and scriptures function differently in each religion. Students of world religions must take note of these variations and learn to look at each religion's scriptures in a fresh way. Readers of scripture who come from a "religion of the book" must especially try to lay aside their preconceptions. Protestant Christians, for example, must beware of assuming that certain qualities of scripture and its function to which they are accustomed (e.g., that scripture is best absorbed by individual silent reading and meditation) will be true of every religion's scripture. Moreover, the use of new scriptures in new religious movements such as the Church of Jesus Christ of Latter-day Saints (the "Mormons") and the Unification Church will often differ from usage in older, classical religious movements. The more we genuinely encounter world scriptures in their full range of reception and use, the less likely we will be to inject our own bias into the scriptures of others. Then "scripture" itself will become a fuller, more useful category.

A third disadvantage is that we must *read translations,* which cannot fully capture the literary characteristics or meaning of the original. An old Italian proverb says, "Translators are traitors," and all scriptures are betrayed in some way by translation. Some religions are acutely aware of this betrayal. Islam, for example, holds that use of the *Quran* must be in Arabic; a translation is no longer the *Quran* itself. Among Brahmanic Hindus, the oral power of the *Vedas* in their Sanskrit language is such that it would be unthinkable to translate them into another language for use in worship. Brahmins use them in that ancient language even though they do not fully understand the words. As we read in translation, we must remember that some of the original meaning and resonance of the words is thereby lost.

A fourth disadvantage is that scriptures tend to *reflect only the patriarchal and elite perspectives* of their traditions. They come from times and cultures that are more or less patriarchal, where the voices of women are muted and filtered.[34] Scriptures strongly tend to embody official and elite ideas, the "mainstream" that feminist scholars call "malestream." Comparatively little of popular religion can be found in them. Although the contents of scripture are patriarchal and elitist, feminist scholars today in many religions are working to make contemporary understanding and use of these scriptures more equalitarian. This book will offer some coverage of social justice and the role of women, but the perspective through which these scriptures are filtered is necessarily that of the elite male.[35]

Finally, and perhaps most seriously, we *lack the living context* of scripture when we encounter only its textual form. Scripture, which for most traditions (except new religious movements, of course) comes from ancient times, comes alive as it is appropriated in the life of religious communities. Despite growing religious pluralism, many North American readers of scripture do not have access to these communities. They cannot visit a mosque, see the ritual of a Hindu home or temple, or live for a time in a Buddhist monastery. They cannot directly see the broad ways that scripture is reflected in religious life, or the more specific ways it is used in worship, devotion, or law. What can be reproduced in a book like this is primarily the written text itself. The uses of scripture can be outlined here, but a printed book will inevitably emphasize the written, textual aspects of scripture over the oral and living.

These disadvantages might seem strong enough to cause the reader to give up the encounter with world scriptures. The advantages of studying religions through their scripture are compelling, however. By working from the strengths of this approach, the reader can overcome the weaknesses to some extent and use scripture appropriately to enter the world of other religions.

The first advantage of this approach is that scripture is *widespread* among religions. Even though it is not fully universal, each "major" (to use a traditional but rather prejudicial term) living religion has a scripture. Scriptures naturally vary in form, content, and usage, but they are usually present in a religion. As we have seen, recent researchers emphasize that they form a distinct and important element in the life of most religions. The tendency to *scripturalize,* to make and use scriptures, is strong among religions. Indeed, almost every contemporary religion that is based in a literate culture produces and uses scriptures of some sort.[36] New religious movements also express themselves in writings that have a scriptural status.

Second, scriptures tend to be *comprehensive* for their faiths. Matters that a religion considers of great importance for its life are generally written down for the continu-

---

[34]See the introductory section of Serinity Young, ed., *An Anthology of Sacred Texts by and about Women* (New York: Crossroad, 1993), for good treatment of this issue.

[35]An excellent new series edited by Donald S. Lopez, Jr., "Princeton Readings in Religions," seeks to rectify this male-elite perspective with anthologies that draw on more popular writings and anthropological field reports. Its first volume, *Religions of India in Practice* (Princeton: Princeton University Press, 1995), deals with Hinduism, Sikhism, Islam, and Jainism. The second volume is *Buddhism in Practice* (1995), the third is *Religions of China in Practice* (1996); the fourth is *Religions of Tibet in Practice* (1997). Other volumes are planned for the religions of Japan, Islam, Africa, Judaism, and Christianity.

[36]Only Shinto does not treat its holy books as scripture in the full sense. Thus Shinto is "the exception that proves the rule" that religions based in literate cultures produce and use scriptures.

ing community. "The sacred writings provide not only the essence of each particular religious tradition, but also the archetypal experiences which stir in the depths of all human lives . . . death, trust, anxiety, wonder, loyalty to a cause greater than oneself, fascination, healing, fulfillment, peace."[37] Of course, what religions view as important does vary, and scriptures reflect this variety. For example, the Jewish scriptures regulate a multitude of aspects of life considered significant, from worship to ethics to diet. But the Confucian *Analects* deals almost exclusively with the moral virtues that can make one "superior." What each religion considers of paramount importance will be strongly reflected in its scriptures. They offer comprehensive insight into the key characteristics of their faiths.

Third, scriptures are *authoritative* for their religions. Because they are believed to come from God or the gods, an enlightened teacher, or a wise sage, and because they bear witness to an ultimate reality, the truth contained in scriptures is recognized and lived out by believers. To read a scripture is to discover what is of primary value in the world's religions. And because scriptures are authoritative, they typically reflect the distinctive main aspects of each tradition. As one commentator has noted, "Despite the variety of attitudes to scriptural works [in the world's religions], there is a continuing tendency to find in a sacred text . . . the primary source for true doctrine, correct ritual, [and] appropriate conduct."[38]

The fourth advantage of studying scriptures lies in their *ancient or foundational* character. They or the oral tradition on which they are based arise soon after the beginning of a religion and often signal important stages in its early development. Chinese religions call their oldest scriptures the *Classics,* and in a sense all world scriptures are classic treatments of their religious tradition. Where a religion has a founder(s), scriptures usually give deep insight into the life of the founder(s) from the perspective of later followers. The foundational character of scriptures thus makes them valuable as a primary source for the history of religions. In the new religious movements we will treat in Chapter 13, scriptural books were completed and published by the founder himself or herself, at the very beginning of the movement.

Furthermore, because the traditional religions of the world have so richly influenced and been influenced by their cultures, scriptures are among the most important literary sources for the understanding of world cultures. Though scriptures are indeed ancient and important, it is usually erroneous to argue, as does Charles Braden, that religion is somehow "founded on" scriptures.[39] Rather, as T. W. Hall puts it so well, "Historical investigations show that the religious communities existed prior to the writing of their scripture . . . religions produced scripture and scripture did not produce religion."[40] However, this conclusion is not accurate when applied to new religious movements, because among them scriptures often did precede or coincide with the beginnings of the movement. We will examine the reasons for this phenomenon in Chapter 13.

---

[37]Leonard J. Biallas, "Teaching World Religions through their Scriptures," *Horizons* 17 (1990): 80.
[38]K. Yates et al., *The Religious World: Communities of Faith,* 2d ed. (New York: Macmillan, 1988), p. 3.
[39]Charles Braden, *The Scriptures of Mankind: An Introduction* (New York: Macmillan, 1952), p. 8.
[40]Hall et al., *Religion,* p. 109.

Fifth, scriptures are *accessible* in translation to English-language readers. Most of the important religious books of the world have been translated into English, and many of those that have not are now being translated. Sometimes the translations of a certain scripture are few, but others can boast a virtual riot of English versions. The *Tao Te Ching*, for example, had more than twenty English versions in print in 2001. Although no translation can convey the full meaning and feeling of the original, a good translation can suggest it.

Finally, scriptures as literary texts are *open to critical analysis.* Both the specialist scholar and the beginning reader can analyze them directly or, better yet, enter a conversation with them. Although most religious texts will range from mildly strange to completely baffling for those who come from other cultures and religious traditions, the same intellectual and scholarly skills used to read any other text can be put to use on world scriptures. With some effort, the North American reader can understand scriptures and use them as a pathway into other faiths.

WORLD SCRIPTURES AND MODERN SCHOLARSHIP

The earlier discussion of critical analysis of scripture leads us to an important but often neglected topic. How does the modern academic study of scripture influence how religions use world scriptures and how we read them?

Historical and critical literary scholarship is largely Western and European in origin, stemming from various methods of interpreting literature developed in the Renaissance. Textual criticism methodically judges manuscripts to find the likely original reading; grammatical criticism analyzes the content and style of the wording of a work in its original language; literary criticism studies genres. Most important is historical criticism, which probes the developmental genesis of works from the past, their original meaning and authenticity.[41] In the early nineteenth century this approach began to be applied to the *Bible*. Critical study of the Christian scripture has uncovered development, diversity, and even some disagreement within it. Christianity's effort to understand the *Bible* critically has suffered reversals from time to time. Yet many Protestant groups accept this critical study, perceiving that it offers a fuller understanding of scripture that is compatible with faith.

In the early twentieth century biblical criticism spread to Judaism, and today Conservative and Reform Jews widely accept it, with only Orthodox Jews still opposing it. Since the Second Vatican Council (1962–1965), Roman Catholics have also embraced the **historical-critical method** of biblical study, which derives meaning from the earliest phases of the Bible's literature.[42] Today the basic methods of literary study still are largely European academic methods. Scholars and students read sacred texts through Western eyes and by Western methods.

---

[41]See the essay "Modern Approaches to Biblical Study" in the *New Oxford Annotated Bible* (New York: Oxford, 1990) for a brief discussion of how these and other methods are applied to the study of the Hebrew Scriptures and the New Testament.

[42]See G. P. Fogarty, *American Catholic Biblical Scholarship* (San Francisco: Harper/Collins, 1989), and R. B. Robinson, *Roman Catholic Exegesis since* Divino Afflante Spiritu (Atlanta: Scholars Press, 1988).

The effort to collect, edit, and publish the literature of world religions is also a Western academic enterprise. It had its roots in the eighteenth century, when the first copies of Chinese and Indian scripture made their way to Europe and were greeted with great interest, even enthusiasm, in some circles. A part of this enthusiasm was an Enlightenment hope that these scriptures might be a religious or philosophical alternative to what some saw as the hidebound clericalism of Christianity. The *Vedas*, for example, were at first viewed as religious expressions from near the dawn of time, pristine and unspoiled by priestcraft. Gradually Europeans realized that they reflect a priestly system as traditional as that of Christianity, and even older. By the middle of the nineteenth century, as we saw, a more mature scholarly interest in world scripture blossomed into a systematic effort to publish reliable translations of scriptures. The editing and publishing of sacred texts continue today, especially with religions that have large canons. The methods used to edit, translate, publish, and interpret these scriptures draw generally from the Western tradition.

With scholarship in comparative religion coming from a background that was largely Protestant in orientation, over the last century an inevitable "Protestant bias" has crept into the way scholarship has looked at the scriptures of other faiths.[43] Certain mainstream Protestant ideas about the nature of scripture colored the study of the scriptures of other religions and only today are being identified and corrected. They can be listed serially: a preoccupation with textuality to the exclusion of orality, from the Protestant emphasis on the scripture as *written;* an individualistic orientation that assumes that scriptures are to be read mainly by the individual, from Protestant ideas of the "priesthood of all believers" and universal literacy; the notion that scriptures are widely authoritative over every aspect of religious life, from the Protestant assertion that the scriptures are the sole authority in the Christian faith; and the assumption that scriptures are best understood by academically recognized methods of study, from mainstream Protestant attachment to sound academic procedures.

Of course, believers of the other religions of the world do not share this bias, as we can see as we reflect comparatively on each of these assumptions. In some religions, such as Hinduism, the oral dimension dominates the written. In others, such as Islam, written and oral are more in balance. Next, most religions do not share the Protestant notion that scriptures should be read by the individual; rather, their adherents speak and hear their scriptures in groups, usually in worship and ritual. Indeed, it comes as a striking realization for modern North Americans that most followers of many religions throughout history (and even today!) cannot read, and therefore cannot read their sacred texts. For the typical follower of most faiths, texts must be *spoken* (often from memory) and *heard*.

We examined earlier the next Protestant assumption, that scriptures seek to regulate every aspect of religious life, and we concluded that they seek to regulate the center of religious life as their religion conceives that center. For most religions of the world, the Western academic approach to scripture goes against the grain of faith and is consequently viewed as alien. Other literature may be studied critically, but to study scripture historically and critically is to question its sacredness because such study

---

[43]M. Levering, in her introduction to *Rethinking Scripture*, pp. 3–5, has some good comments on this Protestant bias.

employs the same methods used to study other nonsacred literature. For example, Islam forbids going behind the present Uthmanic edition of the Arabic text to inquire about earlier versions. Traditional conservative Muslims also forbid studying or using the *Quran* in such a way to question its unity or divine origin, as Salman Rushdie discovered. Each religion has some systematic study of its sacred texts, but such study usually remains devotional, meditative, and interpretive. Noncritical and unthreatening, it does not question the received beliefs about the origin and standing of the text.

When we read scriptures, then, we must always remember that the way we read is fully conditioned by our cultural background and academic enterprise. Those who read from a religious background must always try to keep their own viewpoint identified and in check. Those with no religious commitments must try to suspend any doubts they may have about religion and scriptures. We read scriptures as *outsiders*, in an objective, scholarly, noncommittal way. This is altogether necessary as a first step in coming to grips with world scriptures. A second step, more difficult than the first but equally necessary, is to read them as much as possible as *insiders*, with the eyes, minds, and hearts of those for whom these scriptures are much more than the object of scholarship.[44]

SCRIPTURES AND THE WORLD WIDE WEB

The last ten years have seen an explosive growth in the World Wide Web, the linked computer system on the Internet. Much information about religion can be found on the Web; it seems to be one of the leading topics of discussion and inquiry. As a part of this interest in religion, many sites on the Web feature scriptures in translation or sometimes in the original.

Many positive features of this new opportunity to encounter world scriptures can be adduced. The access is almost always free. The amount of scripture on the Web is growing rapidly and may someday encompass most world scriptures. The Internet is an appealing way for most young, computer-oriented students (but not always their professors!) to encounter scriptures. It presents different ways of studying and learning—for example, the ability to search a text electronically. The Internet by its structure encourages exploration. Some sites are fully interactive, allowing students to ask questions and participate in online discussion groups. Finally, but not least, when students explore a religion site sponsored by its followers, the encounter is likely to be a bit more that of an "insider" than classroom or textbook descriptions.

The drawbacks of studying world scriptures on the Web are also significant. Some sites are not well constructed; they may have poor layout, little eye appeal, out-of-date links, or other technical deficiencies. While Internet coverage of world scripture is growing, it is still largely incomplete. The translations used are usually public-domain works that are out of date. When representatives of religions post that reli-

---

[44]See the excellent remarks by Eric Sharpe in *Encyclopedia of Religion*, vol. 14, p. 85, on "imaginative sympathy" in reading scripture as "insiders." See also Ross N. Reat, "Insiders and Outsiders in the Study of Religious Traditions," *Journal of the American Academy of Religion* 51 (1983): 459–475.

gion's writings for missionary and/or public relations purposes, the "spin" put on them may not agree with the current academic consensus on that religion. Most significantly, these electronic publications are subject to little or no scholarly control, such as editorial or peer review before publication, so their quality varies greatly. Some sites are excellent, some average, and some poor.

The result of this mixed situation is that many students need help in finding, using, and especially analyzing critically these Web-based scripture sites. The few books on this topic are of some value, especially Patrick Durusau's *High Places in Cyberspace.*[45] For readers of this anthology of world scriptures, I have designed a special website to further their use of the Web in religious studies. It has links to short, helpful essays on using the Internet in an academically appropriate way. It also has links to sites that my students and I have found useful in the study of scriptures. This listing cannot pretend to be comprehensive, but it does offer a starting place to surf and learn. The address is: http://religion.wadsworth.com/relinks.html.

THE PLAN OF THIS BOOK

This book contains excerpts of world scriptures in the following order of religions: Hinduism, Buddhism, Jainism, Sikhism, Confucianism, Taoism, Shinto,[46] Zoroastrianism, Judaism, Christianity, Islam, and selected new religious movements. This progression keeps the religions of India, China, Japan, and the Near East together in their family groups. Moreover, the reader can see the relationships among religions and scriptures more easily when related bodies of texts are dealt with in succession. For example, when the Jewish scriptures are followed by the Christian and then the Islamic, the deep relationship among them becomes apparent. The same is true to a significant degree with Hinduism, Buddhism, and Jainism, and to a lesser degree with Confucianism and Taoism. A final chapter, new to this edition, gives excerpts from the scriptures of new religious movements treated in order of their time of origin: Baha'i, the Church of Jesus Christ of Latter-day Saints, Christian Science, the Unification Church, and the Church of Scientology.

Each chapter except the last is structured as follows: An introduction outlines the scriptures included, setting them in the context of the whole religion by examining briefly their name(s), overall structure, origin and growth, and use. The first grouping of scripture passages deals with the history of the religion. If the faith has a founder, special attention will be given to him or her; any subsequent history of the religion that scripture reflects will also be excerpted. Second are passages covering the main doctrinal teaching of the religion. These topics include divine or ultimate reality, creation and the environment, the nature of humanity, and achieving human fulfillment (salvation, release, harmony, etc.). Third are passages about the moral/

---

[45]Patrick Durusau, *High Places in Cyberspace,* 2d ed. (Atlanta: Scholars, 1998). The website containing updates to this book is no longer maintained.

[46]Strictly speaking, Shinto does not have scripture as this term is understood in modern scholarship. However, since the ancient sacred writings of Japan are very instructive for understanding Shinto, we will anthologize them briefly here.

ethical structure of the scriptures: good, evil, and the authentic human life. Personal morality is probably more widely treated in world scriptures, but social ethics are also prominent. Such topics as war and peace, violence and nonviolence, tolerance and intolerance of people of other faiths, the status of women, and a just society will be represented as fully as possible. Fourth are passages about the organization of the religion, either in its internal organization (e.g., monks and laity in Buddhism) or in its attempts to organize its wider culture (e.g., the Hindu caste system in India). Last are passages about religious worship, ritual, devotion, and meditation. Of course, some religions will have more in some of these categories than others, but most do fit into them without significant distortion. Where they do not fully fit, this format will be adapted as necessary to do justice to the particular nature of the texts.

The last chapter of the present book follows a different organization. Because the new religious movements treated there differ significantly from each other, we will not combine their scriptures into categories of "history," "teachings," "ethics," and the rest. Rather, each new religious movement will be treated in a separate section, with as much attention to history, teaching, ethics, organization, and worship as befits each movement.

The predominant rationale for this organization is *pedagogical.* It is meant to further the learning of readers, especially students being introduced to the religions of the world. North American readers are familiar with the categories used here, and both teachers and students of world religions will recognize them as a standard paradigm for research and teaching in religion. Moreover, they are categories that seem to "fit" world scriptures themselves. But why not discard any attempt to use categories of organization and simply provide one or two longer excerpts from each religion's body of scripture? A rather uniform scripture like the *Quran* may be possible to encompass in a few long readings. Even Islamic tradition says that the whole Quranic message is contained in each of its chapters, so to read one is in a sense to read them all! However, what Paul Muller-Ortega says about Hinduism is true of many religions including the new religious movements: "It is not possible to put a single sacred text in the hands of students and expect the reading of that one text to allow students to encompass the tradition. . . . Thus, the preferred method of exposing students to the enormity of the Hindu sacred literature has been by means of anthologies."[47]

A GUIDE TO PRONUNCIATION

The languages in which the scriptures of this book are written include, among others, Sanskrit, Pali, Chinese, Hebrew, Arabic, and Greek. With the single exception of Greek, these languages have scripts very different from our alphabet. Many translations from these languages use a system of diacritical marks to translate proper nouns, especially on the consonants in personal names. For example, in Hinduism

---

[47]Paul Muller-Ortega, "Exploring Textbooks: Introductions to Hinduism," in B. R. Gaventa, ed., *Critical Review of Books in Religion, 1988* (Atlanta: Scholars Press, 1989), p. 71.

one often finds the names *Kṛṣṇa* or *Śiva*. These marks serve to indicate their rather exact pronunciation.

This method, though fully appropriate for scholars, is confusing for most beginning readers. Therefore, this book uses a simplified method of translation with no diacritical symbols or marks. Here each word is spelled in a way that permits the reader to pronounce proper nouns directly and more easily. Instead of *Kṛṣṇa*, the reader will see the more pronounceable *Krishna*; *Śiva* becomes *Shiva*. The pronunciation that results is more approximate, but it is fully appropriate for beginning readers of world scriptures. Of course, students should follow the lead of their teachers in pronouncing these words.

Pronouncing foreign language words correctly is challenging, and here the student needs some specific guidance. In what follows we will proceed religion by religion, beginning with the easiest to pronounce. In this section, we will deal only with the rules that come into play in this anthology.

Judaism and Christianity

The pronunciation of Jewish and Christian personal names is usually apparent to North American readers. Most translations, including those used here, use no diacritical marks, and the words are pronounced the way they look in English. The only slight challenge comes in the chapter on Judaism, when Hebrew words are occasionally not translated but *transliterated*, spelled letter for letter in the English alphabet. In these cases, the following rules apply: (1) ' = the initial throaty sound of escaping breath before a vowel is sounded, as in the English *apple;* (2) the plural suffix -*im* = "eem," as in *Kethuvim*, "Writings."

Islam

Arabic is, like Hebrew, a Semitic language. Therefore the rule just given on the throaty sound also applies to Arabic and is used more often than in English translations of the Hebrew *Bible*. The plural suffix is -*in,* "een." *dh* is pronounced as the English *th,* as in *the. kh* is pronounced as the guttural (throat-clearing sound) *ch,* as in the Scottish *loch* or the German *machen.* All other vowels and consonants in the Arabic proper nouns of this book are similar to their English equivalents.

Hinduism and Buddhism

Sanskrit is the main language of Hindu scripture and of much Buddhist scripture. Buddhism also employs the Pali language, which is closely related to Sanskrit. Sanskrit itself is an Indo-European language and as such is pronounced in much the same way as modern European languages. The main exceptions are as follows: *c* is pronounced *ch,* as in *chair. g* is usually hard, as the first (not second) *g* in *garage. h* is pronounced separately from the preceding consonant, as the second *h* in *hothouse,* not the *h* in *think*. The vowels are much the same as in German or Spanish, except that a short *a* (found in an unstressed syllable) is vocalized as *u* in *but*.

Taoism and Confucianism

The Chinese language presents the most challenge to English speakers. A tonal language, Chinese contains sounds that are difficult to capture in other languages. Chinese words are given here in the Wade-Giles system, which despite the newer and generally more accurate *pinyin* system is still the choice in most scholarly literature and the one students will find in most other books. (Because it is becoming more common, we will note the *pinyin* spelling in the glossaries.) Consonants, especially when not immediately followed by an apostrophe, are as follows: *j = r,* as for example the Chinese word for "humaneness," *jen,* is pronounced *ren. k = g,* as for example the goddess Kwan ("Gwan") Yin. *p,* especially at the beginning of a word, is pronounced *b. ch* is pronounced *j,* as in the word for "classic scripture," Ching ("Jing"). *t* is pronounced *d,* as in Tao ("Dow").

SUGGESTIONS ON HOW TO READ SCRIPTURES

Those who are reading world scriptures for the first time often feel they are entering a strange new world. Sometimes one's preconceived notion of what reading a given scripture will be like turns out to be quite wrong. Students of world religion are especially susceptible to the difficulties of reading scripture. Their textbooks usually try to make scriptures easier to encounter by simplifying and summarizing the contents. To encounter scriptures more directly and in their original form is a harder process. As Mortimer Adler and Charles Van Doren once wrote, "The problem of reading the Holy Book . . . is the most difficult problem in the field of reading."[48] In the end, however, it is more profitable for readers to wrestle as directly as possible with the texts. Of course, an anthology such as this does not present world scriptures in their totality but serves as a bridge to the full scripture text.

Each reader must ultimately find an individually suitable method for reading world scriptures. But these suggestions drawn from my experience and the experience of others may be helpful.

1. Use your knowledge of religion to set these readings in a fuller context. Try to relate scriptures as fully as possible to the life of the religions from which they come. For example, when you are reading a passage about ritual, visualize how the ritual is carried out.

2. Read the introductions to each chapter before you turn to the passages. They will provide an important background for understanding the passages.

3. Next, take a few moments to skim the selections. Having a general feel for the "lay of the land" will help you when you begin to read in detail.

---

[48]Mortimer Adler and Charles Van Doren, *How to Read a Book* (New York: Simon & Schuster, 1940), p. 288.

4. Read the scripture passages with the same intellectual skills as you would any other text, religious or nonreligious. Remember their holy status in their religions, but don't be intimidated by it.

5. Mark the text as you read. Research on reading shows that students who mark the text, underlining or highlighting as few as three or four items per page, understand and remember more than readers who do not mark their text. Marking the text helps to make it your own.

6. Pay attention to literary genre. The form and content of any literary passage will reflect its genre. Read with a feeling for the differences among myth, poetry, narrative, law, and other literary forms.

7. Make a personal glossary of unfamiliar terms and names as you go along. You can do this quite easily by circling them in the text and writing them in the bottom margin. (Use circles or other type of marking that will distinguish them from other marked material.) Then you can go back later to make a short note of their meaning, also in the margin. The unfamiliarity and difficulty of so many words, both technical terms and personal names, is a large obstacle for many students of world religions. With a little extra effort, you can minimize this difficulty.

8. Be careful to pronounce the proper nouns correctly and consistently. Take an extra moment to sound them out and make them familiar. If necessary, use the pronunciation guide in this chapter and the glossary at the end of each chapter.

9. Read each selection repeatedly until you are familiar with it and can identify any problems you have in understanding it. View these problems as opportunities, not roadblocks, to achieving greater understanding.

10. Read the selections aloud as much as possible. This may feel embarrassing at first because you are not accustomed to it. Listen to the sounds of the words, and try to get a sense of the oral dimensions of the text. You cannot reproduce the feeling of the original language, but reading aloud will at least remind you that the text does have an oral dimension.

11. Put yourself, as well as you can, inside the faith of the scripture. What could these writings mean to you if you were among those who first heard them? What could they mean to you today if you were a typical follower of that faith? By using your knowledge and imagination, you can participate in the unique use of scripture in each religion and become—partially and temporarily—an insider.[49]

12. Memorize short, selected passages as a way of internalizing scriptures.

13. If you wish to explore the scriptures more fully, begin by comparing the translations found here with other translations. Next, you can study other books and commentaries about the scriptures, many of which can be found in the Suggestions for Further Reading section of each chapter.

---

[49]"By an act of historical imagination we can actually participate up to a certain point in the aspirations and devotions of other times and places. Yet this truly is only up to a certain point, for the curtain is suddenly lowered and we realize with a shock just how far away those places and times really are. That experience has been called 'the paradox of understanding.'" Jaroslav Pelikan, *On Searching the Scriptures—Your Own or Someone Else's* (New York: Quality Paperback Book Club, 1992), p. 7.

14. As time permits, read other scriptures besides those passages anthologized here. Best of all, read entire texts of scripture.

GLOSSARY

bibliolatry [bib-lee-AHL-ah-tree] excessive veneration of a scripture book.

bibliomancy [BIB-lee-oh-man-see] the use of scripture to foresee future events and guide one's control of them.

canon a more or less fixed collection of books regarded as scriptural.

commentary a book written to explain another book, often passage by passage. Many religions possess commentaries on their scriptures.

genre a type of literary form, such as poetry, proverb, narrative history, philosophical meditation, and so on.

historical-critical method the scholarly study of a text that derives its meaning from its earliest phases and traces its historical development.

icon a holy picture. Metaphorically, scripture is an icon when it is revered as a sacred object apart from its contents.

narrative the telling of an event or series of events in story form.

oral tradition the passing down, usually through many generations, of myths, narratives, poems, and the like by word of mouth.

scripture texts that a religion holds to be especially sacred and authoritative.

QUESTIONS FOR STUDY AND DISCUSSION

1. What does the word *scripture* mean to you?

2. "Scripture is more a Western concept than an Asian concept." To what extent do you agree or disagree with this common statement?

3. What special problems and opportunities are posed by having a very large scripture canon, such as in Taoism or Buddhism?

4. Suppose that a new potential scripture—a new gospel book about Jesus, or a collection of new sayings from Buddha or Confucius—were discovered and shown to be authentic. Would such a potential scripture actually get into the scripture canons of these religions? Why?

5. What uses of scripture seem most important and/or interesting to you? Why?

6. What disadvantages are posed by the ancient character of scriptures? Can these be overcome? If so, how?

7. Reflect on this description of Mohandas Ghandi's teachings on studying others' scriptures: "One should read others' scriptures with respect and reverence even to be enriched in one's own religious convictions."

8. What other advantages and disadvantages to using the Internet in religious studies occur to you, besides the ones given here?

SUGGESTIONS FOR FURTHER READING

L. J. Biallas, "Teaching World Religions through Their Scriptures." *Horizons* (Villanova University) 17 (1990): 76–91. Especially useful to teachers, but students can profit from it as well; centers on narrative forms.

H. Coward, *Sacred Word and Sacred Text: Scripture in World Religions.* Maryknoll, NY: Orbis, 1988. Sound chapter-length treatments (especially of orality) of scripture in Christianity, Islam, Hinduism, Sikhism, and Buddhism. See also Coward's more recent *Experiencing Scripture in World Religions* (Maryknoll, NY: Orbis, 2000).

F. M. Denny and R. L. Taylor, eds., *The Holy Book in Comparative Perspective.* Columbia, SC: University of South Carolina Press, 1985. After an introduction by the editors, this volume features up-to-date treatments of the scriptures of nine major religions, including the Church of Jesus Christ of Latter-day Saints.

W. A. Graham, "Scripture." In M. Eliade, ed., *The Encyclopedia of Religion,* vol. 13, pp. 133–145. New York: Macmillan, 1987. This lucid article is the best short survey of its topic.

P.-L. Kwok and E. Schüssler Fiorenza, eds., *Women's Sacred Scriptures.* London: SCM Press / Maryknoll, NY: Orbis, 1998. A treatment of the scriptures of several world religions with a view to a feminist reclaiming of scripture.

M. Levering, ed., *Rethinking Scripture: Essays from a Comparative Perspective.* Albany: State University of New York Press, 1989. Begins with two excellent essays by W. C. Smith, "The Study of Religion and the Study of the Bible," and "Scripture as Form and Concept: Their Emergence in the Western World." There are chapters on Buddhist scripture by Levering, on Hinduism by T. B. Coburn, on Jainism by K. W. Folkert, and on Judaism by B. A. Holdrege. W. A. Graham also has an essay, "Scripture as Spoken Word."

W. C. Smith, *What Is Scripture? A Comparative Approach.* Minneapolis: Fortress, 1993. A full survey of its topic by the most influential researcher on world scriptures.

S. Young, *An Anthology of Sacred Texts by and about Women.* New York: Crossroad, 1993. A comprehensive selection of scriptures and other important religious writings from Judaism, Christianity, Islam, Hinduism, Buddhism, Confucianism, Taoism, ancient European and Near Eastern religions, shamanism and tribal religions, and new religions of modern times.

⌢ INFOTRAC COLLEGE EDITION

You can locate InfoTrac College Edition articles about this chapter by accessing the InfoTrac College Edition website (http://www.infotrac.collegeedition.com/wadsworth/). Using subject guide, enter the search terms relevant to this chapter, and then read abstracts for relevant articles.

Reading Hindu Scripture
A Hindu woman in Banaras, India reads the *Bhagavad Gita* devotionally. Credit: Photo by
Diana Eck, from the Image Bank of the Center for the Study of World Religions, Harvard
University. Photo courtesy Diana Eck.

CHAPTER TWO

Hinduism

- After the monsoon season, people all over northern India gather outside their cities and villages to celebrate Rama-Lilas, a dramatic reading and reenactment of the *Ramayana,* the epic Hindu scripture. At its decisive point, wood and straw effigies of the demon Ravana are made and stuffed with fireworks. When night falls, the fireworks are set off and the demon is destroyed. Rama and the forces of good have prevailed.

- Just before dawn breaks in India, a householder rises and purifies himself with water. He then stirs back to life the embers of the sacred household fire while chanting sacred verses. Raising his arms to the rising sun, he recites a prayer to the sun god from the most ancient scripture, the *Rig-Veda.* This ritual, called the *Agnihotra,* has been performed continually in India for more than three thousand years.

- In Hardwar, India, people gather in what is billed as the "world's largest religious festival." In 1998, 10 million people have come to this site on the upper Ganges River. According to Hindu scriptures, bathing during this festival is the supreme act of worship. Much of the other activity on this site focuses on scripture: Holy men read scripture aloud, chant their mantras, and teach them to the pilgrims.

- At another popular pilgrimage site, people gather at a booth to hear a holy man recite the *Bhagavad-Gita.* Even though the *Gita* is familiar to them, they are still attracted to its telling. Of special interest is the end of the text, which promises them a blessing. The person who listens in true faith will win release from suffering and rebirth.

INTRODUCTION

Hinduism is one of the oldest of world religions, and certainly the most internally diverse. It encompasses many gods and features many paths to salvation. The scriptures of Hinduism mirror this diversity. Vast in size, varied in usage, and profound in influence, many scriptures have been chanted, heard, taught, and repeated for three thousand years. Generalizations about Hindu scriptures are thus especially difficult; almost every statement has exceptions. Still, the main lines of these scriptures can be reliably traced, and they provide good doors into the many-roomed mansion of Hinduism.

Overview of Structure

Hindus have not given any single comprehensive name to their scriptures. They divide its overall structure into two classes, *Shruti* [SHROO-tee] and *Smriti*

Table 2.1
Hindu Scriptures

	Name	*Translation/Content*	*Size*
Shruti	*Veda-samhitas:*		
	Rig-Veda	Hymn *Veda*	1,028 hymns in 10 books
	Yajur-Veda	Formula *Veda*	
	Sama-Veda	Song *Veda*	1,549 mantras
	Atharva-Veda	Spell *Veda*	731 hymns in twenty books
	Brahmanas	Brahmin Books	Correspond to each *Veda*
	Aranyakas	Forest Books	
	Upanishads	Sittings near a Teacher	123 total; 13 principal
Smriti	*Puranas*	Legends	18 books
	Mahabharata	Great Story of the Bharatas	18 books
	Ramayana	Story of Rama	50,000 lines in 7 books
	Manusmriti	Laws of Manu	12 books
	Vishnusmriti	Institutes of Vishnu	100 chapters
	Tantras	Weavings	Uncertain number of books

[SMRIH-tee] (see Table 2.1). **Shruti,** "what is heard," is the primary revelation. It has no human or divine author but captures the cosmic sounds of truth heard by the ancient seers or **rishis** [REE-shees]. The seers then began a process of oral transmission and practice through priestly families that has continued until today. *Shruti* consists of the four *Vedas* [VAY-duhs], the *Brahmanas* [BRAH-muh-nuhs], the *Aranyakas* [ah-RUN-yah-kuhs], and the *Upanishads* [oo-PAH-nee-shahds]. The canon of *Shruti* has been basically fixed for almost two thousand years, and all of Hinduism is in some sense based on it.

Smriti, "what is remembered," designates all other scripture. The role of *Smriti* is to bring out the meaning of *Shruti* and apply it to later ages. Hindus do not consider *Smriti* revelatory in itself but only as it is grounded in *Shruti*. The *Smriti* literature is vast in size and scope. It ranges from myths and legends of the *Puranas,* epics like the *Mahabharata* and the *Ramayana,* and law codes like the *Laws of Manu* and the *Institutes of Vishnu*. These scriptures have been widely translated from their original Sanskrit into the other languages of the Indian subcontinent, and the canon of *Smriti* is still open. Because of its more popular and ever-developing nature, *Smriti* scripture has had, despite its officially secondary status to *Shruti,* a strong influence on Hindu religion and Indian culture.

We turn now to a fuller treatment of the structure of Hindu scripture. Its development over time and its customary use, both very important in understanding Hindu scripture, will be dealt with more fully later in the chapter. But some mention of applications will be made in this section because an understanding of the meaning of Hindu scripture is impossible without it. We will follow the literature in the rough order of its chronological development.

In the Shruti category, the four **Vedas** (Books of Knowledge) are the foundation of Hindu scripture. They are gathered into **samhitas** [SAHM-hee-tuhs], "collections." The *Rig-*(Hymn) *Veda samhita* has 1,028 hymns divided into ten books. Each hymn is addressed to a single god or goddess. Indra, the sky god and king of gods, and Agni, the god of fire, are most prominent in the *Rig-Veda*. Soma, the god of the hallucinogenic drug from a plant (perhaps a mushroom) consumed during a main sacrifice, is also prominent. When a god is extolled in a hymn, the hymn praises that god above other deities, a form of worship called *henotheism*. For example, the *Rig-Veda* ascribes the creation of the world to almost all the individual gods. Readers of the *Rig-Veda* will note a fairly common sequence in each hymn: It begins with the invocation of a deity; it then makes requests of that deity and offers praises by recounting her or his deeds in myth; it finishes with a brief restatement of the worshippers' request.

The other *Vedas* follow up on the *Rig-Veda*. The *Yajur-Veda* is a collection of mostly prose sacrificial formulas (*yajus*) used by the presiding priest in a sacrifice. The *Sama-Veda* is a collection of songs and melodies (*saman*) used in sacrifice, with most of the words taken from the *Rig-Veda*. The *Rig-*, *Yajur-* and *Sama-Veda* are together known in Hinduism as the "threefold Veda." The *Atharva-Veda* differs remarkably from the others, containing mostly spells, curses, and charms in 731 hymns divided into twenty books. It reflects the everyday religious life of the common person, just as the threefold Veda reflects the religious life of the priestly group.

The next part of *Shruti* to emerge are the **Brahmanas**, (Brahmin Books) that are manuals for sacrifice. They describe ancient Vedic sacrifice in great and fascinating detail and are organized to correspond to the four *Veda samhitas*. They present sacrifice—and especially ritual utterance, the powerful sacrificial word correctly spoken—as the power that strengthens the gods, keeps the universe intact, and brings blessing to the sacrificer. The soma sacrifice is the most prominent. A development of the *Brahmanas* are the **Aranyakas** (Forest Books) containing philosophical speculations on sacrifice, especially the sacrificial fire. Reflections on the New Year festival are also prominent. These speculations were considered unsuitable for open knowledge and so were done in the privacy of the forest. Some *Aranyakas* have been incorporated into the *Upanishads*.

The **Upanishads** (Sittings near a Teacher) form the final part of *Shruti*. One hundred twenty-three *Upanishads* have survived, but only thirteen have been the most influential in Hindu history. The *Upanishads* are philosophical monologues on the nature of cosmic reality and sometimes feature debates between opposing teachers. Their emphasis is on self-denial as a way to find religious truth, the way of asceticism. The ritualism of the *Vedas* and especially the *Brahmanas* is downplayed and even attacked. The *Upanishads* are concerned to find the One, the absolute spiritual reality that lies in and behind all the visible elements and beings of this physical world. As the conclusion of *Shruti* and the Vedic scripture collection, they are also called the *Vedanta* (End of the *Veda*).

We begin describing the *Smriti* with the two main epics, the *Mahabharata* and the *Ramayana*. The *Ramayana*, or "Story of Rama," is traditionally attributed to the poet Valkimi. It was written in the third century B.C.E. Prince Rama was exiled from his kingdom and his wife Sita was kidnapped by the demon Ravana, but Rama was restored to his kingdom and his wife with the help of the monkey god. The *Maha-bharata* is "The Great [Story] of the Bharatas," an early Indian dynasty. The longest epic in the world, it is four times longer than the Christian *Bible*. Its basic story involves the feud and eventual war between two sides of King Bharata's family. The *Mahabharata* is a vast repository of Indian myths and legends, and the **Bhagavad-Gita** is a small part of this larger epic. Both the *Mahabharata* and the *Ramayana* share a common body of myth and folklore.

The *Puranas,* traditionally eighteen in number, are also concerned with myth, lore, and legend. Like the epics (and *Smriti* in general), they are addressed to the common person. Emerging about 400 to 1000 C.E., they stress devotion to a specific divinity as the way to release. Thus some speak of Shiva, some of Vishnu, and some of Shakti, the three main devotional movements of Hinduism. By far the most popular, and influential for medieval and early modern Indian popular literature and painting, is the *Bhagavata-Purana*. This tenth-century work provides background on the Krishna of the *Bhagavad-Gita,* especially his youth among the cowherders of his village and his romantic adventures with the cowherd women.

Tantras are "looms, weavings" that mirror the Hinduism of medieval India. They deal with beliefs, rituals, and yogic meditation in a popular way. Each of the three main devotional movements mentioned earlier have their own official collections of tantras. These tantras tell the exploits of their own gods and bring their powers to the devotee by ritual and yoga.

The final type of *Smriti* to be considered here is the manual of dharma, or law code. Law here is broadly conceived in its social and personal dimensions: it encompasses caste, life stages, diet, government, and other matters. The most important dharma manual is the *Laws of Manu,* composed around 200 C.E. in twelve books. The main concern of *Manu* is the codification and operation of the four-caste system, and its influence on Hindu life has been profound. Indeed, the two things that are most often said to define a practicing Hindu are acceptance of the *Veda* and following caste duty.

Origin and Development

The long history of Hindu scripture parallels to a large degree the history of the religion as a whole. We here will briefly survey how it began, the process of its growth, and how it took its present form. One general principle of Hindu scripture should be kept in mind as we begin this section: The literature grows by association. Earlier works, no matter how sacred, invite and attract later works with related themes and styles, which in turn attract still further sacred literature.

The four *Vedas* have their origin in ritual. Sacrifice itself seems to have come first, as even the earliest *Vedas* presuppose an established sacrifice. Then the songs, melodies, and formal directions for their performance were drawn up soon after the Aryan invasion of India. As mentioned, the *Rig-Veda* contains songs for sacrifice. It began about 2000 B.C.E. The oldest hymns deal with the gods of the Indo-Aryans: the sky god Dyaus Pitar, whom the Greeks knew as Zeus, and the earth goddess Prithivi Mater. In the next stage, these old gods receded and new gods arose: Indra the new sky god, Agni the god of fire, Soma the god of drugged sacrifice. The final hymns written down are found in the present *Rig-Veda* books 1 and 10, which move from polytheistic nature gods to the kind of cosmic speculations that search for the oneness of all being. The final form of the *Rig-Veda* was reached about 1200 B.C.E.

The *Sama-Veda* was composed after the *Rig-Veda* was complete. It has lines from the *Rig-Veda,* chanted to fixed melodies. The melodies are not captured in the written text but are passed on from singing priest to his disciples. The proper lyrics and music were essential to the success of the rite. The *Yajur-Veda* contains directions for sacrifice and also comes after the *Rig-Veda* was established. The *Atharva-Veda* with its magical spells gives a glimpse into the more popular levels of ancient Hinduism. They are not addressed to the great gods, but to the gods and spirits that control everyday life, its cycles and challenges. The first seven books are the earliest, whereas Books 8 through 12 are later and contain cosmological speculations similar to Book 10 of the *Rig-Veda* and the later *Upanishads.*

The four *Vedas* were orally composed and handed down orally for thousands of years. To put them in a book would have seemed absurd, even sacrilegious, because they were in essence a spoken and heard revelation (*Shruti*) and their power was in their spokenness. As a student, each young Brahmin is educated in one of the four *Vedas* and becomes an expert in the use of that *Veda* in sacrifice.

The *Brahmanas* mark the high point of Hindu ritualism. The power of the priesthood steadily grew in Vedic times (2000–1000 B.C.E.), and the focus of the *Brahmanas* is on sacrifice itself, not on the gods. Sacrifice is the power that generates the cosmos and keeps it going. The main group of the *Brahmanas* deals with the *Yajur-Veda* and the ritual process. Sacrifices using soma are prominent, as is the horse sacrifice, which took great expense and an entire year to enact. The *Aranyakas* mark the beginning of a departure from Vedic ritualism. Mixed and disjointed in content, these reflections may have been developed by marginalized Brahmins or members of the warrior caste.

The *Upanishads,* the last of the *Vedas,* are close in style to the *Aranyakas,* from which they are often generically indistinguishable. Most were written from the eighth to the fourth centuries B.C.E. The so-called "Principal" *Upanishads* number about thirteen and are the only *Upanishads* accepted by all Hindus. Some with special devotion to a particular deity date from the beginnings of the Common Era all the way to the sixteenth century C.E. and are accepted only by certain Hindu sects as interest in ritual fades and philosophy/renunciation advances. The oldest of these are the *Chandogya* and *Brihad-Aranyaka Upanishads.*

The *Upanishads,* like most *Shruti,* are not uniform or systematic, but diverse collections of philosophical materials from different teachers over the centuries. The "world-affirming" Vedic religion that originally sought salvation in this world has become a "world-negating" religion that seeks release from the world. These *Upanishads* present the way of knowledge, the search for the eternal One called **Brahman** [BRAH-muhn] as it relates to the eternal Self or **Atman** [AHT-muhn] at the hidden center of every human. They are the beginnings of Hindu philosophy, which has continued and been influential until today, although it has been an option for only a tiny minority of Hindus of any period.

Unlike the *Shruti,* the epics of *Smriti* have very little interest in ritual, and deal with broad religious and cultural topics. The *Mahabharata* was finished by 400 C.E., the *Ramayana* by 200 B.C.E. Both epics have many layers of development: (1) myths of the gods, coming from earliest Hinduism; (2) the central plot of the epic itself; (3) a large bloc of material on religious duty and law. The insertion of this last layer into the epic is typically Indian: to pause at key points in the narrative for a religious discussion. The most famous such insertion is the Bhagavad-Gita [BAH-gah-vahd GEE-tuh] in the *Mahabharata,* which today is reckoned a book in itself. These discussions are precursors of the law books, to which we now turn.

The law codes are called **Dharma-Shastras** [DAHR-muh SHAS-truhs], "Writings on Duty." In the schools in which the *Vedas* and *Brahmanas* were studied, books on duty began to be compiled. These developed into more comprehensive and systematic books that formed the basis of Hindu law. *Manu* was written perhaps about 200 C.E. as a full code for all Hindu society, for every caste, occupation, and stage of life. Like the law books of most religions and civilizations, *Manu* and the other law codes were developed by commentary as the centuries passed, and thus their influence was perpetuated. How deep this influence may have been is unknown, because *Manu* (again like most law codes) gives prescriptions for an ideal society. Real Hindu life no doubt fell short of this ideal.

The ancient stories of the *Puranas* number eighteen important ones. Their themes are creation, re-creation, origins of the gods and sages, eras of common history, and dynastic histories. Some, like the *Upanishads,* are sectarian, appealing to devotees of only one god. They fall into three main categories as they promote the gods Vishnu, Shiva, and others. The most important *Purana* is the *Bhagavata-Purana*, composed about 400–1000 C.E. This *Purana* is based on and furthers the book for which it is named, the *Bhagavad-Gita.*

Tantras, books of mystical teachings, spells, and directions for rituals, arose as a popular supplement to Vedic religion. While acknowledging the truth and authority of the *Vedas,* the tantras go beyond them to provide updated rituals. They perfect the use of specific techniques for the body and the mind. Tantrism is widespread in Hindu religion, but the devotional cult of the goddess Shakti has a special attachment to it. The Shaktic tantras occasionally feature "left-handed" tantrism, which most Westerners wrongly associate with tantrism as a whole: esoteric practices, magic, and sexual practices. The tantras were written in the period 500–1800 C.E.

Use

Hindu scriptures have a wide variety of uses, some of which have already been mentioned. In what follows, we will trace these uses briefly, with a special focus on orality.

The *Vedas* have been used for ritual by the Brahmin priests. The threefold *Veda* has always been the text of this religious aristocracy, never of the people as a whole. From the first, the *sound* of these scriptures was more important than their *content.* Traditionalist Hindus believe that the sounds of the *Veda* were the sounds that the sages heard reverberating from the creation of the universe and that they will be the same sounds used again at the next cycle of re-creation. These sounds were passed on orally from guru to student for thousands of years. Gurus taught their students every element of correct oral usage of the *Veda,* including correct enunciation, poetic meter, volume, pitch, and so on. Those Brahmins who excelled in *Veda* memorization and ritual enactment were known as **pandits.** The *Rig-Veda* itself often ends its hymns with a request to the deity that the sacrificers might "speak as men of power" during the rites. Hindus do not study the content of the *Vedas,* as for example in meditation or doctrinal instruction. Much of the ancient Vedic form of the Sanskrit language has been lost, and much of its meaning is not recoverable. During the last two thousand years, accordingly, Brahmins often do not understand what they are saying as the *Vedas* are chanted in the rituals. This is not important; only the correct sounds matter. Today only a few Brahmin families keep up a ritually correct form of the ancient Vedic sacrifices. However, all domestic rituals are done with Vedic formulas. By speaking and concentrating on the **mantra** [MAHN-truh], the believer taps into the cosmic power of creative speech.

The *Upanishads* became the texts of the philosophers, especially of the Vedanta school of Hindu philosophy. By reflecting on the meaning of this scripture in a life of strict renunciation, the sage will be set free from desire and rebirth. In the last hundred years a neo-Vedantic school has arisen, influenced by Western (especially Christian) religious ideas such as theism, ethics, and tolerance among religions. This school represents a break from traditional Vedanta.

Law codes are used for the ordering of society. They especially reflect the Brahmin caste and its view of Hindu life. How closely these books were followed and enforced in ancient times cannot now be determined, but their broadest aspects have certainly kept much authority. Of all Hindu scripture the epics have been the best known and most loved. The *Bhagavad-Gita,* because of the way it affirms and integrates many main aspects of Hinduism, has been acceptable and influential among most Hindus. For its promotion of one way as the best, however, it remains the special text of the Vishnu-Krishna devotional movement.

For most of Hindu history, the primacy of these works has been in their oral, not their written, form. For example, the *Veda-samhitas* were largely composed and collected probably before writing was known in India. The *Upanishads* were not fully written down until 1656 C.E., and then only at the command of the non-Hindu Sultan Dara Shakoh, a translation of these oral works into Persian. Since then, the *Upanishads* have been translated by Hindus into the other main Indian languages; the original Sanskrit was written down as well.

The Hindu tradition has even regarded writing itself as polluting compared with the sanctity of the spoken word. Now, however, orality is fading, and it is common to see even holy men reading aloud from books instead of "reading" from their memory. Still, the "sound" of the scriptures will continue to be important, as sound is their very essence.

Comparing a typical Hindu attitude toward scripture with Western attitudes, Daniel Gold remarks, "The idea of Vedic authority known to traditional Hindus is much more diffuse and abstract than the idea of a closed biblical canon known to the West. Christians, for example, variously interpret a revealed text to which most people have access and of which they can make some literal sense. For Hindus, by contrast, a reverence for scriptural authority can often mean simply that they think that what they do somehow comes from the Vedas, texts which in their antiquity are very rarely used or understood anymore. . . . They exist now primarily as words of power incorporated into newer rites."[1]

To sum up: Hindus' use of scripture depends on their class and occupation and on the particular type of Hinduism (philosophical, devotional, etc.) they follow. All Hindus have a strong, if vague, reverence for the threefold *Veda,* a feeling for the structure of society as reflected in the law codes, and, in devotional Hinduism, a strong feeling for the literature of one's single chosen god or goddess.

---

[1] D. Gold, "Organized Hinduisms," in M. E. Marty and R. S. Appleby, *Fundamentalisms Observed* (Chicago: University of Chicago Press, 1991), pp. 542–543.

TEACHING

Aditi and the Birth of the Gods*

This hymn presents several different and seemingly contradictory explanations of the creation of the world: It was spoken by the lord of sacred speech; it came from nonexistence; the mother goddess gave birth to it; it was formed from the mutual births of Aditi and Daksa; it was formed from Martanda. These and other various explanations still exist among Hindus today.[2]

Let us now speak with wonder of the births of the gods, so that someone may see them when the hymns are chanted in this later age. The lord of sacred speech, like a smith, fanned them together. In the earliest age of the gods, existence was born from nonexistence. In the first age of the gods, existence was born from nonexistence. After this the quarters of the sky were born from her who crouched with legs spread.

The earth was born from her who crouched with legs spread, and from the earth the quarters of the sky were born. From Aditi, Daksa was born, and from Daksa Aditi was born. [5] For Aditi was born as your daughter, O Daksa, and after her were born the blessed gods, the kinsmen of immortality. When you gods took your places there in the water with your hands joined,[3] a thick cloud of mist arose from you like dust from dancers. When you gods like magicians caused the worlds to swell, you drew forth the sun that was hidden in the ocean. Eight sons are there of Aditi, who were born of her body. With seven she went forth among the gods, but she threw Martanda, the sun, aside. With seven sons Aditi went forth into the earliest age. But she bore Martanda so that he would in turn beget offspring[4] and then soon die.

Rig-Veda 10.72

[2] All selections from the *Rig-Veda* are reprinted from *The Rig Veda, An Anthology,* by Wendy Doniger O'Flaherty (London: Penguin, 1981). Copyright 1981 by Wendy Doniger O'Flaherty. Used by permission.

---

[3] *hands joined:* the typical Indian posture of greeting and respect.

[4] *offspring:* humanity, which begets its offspring and dies.

Two Philosophical Views of Creation*

Many accounts of the origin of the universe are philosophical rather than mythological. Questioning and puzzling, they stir up the listener to reflection. In the first selection, "that one" is the impersonal creator by whom the gods themselves are created. This hymn has been most influential among Hindus. The second selection from an important Upanishad presents a philosophical reflection on the origin of the world. It traces creation to Brahman, *the world soul that is the All in and behind the world. The cosmic Person (*purusha*) identified with the world soul is neither male nor female, despite the references to the Person as "he."*[5]

There was neither nonexistence nor existence then; there was neither the realm of space nor the sky which is beyond. What stirred? Where? In whose protection? Was there water, bottomlessly deep? There was neither death nor immortality then. There was no distinguishing sign of night nor of day. That one breathed, windless, by its own impulse. Other than that there was nothing beyond. Darkness was hidden by darkness in the beginning; with no distinguishing sign, all this was water. The life force that was covered with emptiness, that one arose through the power of heat. Desire came upon that one in the beginning; that was the first seed of mind. Poets seeking in their heart with wisdom found the bond of existence in nonexistence. [5] Their cord[6] was extended across. Was there below? Was there above? There were seed-placers; there were powers. There was impulse beneath; there was giving-forth above. Who really knows? Who will here proclaim it? Where was it produced?

From where is this creation? The gods came afterwards, with the creation of this universe. Who then knows where it has arisen? Where this creation has arisen—perhaps it formed itself, or perhaps it did not—the one[7] who looks down on it, in the highest heaven, only he knows—or perhaps he does not know.

[*Brihad-Aranyaka* Upanishad 1.4.1–7] In the beginning this world was Soul alone, in the shape of a Person. He looked around and saw nothing but himself. He first said, "This is I." Therefore, he became I by name. Therefore even now, if a man is asked he first says, "This is I," and then pronounces his other name. Before [*purva*] all this he burnt down [*ush*] all evils; therefore he was a Person [*purusha*]. Truly he who knows this burns down everyone who tries to be before him.

He feared, and therefore anyone who is lonely fears. He thought, "As there is nothing but myself, why should I fear?" Then his fear passed away. For what should he have feared? But he felt no delight. Therefore a man who is lonely feels no delight. He longed for a second person. As he was as large as a man and woman together, he made his Self to fall in two, and there came husband and wife. Therefore Yajnavalkya said: "We two are thus like half a shell." Therefore the void that was there [in the male] is filled by the wife. He had sexual intercourse with her, and humans were born.

She thought, "How can he have sexual intercourse with me, after having produced me from himself? I shall hide myself." She then became a cow. But he became a bull and had sex with her, and therefore cows were born. Then she became a mare, and he a stallion; then he a male ass, and she a female ass. He had sex with her [in both forms], and therefore one-hoofed animals

---

Rig-Veda 10.129; *Brihad-Aranyaka Upanishad* 1.4.1–7)
[5]This and all other selections from the *Upanishads* are taken, with editing, from F. Max Müller, trans., *The Upanishads, Sacred Books of the East*, vols. 1 and 15 (Oxford: Oxford University Press, 1878, 1884).
[6]*cord:* the bond of existence, extending across the universe.

[7]*the one:* Prajapati, the high god.

were born. He became a she-goat, she a he-goat; he became a ewe, she a ram. He had sex with her, and therefore goats and sheep were born. In this way he created everything that exists in pairs, down to the ants. [5] He knew this: "I indeed am this creation, for I created all this." Therefore he became the creation, and he who knows this lives in this his creation.

Next he thus produced fire by rubbing. From the mouth, as from the fire-hole,[8] and from the hands he created fire. Therefore both the mouth and the hands are hairless inside, for the fire-hole is without hair inside.

People say, "Sacrifice to this god or that god." But each god is his manifestation, for he is all gods.

---

[8] *fire-hole:* Sanskrit *yoni,* the circular religious image of the human vagina symbolizing the female cosmic creative power.

Whatever is moist he created from semen; this is Soma. So this universe is really either food or eaters of food. Soma is food, Agni the eater. This is the highest creation of Brahman, when he created the gods from his better part, and when he who was then mortal created the immortals. Therefore it was the highest creation. He who knows this lives in this highest creation. . . .

He cannot be seen, for when breathing he is called breath. When speaking, he is called speech; when seeing, eye; when hearing, ear; when thinking, mind. All these are only the names of his acts. He who worships him as the one or the other, does not know him. . . . Let men worship him as Soul [Atman], for in the Soul all these are one. This Soul is the footprint of everything, for through it one knows everything. As one can find again by footprints what was lost, he who knows this finds glory and praise.

The God Indra*

Indra is the sky god, the king of the gods. This hymn extols Indra's accomplishments over several opposing gods and for promoting the welfare of the people. It seeks to defend the importance of Indra against those who ignore him or even deny his existence (verse 5). This defense evidently did not succeed, because in post-Vedic Hinduism Indra has largely disappeared.

The god who had insight the moment he was born, the first who protected the gods with his power of thought, before whose hot breath the two world-halves tremble at the greatness of his manly powers—he, my people, is Indra. He who made fast the tottering earth, who made still the quaking mountains, who measured out and extended the expanse of the air, who

propped up the sky—he, my people, is Indra. He who killed the serpent and loosed the seven rivers, who drove out the cows that had been pent up by Vala,[9] who gave birth to fire between two stones, the winner of booty in combats—he, my people, is Indra. He by whom all these changes were rung, who drove the race of Dasas[10] down into obscurity, who took away the flourishing wealth of the enemy as a winning gambler takes the stake—he, my people, is Indra. [5] He about whom they ask, "Where is he?," or they say of him, the terrible one, "He does not exist," he who diminishes the flourishing wealth of the enemy as gambling does—believe in him! He, my people, is Indra. He who

---

[9] *Vala:* Indra's demonic enemy, who penned up the cows.
[10] *Dasas:* literally, "slaves," enemies of the Aryans whom they subjugated; called in verse 10 "Dasyus."

---

*Rig-Veda 2.12

encourages the weary and the sick, and the poor priest who is in need, who helps the man who harnesses the stones to press Soma, he who has lips fine for drinking—he, my people, is Indra.

He under whose command are horses and cows and villages and all chariots, who gave birth to the sun and the dawn and led out the waters, he, my people, is Indra. He who is invoked by both of two armies, enemies locked in combat, on this side and that side, he who is even invoked separately by each of two men standing on the very same chariot, he, my people, is Indra. He without whom people do not conquer, he whom they call on for help when they are fighting, who became the image of everything, who shakes the unshakable—he, my people, is Indra. [10] He who killed with his weapon all those who had committed a great sin, even when they did not know it, he who does not pardon the arrogant man for his arrogance, who is the slayer of the Dasyus, he, my people, is Indra. He who in the fortieth autumn discovered Sambara living in the mountains,

who killed the violent serpent, the Danu, as he lay there, he, my people, is Indra. He, the mighty bull who with his seven reins let loose the seven rivers to flow, who with his thunderbolt in his hand hurled down Rauhina as he was climbing up to the sky, he, my people, is Indra. Even the sky and the earth bow low before him, and the mountains are terrified of his hot breath. He who is known as the Soma-drinker, with the thunderbolt in his hand, with the thunderbolt in his palm, he, my people, is Indra. He who helps with his favor the one who presses and the one who cooks,[11] the praiser and the preparer, he for whom prayer is nourishment, for whom Soma is the special gift, he, my people, is Indra. [15] You who furiously grasp the prize for the one who presses and the one who cooks, you are truly real. Let us be dear to you, Indra, all our days, and let us speak as men of power in the sacrificial gathering.

---

[11] *presses . . . cooks:* in preparation of the soma.

The God Shiva*

Although one of the main branches of devotional Hinduism is Shaivism, Shiva does not have a text to celebrate him as Krishna does in the Bhagavad-Gita. *This late Upanishadic hymn identifies the Vedic god Rudra and the Cosmic Person with Shiva. It is used today by the worshippers of Shiva to express his praise. This hymn shows how the worship of one god characteristic of devotional Hinduism is related to the wider Hindu traditions with many gods.*

The snarer rules alone by his powers, rules all the worlds by his powers. He is the same, while things arise and exist. They who know this are immortal. There is only one Rudra. They do not

allow a second; he rules all the worlds by his powers. He stands behind all persons. Having created all worlds, he, the protector, rolls it up at the end of time. This god has his eyes, his face, his arms, and his feet in every place. When producing heaven and earth, he forges them together with his arms and his wings. He is the creator and supporter of the gods. Rudra is the great seer, the lord of all, who formerly gave birth to Hiranyagarbha. May he endow us with good thoughts.

[5] O Rudra, dweller in the mountains, look upon us with your most blessed form that is auspicious, not terrible, and reveals no evil! O lord of the mountains, make lucky that arrow that you hold in your hand to shoot. Do not hurt man or beast!

Beyond this is the High Brahman, the vast, hidden in the bodies of all creatures. He alone

---

* Shvetashvatara Upanishad 3.1–13

envelops everything, as the Lord. Those who know this become immortal. I know that great Person [*purusha*] of sunlike luster beyond the darkness. A man who truly knows him passes over death; there is no other path to go.

This whole universe is filled by this Person, to whom there is nothing superior, from whom there is nothing different, than whom there is nothing smaller or larger. This Person stands alone, fixed like a tree in the sky. [10] That which is beyond this world is without form and without suffering. They who know this become immortal, but others suffer pain.

The Blessed One exists in the faces, the heads, the necks of all. He dwells in the cave of the heart of all beings. He is all-pervading, and therefore he is the omnipresent Shiva. That Person is the great lord. He is the mover of existence. He possesses the purest power reaching everything. He is light; he is undecaying. The Person, not larger than a thumb, always dwelling in the heart of man, is perceived by the heart, the thought, and the mind. Those who know this become immortal.

"That You Are"*

In this reading, the Oneness that exists in and beyond the world is developed in a dialogue between a son and his father. Popularly known as "The Education of Svetaketu," this story points to the cosmic Self as the inner essence of all that is.

Om.[12] There lived once Svetaketu Aruneya, the grandson of Aruna. To him his father, Uddalaka, the son of Aruna, said: "Svetaketu, go to school. For there is none belonging to our race, who, not having studied the Veda, is, so to speak, a Brahmana by birth only."

Having begun his apprenticeship with a teacher when he was twelve years of age, Svetaketu returned to his father when he was twenty-four, having then studied all the Vedas. But he was conceited, considering himself well read and stern.

His father said to him: "Svetaketu, as you are so conceited, considering yourself so well read, and so stern, my dear, have you ever asked for that instruction by which we hear what cannot be heard? Have you asked for that by which we perceive what cannot be perceived, by which we know what cannot be known?"

"What is that instruction, sir?" he asked.

The father replied: "My dear, as by one clod of clay all that is made of clay is known, the difference being only a name, arising from speech, but the truth being that all is clay. As, my dear, by one nugget of gold all that is made of gold is known, the difference being only a name, arising from speech, but the truth being that all is gold. As, my dear, by one pair of nail scissors all that is made of iron is known, the difference being only a name, arising from speech, but the truth being that all is iron—thus, my dear, is that instruction."

The son said: "Surely those venerable men, my teachers, did not know that. For if they had known it, why should they not have told it me? Sir, tell me that." "Be it so," said the father.

"In the beginning, my dear, there was that only which is, one thing only, without a second. It thought, May I be many, may I grow forth. It sent forth fire. That fire thought, May I be many, may I grow forth. It sent forth water. Therefore whenever anybody anywhere is hot and perspires, water is produced on him from fire alone.

"Water thought, may I be many, may I grow forth. It sent forth earth (food). Therefore whenever it rains anywhere, most food is then

---

*Chandogya Upanishad 6.1–2, 9–11

[12] *Om:* a lesson is often begun with this cosmic sound.

produced. From water alone is eatable food produced. . . .

[9] "As the bees, my son, make honey by collecting the juices of distant trees, and reduce the juice into one form, and as these juices have no discrimination, so that they might say, I am the juice of this tree or that, in the same manner, my son, all these creatures, when they have become merged in the True (either in deep sleep or in death), know not that they are merged in the True. Whatever these creatures are here, whether a lion, or a wolf, or a boar, or a worm, or a midge, or a gnat, or a mosquito, that they become again and again. Now that which is that subtle essence, in it all that exists has its self. It is the True. It is the Self, and that, Svetaketu, you are."

"Please, Sir, inform me still more," said the son.

"Be it so, my child," the father replied.

"These rivers, my son, run, the eastern like the Ganges, toward the east, the western like the Sindhu, toward the west. They go from sea to sea, that is, the clouds lift up the water from the sea to the sky, and send it back as rain to the sea. They become indeed sea. And as those rivers, when they are in the sea, do not know, I am this or that river, in the same manner, my son, all these creatures, when they have come back from the True, know not that they have come back from the True. Whatever these creatures are here, whether a lion, or a wolf, or a boar, or a worm, or a midge, or a gnat, or a mosquito, that they become again and again.

"That which is that subtle essence, in it all that exists has its self. It is the True. It is the Self, and that, Svetaketu, you are."

"Please, Sir, inform me still more," said the son.

"Be it so, my child," the father replied.

"If someone were to strike at the root of this large tree here, it would bleed, but live. If he were to strike at its stem, it would bleed, but live. If he were to strike at its top, it would bleed, but live. Pervaded by the living Self that tree stands firm, drinking in its nourishment and rejoicing; but if the life (the living Self) leaves one of its branches, that branch withers; if it leaves a second, that branch withers; if it leaves a third, that branch withers. If it leaves the whole tree, the whole tree withers.

"In exactly the same manner, my son, know this. This body indeed withers and dies when the living Self has left it; the living Self dies not.

"That subtle essence is the self of all that exists. It is the True. It is the Self, and that, Svetaketu, you are."

ORGANIZATION

The Creation of the Caste System*

*One of the many creation hymns of the Rig, this poem presents the cosmic Man (Sanskrit Purusha) as the one through whose sacrifice the gods fashioned the universe. The making of humanity is presented in terms of the caste system, its first appearance in Hindu literature and the foundation of its later authority. Much of the caste system is undergoing a liberalizing change in modern India, especially in the cities. But it is still impor-*tant and pervasive as a general social structure and cultural inheritance.*

The Man has a thousand heads, a thousand eyes, a thousand feet. He pervaded the earth on all sides and extended beyond it as far as ten fingers. It is the Man who is all this, whatever has been and whatever is to be. He is the ruler of immortality, when he grows beyond everything through food. This is his greatness, and the Man is yet more than this. All creatures are a

---

*Rig-Veda 10.90

quarter of him; three quarters are what is immortal in heaven. With three quarters the Man rose upwards, and one quarter of him remains here.

From this he spread out in all directions, into that which eats and that which does not eat. [5] From him Viraj[13] was born, and from Viraj came the Man. When he was born, he ranged beyond the earth behind and before. When the gods spread the sacrifice with the Man as the offering, spring was the clarified butter, summer was the fuel, autumn was the oblation.[14] They anointed the Man, the sacrifice born at the beginning, upon the sacred grass. With him the gods, Sadhyas,[15] and sages sacrificed. From that sacrifice in which everything was offered, the melted fat was collected. He made it into those beasts who live in the air, in the forest, and in villages. From that sacrifice in which everything was offered, the verses and chants were born, the meters were born from it, and from it the

formulas were born.[16] [10] Horses were born from it, and those other animals that have two rows of teeth; cows were born from it, and from it goats and sheep were born.

When they divided the Man, into how many parts did they apportion him? What do they call his mouth, his two arms and thighs and feet? His mouth became the Brahmin; his arms were made into the Warrior, his thighs the People, and from his feet the Servants were born. The moon was born from his mind; from his eye the sun was born. Indra and Agni came from his mouth, and from his vital breath the Wind was born. From his navel the middle realm of space arose; from his head the sky evolved. From his two feet came the earth, and the quarters of the sky from his ear. Thus they set the worlds in order. [15] There were seven enclosing-sticks for him, and thrice seven fuel-sticks, when the gods, spreading the sacrifice, bound the Man as the sacrificial beast. With the sacrifice the gods sacrificed to the sacrifice. These were the first ritual laws. These very powers reached the dome of the sky where dwell the Sadhyas, the ancient gods.

---

[13] *Viraj:* the female counterpart of the man.
[14] *oblation:* what is sacrificed.
[15] *Sadhyas:* saints, called in the last verse of this hymn "the ancient gods."

[16] *verses, chants, meters, formulas:* the *Vedas.*

The Four Castes*

This passage contains a short description of the main structure of the caste system. The duties and means of livelihood of each caste are indicated. The end of this passage gives the moral duties binding on everyone of whatever caste, gender, or stage of life. These general rules are growing more important in contemporary Hinduism as the caste system fades.[17]

Brahmins, Kshatriyas, Vaishyas, and Shudras are the four castes. The first three of these are called twice-born. They must perform with mantras[18] the whole number of ceremonies, which begin with impregnation and end with the ceremony of burning the dead body. Their duties are as follows. [5] A Brahmin teaches the Veda. A Kshatriya has constant practice in arms. A Vaishya tends cattle. A Shudra serves the twice-born. All the twice-born are to sacrifice and

---

* *Institutes of Vishnu* 2–1.17
[17] Taken, with editing, from Julius Jolly, trans., *The Institutes of Vishnu, Sacred Books of the East,* vol. 7 (Oxford: Oxford University Press, 1880).

[18] *mantras:* sacred words or syllables chanted to create and acquire cosmic spiritual power.

study the Veda. [10] Their modes of livelihood are as follows. A Brahmin sacrifices for others and receives alms. A Kshatriya protects the world. A Vaishya engages in farming, keeps cows, trades, lends money at interest, and grows seeds. A Shudra engages in all branches of crafts. In times of distress, each caste may follow the occupation of that below it in rank. Duties common to all castes are patience, truthfulness, restraint, purity, liberality, self-control, not to kill, obedience toward one's gurus, visiting places of pilgrimage, sympathy, straightforwardness, freedom from covetousness, reverence toward gods and Brahmins,[19] and freedom from anger.

---

[19] *reverence towards . . . Brahmins:* as sacrificers, the Brahmins preserve the order of the universe, and other castes are to honor them. India has seen an almost continuous struggle between the priestly caste and the warrior-ruler caste.

ETHICS

Sin and Forgiveness*

The god Varuna protects the cosmic order and punishes those humans who violate it by misdeeds. This passage presents the heartfelt pleas of the worshipper to Varuna to reveal his unknown sin to him and pardon it.

The generations have become wise by the power of him who has propped apart the two world-halves even though they are so vast. He has pushed away the dome of the sky to make it high and wide; he has set the sun on its double journey and spread out the earth. I ask my own heart, "When shall I be close to Varuna? Will he enjoy my offering and not be provoked to anger? When shall I see his mercy and rejoice?" I ask myself what that transgression was, Varuna, for I wish to understand. I turn to the wise to ask them. The poets have told me the very same thing: "Varuna has been provoked to anger against you."

O Varuna, what was the terrible crime for which you wish to destroy your friend who praises you? Proclaim it to me so that I may has-ten to prostrate myself before you and be free from sin, for you are hard to deceive and are ruled by yourself alone. [5] Free us from the harmful deeds of our fathers, and from those that we have committed with our own bodies. O king, free Vasistha[20] like a thief who has stolen cattle, like a calf set free from a rope. The mischief was not done by my own free will, Varuna; wine, anger, dice, or carelessness led me astray. The older shares in the mistake of the younger. Even sleep does not avert evil. As a slave serves a generous master, so would I serve the furious god and be free from sin. The noble god[21] gave understanding to those who did not understand; being yet wiser, he speeds the clever man to wealth. O Varuna, you who are ruled by yourself alone, let this praise lodge in your very heart. Let it go well for us always with your blessings.

---

* *Rig-Veda 7.86*

[20] *Vasistha:* a wise man who, according to myth, broke into Varuna's house; he was tied up but then freed when he praised Varuna.

[21] *the noble god:* Varuna

The Way of Asceticism*

This reading presents all the ancient practices of Hinduism as necessary. But they are "unsafe boats," and those who trust in them to accomplish release are "fools" and "ignorant." The only effective way of release is the way of knowledge based on renunciation and asceticism. This belief has been a guiding principle for ascetics and holy men from Upanishadic times until today.

This is the truth: the sacrificial works that the poets saw in the hymns [of the Veda] have been performed in many ways in the Vedic age. Practice them diligently, you lovers of truth! This is your path that leads to the world of good works!

When the fire is lighted and the flame flickers, let a man offer his oblations between the two portions of melted butter, as an offering with faith. A man's Agnihotra sacrifice destroys his seven worlds if it is not followed by the new-moon and full-moon sacrifices, by the four-months' sacrifices, and by the harvest sacrifice. It destroys his seven worlds if it is unattended by guests, not offered at all, done without the ceremony to all the gods, or not offered according to the rules. . . .

[5] If a man performs his sacred works when these flames are shining, and the sacrificial offerings follow at the right time, they lead him as sunrays to where the one Lord of the gods dwells. "Come here, come here!", the brilliant offerings say to him. They carry the sacrificer on the rays of the sun, while they utter pleasant speech and praise him: "This is your holy Brahma-world, gained by your good works."

But those boats, the eighteen sacrifices,[22] are truly frail. Fools who praise this as the highest good are subjected again and again to old age and death. Fools dwelling in darkness, wise in their own conceit and puffed up with vain knowledge, go round and round staggering back and forth, like blind men led by the blind. . . . [10] Considering sacrifice and good works as the best, these fools know no higher good. Having enjoyed their reward in the height of heaven, gained by good works, they come back again to this world or a lower one. But those who practice penance and faith in the forest, who are tranquil, wise and live on alms, depart free from passion through the sun to where that immortal Person dwells, whose nature is imperishable.

Let a Brahmin, after he has examined all these worlds that are gained by works, acquire freedom from all desires. Nothing that is eternal can be gained by what is not eternal. To understand this, let him take fuel in his hand[23] and approach a Guru who is learned and dwells entirely in Brahman. The wise teacher truly tells that knowledge of Brahman through which he knows the eternal and true Person. He tells a pupil who has approached him respectfully, whose thoughts are not troubled by any desires and who has obtained perfect peace.

---

*Mundaka Upanishad 2.1–3, 5–8, 10–13

[22]*eighteen sacrifices:* Vedic rituals.
[23]*fuel in hand:* a sign of studentship.

Stages of Life for a Twice-Born Man**

The first stage of Hindu life is that of the student, who lives and studies with his guru (private teacher). The first passage gives the rules for the student's relationship with his teacher, especially

the respect owed to one's teacher. The second stage is that of the householder, when the young man, his studies complete, must marry and father children. Here the rules for whom to marry are presented. The third stage is that of retirement into the forest, and Manu relates the style of life and religious aims of this stage. The fourth stage presented is

---

**Laws of Manu 2.69–74, 191–201; 3.1–19; 6.1–9, 33–49

that of the ascetic who renounces all typical life to find release from rebirth. These laws on the stages of life reflect the situation of about 200 C.E., when Manu was written. Some differ from present practice, notably that asceticism no longer requires a prior retirement stage but can be entered by an adult male at any time. The system presented here is idealized—only a minority of Hindus in the past and present has carried them out fully. Nonetheless, they continue to be influential.[24]

[2.69, The Stage of Studentship] Having performed the rite of initiation,[25] the teacher must first instruct the pupil in the rules of personal purification, conduct, fire-worship, and twilight devotions. [70] A student who is about to begin the study of the Veda shall receive instruction after he has sipped water according to the sacred law, has made the *Brahmangali*,[26] has put on clean clothing, and has brought his sexual organs under due control. At the beginning and at the end of a lesson in the Veda he must always clasp both the feet of his teacher. He must study by joining hands; that is called the Brahmangali [joining the palms for the sake of the Veda]. With crossed hands he must clasp the feet of the teacher, and touch the left foot with his left hand, the right foot with his right hand. The teacher, always unwearied, must say to him who is about to begin studying, "Recite!" He shall stop when the teacher says: "Let a stoppage take place!" Let him always pronounce the syllable "Om" at the beginning and at the end of a lesson in the Veda. Unless the syllable "Om" precedes, the lesson will slip away from him, and unless it follows it will fade away. . . .

[191] Both when ordered by his teacher, and without a command, a student shall always exert himself in studying [the Veda], and in doing what is serviceable to his teacher. Controlling his body, his speech, his organs of sense, and his mind, let him stand with joined hands, looking at the face of his teacher. Let him always keep his right arm uncovered, behave decently, and keep the rest of his body well covered. When he is addressed with the words, "Be seated," he shall sit down, facing his teacher. In the presence of his teacher let him always eat less [than the teacher], and wear less valuable clothing and ornaments. Let him rise earlier and go to bed later. [195] Let him not answer or talk with his teacher while reclining on a bed, or while sitting, or eating, or standing, or with an averted face. Let him talk standing up, if his teacher is seated, advancing toward him when he stands, going to meet him if he advances, and running after him when he runs. . . . When his teacher is near, let his bed or seat be low; but within sight of his teacher he shall not sit carelessly at ease. Let him not pronounce the name of his teacher without adding an honorific title, even when talking about him behind his back. Let him not mimic his gait, speech, or conduct. [200] Wherever people justly criticize or falsely defame his teacher, he must cover his ears or depart to another place. By criticizing his teacher, even though justly, he will become in his next birth an ass. By falsely defaming him, he will become a dog. He who lives on his teacher's belongings will become a worm, and he who is envious of his merit will become a larger insect.

[3.1, The Stage of the Householder] The vow of studying the three Vedas under a teacher must be kept for thirty-six years, or for half that time, or for a quarter, or until the student has perfectly learned them. A student who has studied in due order the three Vedas, or two, or even only one, without breaking the rules of studentship, shall enter the order of householders. He who is famous for the strict performance of his duties and has received his heritage, the Veda, from his father, shall be honored. He will sit on a couch and be adorned with a garland, with the present of a cow and honey-mixture.

With the permission of his teacher, having bathed and performed according to the rule the

---

[24]Selections from *Manu* are taken, with editing, from G. Buhler, trans., *The Laws of Manu, Sacred Books of the East,* vol. 25 (Oxford: Oxford University Press, 1886).

[25]*rite of initiation:* the acceptance of a male into full membership in the Hindu community.

[26]*Brahmangali:* the traditional Indian gesture of greeting and respect, explained more fully in the next verse.

ritual for returning home, a twice-born man shall marry a wife of equal caste who is endowed with auspicious bodily marks. [5] A young woman who is neither a Sapinda[27] on the mother's side nor belongs to the same family on the father's side is recommended to twice-born men for marriage and conjugal union. In connecting himself with a wife, let him carefully avoid the ten following types of families, even if they are great, or rich in cattle, horses, sheep, grain, or other property. He must avoid a family that neglects the sacred rites, one in which no male children are born, one in which the Veda is not studied, one that has thick hair on the body, those that are subject to hemorrhoids, tuberculosis, weakness of digestion, epilepsy, or white and black leprosy. Let him not marry a young woman with reddish hair, nor one who has a redundant body part, nor one who is sickly, nor one either with no hair on the body or too much hair. Let him not marry one who is too talkative or has red eyes. Let him not marry one named after a constellation, a tree, or a river, nor one bearing the name of a low caste, or of a mountain, nor one named after a bird, a snake, or a slave, nor one whose name inspires terror. [10] Let him wed a female free from bodily defects and who has an agreeable name. She must have the graceful gait of a swan or of an elephant, moderate hair on the body and on the head, small teeth, and soft limbs.

For the first marriage of twice-born men, wives of equal caste are recommended. But for those who because of desire marry another woman, the following females are approved. They are chosen according to the order of the castes. It is declared that a Shudra woman alone can be the wife of a Shudra, she and one of his own caste the wives of a Vaisya, those two and one of his own caste the wives of a Kshatriya, those three and one of his own caste the wives of a Brahmin. A Shudra woman is not mentioned even in any ancient story as the first wife of a Brahmin or of a Kshatriya, though they lived in the greatest distress. [15] Twice-born men who foolishly marry wives of the low caste soon degrade their families and their children to the state of Shudras. According to Atri and to Gautama the son of Utathya,[28] he who weds a Shudra woman becomes an outcast. According to Saunaka, he becomes an outcaste on the birth of a son, and according to Bhrigu when he has a male child from a Shudra female. A Brahmin who takes a Shudra wife to his bed will sink into hell. If he begets a child by her, he will lose the rank of a Brahmin. The spirits of deceased ancestors and the gods will not eat the offerings of a man who performs the rites in honor of the gods, of the manes, and of guests with a Shudra wife's assistance. Such a man will not go to heaven. For him who drinks the moisture of a Shudra's lips, who is tainted by her breath, and who begets a son on her, no way of forgiveness is prescribed.

[6.1, The Stage of Retirement] A twice-born Snataka,[29] who has lived according to the law of householders, taking a firm resolution and keeping his organs in subjection, may dwell in the forest. He must duly observe the rules given below. When a householder sees his skin wrinkled, and his hair white, and the sons of his sons, then he may depart to the forest. Abandoning all food raised by cultivation, and all his belongings, he may depart into the forest. He may either commit his wife to his sons or be accompanied by her.[30] Taking with him the sacred fire and the implements required for domestic sacrifices, he may go forth from the village into the forest and reside there, controlling his senses. [5] Let him offer those five great sacrifices according to the rule, with various kinds of pure

---

[27] *Sapinda:* a close relative; literally, a sharer in the funeral feast, an obligation usually considered to go back six generations.

[28] *Gautama:* not Gautama Buddha.

[29] *Snataka:* a Brahmin who has completed his studentship.

[30] *accompanied by her:* Note in the next passage that if the husband chooses the way of ascetic renunciation, the wife cannot accompany him. She is in a difficult situation: her husband, having renounced his old life, no longer belongs to her, but she still belongs to him.

food fit for ascetics, or with herbs, roots, and fruit. Let him wear a skin or a tattered garment; let him bathe in the evening or in the morning. Let him always wear his hair in braids, with the hair on his body, his beard, and his nails uncut. Let him perform the Bali-offering with the kind of food he eats, and give alms according to his ability. Let him honor those who come to his hermitage to give him alms of water, roots, and fruit. Let him always be industrious in privately reciting the Veda. Let him be patient in hardships, friendly toward all, collected in mind, always liberal and never a receiver of gifts, and compassionate toward all living creatures. Let him offer, according to the law, the Agnihotra with three sacred fires, and never omit the new-moon and full-moon sacrifices at the proper time. . . .

[6.33, The Stage of Asceticism] Having passed the third part of his natural term of life in the forest, a man may live as an ascetic during the fourth part of his existence. First he must abandon all attachment to worldly objects. He who . . . offers sacrifices and subdues his senses, busies himself with giving alms and offerings of food, and becomes an ascetic gains bliss after death. [35] When he has paid the three debts,[31] let him apply his mind to the attainment of final liberation. He who seeks it without having paid his debts sinks downwards. Having studied the Vedas according to the rule, having fathered sons according to the sacred law, and having offered sacrifices according to his ability, he may direct his mind to the attainment of final liberation. A twice-born man who seeks final liberation sinks downward if he has not studied the Vedas, fathered sons, and offered sacrifices. Having performed the Ishti, sacred to the Lord of creatures, in which he gives all his property as the sacrificial fee, having reposited the sacred fires in himself, a Brahmin may depart from his house as an ascetic. Worlds, radiant in brilliancy, become his who recites the texts regarding

Brahman and departs from his house as an ascetic, after giving a promise of safety to all created beings.[32] [40] For that twice-born man who causes not even the smallest danger to created beings, there will be no danger from anything after he is freed from his body.

Departing from his house fully provided with the means of purification, let him wander about absolutely silent. He must care nothing for enjoyments that may be offered to him. Let him always wander about alone to attain final liberation. The solitary man, who neither forsakes nor is forsaken, gains his desired result. He shall neither possess a fire nor a dwelling. He may go to a village for his food. He shall be indifferent to everything, firm of purpose, meditating and concentrating his mind on Brahman. The marks of one who has attained liberation are a broken pot instead of an alms-bowl, the roots of trees for a dwelling, coarse wornout garments, life in solitude and indifference toward everything. [45] Let him not desire to die, let him not desire to live. Let him wait for his appointed time as a servant waits for the payment of his wages. Let him put down his foot purified by his sight,[33] let him drink water purified by straining with a cloth, let him utter speech purified by truth, let him keep his heart pure. Let him patiently bear hard words, let him not insult anybody. Let him not become anybody's enemy for the sake of this perishable body. Against an angry man let him not show anger, let him bless when he is cursed, and let him not utter false speech. . . . He shall delight in matters of the Soul, sit in the postures prescribed by the Yoga, be independent of external help, entirely abstain from sensual enjoyments, and have himself for his only companion. He shall live in this world, but desire only the bliss of final liberation.

---

[31]*the three debts:* the three obligations discussed in the next verses: study, having sons, sacrifice. These are similar to the modern Hindu expression "the three debts": to the gods, to the guru, to be a father.

[32]*safety to all created beings:* the vow of *ahimsa*, nonviolence to all creatures.

[33]*put down his foot purified by his sight:* i.e., in a place on the ground with no visible living beings on it; so too he must *drink water purified* of living creatures. This requirement, which follows up on the ascetic's "promise of safety to all created beings" (verse 39), will become more important in Jainism.

The Life of Women*

The first passage is often quoted as an example of a positive Hindu attitude to women. It gives some indication of the respected place of Hindu women in the home (in the context of a strongly patriarchal society, of course). Much of this passage has as its background the participation of the wife in all the sacred rites of the home. The second passage contains rules for the whole life of women, emphasizing respect and obedience to husbands during their life. After her husband's death, she must not remarry and must live an ascetic life.

[3.55] Women must be honored and adorned by their fathers, brothers, husbands, and brothers-in-law, who desire their own welfare. Where women are honored, there the gods are pleased. Where they are not honored, no sacred rite yields rewards. Where the female relations live in grief, the family soon perishes completely. But the family where they are not unhappy always prospers. Female relations pronounce a curse on houses where they are not honored; these houses perish completely, as if destroyed by magic. Men who seek their own welfare should always honor women on holidays and festivals with gifts of jewelry, clothes, and dainty food. [60] In a family where the husband is pleased with his wife and the wife with her husband, happiness will certainly be lasting.

[5.147] Nothing must be done independently by a girl, by a young woman, or by an old woman, even in her own house. In childhood a female must be subject to her father, in youth to her husband, and when her husband is dead to her sons. A woman must never be independent. She must not seek to separate herself from her father, husband, or sons. By leaving them she would make both her own and her husband's families contemptible.

[150] She must always be cheerful, clever in household affairs, careful in cleaning her utensils, and economical in expenditure. She shall obey the man to whom her father may give her . . . as long as he lives. When he is dead, she must not insult his memory. For the sake of getting good fortune for brides, the recitation of benedictory texts and the sacrifice to the Lord of creatures are used at weddings; but the betrothal by the father or guardian is the cause of the husband's dominion over his wife. The husband who wedded her with sacred texts always gives happiness to his wife, both in season and out of season, in this world and in the next. Although he may be destitute of virtue, or seek pleasure elsewhere, or lacking good qualities, yet a husband must be constantly worshipped as a god by a faithful wife. [155] No sacrifice, no vow, no fast must be performed by women apart from their husbands. If a wife obeys her husband, she will for that reason alone be exalted in heaven.[34]

A faithful wife who desires to dwell after death with her husband must never do anything that might displease him, whether he is alive or dead. She may emaciate her body by living on pure flowers, roots, and fruit; but she must never even mention the name of another man after her husband has died. Until death let her be patient in hardships, self-controlled, and chaste. Let her strive to fulfil that most excellent duty that is prescribed for wives who have one husband only. Many thousands of Brahmins who were chaste from their youth have gone to heaven without continuing their race. [160] A virtuous wife who after the death of her husband constantly remains chaste reaches heaven although she has no son, just like those chaste men. But a woman who desires to have offspring violates her duty toward her [deceased] husband. She brings disgrace on herself in this world, and loses her place with her husband in heaven. Offspring begotten by another man is not considered lawful, offspring begotten on another man's wife does not belong to the

---

* *Laws of Manu* 3.55–60; 5.147–165

[34]*heaven:* as elsewhere in Hinduism, usually a temporary reward before reincarnation.

begetter, nor is a second husband anywhere allowed for virtuous women.[35] She who lives with a man of higher caste, forsaking her own husband who belongs to a lower one, will become contemptible in this world, and is called

a remarried woman. By violating her duty toward her husband a wife is disgraced in this world. After death she enters the womb of a jackal, and is tormented by diseases as the punishment of her sin. [165] She who controls her thoughts, words, and deeds, and never slights her husband will reside after death with him in heaven. She is called a virtuous wife.

---

[35]*anywhere allowed . . . women:* no ancient stories or laws permit it.

RITUAL AND MEDITATION

The Gayatri Mantra*

The name of this short prayer means "the savior of the singer." Considered the single most important prayer-formula of Hinduism, pious believers repeat it at least three times a day. On its literal level, this verse is a simple prayer to the sun god Savitar for blessing. On its deeper level, it expresses

---

*Rig-Veda 3.62.10

and applies the power that the god himself holds. Given to a young man at his initiation with the sacred thread, it helps to produce his rebirth. Believers in other Hindu deities have adapted it for their use from early times through today.

May we attain to the excellent glory of Savitar the god; so may he stimulate our prayers.

Devotion to Agni in Prayer and Sacrifice**

Agni is the god of fire, especially the sacrificial fire, and he is the priest among the gods (verse 1). This first hymn of the Rig-Veda *seeks to please Agni by praises and invoke his blessings. Like many other hymns of the Rig, it uses both the second person (e.g., "To you, Agni . . .") and the third person ("Agni earned the prayers . . ."), but all of it is addressed to Agni. The second reading is a good example of the Brahmanic exposition and development of the sacrificial rite. The ritual expounded here is the* agnihotra, *the daily household sacrifice to Agni. The god Prajapati is the precursor of Brahman.[36]*

I pray to Agni, the household priest who is the god of the sacrifice, the one who chants and invokes and brings most treasure. Agni earned the prayers of the ancient sages, and of those of the present, too; he will bring the gods here. Through Agni one may win wealth, and growth from day to day, glorious and most abounding in heroic sons. Agni, only the sacrificial ritual that you encompass on all sides goes to the gods. [5] Agni, the priest with the sharp sight of a poet, the true and most brilliant, the god will come with the gods. Whatever good you wish to do for the one who worships you, Agni, through you, O Angiras,[37] that comes true. To you, Agni, who shine upon darkness, we come

---

**Rig-Veda 1.1; Agni-Brahmana 1.1–19*
[36]Taken, with editing, from Julius Eggeling, trans., *The Satapatha-Brahmana,* part 1, *Sacred Books of the East,* vol. 12 (Oxford: Oxford University Press, 1882.

---

[37]*Angiras:* messenger to the gods and the father of an ancient family of priests.

day after day, bringing our thoughts and homage. [We come to] you, the king over sacrifices, the shining guardian of the Order, growing in your own house. Be easy for us to reach, like a father to his son. Abide with us, Agni, for our happiness.

[*Agni-Brahmana* 1.1–19] Prajapati alone existed here in the beginning. He considered, "How may I be reproduced?" He toiled and performed acts of penance. He generated Agni from his mouth. Because he generated him from his mouth, therefore Agni is a consumer of food. Truly, he who knows Agni to be a consumer of food becomes himself a consumer of food.

He thus generated him first of the gods; and therefore [he is called] Agni, for *agni* [they say] is the same as *agri*. He, being generated, went forth as the first; for of him who goes first, they say that he goes at the head. Such, then, is the origin and nature of that Agni.

Prajapati then considered, "In Agni I have generated a food-eater for myself. But there is no other food here but myself, whom Agni certainly would not eat." Then this earth had been made quite bald; there were neither plants nor trees. This, then, weighed on his mind. Then Agni turned toward him with open mouth. Prajapati was terrified, and his own greatness departed from him. Now his own greatness is his speech; his speech departed from him. He desired an offering in himself and rubbed his hands; and because he rubbed his hands, palms are hairless. He then obtained either a butter-offering or a milk-offering; but they are both made of milk.

[5] But this offering did not satisfy him, because it had hairs mixed with it. He poured it away into the fire, saying, "Drink, while burning!" From it plants sprang; hence their name "plants." He rubbed his hands a second time, and by that obtained another offering, either a butter-offering or a milk-offering. But again they are both milk.

This offering then satisfied him. He hesitated: "Shall I offer it up? Or shall I not offer it up?" he thought. His own greatness said to him, "Offer it up!" Prajapati was aware that it was his own [*sva*] greatness that had spoken [*aha*] to him; and offered it up with the word *svaha!* This is why offerings are made with *svaha!* Then that burning one, the sun, rose; and then that blowing one, the wind, sprang up. Then Agni turned away.

Prajapati, having performed offering, reproduced himself, and saved himself from Agni as he was about to devour him. Truly whoever, knowing this, offers the agnihotra reproduces himself by offspring even as Prajapati reproduced himself. He saves himself from Agni, death, when he is about to devour him.

And when he dies, and when they place him on the fire, then he is born again out of the fire, and the fire only consumes his body. Even as he is born from his father and mother, so is he born from the fire. But he who does not offer the agnihotra does not come into life at all. Therefore the agnihotra must be offered.

Soma*

Soma is here, as elsewhere in the Vedas, at once a plant, a drink, and a god. To judge from this hymn, it had an effect that was hallucinogenic. The term soma *is still used today, but it refers not to a hallucinogenic drug but to a fruit drink made of wild rhubarb. Other religions have words spoken during ritual intoxication. Few, however, are as evocative as this hymn's "We have drunk the Soma; we have become immortal; we have gone to the light; we have found the gods."*

I have tasted the sweet drink of life, knowing that it inspires good thoughts and joyous

---

*Rig-Veda 8.48

expansiveness to the extreme, that all the gods and mortals seek it together, calling it honey. When you penetrate inside, you will know no limits, and you will avert the wrath of the gods. Enjoying Indra's friendship, O drop of Soma, bring riches as a docile cow brings the yoke. We have drunk the Soma; we have become immortal; we have gone to the light; we have found the gods. What can hatred and the malice of a mortal do to us now, O immortal one? When we have drunk you, O drop of Soma, be good to our heart, kind as a father to his son, thoughtful as a friend to a friend. Far-famed Soma, stretch out our lifespan so that we may live.

[5] The glorious drops that I have drunk set me free in wide space. You have bound me together in my limbs as thongs bind a chariot. Let the drops protect me from the foot that stumbles and keep lameness away from me. Inflame me like a fire kindled by friction; make us see far; make us richer, better. For when I am intoxicated with you, Soma, I think myself rich. Draw near and make us thrive. We would enjoy you, pressed with a fervent heart, like riches from a father. King Soma, stretch out our life-spans as the sun stretches the spring days. King Soma, have mercy on us for our well-being. Know that we are devoted to your laws. Passion and fury are stirred up. O drop of Soma, do not

hand us over to the pleasure of the enemy. For you, Soma, are the guardian of our body; watching over men, you have settled down in every limb.

If we break your laws, O god, have mercy on us like a good friend, to make us better. [10] Let me join closely with my compassionate friend so that he will not injure me when I have drunk him. O lord of bay horses, for the Soma that is lodged in us I approach Indra to stretch out our lifespan. Weaknesses and diseases have gone; the forces of darkness have fled in terror. Soma has climbed up in us, expanding. We have come to the place where they stretch out life-spans. The drop that we have drunk has entered our hearts, an immortal inside mortals. O fathers, let us serve that Soma with the oblations and abide in his mercy and kindness. Uniting in agreement with the fathers, O drop of Soma, you have extended yourself through sky and earth. Let us serve him with an obla-tion; let us be masters of riches. You protecting gods, speak out for us. Do not let sleep or harmful speech seize us. Let us, always dear to Soma, speak as men of power in the sacrificial gathering. [15] Soma, you give us the force of life on every side. Enter into us, finding the sunlight, watching over men. O drop of Soma, summon your helpers and protect us before and after.

Marriage*

The first part of this hymn, not given here, recounts the myth of the marriage of Surya the goddess. The part printed here contains the incantations and blessings still spoken at weddings to bring good and repel evil. The bride is compared to Surya, and the wedding of the humans is set in parallel with divine marriage. The words are designed to bring good fortune: that the wife continue to have beauty and passion, and so be loved by her husband; that

both have a long life together; that the marriage produce many sons. The careful reader can discern several different ritual actions of the marriage. First comes leaving the site of the wedding, then traveling to the couple's home, then consummation of marriage, and finally the anointing of the cou-ple. Verses from this hymn are still a part of obser-vant, traditional Hindu weddings.

Mount the world of immortality, O Surya, that is adorned with red flowers and made of fra-grant wood, carved with many forms and

---

*Rig-Veda 10.85.20—47

painted with gold, rolling smoothly on its fine wheels. Prepare an exquisite wedding voyage for your husband. "Go away from here! For this woman has a husband." Thus I implore Visvavasu[38] with words of praise as I bow to him. "Look for another girl who is ripe and still lives in her father's house." That is your birthright; find it. "Go away from here, Visvavasu, we implore you as we bow. Look for another girl, willing and ready. Leave the wife to unite with her husband." May the roads be straight and thornless on which our friends go courting. May Aryaman and Bhaga united lead us together. O Gods, may the united household be easy to manage. I free you from Varuna's snare, with which the gentle Savitr bound you. In the seat of the Law, in the world of good action, I place you unharmed with your husband. [25] I free her from here, but not from there.[39] I have bound her firmly there, so that through the grace of Indra she will have fine sons and be fortunate in her husband's love. Let Pusan lead you from here, taking you by the hand; let the Asvins carry you in their chariot. Go home to be mistress of the house with the right to speak commands to the gathered people. May happiness be fated for you here through your progeny. Watch over this house as mistress of the house.

Mingle your body with that of your husband, and even when you are gray with age you will have the right to speak to the gathered people. The purple and red appears, a magic spirit; the stain is imprinted.[40] Her family prospers, and her husband is bound in the bonds. Throw away the gown, and distribute wealth to the priests. It

becomes a magic spirit walking on feet, and like the wife it draws near the husband. [30] The body becomes ugly and sinisterly pale if the husband with evil desire covers his sexual limb with his wife's robe. The diseases that come from her own people and follow the glorious bridal procession, may the gods who receive sacrifices lead them back whence they have come. Let no highwaymen, lying in ambush, fall upon the wedding couple. Let the two of them on good paths avoid the dangerous path. Let all demonic powers run away. This bride has auspicious signs; come and look at her. Wish her the good fortune of her husband's love, and depart, each to your own house. It burns, it bites, it has claws, it is as dangerous as poison to eat.[41] Only the priest who knows the Surya hymn is able to receive the bridal gown. [35] Cutting, carving, and chopping into pieces—see the colors of Surya, which the priest alone purifies.

I [the husband] take your hand for good fortune, so that with me as your husband you will attain a ripe old age. Bhaga, Aryaman, Savitr, Purandhi—the gods have given you to me to be mistress of the house. Pusan, rouse her to be most eager to please, the woman in whom men sow their seed, so that she will spread her thighs in her desire for us and we,[42] in our desire, will plant our penis in her. To you first of all they led Surya, circling with the bridal procession. Give her back to her husbands, Agni, now as a wife with progeny. Agni has given the wife back again, together with long life and beauty. Let her have a long lifespan, and let her husband live for a hundred autumns. [40] Soma first possessed her, and the Gandharva possessed her second. Agni was your third husband, and the fourth was the son of a man. Soma gave her to the Gandharva, and the Gandharva gave her to Agni. Agni gave me wealth and sons—and her.

Stay here and do not separate. Enjoy your whole lifespan playing with sons and grandsons

---

[38] *Visvavasu:* a demigod who possesses virgins.

[39] *here:* her father's house; *there:* her new house with her husband.

[40] *The purple and red appears . . . imprinted:* In the consummation of the marriage, the bride bleeds on her wedding robe as her hymen is ruptured. The resulting stain becomes a magic spirit with power to curse and destroy the marriage. The procedure for dealing with the robe is given at the end of this paragraph.

[41] *it:* the spirit arising from the stained robe.

[42] *us, we:* the husband, and the gods who are said to have spiritually possessed the wife before her marriage.

and rejoicing in your own home. Let Prajapati create progeny for us; let Aryaman anoint us into old age. Free from evil signs, enter the world of your husband. Be good luck for our two-legged creatures and good luck for our four-legged creatures. Have no evil eye; do not be a husband-killer.[43] Be friendly to animals, good-tempered and glowing with beauty. Bringing forth strong sons, prosper as one beloved of the gods and eager to please. Be good luck for our two-legged creatures and good luck for our four-legged creatures. [45] Generous Indra, give this woman fine sons and

the good fortune of her husband's love. Place ten sons in her and make her husband the eleventh.[44] Be an empress over your husband's father, an empress over your husband's mother; be an empress over your husband's sister and an empress over your husband's brothers. Let all the gods and the waters together anoint our two hearts together. Let Matarisvan[45] together with the Creator and together with her who shows the way join the two of us together.

---

[43]*Have no evil eye . . . husband-killer:* a charm against any evil possibly residing in the wife that may threaten her husband.

[44]*her husband the eleventh:* a common Hindu idea is that the husband is the last son of the wife, perhaps signifying the care given to the husband by his wife.
[45]*Matarisvan:* an assistant of Agni.

Cremation*

Agni is petitioned here to bring a good burning to the body of the dead, strikingly called in sacrificial imagery "a good cooking." The proper funeral ritual enables the dead man to go to his fathers. No mention is made here of heaven or hell, transmigration or reincarnation, important in later Hinduism through today.

Do not burn him entirely, Agni, or engulf him in your flames. Do not consume his skin or his flesh. When you have cooked him perfectly, O knower of creatures, only then send him forth to the fathers. When you cook him perfectly, O knower of creatures, then give him over to the fathers. When he goes on the path that leads away the breath of life, then he will be led by the will of the gods. [To the dead man:] May your eye go to the sun, your life's breath to the wind. Go to the sky or to earth, as is your nature; or go to the waters, if that is your fate. Take root in the plants with your limbs. [To Agni:] The goat is your share; burn him with your heat. Let your

brilliant light and flame burn him. With your gentle forms, O knower of creatures, carry this man to the world of those who have done good deeds. [5] Set him free again to go to the fathers, Agni, when he has been offered as an oblation in you and wanders with the sacrificial drink. Let him reach his own descendants, dressing himself in a lifespan. O knower of creatures, let him join with a body. [To the dead man:] Whatever the black bird has pecked out of you, or the ant, the snake, or even a beast of prey, may Agni who eats all things make it whole, and Soma who has entered the Brahmins. Gird yourself with the limbs of the cow as an armor against Agni, and cover yourself with fat and suet, so that he will not embrace you with his impetuous heat in his passionate desire to burn you up.

[To Agni:] O Agni, do not overturn this cup that is dear to the gods and to those who love Soma, fit for the gods to drink from, a cup in which the immortal gods carouse. I send the flesh-eating fire far away. Let him go to those whose king is Yama, carrying away all impurities. But let that other, the knower of creatures,

---

Rig-Veda 10.16

come here and carry the oblation to the gods, since he knows the way in advance. [10] The flesh-eating fire has entered your house, though he sees there the other, the knower of creatures; I take that god away to the sacrifice of the fathers. Let him carry the heated drink to the farthest dwelling-place. Agni who carries away the corpse, who gives sacrifice to the fathers who are strengthened by truth—let him proclaim the oblation to the gods and to the fathers. [To the new fire:] Joyously would we put you in place, joyously would we kindle you. Joyously carry the joyous fathers here to eat the oblation. Now, Agni, quench and revive the very one you have burnt up. Let Kiyamba, Pakadurva, and Vyalkasa plants grow in this place. O cool one, bringer of coolness; O fresh one, bringer of freshness; unite with the female frog. Delight and inspire this, O Agni.

Charms and Spells*

The first of these incantations is a charm against fever, the second a spell to frustrate the sacrifice of an enemy, the third a charm to induce the sexual passion of a woman (perhaps a wife who comes by an arranged marriage), the fourth a spell for success in business. Note that the main point of the charm is often repeated to increase its power. Ritual actions that accompany the saying of these spells are occasionally suggested in the words.[46]

[6.20, against fever] As if from this Agni [fire], that burns and flashes, the fever comes. Let him pass away like a babbling drunkard! Let him, the impious one, search out another person, not ourselves! Reverence be to the fever with the burning weapon![47] Reverence be to Rudra, reverence to the fever, reverence to the luminous king Varuna! Reverence to heaven, reverence to earth, reverence to the plants! To you that burns through, and turns all bodies yellow . . . to the fever produced by the forest, I render honor.

[7.70, for frustration of sacrifice] Whenever that person over there in his thought and with his speech offers sacrifice accompanied by offerings and benedictions, may Nirriti the goddess of destruction ally herself with death and strike his offering before it takes effect! May the sorcerers Nirriti and Rakshas mar his true work with error![48] May the gods, despatched by Indra, churn up his sacrificial butter! May that which he offers not succeed! . . . I tie back both your arms, I shut your mouth. With the fury of Agni, I have destroyed your sacrifice.

[6.9, for love] Desire my body, my feet, my eyes, my thighs! As you lust after me, your eyes and your hair shall be hot with love! I make you cling to my arm, cling to my heart, so that you shall be in my power and shall come to my wish! The cows, the mothers of the sacrificial butter who lick their young, in whose heart love is planted, shall make this woman love me!

[3.16, for success in business] I urge Indra the merchant, come to us and be our forerunner. Ward off the unpaying one, the cutting beast, and let masterful Indra be a bringer of wealth to me. O Gods! That money with which, desiring more money, I conduct my business, let that multiply and never decrease. O Agni, with this sacrifice frustrate those who would ruin my profit.

Atharva-Veda 6.20, 7.70, 6.9, 3.16

[46]Taken, with editing, from Maurice Bloomfield, trans., *Hymns of the Atharva-Veda, Sacred Books of the East*, vol. 42 (Oxford: Oxford University Press, 1897).

[47]*Reverence:* the spell uses flattering praise, as well as insults, to drive the fever away.

[48]*mar . . . with error:* if an error of word or deed is made in the sacrificial ceremony, it is not effective. Such a belief is common to many religions with well-developed sacrificial systems.

Chanting of *Om**

The udgitha, *or "loud chant," is the important* Om (OHM) *in the Vedic ritual. Members of the various Hindu schools differ on whether Om is Brahman itself or a near verbal expression of Brahman. But for all Hindus it is the most sacred of sounds, the mantra that contains all other mantras, all the Vedas, all the meaning of the universe. Those who chant it with full knowledge will be freed from karma.*

Let a man meditate on the syllable *Om*, called the *udgitha*; for the *udgitha* is sung, beginning with *Om*. The full account of *Om* is this.

The essence of all beings is the earth, the essence of the earth is water, the essence of water the plants, the essence of plants man, the essence of man speech, the essence of speech the *Rig-veda*, the essence of the *Rig-veda* the *Sama-veda*, the essence of the *Sama-veda* the *udgitha*, *Om*. The *udgitha* is the best of all essences, the highest, deserving the highest place, the eighth.

What then is the *Rig*? What is the *Saman*? What is the *udgitha*? This is the question. [5] The *Rig* is speech, *Saman* is breath, the *udgitha* is the syllable *Om*. Now speech and breath, or

*Chandogya Upanishad 1.1.1–10

Rig and *Saman*, form one couple. That couple is joined in the syllable *Om*. When two people come together, they fulfil each other's desire. Thus he who knowing this meditates on the syllable *Om*, the *udgitha*, becomes a fulfiller of desires.

That syllable is a syllable of permission, for whenever we permit anything, we say *Om*, yes. Now permission is gratification. He who knows this and meditates on the syllable *Om* becomes a gratifier of desires.

By that syllable proceeds the threefold knowledge (of the three *Vedas*). When the Adhvaryu priest gives an order, he says *Om*. When the Hotri priest recites, he says *Om*. When the Udgatri priest sings, he says *Om*, all for the glory of that syllable. The threefold knowledge and threefold sacrifice proceed by the greatness of that syllable and by its essence. [10] Therefore it seems that both he who knows this [the true meaning of *Om*], and he who does not, perform the same sacrifice. But this is not so, for knowledge and ignorance are different. The sacrifice that a man performs with knowledge, faith, and the *Upanishad* is more powerful. This is the full account of the syllable *Om*.

The Practice of Yoga**

Yoga is a physical discipline to promote knowledge that the individual soul and the world soul are one. This passage relates some of the main components of yogic meditation.[49]

Holding his body steady with the three [upper parts][50] erect,

—

**Shvetashvatara Upanishad 2.8–15
[49]F. Max Müller, trans., *The Upanishads*, part 2, *Sacred Books of the East*, vol. 15 (Oxford: Oxford University Press, 1884), pp. 241–243.
[50]*the three [upper parts]:* head, neck, and torso.

And causing the senses with the mind to enter
    the heart,
A wise man with the Brahma-boat will cross
All the fear-bringing streams.

Compressing his breathings here in the body,
    and having his movements checked,
One should breathe through his nostrils with
    diminished breath.
Like that chariot yoked with vicious horses,
His mind the wise man should restrain
    undistractedly.

[10] In a clean level spot, free from pebbles,
    fire, and gravel,

By the sound of water and similar things
Favorable to thought, not offensive to the eye,
In a hidden retreat protected from the wind,
   one should practice Yoga.

Fog, smoke, sun, fire, wind,
Fire-flies, lightning, a crystal, a moon—
These are the preliminary appearances,
Producing the manifestation of Brahma in Yoga.

When the fivefold quality of Yoga is produced,
Arising from earth, water, fire, air, and space,
No sickness, no old age, no death has he
Who has obtained a body made out of the fire
   of Yoga.

Lightness, healthiness, steadiness,
Clearness of countenance and pleasantness of
   voice,

Sweetness of odor, and scanty excretions—
These, they say, are the first stage in the
   progress of Yoga.

Even as a mirror stained by dust
Shines brilliantly when it has been cleansed,
So the embodied one, on seeing the nature of
   the Soul,
Becomes unitary, his end attained, from sorrow
   freed.

[15] When with the nature of the self, as with
   a lamp,
One who practices Yoga beholds here the
   nature of Brahma,
Unborn, steadfast, from every nature free—
By knowing God one is released from all
   fetters!

APPENDIX 1: SELECTIONS FROM THE *BHAGAVAD-GITA*

The most famous and influential text of Hinduism is section 6 of the *Mahabharata* epic known as the *Bhagavad-Gita* (Song of the Lord). The *Gita* is especially important for an understanding of the devotional Hinduism that has flourished from about 400 C.E. until today. The background of the *Gita* is the rivalry between the Kaurava brothers and the Pandava brothers for the rule of India. In a game of dice, the leader of the Pandavas loses their claim to the throne. For thirteen years the Pandavas are forced into exile. This results in civil war as the Pandavas return to seize rule. As preparation for war begins, Krishna becomes a charioteer for Arjuna.

But just as the battle is about to begin, Arjuna is appalled at the fratricide that will surely result. Moreover, he is afraid that this great evil will harm his own soul now and, by implication, in its later incarnations. His charioteer, the god Krishna, teaches Arjuna the divine truth that enables him to overcome his doubtings. This teaching forms the content of the *Gita*. First, and most immediately for the plot of the *Mahabharata*, Krishna teaches Arjuna that he must do his caste duty and fight. Arjuna knows that his warfare will not harm the souls of the slain. Second, the several ways to salvation given in the long history of Hinduism—sacrifice (the Vedic path), meditation (Upanishadic and ascetic path), and action (the way of caste duty) —are each only effective if done in a spirit of complete detachment. The *Gita* teaches full involvement in life coupled with inner restraint and indifference. Third, the best way is devotion to Krishna, whom the Gita portrays as the "base of Brahman," yet filled with love for his devotees. In this way, the Gita is typically Hindu—it acknowledges and affirms all Hindu ways to the truth but affirms its own way as the best.

The *Gita* contains 7,000 verses grouped into eighteen chapters. It has no plot, only the setting just outlined that poses the religious problem. Most chapters begin with Arjuna's question, which typically deals with the meaning of previous teachings in the *Gita*; a lengthy answer from Krishna follows. Many chapters end with a call for devotion to Krishna. Much of the content of the *Gita* is repetitious; the key teachings are returned to again and again and examined from different perspectives. The following excerpts attempt to reduce this repetition and present the essence of the *Gita*'s argument. A short paragraph introduces and summarizes the content of each of the selections given here.[51]

[1.20–47] Chapter 1 provides the narrative setting and the religious problem of the Gita. King Dhritarashtra's charioteer, Sanjaya, tells the king what happened before the battle that took place to decide the fate of his kingdom. As Prince Arjuna came onto the battlefield, he was overcome by the horrors of the impending fratricidal war. He expresses his misgivings to his charioteer, Krishna, saying that war will lead to the ruin of the kingdom, its families, and its entire social system. He prefers death to fighting such a war. Then he drops his weapons, waiting for his death at the hands of the enemy.

Sanjaya:

Arjuna, his war flag a rampant monkey,
saw Dhritarashtra's sons assembled as
weapons were ready to clash, and he lifted his
    bow.

He told his charioteer: "Krishna,
halt my chariot between the armies!
Far enough to see these men who lust for war,
ready to fight with me in the strain of battle.
I see men gathered here, eager to fight,
bent on serving the folly of Dhritarashtra's son."

When Arjuna had spoken, Krishna halted
their splendid chariot between the armies.

[25] Facing Bhishma and Drona
and all the great kings, he said,
"Arjuna, see the Kuru men assembled here!"

Arjuna saw them standing there:
fathers, grandfathers, teachers, uncles, brothers,
sons, grandsons, and friends.
He surveyed his companions in both armies,
all his kinsmen assembled together.

Dejected, filled with strange pity, he said this:
"Krishna, I see kinsmen gathered here,
    wanting war.
My limbs sink, my mouth is parched,
my body trembles, the hair bristles on my flesh.

[30] The magic bow slips
from my hand, my skin burns,
I cannot stand still, my mind reels.

I see omens of chaos, Krishna;
I see no good in killing my kinsmen in battle.
Krishna, I seek no victory, kingship or pleasures.
What use are kingship, delights, or life itself?

We sought kingship, delights,
and pleasures for the sake of those
assembled to abandon their lives
and fortunes in battle.

They are teachers, fathers, sons,
and grandfathers, uncles, grandsons,
fathers and brothers of wives,
and other men of our family.

[35] I do not want to kill them
even if I am killed, Krishna;
not for kingship of all three worlds,
much less for the earth!

What joy is there for us, Krishna,
in killing Dhritarashtra's sons?
Evil will haunt us if we kill them,
though their bows are drawn to kill.

Honor forbids us to kill
our cousins, Dhritarashtra's sons;
how can we know happiness
if we kill our own kinsmen?

The greed that distorts their reason
blinds them to the sin they commit
in ruining the family, blinds them
to the crime of betraying friends.

How can we ignore the wisdom
of turning from this evil when we see
the sin of family destruction, Krishna?

---

[51]From *Bhagavad-Gita*, by Barbara Stoler Miller, translation copyright 1986 by Barbara Stoler Miller. Used by permission of Bantam Books, a division of Bantam Doubleday Dell Publishing Group, Inc.

[40] When the family is ruined, the timeless laws
of family duty perish; and when duty is lost,
chaos overwhelms the family.
In overwhelming chaos, Krishna,
women of the family are corrupted;
and when women are corrupted,
disorder is born in society.

This discord drags the violators
and the family itself to hell;
for ancestors fall when rites
of offering rice and water lapse.

The sins of men who violate
the family create disorder in society
that undermines the constant laws
of caste and family duty.

Krishna, we have heard that a place in hell
is reserved for men who undermine family
        duties.

[45] I lament the great sin
we commit when our greed
for kingship and pleasures
drives us to kill our kinsmen.

If Dhritarashtra's armed sons
kill me in battle when I am unarmed
and offer no resistance,
it will be my reward."

Saying this in the time of war,
Arjuna slumped into the chariot
and laid down his bow and arrows,
his mind tormented by grief.

*[2:1–7, 11–27, 31–38, 47–48] In chapter 2,
Krishna rebukes Arjuna and urges him to fight.
Krishna advances several arguments: (1) the soul
is immortal, and all else is impermanent; therefore the battle has no real eternal significance; (2)
Arjuna, a Kshatriya (warrior), must do his caste
duty and fight; (3) he must fight in a contempla-
tive, detached manner; and (4) yoga (discipline)
is the way to such detachment. Verse 38 is the key:
"Impartial to joy and suffering, gain and loss,
victory and defeat, arm yourself for the battle, lest
you fall into evil."*

Sanjaya:

Arjuna sat dejected, filled with pity,
his sad eyes blurred by tears.
Krishna gave him counsel.

Lord Krishna:

Why this cowardice in time of crisis, Arjuna?
The coward is ignoble, shameful,
foreign to the ways of heaven.
Don't yield to impotence!

It is unnatural in you!
Banish this petty weakness
from your heart.
Rise to the fight, Arjuna!

Arjuna:

Krishna, how can I fight Bhishma and Drona
with arrows when they deserve my worship?

[5] Better in this world to beg for scraps of food
than to eat meals smeared with the blood
of elders I killed at the height of their power,
while their goals were still desires.

We don't know which weight is worse to bear—
our conquering them or their conquering us.
We will not want to live if we kill
the sons of Dhritarashtra assembled before us.

The flaw of pity blights my very being;
conflicting sacred duties confound my reason.
I ask you to tell me decisively—Which is better?
I am your pupil. Teach me what I seek! . . .

Lord Krishna:

[11] You grieve for those beyond grief,
and you speak words of insight;
but learned men do not grieve
for the dead or the living.

Never have I not existed,
nor you, nor these kings;
and never in the future
shall we cease to exist.

Just as the embodied self
enters childhood, youth, and old age,
so does it enter another body;
this does not confound a steadfast man.

Contacts with matter make us feel
heat and cold, pleasure and pain.

Arjuna, you must learn to endure
fleeting things—they come and go!

[15] When these cannot torment a man,
when suffering and joy are equal
for him and he has courage,
he is fit for immortality.

Nothing of nonbeing comes to be,
nor does being cease to exist;
the boundary between these two
is seen by men who see reality.

Indestructible is the presence
that pervades all this;
no one can destroy
this unchanging reality.

Our bodies are known to end,
but the embodied self is enduring,
indestructible, and immeasurable;
therefore, Arjuna, fight the battle!

He who thinks this self a killer
and he who thinks it killed,
both fail to understand;
it does not kill, nor is it killed.

[20] It is not born, it does not die;
having been, it will never not be;
unborn, enduring, constant, primordial,
it is not killed when the body is killed.

Arjuna, when a man knows the self
to be indestructible, enduring, unborn,
unchanging, how does he kill
or cause anyone to kill?

As a man discards worn-out clothes
to put on new and different ones,
so the embodied self discards
its worn-out bodies to take on new ones.

Weapons do not cut it, fire does not burn it,
waters do not wet it, wind does not wither it.
It cannot be cut or burned, wet or withered;
it is enduring, all-pervasive, fixed,
immovable, and timeless.

[25] It is called unmanifest,
inconceivable, and immutable;
since you know that to be so,
you should not grieve!

If you think of its birth
and death as ever-recurring,
then too, Great Warrior,
you have no cause to grieve!

Death is certain for anyone born,
and birth is certain for the dead;
since the cycle is inevitable,
you have no cause to grieve! . . .

[31] Look to your own duty;
do not tremble before it;
nothing is better for a warrior
than a battle of sacred duty.

The doors of heaven open for warriors who
    rejoice
to have a battle like this thrust on them by
    chance.
If you fail to wage this war of sacred duty,
you will abandon your own duty
and fame only to gain evil.

People will tell of your undying shame,
and for a man of honor shame is worse than
    death.

[35] The great chariot warriors will think
you deserted in fear of battle;
you will be despised
by those who held you in esteem.

Your enemies will slander you,
scorning your skill
in so many unspeakable ways—
could any suffering be worse?

If you are killed, you win heaven;
if you triumph, you enjoy the earth;
Arjuna, stand up and resolve to fight the battle!

Impartial to joy and suffering,
gain and loss, victory and defeat,
arm yourself for the battle, lest you fall into
    evil. . . .

[47] Be intent on action, not the fruits of action;
avoid attraction to the fruits
and attachment to inaction!

Perform actions, firm in discipline,
relinquishing attachment;
be impartial to failure and success—
this equanimity is called discipline.

[4:1–15] In chapter 4 Krishna tells Arjuna of his many incarnations. The Gita itself does not explicitly state that Krishna is an incarnation of Vishnu, but the Vaishnavites of later devotional Hinduism saw this relationship and developed it fully.

Lord Krishna:

I taught this undying discipline
to the shining sun, first of mortals, who
told it to Manu, the progenitor of man;
Manu told it to the solar king Ikshvaku.

Royal sages knew this discipline,
which the tradition handed down;
but over the course of time
it has decayed, Arjuna.

This is the ancient discipline
that I have taught to you today;
you are my devotee and my friend,
and this is the deepest mystery.

Arjuna:

Your birth followed the birth of the sun;
how can I comprehend that you taught it
in the beginning?

Lord Krishna:

[5] I have passed through many births
and so have you;
I know them all, but you do not, Arjuna.

Though myself unborn, undying,
the lord of creatures, I fashion nature,
which is mine, and I come into being
through my own magic.

When sacred duty decays, chaos prevails;
then I create myself, Arjuna. To protect men
of virtue and destroy evil men, to set the
standard of sacred duty, I appear in every age.

He who really knows my divine
birth and my action, escapes rebirth
when he abandons the body—
and he comes to me, Arjuna.

[10] Free from attraction, fear, and anger,
filled with me, dependent on me,
purified by the fire of knowledge,
many come into my presence.

As they seek refuge in me,
I devote myself to them;
Arjuna, men retrace
my path in every way.

Desiring success in their actions,
men sacrifice here to the gods;
in the world of man success
comes quickly from action.

I created mankind in four classes,
different in their qualities and actions;
though unchanging, I am the agent of this,
the actor who never acts!

I desire no fruit of actions,
and actions do not defile me;
one who knows this about me
is not bound by actions.

[15] Knowing this, even ancient seekers
of freedom performed action—
do as these seers did in ancient times.

[9:16–28] Chapter 9 tells how the universe was spun out of Krishna's body. Next come the attributes of God (Krishna), service of different (Hindu) gods, and a critique of Vedic religion. At the end, devotion to Krishna is emphasized as the part that, in contrast to the Vedic cult, is open to all.

Lord Krishna:

I am the rite, the sacrifice,
the libation for the dead, the healing herb,
the sacred hymn, the clarified butter,
the fire, the oblation.

I am the universal father,
mother, granter of all, grandfather,
object of knowledge, purifier,
holy syllable *Om,* threefold sacred lore.

I am the way, sustainer, lord,
witness, shelter, refuge, friend,
source, dissolution, stability,
treasure, and unchanging seed.

I am heat that withholds
and sends down the rains;
I am immortality and death;
both being and nonbeing am I.

[20] Men learned in sacred lore,
Soma drinkers, their sins absolved,
worship me with sacrifices,
seeking to win heaven.

Reaching the holy world of Indra,
king of the gods,
they savor the heavenly delights
of the gods in the celestial sphere.

When they have long enjoyed the world of
heaven and their merit is exhausted,
they enter the mortal world; following
the duties ordained in sacred lore,
desiring desires, they obtain what is transient.

Men who worship me, thinking solely of me,
always disciplined, win the reward I secure.

When devoted men sacrifice
to other deities with faith,
they sacrifice to me, Arjuna,
however aberrant the rites.

I am the enjoyer and the lord of sacrifices;
they do not know me in reality, so they fail.

[25] Votaries of the gods go to the gods,
ancestor-worshippers go to the ancestors,
those who propitiate ghosts go to them,
and my worshippers go to me.

The leaf or flower or fruit or water
that he offers with devotion,
I take from the man of self-restraint
in response to his devotion.

Whatever you do—what you take,
what you offer, what you give,
what penances you perform—
do as an offering to me, Arjuna!

You will be freed from bonds of action,
from the fruit of fortune and misfortune;
armed with the discipline of renunciation,
your self liberated, you will join me.

[11:1–20, 50–55] In chapter 11, after Arjuna asks to see Krishna's divine form, Krishna shows him all his divine forms at once. Arjuna is filled with awe and praises Krishna. Krishna then returns to his human form. The praise of Krishna expresses the kind of attachment to one god that is characteristic of devotional Hinduism.

Arjuna:

To favor me you revealed
the deepest mystery of the self,
and by your words
my delusion is dispelled.

I heard from you in detail
how creatures come to be and die,
Krishna, and about the self
in its immutable greatness.

Just as you have described yourself,
I wish to see your form in all its majesty,
Krishna, Supreme among Men.

If you think I can see it, reveal to me your
immutable self, Krishna, Lord of Discipline.

Lord Krishna:

[5] Arjuna, see my forms
in hundreds and thousands;
diverse, divine, of many colors and shapes.

See the sun gods, gods of light,
howling storm gods, twin gods of dawn,
and gods of wind, Arjuna,
wondrous forms not seen before.

Arjuna, see all the universe,
animate and inanimate,
and whatever else you wish to see;
all stands here as one in my body.

But you cannot see me with your own eye;
I will give you a divine eye to see
the majesty or my discipline.

Sanjaya:

O King, saying this, Krishna, the lord
of discipline, revealed to Arjuna
the true majesty of his form.

[10] It was a multiform, wondrous vision,
with countless mouths and eyes
and celestial ornaments,
brandishing many divine weapons.

Everywhere was boundless divinity
containing all astonishing things,
wearing divine garlands and garments,
anointed with divine perfume.
If the light of a thousand suns
were to rise in the sky at once, it would
be like the light of that great spirit.

Arjuna saw all the universe
in its many ways and parts, standing
as one in the body of the god of gods.

Then filled with amazement,
his hair bristling on his flesh,
Arjuna bowed his head to the god,
joined his hands in homage, and spoke.

Arjuna:

[15] I see the gods in your body, O God,
and hordes of varied creatures:
Brahma, the cosmic creator,
on his lotus throne, all the seers
and celestial serpents.

I see your boundless form everywhere,
the countless arms, bellies, mouths, eyes;
Lord of All, I see no end,
or middle or beginning to your totality.

I see you blazing through the fiery rays
of your crown, mace, and discus,
hard to behold in the burning light
of fire and sun that surrounds
your measureless presence.

You are to be known as supreme eternity,
the deepest treasure of all that is,
the immutable guardian of enduring duty;
I think you are man's timeless spirit.

I see no beginning, middle or end to you;
only boundless strength in your arms,
the moon and sun in your eyes,
your mouths of consuming flames,
your own brilliance scorching the universe.

[20] You alone fill the space between heaven
and earth and all the directions;
seeing this awesome, terrible form of yours,
Great Soul, the three worlds tremble. . . .

Sanjaya:

[50] Saying this to Arjuna, Krishna again
revealed his intimate form;
resuming his gentle body, the great spirit
let the terrified hero regain his breath.

Arjuna:

Seeing your gentle human form, Krishna,
I recover my nature, my reason is restored.

Lord Krishna:

This form you have seen is rarely revealed;
the gods are constantly craving
for a vision of this form.

Not through sacred lore, penances, charity,
or sacrificial rites can I be seen in the form
that you saw me. By devotion alone can I, as
I really am, be seen and entered into, Arjuna.

[55] Acting only for me, intent on me,
free from attachment, hostile to no creature,
Arjuna, a man of devotion comes to me.

*[16:1–11, 21–24] Chapter 16 is a summary of
general morality suitable for all twice-born Hindus. It first describes the person "born to inherit a
godly destiny," who quickly escapes the process of
rebirth. Then it tells of "human devils," who are
eternally recycling through rebirth.*

Lord Krishna:

Fearlessness, purity, determination
in the discipline of knowledge,
charity, self-control, sacrifice,
study of sacred lore, penance, honesty;

Nonviolence, truth, absence of anger,
disengagement, peace, loyalty,
compassion for creatures, lack of greed,
gentleness, modesty, reliability;

Brilliance, patience, resolve,
clarity, absence of envy and of pride;
these characterize a man
born with divine traits.

Hypocrisy, arrogance, vanity,
anger, harshness, ignorance;
these characterize a man
born with demonic traits.

[5] The divine traits lead to freedom,
the demonic lead to bondage;
do not despair, Arjuna;
you were born with the divine.

All creatures in the world
are either divine or demonic;
I described the divine at length;
hear what I say of the demonic.

Demonic men cannot comprehend

activity and rest; there exists no clarity,
no morality, no truth in them.

They say that the world
has no truth, no basis, no god,
that no power of mutual dependence
is its cause, but only desire.

Mired in this view, lost to themselves
with their meager understanding,
these fiends contrive terrible acts
to destroy the world.

[10] Subject to insatiable desire,
drunk with hypocrisy and pride,
holding false notions from delusion,
they act with impure vows.

In their certainty that life
consists in sating their desires,
they suffer immeasurable anxiety
that ends only with death. . . .

[21] The three gates of hell
that destroy the self
are desire, anger, and greed;
one must relinquish all three.

Released through these three gates
of darkness, Arjuna,
a man elevates the self
and ascends to the highest way.

If he rejects norms of tradition
and lives to fulfill his desires,
he does not reach perfection
or happiness or the highest way.

Let tradition be your standard
in judging what to do or avoid;
knowing the norms of tradition,
perform your action here.

[18:1–9, 41–49, 60–73] In the eighteenth and last chapter of the Gita, *the topics of renunciation and the three constituents of nature are treated for the last time. Krishna summarizes the duties of the castes and stresses the importance of doing one's caste duty in a spirit of detachment. Then comes a short summary of the teaching of the whole book and a description of the merits obtained by reading it. Arjuna is convinced by Krishna and surrenders himself in obedience.*

Arjuna:

Krishna, I want to know the real essence
of both renunciation and relinquishment.

Lord Krishna:

Giving up actions based on desire,
the poets know as "renunciation";
relinquishing all fruit of action,
learned men call "relinquishment."

Some wise men say all action
is flawed and must be relinquished;
others say action in sacrifice, charity,
and penance must not be relinquished.

Arjuna, hear my decision
about relinquishment;
it is rightly declared
to be of three kinds.

[5] Action in sacrifice, charity,
and penance is to be performed,
not relinquished—for wise men,
they are acts of sanctity.

But even these actions
should be done by relinquishing to me
attachment and the fruit of action—
this is my decisive idea.

Renunciation of prescribed action
is inappropriate; relinquished in delusion,
it becomes a way of dark inertia.

When one passionately relinquishes
difficult action from fear
of bodily harm, he cannot win
the fruit of relinquishment.

But if one performs prescribed action
because it must be done,
relinquishing attachment and the fruit,
his relinquishment is a lucid act. . . .

[41] The actions of priests, warriors,
commoners, and servants
are apportioned by qualities
born of their intrinsic being.

Tranquility, control, penance,
purity, patience and honesty,
knowledge, judgment, and piety
are intrinsic to the action of a priest.

Heroism, fiery energy, resolve,
skill, refusal to retreat in battle,
charity, and majesty in conduct
are intrinsic to the action of a warrior.

Farming, herding cattle, and commerce
are intrinsic to the action of a commoner;
action that is essentially service
is intrinsic to the servant.

[45] Each one achieves success
by focusing on his own action;
hear how one finds success
by focusing on his own action.

By his own action a man finds success,
worshipping the source
of all creatures' activity,
the presence pervading all that is.

Better to do one's own duty imperfectly
than to do another man's well;
doing action intrinsic to his being,
a man avoids guilt.

Arjuna, a man should not relinquish
action he is born to, even if it is flawed;
all undertakings are marred by a flaw,
as fire is obscured by smoke.

His understanding everywhere detached,
the self mastered, longing gone,
one finds through renunciation
the supreme success beyond action. . . .

[60] You are bound by your own action,
intrinsic to your being, Arjuna;
even against your will you must do
what delusion now makes you refuse.

Arjuna, the lord resides
in the heart of all creatures,
making them reel magically,
as if a machine moved them.

With your whole being, Arjuna,
take refuge in him alone—
from his grace you will attain
the eternal place that is peace.

This knowledge I have taught
is more arcane than any mystery—
consider it completely,
then act as you choose.

Listen to my profound words,
the deepest mystery of all,
for you are precious to me
and I tell you for your good.

[65] Keep your mind on me,
be my devotee, sacrificing, bow to me—
you will come to me, I promise,
for you are dear to me.

Relinquishing all sacred duties to me,
make me your only refuge; do not grieve,
for I shall free you from all evils.
You must not speak of this to one
who is without penance and devotion,
or who does not wish to hear,
or who finds fault with me.

When he shares this deepest mystery
with others devoted to me,
giving me his total devotion,
a man will come to me without doubt.

No mortal can perform
service for me that I value more,
and no other man on earth
will be more dear to me than he is.

[70] I judge the man who studies
our dialogue on sacred duty
to offer me sacrifice
through sacrifice in knowledge.

If he listens in faith,
finding no fault, a man is free
and will attain the cherished worlds
of those who act in virtue.

Arjuna, have you listened
with your full powers of reason?
Has the delusion of ignorance
now been destroyed?

Arjuna:

Krishna, my delusion is destroyed,
and by your grace I have regained
    memory;
I stand here, my doubt dispelled,
ready to act on your words.

APPENDIX 2: NON-SANSKRIT SOURCES (TWO TAMIL POETS)

Much of the Sanskrit foundation of Hinduism was creatively adapted for the myriad languages of India. These adaptations preserved and extended the basic ideas of the ancient scriptural sources. The first two poems of this appendix will sample the Tamil (south Indian) religious poetry of Appar (seventh century), the best-known of the "Shaivite saints" whose writings are given a scriptural function, if not formal status.[52] The last two poems are by Tukaram (seventeenth century), the greatest Maharashtrian poet. These poems reflect popular *bhakti* tradition, and many of them are recited in the humblest households in India.

---

[52]Taken from F. Kingsbury and G. E. Phillips, *Hymns of the Tamil Shaivite Saints* (Calcutta: Association Press, 1921), pp. 47–51.

Confession of Sin

Evil, all evil, my race, evil my qualities all,
Great am I only in sin, evil is even my good.
Evil my innermost self, foolish, avoiding the pure,
Beast am I not, yet the ways of the beast I can never forsake.

I can exhort with strong words, telling men what they should hate.
Yet can I never give gifts, only to beg them I know.
Ah! wretched man that I am, why did I come to birth?

The Presence of God

No man holds sway over us,
Nor death nor hell fear we;
No tremblings, griefs of mind,
No pains nor cringings see.
Joy, day by day, unchanged
Is ours, for we are His,
His ever, who does reign,
Our Shankara,[53] in bliss.
Here to His feet we've come,
Feet as plucked flow'rets fair;
See how His ears divine
Ring and white conch-shell wear.
He is ever hard to find, but He lives in the thought of the good;

He is innermost secret of Scripture, inscrutable, unknowable;
He is holy and milk and the shining light.
He is the king of the Devas,
Immanent in Vishnu, in Brahma, in flame and in wind,
Yet in the mighty sounding sea and in the mountains.
He is the great One who chooses Shiva's paradise for his own.
If there be days when my tongue is dumb and speaks not of him,
Let no such days be counted in the record of my life.

---

[53]*Shankara:* Shiva.

[Tukaram:] Waiting[54]

With head on hand before my door,
   I sit and wait in vain.
Along the road to Pandhari
   My heart and eyes I strain.
When shall I look upon my Lord?
   When shall I see him come?
Of all the passing days and hours
   I count the heavy sum.
With watching long my eyelids throb,
   My limbs with sore distress,

But my impatient heart forgets
   My body's weariness.
Sleep is no longer sweet to me;
   I care not for my bed;
Forgotten are my house and home,
   All thirst and hunger fled.
Says Tuka,[55] Blest shall be the day—
   Ah, soon may it betide!—
When one shall come from Pandhari
   To summon back the bride.

---

[54]Taken from N. Macnicol, *Psalms of the Maratha Saints* (Calcutta: Association Press, 1920), p. 58.

---

[55]*Tuka:* the poet Tukaram himself.

The Burden of the Past[56]

I have been harassed by the world.
I have dwelled in my mother's womb and
   I must enter the gate of the womb eight
   million times.
I was born a needy beggar and my life is passed
   under a stranger's power.
I am bound fast in the meshes of my past and
   its later influence continues with me,
It puts forth its power and whirls me along.
My stomach is empty and never at rest.
I have no fixed course or home or village.
I have no power, O God, to end my
   wanderings;

My soul dances about like rice in a frying pan.
Ages have passed in this way and I do not know
   how many more await me.
I cannot end my course, for it begins again;
Only the ending of the world can set me free.
Who will finish this suffering of mine?
Who will take my burden on himself?
Your name will carry me over the sea of this
   world,
You run to the help of the distressed.
Now run to me, Narayana,[57] to me, poor and
   wretched as I am.
Consider neither my merits or my faults.
Tukaram implores your mercy.

---

[56]From J. N. Fraser and K. B. Marathe, *The Poems of Tukaram* (Madras: Christian Literature Society, 1909), pp. 114–115.

---

[57]*Narayana:* Vishnu.

GLOSSARY

Aranyakas (ah-RUN-yah-kuhs) "Forest Books," containing a philosophical treatment of sacrifice.

Atman (AHT-muhn) the individual self or soul.

Bhagavad-Gita (BAH-gah-vahd GEE-tuh) "The Song of the Lord."

Brahman (BRAH-muhn) the ultimate, absolute reality of the cosmos; the world soul.

Brahmanas (BRAH-muh-nuhs) "Brahmin Books," Vedic expositions of sacrifice.

Dharma-Shastras (DAHR-muh SHAS-truhs) writings on personal and social duties.

mantra (MAHN-truh) a short sacred formula used in prayer or meditation.

Om (or A'um) (OHM) a syllable symbolizing the fundamental hidden reality of the universe.

pandit Brahmin who specializes in Vedic memorization and ritual enactment. (Compare our word *pundit*.)

rishis (REE-shees) "seers" who heard the sounds of the four *Vedas* and collected them into the Veda *samhitas*.

samhitas (SAHM-hee-tuhs) "collections" of the four *Vedas*.

Shruti (SHROO-tee) "what was heard" by the ancients, the *Vedas*; the first level of scripture, considered of cosmic, not human, authorship.

Smriti (SMRIH-tee) "what was remembered" about divine revelation; the second level of scripture.

Upanishads (oo-PAH-nee-shahds) "sittings near a teacher"; philosophical collections forming the end of the *Veda*.

Vedas (VAY-duhs) the body of *Shruti*, consisting of the four *Vedas*, the *Brahmanas*, the *Aranyakas*, and the principal *Upanishads*.

QUESTIONS FOR STUDY AND DISCUSSION

1. To what degree, if any, can the *Vedas* be described as reflecting a nature worship religion?

2. Compare the use and effects of soma to the modern use of drugs among those who argue that it brings a higher consciousness. What might the similarities and differences be?

3. In what ways did the *Upanishads* both differ from and agree with earlier Vedic literature? Do you agree with those scholars who argue that the differences between the earlier *Vedas* and later writings (including the *Upanishads*) justify calling the first stage "Vedic religion" and only the second stage "Hinduism"?

4. How does the variety of usages of Hindu scripture in the past and present mirror the variety of Hindu religion?

5. If you were to become a Hindu, to which caste would you like to belong? Which sex? Why?

6. How would you characterize the role of women in Hinduism? Are the texts given here reflective of what you see as their actual conditions in India?

7. In what ways and for what reasons does the *Bhagavad-Gita* (Appendix 1) present the path of devotion as the best form of Hinduism?

8. How does the *Bhagavad-Gita* present and answer the problem of war? What is your critique of its answer? To what degree may its answer be applicable to peoples of other cultures and other religions?

9. How do the later devotional songs (Appendix 2) carry forth and develop the traditions of devotional Hinduism?

SUGGESTIONS FOR FURTHER READING

Primary Readings

The most complete and accessible translations of Hindu scripture remain the several volumes in F. Max Müller, gen. ed., *Sacred Books of the East* (Oxford: Oxford University Press, 1879–1910). For more recent translations, begin with the following works.

Thomas B. Coburn, *Encountering the Goddess: A Translation of the Devi-Mahatmya and a Study of its Interpretation*. Albany: State University of New York Press, 1991. A translation and study of the best-known goddess text in modern India.

Robert E. Hume, *The Thirteen Principal Upanishads,* 2d ed. Oxford: Oxford University Press, 1983. Perhaps the best translation of the most important *Upanishads*.

Donald S. Lopez, Jr., *Religions of India in Practice*. Princeton: Princeton University Press, 1995. Contains primary documents, many never translated before, of more recent Hindu literature that has scriptural use. See especially the section "Songs of Devotion and Praise," which treats devotional poetry.

Wendy Doniger O'Flaherty, *The Rig Veda: An Anthology*. London: Penguin, 1981. A selection of 108 hymns, with excellent translations and full annotations.

Wendy Doniger O'Flaherty, ed., *Textual Sources for the Study of Hinduism*. Totowa, N.J.: Barnes & Noble, 1988. A selection of readings from both *Shruti and Smriti*.

Patrick Olivelle, *Samnyasa Upanishads: Hindu Scriptures on Asceticism and Renunciation*. New York: Oxford University Press, 1992. Full introduction, fresh translation, and notes for those *Upanishads* that deal with the stage of renunciation.

Barbara Stoller Miller, *The Bhagavad-Gita: Krishna's Counsel in Time of War*. New York: Columbia University Press, 1986. The most readable recent translation of the *Gita*, and one that suggests its power and literary beauty.

Secondary Readings

A. L. Basham, *The Origins and Development of Classical Hinduism,* ed. K. Zysk. New York: Oxford University Press, 1989. An insightful and concise treatment of Hindu scriptures in the context of a survey of the stages of Hinduism.

Thomas B. Coburn, "'Scripture' in India: Towards a Typology of the Word in Hindu Life." In M. Levering, ed., *Rethinking Scripture*. Albany: State University of New York Press, 1989, pp. 102–128; also published in the *Journal of the American Academy of Religion* 52 (1984), pp. 435–459. Argues that *scripture* is an ill-fitting term for Hinduism and proposes instead a *typology of the word*.

Harold Coward, "Scripture in Hinduism." In *Sacred Word and Sacred Text*. Maryknoll: Orbis, 1988. A survey of the Hindu scriptures with special attention to orality.

Klaus Kostermaier, *Hindu Writings: A Short Introduction to the Major Sources*. Oxford: Oneworld, 2000. Treats Veda to contemporary writings, with emphasis on scripture.

Robert C. Lester, "Hinduism: Veda and Sacred Texts." In F. M. Denny and R. L. Taylor, *The Holy Book in Comparative Perspective*. Charleston: University of South Carolina Press, 1985, pp. 126–147. A good treatment of the relationship of Vedic texts and other Hindu scriptures, especially the *Smriti*.

Krishna Sivaraman, ed., *Hindu Spirituality: Vedas through Vedanta*. New York: Crossroad, 1989. A treatment by mostly Indian scholars of the continuing significance of Vedic and Upanishadic traditions for contemporary Hinduism.

Katherine K. Young, "[Women in] Hinduism." In Arvind Sharma, ed., *Women in World Religions*. Albany: State University of New York Press, 1987, pp. 59–103. This concise but fairly comprehensive survey of its topic has good references to the content and usage of Hindu sacred writings.

INFOTRAC COLLEGE EDITION

You can locate InfoTrac College Edition articles about this chapter by accessing the InfoTrac College Edition website (http://www.infotrac.collegeedition.com/wadsworth/). Using subject guide, enter the search terms relevant to this chapter, and then read abstracts for relevant articles.

Chanting Buddhist Scripture
Japanese Buddhist monks chant scriptures at a Buddhist altar. Credit: Michel Strickmann,
from the Image Bank of the Center for the Study of World Religions, Harvard University.
Used by permission of Mr. and Mrs. Leo Strickmann.

CHAPTER THREE

Buddhism

❖ In a Chinese convent, Buddhist nuns gather daily to read scripture. A low hum fills the reading room as they all recite together. They are "making merit," doing a deed that will wear away karma. This merit will enable them to be reborn after death into a better existence, eventually to achieve Nirvana and be reborn no more.

❖ In Washington, D.C., a new "Dharma Wheel Cutting Karma" has been turning since 1997 in the Asian section of the Library of Congress. The wheel contains 208 repetitions of forty-two Tibetan scriptures, which otherwise fill fifteen Tibetan volumes. The spiritual power generated by the constant electrical turning of the wheel is said to generate compassion, prevent natural disasters, and promote peace in the world.

❖ In Tokyo, worshippers from the Nichiren sect of Buddhism gather in their temple. A steady chant goes up: "Hail to the Lotus Sutra." Like all followers of Nichiren, they constantly recite this formula of devotion to a leading scripture to bring blessing on themselves and ultimately unite with the eternal spirit of the Buddha.

❖ In Maharagama, Sri Lanka, several Buddhist monks work at computer keyboards. They are keying in the complete text of the Pali version of the Buddhist collection of scriptures. After three years of work, the scriptures are to be published on the World Wide Web; later they will be available in a fully searchable CD-ROM. The monks and the private patrons funding this project see it as yet another phase in the preservation of Buddhist scripture from 2,500 years ago.

INTRODUCTION

The Buddhist religion is based on the life and teaching of the Indian sage Siddhartha Gotama (ca. 536–476 B.C.E.), the Enlightened One or **Buddha** [BUHD-ah]. It believes that persons can overcome the misery of the world and reach their own Buddha status by a process of mental and moral purification. Buddhism has spread virtually throughout Asia. With this growth has come a wide diversity within Buddhism that is mirrored in its scriptures. The Buddhist canon has three main forms, hundreds of scriptural texts, and many different types of usage. This assemblage of scriptures provides a fascinating overview of the early history of the Buddhist tradition and insight into the contemporary life of Buddhists everywhere.

Overview of Structure

The scriptures of Theravada (south Asian) Buddhism are known as the **Tipitaka**[1] [tih-pee-TAH-kuh], the "Three Baskets" (see Table 3.1). Tradition says that the early disciples of Buddha wrote his words on palm-leaf manuscripts and collected them into three baskets (*pitakas*). The term *pitaka* as a division of scripture does not occur in the scriptures themselves, but it seems to have arisen around 300 B.C.E. and is now universal among Buddhists. The three *pitakas* are **Vinaya** [vih-NIGH-yuh] *Pitaka* ("Discipline Basket"), the **Sutta** [SUH-tuh] *Pitaka* ("Discourse Basket"), and the **Abhidhamma** [ahb-hee-DAHM-muh] *Pitaka* ("Special Teaching Basket"). We will consider each basket in turn and then survey the structure of the Chinese and Tibetan forms of the canon.

The *Vinaya Pitaka* is so named because it contains the regulations for the communal life of the monks and nuns. All these rules are said to be the words of the Buddha. The *Vinaya* has three divisions: the *Sutta-vibhanga*, "Discourse on Rules"; the *Khandhakas*, "Sections"; and the *Parivaras*, "Accessory," a short summary of the rules and how to apply them. Each of the first two are divided into two other groups. The *Vinaya Pitaka* presents 227 different rules, most of them prohibitions of forbidden activities, which are grouped according to importance. They range from a few offenses that result in permanent expulsion from the order to minor offenses that need only be confessed to one's monastic leader. All the rules for monks apply in a general way to the nuns as well, but a special section of the *Suttavibhanga* gives specific regulations for them. The size of the *Vinaya Pitaka* is indicated by its most recent English translation, which runs to six substantial volumes. That the *Vinaya* is first among the *pitakas* attests to the leading role that monasticism has played in the history of Buddhism as a whole and its scriptures in particular.

The *Sutta Pitaka* contains teachings attributed to Gotama Buddha. Buddhists divide this largest of the baskets into five collections, called *nikayas*: Long Discourses, Medium-Length Discourses, Kindred Discourses, Item-More (or Gradual) Discourses, and Short Texts. Each discourse has many subdivisions, and most follow a common structure. First comes "Thus I have heard [from the Buddha]," second comes a statement of the place and occasion of the hearing, third is the body of the teaching, and last the listener's confession of the truth of the teaching and acknowledgment that he is Buddha's disciple. The Discourse Basket is probably the best-known basket of the *Tipitaka*. For students of Buddhism it provides the best access to the essence of this tradition, with its rationale for the first basket, collections of wise sayings, stories of former lives of the Buddha and other Buddhist worthies, and its general suttas on doctrines and ethics.

The *Abhidhamma Pitaka* contains seven scholastic treatises based on the teachings of Buddha. They deal with advanced, difficult topics that are often highly philosophical. Although the Sanskrit and Pali versions of the first two baskets are similar in content, they vary quite a bit in the third basket. The Pali version, used by South Asian

---

[1]Sanskrit *Tripitaka*. Throughout this chapter, we will generally use the Pali language forms of key Buddhist words, with the Sanskrit equivalents, where necessary, in parentheses. The titles of scripture books will reflect their language of origin, generally Pali.

Table 3.1
The Pali Canon, the *Tipitaka*

Name	Translation	Content/Size
Vinaya Pitaka (Discipline Basket):		
1. *Sutta-vibhanga*	Division of Rules	Monastic rules stated and expanded
a. *Mahavibhanga*	Great Division	227 rules for monks
b. *Bhikkuni-vibhanga*	Division about Nuns	Rules for nuns
2. *Khandhaka*	Sections	
a. *Mahavagga*	Great Group	Main rules
b. *Cullavagga*	Small Group	Miscellaneous rules
3. *Parivara*	Accessory	Summaries of rules
Sutta Pitaka (Discourse Basket):		
1. *Digha-nikaya*	Collection of Long Discourses	34 suttas
2. *Majjhima-nikaya*	Collection of Medium Discourses	152 suttas
3. *Samyutta-nikaya*	Collection of Corrected Discourses	56 groups of suttas
4. *Anguttara-nikaya*	Collection of Item-More Discourses	2308 suttas
5. *Khuddaka-nikaya*	Collection of Little Texts	
a. *Khuddaka-patha*	Little Readings	A meditation book
b. *Dhammapada*	Verses on Teaching	26 chapters
c. *Udana*	Utterances	80 utterances
d. *Itivuttaka*	Thus-saids	112 suttas
e. *Sutta-nipata*	Sutta Collection	71 suttas
f. *Vimana-vatthu*	Tales of Heavenly Mansions	85 poems
g. *Peta-vatthu*	Tales of Ghosts	Rebirth as Ghosts
h. *Thera-Gatha*	Verses of Elder Men	Poems from earliest monks
i. *Theri-Gatha*	Verses of Elder Women	Poems from early nuns
j. *Jataka*	Lives	550 past lives of Gotama
k. *Nidessa*	Exposition	2 commentaries
l. *Patisambhida-magga*	Way of Analysis	Doctrinal exposition
m. *Apadana*	Stories	Saints' past lives
n. *Buddhavamsa*	Lineage of the Buddhas	Stories of 24 pre-Gotama Buddhas
o. *Cariya-pitaka*	Basket of Perfections	35 tales from *Jataka*
Abhidhamma Pitaka (Special Teaching Basket):		
1. *Dhamma-sangani*	Enumeration of Dhammas	
2. *Vibhanga*	Distinctions	
3. *Dhastu-Kadha*	Discussions of Elements	
4. *Puggala-pannatti*	Designation of Persons	
5. *Yamaka*	The Pairs	
6. *Patthama*	Activations	

Tables 3.1 and 3.2 are adapted from Richard H. Robinson, *The Buddhist Religion* (Belmont, CA: Dickenson Publishing Company, 1970), pp. 125–128. Copyright © 1970, Dickenson Publishing Company. Used by permission of Wadsworth Publishing Company, Inc.

Table 3.2

The Mahayana or Chinese Canon, the *San-Ts'ang*

Name of Section	Translation	Size
Agama	Limbs	2 vols., 151 texts
Jatakas	Lives	2 vols., 68 texts
Prajna-Paramita	Perfect Wisdom	4 vols., 42 texts
Saddharma-Pundarika	———	1 vol., 16 texts
Avatamsaka	———	2 vols., 31 texts
Ratnakuta		
Mahaparinirvana	Great Decease	1 vol., 23 texts
———	Great Assembly	1 vol., 28 texts
Sutra-Pitaka	Sutra Collection	4 vols., 423 texts
Tantra	Tantra	4 vols., 572 texts
Vinaya	Discipline	3 vols., 86 texts
———	Commentary on Sutras	3 vols., 31 texts
Adhidharma	Special Teaching	4 vols., 28 texts
Madhyamika		1 vol., 15 texts
Yogacara	Yoga Practice	2 vols., 49 texts
———	Treatises	1 vols., 65 texts
———	Commentaries on Sutras	7 vols.
———	Commentaries on *Vinaya*	1 vol.
———	Commentaries on Shastras	5 vols.
———	Chinese Sectarian Writings	5 vols.
———	History and Biography	4 vols., 95 texts
———	Encyclopedias and Dictionaries	2 vols., 16 texts
———	Non-Buddhist Writings	1 vol., 8 texts
———	Catalogues	1 vol., 40 texts

Theravada Buddhism, tries to adhere conservatively to the exact words of Buddha. Its seven treatises are: "The Summary of **Dhamma** [DAH-muh]," "Divisions," "Discussion of Elements," "The Designation of Person," "Subjects of Discussion," "The Pairs," and "Activations." The Sanskrit *Abhidharma* is important for the growth of Buddhist philosophy because these Sanskrit books deal with the *ideas* of Buddha more than with his words. Like the Pali version, the Sanskrit has seven books, but they are different in names and content, and they vary between the Chinese and Tibetan translations. The seven most commonly recognized are "Method of Knowledge," "Treatise," "Overview of Consciousness," "Collection on the Law [Dharma]," "Treatise on Communication," "Overview of the Elements," and "Discourse on Sacred Beliefs."

The Mahayana canon did not adopt the threefold basket-division of the Pali canon; it has no main divisions (see Table 3.2). But many of the more important books of the Pali canon were incorporated in the Mahayana canon. The Pali and Mahayana canons share such important works as the ***Jatakas*** [JAH-tah-kuhs], the *Death of the Buddha* (*Mahaparinibbana*, Sanskrit *Mahaparinirvana*), Vinaya texts on monastic discipline, various Abhidhamma texts, and others. Some books from the Mahayana canon have even penetrated Theravada Buddhism, recognized and used as scripture while not being formally admitted to the historic Pali canon. In Sri Lanka,

Table 3.3
The Tibetan Canon

Name	Translation	Size
I. *Kanjur:*	Translation of the Ordinances	108 vols.
'*Dul-ba*	Discipline [for monastics]	13 vols.
Shes-rab-kyi-pha-rol-tu-phyin-pa	Supreme Otherworldly Knowledge	21 vols.
Phal-chen	Buddhist Cosmology	6 vols.
dKon-brtsegs	Heap of Jewels	6 vols.
mDo	Teaching Lectures	30 vols.
Mya-ngan-'das	Nirvana	2 vols.
rGyud	Texture [Tantra]	22 vols.
II. *Tanjur:*	Translation of the Doctrine	225 vols.
mDo	Teaching	136 vols.
rGyud	Texture [Tantra]	87 vols.
	A book of Hymns	1 vol.
	An index	1 vol.

for example, the *Buddhacarita* and the *Visuddhimagga* are widely received and used as scripture.

The Mahayana canon also added many other new books, all of them claiming to be the true word of the Gotama Buddha. One of the most important is the group of *Prajna-Paramita,* or "Perfection of Knowledge," sutras. These books discuss philosophically the denial of the reality of existence and nonexistence. They feature an almost constant repetitiveness that has contributed to their great length. Another work is the *Sukhavativyuha,* "Description of the Happy Land" where the gracious Buddha Amitabha rules and invites his followers to share eternal life with him. This text has become important in the Japanese Pure Land Buddhist sect. A third work is the *Saddharmapundarika,* "Lotus of the Good Law." This work has become the leading text of Nichiren Buddhism. In sum, with its adoption of many older books along with an astonishing variety of new books, the literature of Mahayana Buddhism is vast and complex.

The third main Buddhist canon is the Tibetan (see Table 3.3). In the seventh century C.E., Buddhism came to Tibet, where it is known as Lamaism (from the Tibetan *bla-ma,* the "superior" religion). The Tibetan king sent a delegation to India, where an alphabet was devised for the Tibetan language and the entire Buddhist literature translated into it. To this Indian literature, the Tibetans added many books of their own, secular as well as religious. The final and official assembling of these books came in the fourteenth century, when they were fixed into two collections, the *Kanjur* ("Translation of the Ordinances") and the *Tanjur* ("Translation of the Doctrine").

The *Kanjur* (or *bKa'-'gyur*) contains 689 books of various lengths in 100 or 108 volumes. It contains only those texts that the Buddha himself is said to have taught. The first main division is the "Discipline," for monks; the second is the "Supreme

Otherworldly Knowledge"; the third deals with Buddhist cosmology; the fourth is the "Heap of Jewels"; the fifth is the "Teaching Lectures"; the sixth is "Nirvana"; the last is the *Tantra.* The *Tanjur* (or *bsTan-'gur*) is not, as is often stated, a commentary on the *Kanjur.* It contains 225 volumes in two main sections, Sutra and Tantra. The Sutra section includes many translations of Indian commentaries on older scriptures. The *Tanjur* deals in an even wider variety of topics than the *Kanjur:* traditional religious teachings, magical texts drawn mainly from native Tibetan religion, and texts on alchemy and astrology. Today the preservation and further dissemination of Tibetan scriptures is a primary task of Tibetan Buddhist exiles.

Origin and Development

The development of Buddhist scripture begins with Gotama Buddha himself. Buddhists believe that Prince Gotama established among his monk disciples an oral transmission of his teachings on which later written scriptures are based. They trace all the varied scripture collections and their contents back to Buddha; all are his word.

When Gotama died, he had not appointed a human successor. Indeed, he taught instead that the leader of the Buddhists was to be his Teaching (Dhamma) and the monastic order (Sangha) he founded. Soon after his death, his disciples gathered at the first general council of Buddhists, held at Rajagaha in 483, to formalize his teachings. After seven months of work collecting and examining the purported sayings of Buddha for authenticity, they drafted an official version and committed it to memory. His chief disciple Ananda is said to have recited them all. The sayings were written down on palm leaves (more durable than paper or parchment in the hot, humid Indian climate) and then separated into baskets. Mahayana Buddhists believe that all three were developed at this time. Theravada Buddhists believe that the last basket, Special Teaching, was formed at the third general council of Buddhists in 253 B.C.E. Most modern scholars would agree that the nature of this basket seems to suggest a later origin.

Even after this initial conversion to writing, oral transmission continued and was seen as the primary mode of scripture preservation by all early Buddhists. An early Special Teaching Basket text, the *Samuccaya,* indicates the reasons for this preference. Among them are: Memorizing is easy, accumulates merit, aids understanding, brings mental satisfaction, and promotes one's good standing among others. In addition, early Buddhists saw transmission by an exacting oral tradition as more reliable in preserving the exact words of the Buddha than writing.

When Mahayana ("Large Vehicle") Buddhism arose in the first century C.E., it had a new concern for liberation through the **bodhisattva** [bohd-hee-SAHT-vuh], one who postpones his own full enlightenment in order to help others. The older idea of self-redemption characteristic of Theravada Buddhism gave way to redemption through the grace of this Buddha, who postponed enlightenment to aid others. The new movement required a new body of scripture, and so began the Mahayana canon. This collection is typically called the "Chinese canon," but it is important to note that this canon is also used in Japan, usually in its Chinese-language form.

Use

Buddhist usage of scripture centers around monastic activity. Since early times, when the teaching of Buddha was passed along orally and then written down, the role of monks (not nuns) in scriptural activity has been primary. The scriptures themselves bear the marks of this orientation. For example, the first and the third baskets are explicitly for monastics. Other reasons also figure in. The expense in owning such a large canon makes it accessible mainly to monastic orders. Its size demands a lifetime of study to master it; its content is challenging and specialized, calling for special teachers who can only be found among the monks. Buddhism in general demands withdrawal from the distractions of daily life in order to give the scriptures the kind of in-depth study they deserve.

What does this monastic usage entail? First, Buddhism has traditionally distinguished between study monks and meditation monks. The very term *study monk* indicates the first usage of scripture, the study of the content of its teachings. The new monk studies scripture to learn the first and most important of the monastic rules that govern his life. He also studies the most easily understood texts in the *Sutta Pitaka*, such as the *Dhammapada* and the *Jataka* verses. As time progresses and he masters this material, he proceeds to learn the other rules in the *Vinaya Pitaka* and the other texts of the *Sutta Pitaka*. If, at the height of his monastic career, he displays an excellence in study and teaching, he may go on to master the intricacies of the *Abhidhamma Pitaka*, the Special Teaching Basket. Because study of the scriptures is in most forms of Buddhism a prerequisite for becoming a meditation monk, all monks pass through this first phase. Moreover, throughout the history of Buddhism and even today, study monks greatly outnumber meditation monks. This is especially the case in modern times, when the general conviction has grown in many Buddhist circles that one cannot reach enlightenment in this life.

In all this study and teaching, the goal is to realize in one's own life the teachings of the Buddha that lead toward enlightenment. The scripture itself, as a book, is worth little or nothing. The *meaning* of the words, not the words themselves, has value in the search for purification.

Monks also pursue scriptural activity for the laity. At funerals they recite texts for the merit of the deceased. Monks often officiate at wedding ceremonies. They lecture on the scriptures to the laity, both individuals and groups. Some monks will preach the scriptures to the laity, often using such popular material as the *Jataka* tales. Wealthy layfolk will often sponsor long recitations of scripture in the monasteries and will pay for the publication of scriptures, all for the sake of making merit for loved ones. But all these activities with the laity are mostly incidental to a monk's main activity—studying and meditating on scripture in order to travel the road to personal enlightenment.

Of all forms of Buddhism, the Tibetan holds its scriptures in a great ritual esteem. The books are venerated in worship, with incense and prayer offered to them. They are produced in the traditional way, either printed by hand or with woodblocks, and are preserved in the monasteries with great care. Although these books are produced and preserved in Tibet, no scholarly critical edition of them has been compiled, modern language translations are very incomplete, and only a few European libraries possess a complete copy of the *Kanjur* and *Tanjur*.

HISTORY

The Past Lives of Gotama Buddha*

After his enlightenment, the Buddha knew all his past lives. In the Jataka *(Birth Stories), he recounts in detail 550 episodes from as many past lives, each revealing his gradual progress to perfection in his last incarnation as Gotama. These* Jatakas *each teach one point, always to edify the reader. Only the verses at the end are considered inspired, and the stories are built from them. They come from a Mahayana setting that features the bestowal of merit from one person to another, but they are widely known in Theravada lands as well. In this story the layman transfers merit to the barber.*[2]

The Master told this story about a believing layman while staying in Jetavana. This was a faithful, pious soul, and a chosen disciple. One evening, on his way to Jetavana, he came to the bank of the river Aciravati, when the ferrymen had pulled up their boat on the shore in order to attend service. As no boat could be seen at the landing, and our friend's mind was full of delightful thoughts of the Buddha, he walked into the river. His feet did not sink below the water. He got as far as mid-river walking as though he were on dry land, but then he noticed the waves. Then his ecstasy subsided, and his feet began to sink. Again he strung himself up to high tension [by meditation], and walked on over the water. So he arrived at Jetavana, greeted the Master, and took a seat on one side. The Master entered into conversation with him pleasantly. "I hope, good layman, you had no mishap on your way." "O Sir," he replied, "on my way I was so absorbed in thoughts of the Buddha that I set foot upon the river; but I walked over it as though it had been dry ground!" "Ah, friend layman," said the Master, "you are not the only one who has been kept safe by remembering the virtues of the Buddha. In older days pious laymen have been shipwrecked in mid-ocean, and saved themselves by remembering the Buddha's virtues." Then, at the man's request, he told a story from the past.

Once upon a time, in the days when Kassapa was Supreme Buddha, a disciple who had entered on the Paths took passage on board ship in company with a barber of some considerable property. The barber's wife had given him charge of our friend, to look after him in better and in worse.

A week later, the ship was wrecked in mid-ocean. These two persons clinging to one plank were cast up on an island. There the barber killed some birds, and cooked them, offering a share of his meal to the lay brother. "No, thank you," said he, "I have had enough." He was thinking to himself, "In this place there is no help for us except the Three Jewels,"[3] and so he pondered upon the blessings of the Three Jewels. As he pondered and pondered, a Serpent-king who had been born in that isle changed his own body to the shape of a great ship. The ship was filled with the seven kinds of precious things. An ocean god was the helmsman. The three masts were made of sapphire, the anchor of gold, the ropes of silver, and the planks were golden.

The Sea-spirit stood on board, crying, "Any passengers for India?" The lay brother said, "Yes, that's where we are headed." "In with you then, on board with you!" He went aboard, and wanted to call his friend the barber. "You may come," said the helmsman to the lay

---

brother, "but not he." "Why not?" "He is not a man of holy life, that's why; I brought this ship for you, not for him." The lay brother replied, "Very well; the gifts I have given, the virtues I have practiced, the powers I have developed—I give him the fruit of all of them!" "I thank you, master!" said the barber. "Now," said the Sea-spirit, "I can take the barber aboard." So he conveyed them both over sea, and sailed upstream to Benares. There, by his power, he created a store of wealth for both of them, and spoke this to them:

"Keep company with the wise and good. If this barber had not been in company with this pious layman, he would have perished in the midst of the deep." Then he uttered these verses in praise of good company:

"Behold the fruit of sacrifice, virtue, and piety:
A serpent in ship-shape conveys the good man
    o'er the sea.

Make friendship only with the good, and keep
    good company;
Friends with the good, this Barber could his
    home in safety see."

Thus the Spirit of the Sea spoke, poised in mid-
    air. Finally he went to his own abode, taking
    the Serpent-king along with him.

The Master, after finishing this discourse, declared the Truths and identified the [connection to his] Birth. At the conclusion of the Truths the pious layman entered on the Fruit of the Second Path.[4] "On that occasion the converted lay brother attained Nirvana; Sariputta was the Serpent-king, and I myself was the ocean god."

---

[4]*the Fruit of the Second Path:* the path of those who are reborn again only once.

The Life of Gotama Buddha*

The Acts of the Buddha *by Ashvaghosha (first century B.C.E.) is often placed between Theravada and Mahayana Buddhism and is a favorite book in the latter. It deals in poetic form with the life and teachings of the Buddha. This selection recounts the birth of Gotama, the "Four Sights," his "Great Retirement," and his enlightenment. It portrays the life of the Buddha as an example for all Buddhists: all his followers should reach Nirvana in this manner. It opens, as do many Buddhist scriptures, with an invocation to Gotama Buddha.*[5]

Buddhacarita 1.1–2, 9–10, 15–17, 19–21, 23–25, 34, 54, 59, 62, 72–74, 83; 2.24–26, 28–32; 3.1–8, 26–33, 40–44, 53–61; 5.7–20; 12.88–104; 14.1–9, 35–37, 64–68, 79–81.
[5]Taken, with editing, from E. B. Cowell, trans., *Buddhist Mahayana Texts, Sacred Books of the East,* vol. 49 (Oxford: Oxford University Press, 1894), pp. 1–157.

That **Arhat** [a "worthy one" who has achieved enlightenment] is here saluted, who has no counterpart. Bestowing the supreme happiness, he surpasses Brahman the Creator. Driving away darkness, he vanquishes the sun. Dispelling all burning heat, he surpasses the beautiful moon.

There was a city, the dwelling-place of the great saint Kapila, that had its sides surrounded by the beauty of a lofty broad plain like a line of clouds. With its high-soaring palaces, it was immersed in the sky. . . . [9] A king by the name of Suddhodana ruled over the city. He was a relative of the sun, anointed to stand at the head of earth's monarchs. He adorned it as a bee adorns a full-blown lotus. [10] He was the very best of kings, intent on liberality yet empty of pride. . . .

[15] He had a queen named Maya, who was free from all deceit [*maya*]. She was a brilliance proceeding from his brilliance, like the splendor

of the sun when it is free from all the influence of darkness. . . . Truly the life of women is always darkness; yet when it encountered her, it shone brilliantly. . . .

[19] Falling from the host of beings in the Tushita heaven, and illumining the three worlds, the most excellent of Bodhisattvas[6] suddenly entered at a thought into her womb. [20] He assumed the form of a huge elephant as white as Himalaya, armed with six tusks, with his face perfumed with flowing ichor. Then he entered the womb of the queen of king Suddhodana to destroy the evils of the world. The guardians of the world hastened from heaven to watch over the world's one true ruler. . . . [23] Then one day by the king's permission the queen, having a great longing in her mind, went with the residents of the women's apartments into the garden Lumbini. As the queen supported herself by a bough that hung with a weight of flowers, the Bodhisattva suddenly came forth, splitting open her womb. [25] Then the constellation Pushya was auspicious. From the side of the queen, who was purified by her vow, her son was born for the welfare of the world. He was born without pain and without illness [for his mother]. . . . [34] [He said:] "I am born for supreme knowledge, for the welfare of the world. Therefore, this is my last birth. . . ."

[54] The great seer Asita learned by signs and through the power of his penances this birth of him who was to destroy all birth. In his thirst for the excellent Law, he came to the palace of the Sakya king. . . . [59] The sage, being invited by the king, filled with properly intense feeling, uttered his deep and solemn words [to the king] as his large eyes opened wide with wonder: ". . . . [62] Hear now the motive for my coming and rejoice in it. I have heard a heavenly voice in the heavenly path, [saying] that your son has been born for the sake of supreme knowledge. . . ."

[72] Knowing the king to be disturbed through his fear of some impending evil, the sage addressed him: "Let not your mind, O monarch, be disturbed. All that I have said is certainly true. I have no feeling of fear about his being subject to change, but I am distressed for my own disappointment. It is my time to depart, and this child is now born. He knows the mystery hard to attain, the means of destroying rebirth. Having forsaken his kingdom, becoming indifferent to all worldly things, and having attained the highest truth by his strenuous efforts, he will shine forth as a sun of knowledge to destroy the darkness of illusion in the world. . . ."

[83] When he heard these words, the king, his queen and his friends abandoned sorrow and rejoiced. Thinking, "Such is this son of mine," he considered that his son's excellence was his own. But he let his heart be influenced by the thought, "He will travel by the noble path." He was not opposed to religion, yet he still was alarmed at the prospect of losing his child. . . .

[2.24] When the young prince had passed the period of childhood and reached his middle youth, he learned in a few days the various sciences suitable to his race, which generally took many years to master. [25] But remembering what the great seer Asita said about his destined future that was to embrace transcendental happiness, the anxious care of the king . . . turned the prince to sensual pleasures. He sought for him from a family of unblemished moral excellence a bride possessed of beauty, modesty, gentle bearing, and widespread glory. Yasodhara was her name, a name well worthy of her, a very goddess of good fortune. . . .

[28] "He might see some inauspicious sight that could disturb his mind." Reflecting this way, the king had a dwelling prepared for his son in the private recesses of the palace. Then the son spent his time in those royal apartments. They were furnished with the delights proper for every season, gaily decorated like heavenly chariots upon the earth, and bright like the clouds of autumn. He spent time

---

[6] *Boddhisatva:* one who has reached enlightenment but postpones entering nirvana in order to help others reach it.

among the splendid musical concerts of singing women. [30] With the softly-sounding tambourines beaten by the tips of the women's hands, and ornamented with golden rims, and with the dances that were like the dances of the heavenly nymphs, that palace shone like Mount Kailasa. The women delighted him with their soft voices, their beautiful pearl-garlands, their playful intoxication, their sweet laughter, and their stolen glances concealed by their brows. Carried away in the arms of these women well-skilled in the ways of love, and reckless in the pursuit of pleasure, he fell from the roof of a pavilion and yet did not reach the ground, like a holy sage stepping from a heavenly chariot. . . .

[3.1] On a certain day he heard about the forests carpeted with tender grass. They had been all bound up in the cold season, but now their trees resounded with the kokilas birds and they were adorned with lotus-ponds. When he heard of the delightful appearance of these parks beloved by the women, he resolved to go outdoors. He was like an elephant long shut up in a house.

When the king learned the wish expressed by his son, he ordered a pleasure-party to be prepared, one worthy of his own affection and his son's beauty and youth. But he prohibited any encounter with any afflicted common person in the highroad. He said, "Heaven forbid that the prince with his tender nature should even imagine himself to be distressed." [5] Then he removed from the road with the greatest gentleness all those who had mutilated limbs or maimed senses, the decrepit and the sick and all squalid beggars. They made the highway assume its perfect beauty. Along this road made beautiful, the fortunate prince with his well-trained attendants came down one day at a proper time from the roof of the palace and went to visit the king to gain his permission to leave. Then the king, with tears rising in his eyes, smelled his son's head and gazed for a long time upon him. He gave him his permission, saying, "Go." But in his heart he did not want him to depart. . . .

[26] But then the gods, dwelling in their pure abodes, saw the city rejoicing like heaven itself. They created an old man to walk along and to stir the heart of the king's son. The prince saw him overcome with decrepitude and different in form from other men. With his gaze intently fixed on him, he addressed his driver with simple confidence. "Who is this man that has come here, with white hair and his hand resting on a staff, his eyes hidden beneath his brows, his limbs bent down and hanging loose? Is this a change produced in him, or his natural state, or an accident?"

The charioteer revealed to the king's son the secret that should have been kept so carefully. He thought no harm in his simplicity, for those same gods had bewildered his mind, and he said, [30] "Old age has broken him down. It is the ravisher of beauty, the ruin of vigor, the cause of sorrow, the destruction of delights, the affliction of memories, the enemy of the senses. He too once drank milk in his childhood, and in time he learned to crawl on the ground. Having step by step become a vigorous youth, he has step by step in the same way reached old age."

The startled prince spoke these words to the charioteer: "What! Will this evil come to me also?" To him the charioteer spoke again, "It will certainly come in time even to my long-lived lord. All the world knows that old age will destroy their beauty, and they are content to have it so. . . ."

[40] Then the same deities created another man with his body all afflicted by disease. On seeing him the son of Suddhodana addressed the charioteer, having his gaze fixed on the man. "That man with a swollen belly, his whole frame shaking as he pants, his arms and shoulders hanging loose, his body all pale and thin, uttering plaintively the word 'mother' when he embraces a stranger—who is this?"

Then his charioteer answered, "Gentle Sir, it is a very great affliction called sickness that has grown up, caused by the inflammation of the three humors. It has made even this strong man no longer master of himself."

Then the prince again addressed him, looking upon the man compassionately, "Is this evil peculiar to him, or are all people threatened by sickness?" The charioteer answered, "O prince, this evil is common to all. Pressed by diseases, people run to pleasure, though racked with pain. . . ."

[53] When the royal road was especially adorned and guarded, the king let the prince go out once more. He ordered the charioteer and chariot to proceed in a direction different from the previous one. But as the king's son was going on his way, the very same deities created a dead man. Only the charioteer and the prince, and no one else, saw him as he was carried dead along the road. [55] Then the prince spoke to the charioteer, "Who is this carried by four men, followed by mournful companions, who is adorned but no longer breathing?"

Then the driver, whose mind was overpowered by the gods who possess pure minds and pure dwellings, and who knew the truth, uttered to his lord this truth which he had been forbidden to tell. "This is some poor man who, bereft of his intellect, senses, vitality and qualities, lying asleep and unconscious, like mere wood or straw, is abandoned by both friends and enemies after they have carefully swathed and guarded him."

Hearing these words of the charioteer he was startled. He said to him, "Is this an accident peculiar to him alone, or is such the end of all living creatures?" Then the charioteer replied to him, "This is the final end of all living creatures. Be one a poor man, a man of middle state, or a noble, destruction will come to all in this world."

[60] Then the king's son, calm though he was, when he heard of death, immediately sank down overwhelmed. . . . He spoke with a loud voice, "This is the end appointed to all creatures, and yet the world throws off all fear and is infatuated! The hearts of men must be hard, for they can be self-composed in such a situation. . . ."

[5.7] Then he wanted to become perfectly alone in his thoughts, and stopped those friends who were following him. He went to the root of a rose-apple in a solitary spot, with its beautiful leaves all quivering [in the wind]. There he sat on the ground covered with leaves, and with its young grass bright like lapis lazuli. Meditating on the origin and destruction of the world, he laid hold of the path that leads to firmness of mind. [10] Having attained firmness of mind, and being immediately set free from all sorrows such as the desire of worldly objects, he attained the first stage of contemplation.

As he considered thoroughly these faults of sickness, old age, and death that belong to all living beings, all the joy that he had felt in the activity of his vigor, in his youth, and in his life vanished in a moment. [15] He did not rejoice, he did not feel remorse. He suffered no hesitation, indolence, nor sleep. He felt no attraction to the qualities of desire. He neither hated nor scorned another person. This pure, passionless meditation grew within the great-souled one. Then unobserved by the other men with him, a man in a beggar's clothing crept up.

The king's son asked him a question. He said, "Tell me, who are you?" He replied, "O bull of men, I who am terrified at birth and death have become an ascetic for the sake of liberation. Desiring liberation in a world subject to destruction, I seek that happy indestructible abode. I am isolated from mankind. My thoughts are unlike those of others, and my sinful passions are turned away from all objects of sense. Dwelling anywhere, at the root of a tree, or in an uninhabited house, a mountain or a forest, I wander without a family and without home. I am a beggar ready for any food, and I seek only the highest good."

[20] When he had spoken, while the prince was looking on, he suddenly flew up to the sky. This ascetic was a heavenly inhabitant who, knowing that the prince's thoughts were other than what his outward form promised, had come to him to rouse his recollection. When the other man had gone like a bird to heaven, the foremost of men rejoiced and was astonished. Having comprehended the meaning of the term dhamma, he set his mind on how to accomplish his deliverance. . . .

[12.88] Then the saint whose every effort was pure [Gotama] fixed his dwelling on the pure bank of the Nairangana. He wanted a lonely habitation. Five beggars who desired liberation came up to him when they saw him there. . . . [90] He was honored by these disciples who were dwelling in that family. . . . Thinking, "This may be the means of abolishing birth and death," he at once began a series of difficult austerities by fasting. For six years, vainly trying to attain merit, he practiced self-mortification. He performed many rules of abstinence which are hard for a man to carry out. At the hours of eating, longing to cross the world whose farther shore is so difficult to reach, he broke his vow with single jujube fruits, sesame seeds, and rice. But the emaciation that was produced in his body by that asceticism became positive fatness because of his splendor. [95] With his glory and his beauty unimpaired although he was thin, he caused gladness to other eyes, as the autumnal moon in the beginning of her bright fortnight gladdens the lotuses. He had only skin and bone remaining. His fat, flesh and blood had faded completely. Yet, though diminished, he still shone with undiminished grandeur like the ocean.

Then the seer, having his body emaciated to no purpose in a cruel self-mortification, and dreading continued existence, reflected in his longing to become a Buddha. "This is not the way to passionlessness, nor to perfect knowledge, nor to liberation. That was certainly the true way that I found at the root of the Gambu tree. But that cannot be attained by one who has lost his strength." So resuming his care for his body, he next pondered how best to increase his bodily vigor. [100] "Wearied with hunger, thirst, and fatigue, with his mind no longer self-possessed through fatigue, how can one who is not absolutely calm reach the purpose that is to be attained by his mind? True calm is properly obtained by the constant satisfaction of the senses. The mind's self-possession is only obtained when the senses are perfectly satisfied. True meditation is produced in one whose mind is self-possessed and at rest. In one whose thoughts are engaged in meditation the exercise of perfect contemplation begins at once. By contemplation are obtained those conditions through which supreme calm is eventually gained. This is the undecaying, immortal state, which is so hard to be reached." Having thus resolved, "This means is based upon eating food," the wise seer of unbounded wisdom decided to accept the continuance of life. . . .

[14.1] When he attained the highest mastery in all kinds of meditation, he remembered in the first watch the continuous series of all his former births. "In such a place I was so and so by name, and from there I passed and came here." Thus he remembered his thousands of births, experiencing each as it were over again. Having remembered each birth and each death in all those various transmigrations, the compassionate one then felt compassion for all living beings. [5] This world of living beings rolls on helplessly like a wheel, having willfully rejected the good guides in this life and done all kinds of actions in various [previous] lives. As he remembered, in his strong self-control this conviction came to him, "All existence is unsubstantial, like the fruit of a banana plant."

When the second watch came, he was possessed of unequaled energy. He who was the highest of all seeing beings received a preeminent divine sight. By that divine, perfectly pure sight he saw the whole world as in a spotless mirror. He saw the various transmigrations and rebirths of the various beings with their several lower or higher merits from their actions, and compassion grew up more within him. . . .

[35] Having pondered all this, in the last watch he reflected, "Alas for this whole world of living beings who are doomed to misery, all wandering astray! They do not know that all this universe, destitute of any real refuge, is born and decays through that existence which is the site of the skandhas[7] and pain. It dies and passes into a new state and then is born anew. . . ."

---

[7]*skandhas:* the five components that constitute the human person.

[64] The all-knowing Bodhisattva, the illuminated one, after pondering and meditating again came to his conclusion. [65] "This is pain; this also is the origin of pain in the world of living beings; this also is the stopping of pain; this is that course which leads to its stopping."[8] Having determined this, he knew everything as it really was. He, the holy one, sitting there on his seat of grass at the root of the tree, pondered by his own efforts and attained perfect knowledge. Then he bursted the shell of ignorance, and gained all the various kinds of perfect intuition. He attained all the partial knowledge of alternatives that is included in perfect knowledge. He became the perfectly wise, the Bhagavat, the Arhat, the king of the Law, the **Tathagata** [tah-THAH-gah-tuh],[9] the one who has attained the knowledge of all forms, the Lord of all knowledge. . . .

[79] The gods rejoiced, and paid him worship and adoration with divine flowers. All the world, when the great saint had become allwise, was full of brightness. Then the holy one descended and stood on his throne under the tree.[10] There he passed seven days filled with the thought, "I have here attained perfect wisdom." [80] When the Bodhisattva had attained perfect knowledge, all beings became full of great happiness. All the different universes were illumined by a great light. The happy earth shook in six different ways like an overjoyed woman. The Bodhisattvas, each dwelling in his own special abode, assembled and praised him.

[8]*This is pain . . . its stopping:* the Buddhist reader would easily recognize here the Four Noble Truths.
[9]*Bhagavat:* the "Blessed One"; *Arhat:* the "Worthy One"; *Tathagata:* "One who has come (or "gone") thus," a title of Buddha indicating his achievement of nirvana.

[10]*the tree:* the *bo* tree, so called because there Gotama achieved enlightenment (*Bodhi*).

The Death of Gotama Buddha*

In "The Book of the Great Decease," Buddha makes provision for life in the monastic community after his death. The unity and knowledge of the community is stressed—the Buddha leaves it in an ideal state.[11]

The Blessed One addressed the venerable Ananda, and said, "It may be, Ananda, that in some of you the thought may arise, 'The word of the Master is ended, we have a teacher no more!' Do not think this way. The truths and the rules of the order that I have set forth and laid down for you all, let them be your Teacher when I am gone.

"Ananda! When I am gone, do not address one another in the way in which the brothers have until now addressed each other, with the title of 'Avuso' [Friend]. A younger brother may be addressed by an elder with his name, or his family name, or the title 'Friend.' But an elder should be addressed by a younger brother as 'Lord' or as 'Venerable Sir.' And when I am gone, Ananda, let the order, if it should so wish, abolish all the lesser and minor precepts. . . ."[12]

[10] Then the Blessed One addressed the brothers, and said, "Behold now, brothers, I exhort you, saying, 'Decay is inherent in all

Mahaparinibbana Sutta 6.1–12, 33–35, 45–48
[11]Taken, with editing, from T. W. Rhys Davids, trans., *Buddhist Suttas, Sacred Books of the East,* vol. 11 (Oxford: Oxford University Press, 1881), pp. 112–130.

[12]This was not done because the monastic order could not decide between major and minor rules.

component things! Work out your salvation with diligence'!" This was the last word of the Tathagata! . . .

Then the Blessed One, passing out of the state in which both sensations and ideas have ceased to be, entered the state between consciousness and unconsciousness. Passing out of the state between consciousness and unconsciousness, he entered the state of mind to which nothing at all is specially present. Passing out of the consciousness of no special object, he entered the state of mind to which the infinity of thought is the only thing present. Passing out of the mere consciousness of the infinity of thought, he entered the state of mind to which the infinity of space is alone present. Passing out of the mere consciousness of the infinity of space, he entered the fourth stage of deep meditation. Passing out of the fourth stage, he entered the third. Passing out of the third stage, he entered the second. Passing out of the second, he entered the first. Passing out of the first stage of deep meditation, he entered the second. Passing out of the second stage, he entered the third. Passing out of the third stage, he entered the fourth stage of deep meditation. Then he passed out of the last stage of deep meditation, and immediately he died.

When the Blessed One died, at the moment of his passing out of existence, a mighty earthquake arose, terrible and awe-inspiring. The thunders of heaven burst forth. . . .

[33] Then the Mallas of Kusinara said to the venerable Ananda, "What should be done, Lord, with the remains of the Tathagata?"

"As men treat the remains of a king of kings, so should they treat the remains of a Tathagata."

"And how, Lord, do they treat the remains of a king of kings?"

"They wrap the body of a king of kings in a new cloth. When that is done, they wrap it in cotton wool. When that is done, they wrap it in a new cloth, and so on till they have wrapped the body in five hundred successive layers of both kinds. Then they place the body in a vessel of iron, and cover that up with another vessel of iron. They then build a funeral pyre of all kinds of perfumes, and burn the body of the king of kings. Then at the four crossroads they build a dagaba[13] to the king of kings. This is the way in which they treat the remains of a king of kings. As they treat the remains of a king of kings, so should they treat the remains of the Tathagata. At the four crossroads a dagaba should be built to the Tathagata. Whoever shall place garlands or perfumes or paint there, or make salutation there, or become in its presence calm in heart, shall have a profit and a joy for a long time."

Then the Mallas gave orders to their attendants, saying, "Gather all the carded cotton wool of the Mallas!" [35] Then the Mallas of Kusinara wrapped the body of the Blessed One in a new cloth. And when that was done, they wrapped it in cotton wool. And when that was done, they wrapped it in a new cloth, and so on till they had wrapped the body of the Blessed One in five hundred layers of both kinds. Then they placed the body in a vessel of iron, and covered that up with another vessel of iron. Then they built a funeral pyre of all kinds of perfumes, and they placed the body of the Blessed One on it. . . .

[45] Then the venerable Maha Kassapa went . . . to the funeral pyre of the Blessed One. When he had come up to it, he arranged his robe on one shoulder. Bowing down with clasped hands, he walked three times reverently around the pyre. Then, uncovering his feet, he bowed down in reverence at the feet of the Blessed One. Those five hundred brethren arranged their robes on one shoulder. Bowing down with clasped hands, they walked reverently around the pyre three times, and then bowed down in reverence at the feet of the Blessed One. When the homage of the venerable Maha Kassapa and of those five hundred brothers was ended, the funeral pyre of the

---

[13]*dagaba:* a burial mound.

Blessed One caught fire by itself. Now as the body of the Blessed One burned itself away, neither soot nor ash was seen from the skin and the covering, and from the flesh and the nerves and the fluid of the joints. Only the bones remained behind. . . . Of those five hundred pieces of clothing the very innermost and outermost were consumed.

TEACHING

The Sermon on the Four Noble Truths*

This excerpt from the "Turning the Wheel of the Law Sutra" is commonly known as the Benares Sermon. It is an excellent short statement of the essentials of Buddhist teaching, the Four Noble Truths and the Eightfold Path.[14]

Reverence to the Blessed One, the Holy One, the Fully Enlightened One!

Thus have I heard. The Blessed One was once staying at Benares, at the hermitage called Migadaya. The Blessed One addressed the company of the five monks, and said, "There are two extremes, O monks, which the man who has given up the world ought not to follow. The first is the habitual practice of those things whose attraction depends upon the passions. This is especially true of sensuality. It is a low and pagan way, unworthy, unprofitable, and fit only for the worldly-minded. Second is the habitual practice of asceticism, which is painful, unworthy, and unprofitable.

"There is a middle path, O monks, avoiding these two extremes, discovered by the Tathagata. This path opens the eyes, bestows understanding, leads to peace of mind, to the higher wisdom, to full enlightenment, and to Nirvana! What is that middle path, O monks, avoiding these two extremes, discovered by the Tathagata, the path that opens the eyes, and bestows understanding, which leads to peace of mind, to the higher wisdom, to full enlightenment, to Nirvana? Truly, it is this Noble Eightfold Path, that is to say: Right views; Right aspirations; Right speech; Right conduct; Right livelihood; Right effort; Right mindfulness; and Right contemplation. . . .

[5] "Now this, O monks, is the noble truth concerning suffering. Birth brings pain, decay is painful, disease is painful, death is painful. Union with the unpleasant is painful, painful is separation from the pleasant. Any craving that is unsatisfied, that too is painful. In brief, the five aggregates that spring from attachment, the conditions of individuality and their cause, are painful. This, O monks, is the noble truth concerning suffering.

"Now this, O monks, is the noble truth concerning the origin of suffering. Truly, it is the thirst or craving, causing the renewal of existence, accompanied by sensual delight, seeking satisfaction now here, now there. That is to say, it is the craving for the gratification of the passions, or the craving for a future life, or the craving for success in this present life. This, O monks, is the noble truth concerning the origin of suffering.

"Now this, O monks, is the noble truth concerning the destruction of suffering. Truly, it is the destruction, in which no passion remains, of this very thirst. It is the laying aside of, the getting rid of, the being free from, the harboring no longer of this thirst. This, O monks, is the noble truth concerning the destruction of suffering.

"Now this, O monks, is the noble truth concerning the way which leads to the destruction

---

Dhammacakkappavattana Sutta 1–8
[14]Taken, with editing, from Rhys Davids, *Buddhist Suttas,* pp. 146–155.

of sorrow. Truly, it is this Noble Eightfold Path. . . .

[21] "As long, O monks, as my knowledge and insight were not quite clear regarding each of these Four Noble Truths in this triple order, in this twelvefold manner, I was uncertain whether I had attained to the full insight of that wisdom that is unsurpassed in the heavens or on earth, among the whole race of Samanas and Brahmins, or of gods or men. But as soon as my knowledge and insight were quite clear regarding each of these four noble truths, in this triple order, in this twelvefold manner, then I became certain that I had attained to the full insight of that wisdom that is unsurpassed in the heavens or on earth, among the whole race of Samanas and Brahmins, or of gods or men. Now this knowledge and this insight has arisen within me. The emancipation of my heart is immovable. This is my last existence. Now there will be no rebirth for me!"

Thus spoke the Blessed One. The five monks praised the words of the Blessed One and were glad. When the discourse had been uttered, there arose within the venerable Kondanna the eye of truth, spotless, and without a stain. He saw that whatever has an origin also inherently must end.

[25] And when the royal chariot wheel of the truth had been set rolling by the Blessed One, the gods of the earth . . . the attendant gods of the four great kings . . . and the gods in the highest heaven gave forth a shout. They said, "In Benares, at the hermitage of the Migadaya, the supreme wheel of the empire of Truth has been set rolling by the Blessed One. That wheel can never be turned back by any Samana or Brahmin, nor by any god, nor by any Brahma or Mara, not by anyone in the universe!" In an instant, a second, a moment, this sound went up to the world of Brahma. This great ten-thousand-world-system quaked and trembled and was shaken violently. An immeasurably bright light appeared in the universe, beyond even the power of the gods!

The Skandhas and the Chain of Causation*

The skandhas *are the elements that together make up the human personality. They relate to the no-soul doctrine of Theravada Buddhism. This passage outlines these* skandhas *and then traces the chain of causation that leads to suffering.*[15]

The omniscient lion of the Sakyas [i.e., Buddha] then caused all the assembly, headed by those who belonged to the company of Maitriya, to turn the wheel of the Law.[16] . . . [28] The body is composed of the five skandhas, and produced from the five elements. It is all empty and without soul, and arises from the action of the chain of causation. This chain of causation is the cause of coming into existence, and the cessation of this chain is the cause of the state of cessation.

[30] He who knows this wants to promote the good of the world. Let him hold fast the chain of causation, with his mind fixed on wisdom. Let him embrace the vow of self-denial for the sake of wisdom, and practice the four perfections, and go through existence always doing good to all beings. Then having become an Arhat and conquered all the wicked, even the hosts of Mara, and attained the threefold wisdom, he shall enter Nirvana. Whoever has his mind indifferent and is empty of all desire for any further form of existence, let him abolish one by one the several steps of the chain of causation. When these effects of the chain of causation are ended one by one, he at last, being free

---

* Buddhacarita 16.1, 28–50

[15]Taken, with editing, from Cowell, *Buddhist Mahayana Texts*, pp. 174–180.

[16]*turn the wheel of the Law:* give and spread the true teaching.

from all stain and substratum, will pass into a blissful Nirvana.

[35] "Listen, all of you, for your own happiness, with your minds free from stain. I will declare to you step by step this chain of causation. The idea of ignorance is what gives the root to the huge poison-tree of mundane existence with its trunk of pain. The impressions are caused by this, which produce [the acts of] the body, voice, and mind. Consciousness arises from these impressions, which produces the five senses and the mind. The organism that is sometimes called samgna or samdarsana, springs from this; and from this arises the six organs of the senses, including the mind.

"The association of the six organs with their objects is called 'contact.' The consciousness of these different contacts is called 'sensation.' [40] Craving is produced by this, which is the desire of being troubled by worldly objects. 'Attachment to continued existence,' arising from this, sets itself in action towards pleasure and the rest. From attachment springs continued existence, which is sensual, possessing form, or formless. From existence arises birth through a returning to various wombs. On birth is dependent the series of old age, death, sorrow and the like. By putting a stop to ignorance and what follows from it, all these cease successively.

This is the chain of causation, which has many turns, whose sphere of action is created by ignorance. This is to be meditated upon by you who enjoy dwelling tranquilly in lonely woods. He who knows it thoroughly reaches at last to absolute thinness. Then he becomes blissfully extinct.

"When you have learned this, to be freed from the bond of existence you must cut down ignorance with all your efforts, for it is the root of pain. [45] Then, set free from the bonds of the prison-house of existence, you will possess as Arhats natures perfectly pure. You shall attain Nirvana."

Having heard this lesson preached by the chief of saints, all the mendicants understood the course and the cessation of embodied existence. As these five ascetics listened to his words, their intellectual eye was purified for the attainment of perfect wisdom. The eye of dharma was purified in six hundred millions of gods, and the eye of wisdom in eight hundred millions of Brahmans. The eye of dharma was purified in eighty thousand men, and even in all beings an ardor for the Law was made visible. [50] Everywhere all kinds of evil became tranquillized, and everywhere an ardor for all that helps the good Law manifested itself.

The Essence of Buddhism*

With its full title The Heart of Transcendent Wisdom, *this scripture is one of the best known in Buddhism. The* Heart Sutra *personifies wisdom as a woman, especially at its beginning and end. In a religion often given to verbose writings, this one is remarkable for its brevity.*[17]

---

* The Heart Sutra
[17]From Douglas A. Fox, trans., *The Heart of Buddhist Wisdom* (Lewiston, NY: Mellen, 1986). Copyright 1985 by Douglas A. Fox. Used by permission.

Honor to the Omniscient. [or, Honor to the Lady, Noble Transcendent Wisdom.]

The noble bodhisattva Avalokitesvara was brooding in the flowing depths of the course of Transcendent Wisdom. Looking about, he sees the five skandhas to be empty of essence.

Here, Sariputra, form is emptiness, emptiness is form. Form is not other than emptiness, and emptiness is not other than form. That which is form equals emptiness, and that which is emptiness is also form. Precisely the same may be said of form and the other skandhas: feeling, perception, impulse, and consciousness.

Here, Sariputra, all dharmas bear the marks of emptiness, which are: not to have arisen nor to have been suppressed, neither to be corrupt nor pure, and to be neither unfinished nor complete.

Therefore, Sariputra, emptiness is not form, nor feeling, perception, impulse, nor consciousness. It is not the eye, ear, nose, tongue, body, or mind. It is not shape, sound, odor, flavor, nor object of touch or thought. It is not the experience of vision (and so on until we reach) it is not elements of mental discrimination. It is not learning or ignorance, and it is not the elimination of learning or ignorance (and so on until we reach) it is not senility and death, and it is not the elimination of senility and death. It is not suffering, beginning, ceasing, or a path. It is not knowledge, not attainment or realization, and therefore neither is it nonattainment.

[5] The bodhisattva, bound to Transcendent Wisdom, lives with nothing clouding his mind. Lacking confusion, he is intrepid, and having passed beyond error, reaches nirvana.

All Buddhas, of the past, present, or future, bound to irrefutable Transcendent Wisdom, reach completely full understanding and the highest awakening.

Therefore Transcendent Wisdom should be known as the great mantra, the great knowledge mantra, the invincible mantra, the unsurpassable mantra, causing all suffering to cease. It is trustworthy because it is not false. It is the mantra proclaimed in the *Prajnaparamita*, and it is this: Oh, you [Lady] who are gone, gone, gone beyond, gone utterly beyond: Hail Wisdom!

With these words *The Heart of Transcendent Wisdom* is complete.

A Mahayana View of the Buddha*

In Mahayana, the Buddha is a gracious savior who enables both monks and laity to reach nirvana. This first selection from the Lotus Sutra of the True Law *argues that the Mahayana ("Large Vehicle") is in fact the only vehicle in Buddhism. In the second, the* Lotus Sutra *itself is the gift of the Buddha that enables those who read and venerate it to come to nirvana. This veneration is today especially prominent in Nichiren Buddhism.*[18]

Only now and then, Sariputra, does the Tathagata preach such a discourse on the law as this. Just as only now and then is seen the blossom of the fig tree, Sariputra, so does the Tathagata

only now and then preach such a discourse on the law. Believe me, Sariputra. I speak what is real, I speak what is truthful, I speak what is right. It is difficult to understand the exposition of the mystery of the Tathagata, Sariputra. For in explaining the law, Sariputra, I use hundreds of thousands of various skillful means, such as different interpretations, indications, explanations, illustrations. It is not by reasoning, Sariputra, that the law is to be found: it is beyond the pale of reasoning, and must be learned from the Tathagata. For, Sariputra, it is for a sole object, a sole aim, truly a lofty object, a lofty aim that the Buddha, the Tathagata, appears in the world. And what is that sole object, that sole aim, that lofty object, that lofty aim of the Buddha, the Tathagata, appearing in the world? To show all creatures the sight of Tathagata-knowledge, the Buddha, the Tathagata, appears in the world. To open the eyes of

---

* *Saddharma-pundarika Sutra* 2.36; 10.1

[18] Taken, with editing, from H. Kern, trans., *The Saddharma-Pundarika, Sacred Books of the East,* vol. 21 (Oxford: Oxford University Press, 1884), pp. 39–49, 213–214.

creatures for the sight of Tathagata-knowledge, the Buddha, the Tathagata, appears in the world. . . .

For, Sariputra, I show all creatures the sight of Tathagata-knowledge. I open the eyes of creatures for the sight of Tathagata-knowledge. I firmly establish the teaching of Tathagata-knowledge, Sariputra. I lead the teaching of Tathagata-knowledge on the right path, Sariputra. By means of one sole vehicle, namely, the Buddha-vehicle, Sariputra, I teach creatures the law. There is no second vehicle, nor a third. This is the nature of the law, Sariputra, universally in the world, in all directions. For all the Tathagatas, who in times past existed in countless, innumerable spheres in all directions for the welfare of many, the happiness of many, out of pity to the world, for the benefit, welfare, and happiness of the great body of creatures, preached the law to gods and men with able means. These means include several directions and indications, various arguments, reasons, illustrations, fundamental ideas, interpretations. They pay regard to the dispositions of creatures whose inclinations and temperaments are so varied. All those Buddhas and Lords have preached the law to creatures by means of only one vehicle, the Buddha-vehicle, which finally leads to omniscience. It is identical with showing all creatures the sight of Tathagata-knowledge; with opening the eyes of creatures for the sight of Tathagata-knowledge; with the awakening (or admonishing) by the display (or sight) of Tathagata-knowledge; with leading the teaching of Tathagata-knowledge on the right path. Such is the law they have preached to creatures. And those creatures who have heard the law from the past Tathagatas have all reached supreme, perfect enlightenment.

The Tathagatas who shall exist in future, Sariputra, in countless, innumerable spheres in all directions for the weal of many, the happiness of many, out of pity to the world, for the benefit, weal, and happiness of the great body of creatures, shall preach the law to gods and men. . . . Such is the law they shall preach to

creatures. Those creatures, Sariputra, who shall hear the law from the future Tathagatas shall all reach supreme, perfect enlightenment.

The Tathagatas who now are staying, living, existing, Sariputra, in countless, innumerable spheres in all directions preach the law to gods and men. . . . Such is the law they are preaching to creatures. Those creatures, Sariputra, who are hearing the law from the present Tathagatas shall all reach supreme, perfect enlightenment.

I myself also, Sariputra, am at the present period a Tathagata, for the weal of many. . . . I myself, also, Sariputra, am preaching the law to creatures. . . . Such is the law I preach to creatures. Those creatures, Sariputra, who now are hearing the law from me shall all reach supreme, perfect enlightenment. In this sense, Sariputra, it must be understood that nowhere in the world a second vehicle is taught, far less a third.

[10.1] The Lord then addressed the eighty thousand Bodhisattvas Mahasattvas by turning to Bhaishajyaraga as their representative. "Do you see, Bhaishajyaraga, in this assembly the many gods, Nagas, goblins, Gandharvas, demons, Garudas, Kinnaras, great serpents, men, and beings not human, monks, nuns, male and female lay devotees, votaries of the vehicle of disciples, votaries of the vehicle of Pratyekabuddhas, and those of the vehicle of Bodhisattvas, who have heard this teaching from the mouth of the Tathagata?"

'I do, Lord; I do, Sugata.'

The Lord proceeded: "All those Bodhisattvas Mahasattvas who in this assembly have heard well only a single stanza, a single verse [or word], or who even by a single rising thought have joyfully accepted this Sutra, to all of them, Bhaishajyaraga, among the four classes of my audience I predict their destiny to supreme and perfect enlightenment. Whoever after the complete extinction of the Tathagata shall hear this Dharmaparyaya and after hearing, if only a single stanza, joyfully accept it, even with a single rising thought, to those also, Bhaishajyaraga, be they young men or young women of good family,[19] I predict their destiny to supreme and perfect enlightenment. Those young men or women of good family, Bhaishajyaraga, shall be worshippers of many hundred thousand myriads of kotis of Buddhas. Those young men or women of good family, Bhaishajyaraga, shall have made a vow under hundreds of thousands of myriads of Buddhas. They must be considered as reborn among the people of Gambudvipa, out of compassion to all creatures. They shall be reborn who shall take, read, make known, recite, copy, and after copying always

keep in memory and from time to time regard were it but a single stanza of this teaching; who by that book shall feel veneration for the Tathagatas, treat them with the respect due to Masters, honor, revere, worship them; who shall worship that book with flowers, incense, perfumed garlands, ointment, powder, clothes, umbrellas, flags, banners, music, etc., and with acts of reverence such as bowing and joining hands. In short, Bhaishajyaraga, any young men or young women of good family who shall keep or joyfully accept only a single stanza of this teaching, to all of them, Bhaishajyaraga, I predict their destiny of supreme and perfect enlightenment.

---

[19] *Young men or women of good family:* layfolk can also reach nirvana.

ETHICS

Conduct of the Monk*

The Dhammapada *("Path of Teaching") is one of the fifteen books in the* Khuddaka-nikaya *of the* Sutta Pitaka. *A first-century* B.C.E. *collection of wise sayings, it summarizes Buddhist moral wisdom. Monks and nuns often memorize it at the beginning of their training, and it is studied as well by the laity.*[20]

Restraint in the eye is good, restraint in the ear is good, restraint in the nose is good, restraint in the tongue is good. In the body restraint is good, in speech restraint is good, in thought restraint is good. Restraint is good in all things. A monk restrained in all things is freed from all pain.

People call a monk one who controls his hand, who controls his feet, who controls his speech, who is well controlled, who delights inwardly, who is collected, who is solitary and

content. The monk who controls his mouth, who speaks wisely and calmly, who teaches the meaning and the law, his word is sweet.

He who dwells in the law, delights in the law, meditates on the law, follows the law, that monk will never fall away from the true law.

[365] Let him not despise what he has received, nor ever envy others; a mendicant who envies others does not obtain peace of mind. Even the gods will praise a monk who, though he receives little, does not despise what he has received, if his life is pure and if he is not lazy.

He who never identifies himself with his name and form, and does not grieve over what he has left behind, he indeed is called a monk.

The monk who acts with kindness, who is calm in the doctrine of Buddha, will reach the quiet place [Nirvana], cessation of natural desires, and happiness. O monk, empty this boat! If emptied, it will go quickly. When you have cut off passion and hatred, you will go to Nirvana.

[370] Cut off the five senses, leave the five, rise above the five. A monk who has escaped

---

* *Dhammapada* 25:360–382
[20] Taken, with editing, from F. Max Müller, *The Dhammapada, Sacred Books of the East,* vol. 10 (Oxford: Oxford University Press, 1881), pp. 85–88.

from the five fetters is called Oghatinna, "saved from the flood."

Meditate, O monk, and do be not careless! Do not direct your thought to what gives pleasure. Then you may not have to swallow the iron ball (in hell), and that you may not cry out when burning, "This is pain." Without knowledge there is no meditation, without meditation there is no knowledge. He who has knowledge and meditation is near to Nirvana.

A monk who has entered his empty house, whose mind is tranquil, feels a super-human delight when he sees the law clearly. When he has considered the origin and destruction of the elements (skandhas) of the body, he finds happiness and joy that belong to those who know the immortal (Nirvana).

[375] This is the beginning here for a wise monk: watchfulness over the senses, contentedness, restraint under the law; keeping noble friends whose life is pure and who are not lazy.

Let him live in charity, let him be perfect in his duties. Then in the fullness of delight he will put an end to his suffering.

As the Vassika plant sheds its withered flowers, men should shed passion and hatred, O monks! The monk whose body and tongue and mind are quieted, who is collected, and has rejected the baits of the world, he is called quiet.

Rouse yourself by yourself, examine yourself by yourself, thus self-protected and attentive you will live happily, O monk!

[380] The self is the lord of self, self is the refuge of self. Therefore curb yourself as the merchant curbs a good horse.

The monk full of delight, who is calm in the doctrine of Buddha, will reach the quiet place (Nirvana), cessation of natural desires, and happiness.

Even a young monk who applies himself to the doctrine of Buddha will brighten up this world like the moon when free from clouds.

Admonition to Laity*

At the end of a discussion of monastic morality, the Buddha lays down instructions for householders (laity). Note how the rules given are modeled on those given to monks.

I will also tell you about the householder's work. . . .

Let him not kill, nor cause to be killed any living being, nor let him approve of others killing. Let him refrain from hurting all creatures, both those that are strong and those that tremble.

[20] Then let [him] abstain from taking anything in any place that has not been given to him, knowing it to belong to another. Let him not cause anyone to take, nor approve of those that take. Let him avoid all theft.

Let the wise man avoid an unchaste life as a burning heap of coals. If he is not able to live a life of chastity, let him not transgress with another man's wife.

Let no one speak falsely to another in the hall of justice or in the hall of the assembly. Let him not cause anyone to speak falsely, nor approve of those that speak falsely. Let him avoid all sort of untruth.

Let the householder who approves of the Dhamma not give himself to intoxicating drinks. Let him not cause others to drink, nor approve of those who drink, knowing it to end in madness. For through intoxication stupid people commit sins and make other people intoxicated. Let him avoid this seat of sin, this madness, this folly, which is delightful to the stupid.

[25] Let him not kill any living being, let him not take what has not been given [to him], let him not speak falsely, and let him not drink intoxicating drinks, let him refrain from unchaste sexual intercourse, and let him not eat untimely food at night. Let him not wear

---

*Culavagga, Dammikasutta 18–29

wreaths nor use perfumes, let him lie on a couch spread on the earth. They call this the eightfold abstinence (*uposatha*), proclaimed by Buddha, who has overcome pain.

Having with a believing mind kept abstinence (*uposatha*) on the fourteenth, fifteenth, and the eighth days of the half-month, and having kept the complete *Patiharakapakkha*[21] con-

sisting of eight parts, then in the morning, after having kept abstinence, let a wise man with a believing mind make distributions according to his ability. Thus he will gladden the assembly of monks with food and drink.

Let him dutifully maintain his parents, and practice an honorable trade. The householder who observes this strenuously goes to the gods called Sayampabhas.

---

[21] *Patiharakapakkha*: further rules for continual abstinence and self-control.

The Wisdom of the Buddha*

This passage, often called "Twin Verses," is a general treatment of Buddhist morality. Each paragraph has two verses, usually opposites. A second section, from the chapter "On the Self," urges the virtue of self-reliance and self-dedication in the path to enlightenment.[22]

All that we are is the result of what we have thought: it is founded on our thoughts, it is made up of our thoughts. If a man speaks or acts with an evil thought, pain follows him, as the wheel follows the foot of the ox that draws the carriage. All that we are is the result of what we have thought. It is founded on our thoughts, it is made up of our thoughts. If a man speaks or acts with a pure thought, happiness follows him like a shadow that never leaves him.

"He abused me, he beat me, he defeated me, he robbed me"—in those who harbor such thoughts hatred will never cease. "He abused me, he beat me, he defeated me, he robbed me" —in those who do not harbor such thoughts hatred will cease.

[5] For hatred does not cease by hatred at any time. Hatred ceases by love; this is an old rule. The world does not know that we must all come to an end here. But for those who know it, their quarrels cease at once.

He who lives looking for pleasures only, his senses uncontrolled, immoderate in his food, idle, and weak, Mara [the tempter] will certainly overthrow him, as the wind throws down a weak tree. He who lives without looking for pleasures, his senses well controlled, moderate in his food, faithful and strong, him Mara will certainly not overthrow, any more than the wind throws down a rocky mountain.

He who wishes to put on the yellow clothing[23] without having cleansed himself from sin, who disregards also temperance and truth, is unworthy of the yellow clothing. [10] But he who has cleansed himself from sin is well grounded in all virtues, and also keeps temperance and truth, he is worthy of the yellow clothing.

They who imagine truth in untruth, and see untruth in truth, never arrive at truth, but follow empty desires. They who know truth in truth, and untruth in untruth, arrive at truth, and follow true desires.

As rain breaks through a poorly thatched house, passion will break through an unreflecting mind. As rain does not break through a well-thatched house, passion will not break through a well-reflecting mind.

[15] The evildoer mourns in this world, and he mourns in the next; he mourns in both. He

---

* *Dhammapada* 1–20, 157–166
[22] Taken, with editing, from Müller, *The Dhammapada*, pp. 1–8, 45–46.

---

[23] *the yellow clothing:* the saffron gown of the monk.

mourns and suffers when he sees the evil of his own work. The virtuous man delights in this world, and he delights in the next; he delights in both. He delights and rejoices when he sees the purity of his own work.

The evildoer suffers in this world, and he suffers in the next; he suffers in both. He suffers when he thinks of the evil he has done. He suffers more when going on the evil path. The virtuous man is happy in this world, and he is happy in the next; he is happy in both. He is happy when he thinks of the good he has done. He is still more happy when going on the good path.

The thoughtless man, even if he can recite a large portion [of the law], but is not a doer of it, has no share in the priesthood. He is like a cowherd counting the cows of others. [20] The follower of the law, even if he can recite only a small portion [of the law], but, having forsaken passion and hatred and foolishness, possesses true knowledge and serenity of mind, he, caring for nothing in this world or that to come, has a share in the order of monks.

[157, On the Self] If a man hold himself dear, let him watch himself carefully. During at least one out of the three watches [of the night] a wise man should be watchful.

Let each man direct himself first to what is proper, then let him teach others. Thus a wise man will not suffer.

If a man make himself as he teaches others to be, being himself well subdued, he may subdue [others]. One's own self is indeed difficult to subdue.

[160] The self is the lord of self; who else could be the lord? With self well subdued, a man finds a lord such as few can find. The evil done by oneself, self-begotten, self-bred, crushes the foolish, as a diamond breaks a precious stone.

He whose wickedness is very great brings himself down to that state where his enemy wishes him to be, as a creeping vine does with the tree that it surrounds. Bad deeds and deeds hurtful to ourselves are easy to do. What is beneficial and good is very difficult to do.

The foolish man who scorns the rule of the venerable [Arhat], of the elect [Ariya], of the virtuous, and follows false doctrine, bears fruit to his own destruction, like the fruits of the Katthaka reed.

[165] By oneself evil is done, by oneself one suffers. By oneself evil is left undone, by oneself one is purified. Purity and impurity belong to oneself; no one can purify another.

Let no one forget his own duty for the sake of another's, however great. Let a man, after he has discerned his own duty, always be attentive to his duty.

ORGANIZATION

Founding of the Order*

After his enlightenment, the Buddha converts the five Hindu ascetics who earlier had left him when he had given up his practice of extreme asceticism. This Vinaya Pitaka *selection offers a succinct view of general Buddhist teaching. Just as important, it offers a good view of the founding of the*

Buddhist order of monks, and therefore of the Buddhist tradition itself.[24]

The Blessed One, wandering from place to place, came to Benares, to the deer park Isi-

---

Mahavagga 1.6.10, 11–16, 27–30, 32, 34, 37

[24]Taken, with editing, from T. W. Rhys Davids and Hermann Oldenberg, trans., *Vinaya Texts*, part 1, *Sacred Books of the East*, vol. 13 (Oxford: Oxford University Press, 1881), pp. 91–102.

patana, to the place where the five monks were. The five monks saw the Blessed One coming from a distance. When they saw him, they agreed with each other, saying, "Friends, there comes Gotama. He lives in abundance, has given up his exertions, and has turned to an abundant life. Let us not salute him, nor rise from our seats when he approaches, nor take his bowl and his robe from his hands. But let us put there a seat; if he likes, let him sit down. . . ."

When they spoke to him, the Blessed One said to the five monks, "Monks, do not address the Tathagata by his name or with the appellation 'Friend.' The Tathagata is the holy, absolute Sambuddha.[25] Give ear, O monks! Immortality has been won by me. I will teach you; I will preach the doctrine to you. If you walk in the way I show you, you will, before long, have penetrated to the truth. You yourselves will know it and see it face to face. You will live with the highest goal of the holy life, for which noble youths give up the world completely and go forth into the houseless state."

When he had spoken, the five monks said to the Blessed One, "Friend Gotama, by those observances, by those practices, and by those austerities you have not been able to obtain power surpassing that of other men. You have not obtained the superiority of full and holy knowledge and insight. Now that you are living in abundance, have given up your exertions, and have turned to an abundant life, how will you be able to obtain power surpassing that of men? How will you obtain the superiority of full and holy knowledge and insight? . . ."

[15] The five monks spoke to the Blessed One a second time as before. And the Blessed One replied to the five monks a second time as before. And the five monks spoke to the Blessed One a third time as before. When they had spoken thus, the Blessed One said to the five monks, "Do you admit, O monks, that I have never spoken to you in this way before this day?"

"You have never spoken so, Lord."

"The Tathagata, O monks, is the holy, absolute Sambuddha. Give ear, O monks. . . ."

The Blessed One was able to convince the five monks. The five monks listened willingly to the Blessed One. They gave ear, and fixed their mind on the knowledge which Buddha imparted to them. . . . [There follows a statement of the Four Noble Truths and the Eightfold Path.]

[27] "O monks, as long as I did not possess with perfect purity this true knowledge and insight into these four Noble Truths . . . I knew that I had not yet obtained the highest, absolute Sambodhi in the world of men and gods, in Mara's and Brahma's world, among all beings, Samanas and Brahmanas, gods and men. But when I possessed with perfect purity this true knowledge and insight into these four Noble Truths . . . then I knew that I had obtained the highest, universal Sambodhi in the world of men and gods. . . . This knowledge and insight arose in my mind: This emancipation of my mind cannot be lost. This is my last birth; I shall not be born again!"

Thus the Blessed One spoke. The five monks were delighted, and they rejoiced at the words of the Blessed One. When this exposition was given, the venerable Kondanna obtained the pure and spotless Eye of this truth: "Whatever is subject to the condition of origination, is subject also to the condition of cessation."

[30] And when the Blessed One had founded the Kingdom of Truth by propounding the Four Noble Truths, the earth-inhabiting gods shouted, "Truly the Blessed One has founded at Benares, in the deer park Isipatana, the highest kingdom of Truth, which may be opposed neither by a Samana nor by a Brahmana, neither by a deva, nor by Mara, nor by Brahma, nor by any being in the world." . . .

[32] The venerable Kondanna . . . overcame uncertainty, dispelled all doubts, and gained full knowledge. He was dependent on nobody else for knowledge of the doctrine of the teacher. He

---

[25]*Sambuddha:* one who has reached the insight essential to the higher stages of arhatship.

said to the Blessed One, "Lord, let me receive the pabbajja and upasampada ordinations from the Blessed One."

"Come, monk," said the Blessed One, "for the doctrine is well taught. Lead a holy life for the sake of the complete extinction of suffering." Then this venerable person received the ordination. . . .

[34] Then [the other monks] spoke to the Blessed One: "Lord, let us receive the pabbajja and upasampada ordinations from the Blessed One."

"Come, monks," said the Blessed One, "for the doctrine is well taught. Lead a holy life for the sake of the complete extinction of suffering." Thus these venerable persons received ordination. . . .

[47] Thus the Blessed One spoke. The five monks were delighted, and rejoiced at the words of the Blessed One. When this exposition had been given, the minds of the five monks became free from attachment to the world, and were released from the Asavas.[26] Then there were six arhants in the world.

---

[26]*Asavas:* mental defilement; the four asavas are sensuality, lust for life, false views, and ignorance.

The Rules of Defeat*

In this scripture from the Vinaya Pitaka, *the "rules of defeat" are given and explained. "Defeat" means expulsion with no possibility of return. These rules govern the life of nuns as well as monks. Note at the end of the passage the ritual for confession of these faults in the monastery, the basic method of which is similar for confession of all other faults. The four prohibitions here— against sexual intercourse, theft, killing, and lying—form the basis of Buddhist morality for the laity. The only qualification is that the prohibition of sexual intercourse is modified to a prohibition of intercourse outside marriage.[27]*

The four Rules concerning those acts that cause Defeat now come into recitation.

If any monk who has taken upon himself the monks' system of self-training and rule of life and has not after that withdrawn from the training, or declared his weakness, shall have sexual intercourse with anyone, down even to an animal, he has fallen into defeat; he is no longer in communion.

If any monk shall take, from village or from forest, anything not given—what men call "theft"—he, too, has fallen into defeat; he is no longer in communion.

If any monk shall knowingly deprive a human being of life, or shall seek out an assassin against a human being, or shall utter the praises of death, or incite another to self-destruction, saying, "Ho, my friend! What good do you get from this sinful, wretched life? Death is better to you than life!"—he, too, is fallen into defeat; he is no longer in communion.

A monk, without being clearly conscious of possessing extraordinary qualities, may perhaps pretend that he has gained insight into the knowledge of the noble ones, saying, "Thus I know, thus I perceive." At some subsequent time whether on being pressed, or without being pressed he feel guilty and may want to be cleansed from his fault. He shall say, "Brothers, when I did not know, I said that I knew; when I did not see, I said that I saw—telling a fruitless

---

* *Patimokkha, Parajika Dhamma* 1–4
[27]Taken, with editing, from Davids and Oldenberg, *Vinaya Texts,* part 1, pp. 3–6.

falsehood." Then, unless he spoke through undue confidence he has fallen into defeat; he is no longer in communion.

Venerable Sirs, the four Conditions of Defeat have been recited. When a monk has fallen into one or other, he is no longer allowed to reside with the monks. As before, so afterwards, he is defeated; he is not in communion.

Rules Requiring Formal Meetings*

The next set of monastic rules covers thirteen matters for which a formal meeting of the order (samghadisesa) *is required. The precise punishment, to be decided at a meeting of the whole monastic assembly, amounts to something less than permanent expulsion, often suspension for one month. All the rules are given here.*[28]

The thirteen things which in their earlier and in their later stages require formal meetings of the Order now come into recitation.

1. If a monk intentionally emits his semen, except while sleeping.
2. If a monk, being degraded with perverted mind, comes into bodily contact with a woman by taking hold of her hand or her hair, or by touching any part of her body.
3. If a monk, being degraded with perverted mind, addresses a woman with wicked words, exciting her to passion as young men do to young women.
4. If a monk, being degraded with perverted mind, magnifies service to himself in the hearing of a woman, saying, "This, Sister, would be the noblest of services, that to so righteous and exalted a religious person as myself you should serve by that act," meaning sexual intercourse.
5. If a monk acts as a go-between for a woman to a man, or for a man to a

Concerning them I ask the venerable ones, "Are you pure in this matter?" A second time I ask, "Are you pure in this matter?" A third time I ask, "Are you pure in this matter?" The venerable ones are pure. Therefore they keep silence. Thus I understand.

woman, or for a wife, or for a mistress, or even for a prostitute.
6. If a monk, at his own request, has a hut put up on a dangerous site, without the open space around it, or does not bring the monks to approve the site, or exceeds the due measure.
7. If a monk has a large house made on a dangerous site, without the open space around it, or does not bring the monks to the place to approve the site.
8. If a monk, in harshness, malice, or anger, harasses another monk by a groundless charge of having committed a Parajika offence, thinking to himself, "Perhaps I may get him to fall from this religious life" —and then later, either when he is pressed, or without his being pressed, the case turns out to be groundless, and the monk confesses his malice.
9. If a monk, in harshness, malice, or anger, harasses another monk by a groundless charge of having committed a Parajika offence, supporting himself by some point or other of no importance in a case that really rests on something of a different kind; thinking to himself, "Perhaps I may get him to fall from this religious life"— and then later, either when he is pressed, or without his being pressed, the case turns out to rest on something of a different kind, and that monk confesses his malice.
10. If a monk causes division in a community that is at union, or persists in calling attention to some matter calculated to cause

Patimokkha, Samghadisesa Dhamma 1–13
[28]Taken, with editing, from Davids and Oldenberg, *Vinaya Texts,* part 1, pp. 7–14.

division, that monk should be addressed by the monks, "Sir, do not go around causing division in a community that is at union"; if that monk, when he has thus been spoken to by the monks, should persist as before, then let that monk be [formally] admonished about it by the monks as a body, even to the third time, to the intent that he abandon that course. If, while being so admonished up to the third time, he abandons that course, it is well; if he does not abandon it, it is a Samghadisesa.

11. Now other monks, one, two, or three, may become adherents of that monk, and may raise their voices on his side. If they should say this, "Do not say, Sirs, anything against that monk! That monk speaks according to the Dhamma, and he speaks according to the *Vinaya;*—then let those monks be addressed by the other monks in this way, "Do not say this, Sirs! That monk does not speak according to the Dhamma, neither does he speak according to the *Vinaya*. Let not the causing of division in the community be pleasing to you!" If those monks, when they have thus been spoken to by the monks, should persist as before, those monks should be formally judged by the monks, as a body, even to the third time, so that they abandon that course. If, while being judged up to three times they abandon that course, it is well. If they do not abandon it, it is a Samghadisesa.

12. A monk may refuse to listen to what is said to him. When spoken to by the monks, according to the Dhamma, about the precepts handed down in the body of recited law, he will allow nothing to be said to him, objecting, "Say nothing to me, Sirs, either good or bad; and I will say nothing, either good or bad, to you. Be good enough, Sirs, to refrain from speaking to me!" Then let that monk be addressed by the monks, "Do not, Sir, make yourself a person who cannot be spoken to. Make yourself a person to whom we can speak. Speak to the monks, Sir, according to the Dhamma; and the monks, Sir, will speak to you according to the Dhamma. For the society of the Blessed One grown large by mutual discussion and by mutual help." If that monk, when he has thus been spoken to by the monks, should persist as before, then let that monk be formally judged by the monks as a body as many as three times, so that he may abandon that course. If, while being judged up to the third time, he abandons that course, it is well. If he does not abandon it, it is a Samghadisesa.

13. If a monk dwells near a certain village or town, leading a life hurtful to the laity and devoted to evil, so that his evil deeds are seen and heard, and the families led astray by him are seen and heard, let that monk be spoken to by the monks. The monks must say, "Your life, Sir, is hurtful to the laity, and evil. Your evil deeds, Sir, are seen and heard; and families are seen and heard to be led astray by you. Be so good, Sir, as to depart from this residence; you have lived here long enough." If that monk, when thus spoken to by the monks, should persist as before, that monk should be formally judged by the monks as a body as many as three times, so that he abandon that course. If, while being so judged up to three times, he abandons that course, it is well. If he does not abandon it, it is a Samghadisesa.

The Order of Nuns*

This selection narrates the story about how women were admitted into the monastic order as nuns. The Buddha was at first very reluctant to admit them, but he relented, giving special rules for an order of nuns. These nuns have historically played a much smaller role in Buddhism than the order of monks, a situation that continues today.[29]

Now at that time the Blessed Buddha was staying among the Sakyas in Kapilavatthu, in the Nigrodharama. And Maha-pajapati the Gotami[30] went to the place where the Blessed One was. When she arrived there, she bowed down before the Blessed One, and remained standing to one side. She said to the Blessed One, "It would be well, Lord, if women should be allowed to renounce their homes and enter the homeless state under the doctrine and discipline proclaimed by the Tathagata."

The Buddha replied, "Enough, O Gotami! Let it not please you that women should be allowed to do so." A second and a third time Maha-pajapati made the same request in the same words, and received the same reply. Then Maha-pajapati, sad and sorrowful that the Blessed One would not allow women to enter the homeless state, bowed down before the Blessed One. Keeping him on her right hand as she passed him, she departed weeping and in tears.

Now when the Blessed One had remained at Kapilavatthu as long as he thought fit, he set out on his journey towards Vesali. Traveling straight on, in due course he arrived there. The Blessed One stayed there in the Mahavana, in the Kuta-gara Hall.

Maha-pajapati cut off her hair, and put on orange-colored robes. She set out, with several women of the Sakya clan, towards Vesali. In due course she arrived at Vesali, at the Mahavana, at the Kutagara Hall. And Maha-pajapati, with swollen feet and covered with dust, sad and sorrowful, weeping and in tears, took her stand outside under the entrance porch.

The venerable Ananda saw her standing there, and on seeing her so, he said to Maha-pajapati, "Why do you stand there, outside the porch, with swollen feet and covered with dust, sad and sorrowful, weeping and in tears?"

"Because, Ananda, the Lord and Blessed One does not allow women to renounce their homes and enter the homeless state under the doctrine and discipline proclaimed by the Tathagata."

Then the venerable Ananda went up to the place where the Blessed One was. Bowing down before the Blessed One, he took his seat on one side. And, so sitting, the venerable Ananda said to the Blessed One: "Behold, Lord, Maha-pajapati is standing outside under the entrance porch. She has swollen feet and is covered with dust. She is sad and sorrowful, weeping and in tears, because the Blessed One does not allow women to renounce their homes and enter the homeless state under the doctrine and discipline proclaimed by the Blessed One. It would be well, Lord, if women were to have permission granted to them to do as she desires."

The Buddha replied, "Enough, Ananda! Let it not please you that women should be allowed to do so." A second and a third time Ananda made the same request, in the same words, and received the same reply.

Then the venerable Ananda thought, "The Blessed One does not give his permission. I will now ask the Blessed One on another ground." And the venerable Ananda said to the Blessed One, "Lord, can women—when they have gone

---

Cullavagga 10.1.1–6

[29]Taken, with editing, from T. W. Rhys Davids and Hermann Oldenberg, trans., *Vinaya Texts,* part 3, *Sacred Books of the East,* vol. 20 (Oxford: Oxford University Press, 1885), pp. 320–326.

[30]*the Gotami:* a relative of Gotama, and his nurse when he was an infant.

forth from the household life and entered the homeless state, under the doctrine and discipline proclaimed by the Blessed One—can they gain the fruit of conversion, or of the second Path, or of the third Path, or of Arhatship?"

"They are capable, Ananda."

"Lord, Maha-pajapati has proved herself of great service to the Blessed One, when as aunt and nurse she nourished him and gave him milk, and on the death of his mother she nursed the Blessed One at her own breast. It would be well, Lord, that women should have permission to go forth from the household life and enter the homeless state, under the doctrine and discipline proclaimed by the Tathagata."

"Ananda, if Maha-pajapati takes upon herself the Eight Chief Rules, let that be reckoned as her initiation. (1) Even if a woman has been a nun for a hundred years, she shall make salutation to, shall rise in the presence of, shall bow down before, and shall perform all proper duties towards a monk, even if he is only just initiated. (2) A nun is not to spend the rainy season in a district in which there is no monk. (3) Every half month a nun is to await from the monks two things, the request about the date of the Uposatha ceremony, and the time when the monk will come to give the Exhortation. (4) After keeping the rainy season, the nun is to inquire whether any fault can be laid to her charge before both Samghas—of monks and of nuns—with respect to three matters: what has been seen, what has been heard, and what has been suspected. (5) A nun who has been guilty of a serious offence is to undergo the Manatta discipline towards both the Samghas. (6) When a nun, as novice, has been trained for two years in the Six Rules, she is to ask permission for the upasampada initiation from both Samghas. (7) A nun is never to revile or abuse a monk. (8)

From this time on, nuns are forbidden to admonish monks, but the official admonition of nuns by monks is not forbidden. . . .

[5] Then the venerable Ananda, when he had learned from the Blessed One these Eight Chief Rules, went to Maha-pajapati and told her all that the Blessed One had said. She replied, "A man or a woman, when young and of tender years, accustomed to adorn himself, would bathe his head and receive with both hands a garland of lotus or jasmine or atimuttaka flowers, and place it on the top of his head. In the same way, I take upon myself these Eight Chief Rules, never to be transgressed my life long."

Then the venerable Ananda returned to the Blessed One, and bowed down before him, and took his seat on one side. So sitting, the venerable Ananda said to the Blessed One, "Lord, Maha-pajapati has taken upon herself the Eight Chief Rules; the aunt of the Blessed One has received the upasampada initiation."

Then the Buddha said, "Ananda, if women had not received permission to go out from the household life and enter the homeless state under the doctrine and discipline proclaimed by the Tathagata, then the pure religion would have lasted long; the good law would have stood fast for a thousand years. But since women have now received that permission, the pure religion will not now last so long, and the good law will now stand fast for only five hundred years. Houses in which there are many women but only a few men are easily violated by robber burglars. In the same way, Ananda, under whatever doctrine and discipline women are allowed to go out from the household life into the homeless state, that religion will not last long. So, Ananda, in anticipation I have laid down these Eight Chief Rules for the nuns, never to be transgressed for their whole life."

RITUAL AND MEDITATION

The Relics of the Buddha*

One of the most important features of Buddhist worship has been veneration of the relics (physical remains, mostly bones) of the Buddha. To a Buddhist, these are the holiest physical objects in the world. This selection from The Book of the Great Decease *tells the story of how the followers of the Buddha settled many arguments about how the relics of the cremated body of the Buddha should be distributed.*[31]

When they heard these things, the Mallas of Kusinara spoke to the assembled brothers. "The Blessed One died in our village domain. We will not give away any part of the remains of the Blessed One!"

When they had thus spoken, Dona the Brahmin addressed the assembled brothers. He said, "Hear, reverend sirs, one word from me. Our Buddha was accustomed to teach moderation. It is unseemly that strife should arise, and wounds, and war, over the distribution of the remains of him who was the best of beings! Let us all, sirs, unite in friendly harmony to make eight portions. Let thupas[32] arise widespread in every land, that humanity may trust in the Enlightened One! Brahmin, divide the remains of the Blessed One equally into eight parts, with fair division."

"Let it be so, sir!" Dona said in assent to the assembled brothers. He divided the remains of the Blessed One equally into eight parts, with fair division. He said to them, "Give me, sirs, this vessel, and I will set up over it a sacred memorial mound, and in its honor I will establish a feast." And they gave the vessel to Dona the Brahmin.

Mahaparinibbana Sutta 6.58–60

[31]Taken, with editing, from Davids, *Buddhist Suttas*, pp. 133–134.

[32]*thupas* (or *stupas*): a house of worship enshrining relics of the Buddha.

Mindfulness in Meditation**

Buddhist monks must have a powerful concentration to fix their minds on the abstract processes and products of meditation. This passage from an influential Theravada meditation scripture discusses the way to full mindfulness.[33]

Monks, there is one road, one path for beings to purify themselves, to transcend sorrow and grief, to overcome suffering and melancholy, to attain the right way, to realize nirvana: that is the fourfold establishment of mindfulness. What are the four mindfulnesses? They are the mindful contemplation of the body, the mindful contemplation of the feelings, the mindful contemplation of thoughts, and the mindful contemplation of the elements of reality.

How does a monk practice the mindful contemplation of the body? In this way: He goes to the forest, or to the foot of a tree, or to an empty room, and he sits down, cross-legged, keeps his back straight, and directs his mindfulness in front of him. Mindfully, he breathes in, mindfully, he breathes out; breathing in a long

---

**Majjhima-Nikaya, Satipatthanasutta* 10.1–9

[33]Taken, with editing, from V. Trenckner, *The Majjhima-Nikaya*, vol. 1 (London: Pali Text Society, 1888) pp. 55–63.

breath, he knows "I am breathing in a long breath"; breathing out a long breath, he knows "I am breathing out a long breath"; breathing in a short breath, he knows "I am breathing in a short breath"; breathing out a short breath, he knows "I am breathing out a short breath." He should be like a lathe operator who knows that "I am making a long turn" when he is making a long turn and that "I am making a short turn" when he is making a short turn. Thus a monk practices mindfully contemplating his body.

Furthermore, when a monk is walking, he knows "I am walking," and when he is standing, knows "I am standing," and when he is sitting, knows "I am sitting," and when he is lying down, knows "I am lying down." Whatever posture his body may take, he knows that he is taking it. Thus a monk practices mindfully contemplating his body.

And also, a monk is fully mindful of what he is doing, both going and coming, looking straight ahead and looking away, holding out his bowl or retracting it, putting on his robes, carrying his bowl, eating, drinking, chewing, tasting, defecating, urinating, moving, standing, sitting, sleeping, waking, talking, being quiet. Thus a monk practices mindfully contemplating his body.

And also, a monk considers his body itself, from the soles of his feet upward and from the top of his head downward, wrapped as it is in skin and filled with all sorts of impurities. He reflects, "In this body, there is hair, body-hair, nails, teeth, skin, flesh, sinews, bones, marrow, kidneys, heart, liver, pleura, spleen, lungs, colon, intestines, stomach, feces, bile, phlegm, pus, blood, sweat, fat, tears, lymph, saliva, snot, synovia, and urine." Thus a monk practices mindfully contemplating his body.

And also, a monk considers his body with regard to the elements that compose it. He reflects, "In this body, there is earth, water, fire, and air." He should think of these elements that make up the body as though they were pieces of the carcass of a cow that a butcher had slaugh-

tered and displayed in a market. Thus a monk practices mindfully contemplating his body.

And also, if a monk should see a corpse abandoned in a cemetery, dead one day or two or three, swollen, turning blue, and beginning to fester, he should concentrate on his own body and think, "This body of mine is just like that one; it has the same nature, and it will not escape this fate." And should he see a corpse abandoned in a cemetery, being eaten by crows, hawks, vultures, dogs, jackals, or various kinds of vermin, he should concentrate on his own body and think, "This body of mine is just like that one; it has the same nature, and it will not escape this fate." And should he see a corpse abandoned in a cemetery, a skeleton still covered with some flesh and blood and held together by tendons, or without flesh but smeared with blood and still held together, or without flesh or blood but still held together, or just bones no longer held together but scattered in different directions—here the bones of a hand, there the bones of a foot, here a tibia, there a femur, here a hipbone, there a backbone, over there a skull—he should concentrate on his own body and think, "This body of mine is just like that; it has the same nature, and it will not escape this fate." And should he see a corpse abandoned in a cemetery, bones bleached white as shells, old bones in a heap, bones that have completely decayed and become dust—he should concentrate on his own body and think, "This body of mine is just like that; it has the same nature, and it will not escape this fate." Thus a monk keeps mindfully contemplating his body.

And how, monks, does a monk practice the mindful contemplation of feelings? In this way: Experiencing a pleasant feeling, he knows "I am experiencing a pleasant feeling"; experiencing an unpleasant feeling, he knows "I am experiencing an unpleasant feeling." Experiencing a feeling that is neither pleasant nor unpleasant, he knows "I am experiencing a feeling that is neither pleasant nor unpleasant." Experiencing a pleasant physical feeling, he knows "I am experiencing a pleasant physical feeling"; experiencing a pleasant spiritual feeling, he knows "I am experiencing a pleasant spiritual feeling"; experiencing an unpleasant physical feeling, an unpleasant spiritual feeling, a physical feeling that is neither pleasant nor unpleasant, a spiritual feeling that is neither pleasant nor unpleasant, he knows he is experiencing those feelings. Thus a monk practices mindfully contemplating his feelings.

And how, monks, does a monk practice the mindful contemplation of thoughts? In this way: He knows a passionate thought to be a passionate thought; he knows a passionless thought to be a passionless thought; he knows a hate-filled thought to be a hate-filled thought; he knows a hate-free thought to be a hate-free thought; he knows a deluded thought, an undeluded thought, an attentive thought, a distracted thought, a lofty thought, a lowly thought, a mediocre thought, a supreme thought, a concentrated thought, a diffused thought, a thought that is free, a thought that is still bound, to be such thoughts as they are. Thus a monk practices mindfully contemplating his thoughts.

And how, monks, does a monk practice the mindful contemplation of the elements of reality? In this way: He practices the mindful contemplation of the elements of reality with regard to the five hindrances. And how does he do that? In this way: When there is within him sensual excitement, he knows that "sensual excitement is occurring within me"; when there is within him no sensual excitement, he knows that "sensual excitement is not occurring within me." When there is within him some ill will, he knows that "ill will is occurring within me"; when there is within him no ill will, he knows "ill will is not occurring within me." And similarly he knows the presence and the absence within himself of laziness and lethargy, agitation and worry, and doubt. Thus he practices mindfully contemplating elements of reality within

himself, he practices mindfully contemplating elements of reality outside of himself and he practices mindfully contemplating elements of reality as they arise and as they pass away. And thinking that "this is an element of reality," he is concerned with it only insofar as he needs to be for the sake of knowledge and recognition; so he abides free from attachment and does not cling to anything in this world.

A monk also practices the mindful contemplation of the elements of reality with regard to the five aggregates of attachment. And how does he do that? In this way: He reflects "Such is physical form, such is the origin of physical form, such is the passing away of physical form." "Such is feeling, such is the origin of feeling, such is the passing away of feeling." "Such is perception, such is the origin of perception, such is the passing away of perception." "Such are karmic constituents, such is the origin of karmic constituents, such is the passing away of karmic constituents." "Such is consciousness, such is the origin of consciousness, such is the passing away of consciousness."

A monk also practices the mindful contemplation of the elements of reality with regard to the six senses and sense-objects. How does he do this? In this way: He knows his eyes, he knows visible forms, and he knows the attachments that develop in connection with the two of them. Similarly he knows his ears, and he knows sounds. He knows his nose and he knows smells. He knows his tongue and he knows tastes. He knows his body and he knows tactile things. He knows his mind and he knows thoughts. And he knows the attachments that develop in connection with any of them.

A monk also practices the mindful contemplation of the elements of reality with regard to the seven factors of enlightenment. How does he do that? In this way: When the first factor of enlightenment, which is mindfulness, is within him, he knows it to be present; when it is not within him, he knows it to be absent. And similarly, he knows the presence and absence within himself of the other factors of enlightenment: the investigation of Dharma, energetic effort, enthusiasm, serenity, meditative concentration, and equanimity.

A monk also practices the mindful contemplation of the elements of reality with regard to the Four Noble Truths. How does he do that?

In this way: He knows "suffering" the way it really is, and he knows "the origination of suffering" the way it really is, and he knows "the cessation of suffering" the way it really is, and he knows "the way leading to the cessation of suffering" the way it really is.

The Merit of Making Images
(The Meritorious Virtue of Making Images)*

Another prominent (and much more widespread than relic veneration) feature of Buddhist worship is using statues of the Buddha to focus one's thoughts toward enlightenment. In this passage from the Mahayana Buddhist canon, the Buddha is said to lavish great merit on those who make his images. The belief that the Buddha gives his gracious blessing to those who seek it is a prominent theme in Mahayana Buddhism.[34]

And the Blessed One sat upon his lotus throne, upon the terrace of enlightenment; and each person in the four assemblies thought to himself: "Truly we wish to hear the Blessed One teach us the meritorious virtue of making images of the Buddha. For what blessings could we gain if we made an image in the form of the Buddha, yet with our meager talent failed to capture his likeness?"

And the bodhisattva Maitreya knew their thoughts: he arose from his seat, placed his robe over his right shoulder, and knelt upon the ground. He joined his palms together, and said to the Blessed One: "King Udayana has made an image of the Buddha. Whether the Buddha is in the world or has passed away into nirvana, how much merit does one gain who follows the dictates of a faithful heart and builds an image such as his? My one wish is that the Blessed One explain this thing to me."

And the Buddha said to the bodhisattva Maitreya: "Listen attentively! Listen attentively, and ever bear in mind what I shall explain to you.

"Let a son of good family or a daughter of good family but be pure and faithful, and fix his mind solely upon the virtues of the Buddha, and meditate unceasingly upon his awe-inspiring virtue and majesty. Let him think upon the ten powers of the Buddha, and upon his fourfold fearlessness; upon his eighteen special qualities, and upon his great love and compassion; upon his omniscience, and upon all his signs of greatness.

"Let him see how every single pore of the Buddha's body glows with measureless multicolored brilliant light, with immensities of surpassing blessings and adornments and accomplishments, with measureless insight and perfect enlightenment, with measureless meditation and forbearance, with measureless magic and spiritual power.

"Let him meditate upon the infinitude of all the virtues of the Buddha, upon his far removal from all the hosts of error, and upon his splendor unequaled in all the world. And let him fix his mind in this manner, and awaken deep faith and joy, and make an image of the Buddha with

---

*Taisho Shinshu Daizokyo, 16, no. 694

[34]From Stephan Beyer, *The Buddhist Experience: Sources and Interpretations* (Belmont, CA: Dickenson, 1974), pp. 47–50, 54–55. Copyright 1974, Dickenson Publishing Company. Used by permission of Wadsworth Publishing Company, Inc.

all its signs. Then he gains merit which is vast, and great, and measureless, and limitless, and which can be neither weighed nor counted.

"Maitreya, should a man draw and adorn an image with a host of varied colors; or cast an image of silver, or bronze, or iron, or lead, or tin; or carve an image of fragrant sandalwood; or cover an image with pearls, or shell, or well-woven and embroidered silk; or cover a wooden image with red earth and white lime plaster; or build an image to the best of his ability, even if it be so small as the size of a finger, as long as those who see it can see that it is in the form of the Blessed One—I shall now tell you what his blessed reward will be, and how he will fare in his next life.

"For a man who does these things may be born again into this world, but he will not be born into a poor family, nor will he be born in a barbarian border kingdom, nor into a lowly clan, nor as an orphan; he will not be born stupid or fierce, nor as a merchant or peddler or butcher; truly he will not be born into any low mean craft or impure caste, into any heretical practices or heretical views.

"For by the power of his intention he has cast aside the cause for such rebirth, and he will not be born into such states; but rather he will always be born into the household of a universal emperor, having powerful clansmen, or perhaps into the household of a Brahmin of pure practices, rich and honorable, lordly and without error.

"And the place where he is born will always be where Buddhas are served and worshipped; and perhaps there he shall be a king, able to maintain and establish the Law, teaching the Law which converts those of evil practices; and perhaps he shall be a universal emperor, having the seven jewels, bringing forth a thousand sons, and mounting into the sky to convert the four corners of the world.

"And when his length of days has been exhausted, the lord will be abundantly joyful, perhaps to rule as the king of the gods, or as lord of the Heaven of Delights, or of the Heaven of Power; for there will be no joy either of gods or of men which he will not taste. And thus his blessed reward will continue in heaven and will not be cut off when he dies.

"And he will always be born as a man: he will not take on the body of a woman, or of a eunuch, or of a hermaphrodite.[35] The body which he takes will be without defect or deformity: neither one-eyed nor blind; his ears not deaf; his nose not bent or twisted; his mouth not large or crooked; his lips not hanging down or wrinkled or rough; his teeth not broken or missing, not black or yellow; his tongue not slow; the back of his neck without tumor or boil; his form not hunched; his color not splotched; his arms not weak; his feet not large; and he will be neither too thin nor too tall, neither too fat nor too thin. . . .

"Maitreya, if there is a man who, in the midst of this world, can awaken his faith and build an image of the Buddha, then between his having done so and his not having done so the difference is . . . great: for anywhere this man is born, he is purified and free of all his past sins, and by all his skill may gain liberation even without a teacher. . . ."

And then the bodhisattva Maitreya said to the Buddha: "Blessed One, you have always said that good or evil deeds are never lost. Any being who has done such grievous sins should be born in a mean, low class and household, be poor and sick and die a speedy death. But if he can awaken his faith and build an image of the Buddha, then will he still experience the retribution for his host of sins?"

And the Buddha said to the bodhisattva Maitreya: "Maitreya, listen attentively, and I shall explain it to you. Should this being, who has done all those sins, put forth his heart to build a Buddha image, seek to wail and repent, take himself strongly in hand and vow to transgress no more, then everything that he has done before is all annulled. . . .

---

[35]*hermaphrodite*: a person with male and female sexual organs and characteristics.

"And why is that? It is because all Buddhas have the measureless limitless blessed virtues of their Buddhahood: measureless limitless great insight, measureless limitless meditation and freedom, and all manner of superlative qualities of meritorious virtue. . . . The virtue of the Blessed Buddha is without limit or measure, and it cannot even be thought or talked of. And that

is why, if a man awakens his faith and builds a Buddha image, every single one of his evil deeds will be exhausted and annulled; and from the store of the Buddhas he gains meritorious virtue without limit or measure, until he himself gains Buddhahood, and himself saves beings from all their suffering and woe forever."

Scripture to Guide the Soul after Death*

Probably the most famous Tibetan scripture is the Bardo Thodol *(or* Bar-do thos-grol*), popularly known as the* Tibetan Book of Dead *but more accurately translated "Listen and Be Liberated from the Intermediate State." This book provides readings done at and after death to guide the soul of the deceased through the intermediate ("Bardo") state to a happy reincarnation. This key reading at the point of death first speaks of the "clear light" of pure Nirvana; the person cannot reach it, and guidance is given to lead the soul through demonic nightmares to shelter in the womb of a being who will later give birth to the dead person's reincarnation.*[36]

"Noble person, (his/her name), now the time has come for you to seek a path [through the Bardo]. After your breath has almost ceased, that which is called the Clear Light of the first phase of the Intermediary State will dawn upon you. Its meaning was explained to you by your lama. It is existence as such, empty and bare like the sky; it will appear to you as the stainless and bare mind, clear and empty, without limitations or a center. At this moment you should recognize this and remain therein. I shall guide you to this insight." Before the physical breath has

totally ceased one should repeat this close to the dying person's ear many times so that it is imprinted on the mind. . . .

"Noble son, (name), listen! The intrinsic light of true being will now become apparent to you. This you must recognize! Noble son, the innate being of your present cognition is this very naked voidness, which does not exist as a thing, phenomenon, or color; it is mere voidness. This is the absolute reality of the female Buddha Samantabhadra.[37] As your cognition consists in voidness, don't let this opportunity become meaningless. . . . The nature of your own mind is void of an inherent being and of any substance, but your intelligence is crystal clear. This nature of your mind is inseparable from your intelligence; together they are the true being, the Buddha. The nature of your mind, equally clear and void, consists in a mass of light, and because of being free of becoming and decaying it is the Buddha of boundless light. This you must recognize! . . .

"Noble son, for three and a half days you will be unconscious. When you awake from the coma you will think: 'What happened to me?' For this reason, you have to recognize that you are now in the intermediate state. At this time, when you depart from the world, all things will appear to you as light, and as celestial beings. The entire sky will shine with bright blue. . . .

---

*Bardo Thodol 1.1–2
[36]From H. Coward, E. Dargyay and R. Neufeldt, *Readings in Eastern Religion* (Waterloo, Ontario: Wilfred Laurier University Press, 1988). Copyright 1988 by Wilfred Laurier University Press. Used by permission.

[37]*Samantabhadra*: As in Buddhist tantric texts, the feminine here represents perfect wisdom.

"You should yearn for the light blue light, which is so brilliant and clear; and full of devotion you should address Vairocana with this prayer which you should repeat after me: 'Alas! At this time I am wandering through the world because of my great ignorance. I beg you, Vairocana, to guide me on the bright path of the primordial wisdom of the sphere being-as-such, the right path. May the divine mother, Akasheshvari (Protector of the heavens) protect me from behind. I beg you, rescue me from the abyss of the intermediate state and guide me to perfect buddhahood.'

"Noble son, (name), hear me! You have not understood me even though I have directed you toward the right insight according to the instructions of this text. Now when you can't close the womb, then the time has truly come when you have to acquire a new body. There is more than only one profound and authentic instruction for closing the door of the womb. Remember them, be not distracted; imprint them on your mind.

"Noble son, although you are reluctant to go, torturers—which are evil deeds—chase you. Powerless, you have to go where you don't want to. Torturers and executioners pull you and you feel as if you are running away from darkness, tornadoes, cries of war, snow, rain, hail, and blizzards. In your anxiety you are looking for a refuge, and you escape and hide—as I have said before—in mansions, rock crevasses, caves, thick undergrowth, or in lotus flowers which close over you. You ask yourself whether they will get you there. 'If they detect me here, then everything is lost,' and while questioning whether you have escaped you cling to this spot. If they take you from there you are afraid of being overcome by the anxieties and terrors of the intermediate state. Thus you feel fear and anxiety and you hide in the middle of these burrows. Therein you seize a bad body that did not exist before, and you will suffer from various ills. This is a sign that the devils and demons have prevented your escape.

"Listen and memorize this instruction suitable for such an occasion! When the torturers chase you into a state of helplessness, or when fear and anxiety threaten you then you should visualize a wrathful deity who destroys all these forms of threat. Quickly perfect your vision of the deity with all his limbs. . . . Through their blessing and compassion you will rid yourself from the torturers and will have the strength to close the door of the womb. This profound and accurate instruction you should keep in mind!"

GLOSSARY

Abhidhamma (ahb-hee-DAHM-muh) "Special Teaching," the third basket of the Buddhist canon [Sanskrit: *Abhidharma*].

arhat (AHR-haht) "Worthy One," a title of those who achieve enlightenment [Sanskrit: *Arhant*].

bodhisattva (bohd-hee-SAHT-vuh) one who comes very close to Buddha nature (enlightenment) but postpones it for the sake of helping others to reach it.

Buddha (BUHD-ah) one who has reached enlightenment; although Gotama is the Buddha *par excellence*, this term applies to all others who attain this state.

dhamma (DAH-muh) teaching, path, way [Sanskrit: *dharma*].

Jatakas (JAH-tah-kuh) the book of tales of Gotama Buddha's previous lives.

sutta (SUH-tuh) a writing, a scripture; *Sutta Pitaka,* the second basket of the canon, featuring the basic teachings of Buddhism [Sanskrit: *sutra*].

tathagata (tah-THAH-gah-tuh) "One who has come/gone thus," one who has reached enlightenment.

Tipitaka (tih-pee-TAH-kuh) "Three Baskets," the main internal divisions of the canon [Sanskrit: *Tripitaka*].

Vinaya (vih-NIGH-yuh) "Discipline," the first basket of the canon, which deals with the rules of monastic life.

QUESTIONS FOR STUDY AND DISCUSSION

1. What are the main features of the Buddhist scripture canon?

2. How is the life of Gotama Buddha an example for all Buddhists? Is it true to say that most of Buddhism is founded on the life of Gotama?

3. In what sense are the Four Noble Truths the essence of Buddhism?

4. What are the characteristics of monasticism as described in scripture?

5. To what degree is Buddhism a religion made for monastics?

6. How is the role of women in Buddhism described in its scripture? Consider especially the role of nuns.

7. In what ways do the scriptures reflect the basic differences (and the similarities) between southern (Theravada) and northern (Mahayana) Buddhism? Consider both canon and content.

8. Based on your understanding of Buddhist scripture, how would you describe nirvana?

9. What are some basic similarities and differences between Hinduism and Buddhism?

SUGGESTIONS FOR FURTHER READING

Primary Readings

The *Sacred Books of the East* series is still the fullest and most accessible collection of Buddhist scripture in English translation. Its volume 10 contains the *Dhammapada*, translated by F. Max Müller, and the *Sutta-Nipata*, by V. Fausboll; vol. 11, various suttas by T. W. Rhys Davids; vols. 13, 17, and 20, the most important *Vinaya* texts, by Rhys Davids and H. Oldenberg; vol. 19, a translation of the Chinese version of the *Acts of the Buddha*; vol. 21, the *Lotus Sutra*, by H. Kern; vols. 35 and 36, the *Questions of King Milinda*; and vol. 49, various Mahayana texts, prominently the *Acts of the Buddha*, by E. B. Cowell, Müller, and J. Takakusu.

E. Conze, *Buddhist Scriptures.* London: Penguin, 1959. An excellent anthology by a leading expert on Buddhism.

W. T. de Bary, *The Buddhist Tradition in India, China and Japan.* New York: Vantage Books, 1972. Of all the anthologies of the three major traditions of Buddhism, this one is the finest.

J. Strong, *The Experience of Buddhism: Sources and Interpretations.* Belmont, CA: Wadsworth, 1995. A comprehensive anthology of Buddhist scripture and other literature.

Secondary Readings

N. S. Barnes, "[Women in] Buddhism." In A. Sharma, ed., *Women in World Religions.* Albany: State University of New York Press, 1987. Gives good attention to the historical witness of Buddhist scriptures to this topic.

M. Levering, ed., "Scripture and Its Reception: A Buddhist Case." In *Rethinking Scripture.* Albany: State University of New York Press, 1989, pp. 58–101. A fascinating glimpse of the use of scripture in a Buddhist nunnery.

Donald S. Lopez, Jr., *Elaborations on Emptiness: Uses of the* Heart Sutra. Princeton: Princeton University Press, 1996. Explores the philosophical and ritual uses of this most important text.

R. A. Ray, "Buddhism: Sacred Text Written and Realized." In F. M. Denny and R. L. Taylor, *The Holy Book in Comparative Perspective* (Gives very good attention to orality.)

K. A. Tsai, *Lives of the Nuns: Biographies of Chinese Buddhist Nuns from the Fourth to Sixth Centuries.* Honolulu: University Press of Hawaii, 1995. A translation and commentary of a Chinese book written to demonstrate the power of Buddhist scripture in the lives of female monastics.

INFOTRAC COLLEGE EDITION

You can locate InfoTrac College Edition articles about this chapter by accessing the InfoTrac College Edition website (http://www.infotrac.collegeedition.com/wadsworth/). Using subject guide, enter the search terms relevant to this chapter, and then read abstracts for relevant articles.

Illustrated Folio from a Jain Kalpasutra Palm-Leaf Manuscript
This thirteenth-century manuscript shows a Shvetambara monk preaching to a prince, who raises his hands in reverence; the scriptures are open before them on a reading stand. Note the hole for threading the binding string at the center of the folio. Credit: Edwin Binney 3rd Collection, San Diego Museum of Art

CHAPTER FOUR

Jainism

❖ A Jaina man makes his way into a temple in Calcutta. He stands reverently before a life-sized statue of a naked man who in ancient times attained nirvana. As other worshippers walk respectfully around the statue several times, he stands still at its base and reads from the Jaina scriptures.

❖ A group of Jaina nuns walks slowly and carefully down a dirt road in northern India. Dressed in white, they have muslin cloths over their mouths to keep out flying insects. They use small brooms to gently sweep the ground in front of them as they walk, looking for even the smallest visible creatures. They are practicing the first and most important of their vows, noninjury to any living thing.

INTRODUCTION

Jainism was founded by Mahavira ("Great Hero") in the sixth century B.C.E. Mahavira taught a stricter version of the Hindu Upanishadic way, giving special emphasis to **ahimsa** [ah-HIM-suh], "noninjury" to all living beings. Rejecting belief in a supreme god, Jains seek release from endless reincarnation through a life of strict self-denial. Two million Jains in India have had an influence all out of proportion to their comparatively small numbers. Gandhi, for example, drew inspiration from their teaching of nonviolence. The Jaina scriptures, despite their fragmentary state, afford an excellent glimpse into this tenacious religion, especially its main teachings and monastic life.

Overview of Structure

Jaina scripture is known in religious scholarship as the *Agama* [ah-GAH-muh], "tradition." Most Jains call it the *Siddhanta* [sid-DAHN-tuh], "Doctrine." The two main branches of Jainism, the Shvetambaras and the Digambaras, share a few books, but for the most part they have different canons. Shvetambara ("white-clad" monastics) is the larger group. It teaches that a woman can achieve nirvana without having to be reborn as a man and therefore this group has an order of nuns. Digambara (with "sky-clad" or naked monks) teaches that women cannot achieve nirvana.

The Shvetambara canon is commonly said by Western scholars to have forty-five books in six sections: *Angas* [AHN-guhs] (Limbs), *Upangas* (Sub-*Angas*), *Prakirnakas* (mixed texts), *Chedasutras* (on authority and discipline), *Culikasutras* (Appendices), and *Mulasutras* ("basic texts"). The *Angas* are the oldest part of the canon. The first *Anga* is the *Acarangasutra,* containing the most reliable Jain story of Mahavira and laws for monks and nuns. The second *Anga* is the *Sutrakritanaga,* which contains the main Jain teachings. The best-known *mulasutra* is the *Uttaradhyayana Sutra,* teachings believed by Jains to be the last words of Mahavira. Besides these books, Jains also say that their original and pure teachings were contained in fourteen *Purvas* (Foundations), now all lost. The difficulties among the two sects and within each sect's canon are traced to the loss of these books. (The least of the Jaina sects, the Sthanakavasis, deny the existence of any scripture.)

The Digambaras accept as canonical the ancient *Purvas* that survive. They also accept the **Prakaranas** which form the main part of their canon: the *Mulacara* (on conduct), the *Samayasara* (on doctrine), the *Pravancanasara* (teaching), and the *Aradhana* ("Accomplishment"). They also treat as scripture many scholastic commentaries on the scriptures (*anuyoga*), which range from the first to the ninth centuries C.E. Both Jain groups accept the important *Tattvarthadhigama Sutra* ("Book for Attaining the Meaning of Principles") by Umasvamin, the first work on Jaina philosophy to be written in Sanskrit. The fixing of the number of Shvetamabara texts at forty-five, and their subdivision into six groups, was largely the work of the nineteenth-century German scholar Georg Buhler. Recently this partition has been called into question as too simplistic and not reflecting actual Jain usage. Kendall Folkert, for example, has stated, "When one asks contemporary Jains what their scriptures are, one receives widely varying answers, responses that vary not because of ignorance, but because there does not appear to be a wholly accepted body of scripture that is of equal value to the entire community." Folkert also states that Digambaras sometimes accept Shvetambara texts.[1]

The *Agama* discusses a vast number of subjects, with books written by many Jain leaders over a long period. Some of it is in prose, some in verse, and some mixed prose and verse. Its content, though frequently repetitious and diffuse, at times can be succinct and systematic.

Origin, Development, and Use

Jains believe that, when he achieved nirvana, Mahavira emitted a "sacred sound" that his followers translated into words. Thus the authority for the most ancient scriptures of both Jain sects is Mahavira himself, but (in typical Indian fashion) he is not thought to have written them. Some of them claim to be speeches given by Mahavira to Gautama Indrabhuti, whose disciple Sudharman gave them in turn to his pupil Jambusvamin. The types of literature mentioned earlier developed over time, all of it handed on orally in the monastic community until about 500 C.E., when it was edited and written down.

Like Theravada Buddhism, which it resembles, Jainism has put monks in control of the development and usage of its scriptures. Mahavira gave the holy teaching as an ascetic. He gave it to his monk followers, who passed it down through the ages for a thousand years until other monks wrote it down. Thus it is not surprising that the content of Jain scripture is dominated by monastic teachings, ideals, and rules. The *Agama* was never intended for a popular audience but for monks (and, to a much lesser degree, nuns), who have much time to study it, learn it, and teach it to one

---

[1] K. Folkert, "The 'Canons' of 'Scripture,'" in M. Levering, *Rethinking Scripture* (Albany: State University of New York Press, 1979), p. 175.

another. Typically, the monk studies the four *Mulasutras* at the beginning of his career. If he masters them, he goes on to other more difficult texts and can perhaps become one of the highly respected monks who is a teacher of scripture in the monastery. Study of scripture is commanded in the rules for monks, and knowledge derived from the sacred books is typically the first step to release. This monastic orientation of scripture explains to a large degree their repetition, many lists of various items, and other features that make them more difficult for the layperson to comprehend.

Nevertheless, the Jain laity also uses its scriptures extensively. Literacy rates are high among Jains, who tend to be more well educated than the average Indian, and this has made its scriptures more accessible. Believers read and reflect upon them in houses of worship. Usage at festivals is also striking. For example, the *Kalpa Sutra* is formally read aloud at Paryusana, the end-of-the-year festival of confession and rededication.

HISTORY

The Life of Mahavira*

*This passage tells the story of Mahavira as an example for believers, and especially for monks and nuns, of one who has achieved nirvana. Mahavira renounced the world, gave away his property, pulled out his hair, and finally starved himself to death. The gods who see and admire these feats are not supreme gods, and Mahavira shows himself superior to them as a **jina** [GEE-nuh] (one who has achieved nirvana). The* Kalpa Sutra *contains a story of Mahavira more legendary than this.*[2]

In that period, in that age, once upon a time, after the lapse of nine complete months and seven and a half days, in the first month of summer . . . on its thirteenth day . . . the Kshatriya woman Trisala, perfectly healthy herself, gave birth to a perfectly healthy boy, the Venerable Ascetic Mahavira.

In that night in which the Kshatriya woman Trisala, perfectly healthy herself, gave birth to a perfectly healthy boy, the Venerable Ascetic Mahavira, there was a great divine, godly luster originated by descending and ascending gods and goddesses. They were of the four orders of Bhavanapatis, Vyantaras, Gyotishkas, and Vimanavasins. In the meeting of the gods their bustle amounted to confusion.

In that night . . . the gods and goddesses rained down a great shower of nectar, sandal powder, flowers, gold, and pearls. In that night the gods and goddesses performed the customary ceremonies of auspiciousness and honor, and anointed Mahavira as a **Tirthankara** [tihr-TAHN-kah-ruh][3]. . . .

[14] Then the Venerable Ascetic Mahavira, after his intellect had developed and his childhood had passed away, lived in the enjoyment of the allowed, noble, fivefold joys and pleasures: sound, touch, taste, color, and smell . . .

Acaranga Sutra 2.15.6–9, 14, 16–20, 22–25, 27
[2]All scripture selections in this chapter are taken, with editing, from Hermann Jacobi, *Jaina Sutras, Sacred Books of the East*, vols. 22, 45 (Oxford: Oxford University Press, 1884, 1895).

---

[3]*Tirthankara:* a "ford-finder" who goes across the river of the world's misery to nirvana. Jains believe that Mahavira was the last of twenty-four Tirthankaras.

[16] The Venerable Ascetic Mahavira's parents were worshippers of Parsva and followers of the Sramanas.[4] For many years they were followers of the Sramanas, and for the sake of protecting the six classes of lives they observed, blamed, repented, confessed, and did penance for their sins. On a bed of Kusa-grass they rejected all food, and their bodies dried up by the last mortification of the flesh, which is to end in death. Thus they died in the proper month, and, leaving their bodies, were born as gods in Adbhuta Kalpa. Descending after the end of their allotted length of life, with their departing breath they will reach absolute perfection in Mahavideha. They will reach wisdom, liberation, final Nirvana, and the end of all misery.[5]

In that period, in that age the Venerable Ascetic Mahavira . . . lived thirty years among the householders under the name of Videha.

After his parents had gone to the worlds of the gods . . . he gave up his gold and silver, his troops and chariots. He distributed, portioned out, and gave away his valuable treasures consisting of riches, plants, gold, pearls, etc., and distributed among those who wanted to make presents to others. Thus he gave away his possessions for a whole year. In the first month of winter, in the first fortnight, in the dark fortnight of Margasiras, on its tenth day, while the moon was in conjunction with Uttaraphalguni, he decided to retire from the world. . . .

Then the four orders of gods awakened the best of Jinas, the Venerable Mahavira, saying, "Arhat [AHR-haht]![6] Propagate the religion which is a blessing to all creatures in the world!"

When the gods and goddesses . . . had become aware of the Venerable Ascetic Mahavira's intention to retire from the world, they assumed their proper form, dress, and ensigns. They ascended their own vehicles and chariots with their proper pomp and splendor, together with their whole retinue. Rejecting all large matter, they retained only tiny matter.[7] Then they rose up, and with that excellent, quick, swift, rapid, divine motion of the gods they came down again. They crossed numberless continents and oceans till they arrived in Gambudvipa at the northern Kshatriya part of the place called Kundapura. In the northeastern quarter of it they suddenly halted. . . .

At that period, in that age, in the first month of winter . . . on its tenth day . . . fasting three days without taking water, having put on one garment, the Venerable Ascetic Mahavira with a train of gods, men, and Asuras[8] left the northern Kshatriya part of the place Kundapura by the high way for the park Gnatri Shanda. There, just at the beginning of night, he caused his palankin to stop quietly on a slightly raised untouched ground. He quietly descended from it, sat quietly on a throne with the face toward the east, and took off all his ornaments and finery.[9] . . .

When the Venerable Ascetic Mahavira had adopted the holy conduct which produced that state of soul in which the reward of former actions is temporarily counteracted, he reached the knowledge called Manahparyaya, by which he knew the thoughts of all sentient beings. . . . Then he formed the following resolution: "I shall for twelve years neglect my body and abandon the care of it. I shall with a right disposition bear, undergo, and suffer all calamities arising from divine powers, men or animals."

The Venerable Ascetic Mahavira formed this resolution. Neglecting his body, he arrived in the village Kummara when only one division of the day remained. Neglecting his body, the Venerable Ascetic Mahavira meditated on his Self in

---

[4] *Sramanas:* monks.

[5] *Descending . . . misery:* they will in their next incarnation achieve nirvana and be reborn no more.

[6] *Arhat:* "worthy one," another name for one who has reached nirvana.

[7] *large matter . . . tiny matter:* the gods change their physical form to a more spiritual and less physical state.

[8] *Asuras:* spirits.

[9] *took off . . . finery:* yet he is not naked, as he wears a cloth underneath. This reflects the Shvetambara orientation of this book.

blameless lodgings, in blameless wandering, in restraint, in kindness, in avoidance of sinful influence, in a chaste life, in patience, in freedom from passion, in contentment, in control, and in correctness, all while practicing religious postures and acts. He walked the path of Nirvana and liberation, which is the fruit of good conduct. With right disposition he bore, endured, sustained, and suffered all calamities arising from divine powers, men, and animals. With undisturbed and unaffected mind, he was careful in body, speech, and mind.

The Venerable Ascetic Mahavira passed twelve years in this way of life. During the thirteenth year in the second month of summer . . . on its tenth day, on the northern bank of the river Rigupalika, in the field of the householder Samaga, in a north-eastern direction from an old temple, not far from a Sal tree, in a squatting position with joined heels exposing himself to the heat of the sun, with the knees high and the head low, in deep meditation, in the midst of abstract meditation, he reached Nirvana. He reached the complete and full, unobstructed, unimpeded, infinite and supreme, best knowledge and intuition, called Kevala.[10] [25] When the Venerable One had become an Arhat and Jina, he was a Kevalin, omniscient and comprehending all objects. He knew all conditions of the world, of gods, men, and demons. He knew from where they come, where they go, whether they are born as men or animals, or become gods or hell-beings. He knew their food, drink, doings, desires, open and secret deeds, their conversation and gossip, and the thoughts of their minds. He saw and knew all conditions in the whole world of all living beings. . . . [27] On the day when the Venerable Ascetic Mahavira had reached the highest knowledge and intuition, he reflected on himself and the world. First he taught the law to the gods, and then to men.

---

[10]*Kevala:* knowledge that frees one from the cycle of rebirth.

TEACHING

The Causes of Sin*

This reading teaches the understanding of all that hurts other beings and renunciation of it. The first section deals with reincarnation, the second with ahimsa *as the path out of it.*

O long-lived Gambusvamin! I Sudharman[11] have heard the following discourse from the venerable Mahavira:

Many do not remember whether they have descended in an eastern direction when they were born in this world, or in a southern, or in a western, or in a northern direction. . . . Similarly, some do not know whether their soul is born repeatedly or not. They do not know what they were before, nor what they will become after they die and leave this world. Now this is what one should know, either by one's own knowledge or through the instruction of the highest [i.e., a Tirthankara], or having heard it from others: that he descended in an eastern direction, or in any other direction. Similarly, some know that their soul is born repeatedly, that it arrives in this or that direction, whatever direction that may be. [5] He believes in soul, believes in the world, believes in reward, believes in action (acknowledged to be our own doing in such judgments as these): "I did it"; "I shall cause another to do it"; "I shall allow

---

*Acaranga Sutra 1.1–2

[11]*Gambusvamin* was the pupil of Sudharman.

another to do it." In the world, these are all the causes of sin, which must be comprehended and renounced. A man that does not comprehend and renounce the causes of sin . . . is born repeatedly in manifold births, experiencing all painful feelings. . . . He who . . . comprehends and renounces these causes of sin is called a karma-knowing sage. Thus I say.

[2:1] The living world is afflicted, miserable, difficult to instruct, and without discrimination. In this world full of pain, with beings suffering by their different acts, benighted ones cause great pain. See! there are beings individually embodied.[12] See! there are men who control themselves, while others only pretend to be houseless.[13] One destroys this earth-body[14] by

[12]*beings individually embodied:* individual souls exist as absolute realities, not as a part of one world soul.
[13]*pretend to be houseless:* unfaithful monks.
[14]*earth-body:* all lives composed of the elements of the earth.

bad and injurious acts. He hurts many other beings besides, by means of earth, through his doing acts relating to earth. About this the Revered One has taught the truth. For the sake of the splendor, honor, and glory of this life, for the sake of birth, death, and final liberation, for the removal of pain, man acts sinfully toward earth, or causes others to act so, or allows others to act so. This deprives him of happiness and perfect wisdom. He is informed about this when he has understood or heard, either from the Revered One or from the monks, the faith to be coveted. Some truly know this injuring to be bondage, delusion, death and hell. A man is longing for this when he destroys this earth-body by bad, injurious acts. He destroys many other beings as well, which he hurts by means of earth, through his deeds relating to earth. Thus I say.

The Road to Final Deliverance*

This passage presents a summary of the way to salvation. The four main steps are by knowledge, faith, conduct, and ascetic practice ("austerities"). Note the Indian penchant to number things up, useful in monastic teaching.

Learn the true road leading to final deliverance, which the Jinas have taught. It depends on four causes and is characterized by right knowledge and faith. Right knowledge, Faith, Conduct, and Austerities; this is the road taught by the Jinas who possess the best knowledge. Right knowledge, faith, conduct, and austerities—beings who follow this road will obtain beatitude.

Knowledge is fivefold: (1) knowledge derived from the sacred books; (2) perception; (3) supernatural knowledge; (4) knowledge of the

thoughts of other people; (5) the highest, unlimited knowledge. [5] This is the fivefold knowledge. The wise ones have taught the knowledge of substances, qualities, and all developments.

Substance is the substrate of qualities; the qualities are inherent in one substance; but the characteristic of developments is that they inhere in either substances or qualities. Dharma, Adharma,[15] space, time, matter, and souls are the six kinds of substances. They make up this world, as has been taught by the Jinas who possess the best knowledge. Dharma, Adharma, and space are each one substance only; but time, matter, and souls are an infinite number of substances. The characteristic of Dharma is motion, that of Adharma immobility, and that of space,

* *Uttaradhyayana* 28

[15]*Dharma, Adharma:* good and evil, respectively.

which contains all other substances, is to make room (for everything).

[10] The characteristic of time is duration, that of soul the realization of knowledge, faith, happiness, and misery. The characteristic of Soul is knowledge, faith, conduct, austerities, energy, and realization of its developments. The characteristic of matter is sound, darkness, luster, light, shade, sunshine, color, taste, smell, and touch. The characteristic of development is singleness, separateness, number, form, conjunction, and disjunction.

The nine truths are: (1) Soul; (2) the inanimate things; (3) the binding of the soul by Karma;[16] (4) merit; (5) demerit; (6) that which causes the soul to be affected by sins; (7) the prevention of asrava by watchfulness; (8) the annihilation of Karma; (9) final deliverance. He who truly believes the true teaching of the fundamental truths possesses righteousness.

Faith is produced by (1) nature; (2) instruction; (3) command; (4) study of the Sutras; (5) suggestion; (6) comprehension of the meaning of the sacred lore; (7) complete course of study; (8) religious exercise; (9) brief exposition; (10) the Law.

He who believes by nature truly comprehends, by a spontaneous effort of his mind, the nature of soul, inanimate things, merit, and demerit. He puts an end to sinful influences. He who spontaneously believes the four truths (explicitly mentioned in the last verse), which the Jinas have taught, thinking they are of this and not of a different nature, believes by nature. But he who believes these truths, having learned them from somebody else, either a Khadmastha[17] or a Jina, believes by instruction. [20] He who has gotten rid of love, hate, delusion, and ignorance, and believes because he is told to do so, believes by command.

He who obtains righteousness by the study of the Sutras, either Angas or other works, believes by the study of Sutras. He who by correctly comprehending one truth arrives at the comprehension of more—just as a drop of oil expands on the surface of water—believes by suggestion. He who truly knows the sacred lore, namely the eleven Angas, the Prakirnas, and the Drishtivada, believes by the comprehension of the sacred lore. He who understands the true nature of all substances by means of all proofs and nayas,[18] believes by a complete course of study.

[25] He who sincerely performs all duties implied by right knowledge, faith, and conduct, by asceticism and discipline, and by all Samitis and Guptis,[19] believes by religious exercise.

He who holds no wrong doctrines though he is not versed in the sacred doctrines nor acquainted with other systems, believes by brief exposition. He who believes in the truth of the realities, the Sutras, and conduct, as it has been explained by the Jinas, believes by the Law.

Right belief depends on the acquaintance with truth, on the devotion to those who know the truth, and on the avoiding of schismatic and heretical tenets. There is no right conduct without right belief, and it must be cultivated for obtaining right faith. Righteousness and conduct originate together, or righteousness precedes conduct. [30] Without faith there is no knowledge, without knowledge there is no virtuous conduct, without virtues there is no deliverance, and without deliverance there is no perfection.

The excellence of faith depends on the following eight points: (1) that one has no doubts

---

[16]*karma:* fruit of evil deeds, viewed by Jains as a physical accretion on the soul.
[17]*Khadmastha:* one who is advanced in knowledge, but not to the full knowledge of nirvana.

[18]*nayas:* literally, "leadings," probably referring to logical arguments.
[19]The five *Samitis,* rules for monks, are: how to walk in a noninjurious manner; how to speak; how to beg for food; how to relieve oneself in a noninjurious manner; how to use the few possessions allowed a monk. The three *Guptis* regulate thought, speech, and the body.

(about the truth of the tenets); (2) that one has no preference (for heretical tenets); (3) that one does not doubt its saving qualities; (4) that one is not shaken in the right belief (because heretical sects are more prosperous); (5) that one praises the pious; (6) that one encourages weak brethren; (7) that one supports or loves the confessors of the Law; (8) that one tries to exalt it.

Conduct, which produces the destruction of all Karma, is (1) the avoidance of everything sinful; (2) the initiation of a novice; (3) purity produced by peculiar austerities; (4) reduction of desire; (5) annihilation of sinfulness according

to the precepts of the Arhats, as well in the case of a Khadmastha[20] as of a Jina.

Austerities are twofold, external and internal. Both external and internal austerities are sixfold. By knowledge one knows things, by faith one believes in them, by conduct one gets freedom from Karma, and by austerities one reaches purity. Having by control and austerities destroyed their Karma, great sages go to perfection and get rid of all misery. Thus I say.

---

[20] *Khadmastha:* one who does not have full knowledge.

ORGANIZATION

The Five Great Vows*

These solemn, final vows are taken by a monk or nun entering the life of renunciation. Note that the vow of ahimsa comes first. The ideals of these vows are also influential among the laity, and they take "Lesser Vows" modeled on the full monastic vows, but not as strict. Because of faithfulness to their vows, Jains have a strong reputation in India for truthfulness (vow 2 below) and honesty (vow 3). The vows themselves are given, but their "clauses" (explanations) are omitted.

The Venerable Ascetic Mahavira, endowed with the highest knowledge and intuition, taught the five great vows, with their clauses . . . to the Sramanas and Nirgranthas,[21] to Gautama, etc.

The first great vow, Sir, is this. I renounce all killing of living beings, whether tiny or large, whether movable or immovable. I myself shall not kill living beings nor cause others to do it, nor consent to it. . . .

The second great vow is this. I renounce all vices of lying speech arising from anger or greed or fear or mirth. I shall neither myself speak lies, nor cause others to speak lies, nor consent to the speaking of lies by others. . . .

The third great vow is this. I renounce all taking of anything not given, either in a village or a town or a wood, either of little or much, of small or great, of living or lifeless things. I shall neither take myself what is not given, nor cause others to take it, nor consent to their taking it. . . .

The fourth great vow is this. I renounce all sexual pleasures, either with gods or men or animals. I shall not give way to sensuality, nor cause others to give way to it, nor consent to their giving way. . . .

The fifth great vow is this. I renounce all attachments, whether little or much, small or great, living or lifeless. I myself shall not form such attachments, nor cause others to do so, nor consent to their doing so. As long as I live, I confess and blame, repent and exempt myself [of these].

---

*Acaranga Sutra 2.15.i–v
[21] *Sramanas and Nirgranthas:* Jaina monks.

ETHICS

Ahimsa*

This selection details the duty of noninjury, the first vow of monastics. This is one of the leading duties of the laity as well. For example, observant Jains do not eat after sunset because they are less able to see any insects then.

These classes of living beings have been declared by the Jinas: earth, water, fire, wind; grass, trees, and plants; and the moving beings, both the egg-bearing and those that bear live offspring, those generated from dirt and those generated in fluids. Know and understand that they all desire happiness. By hurting these beings, people do harm to their own souls, and will repeatedly be born as one of them.

Every being born high or low in the scale of the living creation, among movable and immovable beings, will meet with its death. Whatever sins the evildoer commits in every birth, for them he must die.

In this world or in the next the sinners suffer themselves what they have inflicted on other beings, a hundred times, or suffer other punishment. Living in the Samsara[22] they always acquire new Karma, and suffer for their misdeeds.

[5] Some leave their mother and father to live as Sramanas, but they use fire. The prophet [Mahavira] says, "People are wicked who kill beings for the sake of their own pleasure." He who lights a fire kills living beings; he who extinguishes it kills the fire. Therefore a wise man who well considers the Law should light no fire. Earth contains life, and water contains life; jumping or flying insects fall in the fire; dirt-born vermin and beings live in wood. All these beings are burned by lighting a fire.

Plants are beings possessed of natural development. Their bodies require nourishment, and they all have their individual life. Reckless men who cut them down for their own pleasure destroy many living beings. By destroying plants, when young or grown up, a careless man does harm to his own soul. The prophet says, "People are wicked who destroy plants for their own pleasure."

---

*Sutrakritanga 1.7.1–9

[22]*Samsara:* the wheel of rebirth.

Rules for Monastic Life**

Rules for both conduct and thought govern the life of a monk or a nun. While the passage speaks of "compassion for living things" as a motivation for noninjury, the main motivation is less altruistic—to avoid as much as possible one's collection of karma.

Learn from me, with attentive minds, the road shown by the wise ones. This road leads a monk who follows it to the end of all misery.

Giving up the life in a house, and taking Pravragya,[23] a sage should know and renounce those attachments that take hold of men. A

**Uttaradhyayana 35

[23]*Pravragya:* the vow of the monk's wandering way of life.

restrained monk should abstain from killing, lying, stealing, sexual intercourse, from desire, love, and greed.

Even in his thoughts, a monk should not long for a pleasant painted house filled with the fragrance of garlands and frankincense, secured by doors, and decorated with a white ceiling-cloth. [5] For in such a dwelling a monk will find it difficult to prevent his senses from increased desire and passion. He should be content to live on a burial-place, in a deserted house, below a tree, in solitude, or in a place that had been prepared for the sake of some-body else. A well-controlled monk should live in a pure place that is not too crowded, and where no women live. He should not build a house, nor cause others to erect one. Many living beings both movable and immovable, both tiny and large, are killed when a house is being built; therefore a monk should abstain from building a house.

[10] The same holds good with the cooking of food and drink, or with one's causing them to be cooked. Out of compassion for living beings one should not cook nor cause another to cook. Beings which live in water, plants, or in earth and wood are destroyed in food and drink; therefore a monk should cause nobody to cook. Nothing is so dangerous as fire, for it spreads in all directions and is able to destroy many beings. One should not light a fire.

Even in his thoughts a monk should not long for gold and silver. Indifferent alike to dirt and gold, he abstains from buying and selling. If he buys, he becomes a buyer; if he sells, he becomes a merchant. A monk is not to engage in buying and selling. [15] A monk who is to live on alms should beg and not buy. Buying and selling is a great sin; but to live on alms is befitting. He should collect his alms in small parts according to the Sutras and to avoid faults. A monk should contentedly go on his begging-tour, whether he gets alms or not.

A great sage should not eat for the sake of the pleasant taste [of the food] but for the suste-nance of life. He should not be dainty or eager for good fare, he should restrain his tongue, and be without desire. Even in his thoughts he should not desire to be presented with flow-ers,[24] to be offered a seat, to be eloquently greeted, to be offered presents, or to get a mag-nificent welcome and treatment. He should meditate on true things only, committing no sins and having no property.

He should walk about careless of his body until his end draws near. [20] Rejecting food when the time of his death is near, and leaving the human body, he becomes his own master, and is liberated from misery. Without property, without egoism, free from passions. . . . he obtains absolute knowledge, and reaches eternal blessedness. Thus I say.

[24]*presented with flowers:* these and the following special treatments would come when a monk visits layfolk in public or their homes.

GLOSSARY

Agama (AH-gah-muh) "tradition," the Western name for the Jain canon.

ahimsa (ah-HIM-suh) "noninjury" to any living being.

Angas (AHN-guhs) "limbs," the first and main section of the Shvetambara canon.

arhat (AHR-haht) one who has reached nirvana.

jina (GEE-nuh) a "conqueror," one who has reached nirvana.

Prakaranas (prah-KAR-ah-nuhs) the main section of the Digambara canon.

Siddhanta (sid-DAHN-tuh) "doctrine, teaching," the name that Jains use for their scripture.

tirthankara (tihr-TAHN-kah-ruh) "ford-finder," one who has traveled from the misery of this world across the river of existence to liberation, and who enables others to do so by teach-ing and example.

QUESTIONS FOR STUDY AND DISCUSSION

1. Compare the life of Mahavira and Siddharta Gotama (the Buddha). How are they remarkably alike, and what might their dissimilarities be?

2. One scholar has called Jainism the "unhappy face of Buddhism." Judging from their scriptures, would you agree or disagree? Why?

3. Discuss the division between the Shvetambara and Digambara sects on the place of women as monastics. To what degree may this issue be reflected in arguments over the role of women in the monastics or clergy of other faiths?

4. Discuss the basic idea of *ahimsa* in Jainism. Why has it been influential in the wider Indian tradition? How might it be applicable to the peoples of other, non-Indian faiths?

SUGGESTIONS FOR FURTHER READING

Primary Readings

L. Basham, "Jainism and Buddhism." In W. T. deBary, ed., *Sources of Indian Tradition*. New York: Columbia University Press, 1958, pp. 39–92. Excellent translations with introductions of about twenty short but important passages in Jain religion and philosophy.

Hermann Jacobi, trans., *Gaina Sutras*. In F. M. Müller, gen. ed., *Sacred Books of the East*, vols. 22 and 45. Oxford: Oxford University Press, 1884, 1895. Reprinted, Delhi: Motilal Banarsidass, 1964. Contains selections of two *angas*, a *mulasutta* and a *cheyasutta;* still the fullest English translation.

Secondary Readings

Paul Dundas, *The Jains*. London: Routledge, 1993. The best and most recent introduction to Jainism, with an excellent examination of Jain attitudes to scripture.

Kendall W. Folkert, "The 'Canons' of 'Scripture'." In M. Levering, ed., *Rethinking Scripture*. Albany: State University of New York Press, 1989, pp. 170–179. A thought-provoking analysis of the present reception of Jaina scriptures in light of the comparative study of world scriptures.

Kendall W. Folkert, *Scripture and Community: Collected Essays on the Jains,* ed. J. E. Cort. Studies in World Religions Series. Cambridge: Harvard University Center for the Study of World Religions, 1995. Treats the various aspects of Jain tradition, with special attention to scriptures and monastic practice.

⟨ INFOTRAC COLLEGE EDITION

You can locate InfoTrac College Edition articles about this chapter by accessing the InfoTrac College Edition website (http://www.infotrac.collegeedition.com/wadsworth/). Using subject guide, enter the search terms relevant to this chapter, and then read abstracts for relevant articles.

Recitation of the Guru Granth Sahib
An official reader recites the holy book in the Golden Temple of Amritsar, India, while an attendant behind him waves a horse-hair fan to venerate the book. Credit: Gunter Reitz/ Mary Evans Picture Library

CHAPTER FIVE

Sikhism

❖ A turbaned man walks down a bridge to the gate of the Golden Temple of Amritsar, India. Once inside, he approaches the central and only object of veneration, the large scripture book called the *Adi Granth*. Placed on cushions on a raised platform under a richly ornamented canopy, the *Granth* is read by an official reader as an attendant waves a ceremonial whisk over it. The worshipper bows reverently before the book with folded hands, listening to the melodious reading.

❖ Worshippers at a Sikh temple see, in quick succession, three life-cycle ceremonies. First, a baby is brought in for naming; as the *Adi Granth* is opened at random, the first letter on the left-hand page becomes the first letter in the child's first name. Second, a young couple comes to be married; during the ceremony, the couple circles the *Granth* several times to the accompaniment of verses from its marriage hymns. Third, the relatives of a recently deceased Sikh come for the conclusion of funeral rites; a prominent feature is the continuous reading of the entire *Granth,* and they are present for the solemn conclusion of the reading.

INTRODUCTION

The Sikh religion was founded about 1500 C.E. by Guru Nanak. It has made its home in the Punjab of northern India, where today it numbers more than 9 million believers. Sizeable Sikh communities are also found in Canada and Great Britain. Designed to appeal to Hindus and Muslims, it contains elements of both faiths. With Hinduism, it shares mysticism and devotion; with Islam, a rigid monotheism. Yet it rejects elements of both these traditions, especially their leaders and rituals. Sikhism grew through a line of ten gurus until it reached its present form as expressed in its scripture, considered the successor of this line. In its veneration of scripture, Sikhism is unsurpassed among world religions.

Overview of Structure

The *Adi Granth* [AH-dee GRAHNTH] has three main parts, arranged in order of their importance. First is the *Japji* [JAHP-jee], written by Guru Nanak, which the faithful consider a summary and capstone of Sikhism. Teaching in the form of a poem, it differs from the rest of the *Adi Granth* by having no hymn tune. Appended to the *Japji* are fourteen hymns, all of which are found later in the *Adi Granth*. The second part, by far the longest, is the collection of **Rags** [rahgs] ("tunes"), thirty-nine in all. Each rag is divided by different poetic meters and lengths. These divisions are further divided by guru author, proceeding chronologically through the line of gurus. Each guru calls himself "Nanak," usually at conclusion of the hymn, but the different guru authors are noted by the numbered use of the term **Mahala** [ma-HAH-luh]. Mahala 1 denotes the compositions of Guru Nanak; Mahala 2, of Guru Angad, etc.; up to Mahala 5 for Guru Arjan. The third part is a mixed collection of twenty-six small books, most elaborating on the rags. It also features hymns of many *bhakti* (Hindu) saints and Sufi (Muslim) mystics, which early Sikhs found congenial, and which Sikhs have always seen as proof of the universality of their tradition. As it now stands, the *Adi Granth's* material ranges in time from the twelfth-century hymns of Jaidev to the hymns of the ninth guru, Tegh Bahadur, who died in 1675.

The **Dasam Granth,** or "Tenth Book," is mostly composed of legendary narratives, which are not to be found in the *Adi Granth*. Modern scholarship has traced many of them to Hindu Puranic sources. But certain parts of the *Dasam Granth* are well known and much used among Sikhs, especially the teachings of the tenth guru, Gobind Singh. Often quoted is his famous statement, "The temple and the mosque are one; so too are puja [Hindu worship] and [Muslim] prostration. All men are one though they seem to be many." Coupled with these more ecumenical sayings are statements of the rising militancy of the Sikhs.

The content of the *Adi Granth* states in hymnic form the main beliefs of the Sikhs. The *Adi Granth* rejects what it perceives as the ritualism and formalism of Islam and especially of Hinduism, arguing for moral purity as the chief basis of religion. Hindu caste structure is repeatedly rejected; all men are to live as equals. Karma and reincarnation are accepted, but the practice of the Sikh religion will release one from rebirth and lead to blessedness in heaven. Above all, the *Adi Granth* promotes the strict doctrine of one God and mystical devotion to his name. This loving God offers salvation by his grace to those who meditate on him and live in his truth. The reader looks in vain for stories about the life of the founder or other gurus. These have been collected instead into the **janam-sakhis** [JAH-num SAH-kees], traditional narratives that are highly legendary. The *janam-sakhis* have a semicanonical status among devout Sikhs.

The main language of the *Adi Granth* is Punjabi, written in the Gurmukhi ("mouth of the Guru") script. It also shows strong traces of influence from the Hindi language and from several other north Indian languages. The *Adi Granth* employs the Sadhukari (or Sant-Basha) dialect, which was used by religious poets in North India in the fifteenth and sixteenth centuries. Its language is complicated enough to necessitate special training for the **granthis** [GRAHN-thees], official readers, but most observant Sikhs can understand the scripture well enough to read it on their own.

Origin and Development

The overall structure of the *Adi Granth* suggests its origins and growth. Guru Nanak (1469–1539), in a typical Hindu attitude, rejected the authority of the written word, stressing instead the interior meditation on the "holy [oral] word." The *Japji* and the various hymns he composed were passed along orally. Guru Angad, whom Nanak made his successor, devised a Punjabi alphabet for the Gurmukhi language, and the *Adi Granth* was later written in this script. Guru Amar Das, third in the line, compiled a hymnal of his own poems, the poems of his two predecessors, and poems from pre-Sikh mystics. The fifth guru, Arjan, revised this hymnal and compiled the oral and written work of all his predecessors into the *Adi Granth* in 1603–1604. Tradition says that Arjan's opponents were writing and circulating books falsely attributed to Nanak in an effort to corrupt Sikhism and turn it away from Arjan's leadership. In response, Arjan compiled the *Adi Granth*.

The sixth guru, Arjan's son Har Gobind, altered the Sikh movement's original pacifism to a newfound militancy. The final guru, Gobind Singh, is considered by Sikhs to be, after Nanak, their most important leader. Before his death in 1708, he declared that the line of gurus was complete. From this time on, the only guru of the community was to be the *Adi Granth,* which Gobind edited in its final, present form. (He himself wrote portions of the *Dasam Granth,* as mentioned earlier.) Therefore, the *Adi Granth* has served as the teacher and authority for Sikhs, quite literally as the book containing the soul of the gurus. Nothing expresses this as well as the Sikh daily prayer, the *Ardas:* "From the Timeless One [God] there came the bidding, in accordance with which was established the Panth [Sikh community]. To all Sikhs there comes this command: acknowledge as the Guru the *Granth*. Acknowledge the *Granth* as Guru, for it is the manifest body of the Masters. Ye whose hearts are pure, seek Him in the Word!"[1]

Use

All Sikh usage of the *Adi Granth* is steeped in an attitude of profound respect. Devout Sikhs generally refer to the *Adi Granth* by a more venerable name, the *Sri Guru Granth Sahib* (*Guru Granth* for short), or "Revered Teacher Granth." This name is based on the origin of the Sikh scripture. Sikhs believe that each of their ten gurus had the same soul, the soul of Nanak. The last guru bestowed this soul and its guru status on the *Granth*. It became the book embodiment of the soul of the gurus, the statement of the essence of Sikhism and the final authority for its continuing life.

Sikhs also call the *Adi Granth* the "living embodiment of the Guru." One of their leading theologians has claimed, "This is the only scripture of the world which was compiled by one of the founders of a religion himself and whose authenticity has never been questioned."[2] Moreover, the *Adi Granth* has served for almost three hundred years as a force for unity in Sikhism. Doctrinal disputes are traditionally ended by consulting it, at random if need be. Sikhs have a strong mystical feeling for the *Granth* and treat it as an icon. No doubt the musical nature of its recitation contributes to its emotive power. Nevertheless, Sikhism also stresses the importance of meditating on and comprehending the meaning of its scripture.

The Sikh temple is in essence a shrine for the *Adi Granth*. Temple officials ceremoniously close it and "put it to bed" at night. Before dawn they bring it out again, install it in its place, and open it. All this is done to the accompaniment of hymns from the *Adi Granth's* pages. Despite its large-format size, Sikhs carry their guru

---

[1] W. H. McLeod, *The Evolution of the Sikh Community* (Oxford: Clarendon Press, 1976), p. 66.
[2] Gopal Singh, ed., *Sri Guru Granth Sahib* (Calcutta: M. P. Birla, 1989), p. 1.

above their heads, and those who carry it must wear gloves. When open, the *Granth* is draped in fine silk and placed on a special cot under a rich canopy at the focal point of the temple. Worshippers come to walk around it, bow to it, listen to its reading, and sometimes even pray to it. They must never turn their back on it. The official readers or granthis (often mistaken for "priests" by outsiders) wear white scarves to cover their mouths as they read so that their breath will not touch the holy book. Sikh men take turns fanning it with a horsehair whisk (the **chaur** [chowr], one of the symbols of Sikhism). This scripture-centered activity goes on every day at the temple; there is no weekly service. At special festivals, a nonstop oral reading by a team of granthis is held that lasts two days and nights. Every life-cycle celebration centers in some way around the *Adi Granth*. In sum, it is no exaggeration to say that all the worship of the Sikhs centers on and originates in the *Adi Granth*.

This usage also carries over into the Sikh home. A prosperous Sikh household has a special room solely for the prominent placement of the *Granth*. Almost every other Sikh household has a **gutka** [GUHT-kuh], an anthology of the *Adi Granth* with a few passages from the *Dasam Granth*. Daily readings are held in the home. Early-morning recitation by memory of the *Japji* and other long sections is common, often lasting for more than an hour. Devout Sikhs have committed large portions of the *Adi Granth* to memory, and it is constantly on their lips during the day and night, especially in the five required daily prayers.

A memorable feature of Sikh scripture usage is **vak lao** [vahk low], "taking (God's) word." In the home or in the temple, the scripture is always opened at random, and the reading begins from the top of the lefthand page. This reading is thought to hold special significance for the occasion; it is God's word for the moment, which must be "taken" into the believer's life.

TEACHING

Selections from the *Japji**

This entire poem is repeated from memory by practicing Sikhs every morning during prayers—no small feat, as it is almost twice as long as the excerpts given here. They consider it the essence and epitome of their faith. The Japji *moves back and forth between several topics: (1) God's name, greatness, and power; (2) God's creation of the world; (3) the way of salvation by meditating on God's name; (4) good and evil; (5) relations with Hinduism and Islam. The rich sonority of the* Japji's *poetry comes through in this translation. It begins with the* **Mul** *("root")* **Mantra** *[mool MAHN-truh], a confession of faith considered the capstone of the whole composition.*[3]

There is only one God whose name is true, the Creator, devoid of fear and enmity, immortal, unborn, self-existent; by the favor of the Guru.[4] Repeat His Name!

---

*1–3, 5–6, 9–10, 12–13, 15, 17–18, 20–22, 25, 28–29, 33, 37–Epilogue

---

[3]All selections from the Sikh scriptures are taken from Max A. Macauliffe, *The Sikh Religion: Its Gurus, Sacred Writings and Authors* (Oxford: Oxford University Press, 1909).
[4]*by the favor of the Guru:* known through the Guru.

The True One was in the beginning; the True One was in the primal age.

The True One is now also, O Nanak; the True One also (forever) shall be.

[1] By thinking I cannot obtain a conception of Him, even though I think hundreds of thousands of times.

Though I be silent and keep my attention firmly fixed on Him, I cannot preserve silence.

The hunger of the hungry for God does not subside, though they obtain the load of the worlds.

If man should have thousands and hundreds of thousands of devices, even one would not assist him in obtaining God.

How shall man become true before God? How shall the veil of falsehood be torn?

By walking, O Nanak, according to the will of the Commander as preordained.

By His order bodies are produced; His order cannot be described.

By His order souls are infused into them; by His order greatness is obtained.

By His order men are high or low; by His order they obtained preordained pain or pleasure.

By His order some obtained their reward; by His order others must ever wander in transmigration.

All are subject to His order; none is exempt from it.

He who understands God's order, O Nanak, is never guilty of egoism. . . .

Millions of men give millions upon millions of descriptions of Him, but they fail to describe Him.

The Giver gives; the receiver grows weary of receiving.

In every age man subsists by His bounty.

The Commander by His order has laid out the way of the world.

Nanak, God the unconcerned[5] is happy. . . .

[5] He is not established, nor is He created.

The Pure One exists by Himself.

They who worshipped Him have obtained honor.

Nanak, sing His praises who is the Treasury of excellences.

Sing and hear and put His love into your hearts.

Thus shall your sorrows be removed, and you shall be absorbed in Him who is the abode of happiness.

Under the Guru's instruction God's word is heard; under the Guru's instruction its knowledge is acquired; under the Guru's instruction man learns that God is everywhere contained. . . .

[9] By hearing the Name man becomes as Shiva, Brahma, and Indra.

By hearing the Name even the low become highly lauded.

By hearing the Name the way of Yoga and the secrets of the body are obtained.

By hearing the Name man understands the real nature of the Shastras, the Smritis, and the Vedas.

Nanak, the saints are ever happy.

By hearing the Name sorrow and sin are no more.

[10] By hearing the Name truth, contentment, and divine knowledge are obtained.

Hearing the Name is equal to bathing at the sixty-eight places of pilgrimage.

By hearing the Name and reading it man obtains honor.

By hearing the Name the mind is composed and fixed on God.

Nanak, the saints are always happy.

By hearing the Name sorrow and sin are no more. . . .

[12] The condition of him who obeys God cannot be described.

Whoever tries to describe it shall afterward repent.

There is no paper, or pen, or writer

To describe the condition of him who obeys God.

---

[5]*unconcerned:* free of care.

So pure is His name—
Whoever obeys God knows the pleasure of it in
his own heart.
By obeying Him wisdom and understanding
enter the mind;
By obeying Him man knows all worlds;
By obeying Him man suffers no punishment;
By obeying Him man shall not depart with
Jam[6]—
So pure is God's name—
Whoever obeys God knows the pleasure of it in
his own heart. . . .

[15] By obeying Him man attains the gate of
salvation;
By obeying Him man is saved with his family;
By obeying Him the Guru is saved, and saves
his disciples;
By obeying Him, O Nanak, man wanders not
in quest of alms—
So pure is God's name—
Whoever obeys God knows the pleasure of it in
his own heart. . . .

[17] Numberless Your worshippers, and num-
berless Your lovers;
Numberless adorers, and numberless they who
perform austerities for You;
Numberless the reciters of sacred books and
Vedas;
Numberless Your Yogins whose hearts are indif-
ferent to the world;
Numberless the saints who ponder on attrib-
utes and divine knowledge;
Numberless Your true men; numberless alms-
givers;
Numberless Your heroes who face the steel of
their enemies;
Numberless Your silent worshippers who lov-
ingly fix their thoughts upon You.
What power have I to describe You?
So lowly am I, I cannot even once be a sacrifice
to You.
Whatever pleases You is good.

O formless One, You are always secure.

Numberless are the fools appallingly blind;
Numberless are the thieves and devourers of
others' property;
Numberless those who establish their sover-
eignty by force;
Numberless the cut-throats and murderers;
Numberless the sinners who pride themselves
on committing sin;
Numberless the liars who roam about lying;
Numberless the filthy who enjoy filthy gain;
Numberless the slanderers who carry loads of
calumny on their heads;
Nanak thus describes the degraded.
So lowly am I, I cannot even once be a sacrifice
to You.
Whatever pleases You is good.
O Formless One, You are always secure. . . .

[21] Pilgrimage, austerities, mercy, and alms-
giving on general and special occasions
Whoever performs, may obtain some little
honor;
But he who hears and obeys and loves God in
his heart
Shall wash off his impurity in the place of pil-
grimage within him.
All virtues are Yours, O Lord; none are mine.
There is no devotion without virtue.
From the Self-existent proceeded Maya,[7]
whence issued a word which produced Brahma
and the rest—
"You are true, You are beautiful, pleasure is
ever in Your heart!"
What the time, what the epoch, what the lunar
day, and what the week-day,
What the season, and what the month when the
world was created,
The Pandits[8] did not discover; had they done
so, they would have recorded it in the
Puranas.

---

[6]*Jam:* the god of death. By obeying God, a person will not
be reborn to die again.

[7]*Maya:* "deceit, illusion," God's mystical power by which he
created matter.
[8]*Pandits:* highly learned Brahmins.

Nor did the Qazis[9] discover it; had they done
so, they would have recorded it in the
Quran.

Neither the Yogi nor any other mortal knows
the lunar day, or the week-day, or the season,
or the month.

Only the Creator who fashioned the world
knows when He did so.

How shall I address You, O God? How shall I
praise You? How shall I describe You? And
how shall I know You?

Says Nanak, everybody speaks of You, one wiser
than another.

Great is the Lord, great is His name; what He
does comes to pass.

Nanak, he who is proud shall not be honored
on his arrival in the next world.

There are hundreds of thousands of nether and
upper regions.

Men have grown weary at last of searching for
God's limits; they say one thing, that God
has no limit.

The thousands of Puranas and Muslim books
tell that in reality there is but one principle.

If God can be described by writing, then
describe Him; but such description is
impossible.

O Nanak, call Him great; only He Himself
knows how great He is. . . .

[25] His many bounties cannot be recorded,

He is a great giver and has not a particle of
covetousness.

How many, yes countless heroes beg of Him!

How many others whose number cannot be
conceived!

How many persons receive yet deny God's
gifts!

How many fools there are who merely eat!

How many are ever dying in distress and
hunger!

O Giver, these are also Your gifts.

Rebirth and deliverance depend on Your will:
Nobody can interfere with it.

If any fool tries to interfere with it,

He himself shall know the punishment he shall
suffer.

God himself knows to whom He may give, and
He Himself gives:

Very few acknowledge this.

He to whom God has given the boon of praising and lauding Him,

O Nanak, is the King of kings. . . .

[28] Make contentment and modesty your ear-
rings, self-respect your wallet, meditation the
ashes to smear on your body;

Make your body, which is only a morsel for
death, your beggar's coat, and faith your
rule of life and your staff.

Make association with men your Ai Panth,[10]
and the conquest of your heart the conquest
of the world.

The primal, the pure, without beginning, the
indestructible, the same in every age!

Make divine knowledge your food, compassion
your storekeeper, and the voice that is in
every heart the pipe to call to feast.

Make Him who has strung the whole world on
His string your spiritual Lord; let wealth and
supernatural power be relishes for others.

Union and separation is the law that regulates
the world. By destiny we receive our
portion.

Hail! Hail to Him, the primal, the pure, without beginning, the indestructible, the same
in every age! . . .

[Epilogue] The air is the guru, water our
father, and the great earth our mother;

Day and night are our two nurses, male and
female, who set the whole world playing.

Merits and demerits shall be read out in the
presence of the Judge.

According to men's acts, some shall be near,
and others distant from God.

They who have pondered on the Name and
departed after the completion of their toil,

Shall have their countenances made bright,
O Nanak; how many shall be emancipated in
company with them!

---

[9] *Qazis:* Islamic judges.

[10] *Ai Panth:* a sect of (Hindu) yogins.

Remembering God*

In Sikhism, the way of salvation is by profound reflection on, and commitment to, God's name. "Remembering" is not the opposite of "forgetting," but a way to deep reflection. These are the words of Guru Arjan, often repeated after the Japji *in the morning prayer service.*

I bow to the primal Guru;
I bow to the Guru of the primal age;
I bow to the true Guru;
I bow to the holy divine Guru.

Remember, remember God;
By remembering Him you shall obtain happiness,
And erase from your hearts trouble and affliction.
Remember the praises of the one all-supporting God.
Numberless persons utter God's various names.
Investigating the Vedas, the Puranas, and the Smritis,
Men have made out the one word that is God's name.
His praises cannot be recounted,
Who treasures God's name in his heart even for a moment.
Says Nanak, save me, O Lord, with those who are desirous of one glance of You.
In this Sukhmani is the name of God which like ambrosia bestows happiness,
And gives peace to the hearts of the saints.

By remembering God man does not again enter the womb;
By remembering God the tortures of Death disappear;
By remembering God death is removed;
By remembering God enemies retreat;
By remembering God no obstacles are met;
By remembering God we are watchful night and day;
By remembering God fear is not felt;
By remembering God sorrow troubles not:
Men remember God in the company of the saints.
Nanak, by the love of God all wealth is obtained.

By remembering God we obtain wealth, super-natural power, and the nine treasures;
By remembering God we obtain divine knowl-edge, meditation, and the essence of wisdom;
Remembrance of God is the real devotion, penance, and worship;
By remembering God the conception of duality is dispelled;
By remembering God we obtain the advantages of bathing at places of pilgrimage;
By remembering God we are honored at His court;
By remembering God we become reconciled to His will;
By remembering God men's lives are very profitable;
They whom He has caused to do so remember Him.
Nanak, touch the feet of such persons.[11]

---

*Gauri Sukhmani, Mahala 5

[11]*touch the feet of such persons:* Nanak approves of them.

Creation of the World**

The world was directly and purposefully created by God; it still reflects God's goodness. This composition by Guru Nanak extolling God's creation is sung in every Sikh temple in the morning.

**Asa Ki Var, Mahala 1

Wonderful Your word, wonderful Your knowledge;
Wonderful Your creatures, wonderful their species;
Wonderful their forms, wonderful their colors;
Wonderful the animals which wander naked;

Wonderful Your wind; wonderful Your water;
Wonderful Your fire which sports wondrously;
Wonderful the earth, wonderful the sources of
  production;
Wonderful the pleasures to which mortals are
  attached;
Wonderful is meeting, wonderful parting from
  You;
Wonderful is hunger, wonderful repletion;
Wonderful Your praises, wonderful Your
  eulogies;
Wonderful the desert, wonderful the road;
Wonderful Your nearness, wonderful Your
  remoteness;
Wonderful to behold You present.
Beholding these wonderful things I remain
  wondering.
Nanak, they who understand them are
  supremely fortunate.
By Your power we see, by Your power we hear,
  by Your power we fear, or enjoy the highest
  happiness;

By Your power were made the nether regions
  and the heavens; by Your power all creation;
By Your power were produced the Vedas, the
  Puranas, the Muslim books, and by Your
  power all compositions;
By Your power we eat, drink, and clothe ourselves; by Your power springs all affection;
By Your power are the species, classes, and colors of creatures; by Your power are the animals of the world.
By Your power are virtues; by Your power are
  vices: by Your power, honor and dishonor;
By Your power are wind, water, and fire; by
  Your power is the earth.
Everything exists by Your power; You are the
  omnipotent Creator; Your name is the holiest of the holy.
Says Nanak, You behold and pervade all things
  subject to Your command: You are altogether unrivaled.

Dancing for Krishna*

*Sikhism developed out of devotional Hinduism.
Here Guru Amar Das rejects the Krishnavites'
idea that merit is earned by participation in the
dancing for Krishna that occurs at his festivals. In
typical* Guru Granth *style, it adapts the practices
of other religions to Sikhism by reinterpreting
them for the new faith.*

I dance, but it is my heart I cause to dance;
By the favor of the Guru I have effaced myself.
He who keeps his mind firmly fixed on God
  shall obtain deliverance and the object of his
  desires.
Dance, O man, before your Guru;
He who dances as it pleases the Guru shall
  obtain happiness, and at the last moment the
  fear of Death shall forsake him.

He whom God causes to dance and whom He
  loves is a saint.
He himself sings, he himself instructs, and puts
  ignorant man on the right way.
He who banishes worldly love shall dance day
  and night in God's house and never sleep.

Every one who dances, leaps, and sings of other
  gods is lulled to sleep in the house of riches;
  such are the perverse who have no devotion.
Demigods and men who abandon the world
  dance in religious works; Munis and men
  dance in the contemplation of divine
  knowledge.
The Sidhs, Strivers, and holy men who have
  acquired wisdom to meditate on God dance
  in God's love.
The regions, worlds, beings endowed with the
  three qualities, and they who love You,
  O God, dance.

---

* Rag Gurji, Mahala 3

Men and the lower animals all dance, the four
sources of life dance.
They who please You dance, the pious who love
the Word. . . .
He to whom You are gracious shall obtain You
by the favor of the Guru.
If I forget the True One even for a moment,
that moment passes in vain.

Remember Him at every breath and He will
pardon you from His own grace.
It is they who please You, O God, and who
meditate on the Word, who really dance.
Says Nanak, they to whom You are merciful
shall easily obtain bliss.

The Hindu Thread*

This passage from Guru Nanak *features a strong
rejection of Hindu ritual practices, especially those
of the Brahmin (priestly) caste. As in the previous
selection, Hindu practice is reinterpreted for
Sikhs: "Make a sacred thread for the soul."*

Make mercy your cotton, contentment your
thread, continence its knot, truth its twist.
That would make a sacred thread for the soul;
if you have it, O Brahmin, then put it on me.
It will not break, or become soiled, or be
burned, or lost.
Blest is the man, O Nanak, who has such a
thread on his neck.
You purchase a sacred thread for four damris,
and seated in a square[12] put it on;
You whisper instruction that the Brahmin is the
guru—
Man dies, the sacred thread falls, and the soul
departs without it.
Though men commit countless thefts, countless adulteries, utter countless falsehoods and
countless words of abuse;
Though they commit countless robberies and
villainies night and day against their fellow
creatures;

Yet the cotton thread is spun, and the Brahmin
comes to twist it.
For the ceremony they kill a goat and cook and
eat it, and everybody then says, "Put on the
sacred thread."
When it becomes old, it is thrown away and
another is put on.
Nanak, the string does not break if it is strong.
By adoring and praising the Name honor and a
true thread are obtained.
In this way a sacred thread shall be put on
which will not break, and which will be fit
for entrance into God's court.
There is no string for the sexual organs
(to wear), no string for women;
There is no string for the impure acts which
cause your beards to be daily spat upon.
There is no string for the feet, no string for the
hands,
No string for the tongue, no string for the eyes.
Without such strings the Brahmin wanders
astray,
Twists strings for the neck, and puts them on
others.
He takes a fee for marrying;
He pulls out a paper, and shows the fate of the
wedded pair.[13]
Hear and see, you people; it is strange
That, while mentally blind, a man is named wise.

---

*Asa Ki Var, Mahala 1
[12]*seated in a square:* a square drawn on the ground in which
the thread ceremony occurs.

---

[13]*He pulls . . . pair:* shows them an astrological prediction,
still an important part of Hindu marriage.

ETHICS

Prayer for Forgiveness*

This lyrical prayer by Guru Arjan expresses the moral structure of Sikhism. God is holy and forgives those who confess their sin. The prayer ends with the worshipper assured of forgiveness.

Hear my supplication, O my Lord God,
Though I am full of millions of sins, nevertheless I am Your slave.
O You Dispeller of grief, merciful, fascinating,
Destroyer of trouble and anxiety,
I seek Your protection; protect my honor.
You are in all things, O spotless One;
You hear and behold us; You are with us all, O God;
You are the nearest of all to us.
O Lord, hear Nanak's prayer; save the slave of Your household.
You are ever omnipotent; we are poor and beggars.
O God, save us who are involved in the love of money.
Bound by covetousness and worldly love, we have committed various sins.
The Creator is distinct and free from entanglements; man obtains the fruit of his acts.
Show us kindness, You purifier of sinners; we are weary of wandering through many a womb.

Nanak represents—I am the slave of God who is the support of the soul and life.
You are great and omnipotent; my understanding is feeble.
You cherish even the ungrateful; You look equally on all.
Unfathomable is Your knowledge, O infinite Creator;
I am lowly and know nothing.
Having rejected the gem of Your name, I have amassed kauris;[14]
I am a degraded and silly being.
By the commission of sin I have amassed what is very unstable and forsakes man.
Nanak has sought Your protection, O omnipotent Lord; preserve his honor.
When I sang God's praises in the association of the saints,
He united me, who had been separated from Him, with Himself.
By ever thoroughly singing God's praises, He who is happiness itself becomes manifest.
My couch, when God accepts me as His own, is adorned by Him.
Having dismissed anxiety I am no longer anxious, and suffer no further pain.
Nanak lives beholding God and singing the praises of the Ocean of excellences.

---

* Rag Bihagra, Mahala 5

[14]*kauris:* human money, worthless with God.

Against the Use of Wine**

Although the Sikh scriptures contain no formal listing of ethical commands, one of the firmest and most explicit moral commands of Sikhism is the prohibition of alcoholic beverages. Note once again the reinterpretation of an evil practice: "Make . . . God's name your wine."

The barmaid is misery, wine is lust; man is the drinker.
The cup filled with worldly love is wrath, and it is served by pride.

** Rag Bihagra, Mahala 1

The company is false and covetous, and is ruined by excess of drink.

Instead of such wine make good conduct your yeast, truth your molasses, God's name your wine;

Make merits your cakes, good conduct your clarified butter, and modesty your meat to eat.

Such things, O Nanak, are obtained by the Guru's favor; by partaking of them sins depart.

RITUAL

Hymn for the Installation of the *Guru Granth**

Although the content of this hymn seems to be unrelated to the Guru Granth, *it is sung by Sikhs in the temple as the holy book is brought out in the morning and put to rest at night.*

O God, this is the desire of my heart:

That You, the Treasure of mercy, the Compassionate, should make me the slave of Your saints;

That I should devote my body and soul to their service and sing God's praises with my tongue;

That I should ever abide with the saints and remember You at every breath I draw.

The Name is my sole support and wealth; from it Nanak obtains delight.

* Rag Devgandhari, Mahala 5

A Marriage Hymn**

Here is a hymn typically sung at Sikh weddings. Devotion to God and to one's spouse are masterfully blended. The believer is represented as the bride, God as the groom.

The stars glitter on a clear night.

Holy men, the beloved of my Lord, are awake;

The beloved of my Lord are ever awake, and remember His name night and day.

They meditate in their hearts on His lotus feet, and forget Him not for a moment.

They renounce the mental sins of pride and worldly love, and efface the pain of wrongdoing.

Nanak represents, the servants of God, the dear saints are ever awake.

My couch has splendid trappings.

In my heart joy has sprung up since I heard that my Lord was approaching.

On meeting my Lord I have entered on happiness and am filled with the essence of joy and delight.

He embraced me; my sorrows fled; my soul, mind, and body all bloomed afresh.

I have obtained my heart's desires by meditating on God; the time of my union with Him I account auspicious.

Nanak testifies, when he met the Bearer of prosperity, the essence of all pleasure was prepared for him.

My companions meeting me asked me to describe my Spouse.

I was so filled with the sweets of love that I could not speak.

The attributes of the Creator are deep, mysterious, and boundless; the Vedas have not found His limit.

** Rag Asa, Mahala 5

She who meditates on the Lord with devotion
   and love, who ever sings His praises,
And is pleasing to her God, is full of all virtues
   and divine knowledge.
Nanak testifies, she who is dyed with the color
   of God's love shall be easily absorbed in Him.
When I began to sing songs of joy to God,
My friends became glad, my troubles and my
   enemies fled away,

My happiness and comfort increased, I rejoiced
   in God's name, and He Himself bestowed
   mercy on me.
I clung to His feet, and being ever wakeful
   I met Him.
Happy days came, I obtained peace with all
   treasures and was blended with God.
Nanak testifies, the saints of God are ever steadfast in seeking His protection.

ORGANIZATION

The Guru*

*This hymn by Guru Amar Das expresses the char-
acteristic attitude of later Sikhs toward the line of
the gurus. Though the* Sri Guru Granth *Sahib is
not explicitly mentioned, Sikhs hearing this hymn
would think that everything said about the guru
applies to their* Guru Granth, *in which the soul of
the guru is incarnated.*

Through the Guru a few obtain divine knowledge;
He who knows God through the Guru shall be
   acceptable.
Through the Guru there results divine knowledge and meditation on the True One;
Through the Guru the gate of deliverance is
   attained.
It is only by perfect good fortune the Guru
   comes in one's way.

The true become easily absorbed in the True
   One.
On meeting the Guru the fire of avarice is
   quenched.
Through the Guru peace dwells in the heart.
Through the Guru man becomes pure, spot-
   less, and immaculate.
Through the Guru the Word which unites man
   with God is obtained.
Without the Guru every one wanders in doubt.
Without the Name great misery is suffered.
He who is pious meditates on the Name.
On beholding the True One, true honor is
   obtained.
Whom shall we call the giver? The One God.
If He be gracious, the Word by which we meet
   Him is obtained.
May Nanak meet the beloved Guru, sing the
   True One's praises,
And becoming true be absorbed in the True
   One!

* Rag Gauri, Mahala 3

God's Power in the Sikh Community**

The final shape of the Sikh community (panth)
*was established by the tenth guru, Gobind Singh.
This hymn by Guru Arjan contains a line, "Victory be ever to the society of the saints," very remi-*
*niscent of the shout used to close almost every Sikh
service, "The Khalsa shall rule!"*

There is none beside Him,
In whose power are lords and emperors;
In whose power is the whole world;
Who has created everything.

** Rag Gauri, Mahala 5

Address your supplication to the true Guru,
That he may arrange all your affairs.
His court is the most exalted of all;
His name is the prop of all the saints.
The Lord whose glory shines in every heart
Is contained in everything, and fills creation.
By remembering Him the abode of sorrow is
    demolished;
By remembering Him Death molests us not;

By remembering Him what is withered
    becomes green;
By remembering Him the sinking stone floats.
Victory be ever to the society of the saints!
God's name is the support of the lives of His
    servants.
Says Nanak, hear, O God, my supplication—
By the favor of the saints, grant me to dwell in
    Your name.

APPENDIX: SELECTIONS FROM THE *DASAM GRANTH*

A. Guru Gobind Singh's Story*

*Guru Gobind tells not just his own story, but the
story of the one soul of the line of Gurus.*[15]

I shall now tell my own history,
How God brought me into the world as I was
    performing penance
On the mountain of Hem Kunt,
Where the seven peaks are conspicuous—
The place is called the Sapt Shring—
Where King Pandu practiced Yoga.
There I performed very great austerities
And worshipped Great-death.
I performed such penance
That I became blended with God.
My father and mother had also worshipped the
    Unseen One,
And strove in many ways to unite themselves
    with Him.
The Supreme Guru was pleased
With their devotion to Him.
When God gave me the order
I assumed birth in this age.
I did not desire to come,
As my attention was fixed on God's feet.
God remonstrated earnestly with me,

And sent me into this world with the following
    orders:
"When I created this world
I first made the demons, who became enemies
    and oppressors.
They became intoxicated with the strength of
    their arms,
And ceased to worship Me, the Supreme Being.
I became angry and at once destroyed them.
In their places I established the gods.
They also busied themselves receiving sacrifices
    and worship,
And called themselves supreme beings.
Mahadev called himself the imperishable God.
Vishnu too declared himself to be God;
Brahma called himself the supreme Brahma,
And nobody thought Me to be God . . .
Brahma made the four Vedas
And caused all to act according to them;
But they whose love was attached to My feet
Renounced the Vedas.
They who abandoned the tenets of the Vedas
    and other books
Became devoted to Me, the supreme God.
They who follow true religion
Shall have their sins of various kinds blotted out.
They who endure bodily suffering
And cease not to love Me,
Shall all to go paradise,

---

* *Vichitar Natak*, 6
[15]From Max Macauliffe, *The Sikh Religion*, vol. 5 (Oxford:
Oxford University Press, 1909), pp. 296–300.

And there shall be no difference between Me
   and them.
They who shrink from suffering,
And, forsaking Me, adopt the way of the Vedas
   and Smritis shall fall into the pit of hell,
And continually suffer transmigration. . . .
I then created Muhammad,
And made him king of Arabia.
He too established a religion of his own,
Cut off the foreskins of all his followers,
And made every one repeat his name;[16]
But no one fixed the true Name in man's
   heart. . . .
I have cherished you as My son,
And created you to extend My religion.

---

[16]*repeat his name:* in the confession of Islam, "There is no
God but God, and Muhammad is his prophet."

Go and spread My religion there,
And restrain the world from senseless acts."
I stood up, clasped my hands, bowed my head,
   and replied:
"Your religion shall prevail in the world when
   You assure me your assistance."
On this account God sent me.
I took birth and came into the world.
As He spoke to me so I speak unto men.
I bear no enmity to any one.
All who call me the Supreme Being
Shall fall into the pit of hell.
Recognize me as God's servant only:
Have no doubt whatever of this.
I am the slave of the Supreme Being,
Come to behold the wonders of the world.
I tell the world what God told me,
And will not remain silent through fear of
   mortals.

B. God as the Holy Sword*

*One of the most important developments in the
early history of Sikhism was the shift from pacifism
to militancy. This famous hymn expresses this militancy with its personification of the sword as God.
Today the Sikh child is baptized with water that
has been stirred by a two-edged sword, and the
dagger between two swords is a prominent symbol
of modern Sikhism.[17]*

I bow with love and devotion to the Holy
   Sword.
Assist me that I may complete this book.
You are the Subduer of countries, the
   Destroyer of the armies of the wicked, in the
   battlefield You greatly adorn the brave.
Your arm is unbreakable, Your brightness
   resplendent, Your radiance and splendor
   dazzle like the sun.

You bestow happiness on the good, You terrify
   the evil, You scatter sinners, I seek Your
   protection.
Hail! hail to the Creator of the world, the Sav-
   ior of creation, my Cherisher, hail to You,
   O Sword!
I bow to Him who holds the arrow in His
   hand; I bow to the Fearless One;
I bow to the God of gods who is in the present
   and the future.
I bow to the Scimitar, the two-edged Sword,
   the broad-bladed sword, and the Dagger.
You, O God, always have one form; You are
   always unchangeable.
I bow to the Holder of the mace,
Who diffused light through the fourteen
   worlds.
I bow to the Arrow and the Musket,
I bow to the Sword, spotless, fearless, and
   unbreakable;
I bow to the powerful Mace and Lance
To which nothing is equal.

---

* *Vichitar Natak,* 1
[17]From Macauliffe, *Sikh Religion,* vol. 5, pp. 286–287.

I bow to Him who holds the discus,
Who is not made of the elements and is terrible.
I bow to Him with the strong teeth;
I bow to Him who is supremely powerful,
I bow to the Arrow and the Cannon
Which destroy the enemy.

I bow to the Sword and the Rapier
Which destroy the evil.
I bow to all weapons called Shastar, which may
    be held.
I bow to all weapons called Astar, which may be
    hurled or discharged.

GLOSSARY

Adi Granth (AH-dee GRAHNTH) "the first/original book," the primary scripture of Sikhism, consisting primarily of the words of the first five gurus; also known as the Sri Guru Granth Sahib or Guru Granth.

chaur (chowr) a horsehair whisk used to venerate the *Adi Granth* by waving it over the scripture to cool the book and repel flies.

Dasam Granth (DAH-sum GRAHNTH) the "tenth book," the secondary scripture consisting mostly of the words of the tenth guru, Gobind Singh.

gutka (GUHT-kuh) an anthology for private use of the most important passages from the *Adi Granth* and a few from the *Dasam Granth*.

granthi (GRAHN-thee) an official reader of the *Guru Granth*.

janam-sakhis (JAH-num SAH-kees) literally, "birth stories" or traditional narratives about the lives of the gurus, especially Nanak.

Japji (JAHP-jee) the first main section of the *Adi Granth*, a poem by Nanak considered to express the essence of Sikhism.

Mahala (ma-HAH-luh) a term used by the *Adi Granth* to differentiate the contributions of the five gurus.

Mul Mantra (mool MAHN-truh) "root formula," the opening of the *Japji*.

Rags (rahgs) the thirty-one rudimentary "tunes" on which melodies used for singing the *Adi Granth* are based.

vak lao (vahk low) "taking (God's) word" by opening the *Granth* at random and beginning the reading from the top of the left-hand page.

QUESTIONS FOR STUDY AND DISCUSSION

1. Describe the main teachings of the *Adi Granth*. Which do you see as most important, and why?

2. "Of all the religions of the world, Sikhism has the best claim to be 'a religion of the book.'" Do you agree or disagree? Why or why not?

3. Which attitudes, teachings, and practices of Sikhism seem to you to resemble Hinduism? Which seem to resemble Islam? Which seem to be distinct?

4. How does Sikh tradition, as expressed in its scriptures, vary between inclusiveness to other faiths and exclusiveness toward them?

5. Describe the shift from pacifism to militarism in Sikh tradition. Can you think of similar shifts in other religions?

SUGGESTIONS FOR FURTHER READING

Primary Readings

M. Dass, *Songs of the Saints from the* Adi Granth. Albany: State University of New York Press, 2000. A fresh, complete translation of the songs of the saints (*sants*), important for the pre-history of Sikhism and its links to devotional Hinduism.

Max A. Macauliffe, *The Sikh Religion: Its Gurus, Sacred Writings and Authors.* 6 vols. Oxford: Oxford University Press, 1909. Reprinted New Delhi: S. Chand, 1963. Provides full selections from the Sikh scriptures, with good, literal translations.

W. H. McLeod, *Textual Sources for the Study of Sikhism.* Totowa, NJ: Barnes & Noble, 1984. An excellent anthology of Sikh scriptures and more recent writings.

Trilochan Singh et al., eds., *Selections from the Sacred Writings of the Sikhs.* London: Allen & Unwin, 1960. Generous selections from the *Adi Granth* and the *Dasam Granth.*

Secondary Readings

M. Juergensmeyer and N. G. Barrier, eds., *Sikh Studies.* Berkeley: Graduate Theological Union, 1979. This volume contains the papers from the Berkeley Conference on Sikh Studies; see especially the essays on scripture by W. McLeod, S. Singh, and F. Staal.

Surindar Singh Kohli, *A Critical Study of the* Adi Granth. New Delhi: Punjabi Writers' Cooperative Industrial Society, 1961. A study of its structure and theology.

H. McLeod, "The Sikh Scriptures." In H. McLeod, *Evolution of the Sikh Community.* Oxford: Clarendon Press, 1976, pp. 59–82. A succinct survey of the origin, development, and use of Sikh scriptures, with special emphasis on textual problems.

T. N. Madan, "The Double-Edged Sword: Fundamentalism and the Sikh Religious Tradition." In M. E. Marty and R. S. Appleby, eds., *Fundamentalisms Observed.* Chicago: University of Chicago Press, 1991, pp. 594–627. A study of the "fundamentalist" dimensions of the movement led by J. S. Bhindranwale, with good attention to its approach to scripture.

⏣ INFOTRAC COLLEGE EDITION

You can locate InfoTrac College Edition articles about this chapter by accessing the InfoTrac College Edition website (http://www.infotrac.collegeedition.com/wadsworth/). Using subject guide, enter the search terms relevant to this chapter, and then read abstracts for relevant articles.

Confucius and His Books
Confucius appears in rich robes on the title page of this modern Taiwanese edition of the *Four Books.* Credit: David Alexander

CHAPTER SIX

Confucianism

* In a high school in Beijing, China, students read and consider the meaning of the main Confucian book, the *Analects*. They read aloud, listen to their teacher's lecture, and discuss its meaning for China today. This study of Confucian scripture is undertaken by many Chinese throughout the world, but its recent revival in communist China heralds the return of classic Chinese values and the waning, some hope, of Communist ideology.

* In Hong Kong, a solitary sage studies ancient Chinese poems. He pauses to reflect on their meaning, especially on how they relate to his Confucian beliefs. After reflecting, he writes out the passage calligraphically. He is practicing self-cultivation toward becoming a "superior man," the highest goal of the Confucian tradition, and his study of the ancient classics is a key ingredient in bringing about this perfection.

* In Los Angeles, a sociologist researches the extraordinary success of Chinese-American students in the University of California system. Her conclusion: The social and intellectual values of these students' Confucian tradition—family loyalty, love of learning, self-cultivation, all values of the Confucian scriptures—have produced a remarkable academic achievement.

INTRODUCTION

Confucianism is the system of religion and philosophy begun by the sage Kung Fu-tzu ("Master Kung," died 479 B.C.E.), known to the Western world as Confucius. Although his teachings had little impact during his lifetime, they were kept alive by the efforts of his disciples. In the second century B.C.E., Confucianism became the official religion of China. Since then it has been closely identified with the essence of traditional Chinese culture, forming the basis of Chinese education, ethics, and statecraft and influencing some of the lands surrounding China, especially Korea and Japan. In Taiwan, study of the Confucian books is required in schools. No longer the state religion of China since the communist takeover in 1949, Confucianism has experienced a rebirth of sorts in other parts of Asia. It teaches a personal and social morality stressing the practice of key virtues such as filiality, humaneness, propriety, and faithfulness. Its full and well-defined scriptural canon, reflecting the Chinese love of books and learning, provides excellent insight into Confucianism.

Overview of Structure

Confucianists call their earlier scriptures the *Classics* or *Ching* [jing]. In Chinese as in English, "classic" suggests a literary work that embodies principles accepted as authoritative over a long time up through the present. The Confucian canon is divided into two parts, the earlier *Five Classics* (*Wu Ching*) and the later *Four Books* (*Ssu Shu*). The *Five Classics* form the foundation of the later works written by Confucius and his followers. These early books were known, respected, and authoritative hundreds of years before the birth of Confucius. According to some lists, they number as many as thirteen, but the best-known list has five books. Confucianists believe that Confucius edited all these classics and wrote commentaries for some. Though this is doubtful as fact, most scholars do hold that the early Confucian tradition played a strong role in shaping and transmitting these books when it took them into its canon. This claim does express the high value the Confucian tradition placed on the ancient classics. As Confucius himself once said, "It is by the *Poetry* that the mind is aroused; by the *Rites* that the character is established; by the *Music* [now lost, but perhaps incorporated in part into the *Rites*] that the finish is received" (*Analects* 8.8). We now will deal briefly with each.

First and oldest is the *I Ching* [ee jing], the "Classic of Changes," a diviner's manual that developed over several hundred years, beginning with the early part of the Chou dynasty (1120–221 B.C.E.). The book contains pairs of eight basic trigrams (combinations of three horizontal lines) used to provide information on the future and recommend a course of action to meet it. The *I Ching* is built on the **yin-yang,** the two great interactive cosmic forces of passive-active, dark-light, and other opposing pairs. This cosmology has given the book great popularity among more educated Chinese. In Confucian history it was also sometimes used philosophically, especially because of the "wings," or commentary appended to the hexagrams. Of all Chinese literature, the *I Ching* has been the most often translated into English and other modern European languages, because of its cosmological appeal rather than as a book of divination; currently more than twenty translations are in print. In China, however, the religio-magical use has tended to predominate. (This book is important for Taoists as well and is a prominent part of their canon.)

Second is the *Shu Ching,* the *Classic of History/Documents.* It consists of royal chronicles, narratives, decrees, and the like from the early Chou dynastic period, a period Confucius looked on as an ideal age. Much of its contents are later, forged additions.

Third is the *Shih Ching* [shir jing], the *Classic of Poetry.* It consists of 305 relatively short poems from the tenth to the seventh centuries B.C.E., all set to music. These songs deal with love, rituals, family relations, and government. The religious songs were sung in worship services, especially in sacrifice to ancestors. The *Poetry* became, even by the time of Confucius, the leading model of Chinese literary expression. The writings of Confucius are filled with allusions to this classic.

Fourth is the *Ch'un ch'iu,* the *Spring and Autumn Annals.* "Spring and Autumn" is an expression that stands for the entire year, not just for those seasons. The *Annals* is a sober and rather reliable chronological account of events in the state of Lu, Confucius' home state, from 720 to 480 B.C.E. Its ideas of respect for law and custom in government are only implicitly Confucian.

Last is the *Li Chi* [lee kee], the *Classic of Rites.* This collection features rituals and ceremonies of ancient China, both public and private. The *Li Chi* was probably collected in the second century B.C.E. *Li* can be variously translated "ritual," "propriety," or "manners," and all these ideas are important in the *Li Chi*.

The *Four Books* are built on what Confucius and his followers saw as the main teachings of this earlier canon. First among them is the *Lun yu*, or *Analects* (collected sayings) of Confucius. The *Analects* is by far the most important text in the history of Confucianism and our most reliable source for a knowledge of Confucius himself. It contains sayings of the Master, and occasionally anecdotes about him, as remembered by his disciples and recorded after his death. The *Analects* contains 12,700 characters (ideograms) in twenty short books. Like most other collections of sayings, the *Analects* is loosely organized and repetitive at times. Yet it treats well all the important concepts of the Confucian tradition: the cardinal virtues of humanity, propriety, respect for parents; becoming a superior man; and proper government.

The second of the *Four Books* is the *Meng-tzu* or *Mencius*. This book is named for its author, who, after Confucius, was the most significant figure in Confucian tradition. Mencius lived in the fourth century B.C.E., and his disciples compiled this book after his death. More than twice as long as the *Analects*, the *Mencius* has well-developed treatments of several important topics, especially proper government. Mencius saw filiality as the greatest of the virtues and held strongly to the teaching of innate human goodness.

Third is the *Ta hsueh*, the *Great Learning*. This short book is an excerpt on virtuous government from the *Li Chi*, where it is chapter 39 in Legge's translation. Its first, short chapter is held to be the work of Confucius. The next ten chapters are a commentary on the first by Tseng-tzu, one of Confucius' disciples. The *Great Learning* teaches that rulers govern by example. If the ruler is morally good, so will be his government and his subjects; if he is not good, his subjects will incline to evil and his rule, along with the Mandate of Heaven to govern, will collapse.

Fourth is the *Chung yung*, or the *Doctrine of the Mean*. Like the *Great Learning*, it was originally a chapter (31) in the *Li Chi*. "Mean" is a broad concept embracing many aspects of virtue: moderation, right conduct, decorum, sincerity. The good Confucianist is expected to "keep to the middle" between emotional and intellectual extremes. It is in the middle that the superior man is formed and comes into harmony with the **Tao** [dow], the cosmic "Way" of life. This book was important in the neo-Confucian movement that arose in the twelfth century.

Origin and Development

We have already discussed briefly the older Classics. We will treat briefly here the two main Confucian works, the *Analects* and the *Mencius,* and the development of the Confucian canon as a whole.

The Confucian canon has not come down to us in an easy chain of tradition. The *Analects* and the *Mencius* were probably first written down in the century following the deaths of their authors. The *Great Learning* and *Doctrine of the Mean* were separated from the *Classic of Rites* and made independent books. But in 213 B.C.E., Emperor Shih Huang-ti, who as a radical innovator was opposed to ancient traditions, gave orders that all Confucian books be destroyed. This famous "Burning of the Books" resulted in the loss of several versions of the Confucian books, but most books survived in some form. The Confucian canon was reedited and republished under the next dynasty, the Han (206 B.C.E. to 220 C.E.). During this dynasty, Confucianism was made the official state religion and the Confucian canon was officially adopted as the basis of thought and conduct—indeed, of all official Chinese culture. In the twelfth century, the *Four Books* were recognized as an independent collection, and they soon became more central to Confucian life than the older *Classics*, which came to be interpreted through the *Four Books*. The state sanction for the Confucian scriptures lasted until 1905, when China abolished the civil service system as based on the canon.

Use

The official use of the Confucian scriptures flows from its adoption as the state literature of China. For more than two thousand years, all education was based either directly or indirectly on them. The first books a child studied and memorized in elementary school were the *Four Books,* especially the *Analects* and *Great Learning*. The rigorous civil service exams to become a government official, whether on the county, provincial, or national level, were also based on the scriptures. Each county in China had a school where the scriptural lore was taught. Those who became unusually expert in the scriptures as applied to government were known as *mandarins;* the last known mandarin died in 1991. The imperial university in Beijing had five professorial posts in scripture that were designed to promote the excellence of the whole system. The personal intention of Confucius was thus fulfilled, not during his lifetime but after it, when the government of China came to be based on his leading ideas.

But Confucius' ideal of providing education to all who desired and could master it fell by the wayside as this training for government became limited to the upper classes who could pay for it. Although only a small percentage of the population of China has been able to read, the influence of the Confucian scriptures through oral teaching and general cultural transmission has been so thorough that the social relationships and cultural attitudes of most Chinese have become essential Confucian. It is often remarked that no matter the specific religion of the Chinese—Buddhist, Taoist, Muslim, Christian, or whatever—they are also Confucian. Thus, largely through the influence of its scripture, Confucianism has taken its place as the leading historic religion of China. Now that communist values are waning in the People's Republic of China, educators are returning to Confucian scriptures to provide a core moral education, especially the values of civility and obedience to law.

The Confucian approach to its scripture is almost exclusively cognitive. Confucius and his followers rejected mysticism, and in subsequent centuries the sometimes bitter struggle with the more mystical Taoist tradition reinforced this cognitive orientation. Teacher and student discuss scriptural meaning in an orderly, rational way. The individual scholar often practices "quiet sitting," solitary study that involves recitation of the text, meditation on its meaning, and often calligraphic reproduction of the text itself.

The literary style of the Confucian canon influences this use. Confucian scriptures share a basic literary style known as **wen-yen** (roughly translated as "formal-classical"). This style is known for brief, even compressed composition. Each Chinese ideogram character must be considered carefully to bring out the meaning. This style is one reason why Confucianists have generated a massive commentarial literature that seeks to shed more light on the canon itself. In the Confucian tradition, these commentaries have become accepted works in understanding the canon. Moreover, this formal-classical style means that translations of Confucian scripture will often vary greatly among themselves. This compressed style invites the reader of both the Chinese original and the English translation to meditate carefully and deeply about its meaning.

HISTORY

The Character of Confucius*

The Analects *depicts Confucius as a model of the "superior man." By following his own teaching, he became an example to his followers. The first passage is Confucius' own summary of his progress in self-cultivation. The second describes key elements in his character. The third gives fascinating detail on some of his daily habits.*[1]

[2.4] The Master said, "At fifteen, I had my mind bent on learning. At thirty, I stood firm. At forty, I had no doubts. At fifty, I knew the decrees of Heaven.[2] At sixty, my ear was an obedient organ for the reception of truth. At seventy, I could follow what my heart desired, without transgressing what was right."

[7.1] The Master said, "A transmitter and not a maker, believing in and loving the ancients, I venture to compare myself with our old P'eng."[3]

The Master said, "The silent treasuring up of knowledge; learning without tiring; and instructing others without being wearied— which one of these things belongs to me?"

The Master said, "Leaving virtue without proper cultivation; not thoroughly discussing what is learned; not being able to move towards righteousness of which a knowledge is gained; and not being able to change what is not good —these are the things which cause me much concern."

When the Master was unoccupied with business, his manner was easy, and he looked pleased.

[5] The Master said, "My decline is extreme. For a long time, I have not dreamed, as I used to do, that I saw the duke of Chou."[4]

The Master said, "Let the will be set on the path of duty. Let every attainment in what is good be firmly grasped. Let perfect virtue be accorded with. Let relaxation and enjoyment be found in the arts."

The Master said, "From the man bringing his bundle of dried meat[5] for my teaching, or more than that, I have never refused instruction to any one."

The Master said, "I do not open up the truth to one who is not eager to get knowledge, nor help out any one who is not anxious to explain himself. When I have presented one corner of a subject to any one, and he cannot from it learn the other three, I do not repeat my lesson."

When the Master was eating by the side of a mourner, he never ate to the full. He did not

---

*Analects 2.4, 7.1–9, 19–24; 10.1–4, 8–12

[1] All selections from the *Analects* and the *Mencius* are taken from James Legge, trans., *The Chinese Classics* (Oxford: Oxford University Press, 1893).

[2] *decrees* (or "mandates") *of Heaven:* understood today by most Confucianists as the working of Nature in people and events, not primarily as the working of God.

[3] *old P'eng:* a sage from ancient times.

[4] *duke of Chou:* in Confucius's view, one of the greatest of the early Chinese sage kings.

[5] *dried meat:* the smallest possible payment for instruction. Confucianism believes that learning and self-cultivation should be open to all who desire it.

sing on the same day in which he had been weeping. . . .

[19] The Master said, "I am not one who was born in the possession of knowledge; I am one who is fond of antiquity,[6] and earnest in seeking it there."

[20] The subjects on which the Master did not talk were extraordinary things,[7] feats of strength, disorder, and spiritual beings.

The Master said, "When I walk along with two others, they may serve me as my teachers. I will select their good qualities and follow them, their bad qualities and avoid them."

The Master said, "Heaven produced the virtue that is in me. What can Hwan T'ui[8] do to me?"

The Master said, "Do you think, my disciples, that I have any concealments? I conceal nothing from you. There is nothing which I do that is not shown to you, my disciples. That is my way."

There were four things which the Master taught—letters, ethics, devotion of soul, and truthfulness.

[10.1] Confucius, in his village, looked simple and sincere, and as if he were not able to speak. When he was in the prince's ancestral temple, or in the court, he spoke minutely on every point, but cautiously.

When he was on duty at court, in speaking with the great officers of the lower grade he spoke freely, but in a straightforward manner. In speaking with those of the higher grade, he did so mildly, but precisely. When the ruler was present, his manner displayed respectful uneasiness; it was serious, but self-possessed.

When the prince called on him to receive a visitor, his countenance appeared to change, and his legs to move forward with difficulty. He

inclined himself to the other officers among whom he stood, moving his left or right arm, as their position required, but keeping the skirts of his robe before and behind evenly adjusted. He hastened forward, with his arms like the wings of a bird. When the guest had left, he would report to the prince, "The visitor is not looking back any more."

When he entered the palace gate, he seemed to bend his body, as if it were not sufficient to admit him. When he was standing, he did not occupy the middle of the gateway; when he passed in or out, he did not tread upon the threshold. When he was passing the vacant place of the prince, his countenance appeared to change, and his legs to bend under him, and his words came as if he hardly had breath to speak them. He ascended the reception hall, holding up his robe with both his hands, and his body bent. He held in his breath also, as if he dared not breathe.

[8] He liked to have his rice finely cleaned, and to have his minced meat cut quite small. He did not eat rice which had been injured by heat or damp and turned sour, nor fish or meat which was gone. He did not eat what was discolored, or what was of a bad flavor, nor anything which was badly cooked, or was not in season. He did not eat meat which was not cut properly, nor what was served without its proper sauce. Though there might be a large quantity of meat, he would not allow what he took to exceed the due proportion for the rice. It was only in wine that he laid down no limit for himself, but he did not allow himself to be confused by it. He did not partake of wine and dried meat bought in the market. He was never without ginger when he ate. He did not eat much. When he had been assisting at the prince's sacrifice, he did not keep the meat which he received overnight. The meat of his family sacrifice he did not keep over three days. If kept over three days, people could not eat it. When eating, he did not converse. When in bed, he did not speak. Although his food might be coarse rice

---

[6]*antiquity:* Confucianists emphasize the Chinese custom of seeking direction from the ancient writings.

[7]*extraordinary things:* strange events in nature.

[8]*Hwan T'ui:* an army officer who had attempted to kill Confucius.

and vegetable soup, he would offer a little of it in sacrifice with a serious, respectful air.

If his mat was not straight, he did not sit on it.

[10] When the villagers were drinking together, after those who carried walking staffs left, he went out immediately. When the villagers were going through their ceremonies to drive away pestilential influences, he put on his court robes and stood on the eastern steps.

When he was sending complimentary inquiries to any one in another state, he bowed twice as he escorted the messenger away.

When Chi K'ang sent him a present of medicine, he bowed and received it, saying, "I do not know it. I dare not taste it."

The stable burned down when he was at court, and on his return he said, "Has any person been hurt?" He did not ask about the horses.

ETHICS

The Virtues of the Superior Man*

Confucius taught self-cultivation in knowledge and virtue. When one reaches moral and intellectual maturity, he is a "superior man." The Chinese phrase for "superior man," chun-tzu [jun-tzoo], literally means "prince's son," but Confucius taught that by education even a common man could become superior. (The noninclusive language is intentional—women were not expected or encouraged to pursue this self-cultivation.) Neo-Confucianism applies these passages to the closely related goal of becoming a sage.

[1.1] The Master said, "Is it not pleasant to learn with a constant perseverance and application? Is it not delightful to have friends coming from distant quarters? Is he not a man of complete virtue, who feels no discomposure though men may take no note of him?"

The philosopher Yu said, "Few are those who, being filial and fraternal, are fond of offending their superiors. There have been none, who, not liking to offend their superiors, have been fond of stirring up confusion. The superior man bends his attention to the foundation. That being established, all practical courses naturally grow up. Filiality and fraternal submis-

sion—are they not the root of all benevolent actions?"

The Master said, "Fine words and an insinuating appearance are seldom associated with true virtue."

The philosopher Tsang said, "I daily examine myself on three points: whether, in transacting business for others, I have been faithful; whether, in dealings with friends, I have been sincere; whether I have mastered and practiced the instructions of my teacher.". . .

[6] The Master said, "A youth, when at home, should be filial, and away from home he should be respectful to his elders. He should be earnest and truthful. He should overflow in love to all, and cultivate the friendship of good people. When he has time and opportunity, after the performance of these things, he should employ them in the arts."

Tsze-hsia said, "If a man withdraws his mind from the love of beauty, and applies it as sincerely to the love of the virtuous; if, in serving his parents, he can exert his utmost strength; if, in serving his prince, he can devote his life; if, in his dealings with his friends, his words are sincere—although men say that he has not learned, I will certainly say that he has."

The Master said, "If the scholar is not serious, he will not call forth any veneration, and

---

* *Analects* 1.1–4, 6–9, 14; 15.17–23

his learning will not be solid. Hold faithfulness and sincerity as first principles. Have no friends not equal to yourself. When you have faults, do not fear to abandon them."

The philosopher Tsang said, "Let there be a careful attention to perform the funeral rites to parents, and let them be followed when long gone with the ceremonies of sacrifice. Then the virtue of the people will resume its proper excellence.". . .

[14] The Master said, "He who aims to be a man of complete virtue in his food does not seek to gratify his appetite, nor in his dwelling place does he seek the appliances of ease. He is earnest in what he does, and careful in his speech. He frequents the company of men of principle that he may be rectified. Such a person may be said indeed to love to learn."

[15.17] The Master said, "The superior man considers righteousness to be essential in everything. He performs it according to the rules of propriety. He brings it forth in humility. He completes it with sincerity. This is indeed a superior man."

The Master said, "The superior man is distressed by his lack of ability. He is not distressed by his lack of fame."

The Master said, "The superior man dislikes the thought of his name not being mentioned after his death."

[20] The Master said, "What the superior man seeks is in himself. What the inferior man seeks is in others."

The Master said, "The superior man is dignified, but does not wrangle. He is sociable, but not a partisan."

The Master said, "The superior man does not promote a man simply on account of his words, nor does he put aside good words because of the man."

Tsze-kung asked, saying, "Is there one word which may serve as a rule of practice for all one's life?" The Master said, "Is not Reciprocity[9] such a word? What you do not want done to yourself, do not do to others."

---

[9] *Reciprocity:* the virtue *shu.*

Benevolence*

*Benevolence (**jen** [ren]) is the chief of the Confucian virtues. It denotes humaneness, fellow feeling, even love; in this translation it is rendered by "virtue." Confucianists, especially those aspiring to sagehood, have trained themselves in benevolence by reflecting on their lives in the light of the scriptures.*

The Master said, "Virtuous manners constitute the excellence of a neighborhood. If a man in selecting a residence does not fix on one where such manners prevail, how can he be wise?"

The Master said, "Those who are without virtue cannot abide long either in a condition of

poverty and hardship, or in a condition of enjoyment. The virtuous rest in virtue; the wise desire virtue."

The Master said, "It is only the [truly] virtuous man who can love, or who can hate, others."

The Master said, "If the will is set on virtue, there will be no practice of wickedness."

[5] The Master said, "Riches and honors are what men desire. If it cannot be obtained in the proper way, they should not be held. Poverty and a low condition are what men dislike. If it cannot be obtained in the proper way, they should not be avoided. If a superior man abandons virtue, how can he fulfill the requirements of that name? The superior man does not, even for the space of a single meal, act contrary to

---

*Analects 4.1–6

virtue. In moments of haste, he clings to it. In seasons of danger, he clings to it."

The Master said, "I have not seen a person who loved virtue, or one who hated what was not virtuous. He who loved virtue would esteem nothing above it. He who hated what is not virtuous would practice virtue in such a way that he would not allow anything that is not virtuous to approach his person. Is any one able for one day to apply his strength to virtue? I have not seen the case in which his strength would be sufficient. Should there possibly be any such case, I have not seen it."

The Actions and Attitudes of Filiality*

Filiality (hsiao), called filial piety in the older literature, is reverence for one's living ancestors, and extends itself to worship of one's dead ancestors. The Classic of Rites *passage goes into great detail in laying down rules for proper filial conduct. It stresses deference, obedience, and faithfulness to one's parents.[10] In the second reading, Confucius stresses not only the actions of filiality, but much more the attitude with which these acts are carried out. This attitude must be one of the genuine reverence implied in* hsiao *or "piety."*

The sovereign king orders the chief minister to send down his lessons of virtue to the millions of the people. . . .

[4] [After getting properly] dressed [in the morning], [sons] should go to their parents and parents-in-law.[11] On getting to where they are, with bated breath and gentle voice they should ask if their clothes are too warm or too cold, whether they are ill or pained, or uncomfortable in any part. If they are, they should proceed reverently to stroke and scratch the place. They should in the same way, going before or following after, help and support their parents in leaving or entering the apartment. In bringing in the basin for them to wash, the younger will carry the stand and the elder the water. They will beg to be allowed to pour out the water, and when the washing is concluded, they will hand them the towel. They will ask whether they want anything, and then respectfully bring it. All this they will do with an appearance of pleasure to make their parents feel at ease. They should bring gruel, thick or thin, spirits or juice, soup with vegetables, beans, wheat, spinach, rice, millet, maize, and glutinous millet—whatever they wish, in fact. They should bring dates, chestnuts, sugar and honey to sweeten their dishes; the ordinary or the large-leaved violets, leaves of elm-trees, fresh or dry, and the most soothing rice-water to lubricate them; and fat and oil to enrich them. The parents will be sure to taste them, and when they have done so, the young people should withdraw. . . .

From the time that sons receive an official appointment,[12] they and their father occupy different parts of their residence. But at dawn, the son will pay his respects, and express his affection by the offer of pleasant delicacies. At sunrise he will retire, and he and his father will attend to their different duties. At sundown, the son will pay his evening visit in the same way. . . .

---

*Classic of Rites 10.1, 4, 7, 10–11, 13–15; Analects 2.5–8; 4.18–21; 13.18

[10]Taken, with editing, from James Legge, trans., *The Sacred Books of China: The Texts of Confucianism*, part 3, *Sacred Books of the East*, vol. 27 (Oxford: Oxford University Press, 1885), pp. 449–457.

[11]The passage presupposes that one's parents have an apartment or room in one's house, typically the case in traditional China.

[12]*official appointment:* in a government position.

[10] While the parents are both alive, at their regular meals, morning and evening, the eldest son and his wife will encourage them to eat everything, and what is left after all, they themselves will eat. When the father is dead, and the mother still alive, the eldest son should wait upon her at her meals. The wives of the other sons will do with what is left as in the former case. The children should have the sweet, soft and oily things that are left.

When sons and their wives are ordered to do anything by their parents, they should immediately respond and reverently proceed to do it. In going forward or backward, or turning round, they should be careful and serious. While going out or coming in, while bowing or walking, they should not presume to belch, sneeze, or cough, to yawn or stretch themselves, to stand on one foot, or to lean against anything, or to look askance. They should not dare to spit or snivel, nor if it is cold to put on more clothes, nor if they itch anywhere, to scratch themselves. Unless for reverent attention to something, they should not presume to bare their [parents'] shoulders or chest. Unless it be in wading, they should not hold up their clothes. Of their private dress and coverlet, they should not display the inside. They should not allow the spittle or snivel of their parents to be seen. They should ask leave to rinse away any dirt on their caps or girdles, and to wash their clothes that are dirty with lye that has been prepared for the purpose; and to stitch together, with needle and thread, any tear. . . .

Sons and sons' wives, who are filial and reverential, when they receive an order from their parents should not refuse or delay executing it. When their parents give them anything to eat or drink, which they do not like, they will nevertheless taste it and wait for their further orders. When they give them clothes which are not to their liking, they will put them on, and wait in the same way. If their parents give them anything to do, and then employ another to take their place, although they do not like the arrangement, they will in the meantime give it

into his hands and let him do it, doing it again, if it is not done well. . . .

When sons and their wives have not been filial and reverential, the parents should not be angry and resentful with them, but endeavor to instruct them. If they will not receive instruction, they should then be angry with them. If that anger does no good, they can then drive out the son, and send the wife away, yet not publicly showing why they have treated them so.

[15] If a parent has a fault, the son should admonish him with bated breath, and bland aspect, and gentle voice. If the admonition does not take effect, he will be more reverential and more filial; and when the father seems pleased, he will repeat the admonition. If he should be displeased with this, rather than allow him to commit an offense against anyone in the neighborhood or countryside, the son should strongly protest. If the parent is angry and more displeased, and beat him till the blood flows, he should not presume to be angry and resentful, but be still more reverential and more filial.

[*Analects* 2.5] Mang asked what filiality was. The Master said, "It is not being disobedient." Soon after, as Fan Ch'ih was driving him, the Master told him, saying, "Mang-sun asked me what filiality was, and I answered him—'not being disobedient'." Fan Ch'ih said, "What did you mean?" The Master replied, "That parents, when alive, should be served according to propriety; that, when dead, they should be buried according to propriety; and that they should be sacrificed to according to propriety."

Mang Wu asked what filiality was. The Master said, "Do not make your parents anxious about anything else than your being sick."

Tsze-yu asked what filiality was. The Master said, "Filial piety nowadays means the support of one's parents. But dogs and horses likewise are able to do something in the way of support. Without reverence, what is there to distinguish the one support given from the other?"

Tsze-hsia asked what filiality was. The Master said, "The difficulty is with the countenance.

When their elders have any troublesome affairs and the young do their work, and when the young have plenty of wine and food to set before their elders, how can this be considered filiality?" . . .

[4.18] The Master said, "In serving his parents, a son may protest to them, but gently; when he sees that they do not incline to follow his advice, he shows an increased degree of reverence, but does not abandon his purpose; and should they punish him, he does not allow himself to murmur."

The Master said, "While his parents are alive, the son may not leave his home area to a far distance. If he does go away, he must have a fixed place to which he goes."[13]

[20] The Master said, "If the son for three years[14] does not alter from the way of his father, he may be called filial."

The Master said, "The age of one's parents should always be kept in the memory, as a reason for joy and for fear." . . .

[13.18] The duke of Sheh informed Confucius, saying, "Among us here are those who may be styled upright in their conduct. If their father stole a sheep, they will bear witness to the fact." Confucius said, "Among us, in our part of the country, those who are upright are different from this. The father conceals the misconduct of the son, and the son conceals the misconduct of the father. Uprightness is to be found in this."

---

[13]*a fixed place:* so his parents know where he is.

[14]*for three years:* after the death of the father.

Propriety*

Li, "propriety," can also be translated as "ritual correctness" or "good manners." The following selection highlights the traditional Confucian connection between propriety in the rites and in everyday life. In typically Confucian style, the Poetry *is quoted to illustrate the point. Confucian rituals carried out in the temples of Korea, Taiwan, and other lands still keep to the meticulous care prescribed here. Just as important, emphasis on li has given Chinese peoples their highly developed sense of politeness.*

The Master said, "If a man lacks the virtues proper to humanity, what has he to do with the rites of propriety? If a man is without the virtues proper to humanity, what has he to do with music?"

Lin Fang asked what was the first thing to be attended to in ceremonies. The Master said, "A great question indeed! In festive ceremonies, it is better to be sparing than extravagant. In the ceremonies of mourning, it is better that there be deep sorrow than a minute attention to observances." . . .

[8] Tsze-hsia asked, "What is the meaning of the passage, 'The pretty dimples of her artful smile! The well-defined black and white of her eye! The plain ground for the colors'?"[15] The Master said, "The business of laying on the colors follows [the preparation of] the plain ground." "Ceremonies then are a subsequent thing?" The Master said, "It is you, Shang, who can bring out my meaning. Now I can begin to talk about the *Poetry* with you."

---

*Analects 3.3–4, 8–9, 12–14, 17–19

[15]A poem from the *Classic of Poetry.*

The Master said, "I could describe the ceremonies of the Hsia dynasty, but Chi cannot sufficiently attest my words. I could describe the ceremonies of the Yin dynasty, but Sung cannot sufficiently attest my words. [They cannot do so] because of the insufficiency of their records and wise men. If those were sufficient, I could adduce them in support of my words.". . .

[12] He sacrificed to the dead as if they were present. He sacrificed to the spirits as if the spirits were present. The Master said, "I consider my not being present at the sacrifice as if I did not sacrifice."

Wang-sun Chia asked, "What is the meaning of the saying, 'It is better to pay court to the furnace than to the southwest corner'?"[16] The Master said, "Not so. He who offends against Heaven has none to whom he can pray."

The Master said, "Chou had the advantage of viewing the two past dynasties. How complete and elegant are its regulations! I follow Chou.". . .

[17] Tzu-kung wished to do away with the offering of a sheep connected with the inauguration of the first day of each month. The Master said, "Tzu, you love the sheep; I love the ceremony."[17]

The Master said, "The full observance of the rules of propriety in serving one's prince is accounted by people to be flattery."

The duke Ting asked how a prince should employ his ministers, and how ministers should serve their prince. Confucius replied, "A prince should employ his minister according to the rules of propriety; ministers should serve their prince with faithfulness."

---

[16]A traditional saying, meaning that it is better to serve the gods of food than the ancestral spirits of the shrine (at the southwest corner of the Chinese house).

[17]Also translated, "Tzu, you love the sheep, but I love the sacrifice."

The Way*

The "Way" (Tao) is an ancient idea in Chinese tradition. In Confucianism, it is understood as the moral way of heaven, to which the ruler as a superior man should aspire. In this selection, the relationship of the Way and good government is brought out.

Confucius said, "When good government prevails in the empire, ceremonies, music, and punitive military expeditions proceed from the son of Heaven. When bad government prevails in the empire, ceremonies, music, and punitive military expeditions proceed from the princes. When these things proceed from the princes, as a rule, the cases will be few in which they do not lose their power in ten generations. When they proceed from the great officers of the princes, as a rule, the cases will be few in which they do not lose their power in five generations. When the subsidiary ministers of the great officers hold in their grasp the orders of the state, as a rule, the cases will be few in which they do not lose their power in three generations. When right principles prevail in the kingdom, government will not be in the hands of the great officers. When right principles prevail in the kingdom, there will be no discussions among the common people."

Analects 16.2

The Love of Learning*

The love of learning is a leading moral quality among anyone who aspires to moral and intellectual superiority. Here Confucius explains its relationship to other prominent virtues.

The Master said, "Yu, have you heard the six words to which are attached six faults?" Yu replied, "I have not." "Sit down, and I will tell them to you. There is the love of being benevolent without the love of learning; the fault here leads to a foolish simplicity. There is the love of knowing without the love of learning; the fault here leads to dissipation of mind. There is the love of being sincere without the love of learning; the fault here leads to an injurious disregard of consequences. There is the love of straightforwardness without the love of learning; the

fault here leads to rudeness. There is the love of boldness without the love of learning; the fault here leads to insubordination. There is the love of firmness without the love of learning; the fault here leads to extravagant conduct."

The Master said, "My children, why do you not study the *Book of Poetry?* The poems serve to stimulate the mind. They may be used for purposes of self-contemplation. They teach the art of sociability. They show how to regulate feelings of resentment. From them you learn the more immediate duty of serving one's father, and the remoter duty of serving one's prince. From them we become largely acquainted with the names of birds, beasts, and plants.". . .

[12] The Master said, "He who puts on an appearance of stern firmness, while inwardly he is weak, is like one of the small, common people. Yes, is he not like the thief who breaks through, or climbs over, a wall?"

___
*Analects 17.8–9, 12

The Goodness of Human Nature**

Although Confucius did not discuss the question of goodness and evil in the human personality, Mencius took up this topic. He argued the optimistic idea that all people are by nature good. Therefore, the ruler must only be good himself and bring out the innate goodness of his subjects in order to establish his rule. In this selection, the philosopher Kao Tzu serves as a foil for the thoughts of Mencius.

The philosopher Kao said, "Man's nature is like the ke willow, and righteousness is like a cup or a bowl. The fashioning benevolence and righteousness out of man's nature is like the making cups and bowls from the ke willow." Mencius

replied, "Can you, leaving untouched the nature of the willow make with it cups and bowls? You must do violence and injury to the willow before you can make cups and bowls with it. If you must do violence and injury to the willow in order to make cups and bowls with it, on your principles you must in the same way do violence and injury to humanity in order to fashion from it benevolence and righteousness! Your words, alas! would certainly lead all men on to reckon benevolence and righteousness to be calamities."

The philosopher Kao said, "Man's nature is like water whirling round in a corner. Open a passage for it to the east, and it will flow to the east; open a passage for it to the west, and it will flow to the west. Man's nature is indifferent to good and evil, just as the water is indifferent to

___
**Mencius 6.1.1–4, 6

the east and west." Mencius replied, "Water indeed will flow indifferently to the east or west, but will it flow indifferently up or down? The tendency of man's nature to good is like the tendency of water to flow downwards. There are none but have this tendency to good, just as all water flows downwards. Now by striking water and causing it to leap up, you may make it go over your forehead, and, by damming and leading it, you may force it up a hill—but are such movements according to the nature of water? It is the force applied which causes them. When men are made to do what is not good, their nature is dealt with in this way."

The philosopher Kao said, "Life is what is to be understood by nature." Mencius asked him, "Do you say that by nature you mean life, just as you say that white is white?" "Yes, I do," was the reply. Mencius added, "Is the whiteness of a white feather like that of white snow, and the whiteness of white snow like that of a white gem?" Kao again said "Yes." "Very well," pursued Mencius. "Is the nature of a dog like the nature of an ox, and the nature of an ox like the nature of a man?"

The philosopher Kao said, "To enjoy food and delight in colors is nature. Benevolence is internal and not external; righteousness is external and not internal." Mencius asked him, "What is the ground of your saying that benevolence is internal and righteousness external?" He replied, "There is a man older than I, and I give honor to his age. It is not that there is first in me a principle of such reverence to age. It is just as when there is a white man, and I consider him white—according as he is so externally to me. On this account, I pronounce of righteousness that it is external." Mencius said, "There is no difference between our pronouncing of a white horse to be white and our pronouncing a white man to be white. But is there no difference between the regard with which we acknowledge the age of an old horse and that with which we acknowledge the age of an old man? And what is it which is called righ-

teousness?—the fact of a man's being old? or the fact of our giving honor to his age?" Kao said, "There is my younger brother—I love him. But the younger brother of a man of Ts'in I do not love; that is, the feeling is determined by myself, and therefore I say that benevolence is internal. On the other hand, I give honor to an old man of Ts'oo, and I also give honor to an old man of my own people: that is, the feeling is determined by the age, and therefore I say that righteousness is external." Mencius answered him, "Our enjoyment of meat roasted by a man of Ts'in does not differ from our enjoyment of meat roasted by ourselves. Thus, what you insist on takes place also in the case of such things, and will you say likewise that our enjoyment of a roast is external?" . . .

The disciple Kung-too said, "The philosopher Kao says, 'Man's nature is neither good nor bad.' Some say, 'Man's nature may be made to practice good, and it may be made to practice evil,' and accordingly, under Wan and Woo, the people loved what was good, while under Yew and Le, they loved what was cruel. Some say, 'The nature of some is good, and the nature of others is bad.' Hence it was that under such a sovereign as Yaou there yet appeared Seang; that with such a father as Koo-sow there yet appeared Shun; and that with Chow for their sovereign, and the son of their elder brother besides, there were found K'e, the viscount of Wei, and the prince Pe-kan. And now you say, 'The nature is good.' Then are all those wrong?" Mencius said, "From the feelings proper to it, it is constituted for the practice of what is good. This is what I mean in saying that the nature is good. If men do what is not good, the blame cannot be imputed to their natural powers. The feeling of commiseration belongs to all men; so does that of shame and dislike; and that of reverence and respect; and that of approving and disapproving. The feeling of commiseration implies the principle of benevolence; that of shame and dislike, the principle of righteousness; that of reverence and respect, the principle of propriety; and that of approving and disapproving, the principle of knowledge. Benevolence, righteousness, propriety, and knowledge are not infused into us from without. We are certainly furnished with them. And a different view is simply from want of reflection. Hence it is said: 'Seek and you will find them. Neglect and you will lose them.' Men differ from one another in regard to them—some as much again as others, some five times as much, and some to an incalculable amount—it is because they cannot carry out fully their natural powers. It is said in the *Book of Poetry:*

'Heaven, in producing mankind,
Gave them their various faculties and relations
    with their specific laws,
These are the invariable rules of nature of all
    to hold,
And all love this admirable virtue.'

Confucius said, 'The maker of this ode knew indeed the principle of our nature!' We may thus see that every faculty and relation must have its law, and since there are invariable rules for all to hold, they consequently love this admirable virtue."

The Basis of Good Government*

The text of Confucius is given in sections 1–7; what follows is from the ninth chapter of the commentary by the philosopher Tsang, which is appended to the Great Learning. *This passage, originally a chapter in the* Classic of Rites, *was made a classic by itself in one of the* Four Books *and has had a great influence on the idea and practice of government in China and other lands influenced by it.*[18]

What the Great Learning teaches is to illustrate illustrious virtue, to love people, and to rest in the highest excellence.

The point where to rest being known, the object of pursuit is then determined; and, that being determined, a calm unperturbedness may be attained to. To that calmness there will succeed a tranquil repose. In that repose there will be careful deliberation, and that deliberation will be followed by the attainment of the desired end. Things have their root and their branches; affairs have their end and their beginning. To know what is first and what is last will lead near to what is taught in the Great Learning.

The ancients, who wished to illustrate illustrious virtue throughout the kingdom, first ordered well their states. Wishing to order well their states, they first regulated their families. Wishing to regulate their families, they first cultivated their persons. Wishing to cultivate their persons, they first rectified their hearts. Wishing to rectify their hearts, they first sought to be sincere in their thoughts. Wishing to be sincere in their thoughts, they first extended to the utmost their knowledge.

The extension of knowledge is by the investigation of things. [5] Things being investigated, knowledge became complete. Their knowledge being complete, their thoughts were sincere. Their thoughts being sincere, their hearts were then rectified. Their hearts being rectified, their persons were cultivated. Their persons being cultivated, their families were regulated. Their families being regulated, their states were rightly governed. Their states being rightly governed, the whole kingdom was made tranquil and happy.

The Great Learning 1–7; 9.1, 3–5
[18]Taken, with editing, from James Legge, trans., *The Sacred Books of China: The Texts of Confucianism*, part 4, *Sacred Books of the East* vol. 28 (Oxford: Oxford University Press, 1885), pp. 411–413, 417–419.

From the son of Heaven down to the multitudes of the people, all considered the cultivation of the person to be the root of everything else. It cannot be, when the root is neglected, that what should spring from it will be well ordered. It never has been the case that what was of great importance has been slightly cared for, and at the same time what was of slight importance has been greatly cared for. . . .

[9.1, from the commentary] What is meant by "In order rightly to govern the state, it is necessary first to regulate the family,"[19] is this. It is not possible for one to teach others, while he cannot teach his own family. Therefore, the ruler, without going beyond his family, completes the lessons for the state. There is filiality, with which the sovereign should be served.

There is fraternal submission, with which elders and superiors should be served. There is kindness, with which the multitude should be treated. . . .

[3] From the loving example of one family a whole state becomes loving, and from its courtesies the whole state becomes courteous, while, from the ambition and perverseness of the one man [the emperor], the whole state may be led to rebellious disorder—such is the nature of the influence. . . . On this account, the ruler must himself be possessed of good qualities, and then he may require them in the people. He must not have bad qualities in himself, and then he may require that they shall not be in the people. Never has there been a man who, not having reference to his own character and wishes in dealing with others, was able effectually to instruct them. [5] Thus we see how the government of the state depends on the regulation of the family.

---

[19]Not a direct quote from the text of Confucius above, but a good statement of an idea that occurs there.

Confidence and Prosperity in Government*

The Mencius *has much to say about good government. The first excerpt deals with the need of the rulers to keep the confidence of the people. The second deals with the need for some level of economic prosperity so that both ruler and people may flourish.*

Mencius said, "It was by benevolence that the three dynasties gained the empire, and by not being benevolent that they lost it. It is by the same means that the decaying and flourishing, the preservation and perishing, of states are determined. If the emperor is not benevolent, he cannot preserve the empire from passing from him. If the sovereign of a state is not

benevolent, he cannot preserve his kingdom. If a high noble or great officer is not benevolent, he cannot preserve his ancestral temple. If a scholar or common man is not benevolent, he cannot preserve his four limbs. Hating death and ruin, and yet delighting in being unbenevolent is like hating to be drunk, and yet loving to drink wine.". . .

Mencius said, "Chieh and Chou's losing the empire arose from their losing the people, and to lose the people means to lose their hearts. There is a way to get the empire: get the people, and the empire is obtained. There is a way to get the people: get their hearts, and the people are obtained. There is a way to get their hearts: collect for them what they like, and do not lay on them what they dislike. The people turn to a benevolent rule as water runs downward, and as wild beasts run to the wilderness."

---

*Mencius 4.3, 9; 1.6.20–24

[1.6.20–24] Mencius said [to King Hsuan of Ch'i] . . . "Only men of education are able to maintain a fixed heart without a fixed means of livelihood. As to the people, if they do not have a certain livelihood, then they will not have a fixed heart. And if they do not have a fixed heart, there is nothing which they will not do. They will go the way of self-abandonment, of moral deflection, of depravity, and of wild license. When they have been involved in these crimes, to follow them up and punish them is to entrap the people. How can such a thing as entrapping the people be done under the rule of a benevolent man?

"Therefore an intelligent ruler will regulate the livelihood of the people, so as to make sure that they shall have enough to serve their parents, and enough to support their wives and children. He insures that in good years they shall always be abundantly satisfied, and that in bad years they shall escape the danger of perishing. Then he may urge them to what is good, and they will do it, for in this case the people will follow after the good with ease. But now the livelihood of the people is so regulated that they do not have enough to serve their parents, and enough to support their wives and children. Even though they may have good years, their lives are continually embittered, and in bad years they do not escape perishing. In such circumstances they only try to save themselves from death, and they are afraid they will not succeed. What leisure do they have to cultivate propriety and righteousness?

"If Your Majesty wishes to govern humanely the livelihood of the people, why not turn to that which is the essential step to it? Let mulberry trees be planted about the homesteads with their five sections of land, and persons of fifty years may then be clothed with silk. In keeping fowls, pigs, and swine, let not their times of breeding be neglected, and persons of seventy years may eat meat. Let there not be taken away the time that is proper for the cultivation of the farm with its hundred sections of land, and the family of eight that is supported by it shall not suffer from hunger. Let careful attention be paid to education in schools, especially its education of the filial and fraternal duties, and gray-haired men will not be seen upon the roads carrying burdens on their backs or on their heads. It never has been that the ruler of a state where such results were seen—the old wearing silk and eating meat, and the black-haired people suffering neither from hunger nor cold—did not attain to the office of emperor."

RITUAL

Divination*

The Classic of Changes (I Ching) *has been used for philosophical meditation, but its main use has been in divination. The traditional ceremony with milfoil sticks is often used, but dice or any other method of selecting numbers can be employed. When the hexagram that matches the numbers thrown is located, it is read and applied to the inquirer's situation, giving the inquirer insight and foresight into the future.[20]*

* *Classic of Changes* 1, 47, 54

[20]Taken, with editing, from James Legge, trans., *The Sacred Books of China: The Texts of Confucianism,* part 2, *The Yi King, Sacred Books of the East* vol. 16 (Oxford: Oxford University Press, 1882), pp. 57–58, 161–163, 180–182.

THE CH'IEN HEXAGRAM:

Ch'ien [represents] what is great and originating, penetrating, advantageous, correct and firm.

In the first [or lowest] line, undivided, [we see] the dragon lying hidden [in the deep]. It is not the time for active doing.

In the second line, undivided, [we see] the dragon appearing in the field. It will be advantageous to meet with the morally great man.

In the third line, undivided, [we see] the superior man active and vigilant all day, and in the evening still careful and apprehensive. [There is] danger, but there will be no mistake.

In the fourth line, undivided, [we see the dragon looking] as if he were leaping up, but still in the deep. There will be no mistake.

In the fifth line, undivided, [we see] the dragon flying in the sky. It will be advantageous to meet with the great man.

In the sixth [or topmost] line, undivided, [we see] the dragon exceeding the proper limits. There will be occasion for repentance.

[The lines of this hexagram are all strong and undivided, as appears from] the use of the number nine. If the host of dragons [thus] appearing were to divest themselves of their heads, there would be good fortune.[21]

THE K'UN HEXAGRAM:

In [the condition denoted by] K'un there may [yet be] progress and success. For the firm and correct, the [really] great man, there will be good fortune. He will fall into no error. If he make speeches, his words cannot be made good.

The first line, divided, shows its subject with bare buttocks in difficulty under the stump of a tree. He enters a dark valley, and for three years has no prospect [of deliverance].

The second line, undivided, shows its subject in difficulty amid his wine and food. Then comes to him the red knee-covers [of the ruler]. It will be well for him [to maintain his sincerity] in sacrificing. Active operations [on his part] will lead to evil, but he will be free from blame.

The third line, divided, shows its subject in difficulty before a [frowning] rock. He lays hold of thorns. He enters his palace, and does not see his wife. There will be evil.

The fourth line, undivided, shows its subject proceeding very slowly [to help the subject of the first line], who is in difficulty by the carriage adorned with metal in front of him. There will be occasion for regret, but the end will be good.

The fifth line, undivided, shows its subject with his nose and feet cut off. He is in difficulty by [his ministers in their] scarlet aprons. He is leisurely in his movements, however, and is satisfied. It will be well for him to be [sincere] in sacrificing [to spiritual beings].

The sixth line, divided, shows its subject in difficulty, as if bound with creepers; or in a high and dangerous position, and saying [to himself], "If I move, I shall regret it." If he does repent of former errors, there will be good fortune in his going forward.[22]

THE KUEI MEI HEXAGRAM:

Kuei Mei indicates that [under the conditions which it denotes] action will be evil, and in no way advantageous.

---

[21]The point of this hexagram is that mildness of action plus firmness of decision leads to good fortune.

[22]The point of this hexagram is that the person beset by problems can move out of them with a grasp of the situation and a change of attitude.

The first line, undivided, shows the younger woman married off in a position ancillary to the real wife.[23] [It suggests the idea of] a person lame on one leg who yet manages to tramp along. Going forward will be fortunate.

The second line, undivided, shows her blind in one eye, and yet able to see. There will be advantage in her maintaining the firm correctness of a solitary widow.

The third line, divided, shows the younger woman who was to be married off in an inferior position. She returns and accepts an ancillary position.

The fourth line, undivided, shows the younger woman who is to be married off pro-tracting the time. She may be late in being married, but the time will come.

The fifth line, divided, reminds us of the marrying of a younger woman to [king] Ti-yi, when the sleeves of the princess were not equal to those of the [still] younger woman who accompanied her in an inferior capacity. [The case suggests the thought of] the moon almost full. There will be good fortune.

The sixth line, divided, shows the young lady bearing the basket [of harvest offerings], but without anything in it, and the gentleman slaughtering the sheep, but without blood flowing from it. There will be no advantage in any way.[24]

---

[23] *younger woman . . . real wife:* the symbolism here draws on the ancient Chinese custom of a man taking a concubine.

[24] The point of this hexagram is that new undertakings are not advantageous, especially for those who, like the young woman, have difficulty accepting a low social role.

Songs for Sacrifice*

These selections from the Classic of Poetry *show the deep connection of ritual and virtue in Confucianism. The first song is for a sacrifice to an ancestor, and the second is a complaint to Heaven about the rule of an unjust king. The last song provides fascinating details on the sacrificial service in the temple.[25]*

---

*Classic of Poetry, Kau 7; Minor Odes 10.1, 3; 5

---

[25] Taken, with editing, from James Legge, trans., *The Sacred Books of China: The Texts of Confucianism*, part 1, vol. 3, *Sacred Books of the East* (Oxford: Oxford University Press, 1879), pp. 304–305, 325–326, 357–358, 365–368.

SACRIFICIAL ODES OF KAU, ODE 7

They come full of harmony;
They are here in all gravity—
The princes assisting,
While the Son of Heaven[26] looks profound.
[He says], "While I present [this] noble bull,
And they assist me in setting forth the sacrifice,
O great and august Father,

Comfort me, your filial son.

With penetrating wisdom you played the man,
A sovereign with the gifts both of peace and war,
Giving rest even to great Heaven,
And ensuring prosperity to your descendants.

You comfort me with the eyebrows of
     longevity;
You make me great with manifold blessings.
I offer this sacrifice to my meritorious father,
And to my accomplished mother."

---

[26] *Son of Heaven:* the king or emperor.

MINOR ODES OF THE KINGDOM, ODE 10.1, 3

Great and wide Heaven,
How is it you have contracted your kindness,
Sending down death and famine,
Destroying all through the kingdom?
Compassionate Heaven, arrayed in terrors,
How is it you exercise no forethought, no care?
Let the criminals alone;
They have suffered for their guilt.
But those who have no crime
Are indiscriminately involved in ruin.

How is it, O great Heaven,
That the king will not listen to the most just
    words?
He is like a man going [astray],
Who knows not where he will proceed to.
All you officers,
Let each of you attend to his duties.
How do you not stand in awe of one another?
You do not stand in awe of Heaven.

MINOR ODES OF THE KINGDOM, ODE 5

Thick grew the tribulus [on the ground],
But they cleared away its thorny bushes.
Why did they do this of old?
That we might plant our millet and sacrificial
    millet;
That our millet might be abundant,
And our sacrificial millet luxuriant.
When our barns are full,
And our stacks can be counted by tens of
    myriads,
We proceed to make drinks and prepare grain,
For offerings and sacrifice.
We seat the representatives of the dead, and
    urge them to eat,[27]
Thus seeking to increase our bright happiness.

With correct and reverent deportment,
The bulls and rams all pure,
We proceed to the winter and autumnal
    sacrifices.
Some arrange [the meat]; some adjust [the
    pieces of it].[28]
The officer of prayer[29] sacrifices inside the tem-
    ple gate,
And all the sacrificial service is complete and
    brilliant.

Grandly come our ancestors;
Their spirits happily enjoy the offerings;
Their filial descendant receives blessing.
They will reward him with great happiness,
With myriads of years, life without end.

They attend to the furnaces with reverence;
They prepare the trays, which are very large—
Some for the roast meat, some for the broiled.
Wives presiding are still and reverent,
Preparing the numerous [smaller] dishes.
The guests and visitors
Present the cup all around.
Every form is according to rule;
Every smile and word are as they should be.
The spirits quietly come,
And respond with great blessings—
Myriads of years as the [fitting] reward.

We are very much exhausted,
And have performed every ceremony without
    error.
The able officer of prayer announces [the will
    of the spirits],
And goes to the filial descendant to convey it—
"Fragrant has been your filial sacrifice,
And the spirits have enjoyed your drinks and
    food.
They confer on you a hundred blessings;
Each as it is desired,
Each as sure as law.
You have been exact and expeditious;

---

[27] *We seat . . . eat:* people who, in the ceremony, represent
the deceased ancestors are seated and feted.
[28] In Confucian sacrifice, the animals are killed before the
ceremony, not as a part of it.
[29] *officer of prayer:* the chief officiant.

You have been correct and careful;
They will always confer on you the choicest
  favors,
In myriads and tens of myriads."

The ceremonies having thus been completed,
And the bells and drums having given their
  warning,
The filial descendant goes to his place,
And the able officer of prayer makes his
  announcement,
"The spirits have drunk to the full."
The great representatives of the dead then rise,
And the bells and drums escort their withdrawal,
[On which] the spirits tranquilly return.
All the servants, and the presiding wives,
Remove [the trays and dishes] without delay.
The [sacrificer's] uncles and cousins

All repair to the private feast.[30]
The musicians all go in to perform,
And give their soothing aid at the second
  blessing.
Your foods are set forth;
There is no dissatisfaction, but all feel happy.
They drink to the full, and eat to the full;
Great and small, they bow their heads, [saying],
"The spirits enjoyed your drinks and foods.
They will cause you to live long.
Your sacrifices, all in their seasons,
Are completely discharged by you.
May your sons and your grandsons
Never fail to perpetuate these services!"

---

[30]*private feast:* where the remainder of the sacrificial food and drink is consumed.

Music and Morality*

Music has played a large role in Chinese culture and religion. One of the ancient Classics *dealt exclusively with music. Although this text has unfortunately been lost, some of it probably has survived in the* Li Chi *or* Classic of Rites. *Note here how music expresses the cosmic forces of the universe, and how its extensive use in sacrifice furthers the meaning of the ceremony.*[31]

Therefore the ancient kings in framing their music laid its foundation in the feelings and nature of men; they examined the notes by the measures for the length and quality of each; and adapted it to express the meaning of the ceremonies in which it was to be used. They brought it into harmony with the energy that produces life, and to give expression to the performance of the five regular constituents of moral worth. They made it indicate that energy in its Yang or phase of vigor, without any dissipation of its power, and also in its Yin or phase of remission, without the vanishing of its power. The strong phase showed no excess like that of anger, and the weak no shrinking like that of pusillanimity. These four characteristics blended harmoniously in the minds of men, and were similarly manifested in their conduct. Each occupied quietly its proper place, and one did not interfere injuriously with another.

After this they established schools for teaching their music, and different grades for the learners. They marked most fully the divisions of the pieces, and condensed into small compass the parts and variations giving beauty and elegance, in order to regulate and increase the inward virtue of the learners. They gave laws for the great and small notes according to their names, and harmonized the order of the beginning and the end, to represent the doing of things. Thus they made the underlying principles of the relations between the near and distant relatives, the noble and inferior, the old and young, males and females, all to appear manifestly in the music. Hence it is said that "In music we must endeavor to see its depths."

---

* *Classic of Rites* 17.2.10–11, 15–16, 18

[31]Taken, with editing, from James Legge, trans., *The Sacred Books of China: The Texts of Confucianism*, part 4, vol. 28, *Sacred Books of the East* (Oxford: Oxford University Press, 1885), pp. 108–112.

[15] Hence the superior man returns to the good affections in order to bring his will into harmony with them, and compares the different qualities of actions in order to perfect his conduct. Notes that are evil and depraved, and sights leading to disorder and licentiousness are not allowed to affect his ears or eyes. Licentious music and corrupted ceremonies are not admitted into the mind to affect its powers. The spirit of idleness, indifference, depravity, and perversity finds no exhibition in his person. And thus he makes his ears, eyes, nose, and mouth the apprehensions of his mind, and the movements of all the parts of his body, follow the course that is correct, and do that which is right.

After this there ensues the manifestation of the inward thoughts by the modulations of note and tone, the elegant accompaniments of the lutes, small and large, the movements with the shield and battle-axe, the ornaments of the plumes and ox-tails,[32] and the concluding with the pipes and flutes. All this has the effect of exhibiting the brilliance of complete virtue, stirring up the harmonious action of the four seasonal energies, and displaying the true natures and qualities of all things. . . .

[18] Therefore, when the music has full course, the different relations are clearly defined by it; the perceptions of the ears and eyes become sharp and distinct; the action of the blood and physical energies is harmonious and calm; bad influences are removed, and manners changed; and all under heaven there is complete repose.

[32] *movements . . . ox-tails:* pantomime dancing often accompanies the important rituals; both military dances (with *shield and battle-axe*) and civilian dances (with *plumes and ox-tails*) are performed by the dancers.

GLOSSARY

(Pinyin spelling, where it differs from Wade-Giles, is given in brackets before the pronunciation.)

Ching [jing] (jing) the *Classics,* books that make up part of the early Confucian canon.

chun-tzu [jun-zi] (jun-tzoo) literally, "prince's son"; in the teaching of Confucius, a "superior man" made so by the study and practice of virtue.

hsiao [xiao] (syow), the virtue of filiality; love for and service of one's parents and deceased ancestors.

I Ching [Yi Jing] (ee jing) the *Classic of Changes,* a diviner's manual; earliest of the Confucian scriptures.

jen [ren] (ren) the virtue of benevolence or humaneness.

li (lee) the virtue of propriety, decorum, both in the rites and in everyday life.

Tao [Dao] (dow) the cosmic Way, way of life; in Confucian scripture, often related to heaven (e.g., the "Way of Heaven").

wen-yen the formal-classical style in which the Confucian classics are written.

yin-yang the two great interactive cosmic forces of passivity and activity, darkness and light, and other opposing pairs.

QUESTIONS FOR STUDY AND DISCUSSION

1. Compare and contrast the earlier Confucian canon, the *Five Classics,* with the later canon, the *Four Books.* What are their commonalities and differences?

2. How do the Confucian scriptures bear witness to the importance of three elements often held to be common to all traditional Chinese religion: heaven, earth, and ancestor worship?

3. Reflect on the lively political issue of the personal character of candidates for public office in contemporary North America. To what degree does Confucius' counsel about a morally superior ruler apply in our society?

4. To what degree may filiality be a prescription for social pressures on the modern Western family?

5. What is the continuing significance of the Confucian scriptures in modern life outside China?

6. Do you think, with Mencius, that human nature is innately good? Why, or why not?

7. After having read these Confucian scriptures, what is your own conclusion on this often discussed issue: Is Confucianism a religion or a philosophy?

SUGGESTIONS FOR FURTHER READING

Primary Readings

The fullest English translation of the Confucian canon continues to be by James Legge and others in F. Max Müller, gen. ed., *Sacred Books of the East*. Volume 3 is the *Shu Ching*, the religious portions of the *Shih Ching*, and the *Hsiao Ching*; volume 16 is the *I Ching*; volumes 27 and 28 are the *Li Chi*.

R. M. Barnhart, *Li Kung-lin's Classic of Filial Piety*. New York: Metropolitan Museum of Art, 1993. Features the paintings of Li Kung-lin (1041–1106) illustrating the *Filial Piety;* Li's paintings are some of the most important works of art in Chinese cultural history.

Wing-tsit Chan, *A Source Book in Chinese Philosophy*. Princeton: Princeton University Press, 1963. Full selections from religious-philosophical Confucian books and older classics, from a leading interpreter of Chinese religious literature to the West.

D. C. Lau, trans., *The* Analects. London: Penguin, 1979. An excellent contemporary translation, with good notes.

D. C. Lau, trans., *The* Mencius. London: Penguin, 1983. The same standard and format as in his translation of the *Analects*.

R. Wilhelm, trans., *The I Ching*. Bollingen Series, no. 19. New York: Pantheon, 1961. Perhaps the best current translation of the *Book of Changes*.

Secondary Readings

J. B. Henderson, *Scripture, Canon, Commentary: A Comparison of Confucian and Western Exegesis*. Princeton: Princeton University Press, 1991. An excellent treatment of the important question of the relationship and explanation of scripture and commentary, with valuable comparative analysis of Chinese commentary and the Western (mainly Christian) commentarial tradition.

T. Kelleher, "[Women in] Confucianism." In A. Sharma, ed., *Women in World Religions*. Albany: State University of New York Press, 1989, pp. 135–159. An insightful essay on the influence of Confucian scripture on the roles of women in China.

R. L. Taylor, "Confucianism: Scripture and Sage." In F. M. Denney and R. L. Taylor, *The Holy Book in Comparative Perspective*. Columbia, SC: University of South Carolina Press, 1985, pp. 181–203. An excellent recent study of the use of scripture to achieve sagehood.

R. L. Taylor, *The Way of Heaven: An Introduction to Confucian Religious Life*. Leiden: Brill, 1986. A fine introduction to Confucian scripture in the context of religious life; many photographic illustrations of Confucian iconography and rituals.

⌕ INFOTRAC COLLEGE EDITION

You can locate InfoTrac College Edition articles about this chapter by accessing the InfoTrac College Edition website (http://www.infotrac.collegeedition.com/wadsworth/). Using subject guide, enter the search terms relevant to this chapter, and then read abstracts for relevant articles.

Scripture in a Chinese Funeral
A Taoist priest in the Sichwan province of China reads a funeral text, and the men sitting around respond, to enable the soul of the deceased to pass successive judgments on its way to final blessing. Credit: Stevan Harrell, from the Image Bank of the Center for the Study of World Religions, Harvard University. Used by permission of Stevan Harrell.

CHAPTER SEVEN

Taoism

❖ A young man visits a Taoist temple in Hong Kong. He is puzzled about the course of his life and consults with a priest. They talk about the great Way and how he relates to it. The priest reminds him of several passages in the Taoist scriptures and explains their meaning. After some minutes of conversation, the young man goes away smiling, now more certain about the future.

❖ In a temple in Kaoshiung, Taiwan, a medium known as a "spirit writer" falls under the possession of the temple's god. As he speaks the words of the god, a scribe standing near writes down the words. These words will be published in the temple's magazine and may perhaps form the basis of new Taoist scripture.

❖ At the Hsing T'ien Temple in Taipei, Taiwan, the temple courtyard is filled with blue-robed women carrying out the faith healing for which the temple has gained its reputation. They lay hands on the sick or on clothing brought by the families of those too sick to come in person.[1] In this way they carry out an ancient tradition of Taoism as discussed in many of its scriptures, that of healing and longevity.

INTRODUCTION

Taoism is, after Confucianism, the most influential religion among Chinese people. According to Taoists, their faith was founded by Lao Tzu in the sixth century B.C.E. Since ancient times, the Taoist tradition has had two interacting parts: philosophical Taoism, rich in cosmological meditation and speculation; and religious (sometimes called "esoteric") Taoism, with its emphasis on exorcism, astrology, and gaining long life or even immortality. Although Taoism has had an important influence through history, its future is cloudy. Some scholars hold it to be a dying tradition. This only time will tell, but the scriptures of Taoism, especially the *Tao Te Ching* [DOW deh jing], or "Classic of the Way and Its Working," and the *Chuang-tzu* [jwahng tzoo], have earned an undying place in the history of the world's cultures and are still influential today.

Overview of Structure

The name of the Taoist scripture as a whole is the *Tao Tsang* [dow tsahng], or "Taoist canon/collection." Its last main printing in 1926 had 1,120 volumes. The *Tao Tsang* has traditionally been grouped into the *Three Caverns (San-Tung)*. The

---

[1] B. E. Reed, "[Women in] Taoism." In A. Sharma, ed., *Women in World Religions* (Albany: State University of New York Press, 1989), p. 180.

Three Caverns reflect three distinct historic traditions within Taoism. The first section is associated with the Supreme Clarity school, the second with the Numinous Treasure school, and the third with the Three Sovereigns school. Each one of the *Three Caverns* is itself divided into twelve sections, the names of which give a good indication of the overall contents of the Taoist scriptures. They are: "Original Revelations"; divine talismans; interpretations; diagrams; chronologies and genealogies; moral codes; ceremonial decorum; rituals; esoteric techniques (alchemy, astrology, exorcism, etc.); lives of past Taoist worthies; hymns; messages to the dead. To this basic tripartite form was added a later addition, the "Four Supplements," itself as mixed in contents as the caverns.

Origin, Development, and Use

Critical study of the history of the Taoist canon is still in its beginning stages, and its massive nature makes the task even more challenging. Certain conclusions, however, have been reached by scholarship. We will relate here those main points most important for understanding the scripture selections in this chapter.

Taoists trace the origins of their religion and scriptures to the claimed founder of their tradition, Lao Tzu. They hold that his disciples wrote down the first and most important work of the canon, the *Tao Te Ching*, shortly after his death. (Taoists often refer to the *Tao Te Ching* as the "Lao-Tzu.") Recent critical scholarship, however, has concluded that even though it may have begun at this time, this book is a collection of material from different authors finally assembled in the third century B.C.E. Despite this later date, the *Tao Te Ching* is in fact the fountainhead of most of the Taoist scripture that followed. Its reflections on the **Tao** [dow] ("Way") and its **te** [duh] ("power") in eighty-one brief sections are written in a highly compressed style. The Chinese original features much parallelism among the lines of poetry, and also a good deal of rhyme, lost in most translations. It points to a Tao that is cosmic, the origin of heaven and earth. This Tao is a part of each individual's existence, and it is a social ideal as well.

Probably because of its cryptic quality and mixed contents, the *Tao Te Ching* was scripture that could be appealed to by all Taoists to come. Indeed, it is one of the few scripture books to be extensively used in both philosophical Taoism and religious Taoism. To judge from the frequency with which it has been translated into English (more than one hundred times) and other European languages, the *Tao Te Ching* has had a significant appeal to peoples of other religions and cultures. The appeal of this book in the United States, for example, is echoed in the titles of more than fifty books in print in 1998, including *The Tao of: Parenting, Dialogue, Spycraft, Coaching, Sales, Golf,* and even *Jesus* and *Islam.*

The next main text of Taoism is the *Chuang-tzu,* named for its author. This book is far removed from the *Tao Te Ching.* Full of anecdote and allegory, it challenges the reader with provocative style and contents. It stresses the illusory nature of knowledge and the difficulty, if not impossibility, of separating right and wrong. Nevertheless, the *Chuang-tzu* does include specific moral guidelines that proceed from the "two great sanctions," the requirement planted in nature and the inner conviction of what is right and wrong. Both of these principles are grounded in the great Tao.

Other important Taoist texts can only be mentioned here in passing. The *T'ai-shang* tractate deals with retribution on sin and reward for evil. If persons live a good life in harmony with the Tao, their lifespan will be lengthened; if an evil life, they will die early or have their punishment passed on to descendants. The *Tao-fa hui-yuan,* "Group of Taoist Rites," is a book of ceremonies to control demonic forces, both in nature and in the individual, when they result in sickness. The *Shang-ching hou-shen tao-chun lieh-chi,* or "Annals of the Lord of the Tao, the Sage-to-Come of Shang-ching," contains information on how certain Taoist masters (often called "adepts") used respiration techniques, alchemy, and other esoteric techniques to feed on astral powers and become immortal or even divine. But many texts of religious/esoteric Taoism are written in a special script taught only to initiates into special sects, and Taoists have in general been very secretive about sharing this literature.

TEACHING

The Nature of the Tao*

The leading themes in the Tao Te Ching *are the nature of the Tao and how one follows it. These passages present the way as unnameable (chapter 1), female in quality (6), the "mother" of heaven and earth (25), and accomplishing great things by means of small things (34). In the* Chuang-tzu, *the sage discusses the Tao in a more philosophic way, yet also in the playful and challenging manner so typical of the* Chuang-tzu.[2]

[1] Tao called Tao is not Tao.
Names can name no lasting name.

Nameless: the origin of heaven and earth.
Naming: the mother of ten thousand things.

Empty of desire, perceive mystery.
Filled with desire, perceive manifestations.

These have the same source, but different names.
    Call them both deep—
        Deep and again deep:
The gateway to all mystery.

[6] The Valley Spirit never dies.
It is called the Mysterious Female.

The entrance to the Mysterious Female
Is called the root of Heaven and Earth,

Endless flow
Of inexhaustible energy.

[25] Something unformed and complete
Before heaven and earth were born,
Solitary and silent,
Stands alone and unchanging,
Pervading all things without limit.
It is like the mother of all under heaven,
But I don't know its name—
    Better call it Tao.
    Better call it great.

Great means passing on.
Passing on means going far.
Going far means returning.

Therefore,
    Tao is great,
    And heaven,
    And earth,
    And humans.

Four great things in the world.
Aren't humans one of them?

Humans follow earth
Earth follows heaven
Heaven follows Tao.
Tao follows its own nature.

---

*Tao Te Ching, 1, 6, 25, 34; Chuang-tzu 29
[2]All readings from the *Tao Te Ching* are taken from Stephen Addiss and Stanley Lombardo, *Lao-Tzu, Tao Te Ching* (Cambridge, MA: Hackett, 1993). Copyright, 1993, Hackett Publishing Co., Inc. Used by permission. Selections from the *Chuang Tzu* are from James Legge, *The Texts of Taoism, Sacred Books of the East,* vols. 39 and 40 (Oxford: Oxford University Press, 1891).

[34] Great Tao overflows
To the left   To the right.

All beings owe their life to it
And do not depart from it.
It acts without a name.
It clothes and nourishes all beings
But does not become their master.

Enduring without desire,
It may be called slight.
All beings return to it,
But it does not become their master.

It may be called immense.
By not making itself great,
It can do great things.

[*Chuang-tzu* 29] Tung-kwo tze asked Chuang Tzu, saying, "Where is what you call the Tao to be found?" Chuang Tzu replied, "Everywhere." The other said, "Specify an instance of it. That will be more satisfactory." "It is here in this ant." "Give a lower instance." "It is in this earthenware tile." "Surely that is the lowest instance?" "It is in that excrement." To this Tung-kwo tze gave no reply.

Chuang Tzu said, "Your questions, my master, do not touch the fundamental point of the Tao. They remind me of the questions addressed by the superintendents of the market to the inspector about examining the value of a pig by stepping on it, and testing its weight as the foot descends lower and lower on the body. You should not specify any particular thing. There is not a single thing without the Tao. So it is with the Perfect Tao. And if we call it the Great Tao, it is just the same. It has the three terms, "Complete," "All-embracing," "the Whole." These names are different, but the reality sought in them is the same; referring to the One thing.

"Suppose we were to try to roam about in the palace of Nowhere. When met there, we might discuss the subject without ever coming to an end. Or suppose we were to be together in the region of Non-action. Should we say that the Tao was Simplicity and Stillness? or Indifference and Purity? or Harmony and Ease? My will would be aimless. It went nowhere, I would not know where it had gone; it went and came again, I wouldn't know where it had stopped; if it went on going and coming, I would not know when the process would end. In vague uncertainty, I would be in the vastest waste. Though I entered it with the greatest knowledge, I would not know how inexhaustible it was. That which makes things what they are does not have the limit which belongs to things; and when we speak of things being limited, we mean that they are so in themselves. The Tao is the limit of the unlimited, and the boundlessness of the unbounded.

"We speak of fullness and emptiness; of withering and decay. It produces fullness and emptiness, but is neither fullness nor emptiness; it produces withering and decay, but is neither withering nor decay. It produces the root and branches, but is neither root nor branch; it produces accumulation and dispersion, but is itself neither accumulated nor dispersed."

The World*

The typical Chinese expression for the world is "Heaven and Earth." These passages present the world, composed of the "ten thousand things," as proceeding from the Tao and holding to the way of inactivity. Wise persons will pattern their lives on the Tao that has made Heaven and Earth.

[7] Heaven is long, Earth enduring.
Long and enduring
Because they do not exist for themselves.

Therefore the Sage

Tao Te Ching 7, 42, 52

Steps back, but is always in front,
Stays outside, but is always within.

No self interest?
Self is fulfilled.

[42] Tao engenders One,
One engenders Two,
Two engenders Three,[3]
Three engenders the ten thousand things.

The ten thousand things carry shade
And embrace sunlight.
     Shade and sunlight, yin and yang,[4]
Breath blending into harmony.[5]

Humans hate
To be alone, poor, and hungry.
Yet kings and princes
Use these words as titles.
     We gain by losing,
     Lose by gaining.

What others teach, I also teach:

---

[3]*the One* is *ch'i*, the primordial, cosmic breath; *the Two* are
yin and yang; *the Three* are the waters under the earth, the
earth, and heaven.
[4]*Yin* and *Yang* are the cosmic principles or dualities: passive
and active, earth and heaven, dark and light, etc.
[5]*breath: ch'i*, the cosmic breath/wind.

A violent man does not die a natural death.
This is the basis of my teaching.

[52] The world has a source: the world's
          mother.
Once you have the mother,
     You know the children.
Once you know the children,
     Return to the mother.

Your body dies.
There is no danger.

Block the passage,
Bolt the gate:
     No strain
Until your life ends.

Open the passage,
Take charge of things:
     No relief
Until your life ends.

Seeing the small is called brightness.
Maintaining gentleness is called strength.
Use this brightness to return to brightness.

Don't cling to your body's woes.
Then you can learn endurance.

ETHICS

Nonaction*

*The leading ethical ideal of Taoism is **wu-wei**
[woo-WAY], nonaction or "active nonstriving."
By nonaction, the sage seeks to come into harmony
with the great Tao, which itself accomplishes by
nonaction.*

Nonaction makes its exemplifier the lord of all
fame; nonaction serves him as the treasury of all
plans; nonaction fits him for the burden of

all offices; nonaction makes him the lord of all
wisdom. The range of his action is inexhaustible, but there is nowhere any trace of his
presence. He fulfills all that he has received from
Heaven, but he does not see that he was the
recipient of anything. A pure vacancy of all purpose is what characterizes him. When the perfect man employs his mind, it is a mirror. It
conducts nothing and anticipates nothing; it
responds to what is before it, but does not
retain it. Thus he is able to deal successfully with
all things, and injures none.

---

* *Chuang-tzu*, book 7

Individual Life in Harmony with the Tao*

These selections, which emphasize the necessity of bringing individual life into accord with the Tao, give advice on how to accomplish this through non-action and indirection.

[16] Attain complete emptiness,
Hold fast to stillness.

The ten thousand things stir about;
I only watch for their going back.

Things grow and grow,
But each goes back to its root.
Going back to the root is stillness.
This means returning to what is.
Returning to what is
Means going back to the ordinary.

Understanding the ordinary:
    Enlightenment.
Not understanding the ordinary:
    Blindness creates evil.
Understanding the ordinary:
    Mind opens.

Mind opening leads to compassion,
Compassion to nobility,
Nobility to heavenliness,
Heavenliness to Tao.

    Tao endures.
    Your body dies.

There is no danger.

[22] Crippled becomes whole,
Crooked becomes straight,
Hollow becomes full,
Worn becomes new,
Little becomes more,
Much becomes delusion.

Therefore Sages cling to the One
    And take care of this world;
Do not display themselves
    And therefore shine;
Do not assert themselves
    And therefore stand out;
Do not praise themselves
    And therefore succeed;
Are not complacent
    And therefore endure;
Do not contend
    And therefore no one under heaven
        Can contend with them.

The old saying
Crippled becomes whole
Is not empty words.

It becomes whole and returns.

[33] Knowing others is intelligent.
Knowing yourself is enlightened.

Conquering others takes force.
Conquering yourself is true strength.

Knowing what is enough is wealth.
Forging ahead shows inner resolve.

Hold your ground and you will last long.
Die without perishing and your life will endure.

[44] Name or body: which is closer?
Body or possessions: which means more?
Gain or loss: which one hurts?

Extreme love exacts a great price.
Many possessions entail heavy loss.

Know what is enough—
    Abuse nothing.
Know when to stop—
    Harm nothing.

This is how to last a long time.[6]

---

* *Tao Te Ching* 16, 22, 33, 44

[6] *last a long time:* lines like these in the *Tao Te Ching* encouraged later Taoist esoteric practices about gaining long life and even immortality through religious practices.

The Superior Man*

Here is a characteristically Taoist presentation of the superior man, designed of course to provide an alternative to the Confucian idea of superiority. The Taoist superiority comes not through self-cultivation in the virtues, but by tapping through inactivity into the superiority of the Tao. The full descriptions of the Taoist superior man form a complete list of the type of person that Taoists, especially philosophically oriented ones, seek to become.

The Master said, "The Tao overspreads and sustains all things. How great it is in its overflowing influence! The superior man ought by all means to remove from his mind all that is contrary to it. Acting without action is what is called Heaven-like. Speech coming forth of itself is what is called a mark of the true Virtue. Loving men and benefiting things is what is called Benevolence. Seeing wherein things that are different yet agree is what is called being Great. Conduct free from the ambition of being distinguished above others is what is called being Generous. The possession in himself of a myriad points of difference is what is called being Rich. Therefore to hold fast the natural attributes is what is called the Guiding Line of government; the perfecting of those attributes is what is called its Establishment; accordance with the Tao is what is called being Complete; and not allowing anything external to affect the will is what is called being Perfect.

"When the superior man understands these ten things, he keeps all matters as it were sheathed in himself, showing the greatness of his mind; and through the outflow of his doings all things move and come to him. Being such, he lets the gold lie hid in the hill, and the pearls in the deep; he considers not property or money to be any gain; he keeps aloof from riches and honors; he rejoices not in long life, and grieves not for early death; he does not account prosperity a glory, nor is ashamed of indigence; he would not grasp at the gain of the whole world to be held as his own private portion; he would not desire to rule over the whole world as his own private distinction. His distinction is in understanding that all things belong to the one treasury, and that death and life should be viewed in the same way."

The Master said, "How still and deep is the place where the Tao resides! How limpid is its purity! Metal and stone without It would give forth no sound. They have indeed the power of sound in them, but if they be not struck, they do not emit it. Who can determine the qualities that are in all things?

"The man of kingly qualities holds on his way unoccupied, and is ashamed to busy himself with the conduct of affairs. He establishes himself in what is the root and source of his capacity, and his wisdom grows to be spiritlike. In this way his attributes become more and more great, and when his mind goes forth, whatever things come in his way, it lays hold of them and deals with them. Thus, if there were not the Tao, the bodily form would not have life, and its life, without the attributes of the Tao, would not be manifested. Is not he who preserves the body and gives the fullest development to the life, who establishes the attributes of the Tao and clearly displays It, possessed of kingly qualities? How majestic is he in his sudden issuings forth, and in his unexpected movements, when all things follow him! —This we call the man whose qualities fit him to rule.

"He sees where there is the deepest obscurity; he hears where there is no sound. In the midst of the deepest obscurity, he alone sees and can distinguish various objects; in the midst of a soundless abyss, he alone can hear a harmony of notes. Therefore where one deep is succeeded by a greater, he can people all with things; where

---

*Chuang-tzu, book 12

one mysterious range is followed by another that is more so, he can lay hold of the subtlest character of each. In this way in his dealings with all things, while he is farthest from having any-thing, he can yet give to them what they seek; while he is always hurrying forth, he yet returns to his resting place; now large, now small; now long, now short; now distant, now near."

Government*

The social ethic of Taoism is largely concerned with government. Here it presents a quietistic approach opposite of the activistic approach of Confucian-ism. By inactivity in following the Tao one can bring about the best state. This social ethic has led to several political options for Taoists: withdrawal from public life, mild participation in it, and at times participation in anarchy.

[3] Don't glorify heroes,
And people will not contend.
Don't treasure rare objects,
And no one will steal.
Don't display what people desire,
And their hearts will not be disturbed.

Therefore,
The Sage rules
    By emptying hearts and filling bellies,
    By weakening ambitions and strengthening
    bones;
Leads people
    Away from knowing and wanting;
Deters those who know too much
    From going too far:
Practices non-action
    And the natural order is not disrupted.

[18] Great Tao rejected:
    Benevolence and righteousness appear.

Learning and knowledge professed:
    Great hypocrites spring up.

Family relations forgotten:
    Filial piety and affection arise.

The nation disordered:
    Patriots come forth.

[57] Use the expected to govern the country,
Use surprise to wage war,
Use non-action to win the world
How do I know?

    Like this!

The more prohibitions and rules,
    The poorer people become.
The sharper people's weapons,
    The more they riot.
The more skilled their techniques,
    The more grotesque their works.
The more elaborate the laws,
    The more they commit crimes.

Therefore the Sage says:
    I do nothing
And people transform themselves.
    I enjoy serenity
And people govern themselves.
    I cultivate emptiness
And people become prosperous.
    I have no desires
And people simplify themselves.

[64] At rest is easy to hold.
Not yet impossible is easy to plan.
Brittle is easy to break.
Fine is easy to scatter.

Create before it exists.
Lead before it goes astray.

A tree too big to embrace
    Is born from a slender shoot.
A nine-storey tower
    Rises from a pile of earth.
A thousand-mile journey
    Begins with a single step.

Act and you ruin it.
Grasp and you lose it.

---

*Tao Te Ching 3, 18, 57, 64

Therefore the Sage
　　Does not act
　　And so does not ruin
　　Does not grasp
　　And so does not lose.
People commonly ruin their work
　　When they are near success.
Proceed at the end as at the beginning
　　And your work won't be ruined.

Therefore the Sage
　　Desires no desires
　　Prizes no prizes
　　Studies no studies
　　　　And returns
　　To what others pass by.
The Sage
　　Helps all beings find their nature,
　　But does not presume to act.

On Death*

This often-quoted story is an excellent example of the striking literary features of the Chuang-tzu.

When Chuang Tzu went to Khu, he saw an empty skull, bleached but still retaining its shape. Tapping it with his horse-switch, he asked it, "Did you, Sir, in your greed of life, fail in the lessons of reason, and come to this? Or did you do so, in the service of a perishing state, by the punishment of the axe? Or was it through your evil conduct, reflecting disgrace on your parents and on your wife and children? Or was it through your hard endurance of cold and hunger? Or was it that you had completed your term of life?"

Having given expression to these questions, he took up the skull, and made a pillow of it when he went to sleep. At midnight the skull appeared to him in a dream and said, "What you

said to me was after the fashion of an orator. All your words were about the entanglements of men in their lifetime. There are none of those things after death. Would you like to hear me, Sir, tell you about death?" "I should," said Chuang Tzu, and the skull resumed: "In death there are not the distinctions of ruler above and minister below. There are none of the phenomena of the four seasons. Tranquil and at ease, our years are those of heaven and earth. No king in his court has greater enjoyment than we have." Chuang Tzu did not believe it, and said, "If I could get the Ruler of our Destiny to restore your body to life with its bones and flesh and skin, and to give you back your father and mother, your wife and children, and all your village acquaintances, would you wish me to do so?" The skull stared intently at him, knitted its brows, and said, "How should I cast away the enjoyment of my royal court, and undertake again the toils of life among mankind?"

*Chuang-tzu, book 18

Reward and Retribution**

Although the Tao does not have a strongly moral character, the Taoist tradition nonetheless developed the doctrine of reward for virtue (in long life) and punishment for evil (shortened life or

punishment of descendants). This passage gives a lyrical list of good deeds and excerpts the beginning of an even longer section on evil deeds.

There are no special doors for calamity and happiness; they come as men themselves summon

**T'ai-Shang, book 1

them. Their recompenses follow good and evil as the shadow follows the substance.

Accordingly, in heaven and earth there are spirits that take account of men's transgressions, and, according to the lightness or gravity of their offenses, take away from their term of life. When that term is curtailed, men become poor and reduced, and meet with many sorrows and afflictions. All (other) men hate them; punishments and calamities attend them; good luck and occasions for felicitation shun them; evil stars send down misfortunes on them. When their term of life is exhausted they die.

There also are the Spirit-rulers in the three pairs of the T'ai stars of the Northern Bushel[7] over men's heads, which record their acts of guilt and wickedness, and take away (from their term of life) periods of twelve years or of a hundred days.

There also are the three Spirits of the recumbent body which reside within a man's person. As each appointed day of reporting comes, they ascend to the court of Heaven, and report men's deeds of guilt and transgression. On the last day of the moon, the spirit of the Hearth does the same.

In the case of every man's transgressions, when they are great, twelve years are taken from his term of life; when they are small, a hundred days.

Transgressions, great and small, are seen in several hundred things. He who wishes to seek for long life must first avoid these.

If his way is right, he should go forward in it; if it is wrong, he should withdraw from it.

He will not tread in devious byways; he will not impose on himself in any secret apartment. He will amass virtue and accumulate deeds of merit. He will feel kindly towards all creatures. He will be loyal, filial, loving to his younger brothers, and submissive to his elder. He will make himself correct and so transform others. He will pity orphans, and have compassion on widows; he will respect the old and cherish the young. Even the insects, grass, and trees he should not hurt.

He ought to pity the evil tendencies of others; to rejoice over their excellences; to help them in their difficulties; to rescue them from their perils; to regard their gains as if they were his own, and their losses in the same way; not to publish their shortcomings; not to flaunt his own superiorities; to put a stop to what is evil, and exalt and display what is good; to yield much, and take little for himself; to receive insult without resenting it, and honor with an appearance of apprehension; to bestow favors without seeking for a return, and give to others without any subsequent regret—this is what is called a good man. All other men respect him; Heaven in its course protects him; happiness and financial rewards follow him; all evil things keep far from him; the spiritual Intelligences defend him; what he does is sure to succeed; he may hope to become Immaterial and Immortal.

He who would seek to become an Immortal of Heaven ought to give the proof of 1,300 good deeds; and he who would seek to become an Immortal of Earth should give the proof of three hundred.

But if the movements of a man's heart are contrary to righteousness, and his conduct is in opposition to reason; if he regards his wickedness as a proof of his ability, and can bear to do what is cruel and injurious; if he secretly harms the honest and good; if he treats with clandestine slight his ruler or parents; if he is disrespectful to his elders and teachers; if he disregards the authority of those whom he should serve; if he deceives the simple; if he calumniates his fellow-learners; if he vents baseless slanders, practices deception and hypocrisy, and attacks and exposes his kindred by blood or marriage; if he is hard, violent, and without humanity—in the case of crimes such as these, (the Spirits) presiding over the Life, according to their lightness or gravity, take away the culprit's periods of twelve years or of one hundred days. When his term of life is exhausted, death ensues. If at death there remains any unpunished guilt, judgment extends to his posterity.

---

[7] *Northern Bushel:* a constellation.

RITUAL

Methods of Prolonging Life*

This text, considered the most important in religious Taoism, stresses the esoteric methods of achieving immortality. The first selection discusses the general principles of achieving longevity or immortality; the second points out how scripture texts can aid in this process.[8]

If you are going to do everything possible to nurture your life, you will take the divine medicines. In addition, you will never weary of circulating your breaths; morning and night you will do calisthenics to circulate your blood and breaths and see that they do not stagnate. In addition to these things, you will practice sexual intercourse in the right fashion; you will eat and drink moderately; you will avoid drafts and dampness; you will not trouble about things that are not within your competence. Do all these things, and you will not fall sick.

On the other hand, you are sure to become ill if you are afraid of not always having your own way in society and of instability in your affairs; also, if laxity and lack of diligence trouble you. If all you have is a heart faithful to God and yet do nothing for your own benefit—your predestined life span being defective and your body threatened with harm the Three Corpses[9] will take advantage of your weak months and perilous days, the hours when your longevity could be interrupted or sickness incurred, to summon vicious breaths and bring in any demons they might be able to find to do you injury. The danger is certainly great for any person for whom these six obstacles are grouped and the Three Destructives (from the duodenary cycle) united

in the same quarter. And when this situation intensifies, it produces the various illnesses. But all of this was set in motion by the anxiety that was present in the first place.

Accordingly, those who first did something about God in antiquity exercised all the medical arts at the same time to save themselves from misfortunes that are ever present, but this principle is unknown to ordinary processors who, not understanding what they have been taught, pay no attention to the prescriptions for treating illness. Further, being unable to break with worldly life and live as hermits, and using only personal remedies to drive away illness, they lack all means for combating it and curing themselves. They are by no means as well off as the people in general who use various infusions. . . .

I heard Cheng Yin say that no Taoist book surpasses *San huang nei wen* and *Wu yueh chen hsing t'u*[10] in importance. They were the honored secrets of the genies and superior men of antiquity, and could be taught only by those bearing the title of genie. Those receiving them transmitted them once after forty years, and in doing so oaths were taken by smearing the lips with the blood of a victim,[11] and agreements were entered into by the giving of a present. Writings of this type are to be found in all the famous mountains and the five revered mountains, but they are stored in hidden spots in caves. In response to those who have secured the divine process and entered a mountain to give sincere thought to it, the god of the mountain will automatically open the mountain and let such persons see the texts, just as Po Ho got his in a mountain, and immediately set up an altar, made a present of silk, drew one ordinary copy,[12] and then left with them. A purified place

---

Pao-p'u tzu 15.6b–7a; 19.6b–7a

[8]From James R. Ware, *Alchemy, Medicine, Religion in the China of A.D. 320: The* Nei P'ien *of Ko Hung* (Pao-p'u tzu). Cambridge, MA: Massachusetts Institute of Technology Press, 1966. Copyright, 1966 by The Massachusetts Institute of Technology. Used by permission.

[9]*Three Corpses:* worms in the body causing illness and death.

[10]Both these books were written by Po Ho.

[11]*victim:* a sacrificed animal.

[12]*drew one ordinary copy:* i.e., wrote out a copy.

is always prepared for such texts, and whenever anything is done about them one must first announce it to them, as though one were serving a sovereign or a father.

The classic itself states that if *San huang nei wen* is in a household, it will banish evil and hateful ghosts, soften the effects of epidemics, block calamities, and rout misfortunes. If anyone is suffering from illness or on the point of death, let someone believing in the process with all his heart give this text to the patient to hold, and he will be sure not to die. If a wife is having trouble in childbirth to the point of possible death, let her hold this text, and her son will be born immediately. If pilgrims wishing to seek Fullness of Life will hold this text when entering the mountains, it will rout tigers and wolves, and none of the mountain powers, poisons, or evils will dare approach. When crossing rivers and seas, the processors will be able to dispel crocodiles and dragons, and halt the wind and waves with this book.

With the method taught in this text it is possible to initiate undertakings positively or negatively without inquiring about the correct site or choosing the right day, and one's household will be free from calamities. If you wish to build a new house or tomb, write several dozen copies of the Earth Augustus text and spread them on the site. Look at them on the following day, and if a yellow color is seen adhering to them, one may begin the work there and the household will be sure to become rich and prosperous. When others are being interred, copy the Man Augustus text and include your own full name written on a folded sheet of paper. Insert this in that person's grave without letting others know what you are doing, and you will be free from sudden misfortune and robbers. Anyone plotting against you will be sure to have his harm turned against himself.

GLOSSARY

(Pinyin spelling, where it differs from Wade-Giles, is given in brackets before the pronunciation.)

Chuang-tzu [Zhuangzi] (jwahng tzoo) the second most important book of the Taoist scriptures.

Tao [Dao] (dow) the Way of the cosmos, to be "tuned into" in human life.

Tao Te Ching [Dao De Jing] (dow duh jing) the "Classic of the Way and Its Working," the leading book of the Taoist scriptures.

Tao Tsang [Dao Zang] (dow tsahng) the Taoist canon.

te [De] (duh) virtue, power, working.

wu-wei (woo WAY) nonaction, nonstriving; passivity; the use of the natural power of the Tao in oneself.

QUESTIONS FOR STUDY AND DISCUSSION

1. From your reading of these texts, how would you define or describe the Tao?

2. In what ways is the *Tao Te Ching* the foundation of subsequent Taoist traditions?

3. Compare and contrast the Taoist and Confucian ideas of the sage or superior man.

4. Discuss the remarkable feminine imagery used, especially in the *Tao Te Ching*, to describe the Tao. Has this carried over into later Taoism in the form of a greater role for women in the religion? If not, why?

5. Discuss the Taoist goal of longevity. How is the pursuit of this goal different in religious and philosophical Taoism?

6. How might the perplexing style of the *Chuang-tzu* be particularly well designed to promote its goals?

7. Compare and contrast the Taoist and Confucian ideas of government. How is it possible, as the *Tao Te Ching* claims, to govern by nonaction?

8. Contrast "philosophical Taoism" and "religious Taoism." How are their differences and similarities reflected in their scriptures?

9. One of the most well-known Taoist sayings in North America is the line from the *Tao Te Ching* 64, "A journey of a thousand miles begins with a single step" (see above, p. 170). Given the context of this saying its chapter, and its topic of non-activity, is this saying correctly interpreted by most people as a positive call to long-term action?

SUGGESTIONS FOR FURTHER READING

Primary Readings

S. Addiss and S. Lombardo, *Lao-Tzu, Tao Te Ching*. Cambridge, MA: Hackett, 1993. An excellent translation, characterized by literary grace and terse poetic power.

R. G. Henricks, *Lao Tzu, Te-Tao Ching*. New York: Ballantine, 1989. A lively translation, with full introduction and commentary, of the recently discovered *Ma-wang-tui* texts. (The usual name of this book is reversed in these texts.)

L. Kohn, *Taoist Mystical Philosophy: The Scripture of Western Ascension*. Albany: State University of New York Press, 1991. A translation and commentary of an important early text from philosophical Taoism.

J. Legge, ed., *The Texts of Taoism*. New York: Julian, 1959; first published 1891 by Oxford University Press. A standard rendering of the *Tao Te Ching, Chuang-tzu*, and the *Thai Shang*.

J. R. Ware, *Alchemy, Medicine, Religion in the China of A.D. 320: the* Nei P'ien *of Ko Hung* (Pao-p'u tzu). Cambridge, MA: M.I.T. Press, 1966. A complete and accurate translation of the single most important text in the history of religious Taoism.

Secondary Readings

R. E. Allinson, *Chuang-Tzu for Spiritual Transformation: An Analysis of the Inner Chapters*. Albany: State University of New York Press, 1989. A challenging philosophical analysis of the heart of this classic.

Chih-chung Tsai, *Zhuangzi Speaks: The Music of Nature*. Princeton: Princeton University Press, 1992. A best-selling book in its Chinese original, this volume features line drawing and cartoon interpretations of the *Chuang-Tzu* to express the ineffable Tao.

B. E. Reed, "[Women in] Taoism." In A. Sharma, ed., *Women in World Religions*. Albany: State University of New York Press, 1989, pp. 161–181. An insightful analysis of the role of the feminine in Taoist scripture, especially the *Tao Te Ching*, and their less than prominent role in lived Taoist religion.

M. Saso, *Blue Dragon White Tiger: Taoist Rites of Passage*. Washington, DC: The Taoist Center, 1990. A treatment of various life-cycle rituals.

INFOTRAC COLLEGE EDITION

You can locate InfoTrac College Edition articles about this chapter by accessing the InfoTrac College Edition website (http://www.infotrac.collegeedition.com/wadsworth/). Using subject guide, enter the search terms relevant to this chapter, and then read abstracts for relevant articles.

Izanagi Creating the Japanese Islands
This hanging scroll painting by Kobayashi Eitaku (1843–1890) depicts a leading theme of
the Shinto sacred writings. Credit: William Sturgis Bigelow Collection. Courtesy, Museum
of Fine Arts, Boston

CHAPTER EIGHT

Shinto

INTRODUCTION

Shinto, the ancient Japanese national religion, is unique among the religious traditions of Asia and the world. Of all major faiths based in historically literate cultures, it has no scripture as modern scholars understand that term. Shinto recognizes no book as officially authoritative; it has no canon; and it has no formalized doctrines or ethical systems that could be shaped by a scripture.

Nevertheless, two books in particular have a special standing in Shinto because of their antiquity and unique contents. They are the *Kojiki,* "Record of Ancient Matters," and the *Nihongi,* "Chronicles of Japan." Both written by imperial decree in the eighth century C.E., these books have held a place of honor in Shinto. Since ancient times, the Japanese have looked on them as the story of the foundation of Japan. For a thousand years schoolchildren were taught their stories as an education in patriotism. These books "are regarded as authoritative and provide [Shinto's] historical as well as its spiritual basis."[1]

Although not classified as scripture, these books give good evidence of the leading ideas of the Shinto tradition. First in importance is the existence of the many **kami,** gods and spirits, whom most Japanese view polytheistically. Second, humanity is the offspring of the *kami* and is continually supported by their power. Third, the Japanese nation, especially the imperial family, is the center of humanity. Fourth, a deep reverence is owed the emperor as the one through whom blessings flow to the nation.

Since the disestablishment of Shinto as the official state religion in 1945, however, the *Kojiki* and *Nihongi* are no longer taught in schools. Moreover, as a part of this disestablishment, the Japanese emperor renounced his divinity, which these books are largely designed to buttress. But much of the old feeling still lingers. For example, both pride and protests erupted in 1991 when the new emperor Akihito spent a night in a specially constructed Shinto shrine, a ritual in older days thought to bring about the emperor's rebirth as a child of the sun god Amaterasu. So, even though the imperial claims they were written to support have been officially renounced, these sacred texts still provide valuable insight into the historical essence of Shinto and its traditional relationship to the Japanese national character.

The *Kojiki,* finished in 712 C.E., is the oldest surviving book in Japan. The only knowledge we have of its origin comes from the preface by its author Yasumaro (given in full in the first reading). This preface records that Emperor Temmu

---

[1] Sokyo Ono, *Shinto, The Kami Way* (Rutland, VT: Charles Tuttle, 1962), p. 10.

(reigned 672–687 C.E.) decreed that the falsified genealogical records, much of them mythological, of the leading Japanese families should be corrected by a new book. In this way the genealogical myths of the competing clans were incorporated into and subsumed by the genealogical myth of Temmu's clan. To do this, the *Kojiki* draws on two main works of the time, the *Teiki*, or *Imperial Sun-Lineage*, and the *Honji*, or *Ancient Dicta of Former Ages*. The first was a source of genealogies, the second a collection of myths, legends, and songs; both were probably oral collections. These two sources, when combined and reworked into the *Kojiki*, shape its characteristic emphasis on a reliable genealogy that goes back to the gods. Besides these changes, scholars discern other revisions to more ancient traditions in the *Kojiki*. For example, it is likely that earlier indigenous Japanese traditions on the complementarity of men and women were adapted to more Confucian ideas of male superiority.

The *Kojiki* itself is divided into three books. The first is a statement of early Japanese mythology which proclaims that the emperor's family, as the "offspring of the heavenly deities," is destined to rule Japan. The second and third books contain stories of the ancient emperors and their exploits, most of them legendary, up to the time of writing. Only a few of these stories have any explicit religious significance.

More fully known as the *Nihonshoki*, or *Chronicles of Japan*, the *Nihongi* was written shortly after the *Kojiki*, in 720 C.E. Shotoku Daishi, its traditional author, compiled the *Nihongi* in thirty books. It narrates a closely related version of the same stories of the *Kojiki*, draws on the same sources, and is written in the same Chinese style. Its special concern is to show that the Teika reforms of 645 C.E., in which Shinto was brought under stricter government regulation, resulted in greater obedience to the way of the *kami*.

SELECTIONS FROM THE *KOJIKI*

Preface to the *Kojiki*

This preface is the author's dedicatory address to Gemmei, niece and daughter-in-law of Emperor Kamu-Yamato [Temmu], who commissioned the work but died before its completion. The preface is a summary of much of the contents of the entire Kojiki. *The narrator tells of the creation of the world, the birth of the early gods, and the creation of Japan. The middle sections deal with various emperors, from the first emperor, Jimmu, to Temmu, although the narrative seems to be speaking of Temmu continually through this section. His decision to sponsor the writing of the* Kojiki *is given special attention. The final sections tell the praises of the Empress and provide the only information we have on the writing of this book. The significance of the* Kojiki *is given in this section: it is "the basis of the country, the grand foundation of the monarchy."*[2]

I, Yasumaro, say:

---

[2]All selections from the *Kojiki* are taken, with editing, from Basil Hall Chamberlain, trans., *Ko-ji-ki, Transactions of the Asiatic Society of Japan*, supplement to vol. 10 (Tokyo: Asiatic Society of Japan, 1906).

When chaos had begun to condense, but force and form were not yet manifest, and nothing was named, nothing done, who could know its shape? Nevertheless Heaven and Earth first parted, and the Three Deities[3] performed the commencement of creation. The Passive and Active Essences[4] then developed, and the Two Spirits[5] became the ancestors of all things. Therefore he entered obscurity and emerged into light, and the Sun and Moon were revealed by the washing of his eyes. He floated on and plunged into the sea-water, and Heavenly and Earthly Deities appeared through the washings of his person. So in the dimness of the great commencement, we, by relying on the original teaching, learn the time of the conception of the earth and of the birth of islands. In the remoteness of the original beginning, we, by trusting the former sages, perceive the era of the genesis of Deities and of the establishment of men. Truly, we know that a mirror was hung up,[6] that jewels were spat out, and that then a Hundred Kings succeeded each other. We know that a blade was bitten, and a serpent cut in pieces, so that a Myriad Deities flourished. By deliberations in the Tranquil River the Empire was pacified; by discussions on the Little Shore the land was purified.

Then His Augustness Ho-no-ni-ni-gi first descended to the Peak of Takachi, and the Heavenly Sovereign Kamu-Yamato traversed the Island of the Dragon-Fly. A weird bear put forth its claws, and a heavenly saber was obtained at Takakura. Men with tails obstructed the path, and a great crow guided him to Yeshinu. Dancing in rows, they destroyed the brigands, and listening to a song they vanquished the foemen. Being instructed in a dream, he was reverent to the Heavenly and Earthly Deities, and was therefore styled the Wise Monarch. Having gazed on the smoke, he was benevolent to the people, and is therefore remembered as the Emperor-Sage.

Determining the frontiers and civilizing the country, he issued laws from the Nearer Afumi; reforming the surnames and selecting the gentile names, he held sway at the Further Asuka. Though each differed in caution and in ardor, though all were unlike in accomplishments and in intrinsic worth, yet they all by contemplating antiquity corrected manners that had fallen to ruin; by illumining recent times, they repaired laws that were approaching dissolution.

In the august reign of the Heavenly Sovereign who governed the Eight Great Islands from the Great Palace of Kiyomihara at Asuka, the Hidden Dragon[7] put on perfection, the Reiterated Thunder came at the appointed moment. Having heard a song in a dream, he felt that he should continue the succession; having reached the water at night, he knew that he should receive the inheritance. Nevertheless Heaven's time was not yet, and he escaped like the cicada to the Southern Mountains.[8]

Then[9] both men and matters were favorable, and he marched like the tiger to the Eastern Land. Suddenly riding in the imperial chariot, he forced his way across mountains and rivers. The Six Divisions rolled like thunder, the Three Hosts sped like lightning. The erect spears lifted up their might, and the bold warriors arose like smoke. The crimson flags glistened among the weapons, and the ill-omened crew were shattered like tiles. Before a day had elapsed, the evil influences were purified. Then the cattle were let loose and the horses given repose, and with shouts of victory they returned to the Flowery

---

[3]*Deities:* the Japanese *kami* is translated "Deities" throughout.

[4]*Passive and Active Essences:* yin and yang, respectively.

[5]*The Two Spirits* from which all creation came are Izanagi (the Male-Who-Invites) and Izanami (the Female-Who-Invites).

[6]*mirror:* in many Shinto shrines, a mirror is often the only visible symbol of the *kami*'s presence.

[7]*the Hidden Dragon:* the emperor as the crown prince.

[8]He renounced ordinary life for a time.

[9]This paragraph tells how the emperor crushed an attempt by a rival to gain the emperor's throne by force.

Summer. The flags were rolled up and the javelins put away, and with dances and chants they came to rest in the capital city.

The year was that of the Rooster, and it was the Second Moon. At the Great Palace of Kiyomihara, he ascended to the Heavenly seat. . . .

Then the Heavenly Sovereign commanded, "I hear that the chronicles of the emperors and likewise the original words in the possession of the various families deviate from exact truth, and are mostly amplified by empty falsehoods. If at the present time these imperfections be not amended, before many years shall have elapsed, the purport of this, the great basis of the country, the grand foundation of the monarchy, will be destroyed. So now I desire to have the chronicles of the emperors selected and recorded, and the old words examined and ascertained, falsehoods erased and truth determined, in order to transmit [the latter] to later ages."

At that time there was a retainer whose surname was Hiyeda and his personal name Are. He was twenty-eight years old, and so intelligent that he could repeat with his mouth whatever met his eyes, and record in his heart whatever struck his ears. Then Are was commanded to learn by heart the genealogies of the emperors, and likewise the words of former ages. Nevertheless time elapsed and the age changed, and the thing was not yet carried out.

Prostrate, I consider how Her Majesty the Empress, having obtained Unity,[10] illumines the empire. Being versed in the Triad,[11] she nourishes the people. Ruling from the Purple Palace, her virtue reaches to the utmost limits of the horses' hoof-marks. Dwelling amid the Somber Retinue, her influence illumines the furthest distance attained to by vessels' prows. The sun rises, and the brightness is increased; the clouds disperse, neither is there smoke. The chroniclers

never cease recording the good omens of connected stalks and double rice-ears. Never for a single moon is the treasury without the tribute of continuous beacon-fires and repeated interpretations. In fame she must be pronounced superior to Bum-Mei, in virtue more eminent than Ten-Itsu.[12]

Regretting the errors in the old words, and wishing to correct the misstatements in the former chronicles, on the eighteenth day of the ninth moon of the fourth year of Wa-do, she commanded me, Yasumaro, to select and record the old words learned by heart by Hiyeda no Are according to the Imperial Decree, and dutifully to lift them up to Her.

In reverent obedience to the contents of the Decree, I have made a careful choice. But in high antiquity both speech and thought were so simple, that it would be difficult to arrange phrases and compose sentences in [Chinese] characters. To relate everything in an ideographic transcription would entail an inadequate expression of the meaning. To write according to the phonetic method would make the story of events unduly lengthy. For this reason have I sometimes in the same sentence used the phonetic and ideographic systems conjointly, and have sometimes in one matter used the ideographic record exclusively. Moreover, where the drift of the words was obscure, I have by comments elucidated their meaning. But need it be said that I have nowhere commented on what was easy? Again, in such cases as calling the surname *Kusaka*, and the personal name written with the character *Tarashi*, I have followed usage without alteration. Altogether the things recorded commence with the separation of Heaven and Earth, and conclude with the august reign at Woharida.[13] . . . Altogether I have written three volumes, which I reverently

---

[10]*obtained Unity:* gotten the throne.
[11]*Triad:* heaven, humanity, and earth.

[12]*Bum-mei, Ten-itsu:* ancient Chinese rulers.
[13]*reign at Wohadira:* of the Empress Suiko, who died in 628 C.E.

and respectfully present. I, Yasumaro, with true trembling and true reverence, bow my head, and bow my head again.

Reverently presented by the Court Noble Futo no Yasumaro, an Officer of the Upper Division of the Fifth Rank and of the Fifth Order of Merit, on the 28th day of the first moon of the fifth year of Wa-do.[14]

_____

[14]March 10, 712 C.E.

The Creation of Japan*

In chapter 1 of the Kojiki, *the spontaneous birth of the first gods is described. Although the narration starts at the "beginning of heaven and earth," the myths of the* Kojiki *(and the* Nihongi *as well) are much more stories of the creation of Japan than full-fledged stories of the creation of the world. The reader notices, for example, no mention of the making of humanity in general or of animals. At*

_____

* Kojiki, Chapters 1–5, 11, 33

the end of chapter 2, the key gods Izanagi (the Male-Who-Invites) and Izanami (the Female-Who-Invites) come into being, and they begin to create islands. Chapters 4 and 5 tell the story of the births of their first children, and we can see a concern for proper male-female relationship here. In chapter 33, the culmination of these myths is reached when the grandson of Amaterasu descends from heaven to rule the land that was to become Japan.

CHAPTER 1 THE BEGINNING OF HEAVEN AND EARTH

The names of the Deities that were born in the Plain of High Heaven when the Heaven and Earth began were the Deity Master-of-the-August-Center-of-Heaven, next the High-August-Producing-Wondrous-Deity, then the Divine-Producing-Wondrous Deity. These three Deities were all Deities born alone, and hid their persons. The names of the Deities that were born next from a thing that sprouted up like a reed-shoot when the earth, young and like floating oil, drifted about medusa-like, were the Pleasant-Reed-Shoot-Prince-Elder-Deity and the Heavenly-Eternally-Standing-Deity. These two Deities were likewise born alone, and hid their persons.

The five Deities in the above list are separate Heavenly Deities.

CHAPTER 2 THE SEVEN DIVINE GENERATIONS

The names of the Deities that were born next were the Earthly-Eternally-Standing-Deity, next the Luxuriant-Integrating-Master-Deity. These two Deities were likewise Deities born alone, and hid their persons. The names of the Deities that were born next were the Deity Mud-Earth-Lord, next his younger sister the Deity Mud-Earth-Lady; next the Germ-Integrating-Deity, next his younger sister the Life-Integrating-Deity; next the Deity Elder-of-the-Great-Place, next his younger sister the Deity Elder-Lady-of-the-Great-Place; next the Deity Perfect-Exterior, next his younger sister the Deity Oh-Awful-Lady; next the Deity the Male-Who-Invites, next his younger sister the Deity the Female-Who-Invites. From the Earthly-Eternally-Standing Deity down to the Deity the Female-Who-Invites in the previous list are what are termed the Seven Divine Generations. (The two solitary Deities above [mentioned] are each called one generation. Of the succeeding ten Deities each pair of deities is called a generation.)

CHAPTER 3 THE ISLAND OF ONOGORO

Then all the Heavenly Deities commanded the two Deities His Augustness the Male-Who-Invites and Her Augustness the Female-Who-Invites, ordering them to "make, consolidate, and give birth to this drifting land." Granting to them a heavenly jewelled spear, they charged them thus. So the two Deities, standing upon the Floating Bridge of Heaven, pushed down the jewelled spear and stirred with it. When they had stirred the brine till it went curdle-curdle, and drew [the spear] up, the brine that dripped down from the end of the spear was piled up and became an island. This is the Island of Onogoro.

CHAPTER 4 COURTSHIP OF THE DEITIES, THE MALE-WHO-INVITES AND THE FEMALE-WHO-INVITES

Having descended from Heaven onto this island, they saw to the erection of an heavenly august pillar, and they saw to the erection of a hall of eight fathoms. Then he asked the Female-Who-Invites, "In what form is your body made?" She responded, saying, "My body is formed with one part not fully formed." Then the Male-Who-Invites said, "My body is formed with one part more than fully formed. Therefore, would it not be good to take that part of my body which is more than fully formed and insert it into that part of your body which is less than fully formed, and procreate the land?" The Female-Who-Invites responded, "That would be good." Then the Male-Who-Invites said, "Let us walk in a circle about this heavenly pillar, meet, and have intercourse." Then she said, "You go around from the right, and I will go around from the left." When they agreed and went around, and the Female-Who-Invites said first, "What a charming and lovable male!" Then the Male-Who-Invites said, "What a charming and lovable female!" When each had finished talking, he said to his wife, "It is not fitting that the woman speak first." But they still began procreating, and she gave birth to a leech-child. This child they placed in a boat of reeds, and let it float away. Next they gave birth to the Island of Aha. He also is not reckoned among their children.

CHAPTER 5 BIRTH OF THE EIGHT ISLANDS

Then the two Deities took counsel, saying: "The children to whom we have now given birth are not good. It will be best to announce this in the august place of the Heavenly Deities." They ascended to Heaven and enquired of Their Augustnesses the Heavenly Deities. Then the Heavenly Deities commanded and found out by grand divination, and ordered them, saying: "They were not good because the woman spoke first. Descend back again and amend your words." So descending back, they again went round the heavenly august pillar as before. Then his Augustness the Male-Who-Invites spoke first: "Ah! What a charming and lovely maiden!" Afterwards his younger sister Her Augustness the Female-Who-Invites spoke: "Ah! What a charming and lovely youth!" When these words were said, they had intercourse as before, and procreated the Island of Ahaji, Ho-no-sa-wake. Next they gave birth to the Island of Futa-na in Iyo. This island has one body and four faces, and each face has a name. So the Land of Iyo is called Lovely Princess; the Land of Sanuki is called Prince Good-Boiled-Rice; the Land of Aha is called the Princess-of-Great-Food; the Land of Tosa is called Brave-Good-Youth. . . .

CHAPTER 33 THE AUGUST DESCENT FROM HEAVEN OF HIS AUGUSTNESS THE AUGUST GRANDCHILD

Then the Heaven-Shining-Great-August-Deity and the High-Integrating-Deity commanded and charged the Heir Apparent His Augustness Truly-Conqueror-I-Conquer-Swift-Heavenly-Great-Great-Ears [saying: "The Brave-Awful-Possessing-Male-Deity] says that he has now finished pacifying the Central Land of Reed-Plains. In accordance with our gracious charge, descend to, dwell in, and rule over it." Then the Heir Apparent His Augustness Truly-Conqueror-I-Conquer-Swift-Heavenly-Great-Ears replied, saying: "While I have been getting ready to descend, there has been born [to me] a child whose name is His Augustness Heaven-Plenty-Earth-Plenty-Heaven's-Sun-Height-Prince-Rice-ear-Ruddy-Plenty. This child should be sent down. [As for this august child, he was augustly joined to Her Augustness Myriad-Looms-Luxuriant-Dragon-fly-Island-Princess, daughter of the High-Integrating-Deity, and begot children: His Augustness-Heavenly Rice-ear-Ruddy, and next His Augustness Prince-Rice-ear-Ruddy-Plenty].

Therefore, in accordance with these words, they laid their command on His Augustness Prince Rice-ear-Ruddy-Plenty, charging him with these words, "This Luxuriant Reed-Plain-Land-of-Fresh-Rice-ears is the land over which you shall rule." So [he replied]: "I will descend from Heaven according to your commands." So when His Augustness Prince Rice-ear-Ruddy-Plenty was about to descend from Heaven, there was at the eight-forking road of Heaven a Deity whose refulgence reached upwards to the Plain of High Heaven and downwards to the Central Land of Reed-Plains. So then the Heaven-Shining-Great-August-Deity and the High-Integrating-Deity commanded and charged the Heavenly-Alarming-Female-Deity [saying]: "Though you are a delicate female, you are a Deity who conquers in facing Deities. So be the one to go and ask thus, 'This being the road by which our august child is about to descend from Heaven, who is it that is there'?" So to this gracious question he replied, saying, "I am an Earthly Deity named the Deity Prince of Saruta. The reason for my coming here is that, having heard of the [intended] descent of the august child of the Heavenly Deities, I have come humbly to meet him and respectfully offer myself as His Augustness's vanguard." Then joining to him His Augustness Heavenly-Beckoning-Ancestor-Lord, His Augustness Grand-Jewel, Her Augustness Heavenly-Alarming-Female, Her Augustness I-shi-ko-ri-do-me, and His Augustness Jewel-Ancestor, in all five chiefs of companies, they sent him down from Heaven. Thereupon they joined to him the eight-feet [long] curved jewels and mirror that had allured [the Heaven-Shining-Great-August-Deity from the Rock-Dwelling], and also the Herb-Quelling-Great-Sword, and likewise the Deity Thought-Includer, the Hand-Strength-Male-Deity, and the Deity Heavenly-Rock-Door-Opener of Eternal Night, and charged him, "Regard this mirror exactly as if it were our august spirit, and reverence it as if reverencing us." Next they said, "Let the Deity Thought-Includer take in hand our affairs, and carry on the government." These two Deities are worshipped at the temple of Isuzu. The next, the Deity of Luxuriant-Food, is the Deity dwelling in the outer temple of Watarahi. The next, the Deity Heavenly-Rock-Door-Opener, another name for whom is the Wondrous-Rock-True-Gate-Deity, and another name for whom is the Luxuriant-Rock-True-Gate-Deity—this Deity of the August Gate. The next, the Deity Hand-Strength-Male, dwells in Sanagata.

Emperor Yuryaku and the Story of the Woman Akawi-ko*

Most of the Kojiki *is made up of legendary stories about the Japanese emperors told to extol their greatness. This bittersweet story of the woman Akawi-ko and the emperor Yuryaku, with the poetic songs that conclude it, is indicative of Japanese literary style. In this chapter, the old woman Akawi-ko comes before Emperor Yuryaku to prove her faithfulness to a command he had given her many years before.*

Once when the Heavenly Sovereign, going out for amusement, reached the River Miwa, there was a girl whose appearance was very beautiful washing clothes by the river-side. The Heavenly Sovereign asked the girl, "Whose child are you?" She replied, "My name is Akawi-ko of the Hiketa Tribe." Then he said to her, "Do not marry a husband. I will send for you," and [with these words] he returned to the palace. Then eighty years passed while she reverently awaited the Heavenly Sovereign's commands. Then Akawi-ko thought: "While looking for the [Imperial] commands, I have already passed many years, and as my face and form are lean and withered, there is no longer any hope. Nevertheless, if I do not show [the Heavenly Sovereign] how truly I have waited, my disappointment will be unbearable." She caused merchandise to be carried on tables holding a hundred items, and came forth and presented [these gifts as] tribute. Then the Heavenly Sovereign, who had quite forgotten what he had formerly commanded, asked Akawi-ko, saying: "What old woman are you, and why have you come here?" Then Akawi-ko replied, saying: "Having in such and such a month of such and such a year received the Heavenly Sovereign's commands, I have been reverently awaiting the great command until this day, and eighty years have past by. Now my appearance is quite decrepit, and there is no longer any hope. Nevertheless I have come forth in order to show and declare my faithfulness." Then the Heavenly Sovereign was greatly startled [and exclaimed], "I had quite forgotten the former circumstance; and you meanwhile, ever faithfully awaiting my commands, have vainly let pass by the years of your prime. This is very pitiful." In his heart he wished to marry her, but shrank from her extreme age, and could not make the marriage; but he conferred on her an august Song. That Song said: . . .

"The younger chestnut orchard plain of Hiketa: would I had slept with her in her youth! Oh! How old she has become!"

Then the tears that Akawi-ko wept drenched the red-dyed sleeve that she had on. In reply to the great august Song, she sang, saying:

"Left over from the piling up of the jewel-wall piled up round the august dwelling,—to whom shall the person of the Deity's temple go?". . .

Then the old woman was sent back plentifully endowed. So these three Songs are Quiet Songs.

Kojiki 154

GLOSSARY

kami [KAH-mee] gods or spirits, and their sacred power.

Kojiki [koh-JEE-kee] the "Record of Ancient Matters."

Nihongi [nih-HAWN-gee] the "Chronicles of Japan."

QUESTIONS FOR STUDY AND DISCUSSION

1. Describe the basic structure of Shinto polytheism as reflected in Shinto mythology.

2. Why, in your view, do the Japanese myths place so much emphasis on the creation of Japan instead of on the creation of the world?

3. Compare the status of the emperor in Confucianism and Shinto.

4. To what degree does the *Kojiki* reflect the traditional interpersonal customs of Japan?

5. How might the Emperor's renunciation of divine standing have altered the reading of these texts and their influence in contemporary Japan?

SUGGESTIONS FOR FURTHER READING

W. G. Aston, *Nihongi: Chronicles of Japan from the Earliest Times to* A.D. *697.* London: Kegan Paul, 1896.

B. H. Chamberlain, *Translation of* Ko-ji-ki. 1st ed., Tokyo: Asiatic Society of Japan, 1906; 2d ed., Kobe: Thompson, 1932. The standard translation of the *Kojiki.*

W. Theodore de Bary, *Sources of Japanese Tradition.* New York: Columbia University Press, 1958. Contains fresh translations of many important Shinto texts and a treatment of how early texts were used in Japanese history.

D. Philippi, *The* Kojiki. Tokyo: Princeton University Press and University of Tokyo Press, 1968. Has full and helpful introduction and notes.

INFOTRAC COLLEGE EDITION

You can locate InfoTrac College Edition articles about this chapter by accessing the InfoTrac College Edition website (http://www.infotrac.collegeedition.com/wadsworth/). Using subject guide, enter the search terms relevant to this chapter, and then read abstracts for relevant articles.

Zoroastrian Ritual
A Zoroastrian priest in India offers a sacrifice with the Avesta at his right hand for ready reference. Credit: Jehangir Gazdar/Woodfin Camp & Associates

CHAPTER NINE

Zoroastrianism

❖ In a house in Bombay, India, a seven-year-old girl is being received into the Zoroastrian religion. A priest stands behind her, guiding her hands as she ties a sacred cord around her waist. She will wear this cord, which serves as a belt, for the rest of her life, except while bathing or sleeping. Five times a day she will ceremonially loosen it, say her prayers, and retie it. This cord has seventy-two threads representing the seventy-two chapters of the chief book of the Zoroastrian scripture, the *Yasna*.

❖ As he sits on the floor in a Zoroastrian temple, a priest offers sacrifice. Before him are spread a variety of consecrated objects, mostly fruits, vegetables and herbs, and a small flame. Usually he recites the scriptural words of sacrifice from memory, but today is one of the seven great yearly festivals of the faith, so a large-print *Avesta* book rests on a small stand to his right. He refers to the book from time to time to read some passages aloud and refresh his memory for the recitation of other passages.

INTRODUCTION

Begun perhaps as long as three thousand years ago in ancient Iran by its prophet Zarathushtra, Zoroastrianism was the state religion of the ancient Sassanid Empire. Today its numbers are severely reduced, with no more than 200,000 adherents in the world, clustered now in eastern Iran and near Bombay, India, and a few thousand adherents in North America. The scriptures of Zoroastrianism combine its strong message of living a moral life with concerns for ritual purity in worship and in daily life. Because of their obscure ancient language, troubled history of transmission, and fragmentary character, these scriptures are often difficult to translate and understand. But the main beliefs of Zoroastrianism come through these writings as well today as perhaps as at any time in the three millennia of this religion, and Zoroastrians are as concerned as ever about how the message of their writings is embodied in daily life.

Overview of Structure

The *Avesta* [ah-VES-tuh] has four major divisions, each with a ritual content and orientation. The first and most important is the *Yasna* [YAHZ-nuh], "Sacrifice," composed of hymns for worship in seventy-two chapters. The *Visparad* [VEE-spuh-rahd], "All the [divine] Lords," has hymns in twenty chapters. The *Yashts* [yahshts] are twenty-one "Hymns" to as many divinities. The *Vendidad* [VEN-dih-dahd] of twenty-two chapters is "The Law against Demons." Minor texts include the *Nyay-ishn,* "Litanies" or short prayers to the gods of nature and to angels; *Gahs,* hymns to the spirits of the five periods of the day; two *Sirozahs,* each with thirty paragraphs that invoke the deities of each day of the month; and *Afrigans,* four "Blessings." We now will examine the four major divisions more closely.

The earliest and most important part of the *Yasna* is the collection of seventeen hymns called the **Gathas** [GAH-tuhs]. They now stand in five sections in the *Yasna* as chapters 28–34, 43–51, and 53. Although orthodox Zoroastrians believe the whole of the *Avesta* to be the work of Zarathushtra, they hold these *Gathas* especially as his. Modern scholarship agrees, using the *Gathas* as the primary source for our knowledge of Zarathushtra. Written in an earlier type of Avestan language, the *Gathas* are distinguished from the other hymns of the *Yasna* by their emphasis on ethical dualism and lack of attention to ritual concerns. One main topic of the *Yasna* is the *haoma* ritual, by which the juices of the *haoma* plant are ground out and mixed with milk and herbs (chapters 9–11, 22–27). Other topics include prayer (19–21), a confession of faith (12), and sacrifices to water (45–48). All seventy-two chapters are recited daily by priests (from memory!) during Zoroastrianism's main sacrificial ceremony, the sacrifice of the *haoma* before the fire. This sacrifice is called the Yasna, from which this collection of scripture gets its name.

The *Visparad* is about one-sixth as long as the *Yasna*. It contains poetic invocations, praises, and sacrifices to all the divine lords of Zoroastrianism. Because its words are recited in different parts of the Yasna ceremony, when it is separated into its own collection it seems disjointed. Zoroastrians also recite the *Visparad* during their six holy days of obligation, especially New Year's Day.

The *Yashts* are hymns of praise to twenty-one divinities, angels, and human heroes of ancient Iran. Among the most important are hymns to Mithra, who was to become a god in his own religion of Mithraism (chapter 10), and a hymn to the guardian spirits (Fravashis) of the old saints (13). Much of the material in the *Yashts* is drawn from pre-Zoroastrian religion and provides an interesting glimpse on how later Zoroastrianism (after the prophet himself, who according to the *Gathas* made a clean break with older religion) adapted these older Indo-European religious ideas to its own usage.

The *Vendidad* begins with two myths about the creation and a primeval flood that tell how the divine law came to humans. The remaining sixteen chapters form a law code that prescribes purifications and penalties for priests. Chapters 3 and 5, for example, contain regulations for funerals; chapter 18 deals with the difference between the true and false priest. Like the *Yashts,* the *Vendidad* is inserted into the *Yasna* for ritual reasons.

The meaning of the word *avesta* is uncertain. Usually translated as "injunction, command," it has also been translated as "wisdom, knowledge," as "authoritative utterance," and as "scripture." It probably derives from the Middle Persian word *avastaq,* "law." The "injunction" is that of the god Ahura Mazda through the prophet Zarathushtra. This name is broad enough to encompass all the commands of Zoroastrianism: to serve good and turn from evil; to be both morally and ceremonially pure; and to worship Ahura Mazda and the good spirits by sacrifice and praise.

Origin and Development

The *Avesta* begins with Zarathushtra himself. Though a date for the prophet in the sixth century B.C.E. is still held by most scholars, some (especially Mary Boyce) would push Zarathushtra back to 1400–1000 B.C.E. The oral tradition that was later written down into the *Gathas* as we know them can be traced more or less to Zarathushtra for reasons both of style and content.

Next to arise over probably a millennium were the other poetic sections of the *Avesta*, which scholars today call the "Younger *Avesta*." The rest of the *Yasna* and the *Yashts* are in metrical poetry. Last to be written were the prose portions of the *Avesta*. The whole process was complete, and the canon of the *Avesta* fixed, at about 325 C.E.

In its original form, the *Avesta* was probably about four times larger than it is now. Besides the liturgical texts now in the *Avesta*, it probably treated cosmogony, eschatology, astronomy, natural history, the history of Zarathushtra, and several other topics. The *Zand* contains many references to a large loss of Zoroastrian scripture during the invasions of Alexander the Great (fourth century B.C.E.). What remained from these persecutions was material that was fixed in the memory of the priests, liturgical scripture. A collection was made under the Sassanian dynasty of Iran in the third and fourth centuries C.E. The *Avesta* as we know it comes from this period and was probably first written down at this time. Zoroastrianism was now the state religion of the Sassanid Empire, and a written text may have been viewed as promoting uniformity in religious doctrine and practice.

Islam then pressed hard on the religion of Ahura Mazda. Although it officially tolerated Zoroastrianism as a monotheistic religion, Islam also sought to end the faith by suppressing its temples and burning its scripture books. Some Zoroastrians fled Muslim intolerance for a more congenial life around Bombay in India. During this period the *Avesta* was reduced to its present size, preserved by the small Zoroastrian community left to continue to this day. The oldest manuscript that has survived dates to 1323 C.E.; the entire Avestan collection was printed only in the nineteenth century.

Use

As one can infer from the names of the Avestan books, they are strongly oriented to worship and sacrifice. The scriptures are the hymn texts for sacrifice, and sacrifice is done to the constant accompaniment of scripture recitation, usually by memory. Scripture usage throughout Zoroastrian history has therefore been almost exclusively performative. Scripture is used for the enactment of ritual, not for study, meditation, or the formation and teaching of doctrine. The Avestan language used in formal worship and in the traditional main prayers of the faithful is largely unknown to priest and layperson alike. Thus, Zoroastrians typically have had little knowledge of what their scriptures actually "teach." For example, a nineteenth-century British missionary to Bombay, John Wilson, was able to confuse and embarrass a high-ranking Zoroastrian priest in a public debate when he made it apparent that the priest did not know the contents of the *Avesta* and was not able to defend them.

At the end of nineteenth century, a movement of reform sought to change this age-old usage of the *Avesta*. Under the influence of Western religion and European methods of religious scholarship, reformers claimed that the *Gathas* are the center and only authentic part of the *Avesta*. Everything else is to be judged by its leading ideas. Rituals were regarded as secondary to moral teachings and were interpreted symbolically, altered, or sometimes disregarded altogether. The rational, philosophical, and moral elements of the faith were given priority. This shift from a performative to a cognitive usage among a minority of Zoroastrians in India and North America is the source of one of the chief internal disagreements in Zoroastrianism.

HISTORY

The Call of Zarathushtra*

This gatha is a conversation between four main characters: (1) the collective soul of the cattle, which represents the means of livelihood for the people of the Zoroastrian faith; (2) Asha, or "Righteousness," one of the immortals; (3) Ahura Mazda, the Lord and Creator; and (4) Zarathushtra. It closes with Zarathushtra's prayer for divine aid. This passage is used by worshippers as a prayer for divine help to destroy the powers of deceit and to promote peace and truth.[1]

The Soul of the Cattle and the people cried aloud to you, O Ahura and Asha, "For whom did you create me, and by whom did you fashion me? The assaults of wrath and violent power come upon me, with desolating blows, audacious insolence, and thieving might. I have no other pasture-giver than you. Teach me good cultivation of the fields, which is my only hope of blessing!"

Then the Creator of the Cattle asked Righteousness: "How did you appoint a guardian for the cattle when you made her? How did you secure for her both pasture and a Cattle-chief who was skilled and energetic? Did you select as her master one who might hurl back the fury of the wicked?"

The Divine Righteousness answered in his holiness, "We were very perplexed. We could not obtain a leader who was capable of striking back their fury, and who himself was without hate. We cannot know the influences which approach and move the heavenly fires, fires which reveal the favor and the will of God. God is the mightiest of beings. Those who have performed their actions approach him with invocations. He has no need to ask!"

Zarathushtra said, "The Great Creator is most mindful of the commands that have been fulfilled in the deeds of demon-gods and good or evil men. He knows the commands that they will fulfill. Ahura is the discerning judge. It shall be to us as he desires! [5] Therefore we both, my soul and the soul of the mother Cattle, are making our requests for the two worlds[2] to Ahura. With hands stretched out in entreaty, we pray to the Great Creator with questions in our doubt. He will answer. Destruction will not come to the one who lives righteously, or to the careful farmers of the earth!"

---

* *Yasna* 29
[1] Except where noted, all passages from Zoroastrian scripture are taken, with editing, from J. Darmesteter and L. H. Mills, trans., *The Zend-Avesta*, vols. 4, 23, 31, *Sacred Books of the East* (Oxford: Oxford University Press, 1880–1887).

[2] *the two worlds:* this present world and the world to come at the end of time.

Then the Lord, the Great Creator who understands the mysterious grace by his insight, spoke. "A spiritual master is not found for us in this way. Nor can we find in this way a leader moved by Righteousness and appointed by its spirit. Therefore I have named you as the leader of the diligent tillers of the ground!"

The Amesha-Spentas[3] said, "Mazda has created the inspired Word of reason that is a Mathra[4] of fatness for the offering. The Divine Righteousness consented to Mazda's deed. He has prepared food for the cattle and food for the eaters. He is bountiful with his saving doctrine. But who is endowed with the Good Mind, who can give those teachings by word of mouth to mortals?"

Ahura said, "I have found this man, Zarathushtra Spitama, who alone has listened to our words! He desires to announce our mighty and completed acts of grace, for me the Great Creator, and for Righteousness. Therefore I will give him the good dwelling and the authoritative position of one who speaks for us!"

Then the Soul of the Cattle lamented, "Woe is me, for I have obtained a lord who is powerless to carry out his wish! He is only the voice of a feeble and timid man. I desire one who is lord over his will, one who is able like a king to carry out what he desires." The Amesha-Spentas said, "Yes, when shall one who brings strong help to her[5] ever appear?"

[10] Zarathushtra said, "O Ahura, O Righteousness, grant gladness to these our disciples. Grant them the sovereign kingdom of the Deity, which is established in his Good Mind. This kingdom gives them the peaceful amenities of home and quiet happiness, instead of the terrible ravages that they suffer. O Great Creator, I have always thought You to be the first possessor of these blessings! O Great Creator and Living Lord, when shall the Divine Righteousness, the Good Mind of the Lord, and his Sovereign Power hurry to me? When will they give me strength for my task and my mission? Without this I cannot advance or even undertake my work. Give us your aid in abundance for our great cause. May we partake in the bountiful grace of your equals, your counselors and servants!"

---

[3] *Amesha-Spentas:* "immortal holy ones," seen sometimes as aspects of God's being, or other times as beings in their own right.
[4] *Mathra:* a special sacrificial formula; cf. Sanskrit *mantra*.

[5] *her:* the (female) Soul of the Cattle.

A Hymn of Praise to Zarathushtra*

With this hymn Zoroastrians venerate the memory of Zarathushtra. Note the recurring use of "who/he first." The end of this selection recounts a legend of the cosmic praise offered to the baby Zarathushtra.

We worship the piety and the *Fravashi*[6] of the holy Zarathushtra. He was the first who thought

what is good, the first who spoke what is good, the first who did what is good. He was the first Priest, the first Warrior, the first Plower of the ground. He first knew and first taught. He first possessed and first took possession of the Bull, of Holiness, of the Word, the obedience to the Word, the dominion, and all the good things made by Mazda, the good things that are the offspring of the good Principle.

He was the first Priest, the first Warrior, the first Plower of the ground. He first took the

---

* *Yasht* 24: 87b–94
[6] *Fravashi:* guardian spirit.

turning of the wheel[7] from the hands of the Daeva[8] and the cold-hearted man. He was first in the material world to pronounce the praise of Asha, thus bringing the Daevas to nothing. He confessed himself a worshipper of Mazda, a follower of Zarathushtra. He is one who hates the Daevas, and obeys the laws of Ahura.

[90] He was first in the material world to say the word that destroys the Daevas, the law of Ahura. He was first in the material world to proclaim the words that destroy the Daevas, the law of Ahura. He was the first in the material world to declare all the creation of the Daevas unworthy of sacrifice and prayer. He was strong, giving all the good things of life, and he was the first bearer of the law among the nations.

In him was heard the whole Mathra, the word of holiness. He was the lord and master of the world. He was the praiser of Asha who is the most great, most good and most fair. He had a revelation of the Law, that most excellent of all beings.

For him the Amesha-Spentas longed, in one accord with the sun, in the fullness of the faith of a devoted heart. They longed for him as the lord and master of the world, as the praiser of the most great, most good and most fair Asha. He had a revelation of the Law, that most excellent of all beings.

In his birth and growth the waters and the plants rejoiced. In his birth and growth the waters and the plants grew. In his birth and growth all the creatures of the good creations cried out, "Hail! Hail to us! For he is born, the Athravan,[9] Spitama Zarathushtra. Zarathushtra will offer us sacrifices with drink offerings and bundles of baresma.[10] The good Law of the worshippers of Mazda will come, and it will spread through all the seven Karshvares[11] of the earth."

---

[7] *turning of the wheel:* the life of the created world.
[8] *Daeva:* evil spirit.

[9] *Athravan:* priest.
[10] *baresma:* sandalwood twigs, present at every sacrifice.
[11] *Karshvares:* divisions.

TEACHING

Hymn to Ahura and the Purifying Fire*

This hymn to Ahura Mazda and to the spirit of the fire is set in the fire temple. Note the emphasis on morality in thought, word, and deed. Today the fire is still a symbol of moral purity and the center of every Zoroastrian temple.

[1] We would approach you . . . in the house of this your holy Fire, O Ahura Mazda, most bounteous Spirit! If anyone brings pollutions to this flame, you will cover him with pollutions. O most friendly one, O Fire of the Lord, give us

zeal! Come to us with the loving blessing of one who is most friendly, with the praise of the one most adored. Yes, come to us and aid us in this great task!

You truly are the Fire of Ahura Mazda. Yes, you are the most bounteous one of his Spirit. Therefore yours is the most potent of all names for grace, O Fire of the Lord! Therefore we come to you, O Ahura, with the help of your Good Mind that you implant in us. We come to you with your good Righteousness, and with actions and words implanted by your good wisdom!

[5] We bow before you, and we direct our prayers to you with confessions of our guilt, O

---

* *Yasna 36*

Ahura Mazda! With all the good thoughts that you inspire, with all the words well said, and the deeds well done, with these we come to you. To your most beautiful body we make our deep acknowledgments, O Ahura Mazda. We acknowledge those stars that are your body, and we acknowledge that one star, the highest of the high, as the sun was called!

Hymn to Ahura Mazda the Creator*

This selection is a beautiful expression of faith and devotion to Ahura Mazda the Creator, and the spirits associated with him.

We worship Ahura Mazda, who made the Cattle, Righteousness, the waters, the wholesome plants, the stars, the earth, and all existing things that are good. Yes, we worship him for his Sovereign Power and his greatness. They are full of blessing, and have priority among the Yazads who abide beside the Cattle in protection and support.

We worship him under his name as Lord, Mazda dear, the most gracious of names. We worship him with our bones and with our flesh. We worship the **Fravashis** [guardian spirits] of the saints, of holy men and holy women. We worship Righteousness the Best, the most beautiful, the Bountiful Immortal, who is endowed with light in all things good.

[5] We worship the Good Mind of the Lord, and his Sovereign Power, and the Good Faith, the good law, and Piety the ready mind within your people!

---

* *Yasna 37:1–5*

The Doctrine of Dualism**

This gatha instructs the believer in the basic teachings of Zarathushtra on good and evil. It speaks of the ancient character of good and evil, their role in creation of the world, their present struggle for domination, and their destiny at the end of history. The believer must constantly choose the good and thereby build up its power in the universe. Note the nonritual character of righteousness.

[1] You who are drawing near and want to be taught, now I will proclaim to you my observations about him who knows all things. I will proclaim the praises of Ahura, the sacrifices that spring from the Good Mind, and the blessed meditations inspired by Righteousness. I pray that favorable results may be seen in the lights. Hear then with your ears; see the bright flames with the eyes of the Better Mind. It is a decision about religions, man and man, each individual himself. Before taking up this cause, awake to our teaching!

The primeval spirits as a pair combined their opposite strivings, and yet each is independent in his action. They have long been famous. One is better, the other worse, in thought, in word, and in deed. Let those who act wisely choose correctly between these two. Do not choose as evil-doers choose!

When the two spirits came together at first, they made life and life's absence. They decided how the world shall be ordered at its end. The wicked receive Hell, the worst life; the holy receive Heaven, the Best Mental State. [5] He

---

** *Yasna 30*

who was the evil one chose the evil realm, working the worst possible results. But the more gracious spirit chose the Divine Righteousness. Yes, he who clothes himself with the firm stones of heaven as his robe made this choice. He also chose those who make Ahura happy by their actions, actions performed in accordance with the faith.

The Demon-gods and those who worship them can make no righteous choice between these two spirits, since they have been deceived. As they were questioning and debating in their council, the Worst Mind approached them that he might be chosen. They made their fatal decision. Then they rushed to the Demon of Fury, that they might pollute the lives of mortals.

Then Aramaiti, the personified Piety of the saints, approached. The Sovereign Power, the Good Mind, and the Righteous Order came with her. Aramaiti gave a body to the spiritual creations of good and of evil; she is the abiding and ever-strenuous one. O Mazda, let that body for your people be at the end like it was when you first created it! At the end the great struggle shall be fought out which began when the Daevas first seized the Demon of Wrath as their ally, and then just vengeance shall come upon these wretches.

Then, O Mazda, the Kingdom shall be gained for you by your Good Mind within your people. O living Lord, the Good Mind speaks his command to those who will deliver the Demon of the Lie into the two hands of the Righteous Order, like a captive is delivered to a destroyer.

May we be like those who bring on this great renovation. May we make this world progressive, until its perfection is reached. May we be like the Ahuras of Mazda. Yes, may we be like you, in helpful readiness to meet your people, presenting benefits in union with the Righteous Order. Our thoughts will be where true wisdom shall live in her home.

[10] When perfection will be attained, then the blow of destruction shall fall upon the Demon of Falsehood, and her adherents shall perish with her. But the righteous saints, who walk on earth in good reputation and in honor, will gather swiftly in the happy home of the Good Mind and of Ahura.

Therefore, O mortals, you are learning these religious commands that Ahura gave in our happiness and our sorrow. You are also learning the long punishment of the wicked, and the blessings that are in store for the righteous. When these begin their course, salvation will be yours!

WORSHIP AND RITUAL

The Place of the *Gathas**

This passage, which stands at the end of the Gathas, *serves to show their high place in the Zoroastrian faith.*

As our offering to the bountiful *Gathas* that rule as the leading chants within the appointed times and seasons of our ritual, we present all our

riches of land, and our persons, together with our very bones and tissues. We present our forms and forces, our consciousness, our soul, and Fravashi.

The *Gathas* are our guardians and defenders, and our spiritual food. Yes, they are both food and clothing to our souls. These *Gathas* are guardians and defenders and spiritual food, both food and clothing to our souls. May they be an offering for us. May they give abundant re-

---

* Yasna 55:1–3

wards . . . for the world beyond the present world, after the parting of our consciousness and body. May these Praises of the Offering come forth, and appear for us with power and victory, with health and healing, with progress, with growth, with preparation and protection, and with blessing and holiness. May they abound with gifts for those who can understand. Let them appear with free generosity to the enlightened; let them appear as Mazda, the most beneficial, has produced them. He is the one who is victorious when he strikes. He helps our settlements advance, he protects and guards the religious order of the settlements which are even now being furthered. He guards those who will bring salvation to us, and protects the entire creation of holy and clean things.

The Zoroastrian Confession*

This stately creed of Zoroastrianism is called the Faravane. *Recited daily by every faithful worshipper of Mazda, it outlines an important Zoroastrian doctrine, the dualism of good and evil as cosmic forces. Believers pledge themselves to Mazda and the good, and reject the Daevas [evil spirits] in the universe and their lives.*

[1] I drive the Daevas away. I confess myself a Mazda-worshipper of the order of Zarathushtra. I renounce the Daevas and devote myself to the lore of the Lord. I am a praiser of the Bountiful Immortals. I attribute all things good to Ahura Mazda, the Holy and Resplendent One. To Him belong all things good: the Cattle, Asha, and the stars, in whose lights the glorious beings and objects are clothed. I choose Piety, the generous and the good. I loudly condemn all robbery and violence against the sacred Cattle, and all drought that wastes the Mazdayasnian villages. I put away the thought of wandering at will, of pitching my tent freely like a nomad. I wish to remove all wandering from the Cattle which abide steadfastly on this land. Bowing down in worship to Righteousness, I dedicate my offerings with praise. May I never be a source of decline, may I never be a source of withering to the Mazdayasnian villages, not for the love of body or life.

I renounce the shelter and headship of the Daevas, evil as they are. They are utterly empty of good and void of Virtue. They are deceitful in their wickedness. Of all beings they are most like the Demon of the Lie, the most loathsome of existing things. They are completely empty of good.

[5] I renounce and renounce again the Daevas and all possessed by them, the sorcerers and all who use their methods, and every being of the sort. I renounce their thoughts, their words and actions, and the seed that propagates their sin. I renounce their shelter and their headship. I renounce sinners of every kind who act as Rakhshas[12] act!

Thus indeed might Ahura Mazda have shown to Zarathushtra, answering every question which Zarathushtra asked, in all the consultations in which they conversed together. Thus might Zarathushtra have renounced the shelter and the headship of the Daevas in all the questions, and in all the consultations with which Zarathushtra and the Lord conversed together. And so I myself, in whatever circumstances I may be placed, as a worshipper of Mazda and of Zarathushtra's order, so renounce the Daevas and their shelter. The holy

---

* *Yasna* 12

[12] *Rakhshas:* demons.

Zarathushtra renounced them the same way in old times.

I belong to that religious holiness to which the waters belong, to that holiness to which the plants, to that holiness to which the Cattle of blessed gift, to that religious holiness to which Ahura Mazda, who made both cattle and holy men, belongs. To that holiness I belong. I am of the creed which Zarathushtra held, which Kavi Vistaspa, and those two, Frashaostra and Gamaspa, held.[13] Yes, I am of that religious faith as every **Saoshyant** [future savior] who shall yet come to see us, the holy ones who do truly sig-

nificant things. Of that creed, and of that tradition, am I.

I am a Mazda-worshipper of Zarathushtra's order. So I confess, as a praiser and confessor. I praise aloud the thing well thought, the word well spoken, and the deed well done. Yes, I praise at once the Faith of Mazda, the Faith that has no saying that fails, the Faith that wields the deadly halberd,[14] the Faith of kindred marriage.[15] I praise the holy Creed, which is the most imposing, best, and most beautiful of all religions which exist, and of all that in the future shall come to knowledge. I praise Ahura's Faith, the Zarathushtrian creed. I ascribe all good to Ahura Mazda, and such shall be the worship of the Mazdayasnian belief!

---

[13]King *Kavi Vistaspa* was Zarathushtra's royal patron and protector. *Frashaostra* was an early follower of Zarathushtra, whose daughter Hvovi was Zarathushtra's third wife. *Gamaspa* was the chief counselor of King Vishtaspa and a friend of the new faith.

---

[14]*halberd:* battle axe.
[15]*kindred marriage:* refers to the Zoroastrian practice of marrying distant relatives.

The Four Great Prayers*

These four prayers are the most important in Zoroastrian worship. They are named after their first words.[16]

A. *Ahuna vairyo*

As is the Master, so is the Judge to be chosen in accord with truth. Establish the power of acts arising from a life lived with good purpose, for Mazda and for the lord whom they made pastor for the poor.

B. *Airyema ishyo*

May longed-for Airyaman come to the support of the men and women of Zarathushtra, to the support of our good purpose. The Inner Self earns the reward to be chosen. I ask for it the longed-for recompense of truth, which the Lord Mazda has in mind.

C. *Ashem vohu*

Asha is good, it is best. According to wish it is, according to wish it shall be for us. Asha belongs to Asha Vahishta.

D. *Yenhe hatam*

Those Beings, male and female, whom Lord Mazda knows the best for true worship, we worship them all.

---

*From the *Yasna*
[16]This prayer, and the *Ashem vohu*, are taken from M. Boyce, *A History of Zoroastrianism*, 2 vols. (Leiden: Brill, 1975, 1982).

Disposal of the Dead*

This passage describes the Zoroastrian "towers of silence," in which the dead are exposed to birds of prey so that their ritually defiling bodies may not pollute the sacred earth. First, provision is made for the on-ground exposure of the dead in places where "towers of silence" cannot be built.

"O Maker of the material world, you Holy One! Where shall we bring the bodies of the dead, where shall we lay their bodies, O Ahura Mazda?"

[45] Ahura Mazda answered, "On the highest summits, where you know there are always corpse-eating dogs and corpse-eating birds, O holy Zarathushtra! There the worshippers of Mazda shall secure the corpse by the feet and by the hair. They shall secure it with brass, stones, or lead, lest the corpse-eating dogs and the corpse-eating birds go and carry the bones to the water and to the trees."

"If they shall not secure the corpse, so that the corpse-eating dogs and the corpse-eating birds carry the bones to the water and to the trees, what is the penalty that they shall pay?"

Ahura Mazda answered: "They shall be Peshotanus.[17] They shall receive two hundred stripes with the Aspahe-astra, two hundred stripes with the Sraoshokarana."[18]

"O Maker of the material world, you Holy One! Where shall we bring the bones of the dead, where shall we lay them, O Ahura Mazda?"

[50] Ahura Mazda answered: "The worshippers of Mazda shall build a building out of the reach of the dog, of the fox, and of the wolf, and in which rain water cannot stay. Such a building shall they build, if they can afford it, with stones, mortar, and earth. If they cannot afford it, they shall lay the dead man on the ground, on his carpet and his pillow, clothed with the light of heaven,[19] and beholding the sun."

---

* *Vendidad, Fargard* 6, section 5, 44–51

---

[17] *Peshotanus:* ones subject to punishment.

[18] The same type of whip is probably meant here, so that the total number of lashes would be two hundred.

[19] *Clothed with the light of heaven:* naked. Exposed to the birds of prey, the body will undergo the same ritual disposal as corpses put in towers of silence.

GLOSSARY

Avesta [ah-VES-tuh] the name of the Zoroastrian scriptures.

Fravashis [frah-VAH-shees] guardian spirits.

Gathas [GAH-tuhs] the collection of seventeen hymns in the *Yasna*.

Saoshyant [sa-OSH-yant] a future savior who will help purify the world.

Vendidad [VEN-dih-dahd] The *Law against Demons*, a division of the *Avesta*.

Visparad [VEE-spuh-rahd] "All the [Divine] Lords," a twenty-chapter collection of hymns in the *Avesta*.

Yashts [yahshts] "Hymns," twenty-one in number, a division of the *Avesta*.

Yasna [YAHZ-nuh] "Sacrifice," or hymns for worship; the first and foremost division of the *Avesta*.

QUESTIONS FOR STUDY AND DISCUSSION

1. What, to judge from the *Gathas,* were the main religious ideas of the prophet Zarathushtra?

2. What sort of changes occurred in Zoroastrian religion after the passing of Zarathushtra? For your answer, compare the *Gathas* with the rest of the *Avesta.*

3. Explain how Zarathushtra is worshipped by way of these scriptures.

4. How do the striking funeral and cleanliness rituals reproduced here testify to the strong connection made in Zoroastrianism between ritual and moral purity?

SUGGESTIONS FOR FURTHER READING

Primary Sources

M. Boyce, *Textual Sources for the Study of Zoroastrianism.* Chicago: University of Chicago Press, 1990. A full selection of texts, with introductions but few annotations.

J. Darmesteter and L. H. Mills, *The Zend-Avesta.* In F. Max Müller, ed., *Sacred Books of the East,* vols. 4, 23, and 31. Oxford: Oxford University Press, 1880–87. Its Victorian English often interferes, but this is the only relatively complete translation of the *Avesta* in English.

J. Insler, *The Gathas of Zarathushtra.* Leiden: Brill, 1975. Contains the Avestan text, English translation and notes, and excellent commentary.

Secondary Sources

J. Barr, "The Question of Religious Influence: The Case of Zoroastrianism, Judaism, and Christianity." *Journal of the American Academy of Religion,* 53 (1985): 201–235. A reexamination of the notion, commonly accepted in religious scholarship, that Zoroastrian teachings had a great influence on Judaism and through it on Christianity.

M. Boyce, *A History of Zoroastrianism,* 2 vols. Leiden: Brill, 1975, 1982. The standard history of Zoroastrianism, with comprehensive treatment of the *Avesta* as the main source of our knowledge of early Zoroastrianism.

M. Boyce, *A Persian Stronghold of Zoroastrianism.* Oxford: Oxford University Press, 1977. Though no explicit and extended treatment of scripture is included here, this firsthand report on the life of Iranian Zoroastrians will shed much light on present-day use of the *Avesta.*

J. W. Boyd, "Zoroastrianism: Avestan Scripture and Rite." In F. M. Denny and R. L. Taylor, eds., *The Holy Book in Comparative Perspective.* Charleston: University of South Carolina Press, 1985, pp. 109–125. An excellent discussion of orthodox versus reformist reception and use of the *Avesta.*

INFOTRAC COLLEGE EDITION

You can locate InfoTrac College Edition articles about this chapter by accessing the InfoTrac College Edition website (http://www.infotrac.collegeedition.com/wadsworth/). Using subject guide, enter the search terms relevant to this chapter, and then read abstracts for relevant articles.

Reading the Bible in a Bat Mitzvah
Emily Kopley, using a silver pointer, reads in Hebrew from the Torah scroll in Congregation Brit Shalom synagogue, State College, Pennsylvania. After this high point of her bat mitzvah, she will be pelted with candy by the congregation in a custom found in several different kinds of Judaism. Credit: Amy Golahny.

CHAPTER TEN

Judaism

❖ In New York City, detective Mordacai Dzinkansky sets up a "sting" operation with unsuspecting criminals who are selling *Torah* scrolls. These scrolls, many of which are worth more than $50,000 each, have been stolen from synagogues. A member of the N.Y.P.D. Torah Task force and a Hebrew-speaking Orthodox Jew, Dzinkansky is remarkably effective at winning the confidence of criminals, bringing them to justice, and recovering the stolen Torahs for return to their rightful owners.

❖ Jewish demonstrators surround the parliament building in Jerusalem as its members debate trading land for peace with the Palestinians. Several of the signs carry references to "Eretz Israel," the land of Israel promised by God to Abraham in *Genesis* 15:18–21. Some Israeli rabbis have threatened to excommunicate any soldiers who participate in transferring any part of this land to Palestinian control. This insistence on keeping Eretz Israel complicates the fledgling peace process.

❖ In New York City's Madison Square Garden, a sellout crowd of Orthodox Jews gathers to celebrate *Talmud* scholarship. By prayers, readings, song and dance, they honor a group of men who have completed their study of the *Talmud*, reading and studying a page a day for nearly seven and a half years. Many observers of the Jewish religious scene see this as evidence of an upswing of rigorously traditional Judaism in America.

INTRODUCTION

Judaism is founded on a belief in one personal God who has revealed himself in the early history of the Jewish people, calling them to serve God and spread divine love and justice in the world. The influence of the Jewish scriptures stems directly from a rigorous adherence over more than 2,500 years in ways these sketches can only suggest. The Jewish **Bible** is the foundation of both the Christian and Islamic scriptures as well, and thus its teachings have carried over into the life of the world's two largest religions. Even though some of the importance of the Jewish scriptures has been lost in the modern secularized world, its deep influence on everyday life and patterns of Western thought and culture has abated only a little. Our seven-day week with its day of rest is an inheritance from Jewish scripture; the belief that there is only one God is a gift of these writings as well. That the human race is one family, and that each individual can fully realize the meaning of life regardless of social or economic class, have also come to the Western world from the Jewish scriptures.

Names

Before we treat the structure of the Jewish scriptures, we should deal with its names. The most particularly Jewish name for their scripture is **Tanakh,** an acronym formed from the first letters of the three sections of the scriptures: **Torah** [TOH-rah], "Teaching" or "Law," **Nevi'im** [NEH-vih-eem], "Prophets," and **Kethuvim** [KETH-u-veem], "Writings." This name arose in the Middle Ages and is widely known among European and American Jews. *Tanakh* is not widely known among non-Jews, however, nor is it the most typical academic name for the Jewish scriptures.

Another appellation is the "Hebrew scriptures." "Hebrew" here refers to the language of the Jewish *Bible,* which is Hebrew except for one verse each in the books of *Genesis* and *Jeremiah* and several chapters in *Ezra* and *Daniel.* These are in Aramaic, a language closely related to Hebrew. Christians and Jews accept this name as both descriptively accurate and nonprejudicial. Its wide acceptance is indicated by its use in the *New Revised Standard Version* of the (Christian) *Bible.*

Many people call the Jewish scripture the *Old Testament,* which is its Christian name. (The latter part of the Christian *Bible* is called the *New Testament.*) Because of the predominance of Christianity over Judaism in the West, this name has been traditional even in journalistic and academic circles. (When a prominent university in Pennsylvania renamed its *Old Testament* course "Hebrew Scriptures," enrollment fell off sharply because most students did not understand the new title.) But Jews rightly see the term *Old Testament* and the more kindly "First Testament" as derogatory, and students of religion now avoid it as partisan and inappropriate.

The most common name for the Jewish scriptures, the simple term *Bible* is probably its oldest. This word has its roots in the Hebrew term *Ha-Sefarim,* "The Books" (*Daniel* 9:2), which Greek-speaking Jews by the second century B.C.E. translated as *ta biblia.* The term passed into the Greek New Testament and then through Latin to give us the English word *Bible.* This name stresses the written, textual nature of the Jewish **revelation.** (When Jews refer to the *Bible,* they mean of course *their* scripture, not at all including the Christian *New Testament.*) In sum, though there is and was no single name for the Jewish scripture common to all Jews of yesterday or today, *Bible* is probably the most ancient and the most common, and we will use it here.

Overview of Structure

Reduced to its most basic form, the overall structure of the Jewish *Bible* may be summarized as follows. (The dates provide a timeline for the events narrated in the books but are not to be taken as dates of the writing of the books themselves.) In the first book of the *Torah, Genesis,* God created the world good, but humanity fell into sin and rebellion. After the growth of the human race through many generations, Abraham responded to God's call by migrating from Mesopotamia to Palestine (c. 1750 B.C.E.). He and his main descendants, Isaac and Jacob, moved about in the hills of Palestine; Jacob and his descendants went to Egypt during a famine. In *Exodus* Moses led the Hebrews by God's power from Egypt into the Sinai Peninsula between Egypt and Palestine, where they received the law of God (c. 1280 B.C.E.). In *Leviticus* they received God's instruction for worship and purity, and *Numbers* relates how they wandered in the wilderness until they were ready to enter the Promised Land. In *Deuteronomy*, the people received the law a second time as Moses warns them against serving other gods. These five books are together known as the *Torah*, "teaching, instruction." They are the most important books of the scriptures.

The next section of the *Bible, Prophets*, is subdivided into two parts, *Former* and *Latter*, referring to their position in the canon, not to the time of their composition. The *Former Prophets* include *Joshua, Judges, Samuel*, and *Kings. Joshua* narrates a somewhat idealized version of how the Israelites crossed the Jordan River and conquered the peoples of Palestine (c. 1250 B.C.E.). *Judges* provides another view of how the Israelites engaged in continuing wars to maintain their possession of the land as they are led by charismatic figures against their enemies. *I–II Samuel* relates how a monarchy was established with Saul as the first king and David (crowned 1000 B.C.E.) as his successor. *I–II Kings* tells how, under King Solomon, Israel grew to be a small empire, but when Solomon died, the kingdom split into two nations, the northern kingdom of Israel (or Ephraim) and the southern kingdom of Judah. The northern kingdom was conquered by Assyria in 721 B.C.E., never to reappear; the southern kingdom fell to Babylonia in 590, with many of its people going into captivity in Babylon, a captivity seen as punishment for not serving God alone.

The *Latter Prophets* begin with *Isaiah*, a composite book that contains the words of Isaiah in the eighth century and the messages of "Second Isaiah" and "Third Isaiah" in the sixth century. *Jeremiah* is the message of the mournful prophet who foresaw the destruction of Jerusalem by the Babylonians. *Ezekiel* prophesies hope among the Jewish exiles in Babylon. The last book is *The Twelve*, called in English the *Minor Prophets* because of the relatively small size of their books, formerly written on one scroll, not for the importance of their message. They are *Hosea, Joel, Amos, Obadiah, Jonah, Micah, Nahum, Habakkuk, Zephaniah, Haggai, Zechariah*, and *Malachi*. The careers of these prophets run from the 700s to the 500s B.C.E.

The third section of the Jewish *Bible* is the *Writings*. As this name suggests, the *Writings* are a miscellaneous collection of several types of literature. It begins with the Psalms, (**psalms** are song prayers for temple use). *Proverbs* and *Job* are books that deal with wisdom, the former a collection of wise sayings attributed to Solomon and the latter a drama about the perennial question, "If God is good, why do good people suffer?" *Ruth* tells the beautiful story of how a non-Israelite woman became a part of the people of God and the ancestor of King David. The *Song of Songs* is a collection of poetry that celebrates love between a man and a woman, traditionally interpreted by Jews as symbolic of the relationship of God and Israel. *Ecclesiastes* offers a bittersweet perspective on what wisdom and life have to offer. *Lamentations*, traditionally ascribed to the prophet Jeremiah, mourns the destruction of Jerusalem by the Babylonians. *Esther* is a dramatic story of how a Jewish woman delivers her people from destruction by a Persian king. *Daniel* contains visions of the end of time. *Ezra-Nehemiah* records the return of the Jewish exiles from Babylon at the end of the sixth century B.C.E., the reconstruction of Jerusalem, and the reconstitution of Judaism. Finally, *I–II Chronicles* tell much the same story as *I–II Kings* (in the *Former Prophets*), but from the perspective of the Jerusalem priesthood.

These, then, are the books of the Jewish *Bible*. In Jewish reckoning, they number twenty-four in all, a number obtained by counting as one book each *I–II Samuel*,

I–II Kings, I–II Chronicles, The Twelve, and *Ezra-Nehemiah.* In ancient times they were traditionally written on twenty-four scrolls, and this number was kept even after the two-volume books were separated at the end of the Middle Ages. The content of the Jewish scriptures can be summarized in table form (see Table 10.1).

The order of the books of the Jewish *Bible* more familiar to Christians is based on their Greek translation made before Christianity began. (This translation, known as the *Septuagint,* was the only scripture of early Christianity until the *New Testament* was recognized as scripture in the second and third centuries C.E. We will deal more fully with the relationship of the Jewish and Christian scriptures in the next chapter, on Christianity.) This order is charted in Table 10.2.

Origin and Development

The Jewish *Bible* had a long history of formation in oral tradition, transcription in writing, and editorial polishing. Because this process of development is shrouded in the mists of antiquity, scholarly judgments will vary, but the following summary description has some consensus. The writing probably began about 1100 B.C.E., after the Israelites entered Palestine, when the oldest sections of poetry and historical narratives were written (e.g., the "Songs of Moses and Miriam" in *Exodus* 15; the "Song of Deborah" in *Judges* 5). Under Solomon, the story of his father David began to be written (*II Samuel* 9–*I Kings* 2). One source of the *Torah,* which told of creation and the patriarch as a prelude to the formation of Israel, was written in southern Israel. Another source of the *Torah* was written in northern Israel from a northern religious and political perspective.

The eighth century B.C.E. saw a flowering of literary effort. The disciples of the prophets Amos, Hosea, Isaiah, and Micah began to write down their words. When the north fell in 721 B.C.E., the sources mentioned above were combined into the "Old Epic" narrative to give us much of our present *Genesis.* In 621 B.C.E., the finding of a law scroll in the Jerusalem temple, a scroll probably containing the substance of *Deuteronomy* 12–26, gave an impetus for the writing of the rest of this book.

The exile in Babylon (587–539 B.C.E.) was a fruitful period of literary activity. *Jeremiah, Ezekiel,* and "Second Isaiah" (chapters 40–55) were largely written by their disciples. The Deuteronomic history (*Deuteronomy, Joshua, Judges, I–II Samuel,* and *I–II Kings*) was probably completed at the end of the Exile. Priestly sections of the *Torah* were completed, and many of the *Psalms* were written down.

After the Exile, Jewish scriptural activity centered on Jerusalem and its temple. More prophetic books were completed: "Third Isaiah" (*Isaiah* 56–66), *Malachi,* and *Joel* were written, and *Haggai* was edited to its final form. By the year 400 B.C.E., the *Torah* probably reached its present form as it was finished and edited by the Jerusalem priests, becoming the first and primary section of Jewish scripture. *Genesis* through *Deuteronomy* was labeled *Torah,* and Moses was said to be its author. Around 350 B.C.E., the historical work of the Chronicler, *I–II Chronicles* and *Ezra-Nehemiah,* was completed. The later wisdom books, *Job* and *Ecclesiastes,* were compiled, and two short stories, *Ruth* and *Esther,* appeared. By 200 B.C.E., the eight-book section known as *Prophets* was complete. The final stratum of the Jewish scripture was in the apocalyptic mode: *Isaiah* 24–27, *Ezekiel* 38, and especially the book of *Daniel,* the

Table 10.1

The Books of the Hebrew *Bible*

Division	English Name	Hebrew Name	Chapters
Torah ("Teaching, Law")	*Genesis*	*Bereshith* ("in the beginning")	50
	Exodus	*Shemoth* ("names")	40
	Leviticus	*Wayiqra* ("and he called")	27
	Numbers	*Bemidbar* ("in the wilderness")	36
	Deuteronomy	*Debarim* ("words")	34
Nevi'im ("Prophets")	*Joshua*	*Yehoshua*	24
	Judges	*Shofetim* ("judges")	21
	I–II Samuel	*Shemuel*	31, 24
	I–II Kings	*Melakim* ("kings")	22, 25
	Isaiah	*Yeshayahu*	66
	Jeremiah	*Yirmeyahu*	52
	Ezekiel	*Yehezqel*	48
	The Twelve:		
	Hosea	*Hoshea*	14
	Joel	*Yoel*	3
	Amos	*Amos*	9
	Obadiah	*Obadyahu*	1
	Jonah	*Yonah*	4
	Micah	*Micah*	7
	Nahum	*Nahum*	3
	Habakkuk	*Habaqquq*	3
	Zephaniah	*Zephanyah*	3
	Haggai	*Haggai*	2
	Zachariah	*Zekaryahu*	14
	Malachi	*Malaki*	4
Kethuvim ("Writings")	*Psalms*	*Tehillim* ("Praises")	150
	Job	*Iyyob*	31
	Proverbs	*Mishle* ("Proverbs of")	42
	Ruth	*Ruth*	4
	Song of Songs	*Shir Hashirim* ("Song of Songs")	8
	Ecclesiastes	*Koheleth* ("Preacher")	12
	Lamentations	*Ekah* ("How")	5
	Esther	*Ester*	10
	Daniel	*Daniel*	12
	Ezra-Nehemiah	*Ezra-Nehemyah*	10, 13
	I–II Chronicles	*Dibre Hayamin* ("words of")	29, 36

Table 10.2

The Books of the Greek Version of the Hebrew *Bible*

Genesis	*Proverbs*
Exodus	*Ecclesiastes*
Leviticus	**Wisdom of Solomon*
Numbers	**Wisdom of Sirach*
Deuteronomy	**Psalms of Solomon*
Joshua	*Isaiah*
Judges	*Jeremiah*
Ruth	*Lamentations*
I Kings (I Samuel)	**Baruch*
II Kings (II Samuel)	**Letter of Jeremiah*
III Kings (I Kings)	*Ezekiel*
IV Kings (II Kings)	*Daniel*
I Chronicles	**Susanna*
II Chronicles	**Bel and the Snake*
* I Esdras	*Hosea*
II Esdras (Ezra-Nehemiah)	*Joel*
* Tobit	*Amos*
* Judith	*Obadiah*
Esther	*Jonah*
* I Maccabees	*Micah*
* II Maccabees	*Nahum*
* III Maccabees	*Habakkuk*
* IV Maccabees	*Zephaniah*
Job	*Haggai*
Psalms	*Zechariah*
* Odes	*Malachi*

*These apocryphal, or deutero-canonical, books are not included in the canon of the Hebrew scriptures or in the *Bibles* of most Protestant churches. They are included in the *Bibles* of the Eastern Orthodox and Roman Catholic churches, but the Catholic canon excludes *I Esdras, III* and *IV Maccabees, Odes,* and *Psalms of Solomon.* Some *Bibles* used by Orthodox Christians omit *IV Maccabees, Odes,* and *Psalms of Solomon.*

last book to be written, in 160 B.C.E. The *Writings* section was basically collected by about 100 B.C.E., but the canonical status of some books in it (especially *Esther* and the *Song of Songs*) was debated later.

The full and formal canonization of the entire Jewish *Bible* as we now have it—the *Law (Torah), Prophets,* and *Writings*—took place at the end of the first century C.E. No one disagreed on the books of the *Torah* and the *Prophets*—this canon had been settled for several centuries. The Jewish council at Jamnia (c. 90 C.E.) seems to have ruled on the writings as we have them, but it took some years for this ruling to be widely accepted. The main criterion for canonicity was the recognition that God was revealed in these books and spoke to his people in them. Canonization did not *confer* scripturality on a book. Rather, it was the official and formal recognition of a long-standing reception and use of these books as holy and scriptural by the Jewish community itself. Once it was given, canonization helped reinforce their holiness and authority.

Use

The Jewish *Bible* is built on the foundation of the *Torah,* the written law of God. But ancient law needs interpreting and application to new times and situations, and so arose the concept of "oral Torah." The oral Torah explains, supplements, and applies the commands of the written *Torah.* It is called "oral" because it was believed by the end of the first century C.E. to have been revealed to Moses on Mount Sinai and passed down orally by experts for more than a thousand years. It was also probably kept in oral form so as not to compete in standing and authority with the *Bible,* the written *Torah.* This oral Torah grew so large and authoritative that it had to be written down, first in the *Mishnah* (c. 200 C.E.), then in its commentary, the *Gemara* (c. 450–550 C.E.), and shortly thereafter in the combination of these two in the **Talmud** [TALL-mood]. The *Talmud* has two versions, the short *Jerusalem Talmud* and the longer and more authoritative *Babylonian Talmud.* For almost all Jews from 500 to 1800 C.E., the scripture was understood by way of the oral Torah, the *Talmud,* and Orthodox Jews still understand it this way. For example, it said that the biblical law of "an eye for an eye" was not to be taken literally but meant that one who injures another must pay adequate monetary fines to compensate for the loss.

This was the way in which the *Talmud* was used through the Middle Ages. This period of rabbinic Judaism also saw the rise of the fourfold meaning of the scripture: Midrashic, philosophical, mystical, and literal. "Midrash" was the sermonic, illustrative interpretation of the *Bible,* often quite fanciful. The philosophical meaning practiced by Maimonides and others discovered deep truths in the *Bible* that could be related to the teaching of Plato or Aristotle. The hidden, mystical meaning led to direct experience of God, emotional as well as intellectual or moral; the Kabalists found cryptic meanings in words and letters of scripture while ignoring the other three meanings. The literal meaning explained the plain, grammatical sense; its greatest practitioner was Rashi (Rabbi Solomon Itzchaki) of Troyes, France. The four levels of meaning were often combined in some way, but the literal meaning had gained the upper hand at the end of the Middle Ages and was the most compatible with the developing historical method.

With the emancipation of Judaism from legal restrictions and official discrimination around 1800 C.E., liberalizing Jews applied the historical-critical method of studying texts to the Jewish *Bible.* Accepting the ideas of the Enlightenment, these Jews said that scripture was to be understood like any other book, with supernatural and miraculous elements largely discounted. The Dutch Jewish philosopher Baruch Spinoza (1623–1677), a pre-emancipation scholar, had already introduced and exemplified this approach. In his influential *Tractatus Theologico-Politicus* (Theological-Political Essay), he dismissed the divine inspiration of scripture and Moses' authorship of the *Torah,* advocating a historical interpretation. At first his methods shocked and scandalized the Jewish world, but over the next three hundred years they gained the ascendancy in all but Orthodox Judaism.

By the end of the 1800s, the three main groups of modern Judaism had emerged along with their distinct approaches to scripture. The Reform branch, which largely adopted the historical-critical method, approaches the *Bible* much like mainstream Protestants and Roman Catholics understand it. The Orthodox branch sticks to the traditional and Talmudic views of scripture and methods of interpreting it: for example, that the whole *Torah* was written by Moses, that the *Talmud* is the oral Torah, and that every law of God is to be followed literally as fully as possible. The Conservative branch lies between these two, largely employing modern historical methods in understanding and applying scripture but seeking to preserve much of the essential and traditional meaning.

When Muhammad called the Jews (with Christians) the "people of the Book," he made an accurate assessment of the role of scripture in Judaism. For more than two thousand years the *Bible* has been read, prayed, and taught in the synagogue. It has shaped the doctrine, ethics, and worship of the Jews. Its instruction and inspiration have helped to preserve them through good times and bad, over their wide dispersion through much of the world.

As in most religions, the site where Jews have characteristically met and used their scripture is their place of worship. Synagogue worship is filled with the *Bible;* scripture saturates its prayers, chants, hymns, and liturgies. The main point of the service is the solemn reading of the passages appointed for the day in the prayer books. The entire *Torah* is read at the sabbath services during the course of each year. Special *Torah* readings are fixed for the main festivals and High Holy Days. Related readings from the prophets (called the *Haftorah*) are also fixed in the **lectionary,** or list of readings, for each sabbath and holy day. Some passages from the *Writings* section of the *Bible* are read on five lesser festivals (Sukkot, Passover, Shavu'ot, Purim, the Ninth of Ab) from the five scrolls known as the *Megilloth* (*Ecclesiastes, Song of Songs, Ruth, Esther,* and *Lamentations,* respectively).

The readings themselves are very musical—the words are chanted in Hebrew using accent marks written into the Hebrew text and also employing traditional Hebrew melodies. The special place where the Torah scrolls are kept, called the **ark,** is usually the focal point of the synagogue and often faces Jerusalem. The scrolls themselves are typically covered with richly embroidered cloth, and the upper ends of the wooden rollers are adorned with gold and silver decorations. When the scroll is removed from the ark during the service, everyone in the synagogue stands and special songs are sung. The scroll is placed on a reading desk, and the reader uses a special pointer, often made of solid silver, to keep place in the text. When the reading is complete, the scroll is rolled up, its covers are put back on, and it is placed in the ark with great solemnity. Then a sermon is preached on the basis of the texts read, especially the *Torah* reading.

The *Bible,* together with the *Talmud,* is also the focus of group and individual study. Since ancient times it has been a legal obligation for every Jewish man—and often an option for women—to be able to read and understand scripture. In North America, every synagogue of substance provides after-school classes in Hebrew language and religious studies to children from elementary to high school age. Jewish parochial schools that teach both general and religious subjects, with heavy doses of scripture, can be found in cities with sizable Jewish populations. This emphasis on early education in scripture fosters Jewish adults who are able and willing to study it on an advanced level. Every Jewish home typically possesses a *Bible* in the native language of the family and often one in Hebrew as well.

The daily life of the observant Jew is also immersed in reminders of the *Bible* and its instruction. For example, the mezuzah mentioned earlier contains three short passages from the *Torah,* among them the well-known words of *Deuteronomy* 6:4–9, "Take to heart these instructions with which I charge you this day. Impress them upon your children. Recite them when you stay at home and when you are away, when you lie down and when you get up . . . inscribe them on the doorposts of your house and on your gates." This passage also commands the wearing of **tefillin,** "phylacteries" or small wooden boxes containing tiny scripture scrolls, tied to the forehead and the weaker arm by leather straps. Phylacteries are worn by Orthodox Jews while praying, which is traditionally done three times a day. These outward practices of religion are designed to remind every Jew of the duty to act in obedience to God during every activity in the night or the day, at home or away.

HISTORY

The Call of Abraham*

The history of the Jewish people begins with Abraham, whose name was Abram at first. God calls him to journey to Canaan (ancient Palestine) and promises that Abraham's descendants will form a great nation, will become a source of blessing to the world, and will inherit the land of Canaan. Abraham responds faithfully to God's call. Compare this passage with Genesis *17:1–14, given later in* Ritual.[1]

The Lord said to Abram, "Go forth from your native land and from your father's house to the land that I will show you.
I will make of you a great nation,
And I will bless you;
I will make your name great,

And you shall be a blessing.
I will bless those who bless you
And curse him that curses you;
And all the families of the earth
Shall bless themselves by you."

Abram went forth as the Lord had commanded him, and Lot went with him. Abram was seventy-five years old when he left Haran.[2] [5] Abram took his wife Sarai and his brother's son Lot, and all the wealth that they had amassed, and the persons that they had acquired in Haran; and they set out for the land of Canaan. When they arrived in the land of Canaan, Abram passed through the land as far as the site of Shechem, at the terebinth[3] of Moreh. The Canaanites were then in the land.

---

*Genesis 12:1–9
[1] All passages from the Jewish *Bible* are from *Tanakh: The Holy Scriptures.* Copyright 1985, by the Jewish Publication Society. Used by permission.

---

[2] *Haran:* the city in northern Mesopotamia (modern-day Iraq) where Abraham lived.
[3] *terebinth:* an oak tree, with sacred significance.

The Lord appeared to Abram and said, "I will assign this land to your heirs." And he built an altar there to the Lord who had appeared to him. From there he moved on to the hill country east of Bethel and pitched his tent, with Bethel on the west and Ai on the east; and he built there an altar to the Lord and invoked the Lord by name. Then Abram journeyed by stages toward the Negeb.

The Call of Moses*

Speaking from a burning bush, God called Moses to be God's prophetic agent in liberating the Hebrews from their Egyptian slavery. This passage provides insight into the personality of Moses, the most influential person in the Tanakh and in Jewish history.

Now Moses, tending the flock of his father-in-law Jethro, the priest of Midian, drove the flock into the wilderness, and came to Horeb, the mountain of God. An angel of the Lord appeared to him in a blazing fire out of a bush. He gazed, and there was a bush all aflame, yet the bush was not consumed. Moses said, "I must turn aside to look at this marvelous sight; why doesn't the bush burn up?" When the Lord saw that he had turned aside to look, God called to him out of the bush: "Moses!" He answered, "Here I am." [5] And He said, "Do not come closer. Remove your sandals from your feet, for the place on which you stand is holy ground.[4] I am," He said, "The God of your father, the God of Abraham, the God of Isaac, and the God of Jacob." And Moses hid his face, for he was afraid to look at God.

And the Lord continued, "I have marked well the plight of My people in Egypt and have heeded their outcry because of their taskmasters; yes, I am mindful of their sufferings. I have come down to rescue them from the Egyptians and to bring them out of that land to a good and spacious land, a land flowing with milk and honey, the region of the Canaanites, the Hittites, the Amorites, the Perizzites, the Hivites, and the Jebusites. Now the cry of the Israelites has reached Me; moreover, I have seen how the Egyptians oppress them. [10] Come, therefore, I will send you to Pharaoh, and you shall free My people, the Israelites, from Egypt."

But Moses said to God, "Who am I that I should go to Pharaoh and free the Israelites from Egypt?" And He said, "I will be with you, that shall be your sign that it was I who sent you. And when you have freed the people from Egypt, you shall worship God at this mountain."

Moses said to God, "When I come to the Israelites and say to them 'The God of your fathers has sent me to you,' and they ask me, 'What is His name?' what shall I say to them?" And God said to Moses, "Ehyeh-Asher-Ehyeh."[5] He continued, "Thus shall you say to the Israelites, 'Ehyeh sent me to you.'" [15] And God said further to Moses, "Thus shall you speak to the Israelites: The Lord, the God of your fathers, the God of Abraham, the God of Isaac, and the God of Jacob, has sent me to you: This shall be My name forever, This My appellation for all eternity."

"Go and assemble the elders of Israel and say to them: the Lord, the God of your fathers, the God of Abraham, Isaac, and Jacob, has appeared to me and said, 'I have taken note of you and of

---

*Exodus 3:1–20

[4]*remove your sandals:* the custom in many ancient Near Eastern religions of going barefoot in a holy place, still practiced in Islamic mosques.

[5]*Ehyeh-Asher-Ehyeh:* "I am what I am," based on the holy name YHWH, probably pronounced "YAH-way." This name both reveals and conceals God's nature. It is translated here, as in the ancient synagogues, as "the Lord."

what is being done to you in Egypt, and I have declared: I will take you out of the misery of Egypt to the land of the Canaanites, the Hittites, the Amorites, the Perizzites, the Hivites, and the Jebusites,[6] to a land flowing with milk and honey.' They will listen to you; then you

___

[6]*Canaanites . . . Jebusites:* peoples of Palestine before the Israelite conquest of the Promised Land.

shall go with the elders of Israel to the king of Egypt and you shall say to him, 'The Lord, the God of the Hebrews, manifested Himself to us. Now therefore, let us go a distance of three days into the wilderness to sacrifice to the Lord our God.' Yet I know that the king of Egypt will let you go only because of a greater might. [20] So I will stretch out My hand and smite Egypt with various wonders which I will work upon them; after that he shall let you go."

Crossing the Red Sea*

The dramatic climax of the Exodus is the Israelites' escape through the sea, and the destruction of the Egyptians who pursued them. This tale is told at every Passover feast.

The Lord said to Moses: "Tell the Israelites to turn back and encamp before Pi-hahiroth, between Migdol and the sea, before Baal-zephon;[7] you shall encamp facing it, by the sea. Pharaoh will say of the Israelites, 'They are astray in the land; and wilderness has closed in on them.' Then I will stiffen Pharaoh's heart and he will pursue them, that I may gain glory through Pharaoh and all his host; and the Egyptians shall know that I am the Lord." And they did so.

[5] When the king of Egypt was told that the people had fled, Pharaoh and his courtiers had a change of heart about the people and said, "What is this we have done, releasing Israel from our service?" He ordered his chariot and took his men with him; he took six hundred of his picked chariots, and the rest of the chariots of Egypt, with officers in all of them. The Lord stiffened the heart of Pharaoh king of Egypt,

___

*Exodus 14:1–31
[7]*Pi-hahiroth, Migdol, Baal-zephon:* Egyptian fortified towns. The Israelites were trapped between the Egyptians and the sea.

and he gave chase to the Israelites. As the Israelites were departing defiantly, the Egyptians gave chase to them, and all the chariot horses of Pharaoh, his horsemen, and his warriors overtook them encamped by the sea, near Pi-hahiroth, before Baal-zephon.

[10] As Pharaoh drew near, the Israelites caught sight of the Egyptians advancing upon them. Greatly frightened, the Israelites cried out to the Lord. And they said to Moses, "Was it for want of graves in Egypt that you brought us to die in the wilderness? What have you done to us, taking us out of Egypt? Is this not the very thing we told you in Egypt, saying 'Let us be, and we will serve the Egyptians, for it is better for us to serve the Egyptians than to die in the wilderness'?" But Moses said to the people, "Have no fear. Stand by, and witness the deliverance which the Lord will work for you today; for the Egyptians whom you see today you will never see again. The Lord will battle for you; you hold your peace."

[15] Then the Lord said to Moses, "Why do you cry out to Me? Tell the Israelites to go forward. And you lift up your rod and hold out your arm over the sea and split it, so that the Israelites may march into the sea on dry ground. And I will stiffen the hearts of the Egyptians so that they go in after them; and I will gain glory through Pharaoh and all his warriors, his chariots and his horsemen. Let the Egyptians know

that I am Lord, when I gain glory through Pharaoh, his chariots, and his horsemen."

The angel of God, who had been going ahead of the Israelite army, now moved and followed behind them; and the pillar of cloud shifted from in front of them and took up a place behind them, [20] and it came between the army of the Egyptians and the army of Israel. Thus there was the cloud with the darkness, and it cast a spell upon the night, so that the one could not come near the other all through the night.

Then Moses held out his arm over the sea and the Lord drove back the sea with a strong east wind all that night, and turned the sea into dry ground. The waters were split, and the Israelites went into the sea on dry ground, the waters forming a wall for them on their right and on their left. The Egyptians came in pursuit after them into the sea, all of Pharaoh's horses, chariots, and horsemen. At the morning watch, the Lord looked down upon the Egyptian army from a pillar of fire and cloud, and threw the Egyptian army into panic. [25] He locked the wheels of their chariots so that they moved forward with difficulty. And the Egyptians said, "Let us flee from the Israelites, for the Lord is fighting for them against Egypt."

Then the Lord said to Moses, "Hold out your arm over the sea, that the waters may come back upon the Egyptians and upon their chariots and upon their horsemen." Moses held out his arm over the sea, and at daybreak the sea returned to its normal state, and the Egyptians fled at its approach. But the Lord hurled the Egyptians into the sea. The waters turned back and covered the chariots and the horsemen— Pharaoh's entire army that followed them into the sea; not one of them remained. But the Israelites had marched through the sea on dry ground, the waters forming a wall for them on their right and on their left.

[30] Thus the Lord delivered Israel that day from the Egyptians. Israel saw the Egyptians dead on the shore of the sea. And when Israel saw the wondrous power which the Lord had wielded against the Egyptians, the people feared the Lord; they had faith in the Lord and His servant Moses.

The Covenant with Israel*

*After the Exodus, God renewed the **covenant** or pact made with Abraham. The familiar terms of the covenant from Genesis 17:1–8 are present here: "I will be your God"; "You will be my people"; "you will obey me." These covenant conditions are here prefaced and founded on what God did in liberating the people from Egypt.*

On the third new moon after the Israelites had gone forth from the land of Egypt, on that very day, they entered the wilderness of Sinai. Having journeyed from Rephidim, they entered the wilderness of Sinai and encamped in the wilderness. Israel encamped there in front of the mountain, and Moses went up to God. The Lord called to him from the mountain, saying, "Thus shall you say to the house of Jacob and declare to the children of Israel: 'You have seen what I did to the Egyptians, how I bore you on eagles' wings and brought you to Me. [5] Now then, if you will obey Me faithfully and keep My covenant, you shall be My treasured possession among all the peoples. Indeed, all the earth is Mine, but you shall be to Me a kingdom of priests and a holy nation.' These are the words that you shall speak to the children of Israel."

Moses came and summoned the elders of the people and put before them all that the Lord had commanded him. All the people answered as one, saying, "All that the Lord has spoken we will do." And Moses brought back the people's words to the Lord.

---

*Exodus 19:1–8

A Psalm for David*

The story of David's rule over Israel is told in II Samuel. *Psalm 132 portrays well the significance of David for the continuing life of Judaism. Israel hopes for the coming of its Messiah from the descendants of David to take up again the rule of David. Orthodox Jews look for a literal fulfillment of this hope; more liberal Jews look for a symbolic fulfillment.*

O Lord, remember in David's favor
   his extreme self-denial,
   how he swore to the Lord,
   vowed to the Mighty One of Jacob,
   "I will not enter my house,
   nor will I mount my bed,
   I will not give sleep to my eyes,
   or slumber to my eyelids
   [5] until I find a place for the Lord,
   an abode for the Mighty One of Jacob."

We heard it was in Ephrath;
   we came upon it in the region of Jaar.[8]
Let us enter His abode,
   bow at His footstool.

Advance, O Lord, to Your resting-place,
   You and Your mighty Ark!
Your priests are clothed in triumph;
   Your loyal ones sing for joy.
[10] For the sake of Your servant David
   do not reject Your anointed one.
The Lord swore to David
   a firm oath that He will not renounce,
   "One of your own issue I will set upon your throne.
If your sons keep My covenant
   and My decrees that I teach them,
   then their sons also,
   to the end of time,
   shall sit upon your throne."
For the Lord has chosen Zion;[9]
   He has desired it for His seat.
"This is my resting-place for all time;
   here I will dwell, for I desire it.
[15] I will amply bless its store of food,
   give its needy their fill of bread.
I will clothe its priests in victory,
   its loyal ones shall sing for joy.
There I will make a horn sprout for David;
   I have prepared a lamp for My anointed one.
I will clothe his enemies in disgrace,
   while on him his crown shall sparkle."

---

*Psalm 132

[8]*Ephrath:* David's home city, also known as Bethlehem; *Jaar:* where the Ark of the Covenant was kept from Samuel's time until David moved it to Jerusalem.

---

[9]*Zion:* Jerusalem.

Ezra's Enforcement of *Torah* Observance**

The return of the Jews from Exile in Babylon brought a new dedication to keep the Torah, *as it was widely perceived that God had used the Exile to punish them for their sins. One way that this* Torah *observance was enforced was in the divorce*

of Jewish men from non-Jewish wives. Marriage only within Judaism became the rule in Jewish law and was widely followed in all branches of Judaism until modern times. (See the book of Ruth, *perhaps also written at this time, for a more liberal view of intermarriage.)*

When this was over, the officers approached me, saying, "The people of Israel and the priests and

---

**Ezra 9:1–7, 13–15; 10:1–12

Levites have not separated themselves from the peoples of the land whose abhorrent practices are like those of the Canaanites, the Hittites, the Perizzites, the Jebusites, the Ammonites, the Moabites, the Egyptians, and the Amorites. They have taken their daughters as wives for themselves and for their sons, so that the holy seed has become intermingled with the peoples of the land; and it is the officers and prefects who have taken the lead in this trespass."

When I heard this, I rent my garment and robe, I tore hair out of my head and beard, and I sat desolate.[10] Around me gathered all who were concerned over the words of the God of Israel because of the returning exiles' trespass, while I sat desolate until the evening offering. [5] At the time of the evening offering I ended my self-affliction; still in my torn garment and robe, I got down on my knees and spread out my hands to the Lord my God, and said, "O my God, I am too ashamed and mortified to lift my face to You, O my God, for our iniquities are overwhelming and our guilt has grown high as heaven. From the time of our fathers to this very day we have been deep in guilt. Because of our iniquities, we, our kings, and our priests have been handed over to foreign kings, to the sword, to captivity, to pillage, and to humiliation, as is now the case. . . . [13] After all that has happened to us because of our evil deeds and our deep guilt—though You, our God, have been forbearing, less than our iniquity in that You have granted us such a remnant[11] as this—shall we once again violate Your commandments by intermarrying with these peoples who follow such abhorrent practices?[12] Will You not rage against us till we are destroyed without remnant or survivor? [15] O Lord, God of Israel, You are benevolent, for we have survived as a remnant, as is now the case. We stand before You in all our guilt, for we cannot face You on this account."

[10:1] While Ezra was praying and making confession, weeping and prostrating himself before the House of God, a very great crowd of Israelites gathered about him, men, women, and children; the people were weeping bitterly. Then Shecaniah son of Jehiel of the family of Elam spoke up and said to Ezra, "We have trespassed against our God by bringing into our homes foreign women from the peoples of the land; but there is still hope for Israel despite this. Now then, let us make a covenant with our God to expel all these women and those who have been born to them, in accordance with the bidding of the Lord and of all who are concerned over the commandment of our God, and let the Teaching be obeyed. Take action, for the responsibility is yours and we are with you. Act with resolve!"

[5] So Ezra at once put the officers of the priests and the Levites and all Israel under oath to act accordingly, and they took the oath. Then Ezra rose from his place in front of the House of God and went into the chamber of Jehohanan son of Eliashib; there, he ate no bread and drank no water, for he was in mourning over the trespass of those who had returned from exile. Then a proclamation was issued in Judah and Jerusalem that all who had returned from the exile should assemble in Jerusalem, and that anyone who did not come in three days would, by decision of the officers and elders, have his property confiscated and himself excluded from the congregation of the returning exiles.

All the men of Judah and Benjamin assembled in Jerusalem in three days; it was the ninth month, the twentieth of the month. All the people sat in the square of the House of God, trembling on account of the event and because of the rains. [10] Then Ezra the priest got up and said to them, "You have trespassed by bringing home foreign women, thus aggravating the guilt of Israel. So now, make confession to the Lord, God of your fathers, and do His will, and separate yourselves from the peoples of the land and from the foreign women." The entire congregation responded in a loud voice, "We must surely do just as you say."

---

[10]*I rent my garment . . . sat desolate:* all signs of mourning.
[11]*remnant:* group of survivors.
[12]*such abhorrent practices:* the immoralities and idolatry of other peoples.

TEACHING

The Oneness of God*

*These words of Moses explain the commandment, "You shall have no other gods beside me." In Jewish tradition, the last paragraph of this selection is known as the **Shema**, the Hebrew word meaning "hear" which opens this section. The last sentence has produced the use of the tefillin, small boxes with the* Shema *and three other passages inside that are bound by leather straps to the hand and forehead, and the* mezuzah, *a small box fastened to the doorpost that has the* Shema *and* Deuteronomy 11:13–21 *inside. They are reminders of Jewishness and the duty to love and serve God alone.*

"And this is the Instruction—the laws and the rules—that the Lord your God has commanded to impart to you, to be observed in the land that you are about to cross into and occupy, so that you, your children, and your

*Deuteronomy 6:1–9

children's children may revere the Lord your God and follow, as long as you live, all His laws and commandments that I enjoin upon you, to the end that you may long endure. Obey, O Israel, willingly and faithfully, that it may go well with you and that you may increase greatly a land flowing with milk and honey, as the Lord, the God of your fathers, spoke to you.

"Hear, O Israel The Lord is our God, the Lord alone. [5] You shall love the Lord your God with all your heart and with all your soul and with all your might. Take to heart these instructions with which I charge you this day. Impress them upon your children. Recite them when you stay at home and when you are away, when you lie down and when you get up. Bind them as a sign on your hand and let them serve as a symbol on your forehead; inscribe them on the doorposts of your house and on your gates."

God's Creation of the World**

Two narratives tell the story of God's creation of the world: one from Priestly (P) traditions (1:1–2:3), the other from Old Epic (J and E) traditions (2:4–25). They vary in content and style. In the first, God creates an orderly cosmos out of primeval chaos, with humankind as the capstone of creation. In the second, the creation of humanity is the central topic. Note the different ways the two stories account for the creation of woman.

When God began to create heaven and earth—the earth being unformed and void, with darkness over the surface of the deep and a wind from God sweeping over the water—God said, "Let there be light"; and there was light. God

**Genesis 1:1–31; 2:1–9, 15–25

saw that the light was good, and God separated the light from the darkness. [5] God called the light Day, and the darkness He called Night. And there was evening and there was morning, a first day.

God said, "Let there be an expanse in the midst of the water, that it may separate water from water." God made the expanse, and it separated the water which was below the expanse from the water which was above the expanse. And it was so. God called the expanse Sky. And there was evening and there was morning, a second day.

God said, "Let the water below the sky be gathered into one area, that the dry land may appear." And it was so. [10] God called the dry land Earth, and the gathering of waters He called Seas. And God saw that this was good.

And God said, "Let the earth sprout vegetation: seed-bearing plants, fruit trees of every kind on earth that bear fruit with the seed in it." And it was so. The earth brought forth vegetation: seed-bearing plants of every kind, and trees of every kind bearing fruit with the seed in it. And God saw that this was good. And there was evening and there was morning, a third day.

God said, "Let there be lights in the expanse of the sky to separate day from night; they shall serve as signs for the set times—the days and the years; [15] and they shall serve as lights in the expanse of the sky to shine upon the earth." And it was so. God made the two great lights, the greater light to dominate the day and the lesser light to dominate the night, and the stars. And God set them in the expanse of the sky to shine upon the earth, to dominate the day and the night, and to separate light from darkness. And God saw that this was good. And there was evening and there was morning, a fourth day.

[20] God said, "Let the waters bring forth swarms of living creatures, and birds that fly above the earth across the expanse of the sky." God created the great sea monsters, and all the living creatures of every kind that creep, which the waters brought forth in swarms, and all the winged birds of every kind. And God saw that this was good. God blessed them, saying, "Be fertile and increase, fill the waters in the seas, and let the birds increase on the earth." And there was evening and there was morning, a fifth day.

God said, "Let the earth bring forth every kind of living creature: cattle, creeping things, and wild beasts of every kind." And it was so. [25] God made wild beasts of every kind and cattle of every kind, and all kinds of creeping things of the earth. And God saw that this was good. And God said, "Let us make man in our[13] image, after our likeness. They shall rule the fish of the sea, the birds of the sky, the cattle, the whole earth, and all the creeping things that

creep on earth." And God created man in His image, in the image of God He created him; male and female He created them. God blessed them and God said to them, "Be fertile and increase, fill the earth and master it; and rule the fish of the sea, the birds of the sky, and all the living things that creep on earth."

God said, "See, I give you every seed-bearing plant that is upon all the earth, and every tree that has seed-bearing fruit; they shall be yours for food. [30] And to all the animals on land, to all the birds of the sky, and to everything that creeps on earth, in which there is the breath of life, all the green plants for food." And it was so. And God saw all that He had made, and found it very good. And there was evening and there was morning, the sixth day.

[2:1] The heaven and the earth were finished, and all their array. On the seventh day God finished the work that He had been doing, and He ceased on the seventh day from all the work that He had done. And God blessed the seventh day and declared it holy, because on it God ceased from all the work of creation that He had done.[14] Such is the story of heaven and earth when they were created.

[2:4, the second creation account:] When the Lord God made earth and heaven—when no shrub of the field was yet on earth and no grasses of the field had yet sprouted, because the Lord God had not sent rain upon the earth and there was no man to till the soil, but a flow would well up from the ground and water the whole surface of the earth—the Lord God formed man from the dust of the earth. He blew into his nostrils the breath of life, and man became a living being.

The Lord God planted a garden in Eden, in the east, and placed there the man whom He had formed. And from the ground the Lord God caused to grow every tree that was pleasing to the sight and good for food, with the tree of life in the middle of the garden, and the tree of knowledge of good and bad. . . .

---

[13]*us, our:* God and the beings of the heavenly court. There is probably no idea of the plurality of God here.

[14]*God blessed the seventh day . . . done:* an allusion to the law of rest and renewal on the seventh day, the sabbath.

[2:15] The Lord God took the man and placed him in the garden of Eden, to till it and tend it. And the Lord God commanded the man, saying, "Of every tree of the garden you are free to eat; but as for the tree of knowledge of good and bad, you must not eat of it; for as soon as you eat of it, you shall die."

The Lord God said, "It is not good for man to be alone; I will make a fitting helper for him." And the Lord God formed out of the earth all the wild beasts and all the birds of the sky, and brought them to the man to see what he would call them; and whatever the man called each living creature, that would be its name. [20] And the man gave names to all the cattle and to the birds of the sky and to all the wild beasts; but for Adam no fitting helper was found. So the Lord

God cast a deep sleep upon the man; and, while he slept, He took one of his ribs and closed up the flesh at that spot. And the Lord God fashioned the rib that He had taken from the man into a woman; and He brought her to the man. Then the man said,

"This one at last
Is bone of my bones
And flesh of my flesh.
This one shall be called Woman,
For from man was she taken."

Hence a man leaves his father and mother and clings to his wife, so that they become one flesh. [25] The two of them were naked, the man and his wife, yet they felt no shame.

The Revolt of Humanity*

Humanity falls into sin by rebelling against God's command. Tempted by the serpent (in this story a wily creature, but in later Jewish and then Christian and Islamic tradition thought to be the devil in disguise), first the woman and then the man disobey God. God punishes all the guilty parties in various ways, but humanity's chief punishment is being driven out of the Garden. Orthodox Jews, like fundamentalist Christians and traditional Muslims, regard this as a fully historical event. Many Conservative and most Reform Jews, like more liberal Christians, see it as mythic.

Now the serpent was the shrewdest of all the wild beasts that the Lord God had made. He said to the woman, "Did God really say: 'You shall not eat of any tree of the garden'?" The woman replied to the serpent, "We may eat of the fruit of the other trees of the garden. It is only about fruit of the tree in the middle of the

garden that God said: 'You shall not eat of it or touch it, lest you die.'" And the serpent said to the woman, "You are not going to die, [5] but God knows that as soon as you eat of it your eyes will be opened and you will be like divine beings who know good and bad." When the woman saw that the tree was good for eating and a delight to the eyes, and that the tree was desirable as a source of wisdom, she took of its fruit and ate. She also gave some to her husband, and he ate. Then the eyes of both of them were opened and they perceived that they were naked;[15] and they sewed together fig leaves and made themselves loincloths.

They heard the sound of the Lord God moving about in the garden at the breezy time of day; and the man and his wife hid from the Lord God among the trees of the garden. The Lord God called out to the man and said to him,

---

* Genesis 3:1–24

[15] *naked:* knowledge of their nakedness is a symbol of their loss of goodness and innocence.

"Where are you?" [10] He replied, "I heard the sound of You in the garden, and I was afraid because I was naked, so I hid." Then He asked, "Who told you that you were naked? Did you eat of the tree from which I had forbidden you to eat?" The man said, "The woman You put at my side—she gave me of the tree, and I ate." And the Lord God said to the woman, "What is this you have done?" The woman replied, "The serpent duped me, and I ate." Then the Lord God said to the serpent,

"Because you did this,
More cursed shall you be
Than all cattle
And all the wild beasts:
On your belly shall you crawl
And dirt shall you eat
All the days of your life.
 [15] I will put enmity
Between you and the woman,
And between your offspring and hers;
They shall strike at your head,
And you shall strike at their heel."

And to the woman He said,
"I will make most severe
Your pangs in childbearing;
In pain shall you bear children.
Yet your urge shall be for your husband,
And he shall rule over you."[16]

To Adam He said, "Because you did as your
    wife said and ate of the tree about which
    I commanded you, 'You shall not eat of it,'
Cursed be the ground because of you;
By toil shall you eat of it
All the days of your life:
Thorns and thistles shall it sprout for you.
But your food shall be the grasses of the field;
By the sweat of your brow
Shall you get bread to eat,
Until you return to the ground—
For from it you were taken.
For dust you are,
And to dust you shall return."

[20] The man named his wife Eve, because she was the mother of all the living. And the Lord God made garments of skins for Adam and his wife, and clothed them.

And the Lord God said, "Now that the man has become like one of us, knowing good and bad, what if he should stretch out his hand and take also from the tree of life and eat, and live forever." So the Lord God banished him from the garden of Eden, to till the soil from which he was taken. He drove the man out, and stationed east of the garden of Eden the cherubim[17] and the fiery ever-turning sword, to guard the way to the tree of life.

---

[16]*he shall rule over you:* the original equality between man and woman is lost; the husband now has authority over the wife.

[17]*cherubim:* not "cherubs," but fearsome six-winged angels, half human and half lion.

Prayer for Divine Deliverance*

The Psalms *show a strong personal relationship to God as well as a strong distinction between good and evil, both characteristic of Israelite religion. This psalm, a typical prayer for deliverance, first describes the difficulties of the believer and ends* *with expression of the believer's trust in God to deliver.*

Give ear to my speech, O Lord;
    consider my utterance.
Heed the sound of my cry,
    my king and God,
    for I pray to You.

---

* Psalm 5

Hear my voice, O Lord, at daybreak;
  at daybreak I plead before You, and wait.
[5] For You are not a God who desires
    wickedness;
  evil cannot abide with You;
  wanton men cannot endure in Your sight.
You detest all evildoers;
  You doom those who speak lies;
  murderous, deceitful men the Lord abhors.
But I, through Your abundant love, enter Your
    house;
  I bow down in awe at Your holy temple.
O Lord, lead me along Your righteous
    because of my watchful foes;
  make Your way straight before me.

[10] For there is no sincerity on their lips;
  their heart is malice;
  their throat is an open grave;
  their tongue slippery.
Condemn them, O God;
  let them fall by their own devices;
  cast them out for their many crimes,
  for they defy You.
But let all who take refuge in You rejoice,
  ever jubilant as You shelter them;
  and let those who love Your name exult in
  You.
For You surely bless the righteous man,
    O Lord,
  encompassing him with favor like a shield.

The Messianic King*

This prophetic oracle promises a deliverer of Israel to come from among the descendants of King David. He will bring forth light, joy, peace, and justice. Orthodox Jews look forward to a literal fulfillment of this promise; others interpret it in the sense of progress toward justice in Judaism or in all of humanity.

But a shoot shall grow out of the stump of
    Jesse,
A twig shall sprout from his stock.
The spirit of the Lord shall alight upon him:
A spirit of wisdom and insight,
A spirit of counsel and valor,
A spirit of devotion and reverence for the Lord.
He shall sense the truth by his reverence for
    the Lord:
He shall not judge by what his eyes behold,
Nor decide by what his ears perceive.
Thus he shall judge the poor with equity

And decide with justice for the lowly of the land.
He shall strike down a land with the rod of his
    mouth
And slay the wicked with the breath of his lips.
[5] Justice shall be the girdle of his loins,
And faithfulness the girdle of his waist.
The wolf shall dwell with the lamb,
The leopard lie down with the kid;
The calf, the beast of prey, and the fatling
    together,
With a little boy to herd them.
The cow and the bear shall graze,
Their young shall lie down together;
And the lion, like the ox, shall eat straw.
A babe shall play
Over a viper's hole
And an infant pass his hand
Over an adder's den.
In all of My sacred mount
Nothing evil or vile shall be done;
For the land shall be filled with devotion to
    the Lord
As water covers the sea.

---

* *Isaiah* 11:1–9

The Final Judgment of the World*

The apocalyptic view of the world and history can be richly symbolic, with dreams and visions featuring mixed-form animals, cosmic battles, and other fantastic events. In this passage, the winged lion represents the Babylonian empire, the bear is the Medes, the four-headed leopard is the Persians, and the dragon is the Greeks. The ten horns are the ten rulers succeeding Alexander in the Near East, and the "little horn" is the Syrian king Antiochus Epiphanes, whose brutal persecution of the Jews precipitated a Jewish revolt and whose destruction is foretold here. Although the rich symbolism of apocalyptic scripture did not carry over into later Judaism, an apocalyptic view of the main events at the end of time did: God will someday bring history to an end and judge all peoples and nations.

In the first year of King Belshazzar of Babylon, Daniel saw a dream and a vision of his mind in bed; afterward he wrote down the dream. Beginning the account, Daniel related the following: "In my vision at night, I saw the four winds of heaven stirring up the great sea. Four mighty beasts different from each other emerged from the sea. The first was like a lion but had eagles' wings. As I looked on, its wings were plucked off, and it was lifted off the ground and set on its feet like a man and given the mind of a man. [5] Then I saw a second, different beast, which was like a bear but raised on one side, and with three fangs in its mouth among its teeth; it was told, 'Arise, eat much meat.' After that, as I looked on, there was another one, like a leopard, and it had on its back four wings like those of a bird; the beast had four heads, and dominion was given to it. After that, as I looked on in the night vision, there was a fourth beast—fearsome, dreadful, and very powerful, with great iron teeth—that devoured and crushed, and stamped the remains with its feet. It was different from all the other beasts which had gone before it; and it had ten horns. While I was gazing upon these horns, a new little horn sprouted up among them; three of the older horns were uprooted to make room for it. There were eyes in this horn like those of a man, and a mouth that spoke arrogantly. As I looked on,

Thrones were set in place,
And the Ancient of Days[18] took His seat.
His garment was like white snow,
And the hair of His head was like lamb's wool.
His throne was tongues of flame;
Its wheels were blazing fire.
[10] A river of fire streamed forth before Him;
Thousands upon thousands served Him;
Myriads upon myriads attended Him;
The court sat and the books were opened.[19]

I looked on. Then, because of the arrogant words that the horn spoke, the beast was killed as I looked on; its body was destroyed and it was consigned to the flames. The dominion of the other beasts was taken away, but an extension of life was given to them for a time and season. As I looked on, in the night vision,

One like a human being[20]
Came with the clouds of heaven;
He reached the Ancient of Days
And was presented to Him.
Dominion, glory, and kingship were given to him;
All peoples and nations of every language must serve him.
His dominion is an everlasting dominion that shall not pass away,
And his kingship, one that shall not be destroyed."

---

[18] *the Ancient of Days:* God, the Eternal One.
[19] *books were opened:* books in which the deeds of all people and/or their eternal destiny are written.
[20] *one like a human being:* this human figure represents the faithful Jews; traditionally he is identified as the messiah.

---

*Daniel 7:1–14

Resurrection of the Dead*

One prominent element of apocalyptic scripture is the resurrection of the dead, God's summoning them out of their graves with new, eternal bodies to face a judgment that determines their eternal fate. Although this short passage says that "many" will arise, soon the idea is established in Judaism that all *will arise. This belief is held firmly by the Orthodox; other Jews interpret it metaphorically or discard it. God speaks to Daniel:*

---

* Daniel 12:1–3

"At that time, the great prince, Michael, who stands beside the sons of your people,[21] will appear. It will be a time of trouble, the like of which has never been since the nation came into being. At that time, your people will be rescued, all who are found inscribed in the book. Many of those that sleep in the dust of the earth will awake, some to eternal life, others to reproaches, to everlasting abhorrence. And the knowledgeable will be radiant like the bright expanse of sky, and those who lead the many to righteousness will be like the stars forever and ever."

---

[21] *Michael* is the guardian angel of Israel.

ETHICS

The Ten Commandments**

This is the first section of the law given by God to Israel at Mount Sinai after the Exodus from Egypt. The first group of commandments, up through false swearing, deals with humanity's duty to God; the last group deals with person-to-person obligations. Of all ancient law codes, the Ten Commandments (or the **Decalogue***) is probably the most influential in Western religion and culture. The numbering of the commands varies among Jews and Christians, but all agree on the total of ten.*

God spoke all these words, saying:

I the Lord am your God who brought you out of the land of Egypt, the house of bondage: You shall have no other gods beside Me.

You shall not make for yourself a sculptured image, or any likeness of what is in the heavens

---

** Exodus 20:1–14

above, or on the earth below, or in the waters under the earth. [5] You shall not bow down to them or serve them. For I the Lord your God am an impassioned God, visiting the guilt of the parents upon the children, upon the third and upon the fourth generations of those who reject Me, but showing kindness to the thousandth generation of those who love Me and keep My commandments.

You shall not swear falsely by the name of the Lord your God; for the Lord will not clear one who swears falsely by His name.

Remember the sabbath day and keep it holy. Six days you shall labor and do all your work, [10] but the seventh day is a sabbath of the Lord your God: you shall not do any work—you, your son or daughter, your male or female slave, or your cattle, or the stranger who is within your settlements. For in six days the Lord made heaven and earth and sea, and all that is in them, and He rested on the seventh day; therefore the Lord blessed the sabbath day and hallowed it.

Honor your father and your mother, that you may long endure on the land that the Lord your God is assigning to you.

You shall not murder.

You shall not commit adultery.

You shall not steal.

You shall not bear false witness against your neighbor.

You shall not covet your neighbor's house: you shall not covet your neighbor's wife, or his male or female slave, or his ox or his ass, or anything that is your neighbor's.

Laws on Slaves, Violence, Property*

Following the Ten Commandments is a section of laws also traditionally traced to God's giving of the law to Moses. The laws on slavery reflect the humanitarian concern of Israel in the midst of a slave-owning and patriarchal culture. Although both male and female Hebrew slaves are given some protections, the male has more. The time limits on slavery imply that it is not the proper condition of humankind, or at least of Israelites. In the laws on violence, a distinction is made between intentional and unintentional acts. The law of retribution, "an eye for an eye," is often seen today as a crude and violent method of justice, but it is a humane limitation on the continual violence of blood feuds and private revenge. This selection closes with laws that protect the more vulnerable and helpless members of society.

These are the rules that you shall set before them:

When you acquire a Hebrew slave, he shall serve six years; in the seventh year he shall go free, without payment. If he came single, he shall leave single; if he had a wife, his wife shall leave with him. If his master gave him a wife, and she has borne him children, the wife and her children shall belong to the master, and he shall leave alone. [5] But if the slave declares, "I love my master, and my wife and children: I do not wish to go free," his master shall take him

before God.[22] He shall be brought to the door or the doorpost, and his master shall pierce his ear with an awl; and he shall then remain his slave for life.

When a man sells his daughter as a slave, she shall not be freed as male slaves are. If she proves to be displeasing to her master, who designated her for himself, he must let her be redeemed;[23] he shall not have the right to sell her to outsiders, since he broke faith with her. And if he designated her for his son, he shall deal with her as is the practice with free maidens. [10] If he marries another, he must not withhold from this one her food, her clothing, or her conjugal rights. If he fails her in these three ways, she shall go free, without payment.

He who fatally strikes a man shall be put to death. If he did not do it by design, but it came about by an act of God, I will assign you a place to which he can flee.[24]

When a man schemes against another and kills him treacherously, you shall take him from My very altar to be put to death.

---

[22] *take him before God:* i.e., at the sacred doorpost of the house.

[23] *redeemed:* bought from slavery by a relative or other interested party.

[24] *a place to flee:* a place of safety in which to take refuge, often at an altar of God; hence our word "sanctuary" in the sense of "safe refuge."

---

* *Exodus* 21:1–36; 22:15–26

[15] He who strikes his father or his mother shall be put to death.

He who kidnaps a man—whether he has sold him or is still holding him—shall be put to death.

He who insults his father or mother shall be put to death.

When men quarrel and one strikes the other with stone or fist, and he does not die but has to take to his bed—if he then gets up and walks outdoors upon his staff, the assailant shall go unpunished, except that he must pay for his idleness and his cure.

[20] When a man strikes his slave, male or female, with a rod, and he dies there and then, he must be avenged. But if he survives a day or two, he is not to be avenged, since he is the other's property.

When men fight, and one of them pushes a pregnant woman and a miscarriage results, but no other damage ensues, the one responsible shall be fined according as the woman's husband may exact from him, the payment to be based on reckoning. But if other damage ensues, the penalty shall be life for life, eye for eye, tooth for tooth, hand for hand, foot for foot, [25] burn for burn, wound for wound, bruise for bruise.

When a man strikes the eye of his slave, male or female, and destroys it, he shall let him go free on account of his eye. If he knocks out the tooth of his slave, male or female, he shall let him go free on account of his tooth.

When an ox gores a man or a woman to death, the ox shall be stoned and its flesh shall not be eaten, but the owner of the ox is not to be punished. If, however, that ox has been in the habit of goring, and its owner, though warned, has failed to guard it, and it kills a man or a woman—the ox shall be stoned and its owner, too, shall be put to death. [30] If ransom is laid upon him, he must pay whatever is laid upon him to redeem his life. So, too, if it gores a minor, male or female, shall be dealt with according to the same rule. But if the ox gores a slave, male or female, he shall pay thirty shekels of silver to the master, and the ox shall be stoned.

When a man opens a pit, or digs a pit and does not cover it, and an ox or an ass falls into it, the one responsible for the pit must make restitution; he shall pay the price to the owner, but shall keep the dead animal.

[35] When a man's ox injures his neighbor's ox and it dies, they shall sell the live ox and divide its price; they shall also divide the dead animal. If, however, it is known that the ox was in the habit of goring, and its owner has failed to guard it, he must restore ox for ox, but shall keep the dead animal. . . .

[22:15[25]] If a man seduces a virgin for whom the bride-price has not been paid, and lies with her, he must make her his wife by payment of a bride-price. If her father refuses to give her to him, he must still weigh out silver in accordance with the bride-price for virgins.

You shall not tolerate a sorceress.

Whoever lies with a beast shall be put to death.

Whoever sacrifices to a god other than the Lord alone shall be proscribed.[26]

[20] You shall not wrong a stranger or oppress him, for you were strangers in the land of Egypt.

You shall not ill-treat any widow or orphan. If you do mistreat them, I will heed their outcry as soon as they cry out to Me, and My anger shall blaze forth and I will put you to the sword, and your own wives shall become widows and your children orphans.

If you lend money to My people, to the poor among you, do not act toward them as a creditor: exact no interest from them. [25] If you take your neighbor's garment in pledge, you must return it to him before the sun sets; it is his only clothing, the sole covering for his skin. In what else shall he sleep? Therefore, if he cries out to Me, I will pay heed, for I am compassionate.

---

[25]The verse numbers differ by one between this translation and the Christian translations of this passage.
[26]*proscribed:* put to death.

Justice for All*

Israel's strong sense of equal justice and correct judicial procedure is shown in this selection.

You must not carry false rumors; you shall not join hands with the guilty to act as a malicious witness: You shall neither side with the mighty to do wrong—you shall not give perverse testimony in a dispute so as to pervert it in favor of the mighty—nor shall you show deference to a poor man in his dispute.

When you encounter your enemy's ox or ass wandering, you must take it back to him. When you see the ass of your enemy lying under its burden and would refrain from raising it, you must nevertheless raise it with him.

You shall not subvert the rights of your needy in their disputes. Keep far from a false charge; do not bring death on those who are innocent and in the right, for I will not acquit the wrong-doer. Do not take bribes, for bribes blind the clear-sighted and upset the pleas of those who are in the right.

You shall not oppress a stranger,[27] for you know the feelings of the stranger, having yourselves been strangers in the land of Egypt.

---

* *Exodus* 23:1–9

[27] *stranger:* resident alien in the land.

Holy War**

In holy war, God fights with and for the people against their Canaanite enemies during the conquest of the Promised Land. The people and cities of Canaan are to be sacrificed to God by utter destruction. Note that verses 10–14 specify a more humane method of warfare against non-Canaanite opponents. The last section sets limits on the destruction of the natural environment during warfare.

When you take the field against your enemies, and see horses and chariots—forces larger than yours—have no fear of them, for the Lord your God, who brought you from the land of Egypt, is with you. Before you join battle, the priest shall come forward and address the troops. He shall say to them, "Hear, O Israel You are about to join battle with your enemy. Let not your courage falter. Do not be in fear, or in panic, or in dread of them. For it is the Lord your God who marches with you to do battle for you against your enemy, to bring you victory."

[5] Then the officials shall address the troops, as follows: "Is there anyone who has built a new house but has not dedicated it? Let him go back to his home, lest he die in battle and another dedicate it. Is there anyone who has planted a vineyard but has never harvested it? Let him go back to his home, lest he die in battle and another harvest it. Is there anyone who has paid the bride-price[28] for a wife, but who has not yet married her? Let him go back to his home, lest he die in battle and another marry her." The officials shall go on addressing the troops and say, "Is there anyone afraid and disheartened? Let him go back to his home, lest the courage of his comrades flag like his." When the officials have finished addressing the troops, army commanders shall assume command of the troops.

** *Deuteronomy* 20:1–20

[28] *bride-price:* the husband's payment to the family of the bride.

[10] When you approach a town to attack it, you shall offer it terms of peace. If it responds peaceably and lets you in, all the people present there shall serve you at forced labor. If it does not surrender to you, but would join battle with you, you shall lay siege to it; and when the Lord your God delivers it into your hand, you shall put all its males to the sword. You may, however, take as your booty the women, the children, the livestock, and everything in the town—all its spoil—and enjoy the use of the spoil of your enemy, which the Lord your God gives you.

[15] Thus you shall deal with all towns that lie very far from you, towns that do not belong to nations hereabout. In the towns of the latter peoples, however, which the Lord your God is giving you as a heritage, you shall not let a soul remain alive. No, you must proscribe them—the Hittites and the Amorites, the Canaanites and the Perizzites, the Hivites and the Jebusites—as the Lord your God has commanded you, lest they lead you into doing all the abhorrent things that they have done for their gods and you stand guilty before the Lord your God.

When in your war against a city you have to besiege it a long time in order to capture it, you must not destroy its trees, wielding the ax against them. You may eat of them, but you must not cut them down. Are trees of the field human to withdraw before you into the besieged city? [20] Only trees that you know do not yield food may be destroyed; you may cut them down for constructing siegeworks against the city that is waging war on you, until it has been reduced.

Sexual Love*

The finest literary testimony to sexual love in the Bible *is the* Song of Songs. *Its poems are a dialogue between a man (traditionally Solomon) and a woman who take full delight in both the emotional and physical dimensions of love. Later Judaism, as well as Christianity, made this book symbolic of the love of God for people. (The notes in the brackets are not in the scripture text but are explanations by the editors of the* Tanakh *translation).*

[The woman speaks:] Oh, give me of the kisses
    of your mouth,
For your love is more delightful than wine.
Your ointments yield a sweet fragrance,
Your name is like finest oil—
Therefore do maidens love you.
Draw me after you, let us run
The king has brought me to his chambers.
Let us delight and rejoice in your love,

Savoring it more than wine—
Like new wine they love you!
[5] I am dark, but comely,[29]
O daughters of Jerusalem—
Like the tents of Kedar,
Like the pavilions of Solomon.
Don't stare at me because I am swarthy,
Because the sun has gazed upon me.
My mother's sons quarreled with me,
They made me guard the vineyards;
My own vineyard I did not guard.

Tell me, you whom I love so well;
Where do you pasture your sheep?
Where do you rest them at noon?
Let me not be as one who strays
Beside the flocks of your fellows.
If you do not know, O fairest of women,
Go follow the tracks of the sheep,

---

*Song of Songs 1:1–2:17

[29]The *New Revised Standard Version* of the Bible translates this, "I am black and beautiful."

And graze your kids
By the tents of the shepherds.

[The man speaks:] I have likened you, my
    darling,
To a mare in Pharaoh's chariots:
[10] Your cheeks are comely with plaited
    wreaths,
Your neck with strings of jewels.
We will add wreaths of gold
To your spangles of silver.

[The woman speaks:] While the king was on his
    couch,
My nard gave forth its fragrance.
My beloved to me is a bag of myrrh
Lodged between my breasts.
My beloved to me is a spray of henna blooms
From the vineyards of En-gedi.

[15, The man and woman exchange short com-
    pliments:] Ah, you are fair, my darling,
Ah, you are fair,
With your dove-like eyes
And you, my beloved, are handsome,
Beautiful indeed
Our couch is in a bower;
Cedars are the beams of our house,
Cypresses the rafters.
[2:1] I am a rose of Sharon,
A lily of the valleys.

[The woman speaks:] Like a lily among thorns,
So is my darling among the maidens.
Like an apple tree among trees of the forest,
So is my beloved among the youths.
I delight to sit in his shade,
And his fruit is sweet to my mouth.
He brought me to the banquet room
And his banner of love was over me.
[5] "Sustain me with raisin cakes,
Refresh me with apples,
For I am faint with love."
His left hand was under my head,
His right arm embraced me.
I adjure you, O maidens of Jerusalem,
By gazelles or by hinds of the field:

Do not wake or rouse
Love until it please!

Hark My beloved!
There he comes,
Leaping over mountains,
Bounding over hills.
My beloved is like a gazelle
Or like a young stag.
There he stands behind our wall,
Gazing through the window,
Peering through the lattice.
[10] My beloved spoke thus to me,
"Arise, my darling;
My fair one, come away!
For now the winter is past,
The rains are over and gone.
The blossoms have appeared in the land,
The time of pruning has come;
The song of the turtledove
Is heard in our land.
The green figs form on the fig tree,
The vines in blossom give off fragrance.
Arise, my darling;
My fair one, come away!"

[The man speaks:]
"O my dove, in the cranny of the rocks,
Hidden by the cliff,
Let me see your face,
Let me hear your voice;
For your voice is sweet
And your face is comely."
[15] Catch us the foxes,
The little foxes
That ruin the vineyards—
For our vineyard is in blossom.

[The woman speaks:] My beloved is mine
And I am his
Who browses among the lilies.
When the day blows gently
And the shadows flee,
Set out, my beloved,
Swift as a gazelle
Or a young stag,
For the hills of spices!

God's Call to an Unfaithful People*

In this oracle, Amos pronounces God's judgment on the unfaithful people of Israel. They enjoy worship and sacrifice to God but have neglected the basic commands of the law: justice and mercy. They have ignored God's chastisements, listed here; now God promises a severe final punishment.

Hear this word, you cows of Bashan
On the hill of Samaria—
Who defraud the poor,
Who rob the needy;
Who say to your husbands,
"Bring, and let's carouse!"
My Lord God swears by His holiness:
Behold, days are coming upon you
When you will be carried off in baskets,
And, to the last one, in fish baskets,
And taken out—
Each one through a breach straight ahead—
And flung on the refuse heap[30]
—declares the Lord.
Come to Bethel and transgress;
To Gilgal, and transgress even more:[31]
Present your sacrifices the next morning
And your tithes on the third day;
[5] And burn a thank offering of leavened
    bread;
And proclaim freewill offerings loudly.
For you love that sort of thing, O Israelites
—declares my Lord God.

I, on My part, have given you
Cleanness of teeth in all your towns,
And lack of food in all your settlements.
Yet you did not turn back to Me
—declares the Lord.

I therefore withheld the rain from you
Three months before harvest time:
I would make it rain on one town
And not on another;
One field would be rained upon
While another on which it did not rain
Would wither.
So two or three towns would wander
To a single town to drink water,
But their thirst would not be slaked.
Yet you did not turn back to Me
—declares the Lord.

I scourged you with blight and mildew;
Repeatedly your gardens and vineyards,
Your fig trees and olive trees
Were devoured by locusts.
Yet you did not turn back to Me
—declares the Lord.

[10] I sent against you pestilence
In the manner of Egypt;
I slew your young men with the sword,
Together with your captured horses,
And I made the stench of your armies
Rise in your very nostrils.
Yet you did not turn back to Me
—declares the Lord.

I have wrought destruction among you
As when God destroyed Sodom and
    Gomorrah;[32]
You have become like a brand plucked from
    burning.
Yet you have not turned back to Me
—declares the Lord.

Assuredly,
Because I am doing that to you,
Even so will I act toward you, O Israel—
Prepare to meet your God, O Israel!

---

*Amos 4:1–13
[30]These predictions look forward to the destruction of the northern kingdom of Israel by Assyria in 721 B.C.E.
[31]*Bethel, Gilgal:* Israelite cities with sanctuaries. Note the biting sarcasm of this section.

[32]*Sodom and Gomorrah:* cities destroyed for their wickedness; see *Genesis* 19:1–29.

Behold,
He who formed the mountains,
And created the wind,
And has told man what His wish is,

Who turns blackness into daybreak,
And treads upon the high places of the earth—
His name is the Lord, the God of Hosts.

Two Views of Wisdom*

Of all the types of literature in the Hebrew scriptures, the most international in form and content is the wisdom literature. In the first passage from the beginning of Proverbs, *the first paragraph describes what wisdom can do for its followers— lead to knowledge, mental power, and moral strength. Note in verse 20 and following the personification of wisdom as a woman. The second passage from* Ecclesiastes *gives a more pessimistic outlook on wisdom. Here it cannot answer life's riddles.* Proverbs *and* Ecclesiastes *are attributed to King Solomon, who had an ancient reputation as a sage.*

The proverbs of Solomon, son of David, king
    of Israel:
For learning wisdom and discipline;
For understanding words of discernment;
For acquiring the discipline for success,
Righteousness, justice, and equity;
For endowing the simple with shrewdness,
The young with knowledge and foresight.
[5]—The wise man, hearing them, will gain
    more wisdom;
The discerning man will learn to be adroit;
For understanding proverb and epigram,
The words of the wise and their riddles.

The fear of the Lord is the beginning of
    knowledge;
Fools despise wisdom and discipline.
My son, heed the discipline of your father,
And do not forsake the instruction of your
    mother;

For they are a graceful wreath upon your head,
A necklace about your throat.

[10] My son, if sinners entice you, do not yield;
If they say, "Come with us,
Let us set an ambush to shed blood,
Let us lie in wait for the innocent
[Without cause!]
Like Sheol, let us swallow them alive;
Whole, like those who go down into the Pit.[33]
We shall obtain every precious treasure;
We shall fill our homes with loot.
Throw in your lot with us;
We shall all have a common purse."

[15] My son, do not set out with them;
Keep your feet from their path.
For their feet run to evil;
They hurry to shed blood.
In the eyes of every winged creature
The outspread net means nothing.
But they lie in ambush for their own blood;
They lie in wait for their own lives.
Such is the fate of all who pursue unjust gain;
It takes the life of its possessor.

[20] Wisdom cries aloud in the streets,
Raises her voice in the squares.
At the head of the busy streets she calls;
At the entrance of the gates, in the city, she
    speaks out:
"How long will you simple ones love simplicity,
You scoffers be eager to scoff,
You dullards hate knowledge?
You are indifferent to my rebuke;
I will now speak my mind to you,

---

* *Proverbs* 1:1–33; *Ecclesiastes* 1:1–9

[33] *Sheol, the Pit:* the land of the dead.

And let you know my thoughts.
Since you refused me when I called,
And paid no heed when I extended my hand,
[25] You spurned all my advice,
And would not hear my rebuke,
I will laugh at your calamity,
And mock when terror comes upon you,
When terror comes like a disaster,
And calamity arrives like a whirlwind,
When trouble and distress come upon you.
Then they shall call me but I will not answer;
They shall seek me but not find me.
Because they hated knowledge,
And did not choose fear of the Lord,
[30] They refused my advice,
And disdained all my rebukes,
They shall eat the fruit of their ways,
And have their fill of their own counsels.
The tranquillity of the simple will kill them,
And the complacency of dullards will destroy
    them.
But he who listens to me will dwell in safety,
Untroubled by the terror of misfortune."

[*Ecclesiastes* 1:1–9] The words of Koheleth son
    of David, king in Jerusalem.
Utter futility!—said Koheleth—

Utter futility! All is futile!
What real value is there for a man
In all the gains he makes beneath the sun?

One generation goes, another comes,
But the earth remains the same forever.
[5] The sun rises, and the sun sets—
And glides back to where it rises.
Southward blowing,
Turning northward,
Ever turning blows the wind;
On its rounds the wind returns.
All streams flow into the sea,
Yet the sea is never full;
To the place [from] which they flow
The streams flow back again.
All such things are wearisome:
No man can ever state them;
The eye never has enough of seeing,
Nor the ear enough of hearing.
Only that shall happen
Which has happened,
Only that occur
Which has occurred;
There is nothing new
Beneath the sun!

The Virtuous Wife*

*Given the context of a patriarchal society, the
ideal wife depicted here is remarkably independent, appreciated for her abilities and relationships
rather than for her beauty or her ability to bear
children. The somewhat disjointed style of this
poem is the result of its unique composition—each
line begins with a successive letter of the Hebrew
alphabet.*

What a rare find is a capable wife!
Her worth is far beyond that of rubies.

Her husband puts his confidence in her,
And lacks no good thing.
She is good to him, never bad,
All the days of her life.
She looks for wool and flax,
And sets her hand to them with a will.
She is like a merchant fleet,
Bringing her food from afar.
[15] She rises while it is still night,
And supplies provisions for her household,
The daily fare of her maids.
She sets her mind on an estate and acquires it;
She plants a vineyard by her own labors.
She girds herself with strength,

---

*Proverbs 31:10–31

And performs her tasks with vigor.
She sees that her business thrives;
Her lamp never goes out at night.
She sets her hand to the distaff;
Her fingers work the spindle.
[20] She gives generously to the poor;
Her hands are stretched out to the needy.
She is not worried for her household because
   of snow,
For her whole household is dressed in crimson.
She makes covers for herself;
Her clothing is linen and purple.
Her husband is prominent in the gates,
As he sits among the elders of the land.
She makes cloth and sells it,
And offers a girdle to the merchant.

[25] She is clothed with strength and splendor;
She looks to the future cheerfully.
Her mouth is full of wisdom,
Her tongue with kindly teaching.
She oversees the activities of her household
And never eats the bread of idleness.
Her children declare her happy;
Her husband praises her,
"Many women have done well,
But you surpass them all."
[30] Grace is deceptive,
Beauty is illusory;
It is for her fear of the Lord
That a woman is to be praised.
Extol her for the fruit of her hand,
And let her works praise her in the gates.

ORGANIZATION

The Ordination of Priests*

This passage outlines the sacrificial ceremony by which priests are ordained, that is, consecrated to the service of God. The ceremony here indicates the role of the priesthood in Israel: intermediaries between God and the people. God here speaks to Moses ("you").

This is what you shall do to them in consecrating them to serve Me as priests: Take a young bull of the herd and two rams without blemish; also unleavened bread, unleavened cakes with oil mixed in, and unleavened wafers spread with oil—make these of choice wheat flour. Place these in one basket and present them in the basket, along with the bull and the two rams. Lead Aaron and his sons up to the entrance of the Tent of Meeting, and wash them with water. [5] Then take the vestments, and clothe Aaron with the tunic, the robe of the ephod [the main priestly garment], the ephod, and the breast-piece, and gird him with the decorated band of the ephod. Put the headdress on his head, and place the holy diadem upon the headdress. Take the anointing oil and pour it on his head and anoint him. Then bring his sons forward; clothe them with tunics and wind turbans upon them. And gird both Aaron and his sons with sashes. And so they shall have priesthood as their right for all time.

You shall then ordain Aaron and his sons. [10] Lead the bull up to the front of the Tent of Meeting, and let Aaron and his sons lay their hands upon the head of the bull. Slaughter the bull before the Lord, at the entrance of the Tent of Meeting, and take some of the bull's blood and put it on the horns of the altar with your finger; then pour out the rest of the blood at the base of the altar. Take all the fat that covers the entrails, the protuberance on the liver, and the two kidneys with the fat on them, and turn them into smoke upon the altar. The rest of the flesh of the bull, its hide, and its dung shall be put to the fire outside the camp; it is a sin offering.

* Exodus 29:1–37

[15] Next take the one ram, and let Aaron and his sons lay their hands upon the ram's head. Slaughter the ram, and take its blood and dash it against all sides of the altar. Cut up the ram into sections, wash its entrails and legs, and put them with its quarters and its head. Turn all of the ram into smoke upon the altar. It is a burnt offering to the Lord, a pleasing odor, an offering by fire to the Lord.

Then take the other ram, and let Aaron and his sons lay their hands upon the ram's head. [20] Slaughter the ram, and take some of its blood and put it on the ridge of Aaron's right ear and on the ridges of his sons' right ears, and on the thumbs of their right hands, and on the big toes of their right feet; and dash the rest of the blood against every side of the altar round about. Take some of the blood that is on the altar and some of the anointing oil and sprinkle upon Aaron and his vestments, and also upon his sons and his sons' vestments. Thus shall he and his vestments be holy, as well as his sons and his sons' vestments.

You shall take from the ram the fat parts— the broad tail, the fat that covers the entrails, the protuberance on the liver, the two kidneys with the fat on them—and the right thigh; for this is a ram of ordination. Add one flat loaf of bread, one cake of oil bread, and one wafer, from the basket of unleavened bread that is before the Lord. Place all these on the palms of Aaron and his sons, and offer them as an elevation offering[34] before the Lord. [25] Take them from their hands and turn them into smoke upon the altar with the burnt offering, as a pleasing odor before the Lord; it is an offering by fire to the Lord. . . . The sacral vestments of Aaron shall pass on to his sons after him, for them to be anointed and ordained in. [30] He among his sons who becomes priest in his stead, who enters the Tent of Meeting to officiate within the sanctuary, shall wear them seven days. . . .

[35] Thus you shall do to Aaron and his sons, just as I have commanded you. You shall ordain them through seven days, and each day you shall prepare a bull as a sin offering for expiation; you shall purge the altar by performing purification upon it, and you shall anoint it to consecrate it. Seven days you shall perform purification for the altar to consecrate it, and the altar shall become most holy; whatever touches the altar shall become consecrated.

---

[34]*elevation offering:* a sacrifice of a vegetable product, moved back and forth, and up and down, before the altar.

A Call to Be a Prophet*

This passage from the ninth-century B.C.E. is the fullest prophetic call vision in the Hebrew scriptures, and certainly the most dramatic. Though highly negative in tone—Isaiah's job as a prophet will not be a happy one—the end of the passage (probably added later) promises some hope.

In the year that King Uzziah died, I beheld my Lord seated on a high and lofty throne; and the skirts of His robe filled the Temple. Seraphs stood in attendance on Him. Each of them had six wings: with two he covered his face, with two he covered his legs, and with two he would fly.

And one would call to the other,
"Holy, holy, holy!
The Lord of Hosts!
His presence fills all the earth!"

The doorposts would shake at the sound of the one who called, and the House kept filling with smoke. [5] I cried,

"Woe is me; I am lost!
For I am a man of unclean lips

---

* *Isaiah 6:1–13*

And I live among a people
Of unclean lips;
Yet my own eyes have beheld
The King Lord of Hosts."

Then one of the seraphs flew over to me with a live coal, which he had taken from the altar with a pair of tongs. He touched it to my lips and declared,

"Now that this has touched your lips,
Your guilt shall depart
And your sin be purged away."

Then I heard the voice of my Lord saying, "Whom shall I send? Who will go for us?" And I said, "Here am I; send me." And He said, "Go, say to that people:

'Hear, indeed, but do not understand;
See, indeed, but do not grasp.'
[10] Dull that people's mind,

Stop its ears,
And seal its eyes—
Lest, seeing with its eyes
And hearing with its ears,
It also grasps with its mind,
And repents and saves itself."

I asked, "How long, my Lord?" And He replied:

"Till towns lie waste without inhabitants
And houses without people,
And the ground lies waste and desolate—
For the Lord will banish the population—
And deserted sites are many
In the midst of the land.

"But while a tenth part yet remains in it, it shall repent. It shall be ravaged like the terebinth and the oak, of which stumps are left even when they are felled: its stump shall be a holy seed."

Women as Judges and Prophets*

The leadership of Israel was predominantly male, but occasionally women rose to prominent positions. In the first selection, Deborah the "judge" (national leader) delivers her nation from a military threat. In the second selection, Huldah the prophet speaks the word of God to the king of Judah at a critical time of repentance and reform.

Deborah, wife of Lappidoth, was a prophetess; she led Israel at that time. [5] She used to sit under the Palm of Deborah, between Ramah and Bethel in the hill country of Ephraim, and the Israelites would come to her for decisions.

She summoned Barak son of Abinoam, of Kedesh in Naphtali, and said to him, "The Lord, the God of Israel, has commanded: Go, march up to Mount Tabor, and take with you ten thousand men of Naphtali and Zebulun. And I will draw Sisera, Jabin's army commander, with his chariots and his troops, toward you up to the Wadi Kishon; and I will deliver him into your hands." But Barak said to her, "If you will go with me, I will go; if not, I will not go." "Very well, I will go with you," she answered. "However, there will be no glory for you in the course you are taking, for then the Lord will deliver Sisera into the hands of a woman." So Deborah went with Barak to Kedesh. [10] Barak then mustered Zebulun and Naphtali at Kedesh; ten thousand men marched up after him; and Deborah also went up with him. . . .

Sisera was informed that Barak son of Abinoam had gone up to Mount Tabor. So Sisera ordered all his chariots—nine hundred iron chariots—and all the troops he had to move

---

*Judges 4:4–10, 12–16; II Kings 22:11–20

from Harosheth-goiim to the Wadi Kishon. Then Deborah said to Barak, "Up! This is the day on which the Lord will deliver Sisera into your hands: the Lord is marching before you." Barak charged down Mount Tabor, followed by the ten thousand men, [15] and the Lord threw Sisera and all his chariots and army into a panic before the onslaught of Barak. Sisera leaped from his chariot and fled on foot as Barak pursued the chariots and the soldiers as far as Harosheth-goiim. All of Sisera's soldiers fell by the sword; not a man was left. [The next section recounts how Jael, a Kenite woman allied with Israel, killed Sisera while he was sleeping in her tent.]

[II Kings 22:11] When the king [Josiah] heard the words of the scroll of the Teaching,[35] he rent his clothes. And the king gave orders to the priest Hilkiah, and to Ahikam son of Shaphan, Achbor son of Michaiah, the scribe Shaphan, and Asaiah the king's minister: "Go, inquire of the Lord on my behalf, and on behalf of the people, and on behalf of all Judah, concerning the words of this scroll that has been found. For great indeed must be the wrath of the Lord that has been kindled against us, because our fathers

---

[35] *scroll of the Teaching:* probably an early form of the biblical book of *Deuteronomy.*

did not obey the words of this scroll to do all that has been prescribed for us."

So the priest Hilkiah, and Ahikam, Achbor, Shaphan, and Asaiah went to the prophetess Huldah—the wife of Shallum son of Tikvah son of Harhas, the keeper of the wardrobe—who was living in Jerusalem in the Mishneh, and they spoke to her. [15] She responded: "Thus said the Lord, the God of Israel: Say to the man who sent you to me: Thus said the Lord: I am going to bring disaster upon this place and its inhabitants, in accordance with all the words of the scroll which the king of Judah has read. Because they have forsaken Me and have made offerings to other gods and vexed Me with all their deeds, My wrath is kindled against this place and it shall not be quenched. But say this to the king of Judah, who sent you to inquire of the Lord: Thus said the Lord, the God of Israel: As for the words which you have heard—because your heart was softened and you humbled yourself before the Lord when you heard what I decreed against this place and its inhabitants—that it will become a desolation and a curse—and because you rent your clothes and wept before Me, I for My part have listened—declares the Lord. [20] Assuredly, I will gather you to your fathers and you will be laid in your tomb in peace. Your eyes shall not see all the disaster which I will bring upon this place." So they brought back the reply to the king.

RITUAL

The Establishment of Circumcision*

Circumcision is the sign of the covenant and membership in the people of Israel. As such, it is the primary ritual in Judaism. Here its origins are traced to Abraham.

---

*Genesis 17:9–14, 23–27

God further said to Abraham, "As for you, you and your offspring to come throughout the ages shall keep My covenant. [10] Such shall be the covenant between Me and you and your offspring to follow which you shall keep: every male among you shall be circumcised. You shall circumcise the flesh of your foreskin, and that shall be the sign of the covenant between Me and you. And throughout the generations, every male among you shall be circumcised at the age of eight days. As for the homeborn slave and the one bought from an outsider who is not of your offspring, they must be circumcised, homeborn and purchased alike. Thus shall My covenant be marked in your flesh as an everlasting pact. And if any male who is uncircumcised fails to circumcise the flesh of his foreskin, that person shall be cut off from his kin; he has broken My covenant. . . ."

[23] Then Abraham took his son Ishmael, and all his homeborn slaves and all those he had bought, every male in Abraham's household, and he circumcised the flesh of their foreskins on that very day, as God had spoken to him. Abraham was ninety-nine years old when he circumcised the flesh of his foreskin, [25] and his son Ishmael was thirteen years old when he was circumcised in the flesh of his foreskin. Thus Abraham and his son Ishmael were circumcised on that very day; and all his household, his homeborn slaves and those that had been bought from outsiders, were circumcised with him.

The Establishment of the Passover*

In the first two paragraphs of this selection, the ingredients of the meals itself and the meaning of the Passover are given. In the third and fourth paragraphs, the feast of unleavened bread (mazoh) is treated; originally it was a harvest festival, but now it is incorporated into the Passover.

The Lord said to Moses and Aaron in the land of Egypt: This month shall mark for you the beginning of the months; it shall be the first of the months[36] of the year for you. Speak to the whole community of Israel and say that on the tenth of this month each of them shall take a lamb to a family, a lamb to a household. But if the household is too small for a lamb, let him share one with a neighbor who dwells nearby, in proportion to the number of persons; you shall contribute for the lamb according to what each household will eat. [5] Your lamb shall be without blemish, a yearling male; you may take it from the sheep or from the goats. You shall keep watch over it until the fourteenth day of this month; and all the assembled congregation of the Israelites shall slaughter it at twilight. They shall take some of the blood and put it on the two doorposts and the lintel of the houses in which they are to eat it. They shall eat the flesh that same night; they shall eat it roasted over the fire, with unleavened bread and with bitter herbs. Do not eat any of it raw, or cooked in any way with water, but roasted—head, legs, and entrails—over the fire. [10] You shall not leave any of it over until morning; if any of it is left until morning, you shall burn it.

This is how you shall eat it: your loins girded, your sandals on your feet, and your staff in your hand; and you shall eat it hurriedly: it is a passover offering to the Lord. For that night I will go through the land of Egypt and strike down every first-born in the land of Egypt, both man and beast; and I will mete out punishments to all the gods of Egypt, I the Lord. And the blood on the houses where you are staying shall be a sign for you: when I see the blood I will pass over you, so that no plague will destroy you when I strike the land of Egypt.

This day shall be to you one of remembrance: you shall celebrate it as a festival to the Lord throughout the ages; you shall celebrate it as an institution for all time. [15] Seven days you shall

---

*Exodus 12:1–19, 24–27
[36]*first of months:* Nisan, a spring month that is the first month in the Jewish calendar.

eat unleavened bread; on the very first day you shall remove leaven from your houses, for whoever eats leavened bread from the first day to the seventh day, that person shall be cut off from Israel.

You shall celebrate a sacred occasion on the first day, and a sacred occasion on the seventh day; no work at all shall be done on them; only what every person is to eat, that alone may be prepared for you. You shall observe the [Feast of] Unleavened Bread, for on this very day I brought your ranks out of the land of Egypt; you shall observe this day throughout the ages as an institution for all time. In the first month, from the fourteenth day of the month at evening, you shall eat unleavened bread until the twenty-first day of the month at evening. No leaven shall be found in your houses for seven days. For whoever eats what is leavened, that person shall be cut off from the community of Israel, whether he is a stranger or a citizen of the country. . . .

[24] You shall observe this [Passover] as an institution for all time, for you and for your descendants. And when you enter the land that the Lord will give you, as He has promised, you shall observe this rite. And when your children ask you, 'What do you mean by this rite?' you shall say, 'It is the Passover sacrifice to the Lord, because He passed over the houses of the Israelites in Egypt when He smote the Egyptians, but saved our houses.'

The Observance of the Sabbath*

Throughout Jewish history, keeping the sabbath, or seventh day of the week, has been an important sign of Judaism. In this passage, which expands on the sabbath command in the Decalogue, the penalty for breaking it, like the penalty for breaking the other commandments of the Decalogue, is death.

The Lord said to Moses: Speak to the Israelite people and say: Nevertheless, you must keep My sabbaths, for this is a sign between Me and you throughout the ages, that you may know that I the Lord have consecrated you. You shall keep the sabbath, for it is holy for you. He who profanes it shall be put to death: whoever does work on it, that person shall be cut off from among his kin. [15] Six days may work be done, but on the seventh day there shall be a sabbath of complete rest, holy to the Lord; whoever does work on the sabbath day shall be put to death. The Israelite people shall keep the sabbath, observing the sabbath throughout the ages as a covenant for all time: it shall be a sign for all time between Me and the people of Israel. For in six days the Lord made heaven and earth, and on the seventh day He ceased from work and was refreshed.

*Exodus 31:12–17

Offerings for the Forgiveness of Sin**

The sin offering is a sacrifice of repentance for unintentional sin. It restores the offender to God and secures the well-being of his community. The sections before this passage deal with offerings for the high priest, for the nation of Israel as a whole, and with a ruler. This passage deals with offerings prescribed for a common citizen. Though this passage speaks of the Tent of Meeting that was used immediately after the Exodus, the ceremony described here is more reflective of later temple procedure.

**Leviticus 4:27–5:7

If any person from among the populace unwittingly incurs guilt by doing any of the things which by the Lord's commandments ought not to be done, and he realizes his guilt—or the sin of which he is guilty is brought to his knowledge—he shall bring a female goat without blemish as his offering for the sin of which he is guilty. He shall lay his hand upon the head of the sin offering, and the sin offering shall be slaughtered at the place of the burnt offering. [30] The priest shall take with his finger some of its blood and put it on the horns of the altar of burnt offering; and all the rest of its blood he shall pour out at the base of the altar. He shall remove all its fat, just as the fat is removed from the sacrifice of well-being; and the priest shall turn it into smoke on the altar, for a pleasing odor to the Lord. Thus the priest shall make expiation for him, and he shall be forgiven.

If the offering he brings as a sin offering is a sheep, he shall bring a female without blemish. He shall lay his hand upon the head of the sin offering, and it shall be slaughtered as a sin offering at the spot where the burnt offering is slaughtered. The priest shall take with his finger some of the blood of the sin offering and put it on the horns of the altar of burnt offering, and all the rest of its blood he shall pour out at the base of the altar. [35] And all its fat he shall remove just as the fat of the sheep of the sacrifice of well-being is removed; and this the priest shall turn into smoke on the altar, over the Lord's offerings by fire. Thus the priest shall make expiation on his behalf for the sin of which he is guilty, and he shall be forgiven.

[5:1] If a person incurs guilt: When he has heard a public imprecation and—although able to testify as one who has either seen or learned of the matter—he does not give information, so that he is subject to punishment; or when a person touches any unclean thing—be it the carcass of an unclean beast or the carcass of unclean cattle or the carcass of an unclean creeping thing—and the fact has escaped him, and then, being unclean, he realizes his guilt; or when he touches human uncleanness—any such uncleanness whereby one becomes unclean—and, though he has known it, the fact has escaped him, but later he realizes his guilt; or when a person utters an oath to bad or good purpose—whatever a man may utter in an oath—and, though he has known it, the fact has escaped him, but later he realizes his guilt in any of these matters—[5] when he realizes his guilt in any of these matters, he shall confess that wherein he has sinned. And he shall bring as his penalty to the Lord, for the sin of which he is guilty, a female from the flock, sheep or goat, as a sin offering; and the priest shall make expiation on his behalf for his sin.

But if his means do not suffice for a sheep, he shall bring to the Lord, as his penalty for that of which he is guilty, two turtledoves or two pigeons, one for a sin offering and the other for a burnt offering.

The Day of Atonement*

This selection presents the ceremonies of the Day of Atonement (Yom Kippur). Since the destruction of the Second Temple in 70 C.E., Jews have practiced the spiritual heart of the feast as it is developed at the end of the passage: a day of rest, self-denial, confession, and making amends.

The Lord spoke to Moses after the death of the two sons of Aaron who died when they drew too close to the presence of the Lord. The Lord said to Moses:

Tell your brother Aaron that he is not to come at will into the Shrine behind the curtain, in front of the cover that is upon the ark, lest he die; for I appear in the cloud over the cover. Thus only shall Aaron enter the Shrine: with a

*Leviticus 16:1–5, 11–19, 29–34

bull of the herd for a sin offering and a ram for a burnt offering. He shall be dressed in a sacral linen tunic, with linen breeches next to his flesh, and be girt with a linen sash, and he shall wear a linen turban. They are sacral vestments; he shall bathe his body in water and then put them on. And from the Israelite community he shall take two he-goats for a sin offering and a ram for a burnt offering. . . .

[11] Aaron shall then offer his bull of sin offering, to make expiation for himself and his household. He shall slaughter his bull of sin offering, and he shall take a panful of glowing coals scooped from the altar before the Lord, and two handfuls of finely ground aromatic incense, and bring this behind the curtain. He shall put the incense on the fire before the Lord, so that the cloud from the incense screens the cover that is over [the Ark of] the Pact, lest he die. He shall take some of the blood of the bull and sprinkle it with his finger over the cover on the east side; and in front of the cover he shall sprinkle some of the blood with his finger seven times. [15] He shall then slaughter the people's goat of sin offering, bring its blood behind the curtain, and do with its blood as he has done with the blood of the bull: he shall sprinkle it over the cover and in front of the cover.

Thus he shall purge the Shrine of the uncleanness and transgression of the Israelites, whatever their sins; and he shall do the same for the Tent of Meeting, which abides with them in the midst of their uncleanness. When he goes in to make expiation in the Shrine, nobody else shall be in the Tent of Meeting until he comes out.

When he has made expiation for himself and his household, and for the whole congregation of Israel, he shall go out to the altar that is before the Lord and purge it: he shall take some of the blood of the bull and of the goat and apply it to each of the horns of the altar; and the rest of the blood he shall sprinkle on it with his finger seven times. Thus he shall cleanse it of the uncleanness of the Israelites and consecrate it. . . .

[29] And this shall be to you a law for all time: In the seventh month, on the tenth day of the month, you shall practice self-denial; and you shall do no manner of work, neither the citizen nor the alien who resides among you. For on this day atonement shall be made for you to cleanse you of all your sins; you shall be clean before the Lord. It shall be a sabbath of complete rest for you, and you shall practice self-denial; it is a law for all time. The priest who has been anointed and ordained to serve as priest in place of his father shall make expiation. He shall put on the linen vestments, the sacral vestments. He shall purge the innermost Shrine; he shall purge the Tent of Meeting and the altar; and he shall make expiation for the priests and for all the people of the congregation. This shall be to you a law for all time: to make atonement for the Israelites for all their sins once a year. And Moses did as the Lord had commanded him.

Kosher and Nonkosher Foods*

This passage on dietary law gives a list of clean and unclean foods, the first criterion for cleanness. The types of unclean animals specified here are: (1) four-footed animals that do not chew the cud and have a split hoof, (2) carnivorous birds, (3) *winged insects, (4) water animals lacking fins and scales, and (5) small creeping ("swarming") animals.*

The Lord spoke to Moses and Aaron, saying to them: Speak to the Israelite people thus:

These are the creatures that you may eat from among all the land animals: any animal that has

---

*Leviticus 11:1–31, 41–45

true hoofs, with clefts through the hoofs, and that chews the cud—such you may eat. The following, however, of those that either chew the cud or have true hoofs, you shall not eat: the camel—although it chews the cud, it has no true hoofs: it is unclean for you; [5] the daman [a type of sheep]—although it chews the cud, it has no true hoofs: it is unclean for you; the hare —although it chews the cud, it has no true hoofs: it is unclean for you; and the swine— although it has true hoofs, with the hoofs cleft through, it does not chew the cud: it is unclean for you. You shall not eat of their flesh or touch their carcasses; they are unclean for you.

These you may eat of all that live in water: anything in water, whether in the seas or in the streams, that has fins and scales—these you may eat. [10] But anything in the seas or in the streams that has no fins and scales, among all the swarming things of the water and among all the other living creatures that are in the water— they are an abomination for you and an abomination for you they shall remain: you shall not eat of their flesh and you shall abominate their carcasses. Everything in water that has no fins and scales shall be an abomination for you.

The following you shall abominate among the birds—they shall not be eaten, they are an abomination: the eagle, the vulture, and the black vulture; the kite, falcons of every variety; [15] all varieties of raven; the ostrich, the nighthawk, the sea gull; hawks of every variety; the little owl, the cormorant, and the great owl; the white owl, the pelican, and the bustard; the stork; herons of every variety; the hoopoe, and the bat.

[20] All winged swarming things that walk on fours shall be an abomination for you. But these you may eat among all the winged swarming things that walk on fours: all that have, above their feet, jointed legs to leap with on the ground—of these you may eat the following: locusts of every variety; all varieties of bald locust; crickets of every variety; and all varieties of grasshopper. But all other winged swarming things that have four legs shall be an abomination for you.

And the following shall make you unclean— whoever touches their carcasses shall be unclean until evening, [25] and whoever carries the carcasses of any of them shall wash his clothes and be unclean until evening—every animal that has true hoofs but without clefts through the hoofs, or that does not chew the cud. They are unclean for you; whoever touches them shall be unclean. Also all animals that walk on paws, among those that walk on fours, are unclean for you; whoever touches their carcasses shall be unclean until evening. And anyone who carries their carcasses shall wash his clothes and remain unclean until evening. They are unclean for you.

The following shall be unclean for you from among the things that swarm on the earth: the mole, the mouse, and great lizards of every variety; [30] the gecko, the land crocodile, the lizard, the sand lizard, and the chameleon. Those are for you the unclean among all the swarming things; whoever touches them when they are dead shall be unclean until evening. . . .

[41] All the things that swarm upon the earth are an abomination; they shall not be eaten. You shall not eat, among all things that swarm upon the earth, anything that crawls on its belly, or anything that walks on fours, or anything that has many legs; for they are an abomination. You shall not draw abomination upon yourselves through anything that swarms; you shall not make yourselves unclean therewith and thus become unclean. For I the Lord am your God: you shall sanctify yourselves and be holy, for I am holy. You shall not make yourselves unclean through any swarming thing that moves upon the earth. [45] For I the Lord am He who brought you up from the land of Egypt to be your God: you shall be holy, for I am holy.

APPENDIX: SELECTIONS FROM THE *MISHNAH* AND *TALMUD*

Jews have traditionally held the *Talmud* as an authoritative book. They often understood the *Bible,* and applied it to all the affairs of their daily life, through the *Talmud.* Here are two sample passages from this important writing. In the first, taken entirely from the *Mishnah,* the rabbis explain the chain of transmission of the Oral Torah from Moses to the writing of the *Mishnah.* In the second, the biblical duty to have children is discussed in the *Talmud.*

The Sayings of the Fathers*

This famous passage from the Mishnah, *which was of course incorporated with all the* Mishnah *into the* Babylonian Talmud, *is concerned to trace the transmission of the Torah ("law, instruction") from Moses to the second century* C.E., *when the* Mishnah *was compiled. This* Torah *refers especially to the oral Torah, the body of legal opinions developed by the rabbis and codified in the* Mishnah. *Note the characteristic use of three sayings to sum up the teachings of leading figures in this chain of transmission.*[37]

Moses received the Torah from Sinai and delivered it to Joshua, and Joshua delivered it to the elders, and the elders to the prophets, and the prophets to the men of the great synagogue. They said three things, "Be deliberate in judgment, raise up many disciples, and make a fence around the law."

Simon the Just was one of the last men of the great synagogue. He used to say that the world stood on three things, "On the law, the [temple] service, and the acts of the pious."

Antigonus of Soco received [the Torah] from Simon the Just. He used to say, "Be not like servants who serve their master for the sake of receiving a reward, but be like servants who serve their master without the intent of receiving a reward; and let the fear of heaven be upon you."

Jose, son of Joezer of Zeredah, and Jose, son of Jochanan of Jerusalem, received [the Torah] from him. Jose, son of Joezer of Zeredah, said, "Let your house be a house of assembly for the wise, dust yourself with the dust of their feet, and drink their words in thirstiness."

[5] Jose, son of Jochanan of Jerusalem, said, "Let your house be wide open, and let the poor be your children. Do not talk much with women, not even with your wife, much less with your neighbor's wife." Hence the wise men say, "Whoever converses much with women brings evil on himself, neglects the study of the law, and at last will inherit hell."

Joshua, son of Perechiah, and Natai the Arbelite received the oral law from them. Joshua, son of Perechiah, said, "Get yourself a master, and obtain a companion [in learning], and judge all mankind with favor."

Natai the Arbelite said, "Withdraw from an evil neighbor, and associate not with the wicked, neither flatter yourself to escape punishment."

Judah, son of Tabai, and Simon, son of Shetach, received it from them. Judah son of Tabai said, "Do not consider yourself as the arranger of the law, and when the parties are before you in judgment, consider them as guilty; but when they are departed from you, consider them as innocent, when they have acquiesced in the sentence."

---

*Mishnah, *Aboth* 1.1–18
[37]Taken, with editing, from Joseph Barclay, trans., *Hebrew Literature,* rev. ed. (New York: Colonial Press, 1901).

Simon, son of Shetach, said, "Be extremely careful in the examination of witnesses, and be cautious in your words, lest they [the witnesses] should learn to utter a falsehood."

[10] Shemaiah and Abtalyon received it from them. Shemaiah said, "Love your business and hate power, and keep clear of the government."

Abtalyon said, "You Sages, be cautious of your words, lest you be doomed to captivity, and carried captive to a place of bad waters, and the disciples who follow you should drink of them, by which means the name of God may be profaned."

Hillel and Shammai received it from them. Hillel said, "Be like the disciples of Aaron, who loved peace and pursued peace, so that you love mankind, and allure them to the study of the law."

He used to say, "Whoever aggrandizes his name, destroys his name; he who does not increase his knowledge in the law, shall be cut off; he who does not study the law is deserving of death, and he who serves himself with the crown of the law, will perish."

He also said, "If I do not perform good works myself, who can do them for me?" and "When I consider myself, what am I?" and "If not now, when?"

[15] Shammai said, "Let your study of the law be fixed, say little and do much, and receive all men with an open, pleasant face."

Rabban Gamaliel said, "Get yourself an instructor, that you may not be in doubt, and do not accustom yourself to give [too many] tithes by conjecture."

Simon, his son, said, "All my life I have been brought up among wise men, and never found anything so good for the body as silence; neither is the study of the law the principal thing, but its practice; whoever multiplies words causes sin."

Rabban Simon, son of Gamaliel, said the duration of the world depends on three things, justice, truth, and peace, as is said, "Judge truth, justice, and peace in your gates."[38]

---

[38]*Judge truth . . . gates:* a quotation from *Zechariah* 8:16.

The Duty to Marry and Have Children*

In Jewish reckoning, the first commandment in the Torah *is God's command to the human race, "Be fruitful and multiply." This passage discusses the implications of this command. Like all Talmudic passages, this one relies heavily on the interpretation of scripture, some of it straightforward and some highly creative.*[39]

A man must not abstain from carrying out the obligation to "be fruitful and multiply"[40] unless he already has two children. The School of

Shammai ruled that this means two sons, and the School of Hillel ruled that it means a son and a daughter, because it is written, "Male and female He created them."[41] The duty of procreation applies to a man, but not to a woman. Rabbi Yohanan the son of Seroka said that it applies to both [man and woman], for "God blessed them and said to them, 'Be fruitful and multiply'."[42]

This [Mishnah] passage means that if a man has children he may abstain from the duty of procreation, but he may not abstain from living with his wife. This supports the view of Rabbi

---

*Babylonian Talmud, tractate *Yebamoth* ("Sisters-in-law") 61b–63

[39]This passage, and the following, are translated by the editor.

[40]*Genesis* 1:28.

[41]*Genesis* 1:28, 5:2.

[42]This paragraph is from *Mishnah* 6:6; the rest of the passage is the *Gemara* discussion of it.

Nahman who reported a ruling in the name of Samuel, that even though a man have many children, he may not remain without a wife, for it is written: "It is not good for a man to be alone."[43] Others held the opinion that if a man had children, he may abstain from the duty of procreation and he may also abstain from the duty of living with a wife. Does this contradict what was reported by Rabbi Nahman in the name of Samuel? No. If he has no children, he is to marry a woman capable of having a child, but if he already has children, he may marry a woman who is incapable of having children.

Other rabbis taught that Rabbi Nathan said that according to the School of Shammai, a person satisfies the obligation to "be fruitful and multiply" if he has a son and a daughter, and according to the School of Hillel if he has a son or a daughter. Rabbi [Judah the Prince] said, "Why this view of the School of Hillel? It is written, 'God created it not to be a waste, and he formed it to be inhabited,'[44] and he has already contributed to making it a place of habitation [by having a child].

What if a person had children while he was a pagan, and was later converted? Rabbi Yohanan said that he has already fulfilled the duty of procreation. However, Rabbi Lakish said that he has not fulfilled it, because when a person is converted he is like a born-again child."

The Mishnah disagrees with the view of Rabbi Joshua. Joshua stated that if a person married in his youth he is also to marry in his old age; and if he had children in his youth, he is also to have children in his old age. For it is written: "Sow your seed in the morning and do not withdraw your hand in the evening, for you do not know which will prosper, this or that, or whether both alike will be good."[45]

Rabbi Tanhum said in the name of Rabbi Hanilai that a man who is without a wife has no joy, no blessing, and no good. He has no joy, for it is written: "You shall rejoice, you and your household."[46] He has no blessing, for it is written: "That a blessing may rest on your house."[47] He has no good, for it is written: "It is not good for a man to be alone.". . .[48]

Rabbi Joshua the son of Levi said that a man who knows his wife to be a God-fearing woman and does not have sexual relations with her is a sinner, for it is written: "And you shall visit your habitation and you will not sin."

The rabbis taught that when a man loves his wife as himself, and honors her more than himself, and trains his sons and daughters in the right path and arranges for their marriage at a young age—about this man the verse says, "And you shall know that your tent is at peace."

Rabbi Eleazar said that a man without a wife is not a complete man, for it is written: "Male and female created He them, and He called their name *adam*, 'man'."[49]

Avert your eyes from the charms of another man's wife, or you may be trapped in her snare. Do not become friends with her husband, and drink wine and strong drink with him. Through the appearance of a beautiful woman many men have been destroyed, and she has killed a vast number.

---

43 *Genesis* 2:18.
44 *Isaiah* 45:18.
45 *Ecclesiastes* 11:6.
46 *Deuteronomy* 14:26.
47 *Ezekiel* 44:30.
48 *Genesis* 2:18.
49 *Genesis* 5:2.

GLOSSARY

ark the special closet or recess in the synagogue wall on the side nearest Jerusalem in which *Bible* scrolls used for public worship are stored.

Bible the "Book" of Jewish scripture, numbering twenty-four books by Jewish count. In the Christian framework, it includes the thirty-nine books of the Jewish scripture and the twenty-seven *New Testament* books.

covenant an agreement between God and the people of Israel, with obligations and privileges for each party.

Decalogue literally, the "Ten Words"; also known as the Ten Commandments (*Exodus* 20:1–17, with a restatement in *Deuteronomy* 5:6–21).

Kethuvim [KETH-u-veem] *Writings*, the third division of the Jewish *Bible*.

lectionary a list of scripture readings for divine worship.

mezuzah [meh-ZOO-zah] a small box containing *Bible* verses attached to doorposts of the Jewish house.

Nevi'im [NEH-vih-eem] *Prophets*, the second division of the Jewish *Bible*.

psalm [sahlm] in Judaism and Christianity, a religious song of the style found in the biblical book of Psalms used for divine worship.

revelation the communication of the divine person or truth to humanity.

Shema [sheh-MAH] Judaism's most basic statement of faith, found in *Deuteronomy* 6:4–9 and two shorter passages.

Talmud [TALL-mood] the Jewish law code, a compilation of the "oral Torah."

Tanakh [TAH-nahk] acronymic name for the Jewish *Bible*, formed from the first letters of *Torah, Nevi'im,* and *Kethuvim*.

tefillin [teh-FILL-in] small boxes containing *Bible* verses on tiny scrolls, bound by leather straps on the forehead and weaker arm of the Orthodox Jew during prayers.

Torah [TOH-rah] the first five books of the Jewish *Bible;* more broadly, God's teaching and revelation.

QUESTIONS FOR STUDY AND DISCUSSION

1. In what ways did the Jewish people link their history to their system of morality? Consider two focal points of the *Bible:* (1) the relationship of the Exodus and law; (2) the restoration of the Jews to their land after the Exile and concerns for purity.

2. Explain how the Jewish scripture's three main sections are arranged in order of importance. What has it meant for Judaism that the *Torah* is first, *Prophets* second, and *Writings* third?

3. Discuss the tension in the *Bible* between Israel's call to be a light to the other nations and the demand to be a separate, holy people.

4. How has Judaism adapted its worship and rituals to a time when it has no Temple? Which rituals dealt with in the passages above could be continued essentially as is, which had to be altered greatly, and which had to be discontinued?

5. How could the ancient Israelite ideal of equal justice be seen as an antecedent of modern European and North American ideals of justice?

6. Explain the standing of women in the Jewish *Bible*. To what degree did the Hebrew scriptures ameliorate the condition of women, and to what degree did they reinforce a patriarchal society?

7. Trace the theme of the chosen/covenant people through the Hebrew scriptures.

8. Explain the statement, "Judaism is a religion of the book."

SUGGESTIONS FOR FURTHER READING

Primary Readings

The New English Bible. New York: Oxford, 1970. A fresh, vivid translation by a team of British scholars of both the Jewish *Bible* and the *New Testament.*

The New Revised Standard Version of the Bible. New York: Oxford, 1991. The best one-volume translation of both the Jewish and Christian scriptures, with a Hebrew scripture section widely recognized for its accuracy.

Tanakh: The Holy Scriptures. Philadelphia: Jewish Publication Society, 1988. The most widely recognized Jewish translation of the Jewish *Bible,* known for both accuracy and literary grace.

L. H. Schiffman, ed., *Texts and Traditions: A Source Reader for the Study of Second Temple and Rabbinic Judaism.* New York: KTAV, 1998. A comprehensive collection of primary sources for this formative period, especially *Bible* and *Talmud* selections.

Secondary Readings

R. Alter, *The Art of Biblical Narrative.* New York: Basic Books, 1981. An excellent introduction to the Jewish *Bible* as literature.

B. Anderson, *Understanding the Old Testament,* 4th ed. Englewood Cliffs, NJ: Prentice-Hall, 1986. The standard introductory study.

E. Fackenheim, *The Jewish Bible After the Holocaust—A Rereading.* Indianapolis: Indiana University Press, 1991. A prominent Jewish philosopher contends that the Jewish *Bible* is still the great spiritual resource of the Western religious traditions.

F. Greenspahn, "Does Judaism Have a Bible?" In L. J. Greenspoon and B. F. LeBeau, eds., *Sacred Text, Secular Times: The Hebrew Bible in the Modern World.* Omaha: Creighton University Press, 2000, pp. 1-12. The most up-to-date critical discussion of the Hebrew canon in the life of Judaism.

J. Rosenbaum, "Judaism: Torah and Tradition." In F. M. Denny and R. L. Taylor, *The Holy Book in Comparative Perspective.* Columbia, SC: University of South Carolina Press, 1985, pp. 10–35. Examines the interplay of the *Bible* and other sacred literature of Judaism, especially the *Talmud.*

P. Trible, *Texts of Terror.* Philadelphia: Fortress, 1984. A powerful examination of some biblical passages from a religious and feminist perspective.

B. Visotzky, *Reading the Book: Making the Bible a Timeless Text.* New York: Anchor/Doubleday, 1991. Designed to provide an "introduction to the meaningful reading of Scripture," this book takes account of both rabbinic and modern methods of interpretation.

☿ INFOTRAC COLLEGE EDITION

You can locate InfoTrac College Edition articles about this chapter by accessing the InfoTrac College Edition website (http://www.infotrac.collegeedition.com/wadsworth/). Using subject guide, enter the search terms relevant to this chapter, and then read abstracts for relevant articles.

Reading the Bible in Christian Worship
Father Andrew France reads from the *Bible* during a service at Trinity Episcopal Church,
Williamsport, Pennsylvania. Credit: Craig W. Smith

CHAPTER ELEVEN

Christianity

❖ In a congregation of the Church of Scotland, the bell tolls and the congregation stands out of respect for the Word as a layperson walks solemnly down the center aisle carrying a large *Bible*. When the book is placed on the pulpit, the service begins.

❖ In a village of New Guinea, North American and European missionaries trained in linguistics work to decipher a tribal language, commit it to writing, and educate the tribespeople to read it. The purpose of their work is to translate the *New Testament* into the tribal language for use in training new believers in the faith and as a tool for converting other members of the tribe.

❖ The Council of Bishops of the Evangelical Lutheran Church in America deals with a challenge to the traditional names of God used in baptism—"Father, Son, and Holy Spirit," words taken from the Gospel of *Matthew*. Attacking these names as sexist, some congregations of that church have substituted the words "Creator, Redeemer, and Sanctifier." The bishops reject this move and reaffirm the biblical formula as the only permissible one in the church.

INTRODUCTION

Christianity teaches salvation from sin and the gift of eternal life through the life, death, and resurrection of Jesus, the Son of God. A missionary religion from its beginning, it has become the world's most widespread faith. The *New Testament* has had paramount importance in the history of Christianity from the time of its writing in the century after the death of Jesus in 30 C.E. The church's teaching, ethics, ritual, organization, and mission in the world have been shaped by its scripture. Although Christians differ in language, culture, organization, and the fine points of religious teaching, all believers have the books of the *New Testament* in common. Indeed, it has often been remarked that the *New Testament* is the *only* thing that all Christians have in common! This scripture has played such a prominent role in world events past and present that to know the *New Testament* and its patterns of use is to have a key to the understanding of Western culture as well as Christianity itself.

Names

The common name in Christianity for its scriptures is the **Bible,** composed of both the **Old Testament** (the Hebrew scriptures) and the **New Testament.** As in the Jewish *Bible,* **testament** or its synonym "covenant" refers to the relationship God has established with people. "New" signifies the early Christian belief that in Jesus God has acted in a new way for salvation. This is seen as a fulfillment of the promises made by

God to the Jewish people. In *II Corinthians* 3:6–15, the early Christian missionary Paul calls Christian believers members of the "new covenant" and the books of Moses (the Jewish *Bible*) the "old covenant." The first term echoes *Jeremiah* 31:31, in which God promises, "I will make a new covenant with the house of Israel and the house of Judah." The expression "new covenant" was also used in the early Christian celebration of the ritual of Holy Communion, as its earliest recorded form attests: "In the same way [Jesus] took the cup also, after supper, saying, "This cup is the new covenant in my blood" (*I Corinthians* 11:25). In sum, "new covenant/testament" was a common term in early Christianity, and it did not take long to be formally attached to the body of Christian scripture.

The advantage of *New Testament* as a label is that it suggests the complexity of the early Christian attitude to its relationship with Judaism and the Jewish *Bible*. This relationship has both continuity with Judaism, as expressed by "covenant" or "testament," and discontinuity, as expressed by the qualifier "new." A disadvantage is that it leads to an all-too-easy misunderstanding of the role of the Jewish *Bible* in Christianity—that it is "old," outmoded, and completely replaced by the *New Testament*. This misconception ignores the fact that the Jewish *Bible* is itself a part of the Christian scriptures and that the earliest scripture of Christianity—before its own writings were canonized—was the Jewish *Bible*.

In recent years there has been a growing tendency to counter this disadvantage by labeling the twenty-seven books of the *New Testament* by a different name. Some use the name "Christian scriptures." But this name is even more disadvantageous than "New Testament" because it implies that the Jewish *Bible* is not a part of the Christian scriptures. A few scholars call these books the "Second Testament," with the Hebrew Bible being the "First Testament," but this is vague. In sum, therefore, *New Testament* seems the best choice. Despite its disadvantages, this is the commonly accepted label within the Christian church and in the academic community, and it will be used here.

Overview of Structure

The *New Testament* is organized into two main sections, books about Jesus called *Gospels* and letters of the apostles to early churches.

The **gospels** are "good news" of the story of Jesus. The *Gospel of Matthew* tells the story of Jesus the Savior as the promised Messiah of Israel, going from his conception by the Holy Spirit in the womb of the Virgin Mary through his appearances after his resurrection from the dead. The *Gospel of Mark* tells the story of Jesus from baptism through the resurrection, presenting Jesus as the Savior of the Gentiles (non-Jews). The *Gospel of Luke* also presents Jesus as the savior of the Gentiles, with a secondary theme of God's concern for the poor, women, and outcasts. These three gospels are known as **synoptic** or "seen in one view" because of their parallel structure and content in recounting the story of Jesus. The *Gospel of John* is the story of Jesus as the eternal, divine Son of God who came to earth to show God's glory in his life, death, and resurrection from the dead.

The gospels are followed by the *Acts of the Apostles,* the only book of the *New Testament* devoted to a historical account of the early church and its growth through its first approximately thirty-five years. *Luke* and *Acts* were written as a two-volume work by the same author; unfortunately, *John* now stands between them in the canonical order. The names of all these books were attached in the second century C.E.; when first written, they probably featured no authors' names.

The rest of the *New Testament* is largely composed of **letters** or "epistles" of instruction and correction written by church leaders to various churches. Some scholars dispute the names on these letters, arguing that they are **pseudonymous,** written by someone other than the given author, usually by one of his followers or coworkers after his death. Letters thought to be genuinely written by the stated person are called **authentic.**

The first section of letters are those of the **apostle** ("one sent out" with the message of salvation) Paul, arranged mostly by length from the longest to the shortest, and named according to their destination. *Romans* presents Paul's understanding of Christian teaching in a fairly systematic way to a church that he did not establish but was soon to visit. In *I Corinthians* Paul discusses various issues related to Christian doctrine, morality and worship. In *II Corinthians*—a later letter that is probably, as it now stands, a composite of two or three letters Paul wrote to that church after *I Corinthians*—Paul's main concern is to keep this Gentile-Christian church from straying to Jewish Christianity. *Galatians* has much this same theme—Christians from non-Jewish backgrounds need not be Jewish as well as Christian. *Ephesians,* probably written by a fellow worker of Paul's after his death, presents Jesus Christ as the cosmic savior who unifies races and nations. *Philippians,* a genuine Pauline letter, urges Christians to find joy in Christ. *Colossians,* probably written under Paul's name by a coworker, seeks like *Ephesians* to correct error by presenting Jesus Christ as the all-sufficient savior of the universe, not just of the church. *I Thessalonians* answers questions about what happens when the Lord Jesus returns in glory to judge the world at the end of time. *II Thessalonians,* probably pseudonymously written after the death of Paul, instructs Christians about how to wait for Jesus' return. The next three letters, *I* and *II Timothy* and *Titus,* are called the "Pastoral" letters because they are instructions under Paul's name about pastoral offices and church life at the end of the first century. Finally, *Philemon* is Paul's attempt to reconcile a Christian slaveowner to his runaway Christian slave who now seeks to return to that master.

The next section of the *New Testament* is traditionally known as the "General" or "Catholic" *Letters* (formerly *Epistles*). This name was given to them because church authorities supposed that they were written to all the church, but today scholars view them as having just as specific an audience as the Pauline letters. Like the Pauline letters, these also seem to be arranged by length. It begins with *Hebrews,* an anonymous letter written to encourage Christians not to turn to Judaism. The book of *James* exhorts its audience to live wise, righteous, and socially responsible lives. *I Peter* offers guidelines on Christian behavior, especially to those undergoing persecution for the faith. *II Peter* urges its readers to stay true to traditional Christian teaching and reject false forms of the faith. The three letters of *John* combat false teachers while promoting love and hospitality among Christians. *Jude* is very similar in content and purpose to *II Peter*—defending the faith against falsehoods. Finally, the apocalyptic book, *Revelation* offers visions of God's triumph at the end of the world,

Table 11.1

The Books of the *New Testament*

Book	Traditional and/or Given Author	Date (C.E.)	Genre	Size in Chapters
Matthew	Matthew (disputed)	80s	gospel	28
Mark	Mark (disputed)	70	gospel	16
Luke	Luke (disputed)	80s	gospel	24
John	John (disputed)	90	gospel	21
Acts of the Apostles	Luke (disputed)	80s	history	28
Romans	Paul	55	letter	16
I Corinthians	Paul	53	letter	16
II Corinthians	Paul	55	letter	13
Galatians	Paul	55	letter	6
Ephesians	Paul (disputed)	90	letter	6
Philippians	Paul	61	letter	4
Colossians	Paul (disputed)	80s	letter	4
I Thessalonians	Paul	51	letter	5
II Thessalonians	Paul (disputed)	80s	letter	3
I Timothy	Paul (disputed)	90s	letter	6
II Timothy	Paul (disputed)	90s	letter	4
Titus	Paul (disputed)	90s	letter	3
Philemon	Paul	50s	letter	1
Hebrews	Anonymous	80s	letter-sermon	13
James	James (disputed)	90	letter-sermon	5
I Peter	Peter (disputed)	80	letter	5
II Peter	Peter (disputed)	120	letter	3
I John	John "the Elder"	95	essay	5
II John	John "the Elder"	96	letter	1
III John	John "the Elder"	97	letter	1
Jude	Jude (disputed)	100	letter	1
Revelation	John "the Prophet"	90s	apocalypse	22

delivering believers from persecution by establishing the kingdom of heaven on earth.

For the order, authors (those probably pseudonymous noted as disputed), approximate dates, genres, and size (in number of chapters) of the *New Testament* literature, see Table 11.1.

Origin and Development

At first glance, it would seem that the *New Testament* was written perhaps only one or two generations after the death and resurrection of Jesus and the beginnings of the church. Yet modern biblical scholarship has discovered that its writing was not completed until perhaps ninety years after Jesus' death. (The process of forming the canon was even longer.)

The pace of writing was retarded by several factors. First, the early church, which began as a group within Judaism, already had a complete body of scripture—the Jewish *Bible*. At first it found this scripture sufficient for its life, especially when it could interpret and use the Jewish *Bible* in its own way to bolster its claim that Jesus was the Messiah, the promised deliverer of Israel. Second, the early Christians quite comfortably used the words and deeds of Jesus in primarily oral form. They did not remember Jesus as a writer, and there was no urgency to write down his words. Indeed, they probably looked on the oral words of Jesus as more immediate and potent than words about him written in a book. Third, many early Christians believed that the end of the world was near, and with this expectation the lengthy process of writing, copying (by hand), and distributing books was not to be expected.

How, then, did the process of writing what was to become the *New Testament* begin? The genuine Pauline letters came first. Paul wrote letters to keep in contact with the churches he founded as he traveled around the northeastern Mediterranean provinces of the Roman empire on his missionary travels. He used letters to instruct and exhort his churches and as a substitute for his own personal presence. These letters gained more importance after Paul's death (probably c. 65 C.E.), and after his death his coworkers continued to write letters in his name to perpetuate and adapt his teachings for a new generation. Of course, at this stage there was probably no thought by Paul and his followers that these letters would become a part of a new body of Christian scripture.

After Paul's letters, the gospels began to be written down around 70 C.E. The word *gospel* in English is derived from the Anglo-Saxon "god-spell." The Greek word (all the *New Testament* was written in Greek, the common language of the Mediterranean world) is *euangelion,* "good news," from which we get the word "evangelical." The characteristic structure of the gospel seems to have been invented by Mark: Jesus' ministry in Galilee, his journey to Jerusalem, teaching in Jerusalem, arrest, trial, death, and resurrection. This structure is followed by two other gospels, *Matthew* and *Luke,* which (the vast majority of scholars conclude) use *Mark* as a source. *John* does not use *Mark* as a source, so it differs from this basic outline.

These two parts of the *New Testament,* commonly called "the gospel and the apostle," were the basic building blocks of the canon. Beginning in the second century C.E., Christians began sorting out true Christian writings from ones they considered false and heretical. The details of this process are hazy, but the main features seem clear. First, a canonical writing had to have a claim to apostolic authorship or authority. It had to be seen as either being written by an apostle, one "sent forth" with the Gospel (e.g., Matthew, John, Paul, Peter), or by someone under apostolic authority (Mark, Luke). It had to give the appearance of going back to ancient times. Second, the content of the writings was weighed. In the fight with heresy in the second century, doctrinal content was important because writings the church deemed heretical also claimed to be written by the apostles, and the only way to tell them from false teaching was to compare the content of their teaching to books held to be genuinely apostolic in content. In his *Church History,* for example, Eusebius tells the story of Serapion, the bishop of Antioch in Syria (about 190 C.E.), who heard a reading in church of the *Gospel of Peter,* a work he did not know. At first he accepted it as apostolic, but later he learned that its account of the death of Jesus was being used by heretics to bolster their claim that Jesus did not die on the cross but had already returned to heaven. Therefore, Serapion forbade any further reading of the *Gospel of Peter* in the churches under his authority.

The third main factor in the process of canonization was the actual scripture usage of prominent Christian churches. In the gospels, for example, Antioch promoted *Matthew,* the province of Asia Minor (modern western Turkey) used *John* and *Luke,* and Rome used *Mark.* The support of these large and influential centers of early Christianity was crucial in the formation of the canon. The final factor was the competing canons of groups that the mainstream church considered heretical. Marcion, an early Christian leader who came to Rome about 145 C.E., argued that the God revealed by Jesus was not the creator God revealed in the Jewish *Bible.* As a result, Marcion totally rejected the Jewish *Bible* as canonical and made a special canon of Christian books out of the *Gospel of Luke* only and ten Pauline letters, rejecting everything else. This selection probably spurred the early church to insist on a wider canon: four gospels, all the Pauline letters that looked genuinely apostolic in content, and other letters from the twelve apostles of Jesus to their churches.

Thus, a consensus grew during the third and fourth centuries around the main books of the emerging canon of the *New Testament.* Seven books remained in doubt during this time, accepted by some churches but not by all: *Hebrews, James, II* and *III John, Jude, II Peter,* and *Revelation.* But as the widely scattered churches grew closer together in the third and fourth centuries, they began accepting these disputed books from each other. By 367 C.E., the twenty-seven-book canon was widely accepted, as the *Festal Letter* of Bishop Athanasius of Alexandria, Egypt testifies. The catholic (which means "universal") church had a catholic *New Testament.*

Use

Because Christianity came from a Judaism with well-formed patterns of scripture usage, the use of the *New Testament* in the church strongly reflects the ways in which the Jewish *Bible* is used in Judaism. The first scripture of the church was the Jewish *Bible* in its Greek form, the *Septuagint.* The entire Jewish *Bible* had a strong influence in early Christianity, but certain sections were especially important. Some of these are given in the previous chapter on Judaism because they are important for both Judaism and Christianity. For reasons of space, the important Jewish *Bible* selections cannot be repeated or given here. So the reader should be familiar with the Exodus traditions, including the Passover feast (*Exodus* 12:1–27; 14:1–31); the rising Messianic hope (*Isaiah* 11:1–9; 42:1–7); expectations for the end of time (*Daniel* 7:1–14; 12:1–3); and the passages that the early church used to interpret the person and work of Jesus (e.g., *Psalm* 110; *Isaiah* 52:13–54:12).

As in Judaism, the primary use of the Christian *Bible* has always been in the service of divine worship. Worship in the church is saturated in the *Bible*. One of the high points of the service in all Catholic and most Protestant churches is the reading of a selection from the *Old Testament* and two selections from the *New Testament*, the last always a gospel reading. This lectionary system arose in the early Greek church, probably as an inheritance from Judaism. It quickly passed into Western Catholic Christianity. In the twentieth century, especially in its last quarter, many Protestant and Roman Catholic churches in Europe and North America have adopted basically the same lectionary system, with the result that on any given Sunday most American Christians hear the same scripture readings and sermons based more or less on them. (Independent Protestants, such as fundamentalists and Pentecostalists, do not follow this system.)

The *Bible* itself occupies a privileged place in the physical arrangement of the typical Christian church. In churches of a "higher," more elaborate form of worship, it is often placed on a special ornate lectern. In more formal services, the book of the gospels is often brought before the altar, "incensed," and kissed by the priest(s) as a sign of its holiness before it is read. In both Catholic and Eastern Orthodox traditions, the scripture books are often richly bound and decorated with gold, jewels, and icons. But the *Bible* is also revered even in Protestant churches with less formal worship. In such churches it is often placed on the main pulpit from which the minister conducts the entire service. In churches of the Baptist wing of Protestantism it is not unusual to see the preacher carrying the *Bible* in one hand and referring to it constantly during the sermon.

This formal use of the *Bible* is supplemented by many Christians with private devotional reading. Since the times of the Reformation in the sixteenth century, the Protestant churches have insisted on the right and duty of every Christian to read the *Bible* individually. This reading includes prayerful meditation on the meaning of the words and the implication of this meaning for the life of the reader. Reading is also often done aloud by families as a part of the main meal of the day. Such private and familial use of scripture has formed a large part of Protestant spirituality. In the twentieth century, and especially since the reforms of the Second Vatican Council in the 1960s, Roman Catholics have also recognized the importance of private study and historical study of the Bible. Despite this emphasis on private usage of scripture, however, most Christians throughout the world still come into contact with their *Bible* mostly during church services.

Alongside this devotional use of the *Bible* is academic study by means of the historical-critical method. This method seeks to understand the various parts of the *Bible* in their original historical context and tries to determine what the writings meant to their original readers. It tends to disregard the teachings of the various churches about the content of Scripture. Because it puts the *Bible* in the same analytical framework as any other book from the ancient world, this approach is strongly rejected by fundamentalists, both Protestant and Catholic alike. An indication of the rapid advance that historical-critical study has made in the Roman Catholic church during the twentieth century is that probably the most influential New Testament scholar of the last thirty years, the late Raymond E. Brown, was a Catholic priest.

HISTORY

The Birth of Jesus the Messiah*

The gospels of Matthew and Luke present Jesus as conceived by the action of the Spirit of God in the Virgin Mary. This miraculous conception signifies the divine Sonship of Jesus. The passage also focuses on the name Jesus, which in the Aramaic language of Palestine means "he will save."[1]

Now the birth of Jesus the Messiah took place in this way. When his mother Mary had been engaged to Joseph, but before they lived together, she was found to be with child from the Holy Spirit. Her husband Joseph, being a righteous man and unwilling to expose her to public disgrace, planned to dismiss her quietly. [20] But just when he had resolved to do this, an angel of the Lord appeared to him in a dream and said, "Joseph, son of David, do not be afraid to take Mary as your wife, for the child conceived in her is from the Holy Spirit. She will bear a son, and you are to name him Jesus, for he will save his people from their sins." All this took place to fulfill what had been spoken by the Lord through the prophet: "Look, the virgin shall conceive and bear a son, and they shall name him Emmanuel," which means, "God is with us." When Joseph awoke from sleep, he did as the angel of the Lord commanded him; he took her as his wife, [25] but had no marital relations with her until she had borne a son;[2] and he named him Jesus.

---

*Matthew 1:18–25

[1] All passages from the *New Testament* are from the *New Revised Standard Version of the Bible*. Copyright 1989 by the Division of Christian Education of the National Council of the Churches of Christ in the U.S.A. Used by permission. All rights reserved.

---

[2]*until she had borne a son:* Roman Catholics, who confess the lifelong virginity of Mary, do not interpret this verse to mean that Mary and Joseph did have sexual relations after Jesus' birth.

Jesus Denounces Pharisees and Lawyers**

The Pharisees were a group of Jewish men dedicated to strict observance of the law of Moses and the development of an oral tradition to interpret and apply it. The "lawyers" here are also experts in religious law. Jesus attacks them for emphasizing outward observance; he argues that only purity within leads to proper outward action. The end of this passage indicates the opposition and plotting that develops against Jesus from a group of Jews, primarily some Pharisees and Sadducees.

While he was speaking, a Pharisee invited him to dine with him; so he went in and took his place at the table. The Pharisee was amazed to see that he did not first wash before dinner.[3] Then the Lord said to him, "Now you Pharisees clean the outside of the cup and of the dish, but inside you are full of greed and wickedness. [40] You fools! Did not the one who made the outside make the inside also? So give for alms those things that are within; and see, everything will be clean for you. But woe to you Pharisees! For you tithe mint and rue and herbs of all kinds, and neglect justice and the love of God; it is these you ought to have practiced, without

---

**Luke 11:37–54

[3]*wash before dinner:* not to remove physical dirt, but ceremonial washing to assure religious purity.

neglecting the others. Woe to you Pharisees! For you love to have the seat of honor in the synagogues and to be greeted with respect in the marketplaces. Woe to you! For you are like unmarked graves, and people walk over them without realizing it."[4]

[45] One of the lawyers answered him, "Teacher, when you say these things, you insult us too." And he said, "Woe also to you lawyers! For you load people with burdens hard to bear, and you yourselves do not lift a finger to ease them. Woe to you! For you build the tombs of the prophets whom your ancestors killed. So you are witnesses and approve of the deeds of your ancestors; for they killed them, and you build their tombs. Therefore also the Wisdom of God said, 'I will send them prophets and

apostles, some of whom they will kill and persecute,' [50] so that this generation may be charged with the blood of all the prophets shed since the foundation of the world, from the blood of Abel to the blood of Zechariah, who perished between the altar and the sanctuary.[5] Yes, I tell you, it will be charged against this generation. Woe to you lawyers! For you have taken away the key of knowledge; you did not enter yourselves, and you hindered those who were entering." When he went outside, the scribes and the Pharisees began to be very hostile toward him and to cross-examine him about many things, lying in wait for him, to catch him in something he might say.

---

[4]*unmarked graves:* to walk on a grave is to incur impurity, so an unmarked grave is a hidden pollution.

[5]*Abel . . . Zechariah:* Abel was the victim of the first murder as recorded in the first book of the *Bible, Genesis* (4:8); the murder of Zechariah is written in the last book of the Jewish *Bible, 2 Chronicles* (24:20–22).

Jesus' Miracles*

In the gospels, as in the Hebrew scriptures, miracles signify the inbreaking of God into human life. They are not seen as "violations of natural law," but as acts of divine power for salvation. This selection has two types of miracles characteristic of the ministry of Jesus: exorcism of demons, showing the power of Jesus over supernatural evil; and healing of the sick, showing Jesus' ultimate victory over physical evil and death that is so central to early Christianity.

Then they arrived at the country of the Gerasenes, which is opposite Galilee. As he stepped out on land, a man of the city who had demons met him. For a long time he had worn no clothes, and he did not live in a house but in the tombs. When he saw Jesus, he fell down

before him and shouted at the top of his voice, "What have you to do with me, Jesus, Son of the Most High God? I beg you, do not torment me"—for Jesus had commanded the unclean spirit to come out of the man. (For many times it had seized him; he was kept under guard and bound with chains and shackles, but he would break the bonds and be driven by the demon into the wilds.) [30] Jesus then asked him, "What is your name?" He said, "Legion"; for many demons had entered him. They begged him not to order them to go back into the abyss.[6]

Now there on the hillside a large herd of swine was feeding; and the demons begged Jesus to let them enter these. So he gave them

---

* *Luke 8:26–56*

[6]*abyss:* a section of hell in which demons are confined to await final destruction.

permission. Then the demons came out of the man and entered the swine, and the herd rushed down the steep bank into the lake and was drowned. When the swineherds saw what had happened, they ran off and told it in the city and in the country. [35] Then people came out to see what had happened, and when they came to Jesus, they found the man from whom the demons had gone sitting at the feet of Jesus, clothed and in his right mind. And they were afraid. Those who had seen it told them how the one who had been possessed by demons had been healed. Then all the people of the surrounding country of the Gerasenes asked Jesus to leave them; for they were seized with great fear. So he got into the boat and returned. The man from whom the demons had gone begged that he might be with him; but Jesus sent him away, saying, "Return to your home, and declare how much God has done for you." So he went away, proclaiming throughout the city how much Jesus had done for him.

[40] Now when Jesus returned, the crowd welcomed him, for they were all waiting for him. Just then there came a man named Jairus, a leader of the synagogue. He fell at Jesus' feet and begged him to come to his house, for he had an only daughter, about twelve years old, who was dying. As he went, the crowds pressed in on him. Now there was a woman who had been suffering from hemorrhages for twelve years; and though she had spent all she had on physicians, no one could cure her. She came up behind him and touched the fringe of his clothes, and immediately her hemorrhage

stopped. [45] Then Jesus asked, "Who touched me?" When all denied it, Peter said, "Master, the crowds surround you and press in on you." But Jesus said, "Someone touched me; for I noticed that power had gone out from me." When the woman saw that she could not remain hidden, she came trembling; and falling down before him, she declared in the presence of all the people why she had touched him, and how she had been immediately healed. He said to her, "Daughter, your faith has made you well; go in peace."

While he was still speaking, someone came from the leader's house to say, "Your daughter is dead; do not trouble the teacher any longer." [50] When Jesus heard this, he replied, "Do not fear. Only believe, and she will be saved." When he came to the house, he did not allow anyone to enter with him, except Peter, John, and James, and the child's father and mother. They were all weeping and wailing for her; but he said, "Do not weep; for she is not dead but sleeping."[7] And they laughed at him, knowing that she was dead. But he took her by the hand and called out, "Child, get up." [55] Her spirit returned, and she got up at once. Then he directed them to give her something to eat. Her parents were astounded; but he ordered them to tell no one what had happened.[8]

---

[7] *sleeping:* Jesus knows the girl is dead but soon to be brought to life, so her condition is like sleep from which one awakens.

[8] *tell no one what had happened:* probably connected with the "messianic secret"; see *Matthew* 16:20 (p. 282 in this text).

The Arrest, Trial, and Death of Jesus*

The sufferings of Jesus at the end of his life include betrayal by his disciple Judas, denial by Peter, a trial before the Jews on religious charges, a trial before the Roman governor Pontius Pilate on civil charges, and condemnation to be crucified. Throughout their narration of these sufferings, Mark *and the other gospels portray Jesus gently accepting his suffering as the will of God and his death as a sacrifice for the sin of the world.*

Immediately, while he was still speaking, Judas, one of the twelve, arrived; and with him there

---

*Mark 14:43–50, 53–65; 15:1–41

was a crowd with swords and clubs, from the chief priests, the scribes, and the elders. Now the betrayer had given them a sign, saying, "The one I will kiss is the man; arrest him and lead him away under guard." [45] So when he came, he went up to him at once and said, "Rabbi" and kissed him. Then they laid hands on him and arrested him. But one of those who stood near drew his sword and struck the slave of the high priest, cutting off his ear. Then Jesus said to them, "Have you come out with swords and clubs to arrest me as though I were a bandit? Day after day I was with you in the temple teaching, and you did not arrest me. But let the scriptures be fulfilled." [50] All of them deserted him and fled. . . .

They took Jesus to the high priest; and all the chief priests, the elders, and the scribes were assembled. Peter had followed him at a distance, right into the courtyard of the high priest; and he was sitting with the guards, warming himself at the fire. [55] Now the chief priests and the whole council were looking for testimony against Jesus to put him to death; but they found none. For many gave false testimony against him, and their testimony did not agree. Some stood up and gave false testimony against him, saying, "We heard him say, 'I will destroy this temple that is made with hands, and in three days I will build another, not made with hands.'" But even on this point their testimony did not agree. [55] Then the high priest stood up before them and asked Jesus, "Have you no answer? What is it that they testify against you?" But he was silent and did not answer. Again the high priest asked him, "Are you the Messiah, the Son of the Blessed One?" Jesus said, "I am; and 'you will see the Son of Man seated at the right hand of the Power,' and 'coming with the clouds of heaven.'"[9] Then the high priest tore his clothes and said, "Why do we still need witnesses? You have heard his blasphemy! What is your decision?" All of them condemned him as

deserving death. [65] Some began to spit on him, to blindfold him, and to strike him, saying to him, "Prophesy!" The guards also took him over and beat him.

[15:1] As soon as it was morning, the chief priests held a consultation with the elders and scribes and the whole council. They bound Jesus, led him away, and handed him over to Pilate. Pilate asked him, "Are you the King of the Jews?" He answered him, "You say so." Then the chief priests accused him of many things. Pilate asked him again, "Have you no answer? See how many charges they bring against you." [5] But Jesus made no further reply, so that Pilate was amazed.

Now at the festival he used to release a prisoner for them, anyone for whom they asked. Now a man called Barabbas was in prison with the rebels who had committed murder during the insurrection. So the crowd came and began to ask Pilate to do for them according to his custom. Then he answered them, "Do you want me to release for you the King of the Jews?" [10] For he realized that it was out of jealousy that the chief priests had handed him over. But the chief priests stirred up the crowd to have him release Barabbas for them instead. Pilate spoke to them again, "Then what do you wish me to do with the man you call the King of the Jews?" They shouted back, "Crucify him!" Pilate asked them, "Why, what evil has he done?" But they shouted all the more, "Crucify him!" [15] So Pilate, wishing to satisfy the crowd, released Barabbas for them; and after flogging Jesus, he handed him over to be crucified.

Then the soldiers led him into the courtyard of the palace; and they called together the whole cohort. And they clothed him in a purple cloak; and after twisting some thorns into a crown, they put it on him. And they began saluting him, "Hail, King of the Jews!" They struck his head with a reed, spat upon him, and knelt down in homage to him. [20] After mocking him, they stripped him of the purple cloak and put his own clothes on him. Then they led him out to crucify him. They compelled a passer-by, who was coming in from the country, to carry

---

[9]Quoted from *Daniel* 7:13 in the Hebrew scriptures, with an allusion to *Psalm* 110:1.

his cross; it was Simon of Cyrene, the father of Alexander and Rufus.[10] Then they brought Jesus to the place called Golgotha. And they offered him wine mixed with myrrh; but he did not take it. And they crucified him, and divided his clothes among them, casting lots to decide what each should take. [25] It was nine o'clock in the morning when they crucified him. The inscription of the charge against him read, "The King of the Jews." And with him they crucified two bandits, one on his right and one on his left. Those who passed by derided him, shaking their heads and saying, "Aha! You who would destroy the temple and build it in three days, [30] save yourself, and come down from the cross!" In the same way the chief priests, along with the scribes, were also mocking him among themselves and saying, "He saved others; he cannot save himself. Let the Messiah, the King of Israel, come down from the cross now, so that we may see and believe." Those who were crucified with him also taunted him.

When it was noon, darkness came over the whole land until three in the afternoon. At three o'clock Jesus cried out with a loud voice, "Eloi, Eloi, lema sabachthani?" which means, "My God, my God, why have you forsaken me?"[11] [35] When some of the bystanders heard it, they said, "Listen, he is calling for Elijah."[12] And someone ran, filled a sponge with sour wine, put it on a stick, and gave it to him to drink, saying, "Wait, let us see whether Elijah will come to take him down." Then Jesus gave a loud cry and breathed his last. And the curtain of the temple was torn in two, from top to bottom. Now when the centurion, who stood facing him, saw that in this way he breathed his last, he said, "Truly this man was God's Son!"

[40] There were also women looking on from a distance; among them were Mary Magdalene, and Mary the mother of James the younger and of Joses, and Salome. These used to follow him and provided for him when he was in Galilee; and there were many other women who had come up with him to Jerusalem.

---

[10] *Simon, Rufus:* that these names are given probably indicates that these men were known to the first readers of Mark.

[11] Jesus quotes the words of *Psalm 22.*

[12] *Elijah:* a fairly widespread Jewish belief at this time was that Elijah, the ancient Israelite prophet, would return at the end of time; compare the contemporary Jewish practice of leaving an empty seat at the Passover seder for Elijah.

The Resurrection of Jesus*

After Joseph of Arimathea buried the body of Jesus, three women from among his followers came on Sunday morning to finish the tasks of the funeral. They become the first witnesses of Jesus' resurrection. In this passage, the "young man" is an angel, and his message is that God has raised Jesus from the dead. The resurrection of Jesus and the life it brings became the center of early Christian belief.

When the sabbath was over, Mary Magdalene, and Mary the mother of James, and Salome bought spices, so that they might go and anoint him. And very early on the first day of the week, when the sun had risen, they went to the tomb. They had been saying to one another, "Who will roll away the stone for us from the entrance to the tomb?"[13] When they looked up, they saw

---

* *Mark 16:1–8*

[13] *roll away the stone:* a massive disk-shaped stone has been rolled over the entrance of the tomb.

that the stone, which was very large, had already been rolled back. [15] As they entered the tomb, they saw a young man, dressed in a white robe, sitting on the right side; and they were alarmed. But he said to them, "Do not be alarmed; you are looking for Jesus of Nazareth, who was crucified. He has been raised; he is not here. Look, there is the place they laid him. But go, tell his disciples and Peter that he is going ahead of you to Galilee; there you will see him, just as he told you." So they went out and fled from the tomb, for terror and amazement had seized them; and they said nothing to anyone, for they were afraid.

The Ascension of Jesus*

In Luke and Acts, which are written by the same author, Jesus ascends to heaven forty days after his resurrection. This selection draws a connection between the completion of the earthly ministry of Jesus with the consummation of history: the end is not yet, but in the interim between the present and the end the church is to witness to Jesus throughout the world. This missionary commission began to be carried out in the first century C.E. and has characterized Christianity for several periods of its subsequent history.

So when they had come together, they asked him, "Lord, is this the time when you will

restore the kingdom to Israel?" He replied, "It is not for you to know the times or periods that the Father has set by his own authority. But you will receive power when the Holy Spirit has come upon you; and you will be my witnesses in Jerusalem, in all Judea and Samaria, and to the ends of the earth." When he had said this, as they were watching, he was lifted up, and a cloud took him out of their sight. [10] While he was going and they were gazing up toward heaven, suddenly two men in white robes stood by them. They said, "Men of Galilee, why do you stand looking up toward heaven? This Jesus, who has been taken up from you into heaven, will come in the same way as you saw him go into heaven."

_____

*Acts 1:6–11

The Coming of the Holy Spirit**

In dealing with the "speaking in tongues" that occurs on Pentecost, a Jewish holiday that comes fifty days after Passover, Acts works with two traditions: that the apostles are speaking an actual foreign language; that they speak in a language not human, but one interpreted by the listeners as their own. (Modern Pentecostalism picks up on the second tradition.) Peter's speech on this occasion explains the meaning of the Holy Spirit's coming as the fulfillment of scripture and the divine plan,

bringing the presence and power of God to all in the church regardless of gender or social standing.

When the day of Pentecost had come, they were all together in one place. And suddenly from heaven there came a sound like the rush of a violent wind, and it filled the entire house where they were sitting. Divided tongues, as of fire, appeared among them, and a tongue rested on each of them. All of them were filled with the Holy Spirit and began to speak in other languages, as the Spirit gave them ability. [5] Now there were devout Jews from every nation under heaven living in Jerusalem. And at

_____

**Acts 2:1–21

this sound the crowd gathered and was bewildered, because each one heard them speaking in the native language of each. Amazed and astonished, they asked, "Are not all these who are speaking Galileans? And how is it that we hear, each of us, in our own native language? Parthians, Medes, Elamites, and residents of Mesopotamia, Judea and Cappadocia, Pontus and Asia, [10] Phrygia and Pamphylia, Egypt and the parts of Libya belonging to Cyrene and visitors from Rome, both Jews and proselytes,[14] Cretans and Arabs—in our own languages we hear them speaking about God's deeds of power." All were amazed and perplexed, saying to one another, "What does this mean?" But others sneered and said, "They are filled with new wine."

But Peter, standing with the eleven, raised his voice and addressed them, "Men of Judea and all who live in Jerusalem, let this be known to you, and listen to what I say. [15] Indeed, these are not drunk, as you suppose, for it is only nine o'clock in the morning. No, this is what was spoken through the prophet Joel:

'In the last days it will be, God declares, that
    I will pour out my Spirit upon all flesh, and
    your sons and your daughters shall prophesy,
    and your young men shall see visions, and
    your old men shall dream dreams.
Even upon my slaves, both men and women, in
    those days I will pour out my Spirit; and
    they shall prophesy.
And I will show portents in the heaven above
    and signs on the earth below, blood, fire,
    and smoky mist.
[20] The sun shall be turned to darkness and
    the moon to blood, before the coming of
    the Lord's great and glorious day.
Then everyone who calls on the name of the
    Lord shall be saved.'"

---

[14]*Jews and proselytes:* born Jews and Gentiles converted to Judaism. All the nationalities listed in this "Table of Nations" are Jews now living in Jerusalem.

Persecution of the Apostles*

The early Christian church met opposition from the same forces that acted to do away with Jesus. The apostles' calm and confident attitude to their persecutions is underscored here, and this attitude would remain important in the next few centuries as Roman persecution of the church grew stronger. In verse 29 a theme is sounded that echoes through the history of the church: when the laws of this world and the law of God collide, "we must obey God rather than any human authority."

When they had brought [the apostles], they had them stand before the council. The high priest questioned them, saying, "We gave you strict orders not to teach in this name, yet here you have filled Jerusalem with your teaching and you are determined to bring this man's blood on us." But Peter and the apostles answered, "We must obey God rather than any human authority. [30] The God of our ancestors raised up Jesus, whom you had killed by hanging him on a tree. God exalted him at his right hand as Leader and Savior that he might give repentance to Israel and forgiveness of sins. And we are witnesses to these things, and so is the Holy Spirit whom God has given to those who obey him."

When they heard this, they were enraged and wanted to kill them. But a Pharisee in the council named Gamaliel, a teacher of the law, respected by all the people, stood up and ordered the men to be put outside for a short time. [35] Then he said to them, "Fellow Israelites, consider carefully what you propose

---

*Acts 5:27–42

to do to these men. For some time ago Theudas rose up,[15] claiming to be somebody, and a number of men, about four hundred, joined him; but he was killed, and all who followed him were dispersed and disappeared. After him Judas the Galilean rose up at the time of the census and got people to follow him; he also perished, and all who followed him were scattered. So in the present case, I tell you, keep away from these men and let them alone; because if this

plan or this undertaking is of human origin, it will fail; but if it is of God, you will not be able to overthrow them—in that case you may even be found fighting against God!"

They were convinced by him, [40] and when they had called in the apostles, they had them flogged. Then they ordered them not to speak in the name of Jesus, and let them go. As they left the council, they rejoiced that they were considered worthy to suffer dishonor for the sake of the name. And every day in the temple and at home they did not cease to teach and proclaim Jesus as the Messiah.

---

[15] *Theudas* and *Judas the Galilean* were messianic pretenders whose movements collapsed after they died.

The Council at Jerusalem*

The issue at this council was whether Gentile converts to Christianity should be required to be circumcised and keep at least some of the laws of Moses. Paul and Peter argued no; some conservative Jewish Christians, converts from the Pharisees, said yes. James, kinsman of Jesus and leader of the Jerusalem church at this time, gave the compromise ruling: no circumcision is required of Gentile converts, but certain minimal laws of purity would be imposed. The result of this decision was that Christianity began to separate from its roots in Judaism, becoming a different religion.

Then certain individuals came down from Judea and were teaching the brothers, "Unless you are circumcised according to the custom of Moses, you cannot be saved." And after Paul and Barnabas had no small dissension and debate with them, Paul and Barnabas and some of the others were appointed to go up to Jerusalem to discuss this question with the apostles and the elders. So they were sent on their way by the church, and as they passed through both Phoenicia and Samaria, they reported the conversion of the Gentiles, and brought great joy to all the believ-

ers. When they came to Jerusalem, they were welcomed by the church and the apostles and the elders, and they reported all that God had done with them. [5] But some believers who belonged to the sect of the Pharisees stood up and said, "It is necessary for them to be circumcised and ordered to keep the law of Moses."

The apostles and the elders met together to consider this matter. After there had been much debate, Peter stood up and said to them, "My brothers, you know that in the early days God made a choice among you, that I should be the one through whom the Gentiles would hear the message of the good news and become believers. And God, who knows the human heart, testified to them by giving them the Holy Spirit, just as he did to us; and in cleansing their hearts by faith he has made no distinction between them and us. [10] Now therefore why are you putting God to the test by placing on the neck of the disciples a yoke that neither our ancestors nor we have been able to bear? On the contrary, we believe that we will be saved through the grace of the Lord Jesus, just as they will."

The whole assembly kept silence, and listened to Barnabas and Paul as they told of all the signs and wonders that God had done through them among the Gentiles. After they finished speaking, James replied, "My brothers, listen to me.

---

*Acts 15:1–21

Simeon[16] has related how God first looked favorably on the Gentiles, to take from among them a people for his name. [15] This agrees with the words of the prophets, as it is written, 'After this I will return, and I will rebuild the dwelling of David, which has fallen; from its ruins I will rebuild it, and I will set it up, so that all other peoples may seek the Lord—even all the Gentiles over whom my name has been called. Thus says the Lord, who has been making these things known from long ago.' There-

fore I have reached the decision that we should not trouble those Gentiles who are turning to God, [20] but we should write to them to abstain only from things polluted by idols and from fornication and from whatever has been strangled and from blood.[17] For in every city, for generations past, Moses has had those who proclaim him, for he has been read aloud every sabbath in the synagogues."

---

[16]*Simeon:* Peter.

[17]*from things polluted . . . and from blood:* foods offered to idols in sacrifice, and meat not ritually butchered, respectively.

TEACHING

The Parables of Jesus*

The parables were Jesus' distinctive form of teaching. Parables are stories that compare an experience in everyday life with some aspect of religious life, especially life in the Kingdom of God. Here is a collection of parables gathered by Mark or transmitted to him in the oral tradition. Many scholars view the interpretation of the parable of the sower, found in the third paragraph, as deriving not directly from Jesus, but from the early church.

Again he began to teach beside the sea. Such a very large crowd gathered around him that he got into a boat on the sea and sat there, while the whole crowd was beside the sea on the land. He began to teach them many things in parables, and in his teaching he said to them: "Listen! A sower went out to sow. And as he sowed, some seed fell on the path, and the birds came and ate it up. [5] Other seed fell on rocky ground, where it did not have much soil, and it sprang up quickly, since it had no depth of soil. And when the sun rose, it was scorched; and

since it had no root, it withered away. Other seed fell among thorns, and the thorns grew up and choked it, and it yielded no grain. Other seed fell into good soil and brought forth grain, growing up and increasing and yielding thirty and sixty and a hundred-fold." And he said, "Let anyone with ears to hear listen."

[10] When he was alone, those who were around him along with the twelve asked him about the parables. And he said to them, "To you has been given the secret of the kingdom of God, but for those outside, everything comes in parables; in order that 'they may indeed look, but not perceive, and may indeed listen, but not understand; so that they may not turn again and be forgiven.'"

And he said to them, "Do you not understand this parable? Then how will you understand all the parables? The sower sows the word. [15] These are the ones on the path where the word is sown: when they hear, Satan immediately comes and takes away the word that is sown in them. And these are the ones sown on rocky ground: when they hear the word, they immediately receive it with joy. But they have no

---

* *Mark 4:1–34*

root, and endure only for a while; then, when trouble or persecution arises on account of the word, immediately they fall away. And others are those sown among the thorns: these are the ones who hear the word, but the cares of the world, and the lure of wealth, and the desire for other things come in and choke the word, and it yields nothing. [20] And these are the ones sown on the good soil: they hear the word and accept it and bear fruit, thirty and sixty and a hundredfold."

He said to them, "Is a lamp brought in to be put under the bushel basket, or under the bed, and not on the lampstand? For there is nothing hidden, except to be disclosed; nor is anything secret, except to come to light. Let anyone with ears to hear listen!" And he said to them, "Pay attention to what you hear; the measure you give will be the measure you get, and still more will be given you. [25] For to those who have, more will be given; and from those who have nothing, even what they have will be taken away."

He also said, "The kingdom of God is as if someone would scatter seed on the ground, and would sleep and rise night and day, and the seed would sprout and grow, he does not know how. The earth produces of itself, first the stalk, then the head, then the full grain in the head. But when the grain is ripe, at once he goes in with his sickle, because the harvest has come."

[30] He also said, "With what can we compare the kingdom of God, or what parable will we use for it? It is like a mustard seed, which, when sown upon the ground, is the smallest of all the seeds on earth; yet when it is sown it grows up and becomes the greatest of all shrubs, and puts forth large branches, so that the birds of the air can make nests in its shade."

With many such parables he spoke the word to them, as they were able to hear it; he did not speak to them except in parables,[18] but he explained everything in private to his disciples.

---

[18]*except in parables:* that is, Jesus' teaching was characteristically illustrated by parables, not that the parable was his only form of teaching.

The Word Became Human*

This hymn to Christ as the divine Word made human is perhaps the New Testament's *most exalted view of the savior. Largely on the strength of John's gospel in the early church, with help from some other writers (especially Paul), the early church came to see the divine nature of Jesus as the divine Son from all eternity. This main theme alternates here with a secondary theme, that John the Baptist is not the Messiah.*

In the beginning was the Word, and the Word was with God, and the Word was God. He was in the beginning with God. All things came into being through him, and without him not one thing came into being. What has come into being in him was life, and the life was the light of all people. [5] The light shines in the darkness, and the darkness did not overcome it.

There was a man sent from God, whose name was John. He came as a witness to testify to the light, so that all might believe through him. He himself was not the light, but he came to testify to the light. The true light, which enlightens everyone, was coming into the world. [10] He was in the world, and the world came into being through him; yet the world did not know him. He came to what was his own, and his own people did not accept him. But to all who received him, who believed in his name, he gave power to become children of God, who were born, not of blood or of the will of the flesh or of the will of man, but of God.

---

*John 1:1–18

And the Word became flesh and lived among us, and we have seen his glory, the glory as of a father's only son, full of grace and truth. [15] John testified to him and cried out, "This was he of whom I said, 'He who comes after me ranks ahead of me because he was before me'."

From his fullness we have all received, grace upon grace. The law indeed was given through Moses; grace and truth came through Jesus Christ. No one has ever seen God. It is God the only Son, who is close to the Father's heart, who has made him known.

Nicodemus Visits Jesus*

This selection presents one early Christian view of salvation: a "rebirth" by the power of the Holy Spirit that makes one the child of God. In modern times, a part of evangelical Protestantism has fastened upon this passage, interpreting the "born-again" concept as an emotionally powerful conversion experience. Christians of other Protestant, Roman Catholic, and Orthodox traditions hold that simply to believe in Jesus as Savior and be baptized is to be "born again."

Now there was a Pharisee named Nicodemus, a leader of the Jews. He came to Jesus by night and said to him, "Rabbi, we know that you are a teacher who has come from God; for no one can do these signs that you do apart from the presence of God." Jesus answered him, "Very truly, I tell you, no one can see the kingdom of God without being born from above."[19] Nicodemus said to him, "How can anyone be born after having grown old? Can one enter a second time into the mother's womb and be born?" [5] Jesus answered, "Very truly, I tell you, no one can enter the kingdom of God without being born of water and Spirit. What is born of the flesh is flesh, and what is born of the Spirit is spirit. Do not be astonished that I said to you, 'You must be born from above.' The wind blows where it chooses, and you hear the sound of it, but you do not know where it comes from

or where it goes. So it is with everyone who is born of the Spirit." Nicodemus said to him, "How can these things be?" [10] Jesus answered him, "Are you a teacher of Israel, and yet you do not understand these things? Very truly, I tell you, we speak of what we know and testify to what we have seen; yet you do not receive our testimony. If I have told you about earthly things and you do not believe, how can you believe if I tell you about heavenly things? No one has ascended into heaven except the one who descended from heaven, the Son of Man. And just as Moses lifted up the serpent in the wilderness, so must the Son of Man be lifted up, [15] that whoever believes in him may have eternal life."

"For God so loved the world that he gave his only Son, so that everyone who believes in him may not perish but may have eternal life. Indeed, God did not send the Son into the world to condemn the world, but in order that the world might be saved through him. Those who believe in him are not condemned; but those who do not believe are condemned already, because they have not believed in the name of the only Son of God. And this is the judgment, that the light has come into the world, and people loved darkness rather than light because their deeds were evil. [20] For all who do evil hate the light and do not come to the light, so that their deeds may not be exposed. But those who do what is true come to the light, so that it may be clearly seen that their deeds have been done in God."

---

*John 3:1–21
[19]*born from above:* from the Greek original of the *New Testament* it is possible to translate "from above" as "again."

A Sinful Woman Forgiven*

In this passage Jesus answers a Pharisee's criticism with a parable on the meaning of forgiveness. Jesus teaches the radical nature of God's love and its transforming power.

One of the Pharisees asked Jesus to eat with him, and he went into the Pharisee's house and took his place at the table. And a woman in the city, who was a sinner,[20] having learned that he was eating in the Pharisee's house, brought an alabaster jar of ointment. She stood behind him at his feet, weeping, and began to bathe his feet with her tears and to dry them with her hair. Then she continued kissing his feet and anointing them with the ointment. Now when the Pharisee who had invited him saw it, he said to himself, "If this man were a prophet, he would have known who and what kind of woman this is who is touching him—that she is a sinner." [40] Jesus spoke up and said to him, "Simon, I have something to say to you. . . . A certain

creditor had two debtors; one owed five hundred denarii, and the other fifty.[21] When they could not pay, he canceled the debts for both of them. Now which of them will love him more?" Simon answered, "I suppose the one for whom he canceled the greater debt." And Jesus said to him, "You have judged rightly." Then turning toward the woman, he said to Simon, "Do you see this woman? I entered your house; you gave me no water for my feet, but she has bathed my feet with her tears and dried them with her hair. [45] You gave me no kiss, but from the time I came in she has not stopped kissing my feet. You did not anoint my head with oil, but she has anointed my feet with ointment. Therefore, I tell you, her sins, which were many, have been forgiven; hence she has shown great love. But the one to whom little is forgiven, loves little." Then he said to her, "Your sins are forgiven." But those who were at the table with him began to say among themselves, "Who is this who even forgives sins?" [50] And he said to the woman, "Your faith has saved you; go in peace."

---

*Luke 7:36–50

[20] *a sinner:* a notorious sinner, probably one who made her living by an occupation considered sinful by the law of Moses.

---

[21] A *denarius* was a day's pay for a common laborer.

Results of Justification**

Justification is God's act of making believers righteous through faith in the crucified and resurrected Jesus. In this justification, believers are reconciled to God. Protestant churches have used this and similar passages to support their leading doctrines of justification by faith alone rather than through human obedience to religious law.

Therefore, since we are justified by faith, we have peace with God through our Lord Jesus

Christ, through whom we have obtained access to this grace in which we stand; and we boast in our hope of sharing the glory of God. And not only that, but we also boast in our sufferings, knowing that suffering produces endurance, and endurance produces character, and character produces hope, [5] and hope does not disappoint us, because God's love has been poured into our hearts through the Holy Spirit that has been given to us.

For while we were still weak, at the right time Christ died for the ungodly. Indeed, rarely will anyone die for a righteous person—though perhaps for a good person someone might actually

---

**Romans 5:1–11

dare to die. But God proves his love for us in that while we still were sinners Christ died for us. Much more surely then, now that we have been justified by his blood, will we be saved through him from the wrath of God. [10] For if while we were enemies, we were reconciled to God through the death of his Son, much more surely, having been reconciled, will we be saved by his life.[22] But more than that, we even boast in God through our Lord Jesus Christ, through whom we have now received reconciliation.

_____

[22]*his life:* Jesus' eternal life after his resurrection.

The Resurrection of Christ and the Believer*

Paul writes the believers of Corinth, Greece to correct several problems in their church, most of which center around false beliefs about heavenly perfection. The resurrection of Jesus in history means that believers will also be resurrected at the end of time. They will come back to life with a spiritual body, a body fit for eternal spiritual life.

Now I would remind you, brothers and sisters, of the good news that I proclaimed to you, which you in turn received, in which also you stand, through which also you are being saved, if you hold firmly to the message that I proclaimed to you—unless you have come to believe in vain.

For I handed on to you as of first importance what I in turn had received: that Christ died for our sins in accordance with the scriptures, and that he was buried, and that he was raised on the third day in accordance with the scriptures, [5] and that he appeared to Cephas, then to the twelve. Then he appeared to more than five hundred brothers and sisters at one time, most of whom are still alive, though some have died. Then he appeared to James, then to all the apostles. Last of all, as to one untimely born, he appeared also to me. For I am the least of the apostles, unfit to be called an apostle, because I persecuted the church of God.[23] [10] But by the grace of God I am what I am, and his grace toward me has not been in vain. On the contrary, I worked harder than any of them—though it was not I, but the grace of God that is with me. Whether then it was I or they, so we proclaim and so you have come to believe. . . .

[35] But someone will ask, "How are the dead raised? With what kind of body do they come?" Fool! What you sow does not come to life unless it dies. And as for what you sow, you do not sow the body that is to be, but a bare seed, perhaps of wheat or of some other grain. But God gives it a body as he has chosen, and to each kind of seed its own body. Not all flesh is alike, but there is one flesh for human beings, another for animals, another for birds, and another for fish. [40] There are both heavenly bodies and earthly bodies, but the glory of the heavenly is one thing, and that of the earthly is another. There is one glory of the sun, and another glory of the moon, and another glory of the stars; indeed, star differs from star in glory.

So it is with the resurrection of the dead. What is sown is perishable, what is raised is imperishable. It is sown in dishonor, it is raised in glory. It is sown in weakness, it is raised in power. It is sown a physical body, it is raised a spiritual body. If there is a physical body, there is also a spiritual body. [45] Thus it is written, "The first man, Adam, became a living being;" the last Adam[24] became a life-giving spirit. But

_____

I Corinthians 15:1–11, 35–58
[23]*I persecuted the church:* Paul refers to his activity before his conversion to Christ and call to be a missionary.

_____

[24]*last Adam:* Christ, the man from heaven.

it is not the spiritual that is first, but the physical, and then the spiritual. The first man was from the earth, a man of dust; the second man is from heaven. As was the man of dust, so are those who are of the dust; and as is the man of heaven, so are those who are of heaven. Just as we have borne the image of the man of dust, we will also bear the image of the man of heaven.

[50] What I am saying, brothers and sisters, is this: flesh and blood cannot inherit the kingdom of God, nor does the perishable inherit the imperishable. Listen, I will tell you a mystery! We will not all die, but we will all be changed, in a moment, in the twinkling of an eye, at the last trumpet.[25] For the trumpet will sound, and the dead will be raised imperishable, and we will be changed. For this perishable body must put on imperishability, and this mortal body must put on immortality. When this perishable body puts on imperishability, and this mortal body puts on immortality, then the saying that is written will be fulfilled: "Death has been swallowed up in victory." [55] "Where, O death, is your victory? Where, O death, is your sting?"[26] The sting of death is sin, and the power of sin is the law. But thanks be to God, who gives us the victory through our Lord Jesus Christ. Therefore, my beloved, be steadfast, immovable, always excelling in the work of the Lord, because you know that in the Lord your labor is not in vain.

---

[25]*we will not all die . . . trumpet:* Paul believes that the return of Jesus and the resurrectional transformation of believers ("we will all be changed") will occur during their lifetimes.

[26]Paul quotes from *Isaiah* 25:7 and *Hosea* 13:14.

The End of Time*

Many New Testament *teachings about the end of time are taken from Judaism and adapted to Christianity. In the first passage,* Matthew *relates the teaching of Jesus about his role as the judge at the final judgment. In the second, the author of* Revelation *presents in striking apocalyptic style dreams and visions about the end.*

"When the Son of Man comes in his glory, and all the angels with him, then he will sit on the throne of his glory. All the nations will be gathered before him, and he will separate people one from another as a shepherd separates the sheep from the goats, and he will put the sheep at his right hand and the goats at the left. Then the king will say to those at his right hand, 'Come, you that are blessed by my Father, inherit the kingdom prepared for you from the foundation of the world; [35] for I was hungry and you gave me food, I was thirsty and you gave me something to drink, I was a stranger and you welcomed me, I was naked and you gave me clothing, I was sick and you took care of me, I was in prison and you visited me.'

"Then the righteous will answer him, 'Lord, when was it that we saw you hungry and gave you food, or thirsty and gave you something to drink? And when was it that we saw you a stranger and welcomed you, or naked and gave you clothing? And when was it that we saw you sick or in prison and visited you?' [40] And the king will answer them, 'Truly I tell you, just as you did it to one of the least of these who are members of my family, you did it to me.' Then he will say to those at his left hand, 'You that are accursed, depart from me into the eternal fire prepared for the devil and his angels; for I was hungry and you gave me no food, I was thirsty and you gave me nothing to drink, I was a

---

**Matthew* 25:31–46; *Revelation* 20:1–21:4

stranger and you did not welcome me, naked and you did not give me clothing, sick and in prison and you did not visit me.' Then they also will answer, 'Lord, when was it that we saw you hungry or thirsty or a stranger or naked or sick or in prison, and did not take care of you?' [45] Then he will answer them, 'Truly I tell you, just as you did not do it to one of the least of these, you did not do it to me.' And these will go away into eternal punishment, but the righteous into eternal life."

[*Revelation* 20:1] Then I saw an angel coming down from heaven, holding in his hand the key to the bottomless pit and a great chain. He seized the dragon, that ancient serpent, who is the Devil and Satan, and bound him for a thousand years, and threw him into the pit, and locked and sealed it over him, so that he would deceive the nations no more, until the thousand years were ended. After that he must be let out for a little while.

Then I saw thrones, and those seated on them were given authority to judge. I also saw the souls of those who had been beheaded for their testimony to Jesus and for the word of God. They had not worshiped the beast or its image and had not received its mark on their foreheads or their hands. They came to life and reigned with Christ a thousand years. [5] [The rest of the dead did not come to life until the thousand years were ended.] This is the first resurrection. Blessed and holy are those who share in the first resurrection. Over these the second death has no power, but they will be priests of God and of Christ, and they will reign with him a thousand years.

When the thousand years are ended, Satan will be released from his prison and will come out to deceive the nations at the four corners of the earth, Gog and Magog,[27] in order to gather them for battle; they are as numerous as the sands of the sea. They marched up over the breadth of the earth and surrounded the camp of the saints and the beloved city. And fire came down from heaven and consumed them. [10] And the devil who had deceived them was thrown into the lake of fire and sulfur, where the beast and the false prophet were, and they will be tormented day and night forever and ever.

Then I saw a great white throne and the one who sat on it; the earth and the heaven fled from his presence; and no place was found for them. And I saw the dead, great and small, standing before the throne, and books were opened. Also another book was opened, the book of life. And the dead were judged according to their works, as recorded in the books. And the sea gave up the dead that were in it, Death and Hades[28] gave up the dead that were in them, and all were judged according to what they had done. Then Death and Hades were thrown into the lake of fire. This is the second death, the lake of fire; [15] and anyone whose name was not found written in the book of life was thrown into the lake of fire.

[21:1] Then I saw a new heaven and a new earth; for the first heaven and the first earth had passed away, and the sea was no more. And I saw the holy city, the new Jerusalem, coming down out of heaven from God, prepared as a bride adorned for her husband. And I heard a loud voice from the throne saying,

"See, the home of God is among mortals.
He will dwell with them as their God;
they will be his peoples,
and God himself will be with them;
he will wipe every tear from their eyes.
Death will be no more;
mourning and crying and pain will be no more,
for the first things have passed away."

---

[27] *Gog and Magog:* nations allied with Satan to oppose the coming of God's kingdom. In *Ezekiel* 38–39, these are probably code words for the nation of Babylon, which in the book of *Revelation* is code in turn for Rome.

[28] *Death and Hades* (Hell) are personified here.

ETHICS

The Sermon on the Mount*

The Sermon on the Mount is the gospels' longest collection of the moral teaching of Jesus. It is largely a collection by the gospel writer, probably drawing on an early collection of Jesus' sayings called by modern scholars the Quelle, *"source." The sermon contains his understanding of Jesus' teaching on what it is to follow Jesus. The themes are many and varied: blessings on obedience, the law of Moses, the practice of piety, use of possessions, and following Jesus' words.*

When Jesus saw the crowds, he went up the mountain; and after he sat down, his disciples came to him. Then he began to speak, and taught them, saying:

"Blessed are the poor in spirit, for theirs is the kingdom of heaven.

"Blessed are those who mourn, for they will be comforted.

[5] "Blessed are the meek,[29] for they will inherit the earth.

"Blessed are those who hunger and thirst for righteousness, for they will be filled.

"Blessed are the merciful, for they will receive mercy.

"Blessed are the pure in heart, for they will see God.

"Blessed are the peacemakers, for they will be called children of God.

[10] "Blessed are those who are persecuted for righteousness' sake, for theirs is the kingdom of heaven.

"Blessed are you when people revile you and persecute you and utter all kinds of evil against you falsely on my account. Rejoice and be glad, for your reward is great in heaven, for in the same way they persecuted the prophets who were before you.

"You are the salt of the earth; but if salt has lost its taste, how can its saltiness be restored? It is no longer good for anything, but is thrown out and trampled under foot. You are the light of the world. A city built on a hill cannot be hid. [15] No one after lighting a lamp puts it under the bushel basket, but on the lampstand, and it gives light to all in the house. In the same way, let your light shine before others, so that they may see your good works and give glory to your Father in heaven.

"Do not think that I have come to abolish the law or the prophets; I have come not to abolish but to fulfill. For truly I tell you, until heaven and earth pass away, not one letter, not one stroke of a letter, will pass from the law until all is accomplished. Therefore, whoever breaks one of the least of these commandments, and teaches others to do the same, will be called least in the kingdom of heaven; but whoever does them and teaches them will be called great in the kingdom of heaven. [20] For I tell you, unless your righteousness exceeds that of the scribes and Pharisees, you will never enter the kingdom of heaven.

"You have heard that it was said to those of ancient times, 'You shall not murder'; and 'Whoever murders shall be liable to judgment.' But I say to you that if you are angry with a brother or sister, you will be liable to judgment; and if you insult a brother or sister, you will be liable to the council; and if you say, 'You fool,' you will be liable to the hell of fire. So when you are offering your gift at the altar, if you remember that your brother or sister has something against you, leave your gift there before the altar and go; first be reconciled to your brother or sister, and then come and offer your gift. [25]

---

*Matthew 5–7
[29] *meek:* humble.

Come to terms quickly with your accuser while you are on the way to court with him, or your accuser may hand you over to the judge, and the judge to the guard, and you will be thrown into prison. Truly I tell you, you will never get out until you have paid the last penny.

"You have heard that it was said, 'You shall not commit adultery.' But I say to you that everyone who looks at a woman with lust has already committed adultery with her in his heart. If your right eye causes you to sin, tear it out and throw it away;[30] it is better for you to lose one of your members than for your whole body to be thrown into hell. [30] And if your right hand causes you to sin, cut it off and throw it away; it is better for you to lose one of your members than for your whole body to go into hell.

"It was also said, 'Whoever divorces his wife, let him give her a certificate of divorce.' But I say to you that anyone who divorces his wife, except on the ground of unchastity, causes her to commit adultery; and whoever marries a divorced woman commits adultery.

"Again, you have heard that it was said to those of ancient times, 'You shall not swear falsely, but carry out the vows you have made to the Lord.' But I say to you, Do not swear at all, either by heaven, for it is the throne of God, [35] or by the earth, for it is his footstool, or by Jerusalem, for it is the city of the great King. And do not swear by your head, for you cannot make one hair white or black. Let your word be 'Yes, Yes' or 'No, No'; anything more than this comes from the evil one.

"You have heard that it was said, 'An eye for an eye and a tooth for a tooth.' But I say to you, Do not resist an evildoer. But if anyone strikes you on the right cheek, turn the other also; [40] and if anyone wants to sue you and take your coat, give your cloak as well; and if anyone forces you to go one mile, go also the second mile. Give to everyone who begs from you, and do not refuse anyone who wants to borrow from you.

"You have heard that it was said, 'You shall love your neighbor and hate your enemy.' But I say to you, Love your enemies and pray for those who persecute you, [45] so that you may be children of your Father in heaven; for he makes his sun rise on the evil and on the good, and sends rain on the righteous and on the unrighteous. For if you love those who love you, what reward do you have? Do not even the tax collectors do the same? And if you greet only your brothers and sisters, what more are you doing than others? Do not even the Gentiles do the same? Be perfect, therefore, as your heavenly Father is perfect.[31]

[6:1] "Beware of practicing your piety before others in order to be seen by them; for then you have no reward from your Father in heaven. So whenever you give alms, do not sound a trumpet before you, as the hypocrites[32] do in the synagogues and in the streets, so that they may be praised by others. Truly I tell you, they have received their reward. But when you give alms, do not let your left hand know what your right hand is doing, so that your alms may be done in secret; and your Father who sees in secret will reward you. [5] And whenever you pray, do not be like the hypocrites; for they love to stand and pray in the synagogues and at the street corners, so that they may be seen by others. Truly I tell you, they have received their reward. But whenever you pray, go into your room and shut the door and pray to your Father who is in secret; and your Father who sees in secret will reward you.

"When you are praying, do not heap up empty phrases as the Gentiles do; for they think

---

[30]*tear out your eye,* and the later saying *cut off your hand,* are hyperbole and not to be interpreted literally. Jesus does not advocate self-mutilation; the meaning is that Jesus' followers are to take all necessary measures to avoid adultery.

[31]*perfect:* not sinless, but mature and complete.

[32]*hypocrites:* not those who are evil on the inside and yet act righteously, but those who are basically good yet have moral faults that mar their goodness.

that they will be heard because of their many words. Do not be like them, for your Father knows what you need before you ask him. Pray then in this way:[33]

Our Father in heaven,
hallowed be your name.
[10] Your kingdom come.
Your will be done, on earth as it is in heaven.
Give us this day our daily bread.
And forgive us our debts, as we also have forgiven our debtors.
And do not bring us to the time of trial, but rescue us from the evil one.

For if you forgive others their trespasses, your heavenly Father will also forgive you; [15] but if you do not forgive others, neither will your Father forgive your trespasses.

"And whenever you fast, do not look dismal, like the hypocrites, for they disfigure their faces so as to show others that they are fasting. Truly I tell you, they have received their reward. But when you fast, put oil on your head and wash your face, so that your fasting may be seen not by others but by your Father who is in secret; and your Father who sees in secret will reward you.

"Do not store up for yourselves treasures on earth, where moth and rust consume and where thieves break in and steal; [20] but store up for yourselves treasures in heaven, where neither moth nor rust consumes and where thieves do not break in and steal. For where your treasure is, there your heart will be also.

"The eye is the lamp of the body.[34] So, if your eye is healthy, your whole body will be full of light; but if your eye is unhealthy, your whole body will be full of darkness. If then the light in you is darkness, how great is the darkness!

"No one can serve two masters; for a slave will either hate the one and love the other, or be devoted to the one and despise the other. You cannot serve God and wealth.

[25] "Therefore I tell you, do not worry about your life, what you will eat or what you will drink, or about your body, what you will wear. Is not life more than food, and the body more than clothing? Look at the birds of the air; they neither sow nor reap nor gather into barns, and yet your heavenly Father feeds them. Are you not of more value than they? And can any of you by worrying add a single hour to your span of life? And why do you worry about clothing? Consider the lilies of the field, how they grow; they neither toil nor spin, yet I tell you, even Solomon in all his glory was not clothed like one of these. [30] But if God so clothes the grass of the field, which is alive today and tomorrow is thrown into the oven, will he not much more clothe you—you of little faith? Therefore do not worry, saying, 'What will we eat?' or 'What will we drink?' or 'What will we wear?' For it is the Gentiles who strive for all these things; and indeed your heavenly Father knows that you need all these things. But strive first for the kingdom of God and his righteousness, and all these things will be given to you as well.

"So do not worry about tomorrow, for tomorrow will bring worries of its own. Today's trouble is enough for today.

[7:1] "Do not judge, so that you may not be judged. For with the judgment you make you will be judged, and the measure you give will be the measure you get. Why do you see the speck in your neighbor's eye, but do not notice the log in your own eye? Or how can you say to your neighbor, 'Let me take the speck out of your eye,' while the log is in your own eye? [5] You hypocrite, first take the log out of your own eye, and then you will see clearly to take the speck out of your neighbor's eye.

"Do not give what is holy to dogs; and do not throw your pearls before swine, or they will trample them underfoot and turn and maul you.

---

[33] *pray this way:* Jesus gives this prayer as a model; prayer should be full yet brief. That some English-speaking Christians say "debts" and others "trespasses" comes from different English versions of the Bible.

[34] *eye:* probably the heart as the seat of emotion and thought; perhaps the conscience.

"Ask, and it will be given you; search, and you will find; knock, and the door will be opened for you. For everyone who asks receives, and everyone who searches finds, and for everyone who knocks, the door will be opened. Is there anyone among you who, if your child asks for bread, will give a stone? [10] Or if the child asks for a fish, will give a snake? If you then, who are evil, know how to give good gifts to your children, how much more will your Father in heaven give good things to those who ask him!

"In everything do to others as you would have them do to you; for this is the law and the prophets.[35]

"Enter through the narrow gate; for the gate is wide and the road is easy that leads to destruction, and there are many who take it. For the gate is narrow and the road is hard that leads to life, and there are few who find it.

[15] "Beware of false prophets, who come to you in sheep's clothing but inwardly are ravenous wolves. You will know them by their fruits. Are grapes gathered from thorns, or figs from thistles? In the same way, every good tree bears good fruit, but the bad tree bears bad fruit. A good tree cannot bear bad fruit, nor can a bad tree bear good fruit. Every tree that does not bear good fruit is cut down and thrown into the fire. [20] Thus you will know them by their fruits.

"Not everyone who says to me, 'Lord, Lord,' will enter the kingdom of heaven, but only the one who does the will of my Father in heaven. On that day many will say to me, 'Lord, Lord, did we not prophesy in your name, and cast out demons in your name, and do many deeds of power in your name?' Then I will declare to them, 'I never knew you; go away from me, you evildoers.'

"Everyone then who hears these words of mine and acts on them will be like a wise man who built his house on rock. [25] The rain fell, the floods came, and the winds blew and beat on that house, but it did not fall, because it had been founded on rock. And everyone who hears these words of mine and does not act on them will be like a foolish man who built his house on sand. The rain fell, and the floods came, and the winds blew and beat against that house, and it fell—and great was its fall!"

Now when Jesus had finished saying these things, the crowds were astounded at his teaching, for he taught them as one having authority, and not as their scribes.[36]

---

[35]This is the "Golden Rule." Expressed in its positive form, it is the essence of self-giving love.

[36]*not as their scribes:* Jewish scribes taught on the authority of other scribal experts; Jesus teaches on his own authority.

Directions Concerning Marriage*

Paul here gives detailed directions about marriage. His basic perspective, based mostly on his expectation of the imminent return of Jesus, is that marriage is good, but to remain single is better. In this passage and the next, the quotations are slogans prominent in the church of Corinth to which Paul is responding. Note Paul's distinction between the commands of Jesus and his own preferences. These ideas became influential in the ancient church and continue in churches that practice forms of clerical celibacy.

Now concerning the matters about which you wrote: "It is well for a man not to touch a woman." But because of cases of sexual immorality, each man should have his own wife and each woman her own husband. The husband should give to his wife her conjugal rights, and likewise the wife to her husband. For the

---

*I Corinthians 7:1–16, 25–40

wife does not have authority over her own body, but the husband does; likewise the husband does not have authority over his own body, but the wife does. [5] Do not deprive one another except perhaps by agreement for a set time, to devote yourselves to prayer, and then come together again, so that Satan may not tempt you because of your lack of self-control. This I say by way of concession, not of command. I wish that all were as I myself am. But each has a particular gift from God, one having one kind and another a different kind.

To the unmarried and the widows I say that it is well for them to remain unmarried as I am. But if they are not practicing self-control, they should marry. For it is better to marry than to be aflame with passion.

[10] To the married I give this command— not I but the Lord—that the wife should not separate from her husband, and that the husband should not divorce his wife.

To the rest I say—I and not the Lord—that if any believer has a wife who is an unbeliever, and she consents to live with him, he should not divorce her. And if any woman has a husband who is an unbeliever, and he consents to live with her, she should not divorce him. For the unbelieving husband is made holy through his wife, and the unbelieving wife is made holy through her husband. Otherwise, your children would be unclean, but as it is, they are holy. [15] But if the unbelieving partner separates, let it be so; in such a case the brother or sister is not bound. It is to peace that God has called you. Wife, for all you know, you might save your husband. Husband, for all you know, you might save your wife. . . .

[25] Now concerning virgins,[37] I have no command of the Lord, but I give my opinion as one who by the Lord's mercy is trustworthy. I think that, in view of the impending crisis,[38] it is

well for you to remain as you are. Are you bound to a wife? Do not seek to be free. Are you free from a wife? Do not seek a wife. But if you marry, you do not sin, and if a virgin marries, she does not sin. Yet those who marry will experience distress in this life, and I would spare you that. I mean, brothers and sisters, the appointed time has grown short; from now on, let even those who have wives be as though they had none, [30] and those who mourn as though they were not mourning, and those who rejoice as though they were not rejoicing, and those who buy as though they had no possessions, and those who deal with the world as though they had no dealings with it. For the present form of this world is passing away.

I want you to be free from anxieties. The unmarried man is anxious about the affairs of the Lord, how to please the Lord; but the married man is anxious about the affairs of the world, how to please his wife, and his interests are divided. And the unmarried woman and the virgin are anxious about the affairs of the Lord, so that they may be holy in body and spirit; but the married woman is anxious about the affairs of the world, how to please her husband. [35] I say this for your own benefit, not to put any restraint upon you, but to promote good order and unhindered devotion to the Lord.

If anyone thinks that he is not behaving properly toward his fiancée, if his passions are strong, and so it has to be, let him marry as he wishes; it is no sin. Let them marry. But if someone stands firm in his resolve, being under no necessity but having his own desire under control, and has determined in his own mind to keep her as his fiancée, he will do well. So then, he who marries his fiancée does well; and he who refrains from marriage will do better.

A wife is bound as long as her husband lives. But if the husband dies, she is free to marry anyone she wishes, only in the Lord.[39] But in my judgment she is more blessed if she remains as she is. And I think that I too have the Spirit of God.

---

[37]*virgins:* young women of marriageable age; no other implication is made.

[38]*impending crisis:* troubles for believers at the end of the world.

[39]*only in the Lord:* to a fellow Christian.

Love*

This "Hymn to Love," perhaps written by Paul or adapted by him for use in this letter, extols love as the greatest spiritual gift. It has three distinct themes in these three paragraphs: first, it contrasts love with other spiritual gifts; second, it describes love; third, it extols the persistence of love.

If I speak in the tongues of mortals and of angels, but do not have love, I am a noisy gong or a clanging cymbal. And if I have prophetic powers, and understand all mysteries and all knowledge, and if I have all faith, so as to remove mountains, but do not have love, I am nothing. If I give away all my possessions, and if I hand over my body so that I may boast, but do not have love, I gain nothing.

Love is patient; love is kind; love is not envious or boastful or arrogant [5] or rude. It does not insist on its own way; it is not irritable or resentful; it does not rejoice in wrongdoing, but rejoices in the truth. It bears all things, believes all things, hopes all things, endures all things.

Love never ends. But as for prophecies, they will come to an end; as for tongues, they will cease; as for knowledge, it will come to an end. For we know only in part, and we prophesy only in part; [10] but when the complete comes, the partial will come to an end. When I was a child, I spoke like a child, I thought like a child, I reasoned like a child; when I became an adult, I put an end to childish ways. For now we see in a mirror, dimly, but then we will see face to face. Now I know only in part; then I will know fully, even as I have been fully known. And now faith, hope, and love abide, these three; and the greatest of these is love.

---

* I Corinthians 13:1–13

Ethics in the Christian Household**

This discussion of ethics in the Christian household contains instructions for wives, husbands, children, parents, slaves, and masters. It presupposes the legitimacy of the household structure of the times but seeks to transform it with the Christian ethic.

Be subject to one another out of reverence for Christ.

Wives, be subject to your husbands as you are to the Lord. For the husband is the head of the wife just as Christ is the head of the church, the body of which he is the Savior. Just as the church is subject to Christ, so also wives ought to be, in everything, to their husbands. [25] Husbands, love your wives,[40] just as Christ loved the church and gave himself up for her, in order to make her holy by cleansing her with the washing of water by the word, so as to present the church to himself in splendor, without a spot or wrinkle or anything of the kind—yes, so that she may be holy and without blemish. In the same way, husbands should love their wives as they do their own bodies. He who loves his

---

[40] *Husbands, love your wives:* in ancient societies, as in most societies today where marriage is not based on romantic love, this command would not be seen as essential to marriage.

** Ephesians 5:21–6:9

wife loves himself. For no one ever hates his own body, but he nourishes and tenderly cares for it, just as Christ does for the church, [30] because we are members of his body. For this reason a man will leave his father and mother and be joined to his wife, and the two will become one flesh. This is a great mystery, and I am applying it to Christ and the church. Each of you, however, should love his wife as himself, and a wife should respect her husband.

[6:1] Children, obey your parents in the Lord, for this is right. "Honor your father and mother"—this is the first commandment with a promise: "so that it may be well with you and you may live long on the earth." And, fathers, do not provoke your children to anger, but bring them up in the discipline and instruction of the Lord.

[5] Slaves, obey your earthly masters with fear and trembling, in singleness of heart, as you obey Christ; not only while being watched, and in order to please them, but as slaves of Christ, doing the will of God from the heart. Render service with enthusiasm, as to the Lord and not to men and women, knowing that whatever good we do, we will receive the same again from the Lord, whether we are slaves or free. And, masters, do the same to them. Stop threatening them, for you know that both of you have the same Master in heaven, and with him there is no partiality.

Being Subject to Authorities*

Romans *13 is the most important treatment in the* New Testament *of the relationship of the believer and the government, and the most influential through the history of the church. It couples specific and positive instructions about being subject to governing authorities with more general instructions about social ethics.*

Let every person be subject to the governing authorities; for there is no authority except from God, and those authorities that exist have been instituted by God. Therefore whoever resists authority resists what God has appointed, and those who resist will incur judgment. For rulers are not a terror to good conduct, but to bad. Do you wish to have no fear of the authority? Then do what is good, and you will receive its approval; for it is God's servant for your good.

But if you do what is wrong, you should be afraid, for the authority does not bear the sword in vain. It is the servant of God to execute wrath on the wrongdoer. [5] Therefore one must be subject, not only because of wrath but also because of conscience. For the same reason you also pay taxes, for the authorities are God's servants, busy with this very thing. Pay to all what is due them—taxes to whom taxes are due, revenue to whom revenue is due, respect to whom respect is due, honor to whom honor is due.

Owe no one anything, except to love one another; for the one who loves another has fulfilled the law. The commandments, "You shall not commit adultery; You shall not murder; You shall not steal; You shall not covet;" and any other commandment, are summed up in this word, "Love your neighbor as yourself." [10] Love does no wrong to a neighbor; therefore, love is the fulfilling of the law.

*Romans 13:1–10

The Fall of Rome*

This is the "flip side" of the positive view of civil government presented in Romans 13:1–7. *The city of Rome is depicted symbolically as a "great whore," and the scarlet beast she rides is the Roman empire. This selection concludes with a funeral song sung over the fallen Rome. This approach encourages quiet opposition to idolatrous and persecuting government, longing for its downfall at the coming of God's kingdom.*

Then one of the seven angels who had the seven bowls came and said to me, "Come. I will show you the judgment of the great whore who is seated on many waters, with whom the kings of the earth have committed fornication, and with the wine of whose fornication the inhabitants of the earth have become drunk." So he carried me away in the spirit into a wilderness, and I saw a woman sitting on a scarlet beast that was full of blasphemous names, and it had seven heads and ten horns. The woman was clothed in purple and scarlet, and adorned with gold and jewels and pearls, holding in her hand a golden cup full of abominations and the impurities of her fornication; [5] and on her forehead was written a name, a mystery: "Babylon the great,[41] mother of whores and of earth's abomination." And I saw that the woman was drunk with the blood of the saints and the blood of the witnesses to Jesus.

When I saw her, I was greatly amazed. But the angel said to me, "Why are you so amazed? I will tell you the mystery of the woman, and of the beast with seven heads and ten horns that carries her. The beast that you saw was, and is not, and is about to ascend from the bottomless pit and go to destruction. And the inhabitants of the earth, whose names have not been written in the book of life from the foundation of the world, will be amazed when they see the beast, because it was and is not and is to come.

"This calls for a mind that has wisdom: the seven heads are seven mountains on which the woman is seated; also, they are seven kings, [10] of whom five have fallen, one is living, and the other has not yet come; and when he comes, he must remain only a little while. As for the beast that was and is not, it is an eighth but it belongs to the seven, and it goes to destruction. And the ten horns that you saw are ten kings who have not yet received a kingdom, but they are to receive authority as kings for one hour, together with the beast. These are united in yielding their power and authority to the beast; they will make war on the Lamb,[42] and the Lamb will conquer them, for he is Lord of lords and King of kings, and those with him are called and chosen and faithful."

And he said to me, "The waters that you saw, where the whore is seated, are peoples and multitudes and nations and languages. And the ten horns that you saw, they and the beast will hate the whore; they will make her desolate and naked; they will devour her flesh and burn her up with fire. For God has put it into their hearts to carry out his purpose by agreeing to give their kingdom to the beast, until the words of God will be fulfilled. The woman you saw is the great city that rules over the kings of the earth."

After this I saw another angel coming down from heaven, having great authority; and the earth was made bright with his splendor. He called out with a mighty voice,

"Fallen, fallen is Babylon the great
It has become a dwelling place of demons, a
    haunt of every foul and hateful bird, a haunt
    of every foul and hateful beast.
For all the nations have drunk of the wine of
    the wrath of her fornication,

---

*Revelation 17:1–18:5
[41] *Babylon the great:* a code name for Rome, taken from the name of a great oppressing city-empire in the Jewish *Bible.*

---

[42] *the Lamb:* Jesus Christ, the Lamb of God.

and the kings of the earth have committed fornication with her,
and the merchants of the earth have grown rich
from the power of her luxury."

Then I heard another voice from heaven saying,

"Come out of her, my people, so that you do
not take part in her sins,
and so that you do not share in her plagues; for
her sins are heaped high as heaven,
and God has remembered her iniquities."

ORGANIZATION

The Twelve Apostles and Their Mission*

The apostles, twelve in number to suggest the twelve tribes of ancient Israel, are named and commissioned here. Both the situation of Jesus (the restriction of his mission to the Jews) and the later church (itinerant prophets and evangelists) are reflected. This type of mission was important in the early spread of Christianity through Palestine and Syria.

Then Jesus summoned his twelve disciples and gave them authority over unclean spirits, to cast them out, and to cure every disease and every sickness. These are the names of the twelve apostles: first, Simon, also known as Peter, and his brother Andrew; James son of Zebedee, and his brother John; Philip and Bartholomew; Thomas and Matthew the tax collector; James son of Alphaeus, and Thaddaeus; Simon the Cananaean, and Judas Iscariot, the one who betrayed him.

[5] These twelve Jesus sent out with the fol-
lowing instructions: "Go nowhere among the Gentiles, and enter no town of the Samaritans, but go rather to the lost sheep of the house of Israel. As you go, proclaim the good news, 'The kingdom of heaven has come near.' Cure the sick, raise the dead, cleanse the lepers, cast out demons. You received without payment; give without payment. Take no gold, or silver, or copper in your belts, [10] no bag for your journey, or two tunics, or sandals, or a staff; for laborers deserve their food. Whatever town or village you enter, find out who in it is worthy, and stay there until you leave. As you enter the house, greet it.[43] If the house is worthy, let your peace come upon it; but if it is not worthy, let your peace return to you. If anyone will not welcome you or listen to your words, shake off the dust from your feet as you leave that house or town.[44] [15] Truly I tell you, it will be more tol-
erable for the land of Sodom and Gomorrah[45] on the day of judgment than for that town.

---

[43]*greet it:* give the inhabitants of the house a blessing, such as "peace be to this house."
[44]*shake the dust from your feet:* an action symbolizing con-
demnation for rejecting the message.
[45]*Sodom and Gomorrah:* cities destroyed by God for their wickedness (*Genesis* 19:1–28).

---

*Matthew 10:1–15

Matthew's Church Order*

Matthew is the only gospel with comprehensive instructions for church life. This passage begins with sayings on humility and forgiveness and ends with procedures for dealing with persistent sin among church members.

At that time the disciples came to Jesus and asked, "Who is the greatest in the kingdom of heaven?" He called a child, whom he put among them, and said, "Truly I tell you, unless you change and become like children, you will never enter the kingdom of heaven. Whoever becomes humble like this child is the greatest in the kingdom of heaven. [5] Whoever welcomes one such child in my name welcomes me.

"If any of you put a stumbling block before one of these little ones who believe in me, it would be better for you if a great millstone were fastened around your neck and you were drowned in the depth of the sea. Woe to the world because of stumbling blocks! Occasions for stumbling are bound to come, but woe to the one by whom the stumbling block comes! If your hand or your foot causes you to stumble, cut it off and throw it away; it is better for you to enter life maimed or lame than to have two hands or two feet and to be thrown into the eternal fire. And if your eye causes you to stumble, tear it out and throw it away; it is better for you to enter life with one eye than to have two eyes and to be thrown into the hell of fire.

---

*Matthew 18:1–10, 15-22

[10] "Take care that you do not despise one of these little ones; for, I tell you, in heaven their angels[46] continually see the face of my Father in heaven. . . . [15] "If another member of the church sins against you, go and point out the fault when the two of you are alone. If the member listens to you, you have regained that one. But if you are not listened to, take one or two others along with you, so that every word may be confirmed by the evidence of two or three witnesses. If the member refuses to listen to them, tell it to the church; and if the offender refuses to listen even to the church, let such a one be to you as a Gentile and a tax collector.[47] Truly I tell you, whatever you bind on earth will be bound in heaven, and whatever you loose on earth will be loosed in heaven.[48] Again, truly I tell you, if two of you agree on earth about anything you ask, it will be done for you by my Father in heaven. [20] For where two or three are gathered in my name, I am there among them."

Then Peter came and said to him, "Lord, if another member of the church sins against me, how often should I forgive? As many as seven times?" Jesus said to him, "Not seven times, but, I tell you, seventy-seven times."[49]

---

[46]*their angels:* their guardian angels.

[47]*a gentile and a tax collector:* that is, one to be shunned.

[48]*bind and loose:* forbid an action as sinful, or permit, respectively.

[49]*seventy-seven times:* that is, forgive without limit.

Peter as the Rock**

Jesus here renames Simon as Peter, the rock on which the church is founded. Greek Petros *("Peter") is similar to* petra *("rock"). Jesus gives Peter "the keys of the kingdom of heaven." Catholi-*

**Matthew 16:13–20

cism sees this as establishing the papacy, the bishop of Rome who is the successor of Peter and who holds universal power over the church by these "keys."

Now when Jesus came into the district of Caesarea Philippi, he asked his disciples, "Who do people say that the Son of Man is?" And they said, "Some say John the Baptist, but others Elijah, and still others Jeremiah or one of the prophets." [15] He said to them, "But who do you say that I am?" Simon Peter answered, "You are the Messiah, the Son of the living God." And Jesus answered him, "Blessed are you, Simon son of Jonah! For flesh and blood has not revealed this to you, but my Father in heaven. And I tell you, you are Peter, and on this rock I will build my church, and the gates of Hades will not prevail against it. I will give

you the keys of the kingdom of heaven, and whatever you bind on earth will be bound in heaven, and whatever you loose on earth will be loosed in heaven."[50] [20] Then he sternly ordered the disciples not to tell anyone that he was the Messiah.[51]

---

[50]Compare *Matthew* 18:18 earlier, where the power to bind and loose is given to the apostles as a group.
[51]*not to tell anyone that he was the Messiah:* the reason for this "messianic secret" has been debated for almost a century, with little consensus among scholars.

Qualifications of Bishops and Deacons*

Here we see the beginning of the threefold office in the church: bishop, presbyter (an elder or priest), and deacon. This has been the most common pattern of church office among most Christians even when these particular names are not used. The duties of these offices are not given, but we can infer their duties from the lists of qualifications. The emphasis on skill in family relationships comes in part from the setting of early Christian congregations, which met in believers' homes.

The saying is sure: whoever aspires to the office of bishop desires a noble task. Now a bishop must be above reproach, married only once, temperate, sensible, respectable, hospitable, an apt teacher, not a drunkard, not violent but gentle, not quarrelsome, and not a lover of money. He must manage his own household well, keeping his children submissive and respectful in every way—[5] for if someone does not know how to manage his own household,

how can he take care of God's church? He must not be a recent convert, or he may be puffed up with conceit and fall into the condemnation of the devil. Moreover, he must be well thought of by outsiders, so that he may not fall into disgrace and the snare of the devil.

Deacons likewise must be serious, not double-tongued, not indulging in much wine, not greedy for money; they must hold fast to the mystery of the faith with a clear conscience. [10] And let them first be tested; then, if they prove themselves blameless, let them serve as deacons. Women[52] likewise must be serious, not slanderers, but temperate, faithful in all things. Let deacons be married only once, and let them manage their children and their households well; for those who serve well as deacons gain a good standing for themselves and great boldness in the faith that is in Christ Jesus.

---

*I Timothy 3:1–13

[52]*Women:* historians debate whether this means "wives of deacons" or "women deacons."

Women in the Early Church*

Christianity's traditional attitude to women, which argues for some degree of equality and subjection at the same time, has its roots in the New Testament. In the first passage, Jesus shows that women should participate with men in hearing his teaching, although this might conflict with traditional roles. In the second reading, Paul takes a much more restrictive attitude to the roles of women in the church. The third reading has been very influential in the Christian movement for equality. The last passage features the most patriarchal statement of the place of women in the church, and this passage has been influential in the history of Christianity.

Now as they went on their way, he entered a certain village, where a woman named Martha welcomed him into her home. She had a sister named Mary, who sat at the Lord's feet and listened to what he was saying. [40] But Martha was distracted by her many tasks; so she came to him and asked, "Lord, do you not care that my sister has left me to do all the work by myself? Tell her then to help me." But the Lord answered her, "Martha, Martha, you are worried and distracted by many things; there is need of only one thing. Mary has chosen the better part, which will not be taken away from her."

[*I Corinthians* 11:2] I commend you because you remember me in everything and maintain the traditions just as I handed them on to you. But I want you to understand that Christ is the head of every man, and the husband is the head of his wife, and God is the head of Christ. Any man who prays or prophesies with something on his head disgraces his head, [5] but any woman who prays or prophesies with her head unveiled disgraces her head—it is one and the same thing as having her head shaved. For if a

woman will not veil herself, then she should cut off her hair; but if it is disgraceful for a woman to have her hair cut off or to be shaved, she should wear a veil. For a man ought not to have his head veiled, since he is the image and reflection of God; but woman is the reflection of man. Indeed, man was not made from woman, but woman from man. Neither was man created for the sake of woman, but woman for the sake of man. [10] For this reason a woman ought to have a symbol of authority on her head, because of the angels. Nevertheless, in the Lord woman is not independent of man or man independent of woman. For just as woman came from man, so man comes through woman; but all things come from God. Judge for yourselves: is it proper for a woman to pray to God with her head unveiled? Does not nature itself teach you that if a man wears long hair, it is degrading to him, [15] but if a woman has long hair, it is her glory? For her hair is given to her for a covering. But if anyone is disposed to be contentious —we have no such custom, nor do the churches of God.

[*Galatians* 3:25–28] Now that faith has come, we are no longer subject to a disciplinarian,[53] for in Christ Jesus you are all children of God through faith. As many of you as were baptized into Christ have clothed yourselves with Christ. There is no longer Jew or Greek, there is no longer slave or free, there is no longer male and female; for all of you are one in Christ Jesus.

[*I Timothy* 2:8–15] I desire, then, that in every place the men should pray, lifting up holy hands without anger or argument; also that the women should dress themselves modestly and decently in suitable clothing, not with their hair braided, or with gold, pearls, or expensive clothes, [10] but with good works, as is proper

---

*Luke 10:38–42; I Corinthians 11:2–16; Galatians 3:27–28; I Timothy 2:8–15

[53]*disciplinarian:* The Law of Moses.

for women who profess reverence for God. Let a woman learn in silence with full submission. I permit no woman to teach or to have authority over a man; she is to keep silent. For Adam was formed first, then Eve; and Adam was not deceived, but the woman was deceived and became a transgressor. [15] Yet she will be saved through childbearing, provided they continue in faith and love and holiness, with modesty.

RITUAL

The Eucharist*

The Eucharist ("Thanksgiving") also goes by the names "Lord's Supper" and "Holy Communion." The first passage relates its institution during Jesus' last Passover meal, when he identified the bread and wine of the Passover with his body and blood. These were soon to be shed on the cross for the establishment of a "new covenant" of forgiveness and life. In the second passage, Jesus makes this identification in a symbolic way that has had a strong influence on how Christians view the Eucharist: his body and blood nourish one to eternal life.

On the first day of Unleavened Bread the disciples came to Jesus, saying, "Where do you want us to make the preparations for you to eat the Passover?" He said, "Go into the city to a certain man, and say to him, 'The Teacher says, My time is near; I will keep the Passover at your house with my disciples.'" So the disciples did as Jesus had directed them, and they prepared the Passover meal. . . .

While they were eating, Jesus took a loaf of bread,[54] and after blessing it he broke it, gave it to the disciples, and said, "Take, eat; this is my body." Then he took a cup, and after giving thanks he gave it to them, saying, "Drink from it, all of you; for this is my blood of the covenant, which is poured out for many for the forgiveness of sins. I tell you, I will never again drink of this fruit of the vine until that day when I drink it new with you in my Father's kingdom."

[John 6:22] The next day the crowd that had stayed on the other side of the sea saw that there had been only one boat there. They also saw that Jesus had not got into the boat with his disciples, but that his disciples had gone away alone. Then some boats from Tiberias came near the place where they had eaten the bread after the Lord had given thanks. So when the crowd saw that neither Jesus nor his disciples were there, they themselves got into the boats and went to Capernaum looking for Jesus.

[25] When they found him on the other side of the sea, they said to him, "Rabbi, when did you come here?" Jesus answered them, "Very truly, I tell you, you are looking for me, not because you saw signs, but because you ate your fill of the loaves. Do not work for the food that perishes, but for the food that endures for eternal life, which the Son of Man will give you. For it is on him that God the Father has set his seal." Then they said to him, "What must we do to perform the works of God?" Jesus answered them, "This is the work of God, that you believe in him whom he has sent." [30] So they said to him, "What sign are you going to give us then, so that we may see it and believe you? What work are you performing? Our ancestors ate the manna in the wilderness; as it is written, 'He gave them bread from heaven to eat.'" Then

---

*Matthew 26:17–19, 26-29; John 6:22–40, 52-59
[54]*a loaf of bread:* a large piece of unleavened bread.

Jesus said to them, "Very truly, I tell you, it was not Moses who gave you the bread from heaven, but it is my Father who gives you the true bread from heaven. For the bread of God is that which comes down from heaven and gives life to the world." They said to him, "Sir, give us this bread always."

[35] Jesus said to them, "I am the bread of life. Whoever comes to me will never be hungry, and whoever believes in me will never be thirsty. But I said to you that you have seen me and yet do not believe. Everything that the Father gives me will come to me, and anyone who comes to me I will never drive away; for I have come down from heaven, not to do my own will, but the will of him who sent me. And this is the will of him who sent me, that I should lose nothing of all that he has given me, but raise it up on the last day. [40] This is indeed the will of my Father, that all who see the Son and believe in him may have eternal life; and I will raise them up on the last day.". . .

The Jews then disputed among themselves, saying, "How can this man give us his flesh to eat?" So Jesus said to them, "Very truly, I tell you, unless you eat the flesh of the Son of Man and drink his blood, you have no life in you. Those who eat my flesh and drink my blood have eternal life, and I will raise them up on the last day; [55] for my flesh is true food and my blood is true drink. Those who eat my flesh and drink my blood abide in me, and I in them. Just as the living Father sent me, and I live because of the Father, so whoever eats me will live because of me. This is the bread that came down from heaven, not like that which your ancestors ate, and they died. But the one who eats this bread will live forever." He said these things while he was teaching in the synagogue at Capernaum.

Baptism*

At the conclusion of Matthew, *the triadic divine name—Father, Son, and Holy Spirit—is commanded to be used in the baptism of people from all the nations of the earth. In* Romans 6, *Paul explains that when Christians are baptized they die with Christ to sin and begin to live holy lives for God.* **Baptism,** *a washing with water for forgiveness and new life, became the foundation for the Christian vision of the moral life.*

Now the eleven disciples went to Galilee, to the mountain to which Jesus had directed them. When they saw him, they worshiped him; but some doubted.[55] And Jesus came and said to them, "All authority in heaven and on earth has been given to me. Go therefore and make disci-ples of all nations, baptizing them in the name of the Father and of the Son and of the Holy Spirit, [20] and teaching them to obey everything that I have commanded you. And remember, I am with you always, to the end of the age."

[*Romans* 6:1] What then are we to say? Should we continue in sin in order that grace may abound? By no means! How can we who died to sin go on living in it? Do you not know that all of us who have been baptized into Christ Jesus were baptized into his death? Therefore we have been buried with him by baptism into death, so that, just as Christ was raised from the dead by the glory of the Father, so we too might walk in newness of life.

[5] For if we have been united with him in a death like his, we will certainly be united with him in a resurrection like his. We know that our old self was crucified with him so that the body

---

*Matthew 28:16–20; Romans 6:1–14

[55] *some doubted:* some among the eleven disciples still doubt the reality of Jesus' resurrection.

of sin[56] might be destroyed, and we might no longer be enslaved to sin. For whoever has died is freed from sin. But if we have died with Christ, we believe that we will also live with him. We know that Christ, being raised from the dead, will never die again; death no longer has dominion over him. [10] The death he died, he died to sin, once for all; but the life he lives, he lives to God. So you also must consider yourselves dead to sin and alive to God in Christ Jesus.

---

[56]*the body of sin:* the sinful self, not the physical body.

Therefore, do not let sin exercise dominion in your mortal bodies, to make you obey their passions. No longer present your members[57] to sin as instruments of wickedness, but present yourselves to God as those who have been brought from death to life, and present your members to God as instruments of righteousness. For sin will have no dominion over you, since you are not under law but under grace.

---

[57]*your members:* the different components of the human being.

Confession and Anointing*

This passage is frequently appealed to by those churches—Roman Catholic, Orthodox, and some Protestant—that practice the "anointing of the sick." In the Roman Catholic church, it is one of the seven sacraments, formerly called extreme unction *or (more popularly)* last rites. *The anointing or ritual application with holy oil is connected here with confession of sin, prayer, and the use of the divine name.*

Are any among you suffering? They should pray. Are any cheerful? They should sing songs of

---

*James 5:13–18

praise. Are any among you sick? They should call for the elders of the church and have them pray over them, anointing them with oil in the name of the Lord. [15] The prayer of faith will save the sick, and the Lord will raise them up; and anyone who has committed sins will be forgiven. Therefore confess your sins to one another, and pray for one another, so that you may be healed. The prayer of the righteous is powerful and effective. Elijah was a human being like us, and he prayed fervently that it might not rain, and for three years and six months it did not rain on the earth. Then he prayed again, and the heaven gave rain and the earth yielded its harvest.

GLOSSARY

apostle "one sent out" with the message of salvation, especially the twelve main disciples of Jesus.

authentic writings commonly accepted by most modern biblical scholars as actually written by the persons whose names they bear.

baptism a washing with, or immersion in, water for forgiveness and new, spiritual life.

Bible the scriptures of Christianity, the thirty-nine books of the *Old Testament* and the twenty-seven books of the *New Testament.*

gospel at first, the oral message of "good news" about salvation in Jesus; then, the name given to the books that tell the story of the life, death, and resurrection of Jesus.

letters occasional writings of instruction addressed to churches, so called because they share many or all the features of the common Greco-Roman letter; also called *epistles.*

New Testament the collection of twenty-seven books, mostly gospels and letters, written within the first hundred years of Christianity and constituting the unique, Christian portion of the Christian *Bible.*

Old Testament the name that early Christianity gave to the books of the Jewish *Bible,* which it incorporated into the Christian *Bible.*

pseudonymous writings not commonly accepted by most modern biblical scholars as authentic.

synoptic gospel books that can be "seen in one view" (*synopsis*) because of their parallel structure and content: Matthew, Mark, and Luke.

testament also called *covenant,* the relationship God established with his people. Christians saw a "New Covenant" established in Jesus, leading them to call their new scriptures the *New Testament.*

QUESTIONS FOR STUDY AND DISCUSSION

1. In what ways do the four gospels center on the suffering, death, and resurrection of Jesus?

2. Summarize in your own words the main points of the teaching of Jesus. How does the teaching of Jesus relate to the life, death, and resurrection of Jesus as portrayed in the gospels?

3. In what ways do the acts and teaching of Jesus, the *Acts of the Apostles,* and the letters of Paul show Christianity to be a "missionary religion"?

4. What degree of continuity and discontinuity can be discerned in these readings from the teaching of Jesus to the teaching of Paul?

5. Why is Jesus so harsh toward hypocrisy in the Sermon on the Mount? In what ways could this have been a problem in early Christianity?

6. In what ways does the *New Testament* better the condition of women, and in what ways does it not? Discuss both the first century and today.

7. How does the *New Testament* promote love as the chief virtue in the religious life?

8. To what extent, if any, do the organization of the church and church offices reflect the distinctive teachings of the *New Testament?*

SUGGESTIONS FOR FURTHER READING

Primary Readings

B. M. Metzger and R. E. Murphy, eds., *The New Oxford Annotated Bible.* New York: Oxford University Press, 1991. The standard translation of the *Bible* in an edition with excellent introductions and notes.

The New English Bible. New York: Oxford and Cambridge University Presses, 1970. A translation known for its literary beauty.

D. Senior et al., eds., *The Catholic Study Bible.* New York: Oxford University Press, 1990. An excellent study *Bible* for both Catholics and others who wish to know more about the contemporary Catholic understanding of the *Bible.* Contains the text of the *New American Bible,* which is similar to that of the *New Revised Standard Version.*

Secondary Readings

R. E. Brown, *An Introduction to the New Testament.* New York: Doubleday, 1997. The most recent, and the best, survey of scholarship.

E. P. Sanders, *The Historical Figure of Jesus.* London: Penguin, 1993. Arguably one of the best recent introductions to the "historical Jesus."

E. Schüssler Fiorenza, *In Memory of Her,* rev. ed. Philadelphia: Fortress, 1995. An updating of a classic study of the status and role of women in the *New Testament* from a feminist-liberationist perspective.

B. Witherington, *Women in the New Testament.* Cambridge: Cambridge University Press, 1985. A thorough and readable study of the status and role of women in both the ministry of Jesus and in the early church from a moderate perspective.

$\mathcal{G}$ INFOTRAC COLLEGE EDITION

You can locate InfoTrac College Edition articles about this chapter by accessing the InfoTrac College Edition website (http://www.infotrac.collegeedition.com/wadsworth/). Using subject guide, enter the search terms relevant to this chapter, and then read abstracts for relevant articles.

Private Reading of the Quran
Muhammed Mukti, a teacher of the *Quran*, reads the holy book in the Karanganyar City
Mosque in Central Java, Indonesia. Credit: Joanna Pinneo/Foreign Missions Board, SBC

CHAPTER TWELVE

Islam

❖ In a city in Saudi Arabia, a boy who is auspiciously four years, four months, and four days old celebrates a special event. He goes to the *Quran* school to recite officially his first verse of the *Quran*. The verse is written in honey on a small slate. When the boy finishes practicing the verse, he recites it formally and the honey is dissolved in water. The boy then drinks the water that has been sweetened by the holy words of the *Quran*. The words he has spoken now become a part of him, and he returns home with his family to a celebration.

❖ In a village near Khartoum, Sudan, a large crowd of Muslims has gathered to hear perhaps the most famous healer in Africa, Sheik Abdel Azziz ibn Ali. This Sudanese cleric soon emerges to stand on a platform and sing the Quran. As his chant grows in intensity, the crowd responds in various emotional ways, and some people loudly report that they have now been cured of chronic diseases. The sheik defends himself against occasional charges of charlatanism by saying, "All I do is recite the Quran."

❖ In Philadelphia, Pennsylvania, a recently converted Muslim woman studies the *Quran* as she rides the bus to her job. She looks first at the mostly unfamiliar Arabic original on the right-hand pages, then reads carefully the English interpretation of it on the left-hand pages, and finally looks back at the Arabic. When she leaves the bus, she feels inspired and directed to serve God during that day.

INTRODUCTION

Islam confesses that "there is no God but God" and that Muhammad is God's prophet who has come to teach and spread the way of submission and obedience to God. Muslims believe that the *Quran* was revealed by the angel Gabriel to Muhammad over an approximately twenty-year period, from his call to be a prophet until his death in 632 C.E. It was *given to* Muhammad, not *written by* him—its only author is God, and every word comes from God. The *Quran* is the basic authority for Islamic religious life, Islam's continuing guide during 1,400 years of history. As W. C. Smith has observed, the *Quran* "has fired the imagination, and inspired the poetry, and formulated the inhibitions, and guided the ecstasies, and teased the intellects, and ordered the family relations and the legal chicaneries, and nurtured the piety, of hundreds of millions of people in widely diverse climes and over a series of radically divergent centuries."[1] Therefore, one who understands the *Quran* and its use has been well introduced to Islam.

---

[1] W. C. Smith, "The Study of Religion and the Study of the Bible." In M. Levering, ed., *Rethinking Scripture* (Albany: State University of New York Press, 1987), p. 21.

Name

Quran is Arabic for "recitation, reading." These two meanings suggest the twin aspects of oral and written revelation, both of which are important in understanding the *Quran* and its place in Islam. God gave the message to Muhammad, and Muhammad spoke it to his followers. Indeed, the oral meaning predominates in the *Quran* itself, where *quran* refers primarily to oral revelations, never to the full, written book of human history that we know as the *Quran*. But the oral revelations in turn were based on the heavenly written *Quran*, the "well-preserved tablet" and the "mother of the Book." They began to be recorded in writing during Muhammad's lifetime and were collected into a book, the *Quran*, soon after his death. So the movement of revelation, as Muslims would explain it, goes from the eternal, heavenly *Quran*, to Gabriel's oral revelation of this *Quran* to Muhammad, then orally from Muhammad to his followers, and finally from his followers to the written *Quran*. In each stage, the *Quran* has a strong oral dimension in its formal recitation, called **tilawa,** and (always vocalized) reading. The circle of revelation is complete and perfect—the heavenly *Quran* and the *Quran* on earth are identical.

The usual English spelling of the Muslim scripture is *Quran*. Often the older spelling "Koran" is found, especially in journalism, but more recent scholarship prefers the newer spelling as closer to the Arabic pronunciation. It is pronounced *kuhr-AHN*. Between the two syllables is a glottal stop that is stronger in Arabic than the similar sound speakers of English naturally make when they pronounce the beginning of the second syllable, *-ahn*.

Overview of Structure

The **Quran,** which is approximately the length of the *New Testament,* is divided into 114 chapters called **surahs.** The first surah, *Fatihah* ("Opening"), is a preface to the book. Beginning with Surah 2, these chapters are organized by approximate length, from the longest to the shortest. This means that a new reader of the *Quran* will be faced at first with long chapters that range over many unrelated topics. Also, because the shorter, more poetic surahs typically come from the first part of Muhammad's prophetic career, and the longer, more prosaic surahs from the last part, the *Quran* generally reverses the order in which Muhammad revealed them to his followers. To Muslims, this mixing of sequence is of no importance because the sacredness and authority of the text are based on its origin, not its order. To non-Muslim readers, however, it presents a challenge that often leads them to lay aside the *Quran* out of sheer puzzlement. Some English translations of the *Quran*, trying to make it more intelligible to the non-Muslim reader, rearrange the chapters into an order that more or less follows Muhammad's life.

The internal structure of each surah is as follows (see Table 12.1).

1. A title heads the chapter. Most titles are short, typically two or three words. They are sometimes drawn from the opening words of the chapter; for example, chapter 56, entitled "That Which Is Coming," begins "When that which is coming comes. . . ." More typically, the title is taken from one isolated and sometimes metaphoric word in the chapter, as "The Cave" (18) or "Light" (24). A few surahs

Table 12.1
Structure of a Typical Surah

THE SAND DUNES	← . . . . ←	Title
46:1–11	←	Number
(Mecca)	← . . . . ←	Origin

In the Name of God, the Compassionate, the Merciful _____ *Bismillah*

Ha mim. This Book is revealed by God, the Mighty One, the Wise One.
  It was to manifest the Truth that We created the heavens and   Ayah 1
the earth and all that lies between them; We created them to last for
an appointed term;
Yet the unbelievers give no heed to our warning. _____ Ayah 2

---

are titled after an Arabic letter or letters with which they begin, as chapter 50, *Qaf (K)*. Only occasionally does the title of a surah indicate its main topic, so the new reader of the *Quran* cannot depend on its chapter titles as a guide to its contents. In recent times, the custom has arisen among many Muslims to cite the chapter by its number alone, which is given after the title.

2. The *Quran* then indicates whether the chapter was given to Muhammad while he was in Mecca or Medina. The *Quran* itself mirrors the Islamic division of human history into time before or after the flight to Mecca. As mentioned earlier, the Meccan chapters tend to be found in the second half of the *Quran* and the Medinan chapters in the first half. In reality, though, many passages are of mixed origin, with material from both stages of the Prophet's career. This is recognized by both modern non-Muslim scholars and by Muslim traditionalists. Many English translations omit the notation of Mecca or Medina.

3. Next comes the **Bismillah** (or *Basmallah*), which in full runs *Bismillah al-Rahman, al-Rahim,* "In the name of God, the Compassionate, the Merciful." This sonorous formula, both an invocation of God and a blessing of God, is always spoken before reading a passage as well as at many other times in a Muslim's life. The only chapter with no *Bismillah* is 9, which most Quranic scholars see as a continuation of chapter 8. This is the "exception that proves the rule" that the *Bismillah* marks the beginning of each new chapter. This formula itself likely goes back to the time of Muhammad, but whether it was actually used in his time to mark the head of a chapter is less certain.

4. Each chapter is further divided into **ayahs,** verses. These were added after Muhammad's death for ease in locating passages, especially in the longer chapters. The verses vary greatly in length; one ayah can be as long as several sentences or as short as a few words. *Ayah* literally means "sign," and this meaning is found many times in the *Quran* to denote the signs of nature and history that point to the reality and power of the one God. To Muhammad, the revelation-recital that was to become the written *Quran* was the greatest of God's signs. It was probably for this reason that the verses of the *Quran* are called "signs."

5. The internal content of each chapter has no fixed order or form. As mentioned earlier, several of the chapters begin with one or more Arabic letters, such as *Ta Ha* (chapter 20). Neither Western scholars nor traditional Muslim interpreters have produced a convincing explanation of these mysterious letters. Some have argued that they indicate collections of chapters, others that they have a magical significance; many other explanations have also been put forth. Perhaps, because of lack of evidence on which to base an explanation, there will never be a convincing explanation. Many Muslims say about these letters that "God only knows" what they mean. Another beginning feature of many chapters is an oath, as in chapter 93, which begins "By the light of day, and by the dark of night, your Lord has not forsaken you. . . ." Oaths are sometimes found with the mysterious letters and sometimes without them.

The body of the chapters usually has one or more topics. Generally, the longer the chapter, the more numerous and varied are the topics. Chapter 21, for example, deals successively with themes of creation, God, immortality, prophecy, Abraham, Noah, David, Job, Mary, the end of time, and false gods. Just as they have a variety of topics, the chapters also have a variety of endings. Often there will be a plea to Muhammad to persist in his calling, or a summons for Muslims to persevere, or a promise of reward or punishment in the next life.

The wording of the chapters presents the speech of God. God speaks in a majestic "We," usually capitalized in translations. "You" in the singular refers to Muhammad; at other times, in the plural, it refers to Muhammad's audience. (This will be made explicit in the scripture selections that follow.) Many utterances begin with "Say" and what follows this word is presented as God's revelation to Muhammad's audience. Finally, passages that narrate biblical incidents are frequently related. The way these stories are told seems to imply that the listeners are already familiar with them. The narratives are briefly recounted, with the emphasis on their teaching, not on the story itself.

Origin and Development

As we have seen, the first stage of the *Quran* was its reception as revelation by Muhammad. A few times he heard the audible voice of the angel Gabriel, but usually he received the revelation while in a trance or asleep. Muslims believe that whatever the mode of revelation, Muhammad received the *Quran* from God and that God is its only author. European scholars in the last century searched for literary sources of the *Quran* in the assumption that Muhammad drew on other sources and wrote the *Quran* himself. But recent non-Muslim scholarship recognizes that beyond the question of sources, the *Quran* has its main origin in the internal experience of Muhammad himself. The question of whether his experience has a divine origin is one that historians and scholars of religion cannot answer.

The next stage in the development of the *Quran* was its oral transmission in prophetic utterances to Muhammad's followers. Muhammad spoke to them the words that Gabriel commanded him to speak, which are often introduced in the *Quran* by the imperative "Say." His disciples committed his sayings to memory and spoke them to others, and these early "reciters" of the *Quran* played an important part in its survival and transmission. But, as a *hadith* narrates, Muhammad's followers also wrote them down at his command on "pieces of paper, stones, palm-leaves, shoulder-blade bones and ribs, and bits of leather"—in other words, on any material at hand.

The *Quran* in its final form bears witness to some difficulties in composition: substitution of verses, new revelations that cancel out older ones, and long periods between revelations. A *hadith* even speaks of "Satanic verses" in which Muhammad initially was led by Satan to give a revelation that favored some form of polytheism (the "daughters of Allah"). He later rejected them in favor of the strict monotheism that is the essential element of Islam.

After Muhammad's death in 632 and the battle of Yamamah in 633, it was feared that knowledge of the *Quran* (still mostly recited orally) might die out. The process of recording all of it in writing began under the first caliph, Umar. But different versions arose, with consequent disputes over which *Quran* was better.

To end these troubles, Caliph Uthman (644–656) commissioned respected and learned men to produce a single recognized version using the best manuscripts and the memories of those with recognized knowledge of the *Quran*. This version became the only authorized text recognized by the Muslim community, believed to be a true copy of the "Mother of the Book." Other texts were systematically collected and destroyed. Today almost all Muslims view the Uthmanic edition as identical to the *Quran* of Muhammad. No attempt to go behind this authorized version has been made, as it would be considered blasphemy to suggest that this is not the exact *Quran* that God gave originally to Muhammad.

Finally, the Arabic language in which the *Quran* is written is an important part of its origin and continuing appeal. It is often emphasized that Muhammad gave his followers an "Arabic *Quran*." Just as Jews and Christians had scriptures in their own languages, Arabs have an Arabic book. Muslims view the Arabic style of the *Quran*, especially its poetry, as matchless. Indeed, it is a sin to imitate its style or content in any way. Moreover, the *Quran* itself is not considered translatable into other languages. Though Muslims and non-Muslims alike have translated the *Quran* into many languages, which are typically put interlinearly or on facing pages with the Arabic text, the faithful commonly argue that these translations are only an approximation of the *Quran*, a rough indication of its contents. They are not the scripture itself, which can exist only in Arabic. Even those believers who do not learn Arabic will memorize formulas and passages from the *Quran* in Arabic. Arabic is thus in a limited way the common language of Muslims throughout the world, and the *Quran* contributes to the unity of the Muslim community.

Use

Even before its existence as a text, the *Quran* has enjoyed the standing of the ultimate authority in Islam. Still, from the first generations of Islam arose a second body of authority, first in oral form and then written. This second authority is the **hadith**, narrative "traditions" about Muhammad and the first generation of Muslims. These traditions were meant to form a historical context by which the *Quran* could be interpreted, and they deal especially with the life of Muhammad in a way that the *Quran* does not.

It was almost inevitable that these *hadith* should arise. The *Quran,* with its almost complete lack of any historical framework, needs such a framework by which its difficulties, seeming inconsistencies, and other interpretive issues can be ironed out. Quranic interpretation has been, from the very first, an effort to understand and apply to Muslim life the teachings given through Muhammad (the *Quran*) in the context of the traditions (the *hadith*). The principle arose quickly that every interpretation of the *Quran* must have a tradition to back it up. The collection and preservation of these traditions became a major task of religious scholarship in Islam.

In the Middle Ages (soon after the birth of Islam in the seventh century), the role of commentary became the lens through which the *Quran* was viewed. This commentary, called **tafsir,** became an important branch of Muslim theology. Tafsir combined analysis of both the *Quran* and the relevant *hadith* to produce a detailed and often massive body of literature. The commentary by al-Tabari (839–923 C.E.) and the encyclopedic commentary by Zamakhshari (1075–1143) became authoritative for interpretation. In this period of interpretation, which lasted until the nineteenth century, all higher study of the *Quran* was indirect—the scripture was read only through the commentaries, and the commentaries specified its meaning. Only in the mosques and among the common people was the *Quran* allowed to speak more or less for itself.

In recent times, a period of modernism challenged the monopoly of the commentaries. A movement arose to revive the most ancient forms of Islam and reform it by ending the authority of the medieval commentators. Some methods new to Islam but well known in Europe were introduced to attempt to recover the original meaning of the *Quran*. The Indian Muslim scholar M. Azad, for example, argued that it is necessary to study the life and language of Arabia at the time of Muhammad to understand what the *Quran* meant to its original hearers and readers. D. Rahbar, in his *The God of Justice* (1960), argued that it is more important to compare Quranic passages against each other in determining their meaning than to rely on later commentators. This liberalizing movement was generally confined to the more westernized upper classes. The vast majority of Muslims, common people and scholars alike, never took to it. Since about 1980, the tide of conservatism and anti-Western feeling led by the increasingly influential Shi'ite branch of Islam has effectively limited the movement to modernize the interpretation of the *Quran*.

Among ordinary Muslims during most of Islamic history, the esteem and reverence that is shown to the *Quran* is evidenced in everyday actions. To use the Muslim scripture in any way, one must first ritually wash. Although Muslims often sit on the floor to study the *Quran*, especially in a mosque, the *Quran* itself is never allowed to touch the floor but rests on a short bookstand. A person who carries several books must always place the *Quran* on top. Portions of it are read every day by pious Muslims, and the entire *Quran* is read through during Ramadan, guided by special division marks in the Arabic text. Large portions of it are committed to memory, and it is considered a mark of special piety to memorize the entire *Quran*.

The *Quran* is also used for purposes of magic, especially to ward off evil curses by jinn and humans. Its last two chapters are explicitly countermagical, designed to ward off evil supernatural powers. Verses from other chapters are also copied out and used as amulets to bring blessing and ward off evil.

HISTORY

The Call of Muhammad*

In traditional Muslim understanding, Surah 96 is the story of Muhammad's call vision. A hadith relates that while Muhammad was meditating in a cave, an angel appeared to him and commanded him to recite (iqra', the imperative form of Quran). Muhammad at first refused, but the angel choked and threatened him into submission. This story is told in the first five verses; the rest are said to come from a later time. Most modern scholars identify "The Star," Surah 53, as Muhammad's call vision. It is related as a challenge to those who "question what he sees." Muhammad's vision is inspired and authoritative because it is "received from one who is powerful and mighty." Surah 53 tells of two visions, and Islamic tradition (hadith) says that these are the only two times when Muhammad actually saw Gabriel.[2]

CLOTS OF BLOOD
96
(Mecca)

In the Name of God, the Compassionate, the Merciful

Recite in the name of your Lord who created—created man from clots of blood. Recite Your Lord is the Most Bountiful One, who by the pen[3] [5] taught man what he did not know.

Indeed, man transgresses in thinking himself his own master: for to your Lord all things return.

Observe the man who rebukes Our servant when he prays. [10] Think: does he follow the right guidance or enjoin true piety? Think: if he denies the Truth and gives no heed, does he not know that God observes all things?

[15] No. Let him desist, or We will drag him by the forelock, his lying, sinful forelock. Then let him call his helpmates. We, in Our turn, will call the guards of Hell. No, never obey him. Prostrate yourself and come nearer.

THE STAR
53:1–18
(Mecca)

In the Name of God, the Compassionate, the Merciful

By the declining star, your compatriot[4] is not in error, nor is he deceived He does not speak out of his own fancy. This is an inspired revelation. [5] He is taught by one who is powerful and mighty.

He stood on the uppermost horizon; then, drawing near, he came down within two bows' length or even closer, [10] and revealed to his servant that which he revealed. His[5] own heart did not deny his vision. How can you, then, question what he sees?

He beheld him once again at the sidra tree, beyond which no one may pass.[6] [Near it is the Garden of Repose.] [15] When that tree was covered with what covered it, his eyes did not wander, nor did they turn aside: for he saw some of his Lord's greatest signs.

---

*Quran 96; 53:1–18

[2]Selections are taken from N. J. Dawood, The *Koran* (London: 1990). Copyright N. J. Dawood, 1956, 1959, 1966, 1968, 1974, 1990. Reproduced by permission of Penguin Books Ltd.

[3]*by the pen*: the coming of revelation and its writing down into what was to become the *Quran*.

[4]*Your compatriot*: Muhammad, who was living among his tribe, the Quraysh, at the time of this surah.

[5]*His*: "His" and "he" now refer to Muhammad.

[6]*Sidra tree, Garden of Repose*: the sidra tree is at the border of the highest heaven; the Garden of Repose lies in the presence of God. This second vision is of heaven, which explains why Muhammad saw there "some of his Lord's greatest signs."

The Mission of Muhammad*

Surah 11 describes the tasks of Muhammad as God's prophet. He is a messenger who is to proclaim, "Serve none but God." Submission (islam) to God is the only way to serve him faithfully. Muhammad also warns of the terrors of hell that await those who refuse his message and promises rich rewards to those who obey. Muhammad brings no signs, treasures, or angels; his message itself is the miracle. In the face of opposition, Muhammad received the encouragement recorded in Surah 93. It offers a glimpse into his personal experience: he was an orphan, in error, and poor, from which God delivered him. The surah ends with a call for Muhammad to be faithful to his mission. "You" throughout this passage is Muhammad.

HUD
11:1–16
(Mecca)

In the Name of God, the Compassionate, the Merciful

Alif lam ra'. This Book, whose verses are perfected and made plain, is a revelation from Him who is wise and all-knowing.

Serve none but God. I am sent to you from Him to warn you and to give you good tidings.

Seek forgiveness of your Lord and turn to Him in repentance. A goodly provision He will make for you till an appointed day, and will bestow His grace on those that have merit. But if you give no heed, then beware the torment of a fateful day. To God you shall all return. He has power over all things.

[5] They cover up their breasts to conceal their thoughts from Him. But when they put on their garments, does He not know what they hide and what they reveal? He knows their inmost thoughts. There is not a creature on the earth but God provides its sustenance. He knows its dwelling and its resting-place. All is recorded in a glorious book.

Throned above the waters, He made the heavens and the earth in six days, to find out which of you shall best acquit himself.

[10] When you[7] say: "After death you shall be raised to life," the unbelievers declare: "It is but plain sorcery." And if We put off their punishment till an appointed time, they ask: "Why is it delayed?" On the day it overtakes them, they shall not be immune from it. The terrors at which they scoffed will encompass them.

If We show man Our mercy and then withhold it from him, he yields to despair and becomes ungrateful. And if after adversity We let him taste good fortune, he says: "Gone are my sorrows from me," and grows jubilant and boastful. Not so the steadfast who do good works. Forgiveness and a rich reward await them.

[15] You may chance to omit a part of what is revealed to you and be distressed because they say: "Why has no treasure been sent to him? Why has no angel come with him?" But you are only to give warning. God is the guardian of all things. If they say: "He has invented it himself," say to them: "Produce ten invented chapters like it.[8] Call on whom you will among your idols, if what you say be true. But if they fail you, know that it is revealed with God's knowledge, and that there is no god but Him. Will you then accept Islam?"

DAYLIGHT
93
(Mecca)

In the Name of God, the Compassionate, the Merciful

By the light of day, and by the dark of night, your Lord has not forsaken you, nor does He abhor you.

---

*Quran 11:1–16; 93

[7] *You:* Muhammad.

[8] *Produce ten chapters like it:* this type of response by Muhammad to his opponents is called the **challenge verses.**

The life to come holds a richer prize for you than this present life. [5] You shall be gratified with what your Lord will give you.

Did He not find you an orphan and give you shelter? Did He not find you in error and guide you? Did He not find you poor and enrich you? [10] Therefore do not wrong the orphan, nor chide away the beggar. But proclaim the goodness of your Lord.

Opposition to Muhammad*

Muhammad experienced strong opposition to his ministry, especially in the Meccan phase. The first selection, from Surah 52, catalogues many of the charges of Muhammad's Meccan opponents, who are referred to as "they." Surah 63, the second selection, deals with another type of opposition to Muhammad, from "hypocrites" who seemingly acknowledged Muhammad and accepted Islam, but only for their own advantage. These hypocrites are from the residents of Medina, where Muhammad was widely followed as a religious and political leader.

Do they say: "He is but a poet: we are waiting for some misfortune to befall him"? Say: "Wait if you will; I too am waiting." Does their reason prompt them to say this? Or is it merely that they are wicked men?

Do they say: "He has invented it[9] himself"? Indeed, they have no faith. Let them produce a scripture like it, if what they say be true!

[35] Were they created out of the void? Or were they their own creators? Did *they* create the heavens and the earth? Surely they have no faith! Do they hold the treasures of your Lord, or have control over them? Have they a ladder by means of which they overhear Him? Let their eavesdropper bring a positive proof!

Is He to have daughters and you sons?[10]

[40] Are you demanding payment of them, that they should fear to be weighed down with debts?

Have they knowledge of what is hidden? Can they write it down? Are they seeking to ruin you? They themselves shall be ruined. Have they a god other than God? Exalted be he above their idols!

If they saw a part of heaven falling down, they would still say: "It is but a mass of clouds."

[45] Let them be, until they face the day when they shall stand dumbfounded; the day when their designs will avail them nothing and none will help them. And besides this a punishment awaits the wrongdoers, though most of them do not know it.

Therefore wait the judgment of your Lord: We are watching over you. Give glory to your Lord when you awaken, in the night-time praise Him, and at the setting of the stars.

[Surah 63] When the hypocrites come to you they say: "We bear witness that you are God's apostle." God knows that you are indeed His apostle; and God bears witness that the hypocrites are lying.

They use their faith as a disguise, and debar others from the path of God. Evil is what they do. They believed and then renounced their faith: their hearts are sealed, so that they are devoid of understanding.

When you see them, their good looks please you; and when they speak, you listen to what they say. Yet they are like propped-up beams of timber. Every shout they hear they take to be against them. *They* are the enemy. Guard yourself against them. God confound them! How perverse they are!

---

*Quran 52:30–49; 63
[9]*it:* Muhammad's revelation, on the way to becoming the written *Quran.*
[10]*daughters and sons:* the "daughters of God" were the female deities in the pre-Islamic religions of the Arabs. This charge rests on the higher value that Arabs put on sons than daughters.

[5] When it is said to them: "Come, God's apostle will beg forgiveness for you," they turn their heads and you see them go away in scorn. It is the same whether or not you ask forgiveness for them: God will not forgive them. God does not guide the evil-doers.

It is they who say: "Give nothing to those that follow God's apostle until they have deserted him." God's are the treasures of heaven and earth: but the hypocrites cannot understand. They say: "If we return to Medinah, the strong will soon drive out the weak."

But strength belongs to God and to His apostle and to the faithful: yet the hypocrites do not know it.

Believers, let neither your riches nor your children beguile you of God's remembrance. Those that forget Him shall forfeit all. [10] Give, then, of that which We have given you before death befalls you and you say: "Reprieve me, Lord, awhile, that I may give in charity and be among the righteous."

But God reprieves no soul when its term expires. God has knowledge of all your actions.

The Night Journey*

Surah 17 is entitled "The Night Journey," although only the first two verses deal with this topic. This chapter is also called "The Children of Israel" for one of its later themes. The angel Gabriel took Muhammad to Jerusalem, and most Muslim interpreters and ordinary believers hold that he ascended there to heaven for a brief time. Muhammad's journey to Jerusalem is an important reason for later Islam's viewing it as the third holiest city in the world, after Mecca and Medina.

THE NIGHT JOURNEY
17:1–2
(Mecca)

In the Name of God, the Compassionate, the Merciful

Glory be to Him who made His servant go by night from the Sacred Temple[11] to the farther Temple[12] whose surroundings We[13] have blessed, that We might show him some of Our signs. He alone hears all and observes all.

---

[11] *The Sacred Temple* is the main mosque in Mecca.
[12] *The farther Temple* is the holy mosque of Jerusalem on the site of the ancient Jewish temple. Both these uses of "Temple" are the translation of *masjid*, "mosque."
[13] Note the shift from the third person to the first and then back to the third person in the last sentence.

Quran 17:1–2

The Flight to Medina**

When he was driven out of Mecca by his opponents, Muhammad hid in a cave for three days with his lone companion, Abu Bakr. God's deliverance of the prophet from his threat to his life made a deep impression on him, giving him a sense of confidence that would transform his life.

If you[14] do not help him,[15] God will help him as He helped him when he was driven out by the unbelievers with one other. In the cave he said to his companion: "Do not despair, God is with us." God caused His tranquillity to descend upon him and sent to his aid invisible warriors, so that he routed the unbelievers and exalted the Word of God. God is mighty and wise.

---

[14] *You:* the citizens of Medina.
[15] *him:* Muhammad.

**Quran 9:40

The Wives of Muhammad*

The most extensive view of the personal life of Muhammad that the Quran *offers is on his marriages during the Medinan period. Earlier, in Mecca, the prophet was married only to Kadijah, of whom the* Quran *does not speak. In Medina, Muhammad had many wives and concubines, which became controversial.*

Prophet, say to your wives: "If you seek this life and all its finery, come, I will make provision for you and release you honorably. But if you seek God and His apostle and the abode of the hereafter, know that God has prepared a rich reward for those of you who do good works."

[30] Wives of the Prophet! Those of you who commit a proven sin shall be doubly punished. That is easy enough for God. But those of you who obey God and His apostle and do good works shall be doubly rewarded; for them We have made a generous provision.

Wives of the Prophet, you are not like other women. If you fear God, do not be too complaisant in your speech, lest the lecherous-hearted should lust after you. Show discretion in what you say. Stay in your homes and do not display your finery as women used to do in the days of ignorance.[16] Attend to your prayers, give alms and obey God and His apostle.

Women of the Household, God seeks only to remove uncleanness from you and to purify you. Commit to memory the revelations of God and the wise sayings that are recited in your dwellings. Benevolent is God and all-knowing.

[35] Those who surrender themselves to God and accept the true Faith; who are devout, sincere, patient, humble, charitable, and chaste; who fast and are ever mindful of God—on these, both men and women, God will bestow forgiveness and a rich reward.

It is not for true-believers—men or women—to take their choice in their affairs if God and His apostle decree otherwise. He that disobeys God and His apostle strays far indeed.

You said to the man[17] whom God and yourself have favored: "Keep your wife and have fear of God." You sought to hide in your heart what God was to reveal. You were afraid of man, although it would have been more proper to fear God. And when Zayd divorced his wife, We gave her to you in marriage, so that it should become legitimate for true believers to wed the wives of their adopted sons if they divorced them. God's will must needs be done.

No blame shall be attached to the Prophet for doing what is sanctioned for him by God. Such was the way of God with the prophets who passed away before him; who fulfilled the mission with which God had charged them, fearing God and fearing none besides Him. Sufficient is God's reckoning.

[40] Muhammad is the father of no man among you.[18] He is the Apostle of God and the Seal of the Prophets. God has knowledge of all things. . . .

[48] Prophet, We have made lawful to you the wives to whom you have granted dowries and the slave-girls whom God has given you as booty; the daughters of your paternal and maternal uncles and of your paternal and maternal aunts who fled with you; and any believing woman who gives herself to the Prophet and whom the Prophet wishes to take in marriage.[19] This privilege is yours alone, being granted to no other believer.

---

*Quran 33:28–40, 48–49
[16] *the days of ignorance:* pre-Islamic times.

[17] *the man:* Zayd, an adopted son of Muhammad, was unhappily married to Zainab. He wanted to divorce her, but Muhammad advised him not to. God wished otherwise, and here tells Muhammad to allow the divorce and marry Zainab himself. This provides justification in Islam for marriage to divorced wives of adopted sons.
[18] The Prophet had many wives but no male heirs, seen here as God's will.
[19] The *Quran* elsewhere limits men to four wives at any one time.

The Death of Muhammad*

The Quran *does not narrate the death of Muhammad, but raises it as an issue. Muhammad is indeed mortal, as mortal as any other man. This Medinan passage serves to reinforce the* Quran's *view of Muhammad as a purely human prophet.*

No man before you[20] have We made immortal. If you yourself are doomed to die, will they live for ever?

Every soul shall taste death. We will prove you all with good and evil. To Us you shall return.

When the unbelievers see you, they scoff at you, saying: "Is this the man who fulminates against your gods?" And they deny all mention of the Merciful.

Impatience is the very stuff man is made of. You shall before long see My signs: you need not ask Me to hasten them.

---

*Quran 21:34–37
[20]*you:* In this passage, "you" is Muhammad.

TEACHING

God's Absolute Oneness**

One of the main themes of the Quran *is the absolute oneness of God. The first passage is given against* jinn *(spirits) being considered divine, and against the notion of God having sons and daughters. The wording of Surah 112, entitled "Oneness," seems to suggest that it is specifically anti-Christian, against the Christian belief that God the Father begot the Son, and that the two are equal in being and power. Traditional Muslim interpretation holds it to be both anti-Christian and anti-Arab polytheism. An important* hadith *relates that this chapter is equal in value to two-thirds of the* Quran.

They regard the jinn as God's equals, though He Himself created them, and in their ignorance ascribe to Him sons and daughters. Glory to Him! Exalted be He above their imputations! He is the Creator of the heavens and the earth.

How should He have a son when He had no consort?[21] He created all things and has knowledge of all things.

Such is God, your Lord. There is no god but Him, the Creator of all things. Therefore serve Him. He is the Guardian of all things. No mortal eyes can see Him, though He sees all eyes. He is benevolent and all-knowing.

ONENESS
112
(Mecca)

In the Name of God, the Compassionate, the Merciful

Say: "God is One, the Eternal God. He begot none, nor was He begotten. None is equal to him."

**Quran 6:100–103; 112

[21]"have a son" (singular) might indicate that this is an anti-Christian polemic, countering the Christian belief in Jesus as the Son of God.

God's Names*

"God has the most excellent names," the Quran *affirms (7:17). Two of these names, "compassionate" and "merciful," occur in every* Bismillah *and dozens of times in the chapters proper. God has ninety-nine most gracious names in the* Quran, *as fixed by traditional interpretation (see the appendix at the end of this chapter). The first thirteen are listed here, from "Compassionate" to "Modeler." These names are used in Muslim devotion to express the greatness of God in a very poetic and rhythmic fashion.*

---

*Quran 59:22–24

He is God, besides whom there is no other deity. He knows the unknown and the manifest. He is the Compassionate, the Merciful.

He is God, besides whom there is no other deity. He is the Sovereign Lord, the Holy One, the Giver of Peace, the Keeper of Faith; the Guardian, the Mighty One, the All-powerful, the Most High! Exalted be God above their idols!

He is God, the Creator, the Originator, the Modeller. His are the most gracious names. All that is in heaven and earth gives glory to Him. He is the Mighty, the Wise One.

God's Power**

The first selection sings the praise of God the Creator. It ends, like many other teachings in the Quran, *on a moral note: the creation shows God's truth and the straight (correct) path of life. Creation is here connected to revelation. The second selection ties the power of God in creation firmly to Muhammad's call for repentance and belief.*

Do you not see how God is praised by those in heaven and those on earth? The very birds praise Him as they wing their flight. He notes the prayers and praises of all His creatures, and has knowledge of all their actions.

It is God who has sovereignty over the heavens and the earth. To Him shall all things return.

Do you not see how God drives the clouds, then gathers and piles them up in masses which pour down torrents of rain? From heaven's mountains He sends down the hail, pelting with it whom He will and turning it away from whom He pleases. The flash of His lightning almost snatches off men's eyes. He makes the

---

**Quran 24:41–46; 6:95–99

night succeed the day: surely in this there is a lesson for clear-sighted men.

God created every beast from water. Some creep upon their bellies, others walk on two legs, and others yet on four. God creates what He pleases. He has power over all things.

We have sent down revelations demonstrating the Truth. God guides whom He will to a straight path.

[6:95–99 (Mecca)] It is God who splits the seed and the fruit-stone. He brings forth the living from the dead, and the dead from the living. Such is God. How then can you turn away?

He kindles the light of dawn. He has ordained the night for rest and the sun and the moon for reckoning. Such is the ordinance of the Mighty One, the All-knowing.

It is He that has created for you the stars, so that they may guide you in the darkness of land and sea. We have made plain Our revelations to men of sense. It was He that created you from one being and furnished you with a dwelling and a resting-place. We have made plain Our revelations to men of understanding.

He sends down water from the sky, and with it We bring forth the buds of every plant. From these We bring forth green foliage and close-growing grain, palm-trees laden with clusters of dates, vineyards and olive groves, and pomegranates alike and different. Behold their fruits when they ripen. Surely in these there are signs for true believers.

God's Predestination*

Predestination is God's eternal choice of his own people from among the fallen human race. In the first selection, God is said to predestine many religions for humanity, but only Islam for the saved. The Quran *affirms both the sovereignty of God and human responsibility to live morally, but puts the emphasis on the former. Predestination and fate play a large role in affairs both big and small in Muslim life; in Arab countries, perhaps the most frequently heard expression is* Enshallah, *"if God wills," a word reflected at the beginning of the first passage. The second reading presents a typical Quranic statement of the predestination of individuals. His leading of people into error presents no moral problem, because these are the "heedless," who are and always will be immoral and disobedient. Both passages come from Medina.*

Had it had been God's will, He could have made them all of one religion. But God brings whom He will into His mercy; the wrongdoers have none to befriend or help them.

Have they set up other guardians besides Him? Surely God alone is the Guardian. He resurrects the dead and has power over all things.

Whatever the subject of your disputes, the final word belongs to God. Such is God, my Lord. In Him I have put my trust, and to Him I turn in repentance.

[10] Creator of the heavens and the earth, He has given you wives from among yourselves, and cattle male and female; by this means He multiplies His creatures. Nothing can be compared with Him. He alone hears all and sees all. His are the keys of the heavens and the earth. He gives abundantly to whom He will and sparingly to whom He pleases. He has knowledge of all things.

He has ordained for you the faith which He enjoined on Noah, and which We have revealed to you; which We enjoined on Abraham, Moses, and Jesus, saying: "Observe the Faith and do not divide yourselves into factions." But hard for the pagans is that to which you call them. God chooses for it whom He will, and guides to it those that repent.

[7:177–182] The man whom God guides is rightly guided; but those whom He confounds will surely be lost. We have predestined for Hell many jinn and many men. They have hearts they cannot comprehend with; they have eyes they cannot see with; and they have ears they cannot hear with. They are like beasts—indeed, they are more misguided. Such are the heedless.

God has the Most Excellent Names. Call on Him by His Names and keep away from those that pervert them. They shall be punished for their misdeeds. Among those whom We created there are some who give true guidance and act justly. [180] As for those that deny Our revelations, We will lead them step by step to ruin, whence they cannot tell; for though I bear with them, My stratagem is sure.

---

*Quran 42:8–13; 7:177–182

Jinn*

Like the angels and humanity, jinn are a mixed lot: some are good and some evil. This passage presents the words of a band of formerly evil jinn who hear the message of God in the Quran *and repent, taking up Islam. They serve as a pattern and encouragement for the people to whom Muhammad testifies to do the same. Note the oral nature of* Quran *here—it is the recitation of Gabriel's message to Muhammad.*

THE JINN
72:1–15
(Mecca)

In the Name of God, the Compassionate, the Merciful

Say: "It is revealed to me that a band of jinn listened to God's revelations and said: 'We have heard a wondrous Quran giving guidance to the right path. We believed in it and shall henceforth serve none besides Our Lord. He [exalted be the glory of our Lord!] has taken no wife,[22] nor has He begotten any children. The Blaspheming One among us has uttered a wanton falsehood against God, [5] although we had supposed no man or jinn could tell of Him what is untrue.'"

"'We made our way to high heaven, and found it filled with mighty wardens and fiery comets. We sat eavesdropping, but eavesdroppers find flaming darts in wait for them. [10] We cannot tell if this bodes evil to the inhabitants of earth or whether their Lord intends to guide them.

"'Some of us are righteous, while others are not; we follow different ways. We know we cannot escape on earth from God, nor can we elude His grasp by flight. When we heard His guidance we believed in Him: he that believes in his Lord shall fear neither dishonesty nor injustice. Some of us are Muslims and some are wrongdoers. Those that embrace Islam pursue the right path; [15] but those that do wrong shall become the fuel of Hell.'"

---

*Quran 72:1–15

[22] *He . . . has taken no wife:* The argument of some non-Muslim Arabs and all Christians that God has begotten children or a son implies that God also "has taken a wife," and the *Quran* sees this wife as a goddess who would nullify its preaching of the absolute oneness of God.

Creation**

The Quran *has several poetic recitals of creation, of which Surah 15 is one of the fullest. This passage also tells the origin of Satan as an evil angel and his temptation of humanity to sin. In the second reading, the focus is on the created world familiar to an Arab audience.*

**Quran 15:16–48; 16:1–17

We have decked the heavens with constellations and made them lovely to behold. We have guarded them from every cursed devil. Eavesdroppers are pursued by fiery comets.

We have spread out the earth and set upon it immovable mountains. We have planted it with every seasonable fruit, [20] providing sustenance for yourselves and for those whom you do not provide for. We hold the store of every blessing and send it down in appropriate measure. We let loose the fertilizing winds and bring down water from the sky for you to drink; its stores are beyond your reach.

We ordain life and death. We are the Heir of all things. We know those who have gone before you, and those who will come hereafter. [25] Your Lord will gather them all before Him. He is wise and all-knowing.

We created man from dry clay, from black molded loam, and before him Satan from smokeless fire. Your Lord said to the angels: "I am creating man from dry clay, from black molded loam. When I have fashioned him and breathed of My spirit into him, kneel down and prostrate yourselves before him."

[30] The angels, one and all, prostrated themselves, except Satan. He refused to prostrate himself with the others.

"Satan," said God, "why do you not prostrate yourself?"

He replied: "I will not bow to a mortal whom You created of dry clay, of black molded loam."

[35] "Begone," said God, "you are accursed. My curse shall be on you till Judgment Day."

"Lord," said Satan, "reprieve me till the Day of Resurrection."

He answered: "You are reprieved till the Appointed Day."

"Lord," said Satan, "since You have thus seduced me, I will tempt mankind on earth. [40] I will seduce them all, except those of them who are your faithful servants."

He replied: "This is the right course for Me. You shall have no power over My servants, only the sinners who follow you. They are all destined for Hell. It has seven gates, and through each gate they shall come in separate bands. [45] But the righteous shall dwell among gardens and fountains; in peace and safety they shall enter them. We shall remove all hatred from their hearts, and they shall take their ease

on couches face to face,[23] a band of brothers. Toil shall not weary them, nor shall they ever be driven out."

THE BEE
16:1–17
(Mecca)

In the Name of God, the Compassionate, the Merciful

The Judgment of God will surely come to pass: do not seek to hurry it on. Glory to Him! Exalted be He above their idols!

By His will He sends down the angels with the Spirit to those among His servants whom He chooses, bidding them proclaim: "There is no god but Me: therefore fear Me."

He created the heavens and the earth to manifest the Truth. Exalted be He above their idols! He created man from a little germ:[24] yet is he openly contentious.

[5] He created the beasts which give you warmth and food and other benefits. How pleasant they look when you bring them home and when you lead them out to pasture. They carry your burdens to far-off lands, which you could not otherwise reach except with painful toil. Compassionate is your Lord, and merciful.

He has given you horses, mules, and donkeys, which you may ride or put on show; and He has created other things beyond your knowledge.

God alone points to the right path. Some turn aside but, had He pleased, He would have given you guidance all.

[10] It is He who sends down water from the sky, which provides you with your drink and brings forth the pasturage on which your cattle feed. And with it He brings up corn and olives, dates and grapes and fruits of every kind. Surely

---

[23]*face to face:* in agreement with each other, therefore becoming "a band of brothers."

[24]*a little germ:* human sperm.

in this there is a sign for thinking men. He has forced the night and the day, and the sun and the moon, into your service: the stars also serve you by His leave. Surely in this there are signs for men of understanding.

On the earth He has fashioned for you objects of various hues: surely in this there is a sign for prudent men.

It is He who has subjected to you the ocean, so that you may eat of its fresh fish and bring up from its depths ornaments with which to adorn your persons. Behold the ships plowing their course through its waters. All this He has created, that you may seek His bounty and render thanks to Him.

[15] He set firm mountains upon the earth lest it should move away with you; and rivers, roads, and landmarks, so that you may be rightly guided. By the stars, too, are men directed. Is He, then, who has created, like him who cannot create? Will you not take heed?

Adam, Eve, and the Fall*

Here the fall of humanity into sin and rebellion against God is strongly related to the fall of Satan into sin. Humanity is forgiven when it "receives the revelations of God" and follows them; this is the positive model for those who receive God's revelations through Muhammad and follow them. On the other hand, those who reject these revelations will receive Hell as their punishment (verse 37).

When your Lord said to the angels: "I am placing on the earth one that shall rule as My deputy," they replied: "Will You put there one that will do evil and shed blood, when we have for so long sung Your praises and sanctified Your name?"

He said: "I know what you know not."

He taught Adam the names of all things and then set them before the angels, saying: "Tell Me the names of these, if what you say be true."

[30] "Glory to You," they replied, "we have no knowledge except that which You have given us. You alone are all-knowing and wise."

Then said he: "Adam, tell them their names." And when Adam had named them, He said: "Did I not tell you that I know the secrets of heaven and earth, and all that you hide and all that you reveal?"

And when We said to the angels: "Prostrate yourselves before Adam," they all prostrated themselves except Satan, who in his pride refused and became an unbeliever.

To Adam We said: "Dwell with your wife in Paradise and eat of its fruits to your hearts' content wherever you will. But never approach this tree or you shall both become transgressors." But Satan removed them thence and brought about their banishment. "Go hence," We said, "and be enemies to each other. The earth will for a while provide your dwelling and sustenance."

[35] Then Adam received commandments from his Lord, and his Lord relented towards him. He is the Forgiving One, the Merciful.

"Go down hence, all," We said.[25] "When Our guidance is revealed those that accept it shall have nothing to fear or to regret; but those that deny and reject Our revelations shall be the heirs of Hell, and there they shall abide for ever."

---

*Quran 2:28–37

[25]*go down hence:* leave the Paradise, the ideal Garden of Eden.

The Holy *Quran**

The revelations to Muhammad, which later formed the Quran, *took several forms. The first passage refers to direct, audible speech and to the less direct inspiration that comes "from behind a veil." Whatever the form, Muslims believe that all revelations come from God via his angel Gabriel. The second passage recounts the qualities of the* Quran: *its origin as a revelation from God, its miraculous nature, its connection to the faith of Islam, and its Arabic character. A recurrent theme of this surah is the defense of the Quran against the charge that it is false. In the third passage, the* Quran *claims to be the capstone of the prior scriptures of Judaism and Christianity. It confirms the* Bibles *of these faiths and shares much the same content, but the peoples of these latter books reject Islam.*

It is not given to any mortal that God should speak to him except by revelation, or from behind a veil, or through a messenger sent and authorized by Him to make known His will. Exalted is He, and wise.

Thus have We inspired you[26] with a spirit of Our will when you knew nothing of faith or scripture, and made it a light whereby We guide those of Our servants whom We please. You will surely guide them to the right path: the path of God, to whom belongs all that the heavens and the earth contain. Surely to God all things shall in the end return.

THE SAND DUNES
46:1–11
(Mecca)

In the Name of God, the Compassionate, the Merciful

Ha mim. This Book is revealed by God, the Mighty One, the Wise One.

It was to manifest the Truth that We created the heavens and the earth and all that lies between them; We created them to last for an appointed term. Yet the unbelievers give no heed to Our warning.

Say: "Have you pondered on those whom you invoke besides God? Show me what part of the earth they have created! Have they a share in the heavens? Bring me a scripture revealed before this, or some other vestige of divine knowledge, if what you say be true."

Who is in greater error than the man who prays to idols which will never hear him till the Day of Resurrection—which are, indeed, unconscious of his prayers? [5] When mankind are gathered together upon the Judgment Day, their idols will become their enemies and will disown their worship.

When Our revelations are recited to them, clear as they are, the unbelievers say: "This is plain sorcery." Such is their description of the truth when it is declared to them.

Do they say: "He has invented it himself"?

Say: "If I have indeed invented it, then there is nothing you can do to protect me from the wrath of God. He well knows what you say about it. Sufficient is He as a witness between me and you. He is the Benevolent One, the Merciful."

Say: "I am no prodigy among the apostles; nor do I know what will be done with me or you. I follow only what is revealed to me, and my only duty is to give plain warning."

Say: "Think if this Quran is indeed from God and you reject it; if an Israelite[27] has vouched for it and accepted Islam, while you yourselves deny it with disdain. Truly, God does not guide the wrongdoers."

[10] The unbelievers say of the faithful: "Had there been any good in it they would not

---

*Quran 42:50–53; 46:1–11; 2:81–85
[26]*You:* Muhammad.

[27]*an Israelite:* a Jew who converted to Islam, traditionally identified as Abdullah bin Salam.

have believed in it before us." And since they reject its guidance, they say: "This is an ancient falsehood." Yet before it the Book of Moses was revealed, a guide and a blessing to all men. This Book confirms it. It is revealed in the Arabic tongue, to forewarn the wrongdoers and to give good tidings to the righteous.

[2:81–85 (Medina)] To Moses We gave the Scriptures and after him We sent other apostles.[28] We gave Jesus the son of Mary veritable signs and strengthened him with the Holy Spirit. Will you then scorn each apostle whose message does not suit your fancies, charging some with imposture and slaying others?

---

[28] *other apostles:* not in the *New Testament* meaning of the term "apostle," but the Islamic sense of "messengers, sent ones."

They say: "Our hearts are sealed." But God has cursed them for their unbelief. They have but little faith.

And now that a Book confirming their own has come to them from God, they deny it, although they know it to be the truth and have long prayed for help against the unbelievers. God's curse be upon the infidels! Evil is that for which they have bartered away their souls. To deny God's own revelation, grudging that He should reveal His bounty to whom he chooses from among His servants They have incurred God's most inexorable wrath. An ignominious punishment awaits the unbelievers.

When it is said to them: "Believe in what God has revealed," they reply: "We believe in what was revealed to us." But they deny what has since been revealed, although it is the truth, corroborating their own scriptures.

On Unbelievers, Jews and Christians*

The first reading outlines the Islamic approach to "unbelievers" and "idolaters," those who follow the pre-Islamic religions of Arabia. This passage has no Bismillah; it was probably originally attached to chapter 8. A hadith traced to Caliph Uthman states that it was revealed by Muhammad shortly before his death, and he left no instructions on it. In the second reading, Jesus is presented as a righteous prophet who called his people to submit to the true God. He died, but not by crucifixion, and his death has no saving effect. This sought to undercut the Christian claim that salvation is produced by Jesus' death and resurrection. Nevertheless, Muslims tend to have a positive attitude to Jesus as one of the leading prophets. The last passage indicates how Muhammad hoped to convert the Jews and Christians of Medina to his new faith, but this failed. He then turned overtly hostile to them.

---

*Quran 9:1–7, 3:38–50; 2:111–121, 132–137

They are to convert to Islam or live as subject peoples within the authority of Muslim government.

[9:1-7] A declaration of immunity from God and His apostle to the idolaters with whom you have made agreements: For four months you shall go unmolested in the land. But know that you shall not escape God's judgment, and that God will humble the unbelievers.

A proclamation to the people from God and His apostle on the day of the greater pilgrimage: God and His apostle are under no obligation to the idolaters. If you repent, it shall be well with you; but if you give no heed, know that you shall not be immune from God's judgment.

Proclaim a woeful punishment to the unbelievers, except to those idolaters who have honored their treaties with you in every detail and aided none against you. With these keep faith, until their treaties have run their term. God loves the righteous.

[5] When the sacred months are over slay the idolaters wherever you find them. Arrest them, besiege them, and lie in ambush everywhere for them. If they repent and take to prayer and render the alms levy, allow them to go their way. God is forgiving and merciful.

If an idolater seeks asylum with you, give him protection so that he may hear the Word of God, and then convey him to safety. For the idolaters are ignorant men. God and His apostle put no trust in idolaters, except those with whom you have made treaties at the Sacred Mosque.[29] So long as they keep faith with you, keep faith with them. God loves the righteous.

[3:38–50] And remember the angels' words to Mary. They said: "God has chosen you. He has made you pure and exalted you above womankind. Mary, be obedient to your Lord; bow down and worship with the worshippers."

This is an account of a divine secret. We reveal it to you. You were not present when they cast lots to see which of them should have charge of Mary; nor were you present when they argued about her.

[40] The angels said to Mary: "God bids you rejoice in a word from Him. His name is the Messiah, Jesus the son of Mary. He shall be noble in this world and in the hereafter, and shall be favored by God. He shall preach to men in his cradle and in the prime of manhood, and shall lead a righteous life."

"Lord," she said, "how can I bear a child when no man has touched me?"

He replied: "Such is the will of God. He creates whom He will. When He decrees a thing He need only say: 'Be,' and it is. He will instruct him in the Scriptures and in wisdom, in the Torah and in the Gospel, and send him forth as an apostle to the Israelites. He will say: 'I bring you a sign from your Lord. From clay I will make for you the likeness of a bird. I shall breathe into it and, by God's leave, it shall become a living bird.[30] By God's leave I shall heal the blind man and the leper, and raise the dead to life. I shall tell you what to eat and what to store up in your houses. Surely that will be a sign for you, if you are true believers. I come to confirm the Torah already revealed and to make lawful to you some of the things you are forbidden. I bring you a sign from your Lord: therefore fear God and obey me. God is my Lord and your Lord: therefore serve Him. That is the straight path.'"

When Jesus observed that they had no faith, he said: [45] "Who will help me in the cause of God?" The disciples replied: "We are the helpers of God. We believe in God. Bear witness that we have surrendered ourselves to Him. Lord, we believe in Your revelations and follow Your apostle. Count us among Your witnesses."

They plotted,[31] and God plotted. God is the supreme Plotter. He said: "Jesus, I am about to cause you to die and lift you up to Me. I shall take you away from the unbelievers[32] and exalt your followers above them till the Day of Resurrection. Then to Me you shall all return and I shall judge your disputes. The unbelievers shall be sternly punished in this world and in the world to come; there shall be none to help them. [50] As for those that have faith and do good works, they shall be given their reward in full. God does not love the evil-doers."

[2:111–121,132–137] They declare: "None but Jews and Christians shall be admitted to Paradise." Such are their wishful fancies. Say: "Let us have your proof, if what you say be true." Indeed, those that surrender them-

---

[29] *the Sacred Mosque:* the holy shrine in Mecca.

[30]This story is found in a post–*New Testament* Christian book, the *Apocryphon of James*. It probably came to Muhammad by oral tradition.

[31]*They plotted:* Jesus' opponents seek to bring him to death.
[32]*take you away:* Muslims believe that a lookalike was substituted for Jesus just before his death on the cross, so that he only seemed to die. He was taken up to God before his death. Western scholars commonly hold that this view reflects the views of a Christian group that the mainstream church regarded as heretical.

selves[33] to God and do good works shall be rewarded by their Lord: they shall have nothing to fear or to regret.

The Jews say the Christians are misguided, and the Christians say it is the Jews who are misguided. Yet they both read the Scriptures. And the ignorant say the same of both. God will judge their disputes on the Day of Resurrection.

Who is more wicked than the men who seek to destroy the mosques of God and forbid His name to be mentioned in them, when it behooves these men to enter them with fear in their hearts? They shall be held up to shame in this world and sternly punished in the hereafter.

[115] To God belongs the east and the west. Whichever way you turn[34] there is the face of God. He is omnipresent and all-knowing.

They say: "God has begotten a son." Glory be to Him![35] His is what the heavens and earth contain; all things are obedient to Him. Creator of the heavens and the earth! When He decrees a thing, He need only say "Be," and it is.

The ignorant ask: "Why does God not speak to us or give us a sign?"[36] The same demand was made by those before them: their hearts are all alike. But to those whose faith is firm We have already revealed Our signs. We have sent you forth to proclaim the truth and to give warning. You shall not be questioned about the heirs of Hell.

[120] You will please neither the Christians nor the Jews unless you follow their faith. Say: "God's guidance is the only guidance." And if after all the knowledge you have been given you yield to their desires, there shall be none to help or protect you from the wrath of God. Those to whom We have given the Book, and who read it as it ought to be read, truly believe in it; those that deny it shall assuredly be lost. . . .

[132] Abraham enjoined the faith on his children, and so did Jacob, saying: "My children, God has chosen for you the true faith. Do not depart this life except as men who have submitted to Him."

Were you present when death came to Jacob? He said to his children: "What will you worship when I am gone?" They replied: "We will worship your God and the God of your forefathers Abraham and Ishmael and Isaac: the One God. To Him we will surrender ourselves." . . .

[135] They say: "Accept the Jewish or the Christian faith and you shall be rightly guided." Say: "By no means! We believe in the faith of Abraham, the upright one. He was no idolater." Say: "We believe in God and that which is revealed to us; in what was revealed to Abraham, Ishmael, Isaac, Jacob, and the tribes; to Moses and Jesus and the other prophets by their Lord. We make no distinction among any of them, and to God we have surrendered ourselves."

If they accept your faith, they shall be rightly guided; if they reject it, they shall surely be in schism. Against them God is your all-sufficient defender. He hears all and knows all.

---

[33] *surrender themselves:* accept Islam.

[34] *you turn:* the direction of prayer *(qiblah).*

[35] *Glory be to Him:* i.e., it is not so.

[36] *why no sign:* a complaint against Muhammad that he brings no miracles to authenticate himself as God's prophet as the other biblical prophets had done.

Resurrection and Judgment*

Like Judaism and Christianity, Islam foresees a literal resurrection of the body from death; soul and body are rejoined to face judgment. The Meccan origin of these passages are reflected in their lyrical style and power. The second passage, vivid in its emotional intensity, describes the last judgment that follows the resurrection on the last day. The use of "right" and "left" is reminiscent of the New Testament teaching that at the last judgment the righteous will stand on God's right and the unrighteous at the left.

---

*Quran 75:1–15; 69:14–35

THE RESURRECTION

75:1–15
(Mecca)

In the Name of God, the Compassionate, the Merciful

I swear by the Day of Resurrection, and by the self-reproaching soul!

Does man think We shall never put his bones together again? Indeed, We can remold his very fingers! [5] Yet man would ever deny what is to come. "When will this be," he asks, "this Day of Resurrection?"

But when the sight of mortals is confounded and the moon eclipsed; when sun and moon are brought together—[10] on that day man will ask: "Where shall I flee?"

No, there shall be no refuge. For to your Lord, on that day, all shall return. Man shall on that day be told of all his deeds, from first to last. Indeed, man shall bear witness against himself, plead as he may with his excuses.

[69:14–35 (Mecca)] When the Trumpet sounds a single blast; when earth with all its mountains is raised high and with one mighty crash is shat-tered into dust—[15] on that day the Dread Event will come to pass.

Frail and tottering, the sky will be rent asun-der on that day, and the angels will stand on all its sides with eight of them carrying the throne of your Lord above their heads. On that day you shall be utterly exposed, and all your secrets shall be brought to light.

He who is given his book in his right hand will say: [20] "Here it is, read my book! I knew that I should come to my reckoning!" His shall be a blissful state in a lofty garden, with clusters of fruit within his reach. We shall say to him: "Eat and drink to your heart's content: your reward for what you did in days gone by."

[25] But he who is given his book in his left hand will say: "Would that my book were not given me! Would that I knew nothing of my account! Would that my death had ended all! Nothing has my wealth availed me, and I am bereft of all my power."

[30] We shall say: "Lay hold of him and bind him. Burn him in the fire of Hell, then fasten him with a chain seventy cubits long. For he did not believe in God, the Most High, nor did he care to feed the poor. [35] Today he shall be friendless here; filth shall be his food, the filth which sinners eat."

Heaven and Hell*

The first passage is one of the fullest descriptions in the Quran *of the blessings of heaven. They are phys-ical to the point of sensuousness, with little explicit development of the spiritual blessing or happiness of the residents of heaven. The second passage deals with the two types of heavenly attendants that will be given to the faithful in heaven. "Immortal youths" will wait on them with food and drink, and the houris, beautiful dark-eyed women, will be wed to faithful men (the* Quran *never speaks explicitly about the reward of women in heaven). In the third passage, the punishments of the damned are described in vivid imagery. The pur-pose was to threaten and warn the Arabs against the godless way that leads to eternal destruction, and encourage them in the way of eternal life. All three passages are Meccan.*

[76:1–22] Does there not pass over man a space of time when his life is a blank?[37]

---

*Quran 76:1–22; 56:1–39; 77:1–39

[37]*his life is a blank:* to judge from the next verse, this time is life in the womb before birth.

We have created man from the union of the two sexes, so that We may put him to the proof. We have endowed him with hearing and sight and, be he thankful or oblivious of Our favors, We have shown him the right path.

For the unbelievers We have prepared chains and fetters, and a blazing Fire. [5] But the righteous shall drink of a cup tempered at the Camphor Fountain, a gushing spring at which the servants of God will refresh themselves: they who keep their vows and dread the far-spread terrors of Judgment Day; who, though they hold it dear, give sustenance to the poor man, the orphan, and the captive, saying: "We feed you for God's sake only; we seek of you neither recompense nor thanks. [10] We fear from our Lord a day of anguish and of woe."

God will deliver them from the evil of that day, and make their faces shine with joy. He will reward them for their steadfastness with robes of silk and the delights of Paradise. Reclining there upon soft couches, they shall feel neither the scorching heat nor the biting cold. Trees will spread their shade around them, and fruits will hang in clusters over them.

[15] They shall be served with silver dishes, and beakers as large as goblets; silver goblets which they themselves shall measure: and cups brim-full with ginger-flavored water from a fount called Salsabil.[38] They shall be attended by boys graced with eternal youth, who to the beholder's eyes will seem like sprinkled pearls. When you gaze upon that scene, you will behold a kingdom blissful and glorious.

They shall be arrayed in garments of fine green silk and rich brocade, and adorned with bracelets of silver. Their Lord will give them pure nectar to drink. Thus shall you be rewarded; your high endeavors are gratifying to God.

[56:1–39] When that which is coming comes— and no soul shall then deny its coming—some shall be abased and others exalted.

[5] When the earth shakes and quivers, and the mountains crumble away and scatter abroad into fine dust, you shall be divided into three multitudes: those on the right (blessed shall be those on the right); those on the left (damned shall be those on the left); [10] and those to the fore[39] (foremost shall be those). Such are they that shall be brought near to their Lord in the gardens of delight: a whole multitude from the men of old, but only a few from the later generations.

[15] They shall recline on jewelled couches face to face, and there shall wait on them immortal youths with bowls and ewers and a cup of purest wine (that will neither pain their heads nor take away their reason); [20] with fruits of their own choice and flesh of fowls that they relish. And theirs shall be the dark-eyed houris, chaste as hidden pearls: a reward for their deeds. There they shall hear no idle talk, no sinful speech, but only the greeting, "Peace! Peace!"

[25] Those on the right hand—happy shall be those on the right hand! They shall recline on couches raised on high in the shade of thornless sidrs and clusters of talh; [30] amid gushing waters and abundant fruits, unforbidden, never ending.

[35] We created the houris and made them virgins, loving companions for those on the right hand: a multitude from the men of old, and a multitude from the later generations.

[77:16–39] Would that you knew what the Day of Judgment is! Woe on that day to the disbelievers! [20] Did We not destroy the men of old and cause others to follow them? Thus shall We deal with the guilty.

Woe on that day to the disbelievers! Did we not create you from an unworthy fluid, which

---

[38] *Salsabil:* Arabic for "ginger."

[39] *those to the fore:* the righteous are divided into two groups, the blessed and the more blessed; "those to the fore" are the more blessed.

We kept in a safe receptacle[40] for an appointed time? All this We did; how excellent is Our work!

Woe on that day to the disbelievers! [25] Have We not made the earth a home for the living and for the dead? Have We not placed high mountains upon it, and given you fresh water for your drink?

---

[40]*unworthy fluid . . . safe receptacle:* the fluid is semen, and the receptacle is the womb. One traditional Arab commentator says it is "unworthy" because man is ashamed of the process of procreation by which he comes into being.

Woe on that day to the disbelievers! Begone to that Hell which you deny! [30] Depart into the shadow that will rise high in three columns, giving neither shade nor shelter from the flames, and throwing up sparks as huge as towers, as bright as yellow camels!

Woe on that day to the disbelievers! [35] On that day they shall not speak, nor shall their pleas be heeded.

Woe on that day to the disbelievers! Such is the Day of Judgment. We will assemble you all, together with past generations. If then you are cunning, try your spite against Me!

ETHICS

The Conduct of Believers*

The ethical dimensions of the Islamic life are spread evenly all through the Quran. *Occasional passages summarize the duty of the believer. This selection from Mecca deals comprehensively with the moral structure of Islam. The reader will note its relationship to the Ten Commandments of Judaism.*

Serve no other god besides God, lest you incur disgrace and ruin. Your Lord has enjoined you to worship none but Him, and to show kindness to your parents. If either or both of them attain old age in your dwelling, show them no sign of impatience, nor rebuke them; but speak to them kind words. [25] Treat them with humility and tenderness and say: "Lord, be merciful to them. They nursed me when I was an infant."

Your Lord best knows what is in your hearts; He knows if you are good. He will forgive those that turn to Him.

Give to the near of kin their due, and also to the destitute and to the wayfarers. Do not squander your substance wastefully, for the wasteful are Satan's brothers; and Satan is ever ungrateful to his Lord. [30] But if, while waiting for your Lord's bounty, you lack the means to assist them, then at least speak to them kindly.

Be neither miserly nor prodigal, for then you should either be reproached or be reduced to penury. Your Lord gives abundantly to whom He will and sparingly to whom He pleases. He knows and observes His servants.

You shall not kill your children for fear of want.[41] We will provide for them and for you. To kill them is a great sin.

You shall not commit adultery, for it is foul and indecent.

[35] You shall not kill any man whom God has forbidden you to kill, except for a just cause. If a man is slain unjustly, his heir shall be entitled to satisfaction. But let him not carry his vengeance too far, for his victim will in turn be assisted and avenged.[42]

---

[41]*kill your children:* in pre-Islamic times, unwanted infants, especially females, were killed by being buried alive. The *Quran* views this practice as murder.

[42]*be assisted and avenged:* blood feuds could easily get out of control; this is an effort to limit their scope.

---

*Quran 17:23–29

Do not interfere with the property of orphans except with the best of motives, until they reach maturity. Keep your promises; you are accountable for all that you promise.

Give full measure, when you measure, and weigh with even scales. That is fair, and better in the end.

Do not follow what you do not know. Man's eyes, ears, and heart—each of his senses shall be closely questioned.

Do not walk proudly on the earth. You cannot cleave the earth, nor can you rival the mountains in stature.

Women*

In the Semitic culture of ancient Arabia, society was strongly patriarchal and continues to be so today. This state of affairs is reflected in the first passage, on the general relations between the sexes; and in the second, on marriage, sexual relations, and divorce. Despite this patriarchal structure, women did have some rights, as the beginning of the first reading indicates. Both readings, like most legal material in the Quran, *come from the later, Medinan phase.*

Believers, it is not lawful for you to inherit anything from women against their will. Do not hinder them from remarrying so that you may get part of what you have given them, unless they are openly immoral. Treat them properly, even if you dislike them. [20] If you desire to exchange one wife for another, and you have given one of them a large sum of money, do not hold back any of it. Will you withhold it through slander and open sin? How can you hold it back when you have had intercourse with each other, and they have made a solemn agreement with you? . . .

[34] Men have authority over women because God has made the one superior to the other, and because they spend their wealth to maintain them. Good women are obedient. They guard their unseen parts because God has guarded them. As for those from whom you fear disobedience, admonish them and send them to beds apart and beat them. Then if they obey

you, take no further action against them. God is high, supreme.

If you fear a breach between a man and his wife, appoint an arbiter from his people and another from hers. If they wish to be reconciled God will bring them together again. God is all-knowing and wise.

[2:220–223, 227–233] You shall not wed pagan women, unless they embrace the Faith. A believing slave-girl is better than an idolatress, although she may please you. Nor shall you wed idolaters, unless they embrace the Faith. A believing slave is better than an idolater, although he may please you. These call you to Hell-fire; but God calls you, by His will, to Paradise and to forgiveness. He makes plain His revelations to mankind, so that they may take heed.

They ask you about menstruation. Say: "It is an indisposition. Keep aloof from women during their menstrual periods and do not touch them until they are clean again. Then have intercourse with them in the way God enjoined you. God loves those that turn to Him in repentance and strive to keep themselves clean."

Women are your fields: go, then, into your fields as you please. Do good works and fear God. Bear in mind that you shall meet Him. Give good tidings to the believers. . . .

[227] Those that renounce their wives on oath[43] must wait four months. If they change their minds, God is forgiving and merciful; but

---

*Quran 4:19–22, 34–39; 2:220–223, 227–233

[43]*renounce their wives on oath:* "I divorce you" pronounced twice, temporary and revocable by the husband.

if they decide to divorce them, know that God hears all and knows all.

Divorced women must wait, keeping themselves from men, three menstrual courses. It is unlawful for them, if they believe in God and the last Day, to hide what God has created in their wombs: in which case their husbands would do well to take them back, should they desire reconciliation.

Women shall with justice have rights similar to those exercised against them, although men have a status above women. God is mighty and wise.

Divorce may be pronounced twice, and then a women must be retained in honor or allowed to go with kindness. It is unlawful for husbands to take from them anything they have given them, unless both fear that they may not be able to keep within the bounds set by God; in which case it shall be no offence for either of them if the wife ransom herself. These are the bounds set by God; do not transgress them. Those that transgress the bounds of God are wrongdoers.

[230] If a man divorces[44] his wife, he cannot remarry her until she has wedded another man and been divorced by him; in which case it shall be no offence for either of them to return to the other, if they think that they can keep within the bounds set by God. Such are the bounds of God. He makes them plain to men of understanding.

When you have renounced your wives and they have reached the end of their waiting period, either retain them in honor or let them go with kindness. But you shall not retain them in order to harm them or to wrong them. Whoever does this wrongs his own soul.

Do not make a game of God's revelations. Remember the favors God has bestowed upon you, and the Book and the wisdom He has revealed for your instruction. Fear God and know that God has knowledge of all things.

---

[44]*divorces:* irrevocable divorce, with "I divorce you" pronounced three times.

Against Evil Magic*

Here are formulas to recite against evil magic, the last two chapters in the Quran, *both of which deal with this theme. The traditional explanation of these passages in Muslim interpretation is that they are used to dispel doubt. Used by the ordinary Muslim, however, such a formula often takes on a semimagical character itself. The power of these passages when recited will protect one from evil both human and supernatural.*

DAYBREAK
113
(Mecca)

In the Name of God, the Compassionate, the Merciful

Say: "I seek refuge in the Lord of Daybreak from the mischief of His creation; from the mis-

chief of the night when she spreads her darkness; from the mischief of conjuring witches,[45] from the mischief of the envier, when he envies."

MEN
114
(Mecca)

In the Name of God, the Compassionate, the Merciful

Say: "I seek refuge in the Lord of men, the King of men, the God of men, from the mischief of the slinking prompter who whispers in the hearts of men;[46] from jinn and men."

---

[45]*conjuring witches:* literally, "those who blow on knots," a way to cast an evil spell. Witches here are viewed as conjuring evil on those who follow God.

[46]*the slinking prompter:* the devil or evil jinn.

---

*Quran 113; 114

Holy War*

*The Quran urges holy war (Arabic **jihad**, "struggle") against the unbelievers in order to spread the faith. This struggle includes prayer, study, and the "war" against evil in oneself. A problem arose for Muhammad about what to do with those who refuse to fight in the military aspects of jihad. The answer came by revelation that those who will not fight should have no share in the war booty or in eternal life. The first passage explains this answer and also deals with the spiritual and material blessings of holy war. In the second passage, Muhammad is preparing to sponsor a holy war against Mecca, from which he had fled for his life. In these instructions, the basic guidelines for all holy war in Islam arise: it is obligatory for all who can participate, and its aim is to spread the faith and crush opposition to Islam.*

The desert Arabs who stayed behind[47] will say to you: "We were occupied with our goods and families. Implore God to pardon us." They will say with their tongues what they do not mean in their hearts.

Say: "Who can intervene on your behalf with God if it be His will to do you harm or good? God is cognizant of all your actions."

No. You thought the Apostle and the believers would never return to their people; and with this fancy your hearts were delighted. You harbored evil thoughts and thus incurred damnation.

As for those that disbelieve in God and His apostle, We have prepared a blazing Fire for the unbelievers. God has sovereignty over the heavens and the earth. He pardons whom He will and punishes whom He pleases. God is forgiving and merciful.

[15] When you set forth to take the spoils, those that stayed behind will say: "Let us come with you."

They seek to change the Word of God. Say: "You shall not come with us. So God has said beforehand."

They will reply: "You are jealous of us." But how little they understand! Say to the desert Arabs who stayed behind: "You shall be called upon to fight a mighty nation, unless they embrace Islam. If you prove obedient, God will reward you well. But if you run away, as you have done before this, He will inflict on you a stern chastisement."

It shall be no offence for the blind, the lame, and the sick to stay behind. He that obeys God and His apostle shall be admitted to gardens watered by running streams; but he that turns and flees shall be sternly punished by Him.

God was well pleased with the faithful when they swore allegiance to you under the tree. He knew what was in their hearts. Therefore He sent down tranquillity upon them, and rewarded them with a speedy victory and with the many spoils which they have taken. Mighty is God and wise.

[20] God has promised you rich booty, and has given you this with all promptness. He has stayed your enemies' hands, so that He may make your victory a sign to true believers and guide you along a straight path. And God knows of other spoils which you have not yet taken. God has power over all things.

[2:190–194, 216–218 (Medina)] Fight for the sake of God those that fight against you, but do not attack them first. God does not love the aggressors.

Slay them wherever you find them. Drive them out of the places from which they drove you. Idolatry is worse than carnage. But do not fight them within the precincts of the Holy Mosque unless they attack you there; if they attack you put them to the sword. Thus shall the

---

*Quran 48:11–21; 2:190–194, 216–218

[47]*desert Arabs who stayed behind:* these are certain tribes who refused to participate in a military campaign against Hudaibiyah.

unbelievers be rewarded: but if they mend their ways, know that God is forgiving and merciful.

Fight against them until idolatry is no more and God's religion reigns supreme. But if they mend their ways, fight none except the evil-doers.

A sacred month for a sacred month: sacred things too are subject to retaliation. If anyone attacks you, attack him as he attacked you. Have fear of God, and know that God is with the righteous. . . .

[216] Fighting is obligatory for you, much as you dislike it. But you may hate a thing although it is good for you, and love a thing although it is bad for you. God knows, but you do not.

They ask you about the sacred month. Say: "To fight in this month is a grave offence; but to debar others from the path of God, to deny Him, and to expel His worshippers from the Holy Mosque, is far more grave in His sight. Idolatry is worse than carnage."

They will not cease to fight against you until they force you to renounce your faith—if they are able. But whoever of you recants and dies an unbeliever, his works shall come to nothing in this world and in the world to come. Such men shall be the tenants of Hell, wherein they shall abide for ever.

Those that have embraced the Faith and those that have fled their land[48] and fought for the cause of God may hope for God's mercy. God is forgiving and merciful.

---

[48] *those that have fled their land:* those who fled from Mecca to Medina with Muhammad.

Law Codes*

The Quran *has several developed law codes dealing with various topics of everyday life. As a sample, here is a passage on the treatment of orphans and women. That orphans are treated before women may be an indication that they were more of a problem at the time of Muhammad.*

WOMEN
4:1–10
(Medina)

In the Name of God, the Compassionate, the Merciful

Men, have fear of your Lord, who created you from a single soul. From that soul He created its mate, and through them He filled the earth with countless men and women.

Fear God, in whose name you plead with one another, and honor the mothers who bore you. God is ever watching you.

Give orphans the property which belongs to them. Do not exchange their valuables for worthless things or cheat them of their possessions; for this would surely be a great sin. If you fear that you cannot treat orphans with fairness, then you may marry other women who seem good to you: two, three, or four of them. But if you fear that you cannot maintain equality among them, marry one only or any slave-girls you may own. This will make it easier for you to avoid injustice.

Give women their dowry as a free gift; but if they choose to make over to you a part of it, you may regard it as lawfully yours.[49] [5] Do not give the feeble-minded the property with which God has entrusted you for their support; but maintain and clothe them with its proceeds, and give them good advice.

Put orphans to the test until they reach a marriageable age. If you find them capable of sound judgment, hand over to them their prop-

---

*Quran 4:1–10

[49] *Give . . . yours:* In Islam, a woman continues to own and control her dowry after her marriage.

erty, and do not deprive them of it by squandering it before they come of age.

Let not the rich guardian touch the property of his orphan ward; and let him who is poor use no more than a fair portion of it for his own advantage. When you hand over to them their property, call in some witnesses; sufficient is God's accounting of your actions.

Men shall have a share in what their parents and kinsmen leave; and women shall have a share in what their parents and kinsmen leave:[50]

whether it be little or much, they shall be legally entitled to their share.

If relatives, orphans, or needy men are present at the division of an inheritance, give them, too, a share of it, and speak to them kind words.

Let those who are solicitous about the welfare of their young children after their own death take care not to wrong orphans. Let them fear God and speak for justice.

[10] Those that devour the property of orphans unjustly, swallow fire into their bellies; they shall burn in a mighty conflagration.

---

[50]*women shall have a share . . . leave:* prior to Islam, women could not inherit.

WORSHIP AND RITUAL

The Opening of the *Quran**

The first chapter in the Quran *is its **Fatihah,** "Opening," which stands as a devotional preface to the book. A beautiful poem of praise to God, the* Fatihah *sums up the content of the* Quran: *praise to the one God, and submission to his way. This is by far the most recited chapter in the* Quran.

THE OPENING
1

In the Name of God, the Compassionate, the Merciful

Praise be to God, Lord of the Universe, The Compassionate, the Merciful, Sovereign of the Day of Judgment! You alone we worship, and to You alone we turn for help. Guide us to the straight path, the path of those whom You have favored, not of those who have incurred Your wrath, nor of those who have gone astray.

**Quran 1*

Confession of Faith**

The first pillar of Islam states, "There is no God but God, and Muhammad is God's prophet." This formula does not occur in this developed and exact form in the Quran, *but the two parts of it do occur in early forms. The conclusion of the first selection, "Have faith in God and in his prophet" links the two halves of the confession. In the second selection, the first half of the confession is found in an exact and formal use.*

****Quran 57:1–7; 37:32–39*

IRON
57:1–7
(Mecca)

In the Name of God, the Compassionate, the Merciful

All that is in heaven and earth gives glory to God. He is the Mighty, the Wise One. It is He that has sovereignty over the heavens and the earth. He ordains life and death, and has power over all things. He is the First and the Last, the

Visible and the Unseen. He has knowledge of all things.

He created the heavens and the earth in six days, and then mounted His throne. He knows all that goes into the earth and all that emerges from it, all that comes down from heaven and all that ascends to it. He is with you wherever you are. God is cognizant of all your actions.

[5] He has sovereignty over the heavens and the earth. To God shall all things return. He causes the night to pass into the day, and the day into the night. He has knowledge of the inmost thoughts of men.

Have faith in God and His apostle and give in alms of that which He has made your inheritance; for whoever of you believes and gives in alms shall be richly rewarded.

[37:32–39 (Mecca)] On that day they will all share Our punishment. Thus shall We deal with the evil-doers, for when it was said to them: "There is no god but God," they replied with scorn: "Are we to renounce our gods for the sake of a mad poet?"

Surely he has brought the truth, confirming those who were sent before. You shall all taste the grievous scourge: you shall be rewarded according to your deeds.

Prayer*

At first Muhammad and his followers faced Jerusalem during prayer, as was the Jewish custom. Later, after relations with the Jews of Medina had soured, he changed the direction of prayer (qiblah) to the holy shrine at Mecca. Though the duty and direction of prayer is discussed in the Quran, *the content of prayer is not. Perhaps this is because the* Quran *itself is rich with prayers and other devotional material.*

The foolish will ask: "What has made them turn away from their qiblah?"[51]

Say: "The East and the West are God's. He guides whom He will to the right path."

We have made you a just nation, so that you may testify against mankind and that your own Apostle may testify against you. We decreed your former qiblah only in order that We might know the Apostle's true adherents and those who were to disown him. It was indeed a hard test, but not to those whom God has guided. He was not to make your faith fruitless. He is compassionate and merciful to men.

Many a time have We seen you turn your face towards heaven. We will make you turn towards a qiblah that will please you. Turn your face towards the Holy Mosque; wherever you be, turn your faces towards it.

[145] Those to whom the Scriptures[52] were given know this to be the truth from their Lord. God is never heedless of what they do. But even if you gave them every proof they would not accept your qiblah, nor would you accept theirs; nor would any of them accept the qiblah of the other. If, after all the knowledge you have been given, you yield to their desires, then you will surely become an evil-doer.

Those to whom We gave the Scriptures know Our apostle as they know their own sons. But some of them deliberately conceal the truth. This is the truth from your Lord: therefore never doubt it.

Each one has a goal towards which he turns. But wherever you be, emulate one another in good works. God will bring you all before Him. God has power over all things.

Whichever way you depart, face towards the Holy Mosque. This is surely the truth from your Lord. God is never heedless of what you do.

---

*Quran 2:142–149
[51]*turn away from their* qiblah: that is, change their *qiblah.*

[52]*Scriptures:* Jewish and Christian.

Alms*

In Islam, the giving of alms (zakat) is mandatory; it is more of a tax than an offering, but believers are urged to give fully and willingly. The first passage castigates those who evade the alms tax, the second deals especially with who may receive alms.

ALMS
107
(Mecca: 1–3; Medina: 4–7)

In the Name of God, the Compassionate, the Merciful

Have you thought of him that denies the Last Judgment? It is he who turns away the orphan and has no urge to feed the poor.

Woe to those who pray but are heedless in their prayer; who make a show of piety and give no alms to the destitute.

[9:53–60 (Medina)] Say: "Whether you[53] give willingly or with reluctance, your offerings shall not be accepted from you; for you are wicked men."

Their offerings shall not be accepted from them because they have denied God and His apostle. They pray half-heartedly and begrudge their contributions. [55] Let neither their riches nor their children rouse your envy. Through these God seeks to punish them in this life, so that they shall die unbelievers.

They swear by God that they are believers like you. Yet they are not. They are afraid of you. If they could find a shelter or a cave, or any hiding-place, they would run in frantic haste to seek refuge in it.

There are some among them who speak ill of you[54] concerning the distribution of alms. If a share is given them, they are contented: but if they receive nothing, they grow resentful.

Would that they were satisfied with what God and His apostle have given them, and would say: "God is all-sufficient for us. He will provide for us from His own abundance, and so will His apostle. To God we will submit."

[60] Alms shall be only for the poor and the helpless, for those that are engaged in the management of alms and those whose hearts are sympathetic to the Faith, for the freeing of slaves and debtors, for the advancement of God's cause, and for the traveler in need. That is a duty enjoined by God. God is all-knowing and wise.

---

*Quran 107; 9:53–60
[53]*You:* hypocrites among the Muslims.

[54]*You:* Muhammad.

The Fast**

As the beginning of this Medinan passage indicates, fasting was a pre-Islamic custom among the Arabs. Muhammad here adapts it with his own regulations to Islam, and the reader can easily discern here the transition between pre-Islamic and Islamic fasting.

Believers, fasting is decreed for you as it was decreed for those before you; perchance you will guard yourselves against evil. Fast a certain number of days, but if any one among you is ill or on a journey, let him fast a similar number of days later; and for those that cannot endure it there is a ransom: the feeding of a poor man. He that does good of his own accord shall be well rewarded; but to fast is better for you, if you but knew it.

In the month of Ramadan the Quran was revealed, a book of guidance with proofs of guidance distinguishing right from wrong.

**Quran 2:183–186

Therefore whoever of you is present[55] in that month let him fast. But he who is ill or on a journey shall fast a similar number of days later on.

[185] God desires your well-being, not your discomfort. He desires you to fast the whole month so that you may magnify Him and render thanks to Him for giving you His guidance.

When My servants question you about Me, tell them that I am near. I answer the prayer of the suppliant when he calls to Me; therefore let

them answer My call and put their trust in Me, that they may be rightly guided.

It is now lawful for you to lie with your wives on the night of the fast; they are a comfort to you as you are to them. God knew that you were deceiving yourselves. He has relented towards you and pardoned you. Therefore you may now lie with them and seek what God has ordained for you. Eat and drink until you can tell a white thread from a black one in the light of the coming dawn. Then resume the fast till nightfall and do not approach them, but stay at your prayers in the mosques.

---

[55] *Whoever of you is present:* to judge from the context, "present at home" seems to be meant.

Pilgrimage*

The Sacred Mosque of Mecca, which houses the Kaba (the holy stone) and its shrine, was reclaimed by Muhammad from Arab polytheism with the argument that it was founded by Abraham and Ishmael, the first Muslims. In the second selection, the tribe of the Quraysh, which is Muhammad's own tribe, will receive God's protection in return for keeping the Holy Mosque. In the third, rules for the pilgrimage are given.

We made the House[56] a resort and a sanctuary for mankind, saying: "Make the place where Abraham stood a house of worship." We enjoined Abraham and Ishmael to cleanse Our House for those who walk round it, who meditate in it, and who kneel and prostrate themselves.

[125] "Lord," said Abraham, "make this a land of peace and bestow plenty upon its people, those of them that believe in God and the Last Day."

"As for those that do not," He answered, "I shall let them live awhile, and then shall drag

them to the scourge of the Fire. Evil shall be their fate."

Abraham and Ishmael built the House and dedicated it, saying: "Accept this from us, Lord. You are the One that hears all and knows all. Lord, make us submissive to You; make of our descendants a nation that will submit to You. Teach us our rites of worship and turn to us with mercy; You are forgiving and merciful. Lord, send forth to them an apostle of their own who shall declare to them Your revelations, and shall instruct them in the Book and in wisdom, and shall purify them of sin. You are the Mighty, the Wise One."

QURAYSH
106
(Mecca)

In the Name of God, the Compassionate, the Merciful

For the protection of the Quraysh: their protection in their summer and winter journeyings.[57]

Therefore let them worship the Lord of this House who fed them in the days of famine and shielded them from all peril.

---

*Quran 2:124–130; 106; 2:196–199
[56] *the House:* the Sacred Mosque of Mecca, the holiest site in Islam. It is the house of the Holy Stone and the house of worship for all Muslims.

---

[57] *journeyings:* trade caravans.

[2:196–199 (Medina)] Make the pilgrimage and visit the Sacred House for His sake. If you cannot, send such offerings as you can afford and do not shave your heads until the offerings have reached their destination. But if any of you is ill or suffers from an ailment of the head, he must pay a ransom either by fasting or by alms-giving or by offering a sacrifice.

If in peacetime anyone among you combines the visit with the pilgrimage, he must offer such gifts as he can afford; but if he lacks the means let him fast three days during the pilgrimage and seven when he has returned; that is, ten days in all. That is incumbent on him whose family are not present at the Holy Mosque. Have fear of God: know that He is stern in retribution.

Make the pilgrimage in the appointed months. He that intends to perform it in those months must abstain from sexual intercourse, obscene language, and acrimonious disputes while on pilgrimage. God is aware of whatever good you do. Provide well for yourselves: the best provision is piety. Fear Me, then, you that are endowed with understanding.

It shall be no offence for you to seek the bounty of your Lord. When you come running from Arafat[58] remember God as you approach the sacred monument. Remember Him that gave you guidance when you were in error. Then go out from the place whence the pilgrims will go out and implore the forgiveness of God. He is forgiving and merciful. And when you have fulfilled your sacred duties, remember God as you remember your forefathers or with deeper reverence.

---

[58] *Arafat:* one of the mountains near Mecca, a stop on the pilgrimage.

The Mosque*

"Mosque" in Arabic is masjid, "place of prostration." It is a place of prayer, praise, and hope in the next world. The restrictions on attending mosques are given in the second reading. They are for Muslims only, and Muslims are urged to be faithful as they come to the mosque. These two passages are given from Medina.

God speaks in metaphors to men. God has knowledge of all things.

His light is found in temples which God has sanctioned to be built for the remembrance of His name. In them, morning and evening, His praise is sung by men whom neither trade nor profit can divert from remembering Him, from offering prayers, or from giving alms; who dread the day when men's hearts and eyes shall writhe with anguish; who hope that God will requite them for their noblest deeds and lavish His grace upon them. God gives without measure to whom He will.

[9:15–18] It ill becomes the idolaters to visit the mosques of God, for they are self-confessed unbelievers. Vain shall be their works, and in the Fire they shall abide for ever.

None shall visit the mosques of God except those who believe in God and the Last Day, attend to their prayers and render the alms levy and fear none but God. These shall be rightly guided.

Do you pretend that he who gives a drink to the pilgrims and pays a visit to the Sacred Mosque is as worthy as the man who believes in God and the Last Day, and fights for God's cause? These are not held equal by God. God does not guide the wrongdoers.

---

*Quran 24:36–38; 9:15–18

APPENDIX: SELECTIONS FROM THE *HADITH*

The *hadith* ("traditions") are sayings by Muhammad passed down in early Islam, sayings that did not find their way into the *Quran*. They are called the "unrecited revelation." This rests on the belief common to Muslims that Muhammad's words were divinely inspired, not only when he recited the *Quran*, but in all of his utterances after his prophetic call. The *Quran* and the *hadith* form the basis of the religious law that has governed Islamic societies since early times. Though the *hadith* are not considered scriptural, their high, semicanonical standing leads us to sample them briefly here.

Muslim theologians divide each *hadith* in two parts. First is the **isnad,** the authority on which the tradition stands. This is a list of those who orally passed down the specific tradition, from the one who heard the saying of Muhammad and first framed the story to the last person to report it before it was written down about two hundred to two hundred and fifty years after the Prophet's death. (The whole chain of transmission is not given in the selections here.) For a tradition to be considered authentic, it must show an unbroken chain of transmission and each person in the chain must be reliable and pious. The second part of the *hadith* is the **matn,** the text of the saying itself. Sometimes this is just a short saying, and other times it is framed by a story.[59]

The last four selections deal with jihad, "struggle/warfare" for the faith. In the first, the six privileges of death in combat, called martyrdom, are given. In the second, the Islamic practice of taking captured people and property as plunder is defended against the ancient Israelite prohibition of plunder; for the Hebrew *Bible* story referred to at the end of this selection, see

Chapter 7 in the book of *Joshua.* In the third, a brief command is given forbidding the killing of women and children in jihad. In the last, procedures are laid down for dealing with religious opponents that have come under Muslim control in jihad.

On Innovations: It is related from Irbad bin Sariyah that he said, "On a certain day the Apostle of God said prayers with us; then he drew near to us and gave us eloquent instruction that brought tears to our eyes and by which our hearts were affected. A man said, 'O Apostle of God, this is as if it were a farewell address, therefore give us a command.' He replied, 'I command you the fear of God, and giving ear and obedience even if he is an Abyssinian slave; for those of you who will live after me will see many schisms. Therefore it is your duty to follow my rule of faith and the rule of faith of the rightly guided caliphs. Seize it and hold it fast. Beware of new things, for all new things are an innovation, and all innovation is a going astray.'"

On Ritual Washings: It is related from Othman that he performed his ablutions and poured water on his hands three times, then he washed his mouth, and then cleansed his nose. After that he washed his face three times, then he washed his right arm to his elbow three times, then he washed his left arm to his elbow three times. After that he wiped his hand over his head, then he washed his right foot three times, then the left three times. After that he said, "I saw the Apostle of God perform his ablutions like these ablutions of mine." Then he said, "Whoever performs his ablutions like these ablutions of mine, and then prays two sets of prayers, while his mind speaks nothing the while, all his preceding sins will be forgiven him."

---

[59] The passages that follow are excerpted from W. Goldsack, *Selections from Muhammadan Traditions* (Madras: Christian Literature Society for India, 1923).

On Prayer: It is related from Abdullah bin Omar that, "The Apostle of God said, 'The time for the midday prayer is when the sun declines, and a man's shadow becomes equal to his height, and the afternoon prayer has not arrived. And the time for the afternoon prayer is so long as the sun has not become yellow; and the time for the evening prayer is so long as the ruddy light of twilight has not disappeared; and the time of the night prayer is to the first half of the night; and the time for the morning prayer is from the breaking of the dawn until the sun rises. When the sun rises, then withhold from the morning prayer, for truly it rises between the two horns of Satan.'"

It is related from Ubadah binus-Samit that, "The Apostle of God said, 'There can be no prayer for the one who does not recite the opening chapter of the Book'."

On Alms: It is related from Abu Musaul-Ashari that, "The Apostle of God said, 'Alms are obligatory on every Muslim.' They said 'And if he has nothing?' He replied, 'Then let him work with his hands, and gain something for himself, and give alms.' They said, 'And if he is not able to work, or has not done so?' He replied, 'Then let him assist those who are in need and in distress.' They said, 'And if he does not do that?' He replied, 'Then let him order people to do right.' They said, 'And if he does not do that?' He replied, 'Then let him withhold himself from evil; and truly that will be alms for him.'"

It is related from Abu Umamah that he said, "I heard the Apostle of God say, in his public address, in the year of the farewell pilgrimage,[60] 'Let not a woman spend anything in alms from the house of her husband, except with the permission of her husband.' It was said, 'O Apostle of God, not even food?' He replied, 'That is the best of our property.'"

---

[60]*farewell pilgrimage:* the Prophet's last pilgrimage to Mecca before his death.

On God: It is related from Ubai bin Kab that, "The Apostle of God said, 'O Abu Al Mandhar, do you know which verse from the Book of God most High which is with you is the greatest?' I said, 'God and His Apostle know best.' He said, 'O Abu Al Mandhar, do you know which verse from the Book of God which is with you is greatest?' I said, 'God, there is no God but He, the Living, the Self-subsisting.'" Ubai said, "And he struck me on my breast and said, 'O Abu Al Mandhar, may knowledge be welcome to you.'"

It is related from Abu Hurairah that, "The Apostle of God said, 'Truly God Most High has ninety-nine names. Whoever counts them will enter paradise. He is Allah, than whom there is no other God, the Merciful, the Compassionate, the King, the Holy, the Peace, the Faithful, the Protector, the Mighty, the Compeller, the Proud, the Creator, the Maker, the Fashioner, the Forgiver, the Dominant, the Bestower, the Provider, the Opener, the Knower, the Restrainer, the Speaker, the Abaser, the Exalter, the Honorer, the Destroyer, the Hearer, the Seer, the Ruler, the Just, the Subtle, the Aware, the Clement, the Grand, the Forgiving, the Grateful, the Exalted, The Great, the Guardian, the Strengthener, the Reckoner, the Majestic, the Generous, the Watcher, the Approver, the Comprehensive, the Wise, the Loving, the Glorious, the Raiser, the Witness, the Truth, the Advocate, the Strong, the Firm, the Patron, the Laudable, the Counter, the Beginner, the Restorer, the Quickener, the Killer, the Living, the Subsisting, the Finder, the Glorious, the One, the Eternal, the Powerful, the Prevailing, the Bringer-forward, the Deferrer, the First, the Last, the Evident, the Hidden, the Governor, the Exalted, the Righteous, the Accepter of Repentance, the Avenger, the Pardoner, the Kind, the Ruler of the Kingdom, the Lord of majesty and liberality, the Equitable, the Collector, the Independent, the Enricher, the Giver, the Withholder, the Distresser, the Profiter, the Light, the Guide, the Incomparable, the Enduring, the Inheritor, the Director, the Patient.'"

On the Power of Reading the Quran: It is related from Abu Sa'idu'l-Khudri that Usaid bin Hudair said, "On a certain night when he was reading, and his horse was tethered near him, behold! the horse wheeled round. Then he became silent, and it also became steady. Then he read (again), and it wheeled round. Then he became silent, and it ceased wheeling round. He again read, and the horse wheeled round as before. Then he turned away, and his son Yahya was near it, and he feared that it would injure him. And when he moved the child away he raised his head to the heavens, and behold! something like a cloud and in it objects resembling lamps. And when the morning came he informed the Prophet. . . . "I feared, O Apostle of God, that it would tread on Yahya who was near it, and I moved near to him, and raised my head to the heavens, and behold! something resembling a cloud, in which were objects like lamps, and I went out in order that I should not see them." He replied, "And do you know what that was? He said, "No." He said, "Those were angels which came near at the sound of thy voice, and if you had continued to read, they would have remained until the morning, and men would have seen them. They would not have remained hidden."

On the Martyr in Holy War: It is related from Abu Miqdam bin Madikarib that the Apostle of God said, "The martyr has six privileges near God: he is forgiven his sins on (the shedding of) the first drop of blood; he is shown his resting-place in paradise; he is redeemed from the punishment of the grave; he is made secure from the great fear (of hell); and a crown of glory is placed on his head, one ruby of which is better than the world and all that is therein; and he will marry seventy-two wives of the houris with dark eyes; and his intercession will be accepted for seventy of his relatives."

On Plunder in Holy War: It is related from Abu Hurairah that The Prophet said, "One of the Prophets [Joshua] went out to fight; and he said

to his people, 'Let no man follow me who has married a wife and wishes to take her to his house, but has not yet done so; nor the one who has built a house, but has not yet raised a roof over it; nor the man who has bought a sheep or camel and is expecting it to give birth.' Then he went forth to war. And he drew near a certain village at the time of evening prayer. Then he said to the sun, 'Truly you are under orders, and I am also under orders. O God, restrain it for us.' Then it was restrained (from setting) until God gave him the victory. After that he gathered together the plunder; and a fire came to devour it, but it did not consume it. And he said, 'Truly there is deceit among you with regard to the plunder. Therefore let a man from each tribe pledge his oath.' Then the hand of a certain man stuck to his hand. He said, 'The deceit concerning the plunder is among you.' Then they [the offenders] brought a golden head like the head of a cow. Then he set it down and the fire came and devoured it." And the relater has added in another tradition, "Plunder was not lawful for any one before us. Afterwards God made plunder lawful for us. He saw our weakness and impotence and made it lawful for us."

On Women and Children in Holy War: It is related from Abdullah bin Omar, "The Apostle of God forbade the killing of women and children [in jihad]."

On the Steps for Struggle against Enemies: It is related from Sulaiman bin Buraidah, from his father, that he said, "When the Apostle of God appointed a leader over any army or marauding band, he was in the habit of giving him orders regarding his special duties concerning the fear of God and good behavior towards those Muslims who were with him. After that he would say, 'Go forth to war in the name of God in his road. Fight with those who disbelieve in God. Go forth to war. Do not use deceit or break a covenant, or mutilate [anyone], or kill children. And when you meet your enemy of the polytheists, then invite them to the rights and privileges of Islam or defeat. Then whichever of they give an affirmative answer to, accept if from them and withdraw from them. After that invite them to Islam; and if they give an affirmative answer to you, then accept it from them and withdraw from them. After that invite them to remove themselves from their homes to the homes of the refugees, and inform them that if they do that, then for them is what is given to the refugees; and their duties are the same as those of the refugees. But if they refuse to change from their homes, then inform them that they will remain as the desert Arabs who have embraced Islam. The commands of God will be obligatory upon them which are obligatory upon other believers; but they will get nothing of the plunder and spoils unless they go to fight along with the other Muslims. But if they refuse (to become Muslims) then ask from them the poll-tax. And if they answer thee in the affirmative, then accept it from them, and withdraw from them. But if they refuse (to pay), then seek help from God and fight them.

GLOSSARY

ayah a verse in the *Quran;* literally, "sign."

Bismillah the opening formula for surahs in the *Quran;* literally, "in the name of God."

challenge verses short passages of the *Quran* in which the Prophet calls on his opponents to produce anything like his revelation.

Fatihah the "opening" chapter of the *Quran,* used as a prayer in Islam.

hadith a traditional report recording a saying or action of Muhammad.

isnad the authority on which a section of *Hadith* stands, usually given as a list of names in a chain of tradition.

jihad struggle for Islam, especially armed struggle to promote and defend the faith.

jinn spirits, both good and evil; to be distinguished from angelic beings and the deity.

matn the main text of a *Hadith.*

qiblah the direction Muslims face during prayer.

Quran "recitation, reading"; the scripture of Islam.

surah a chapter of the *Quran.*

tafsir the branch of Islamic scholarship that deals with commentary on the *Quran.*

tilawa ritual recitation of the Quran.

QUESTIONS FOR STUDY AND DISCUSSION

1. How does the *Quran* give both direct (explicit) and indirect (implicit) information about the career of Muhammad?

2. In what sense is Islam especially Arabic? What does it mean for a universal religion like Islam to have a scripture that cannot officially be translated?

3. Explain the statement, "Islam is a religion of the book."

4. Describe the status of women in the *Quran* and Islam in general. To what degree may it be possible to improve this status and still keep within the bounds of the *Quran?*

5. How do the "Pillars of Islam," especially almsgiving, function to promote compassion and social justice?

6. Relate the cognitive to the noncognitive uses of the *Quran*. Which do you see as primary, and why?

7. How does the Quranic view of creation and the world add to the views of Jewish and Christian scripture?

8. Free will and predestination are problems that touch many religions. They even touch other areas, especially philosophy and psychology, with its debate between behaviorists and humanists. Explain your views on this topic, and relate them to the *Quran*.

SUGGESTIONS FOR FURTHER READING

Primary Readings

Alim: version 4.5. ISL Software, 1997. A multimedia CD-ROM featuring Arabic text, recitation, transliteration, translations, and some Hadith text.

A. J. Arberry, ed., *The Koran Interpreted*. New York: Macmillan, 1955. This translation probably does the best job of suggesting in English the literary quality of the original.

K. Cragg, *Readings in the Qur'an*. London: Collins, 1988. An abridgement of the *Quran* to two-thirds its size, arranged by eight themes, with a comprehensive introduction.

N. J. Dawood, trans., *The Koran*. New York: Penguin, 1990. This reliable translation is probably the most widely read edition available.

T. B. Irving, *The Qur'an: The First American Translation*. Brattleboro, Vermont: Amana, 1985. The translation is in good idiomatic English; the notes are from a traditional Muslim perspective and help the reader understand the role of the Quran in Muslim life.

al-Tabari, *The Commentary on the Quran,* vol. 1. Translated, with introduction and notes, by J. Cooper. Oxford: Oxford University Press, 1989. The first of five projected volumes, this book provides a clear insight on Quranic commentary as practiced by its most influential commentator.

M. Sells, *Approaching the Quran: The Early Revelations*. Ashland, Oregon: White Cloud Press, 1999. Fresh, powerful translations of the earlier, more poetic surahs, with a compact disk recording Quranic recitations of several of these surahs.

Secondary Readings

F. M. Denny, "Islam: Qur'an and Hadith." In F. M. Denny and R. L. Taylor, eds., *The Holy Book in Comparative Perspective*. Charleston: University of South Carolina Press, 1985, pp. 84–108. An up-to-date discussion of the relationship of the *Quran* and the *hadith*.

W. A. Graham, "'An Arabic Recital': Qur'an as a Spoken Book." In W. A. Graham, *Beyond the Written Word*. Cambridge: University Press, 1987, pp. 79–115. An excellent treatment of the oral aspects of the *Quran*.

J. D. McAuliffe, *Quranic Christians: An Analysis of Classical and Modern Exegesis*. Cambridge: Cambridge University Press, 1991. An excellent study of the history of Islamic interpretation of the *Quran* by way of an important interreligious question: the meaning of those passages that make ostensibly positive remarks about Christians.

F. Rahman, *The Leading Ideas of the Quran*. Minneapolis: Bibliotheca, 1980. A fine treatment of the most important themes of the *Quran* by a leading Muslim theologian.

J. I. Smith, "Islam." In A. Sharma, ed., *Women in World Religions*. Albany: State University of New York Press, 1987, pp. 235–250. A treatment of the place of women in Islam, with a fine discussion of what the *Quran* says about women and how it is and is not applied in contemporary Muslim societies.

B. Stowasser, *Women in the Quran, Traditions, and Commentaries*. New York: Oxford University Press, 1994. An excellent treatment of the status and role of women in scripture, *Hadith*, and commentary.

W. M. Watt, *Bell's Introduction to the Qur'an*. Edinburgh: Edinburgh University Press, 1970. This is probably the best one-volume introduction to the *Quran*.

⌖ INFOTRAC COLLEGE EDITION

You can locate InfoTrac College Edition articles about this chapter by accessing the InfoTrac College Edition website (http://www.infotrac.collegeedition.com/wadsworth/). Using subject guide, enter the search terms relevant to this chapter, and then read abstracts for relevant articles.

The Grandin Press, Palmyra, New York
The *Book of Mormon* was first published here in 1830. Its first printing was 5,000 copies, unusually large for the time and indicative of the strong initial growth of the Church of Jesus Christ of Latter-day Saints. A unique feature of most scriptures of the new religious movements is their immediate mass publication. Credit: Copyright © 2000 by Intellectual Reserve, Inc. Used by permission.

CHAPTER THIRTEEN

New Religious Movements

❖ A weary business traveler settles into her room in the Marriott Hotel in Chicago. Looking for a bit of inspiration at the end of her day, she opens the top drawer of the nightstand alongside the bed, expecting to find a Christian *Bible*. On top of the Bible, however, is a copy of the *Book of Mormon,* subtitled "Another Testament of Jesus Christ." This puzzles her for a moment, until she remembers that the Marriott family that owns this hotel chain is devoutly Mormon, and like all devout Mormons is eager to spread its scriptures.

❖ In Manhattan's Madison Square Garden, two thousand couples have come to be joined in marriage by the Reverend Sun Myung Moon and his wife Hak Ja Han Moon, the founders of the Unification Church. The Moons have arranged these marriages, and many of the couples have only recently met. As a part of the ceremony, words from the Unification scripture, *Divine Principle,* are intoned over the assembled crowd. These words emphasize one of the key ideas in Unification teaching: under the religious direction of the Moons, the True Parents, the world is saved by its repopulation with true children of God, believing Unificationists.

❖ In Los Angeles, the actor John Travolta gives a press interview at the release of the feature film adapted from L. Ron Hubbard's science fiction novel, *Battlefield Earth.* Attributing his success as an actor, husband, and father to Scientology, he tells about his first experience with reading Hubbard's book *Dianetics,* the main scripture of the Church of Scientology. Travolta is not alone among Hollywood celebrities in adopting Scientology. The church also counts Tom Cruise, Jenna Elfman, and Kirstie Alley among its many celebrity adherents and features them in its publicity.

INTRODUCTION

New religious movements is a recent term in the field of religious studies. While it is somewhat vague, it generally denotes religious groups that arose since the start of the nineteenth century with suficient size, longevity, and cultural impact that they have become important for the academic study of religion. Most recently published encyclopedias, handbooks, and textbooks on religion use this term and give a treatment of the groups in it.[1] "New religious movements" is preferrable in many ways to the other recent terms "alternative religious movements" or "marginal religious movements," and it is clearly preferable to the older "cults" and "sects." While these last two terms have some continuing validity, especially in the sociological study of

---

[1] An excellent treatment of new religious movements can be found in W. H. Swatus, Jr., ed., *Encyclopedia of Religion and Society* (Walnut Creek, CA: AltaMira, 1998), pp. 328–333.

religion where they are used more objectively, they have become so laden with value judgments that most scholars no longer use them to characterize these new religious movements. Hundreds of groups around the world today are in a sense "new religious movements," and each year sees other new religious movements born. Here we are concerned especially with those movements that have become most significant on a world scale, that make and use scriptures, and that are important for students of world religions to encounter. We will deal with them here in their historical order: the Baha'i tradition, the Church of Jesus Christ of Latter-day Saints, the Christian Science Church, the Unification Church, and the Church of Scientology.

Inclusion of these groups together in this chapter does not imply, of course, that they see themselves as new religious movements; often they do not. Neither do they see themselves as related to each other; indeed, they are not. While scholars call these religious movements "new," one must note that they all, with the one exception of Scientology, branch off from older religions. Baha'i arose in the nineteenth century from Shi'ite Islam and sees itself in part as the successor of Islam. The other groups treated here—the Church of Jesus Christ of Latter-day Saints, the Christian Science Church, and the Unification Church—see themselves as Christian, and most experts in comparative religions would view this labeling as basically correct. That they all accept the Christian *Bible* as their first canon is a good indication of this. Moreover, "outsiders" to these three movements, such as Buddhists, would almost certainly recognize them as belonging to the stream of Christian tradition. Only Scientology is truly new, based on a therapeutic self-understanding and self-improvement model not formally based on a prior religion. Scientology calls itself a church, but it is not a part of the Christian movement, nor do most Scientologists see themselves as Christians, at least as that term is traditionally understood. Some of these new religious movements are highly controversial in North America and in other parts of the world. However, many other faiths presented in the present book were also controversial when they were new, and the careful student of religion will want to form a judgment on them based in some measure on encountering what they say about themselves in their own sacred writings.

Because each new religious movement treated here is separate from the others, we will depart from the usual practice of the present book in presenting passages of history, teaching, ethics, and the rest together. Rather, we deal here with each movement separately, keeping its own scriptures together. In the remaining introductory sections, we will also consider briefly the names of their scriptures, their structures, their origin and development, and their use.

Names

The scriptures of the new religious movements were most often written and published by the founders in their lifetime. Thus, unlike most scriptures from the older, traditional faiths, the names of the scriptures of the new religious movements were given by the founding authors themselves.

Baha'i calls its scriptures *Holy Writings*. While this name may seem bland and unilluminating, it does imply something important about Baha'i scriptures: their originally written character. Although the *Quran* ("Recitation") originated orally as the transmission of God's words, the *Holy Writings* are the "Pen of God," a phrase often repeated in the earliest Baha'i scriptures.

The Church of Jesus Christ of Latter-day Saints has a three-part new scripture. The ***Book of Mormon*** is certainly the leading one, and it is from this title that the followers of this movement came to be known as "Mormons." A second, shorter scripture is the ***Pearl of Great Price***, a selection of the inspired translations by Joseph Smith. The final scripture is ***Doctrine and Covenants***, which contains the continuing revelation of God's word through Latter-day Saint prophets, especially Joseph Smith. (The *Book of Mormon*, but not the other two, is also considered scriptural by the Community of Christ, formerly known as the Reorganized Church of Jesus Christ of Latter-day Saints, an early splinter group.) In addition to this "second canon" of scripture, the Latter-day Saint church also has a "first canon" of the Christian *Bible*, in the King James Version of 1611.

The founder of Christian Science, Mary Baker Eddy, was a prolific writer, like many founders of new religious movements. Although new religious movements sometimes consider everything their founder(s) wrote to be scriptural, the Christian Science Church has carefully delineated only one book as its new scripture, ***Science and Health with Key to the Scriptures***. Mrs. Eddy herself guided this delineation. This name accurately suggests its contents: a "science" that uses prayer, Christian scripture (in the King James Version) and Eddy's book itself to heal body, mind and spirit.

The Unification Church's sole scripture, written by its founder Sun Myung Moon, is the ***Divine Principle***. "Principle" here means teaching, and refers to Moon's distinctive reinterpretation of Christianity (the "Divine" of the title) in combination with select Asian teachings such as yin and yang, with devotion to Korea, and with a virulent anticommunism to produce a new religious movement.

Finally, in the Church of Scientology all the writings of L. Ron Hubbard on the faith itself have been explicitly called "scripture" since the Scientology movement became a self-consciously religious movement in the 1950s. In keeping with the technological orientation of Scientology, Hubbard's films and audiotapes are also considered scriptural. This "canon" is a vast one—Scientologists themselves reckon Hubbard's literary output at 35 million words in more than one hundred books. His *Dianetics: The Modern Science of Mental Health* is the basic work, a "canon within the canon" of Scientology scriptures. Scientologists often refer to ***Dianetics*** as "the first book." However, since *Dianetics* is more psychotherapeutic than religious, other, later works by Hubbard have entered the Scientology collection of scripture. Other important writings include his *Scientology: The Fundamentals of Thought* and an anthology of his writings compiled by church officials after his death, *Scientology: Theory and Practice of a Contemporary Religion*. Beyond a firm, consistent description of these books as Scientologist "scripture," Scientology has no overall name for its sacred writings.

Overview of Structure

In general, the scriptures of new religious movements tend to show much less variety in structure and genre than the scriptures of traditional religions. They are usually nonnarrative prose and strongly oriented to teaching the new doctrines of the movement. Three reasons help to explain this internal sameness. First, because they are "second canon" works, following up on the *Quran* (Baha'i) or the Christian *Bible* (with the exception of Scientology), they are more tightly focused than other scriptures. Second, the relatively short period of time in which they were written, compared to the centuries-long process of most other traditions, gives them more focus. (The *Book of Mormon* does claim to have been written by multiple authors over a thousand year period.) Third, they are mostly written by the first founder(s) of the religious movement, not its later leaders.

The *Holy Writings* of Baha'i are organized in four parts corresponding to their four authors. First are the writings of "the Bab" (Gate [to God]), born Sayyid Ali-Muhammad Shiraz (1819–1850). These writings form a sort of preface to Baha'i. Next are the writings of Baha'u'llah, born Mirza Husayn-Ali Nur (1817–1892), the main founder of the faith. In the Baha'i canon, these two groups of writings are considered directly revelatory from God, and hence most authoritative. Next are the writings of Abdu'l-Baha (1843–1921), the third leader, and finally the writings of his grandson Shoghi Effendi (1897–1957), the final leader of Baha'i whose death effectively closed their canon. These writings are a collection of letters, narratives, prayers, and laws. Of the scriptures of new religious movements, those of Baha'i are the most varied.

The scriptures of the Church of Jesus Christ of Latter-day Saints are varied in structure and style, and fairly complex. They record the story of ancient American peoples descended from ancient Hebrews who left Judah around 600 B.C.E., the appearance of the resurrected Jesus Christ to these Americans, and the rebirth of the true Christian church in the nineteenth century with Joseph Smith, Jr. The *Book of Mormon* has fifteen main parts known, with one exception, as books. Like the *Bible*, these books are subdivided into chapters and verses. These are based on four groups of metal plates: those of Nephi, Mormon, and Ether, and the brass plates brought to the Americas by people fleeing Jerusalem in 600 B.C.E. In 421 C.E., Moroni, the last of the Nephite prophets, sealed the sacred plates and hid them by divine instruction. In 1823, this same Moroni visited Joseph Smith as a resurrected prophet, directing him to these sacred plates, which he later translated and published in 1830. The plates themselves eventually were returned to Moroni and then hidden away for all time.

The second Latter-day Saint scripture, *Pearl of Great Price*, was first compiled in 1851 by Franklin Richards, then a member of the church's Council of the Twelve Apostles and in charge of the church's missions in Great Britain. Richards intended to give a wider circulation among Latter-day Saints of Joseph Smith's testimony and translations, which comprise this book. It quickly received wide acceptance, especially in mission fields, and became a scripture of the church by action of its First Presidency (highest official body) in 1880. *Pearl of Great Price* contains five main sections: "Selections From the Book of Moses," an excerpt from Joseph Smith's translation of *Genesis;* "The Book of Abraham," a translation of writings by the patriarch Abraham on Egyptian papyri that Joseph Smith obtained in 1835; "Joseph Smith—Matthew," an excerpt from the testimony of the New Testament's gospel of *Matthew* to Jesus Christ as understood in the church; "Joseph Smith—History," extracts of Joseph Smith's official testimony about his own life; and "Articles of Faith of the Church of Jesus Christ of Latter-day Saints," a statement by Joseph Smith. The third scripture,

Doctrine and Covenants, has 138 sections, plus two "official declarations." It contains revelations on doctrines and community life, some narrative, some theological, and some legal, from 1823 until 1978. Its "official declarations" deal with two controversial topics—the ending of polygamy and the admission of blacks to the priesthood.

The scripture of Christian Science is in two parts, as its title implies. First is "Science and Health," with a preface by the author and fourteen chapters on various topics: Christian doctrines, spiritualism and hypnotism, medicine, and Christian Science practices of prayer and healing. The "Key to Scriptures" section has three chapters, treating Genesis, the *Apocalypse* (*Revelation* in the *New Testament*), and a glossary. A final section appended later to the whole book is "Fruitage," a collection of written testimonies to the healing power of Christian Science, and especially to the role of *Science and Health with Key to the Scriptures* in this healing. This book has not been revised since the last edition of 1910 and has kept in all subsequent printings to the 1910 pagination and line numbers.

The *Divine Principle* of the Unification Church is heavily didactic in content and style, as its abstract title implies. Its organization is also complex. Thirteen chapters are divided into numerous sections and subsections. Topics treated include "Principle of Creation," "The Human Fall," "The Messiah," "Predestination," "Christology," "The Periods in Providential History and the Determination of their Lengths," "Preparation Period for the Second Advent of the Messiah," and "Second Advent." These chapter titles vaguely imply what the contents of this book make plain—Jesus, the first Messiah, did not accomplish God's mission, and a second Messiah has now been born in Korea, God's new chosen nation. *Divine Principle* does not make it explicit, but Moon has in other places proclaimed himself to be this second Messiah.

Since Scientologists consider all religious writings, and even audiotapes and films, by the late L. Ron Hubbard to be scriptural, the structure of their scriptures varies widely. Two types of works predominate: basic teaching on human nature and perfection, and explanatory works based on them. In the first category is *Dianetics,* and the various handbooks for auditors kept under strict control. *Dianetics* is organized into three books ("The Goal of Man," "The Single Source of All Inorganic Mental and Organic Psychosomatic Ills," and "Therapy") and a total of twenty-five chapters. Much of *Dianetics* is revised in the later scriptures. In the second category are the many anthologies of Hubbard's writings along wth his tapes and films. The Religious Technology Center of the Church of Scientology, located in southern California, houses the thousands of Hubbard's manuscripts, books, audiotapes, and films. As the Church's website explains, the Center's special task is also to guard the "advanced religious scriptures" of the church, so that "the materials of each level [of spiritual release] are kept secure . . . and that advanced services are ministered exactly as written by Mr. Hubbard."

Origin and Development

We begin with four general observations. First, scriptures in the older religions generally had a long period of development, both oral and written and stages between, until they reached their final form. The scriptures of the new religious movements have little or no oral tradition behind them, but instead have gone "straight to print." The *Holy Writings* of Baha'i, *Book of Mormon, Dianetics* and the other Scientology scriptures, *Science and Health with Key to the Scriptures,* and the *Divine Principle* were all taken by their authors themselves from composition to publication. Therefore, the scriptures of new religious movements do not reflect a long tradition shaped by community use, but do reflect the mind of the author in giving authoritative written teaching. In all but Scientology scripture, these writings are believed to be revelations of divine truth.

Second, they are "instant scripture" in that they are immediately accepted and used as scripture by their religions. In the traditional faiths, a good deal of time passes —from a generation to many centuries—for writings to be compiled, recognized as scriptural, and put into a canon. In the new movements, as soon as the founder(s) of the movement produces books, the movement itself adopts them as authoritative. As long as the movement endures, these books remain scriptural.

Third, the new religious movements tend to have a remarkably large amount of scriptural literature, compared to the older traditions. Everything the founder wrote for the movement—and often they were very prolific writers—is typically considered scriptural, with special emphasis placed on certain works. For example, L. Ron Hubbard has a vast body of nonfiction work, all of it considered scriptural, but his *Dianetics* is called "the first book." (His science fiction novels are not considered scripturally authoritative, even though most of them written since the founding of the church have broad themes that echo Scientology teaching.) Oral tradition does not sort it out, and the canons become large. In the Latter-day Saint and Baha'i movements, they even grew over time after the death of the first founders of the faith. Moreover, there is a tendency in these movements to have a body of scripture as large as the body of scripture of the more traditional religions they seek to supplant.

Fourth, despite their fixed, published form, most scriptures of the new religious movements are amenable to change. For example, in the Latter-day Saint church, *Doctrine and Covenants* is open ended. An addition to it can change or amplify previous revelation, even previous revelation recorded in the *Book of Mormon*. The Unification Church's *Divine Principle* was revised in 1996, and a careful comparison of this and the previous edition shows a few significant changes in content. The scriptures of the new religious movements are not more amenable to change than the scriptures of the older, traditional religions. But because they were published almost immediately after their writing and the original editions survive, their changes are more noticeable. Now we turn to a brief description of the origin and development of each new movement's scriptures.

The Baha'i scriptures have a fourfold development that corresponds to their current structure as outlined earlier. Each step is built on those that precede it, to make a coherent written tradition and teaching for the faith. First are the writings of "the Bab," a precursor of the formal Baha'i faith. Next are the writings of Baha'u'llah, the main founder of the faith. These writings form the foundation of Baha'i teaching. Next are the writings of Abdu'l-Baha, the third leader, and finally the writings of his grandson Shoghi Effendi, the final leader of Baha'i whose death effectively closed their canon. These writings are a collection of letters, narratives, prayers, and laws.

In the Church of Jesus Christ of Latter-day Saints, the *Book of Mormon*, the main scripture, serves as a basis for the other newer scriptures in the Mormon canon. Ironically, it tends to be more similar than later official church writings and teachings to the mainstream Protestant Christianity against which the movement sprang, especially as regards the controversial doctrines that have tended to set the Latter-day Saint movement apart from other Christians. For example, the *Book of Mormon* promotes monogamy and discourages (but does not forbid) polygamy (e.g., *Jacob* 2:27, 30). This newer teaching comes out in *Doctrine and Covenants,* which preserves both the approval of polygamy (section 132, 37–38, 52, 61–62) and the official disapproval of it ("Official Declaration 1"). While the opponents of the church point to more than three thousand alleged changes in the *Book of Mormon* since its initial publication, the majority of these are corrections and updates of spelling and grammar. In essence, this important book remains as Joseph Smith, Jr., wrote it.

In the development of the new Christian Science scripture, its "Science and Health" section came first and forms the basis of the rest. "Key to the Scriptures" applies the first section to parts of the Christian *Bible,* and the concluding chapter, "Fruitage," was obviously compiled on the basis of earlier editions of the "Science and Health" sections. *Science and Health with Key to the Scriptures* grew in stages from its first publication in 1875 until it reached its final form in 1910, the last edition that Mary Baker Eddy published. Since then, this book has undergone no further development in form, content, or even printing layout.

The Unification Church's *Divine Principle* has gone through three English "editions" since its first publication in 1959. The last of these, in 1996, is a much more fluent translation than the first two editions. However, these three editions are not just new translations of the Korean original, but a few entire sections have been added and deleted, especially from the second to third edition. Because the Unification movement has no other scripture, this book itself shifts as the religion changes.

Finally, the Church of Scientology's foundational scripture, L. Ron Hubbard's *Dianetics,* was published first in 1950. Scientologists typically point to its immediate popularity and impact; for example, its sales placed it on the *New York Times'* bestseller list already in 1950. Soon after this book was published, however, Hubbard included the presence of a soul in his understanding of human beings, and in time he placed this soul (which he called the *thetan*) at the center of human life. This teaching, along with the developing religious organization of Scientology, started the transformation of Scientology into a full-fledged religious movement. Later Hubbard writings would develop this religious aspect, but the basic teachings and practices of the movement were laid out already in the 1950s, and have not been substantively changed since then.

Use

The use of new scripture in the new religious movements is typically more limited than its use in the more traditional religions. Believers within these groups do not regularly use their new scriptures in ritual; they pay them no veneration, and the books themselves are not ornately published or decorated. (Those new religious movements that use the Christian *Bible* alongside their own new scriptures often give it some formal respect short of veneration.) Neither do they typically use their books in organizing the structure of their religious communities.

Instead, they use their scriptures in three key ways. First, believers are expected to study the scriptures, in groups and privately. At times this usage crosses over into meditation. For example, Christian Scientists believe that healing comes from proper meditation on, and use of, Mary Baker Eddy's *Science and Health with Key to the Scriptures.* In the Baha'i faith, the wording of the earlier scriptures, based as it is on lyrical Quranic style, encourages a meditative approach. Second, the scriptures are used in teaching key doctrines. They were written in large measure to teach new religious truth in the context of an older traditional religion, and the continuation of this tradition is important. For example, the Church of Scientology is careful to assure that the teachings of its founder, L. Ron Hubbard, on Scientology's theory and method are exactly taught and carried out by church members authorized to do therapy at various levels of expertise, which the movement calls "auditing." Third, new religious movements typically use their scriptures in missionary activities to spread their faith. Two examples must suffice here. The Christian Science Church widely distributes its *Science and Health with Key to the Scriptures* at a subsidized price. The *Book of Mormon* is strongly advertised on American television and in print advertisements, where people are invited to send for a free copy. Given its role in the missionizing emphasis of the Latter-day Saint church, the *Book of Mormon* has taken its place as one of the world's most important scriptures.

A telling indication of how these groups view their own writings as scriptural is the physical design of the books themselves. Although not ornately published, these books are typically designed to look like the books they supplement or replace. Baha'i publishes its *Holy Writings* to resemble the Quran. The Divine Principle is, like the traditional Christian *Bible,* published in black. The Latter-day Saint church prints its *Book of Mormon* to resemble the physical format of the *Bible* it publishes. Scientology's *Dianetics* has typically been printed as a commercial book, but its special "commemorative edition" of 1986 was printed like an expensive *Bible*: in a leather cover, with gold-edged pages and a silk ribbon for marking one's place.

THE SCRIPTURE OF BAHA'I

The Essence of Baha'i Teaching, and a Sketch of the Life of Baha'u'llah*

Here the last leader of the Baha'i movement gives its definitive teaching. He stresses the oneness of humanity under the oneness of God. This powerful vision for world harmony, here written at the middle of the twentieth century, has become the leading characteristic of the Baha'i movement.[2]

---

*Shoghi Effendi, *The Promised Day Is Come,* Preface
[2]All Baha'i writings are from the website Bahai-library.org. Copyright © 1996 by the National Spiritual Assembly of the Baha'is in the United States. Used by permission.

The fundamental principle enunciated by Baha'u'llah . . . is that religious truth is not absolute but relative, that Divine Revelation is a continuous and progressive process, that all the great religions of the world are divine in origin, that their basic principles are in complete harmony, that their aims and purposes are one and the same, that their teachings are but facets of one truth, that their functions are complementary, that they differ only in the nonessential aspects of their doctrines, and that their missions represent successive stages in the spiritual evolution of human society. . . .

His mission is to proclaim that the ages of the infancy and of the childhood of the human race are past, that the convulsions associated with the present stage of its adolescence are slowly and painfully preparing it to attain the stage of manhood, and are heralding the approach of that Age of Ages when swords will be beaten into plowshares, when the Kingdom promised by Jesus Christ will have been established, and the peace of the planet definitely and permanently ensured. Nor does Baha'u'llah claim finality for his Revelation, but rather stipulates that a fuller measure of the truth He has been commissioned by the Almighty to vouchsafe to humanity, at so critical a juncture in its fortunes, must be disclosed at future stages in the constant and limitless evolution of mankind.

The Baha'i Faith upholds the unity of God, recognizes the unity of His Prophets, and inculcates the principle of the oneness and wholeness of the entire human race. It proclaims the necessity and the inevitability of the unification of mankind, asserts that it is gradually approaching, and claims that nothing short of the transmuting spirit of God, working through His chosen Mouthpiece in this day, can ultimately succeed in bringing it about. It, moreover, enjoins upon its followers the primary duty of an unfettered search after truth, condemns all manner of prejudice and superstition, declares the purpose of religion to be the promotion of amity and concord, proclaims its essential harmony with science, and recognizes it as the foremost agency for the pacification and the orderly progress of human society. . . .

Mirza Husayn-'Ali, surnamed Baha'u'llah (the Glory of God), a native of Mazindaran, Whose advent the Bab [Herald and Forerunner of Baha'u'llah] had foretold . . . was imprisoned in Teheran, was banished, in 1852, from His native land to Baghdad, and thence to Constantinople and Adrianople, and finally to the prison city of Akka, where He remained incarcerated for no less than twenty-four years, and in whose neighborhood He passed away in 1892. In the course of His banishment, and particularly in Adrianople and Akka, He formulated the laws and ordinances of His Dispensation, expounded, in over a hundred volumes, the principles of His Faith, proclaimed His Message to the kings and rulers of both the East and the West, both Christian and Muslim, addressed the Pope, the Caliph of Islam, the Chief Magistrates of the Republics of the American continent, the entire Christian sacerdotal order, the leaders of Shi'ih and Sunni Islam, and the high priests of the Zoroastrian religion. In these writings He proclaimed His Revelation, summoned those whom He addressed to heed His call and espouse His Faith, warned them of the consequences of their refusal, and denounced, in some cases, their arrogance and tyranny. . . .

The Faith which this order serves, safeguards and promotes is essentially supernatural, supranational, entirely non-political, non-partisan, and diametrically opposed to any policy or school of thought that seeks to exalt any particular race, class or nation. It is free from any form of ecclesiasticism, has neither priesthood nor rituals, and is supported exclusively by voluntary contributions made by its avowed adherents. Though loyal to their respective governments, though imbued with the love of their own country, and anxious to promote at all times, its best interests, the followers of the Baha'i Faith, nevertheless, viewing mankind as one entity, and profoundly attached to its vital interests, will not hesitate to subordinate every particular interest, be it personal, regional or national, to the overriding interests of the generality of mankind, knowing full well that in a world of interdependent peoples and nations the advantage of the part is best to be reached by the advantage of the whole, and that no lasting result can be achieved by any of the component parts if the general interests of the entity itself are neglected.

Baha'i, Islam, and Christianity*

The Bab ("Gate" to God) saw himself as the "hidden Imam" (leader) promised in Shi'ite Islam. In this selection from his writings, the forerunner of the faith had to deal with Muslim and Christian opposition and assert the superiority of his faith to theirs. Note how the style of the Bab's writings is very similar to the style of the Quran; *the chapter-and-verse references to the* Quran *are in the original.*

[1] All praise be to God Who hath, through the power of Truth, sent down this Book unto His servant, that it may serve as a shining light for all mankind. . . . Verily this is none other than the sovereign Truth; it is the Path which God hath laid out for all that are in heaven and on earth. Let him then who will, take for himself the right path unto his Lord. . . . This is indeed the eternal Truth which God, the Ancient of Days, hath revealed unto His omnipotent Word—He Who hath been raised up from the midst of the Burning Bush. This is the Mystery which hath been hidden from all that are in heaven and on earth, and in this wondrous Revelation it hath, in very truth, been set forth in the Mother Book by the hand of God, the Exalted. . . . O concourse of kings and of the sons of kings! Lay aside, one and all, your dominion which belongeth unto God. . . . Let not thy sovereignty deceive thee, O Shah,[3] for "every soul shall taste of death," (*Quran* 3:182) and this, in very truth, hath been written down as a decree of God.

[61] Verily, those who ridicule the wondrous, divine Verses revealed through His Remembrance, are but making themselves the objects of ridicule, and We, in truth, aid them to wax in their iniquity. Indeed God's knowledge transcendeth all created things. . . . The infidels, of a truth, seek to separate God from His Remembrance, but God hath determined to perfect His Light through His Remembrance, and indeed He is potent over all things. . . .

Verily, Christ is Our Word which We communicated unto Mary; and let no one say what the Christians term as "the third of three" (*Quran* 5:77) inasmuch as it would amount to slandering the Remembrance Who . . . is invested with supreme authority. Indeed God is but one God, and far be it from His glory that there should be aught else besides Him. All those who shall attain unto Him on the Day of Resurrection are but His servants, and God is, of a truth, a sufficient Protector. Verily I am none other but the servant of God and His Word, and none but the first one to bow down in supplication before God, the Most Exalted; and indeed God witnesseth all things.

[62] O people of the *Quran*! Ye are as nothing unless ye submit unto the Remembrance of God and unto this Book. If ye follow the Cause of God, We will forgive you your sins; but if ye turn aside from Our command, We will, in truth, condemn your souls in Our Book unto the Most Great Fire. We, verily, do not deal unjustly with men, even to the extent of a speck on a date-stone.

---

*The Bab, *Qayyumu'l-Asma*, 1, 61–62
[3] *Shah*: the king of Iran.

Baha'i Laws*

Baha'u'llah's Kitab-I-Aqdas *("Most Holy Book") is the most influential statement of Baha'i laws. From the Muslim background of this new religious movement, great emphasis is placed on knowing and obeying God's laws. The sections given here include treatment of: prayer (12-14), fasting (16), pilgrimage (32), criminals (45), marriage (65), scripture (149–150), and a single language for the world (189).*

In the name of him who is the supreme ruler over all that has been and all that is to be! The first duty prescribed by God for His servants is the recognition of Him Who is the Dayspring of His Revelation and the Fountain of His laws, Who represents the Godhead in both the Kingdom of His Cause and the world of creation. Whoever achieveth this duty hath attained unto all good; and whoever is deprived thereof hath gone astray, though he be the author of every righteous deed. Every one who reacheth this most sublime station, this summit of transcendent glory, must observe every ordinance of Him. . . .

[2] They whom God hath endued with insight will readily recognize that the precepts laid down by God constitute the highest means for the maintenance of order in the world and the security of its peoples. He that turneth away from them is accounted among the abject and foolish. We, verily, have commanded you to refuse the dictates of your evil passions and corrupt desires, and not to transgress the bounds which the Pen of the Most High hath fixed, for these are the breath of life unto all created things. The seas of Divine wisdom and Divine utterance have risen under the breath of the breeze of the All-Merciful. Hasten to drink your fill, O men of understanding! They that have

violated the Covenant of God by breaking His commandments, and have turned back on their heels, these have erred grievously in the sight of God, the All-Possessing, the Most High. . . .

[12] It hath been ordained that obligatory prayer is to be performed by each of you individually. Save in the Prayer for the Dead, the practice of congregational prayer hath been annulled. He, of a truth, is the Ordainer, the All-Wise. God hath exempted women who are in their courses from obligatory prayer and fasting. Let them, instead, after performance of their ablutions, give praise unto God, repeating ninety-five times between the noon of one day and the next "Glorified be God, the Lord of Splendour and Beauty." Thus hath it been decreed in the Book, if ye be of them that comprehend. When travelling, if ye should stop and rest in some safe spot, perform—men and women alike—a single prostration in place of each unsaid Obligatory Prayer, and while prostrating say "Glorified be God, the Lord of Might and Majesty, of Grace and Bounty." Whoso is unable to do this, let him say only "Glorified be God"; this shall assuredly suffice him. . . . Thus doth the Lord make plain the ways of truth and guidance, ways that lead to one way, which is this Straight Path.

[16] O Pen of the Most High! Say: O people of the world! We have enjoined upon you fasting during a brief period, and at its close have designated for you Naw-Rúz as a feast. . . . It befits the people of Baha'i, throughout these days [that preceed the fast], to provide good cheer for themselves, their kindred and, beyond them, the poor and needy, and with joy and exultation to hail and glorify their Lord, to sing His praise and magnify His Name. When they end, let them enter upon the fast. Thus hath it been ordained by Him Who is the Lord of all mankind. The traveler, the ailing, those who are with child, are not bound by the Fast; they have

---

*Baha'u'llah, *Kitab-I-Aqdas*, 1–2, 12–14, 16, 30–34, 45, 49, 56, 63–65, 149–150, 189)

been exempted by God as a token of His grace. . . .

[30] The Lord hath ordained that in every city a House of Justice be established wherein shall gather counsellors. . . . They should consider themselves as entering the Court of the presence of God, the Exalted, the Most High, and as beholding Him Who is the Unseen. It behooveth them to be the trusted ones of the Merciful among men and to regard themselves as the guardians appointed of God for all that dwell on earth. It is incumbent upon them to take counsel together and to have regard for the interests of the servants of God, for His sake, even as they regard their own interests, and to choose that which is meet and seemly. . . .

O people of the world! Build ye houses of worship throughout the lands in the name of Him Who is the Lord of all religions. Make them as perfect as is possible in the world of being, and adorn them with that which befitteth them, not with images and effigies. Then, with radiance and joy, celebrate therein the praise of your Lord, the Most Compassionate. Verily, by His remembrance the eye is cheered and the heart is filled with light.

The Lord hath ordained that those of you who are able shall make pilgrimage to the sacred House, and from this He hath exempted women as a mercy on His part. He, of a truth, is the All-Bountiful, the Most Generous. . . .

Whoever layeth claim to a Revelation direct from God, ere the expiration of a full thousand years, such a man is assuredly a lying impostor. We pray God that He may graciously assist him to retract and repudiate such claim. Should he repent, God will, no doubt, forgive him. If, however, he persisteth in his error, God will, assuredly, send down one who will deal mercilessly with him. Terrible, indeed, is God in punishing! Whoever interpreteth this verse otherwise than its obvious meaning is deprived of the Spirit of God and of His mercy which encompasseth all created things. Fear God, and follow not your idle fancies. Nay, rather, follow the bidding of your Lord, the Almighty, the All-Wise. Before

long clamorous voices will be raised in most lands. Shun them, O My people, and follow not the iniquitous and evil-hearted. . . .

[45] Exile and imprisonment are decreed for the thief, and, on the third offence, place ye a mark upon his forehead so that, thus identified, he may not be accepted in the cities of God and His countries. Beware lest, through compassion, ye neglect to carry out the statutes of the religion of God; do that which hath been bidden you by Him Who is compassionate and merciful. We school you with the rod of wisdom and laws, like unto the father who educateth his son, and this for naught but the protection of your own selves and the elevation of your stations. . . .

[63] God hath prescribed matrimony unto you. Beware that ye take not unto yourselves more wives than two. Whoso contenteth himself with a single partner from among the maidservants of God, both he and she shall live in tranquillity. And he who would take into his service a[nother] young woman may do so with propriety. Such is the ordinance which, in truth and justice, hath been recorded by the Pen of Revelation. . . . . Marriage is dependent upon the consent of both parties. Desiring to establish love, unity and harmony amidst Our servants, We have conditioned it, once the couple's wish is known, upon the permission of their parents, lest enmity and rancor should arise amongst them. In this We have yet other purposes. Thus hath Our commandment been ordained. . . .

[149] Recite ye the verses of God every morn and eventide. Whoso faileth to recite them hath not been faithful to the Covenant of God and His Testament, and whoso turneth away from these holy verses in this Day is of those who throughout eternity have turned away from God. Fear ye God, O My servants, one and all. Pride not yourselves on much reading of the verses or on a multitude of pious acts by night and day; for were a man to read a single verse with joy and radiance it would be better for him than to read with lassitude all the Holy Books of God, the Help in Peril, the Self-Subsisting. . . . Lay not upon your souls that which will weary

them and weigh them down, but rather what will lighten and uplift them, so that they may soar on the wings of the Divine verses towards the Dawning-place of His manifest signs; this will draw you nearer to God, did ye but comprehend. [150] Teach your children the verses revealed from the heaven of majesty and power, so that, in most melodious tones, they may recite the Tablets of the All Merciful. . . .

[189] O members of parliaments throughout the world! Select ye a single language for the use of all on earth, and adopt ye likewise a common script. God, verily, maketh plain for you that which shall profit you and enable you to be independent of others. He, of a truth, is the Most Bountiful, the All-Knowing, the All-Informed. This will be the cause of unity, could ye but comprehend it, and the greatest instrument for promoting harmony and civilization. Would that ye might understand!

Baha'i Prayers*

The Short Obligatory prayer is for use at any time. The Medium Obligatory prayer is to be recited three times a day, at morning, noon and evening. Its italics indicate directions for prayer. The prayer for America was written on the occasion of the visit of Baha'i leaders to the United States early in the twentieth century.

[Short Obligatory Prayer] I bear witness, O my God, that Thou hast created me to know Thee and to worship Thee. I testify, at this moment, to my powerlessness and to Thy might, to my poverty and to Thy wealth. There is none other God but Thee, the Help in Peril, the Self-Subsisting.

[Medium Obligatory Prayer] *Whoever wisheth to pray, let him wash his hands, and while he washeth, let him say:*
Strengthen my hand, O my God, that it may take hold of Thy Book with such steadfastness that the hosts of the world shall have no power over it. Guard it, then, from meddling with whatsoever doth not belong unto it. Thou art, verily, the Almighty, the Most Powerful. I have turned my face unto Thee, O my Lord! Illumine it with the light of Thy countenance. Protect it, then, from turning to anyone but Thee.

Then let him stand up, and facing the Qiblih (Point of Adoration), let him say:
God testifieth that there is none other God but Him. His are the kingdoms of Revelation and of creation. He, in truth, hath manifested Him Who is the Dayspring of Revelation, Who conversed on Sinai, through Whom the Supreme Horizon hath been made to shine, and the [boundary] beyond which there is no passing hath spoken, and through Whom the call hath been proclaimed unto all who are in heaven and on earth: "Lo, the All-Possessing is come. Earth and heaven, glory and dominion are God's, the Lord of all men, and the Possessor of the Throne on high and of earth below!"

Let him, then, bend down, with hands resting on the knees, and say:
Exalted art Thou above my praise and the praise of anyone beside me, above my description and the description of all who are in heaven and all who are on earth!

Then, standing with open hands, palms upward toward the face, let him say:
Disappoint not, O my God, him that hath, with beseeching fingers, clung to the hem of Thy mercy and Thy grace, O Thou Who of those who show mercy art the Most Merciful!

Let him, then, be seated and say:

*Short Obligatory Prayer, Medium Obligatory Prayer, Prayer for America

I bear witness to Thy unity and Thy oneness, and that Thou art God, and that there is none other God beside Thee. Thou hast, verily, revealed thy Cause, fulfilled Thy Covenant, and opened wide the door of Thy grace to all that dwell in heaven and on earth. Blessing and peace, salutation and glory, rest upon Thy loved ones, whom the changes and changes of the world have not deterred from turning unto Thee, and who have given their all, in the hope of obtaining that which is with Thee. Thou art, in truth, the Ever-Forgiving, the All-Bountiful.

[Prayer for America] O Thou kind Lord! This gathering is turning to Thee. These hearts are radiant with Thy love. These minds and spirits are exhilarated by the message of Thy glad-tidings. O God! Let this American democracy become glorious in spiritual degrees even as it has aspired to material degrees, and render this just government victorious. Confirm this revered nation to upraise the standard of the oneness of humanity, to promulgate the Most Great Peace, to become thereby most glorious and praiseworthy among all the nations of the world. O God! This American nation is worthy of Thy favors and is deserving of Thy mercy. Make it precious and near to Thee through Thy bounty and bestowal.

THE SCRIPTURE OF THE CHURCH OF JESUS CHRIST OF LATTER-DAY SAINTS

Joseph Smith's Story*

This autobiographical account tells of Joseph Smith's first vision and angelic visitation, discovery of the Book of Mormon, *and the founding of the church. As the first paragraph indicates, the experience of his vision and conversion was the most contentious point with his opponents, and it continues to be so today.[4]*

Owing to the many reports which have been put in circulation by evil-disposed and designing persons, in relation to the rise and progress of the Church of Jesus Christ of Latter-day Saints, all of which have been designed by the authors thereof to militate against its character as a Church and its progress in the world—I have been induced to write this history, to disabuse the public mind, and put all inquirers after truth in possession of the facts, as they have transpired, in relation both to myself and the Church, so far as I have such facts in my possession. In this history I shall present the various events in relation to this Church, in truth and righteousness, as they have transpired, or as they at present exist, being now [1838] the eighth year since the organization of the said Church.

I was born in the year of our Lord 1805, on the twenty-third day of December, in the town of Sharon, Windsor county, State of Vermont. . . . My father, Joseph Smith, Senior, left the State of Vermont, and moved to Palmyra, in the State of New York, when I was in my tenth year, or thereabouts. In about four years after my father's arrival in Palmyra, he moved with his family into Manchester in the same county of Ontario. . . . [5] Some time in the second year after our removal to Manchester, there was in the place where we lived an unusual excitement on the subject of religion. It commenced with the Methodists, but soon became general

---

*Pearl of Great Price, "Joseph Smith—History 1" 1–22, 25–35, 40–47, 51–54, 59–62, 67–74)

[4]All excerpts from Mormon scriptures are from "The Scriptures—Internet Edition" (http://www.scriptures.lds.org). Copyright © 2000 by Intellectual Reserve, Inc. All rights reserved. Used by permission.

among all the sects in that region of country. Indeed, the whole district of country seemed affected by it, and great multitudes united themselves to the different religious parties, which created no small stir and division amongst the people, some crying, "Lo, here!" and others, "Lo, there!" Some were contending for the Methodist faith, some for the Presbyterian, and some for the Baptist. . . .

I was at this time in my fifteenth year. My father's family was proselyted to the Presbyterian faith, and four of them joined that church, namely, my mother, Lucy; my brothers Hyrum and Samuel Harrison; and my sister Sophronia. During this time of great excitement my mind was called up to serious reflection and great uneasiness; but though my feelings were deep and often poignant, still I kept myself aloof from all these parties, though I attended their several meetings as often as occasion would permit. In process of time my mind became somewhat partial to the Methodist sect, and I felt some desire to be united with them; but so great were the confusion and strife among the different denominations, that it was impossible for a person young as I was, and so unacquainted with men and things, to come to any certain conclusion who was right and who was wrong. . . . [10] In the midst of this war of words and tumult of opinions, I often said to myself: What is to be done? Who of all these parties are right; or, are they all wrong together? If any one of them be right, which is it, and how shall I know it? . . .

So, in accordance with this, my determination to ask of God, I retired to the woods to make the attempt. It was on the morning of a beautiful, clear day, early in the spring of eighteen hundred and twenty. It was the first time in my life that I had made such an attempt, for amidst all my anxieties I had never as yet made the attempt to pray vocally. [15] After I had retired to the place where I had previously designed to go, having looked around me, and finding myself alone, I kneeled down and began to offer up the desires of my heart to God. I had

scarcely done so, when immediately I was seized upon by some power which entirely overcame me, and had such an astonishing influence over me as to bind my tongue so that I could not speak. Thick darkness gathered around me, and it seemed to me for a time as if I were doomed to sudden destruction. But, exerting all my powers to call upon God to deliver me out of the power of this enemy which had seized upon me, and at the very moment when I was ready to sink into despair and abandon myself to destruction. . . . Just at this moment of great alarm, I saw a pillar of light exactly over my head, above the brightness of the sun, which descended gradually until it fell upon me. It no sooner appeared than I found myself delivered from the enemy which held me bound. When the light rested upon me I saw two Personages, whose brightness and glory defy all description, standing above me in the air. One of them spake unto me, calling me by name and said, pointing to the other—"This is My Beloved Son. Hear Him!"

My object in going to inquire of the Lord was to know which of all the sects was right, that I might know which to join. No sooner, therefore, did I get possession of myself, so as to be able to speak, than I asked the Personages who stood above me in the light, which of all the sects was right (for at this time it had never entered into my heart that all were wrong)— and which I should join. I was answered that I must join none of them, for they were all wrong; and the Personage who addressed me said that all their creeds were an abomination in his sight; that those professors[5] were all corrupt; that: "they draw near to me with their lips, but their hearts are far from me, they teach for doctrines the commandments of men, having a form of godliness, but they deny the power thereof." [20] He again forbade me to join with any of them; and many other things did he say unto me, which I cannot write at this time. When I came to myself again, I found myself

---

[5] *Professors:* people who profess a faith.

lying on my back, looking up into heaven. When the light had departed, I had no strength; but soon recovering in some degree, I went home. And as I leaned up to the fireplace, mother inquired what the matter was. I replied, "Never mind, all is well—I am well enough off." I then said to my mother, "I have learned for myself that Presbyterianism is not true."

It seems as though the adversary was aware, at a very early period of my life, that I was destined to prove a disturber and an annoyer of his kingdom; else why should the powers of darkness combine against me? . . . [M]y telling the story had excited a great deal of prejudice against me among professors of religion, and was the cause of great persecution, which continued to increase; and though I was an obscure boy, only between fourteen and fifteen years of age, and my circumstances in life such as to make a boy of no consequence in the world, yet men of high standing would take notice sufficient to excite the public mind against me, and create a bitter persecution; and this was common among all the sects—all united to persecute me. . . .

[O]n the evening of the twenty-first of September, after I had retired to my bed for the night, I betook myself to prayer and supplication to Almighty God for forgiveness of all my sins and follies, and also for a manifestation to me, that I might know of my state and standing before him; for I had full confidence in obtaining a divine manifestation, as I previously had one. [30] While I was thus in the act of calling upon God, I discovered a light appearing in my room, which continued to increase until the room was lighter than at noonday, when immediately a personage appeared at my bedside, standing in the air, for his feet did not touch the floor. . . . When I first looked upon him, I was afraid; but the fear soon left me. He called me by name, and said unto me that he was a messenger sent from the presence of God to me, and that his name was Moroni; that God had a work for me to do; and that my name should be had for good and evil among all nations, kindreds, and tongues, or that it should be both

good and evil spoken of among all people. He said there was a book deposited, written upon gold plates, giving an account of the former inhabitants of this continent, and the source from whence they sprang. He also said that the fulness of the everlasting Gospel was contained in it, as delivered by the Savior to the ancient inhabitants; [35] Also, that there were two stones in silver bows—and these stones, fastened to a breastplate, constituted what is called the Urim and Thummim[6]—deposited with the plates; and the possession and use of these stones were what constituted "seers" in ancient or former times; and that God had prepared them for the purpose of translating the book. . . . Again, he told me that when I got those plates of which he had spoken—for the time that they should be obtained was not yet fulfilled—I should not show them to any person; neither the breastplate with the Urim an Thummim; only to those to whom I should be commanded to show them; if I did I should be destroyed. While he was conversing with me about the plates, the vision was opened to my mind that I could see the place where the plates were deposited, and that so clearly and distinctly that I knew the place again when I visited it. . . .

[59] At length the time arrived for obtaining the plates, the Urim and Thummim, and the breastplate. On the twenty-second day of September, 1827, having gone as usual at the end of another year to the place where they were deposited, the same heavenly messenger delivered them up to me with this charge: that I should be responsible for them; that if I should let them go carelessly, or through any neglect of mine, I should be cut off; but that if I would use all my endeavors to preserve them, until he, the messenger, should call for them, they should be protected. [60] I soon found out the reason why I had received such strict charges to keep

---

[6] *Urim and Thummim:* a device consulted by the chief priest of ancient Israel to determine God's response to a "yes" or "no" question. The Hebrew scriptures do not specify how the device is used; Joseph Smith here uses it as "seer stones" for translating the *Book of Mormon*.

them safe, and why it was that the messenger had said that when I had done what was required at my hand, he would call for them. For no sooner was it known that I had them, than the most strenuous exertions were used to get them from me. Every stratagem that could be invented was resorted to for that purpose. The persecution became more bitter and severe than before, and multitudes were on the alert continually to get them from me if possible. But by the wisdom of God, they remained safe in my hands, until I had accomplished by them what was required at my hand. When, according to arrangements, the messenger called for them, I delivered them up to him; and he has them in his charge until this day, being the second day of May, 1838. . . .

We still continued the work of translation, when, in the ensuing month (May, 1829), we on a certain day went into the woods to pray and inquire of the Lord respecting baptism for the remission of sins, that we found mentioned in the translation of the plates. While we were thus employed, praying and calling upon the Lord, a messenger from heaven descended in a cloud of light, and having laid his hands upon us, he ordained us, saying: "Upon you my fellow servants, in the name of Messiah, I confer the Priesthood of Aaron, which holds the keys of the ministering of angels, and of the gospel of repentance, and of baptism by immersion for the remission of sins; and this shall never be taken again from the earth until the sons of Levi do offer again an offering unto the Lord in righteousness." [70] He said this Aaronic Priesthood had not the power of laying on hands for the gift of the Holy Ghost, but that this should

be conferred on us hereafter; and he commanded us to go and be baptized, and gave us directions that I should baptize Oliver Cowdery, and that afterwards he should baptize me. Accordingly we went and were baptized. I baptized him first, and afterwards he baptized me—after which I laid my hands upon his head and ordained him to the Aaronic Priesthood, and afterwards he laid his hands on me and ordained me to the same Priesthood—for so we were commanded. The messenger who visited us on this occasion and conferred this Priesthood upon us, said that his name was John, the same that is called John the Baptist in the New Testament, and that he acted under the direction of Peter, James and John, who held the keys of the Priesthood of Melchizedek, which Priesthood, he said, would in due time be conferred on us, and that I should be called the first Elder of the Church, and he (Oliver Cowdery) the second. It was on the fifteenth day of May, 1829, that we were ordained under the hand of this messenger, and baptized. Immediately on our coming up out of the water afer we had been baptized, we experienced great and glorious blessings from our Heavenly Father. . . .

Our minds being now enlightened, we began to have the scriptures laid open to our understandings, and the true meaning and intention of their more mysterious passages revealed unto us in a manner which we never could attain to previously, nor ever before had thought of. In the meantime we were forced to keep secret the circumstances of having received the Priesthood and our having been baptized, owing to a spirit of persecution which had already manifested itself in the neighborhood.

The First Description of the *Book of Mormon**

The original title page of the Book of Mormon *(1830) has been printed in every succeeding edition. Written by Joseph Smith, Jr., the title page serves as an apt description of the* Book of Mor-

mon's contents. The original punctuation, replete with dashes, and capitalization, is presented here.

---

* *Book of Mormon*, original title page

THE BOOK OF MORMON, AN ACCOUNT WRITTEN BY THE HAND OF MORMON

UPON PLATES TAKEN FROM THE PLATES OF NEPHI

Wherefore, it is an abridgment of the record of the people of Nephi, and also of the Lamanites —Written to the Lamanites, who are a remnant of the house of Israel; and also to Jew and Gentile—Written by way of commandment, and also by the spirit of prophecy and of revelation —Written and sealed up, and hid up unto the Lord, that they might not be destroyed—To come forth by the gift and power of God unto the interpretation thereof—Sealed by the hand of Moroni, and hid up unto the Lord, to come forth in due time by way of the Gentile—The interpretation thereof by the gift of God.

An abridgment taken from the Book of Ether also, which is a record of the people of Jared, who were scattered at the time the Lord confounded the language of the people, when they were building a tower to get to heaven—Which is to show unto the remnant of the House of Israel what great things the Lord hath done for their fathers; and that they may know the covenants of the Lord, that they are not cast off forever—And also to the convincing of the Jew and Gentile that JESUS is the CHRIST, the ETERNAL GOD, manifesting himself unto all nations—And now, if there are faults they are the mistakes of men; wherefore, condemn not the things of God, that ye may be found spotless at the judgment-seat of Christ.

TRANSLATED BY JOSEPH SMITH, JUNIOR.

The Coming of Jesus Christ in 34 C.E. to the New World*

This reading tells the story of the appearance of Jesus Christ after his resurrection to Americans descended from Israelite settlers. In this account, Jesus uses this appearance to teach the rudiments of true faith.

And now it came to pass that there were a great multitude gathered together, of the people of Nephi, round about the temple which was in the land Bountiful; and they were marveling and wondering one with another, and were showing one to another the great and marvelous change which had taken place. And they were also conversing about this Jesus Christ, of whom the sign had been given concerning his death. And it came to pass that while they were thus conversing one with another, they heard a voice as if it came out of heaven; and they cast their eyes round about, for they understood not the voice which they heard; and it was not a harsh voice, neither was it a loud voice; nevertheless, and notwithstanding it being a small voice it did pierce them that did hear to the center, insomuch that there was no part of their frame that it did not cause to quake; yea, it did pierce them to the very soul, and did cause their hearts to burn. And it came to pass that again they heard the voice, and they understood it not.

[5] And again the third time they did hear the voice, and did open their ears to hear it; and their eyes were towards the sound thereof; and they did look steadfastly towards heaven, from whence the sound came. And behold, the third time they did understand the voice which they heard; and it said unto them: "Behold my Beloved Son, in whom I am well pleased, in whom I have glorified my name—hear ye him." And it came to pass, as they understood they cast their eyes up again towards heaven; and behold, they saw a Man descending out of heaven; and he was clothed in a white robe; and he came down and stood in the midst of them; and the eyes of the whole multitude were turned upon him, and they durst not open their mouths, even one to another, and wist not what it meant, for they thought it was an angel that had appeared unto them. And it came to pass

---

* *Book of Mormon,* "3 Nephi" 11.1–41; 18.36–39

that he stretched forth his hand and spake unto the people, saying: [10] "Behold, I am Jesus Christ, whom the prophets testified shall come into the world. And behold, I am the light and the life of the world; and I have drunk out of that bitter cup which the Father hath given me, and have glorified the Father in taking upon me the sins of the world, in the which I have suffered the will of the Father in all things from the beginning." And it came to pass that when Jesus had spoken these words the whole multitude fell to the earth; for they remembered that it had been prophesied among them that Christ should show himself unto them after his ascension into heaven. . . .

[31] "Behold, verily, verily, I say unto you, I will declare unto you my doctrine. And this is my doctrine, and it is the doctrine which the Father hath given unto me; and I bear record of the Father, and the Father beareth record of me, and the Holy Ghost beareth record of the Father and me; and I bear record that the Father commandeth all men, everywhere, to repent and believe in me. And whoso believeth in me, and is baptized, the same shall be saved; and they are they who shall inherit the kingdom of God. And whoso believeth not in me, and is not baptized, shall be damned. [35] Verily, verily, I say unto you, that this is my doctrine, and I bear record of it from the Father; and whoso believeth in me believeth in the Father also; and unto him will the Father bear record of me, for he will visit him with fire and with the Holy Ghost. And thus will the Father bear record of me, and the Holy Ghost will bear record unto him of the Father and me; for the Father, and I, and the Holy Ghost are one. And again I say unto you, ye must repent, and become as a little child, and be baptized in my name, or ye can in nowise receive these things. . . . Therefore, go forth unto this people, and declare the words which I have spoken, unto the ends of the earth." . . .

Destruction of the Nephites and Burial of the Golden Plates*

The Book of Mormon *relates how the tribe of Nephites was destroyed in warfare in 385 C.E. by their enemies the Lamanites. Approximately twenty years later, the prophet Moroni, Mormon's son, buried the golden plates of scripture in the Hill Cumorah, outside of what is now Palmyra in upstate New York.*

Now I finish my record concerning the destruction of my people, the Nephites. And it came to pass that we did march forth before the Lamanites. And I, Mormon, wrote an epistle unto the king of the Lamanites, and desired of him that he would grant unto us that we might gather together our people unto the land of Cumorah, by a hill which was called Cumorah, and there we could give them battle. And it came to pass that the king of the Lamanites did grant unto me the thing which I desired. . . .

[6] And it came to pass that when we had gathered in all our people in one to the land of Cumorah, behold I, Mormon, began to be old; and knowing it to be the last struggle of my people, and having been commanded of the Lord that I should not suffer the records which had been handed down by our fathers, which were sacred, to fall into the hands of the Lamanites, (for the Lamanites would destroy them) therefore I made this record out of the plates of Nephi, and hid up in the hill Cumorah all the records which had been entrusted to me by the hand of the Lord, save it were these few plates which I gave unto my son Moroni. And it came to pass that my people, with their wives and their children, did now behold the armies of the Lamanites marching towards them; and with that awful fear of death which fills the breasts of all the wicked, did they await to receive them.

And it came to pass that they came to battle against us, and every soul was filled with terror because of the greatness of their numbers. And it came to pass that they did fall upon my people with the sword, and with the bow, and with the

* *Book of Mormon,* "Mormon" 6:1–3, 6–11, 16–22

arrow, and with the ax, and with all manner of weapons of war. [10] And it came to pass that my men were hewn down, yea, even my ten thousand who were with me, and I fell wounded in the midst; and they passed by me that they did not put an end to my life.

And when they had gone through and hewn down all my people save it were twenty and four of us, (among whom was my son Moroni) and we having survived the dead of our people, did behold on the morrow, when the Lamanites had returned unto their camps, from the top of the hill Cumorah, the ten thousand of my people who were hewn down, being led in the front by me. . . .

And my soul was rent with anguish, because of the slaying of my people, and I cried: "O ye fair ones, how could ye have departed from the ways of the Lord! O ye fair ones, how could ye have rejected that Jesus, who stood with open arms to receive you! Behold, if ye had not done this, ye would not have fallen. But behold, ye are fallen, and I mourn your loss. O ye fair sons and daughters, ye fathers and mothers, ye husbands and wives, ye fair ones, how is it that ye could have fallen! [20] But behold, ye are gone, and my sorrows cannot bring your return. And the day soon cometh that your mortal body must put on immortality, and these bodies which are now moldering in corruption must soon become incorruptible bodies; and then ye must stand before the judgment-seat of Christ, to be judged according to your works; and if it so be that ye are righteous, then are ye blessed with your fathers who have gone before you. O that ye had repented before this great destruction had come upon you. But behold, ye are gone, and the Father, yea, the Eternal Father of heaven, knoweth your state; and he doeth with you according to his justice and mercy."

Preparations for the Trek to Utah*

The following account outlines some of the well-planned provisions, both physical and spiritual, for the Latter-day Saints' trek in 1847–48 from Missouri to the Great Salt Lake basin of northern Utah. After years of persecution in New York, Ohio, Illinois, and Missouri, church leaders wanted to move to a location that was promising enough to support their growing community, but not so promising as to attract non-Latter-day Saint settlers. The trek was planned and led by Brigham Young, who succeeded the martyred Joseph Smith.

The Word and Will of the Lord concerning the Camp of Israel in their journeys to the West: Let all the people of the Church of Jesus Christ of Latter-day Saints, and those who journey with them, be organized into companies, with a covenant and promise to keep all the commandments and statutes of the Lord our God. Let the companies be organized with captains of hundreds, captains of fifties, and captains of tens, with a president and his two counselors at their head, under the direction of the Twelve Apostles. And this shall be our covenant—that we will walk in all the ordinances of the Lord.

[5] Let each company provide themselves with all the teams, wagons, provisions, clothing, and other necessaries for the journey, that they can. When the companies are organized let them go to with their might, to prepare for those who are to tarry. Let each company, with their captains and presidents, decide how many can go next spring; then choose out a sufficient number of able-bodied and expert men, to take teams, seeds, and farming utensils, to go as pioneers to prepare for putting in spring crops. Let each company bear an equal proportion, according to the dividend of their property, in taking the poor, the widows, the fatherless, and the families of those who have gone into the army, that the cries of the widow and the fatherless come not up into the ears of the Lord against this people. Let each company prepare houses,

---

*Doctrine and Covenants, 136.1–11, 17–24, 30–42

and fields for raising grain, for those who are to remain behind this season; and this is the will of the Lord concerning his people.

[10] Let every man use all his influence and property to remove this people to the place where the Lord shall locate a stake of Zion. And if ye do this with a pure heart, in all faithfulness, ye shall be blessed; you shall be blessed in your flocks, and in your herds, and in your fields, and in your houses, and in your families. . . . [17] Go thy way and do as I have told you, and fear not thine enemies; for they shall not have power to stop my work. Zion shall be redeemed in mine own due time. And if any man shall seek to build up himself, and seeketh not my counsel, he shall have no power, and his folly shall be made manifest.

[20] Seek ye; and keep all your pledges one with another; and covet not that which is thy brother's. Keep yourselves from evil to take the name of the Lord in vain, for I am the Lord your God, even the God of your fathers, the God of Abraham and of Isaac and of Jacob. I am he who led the children of Israel out of the land of Egypt; and my arm is stretched out in the last days, to save my people Israel. Cease to contend one with another; cease to speak evil one of another. Cease drunkenness; and let your words tend to edifying one another. . . . [30] Fear not thine enemies, for they are in mine hands and I will do my pleasure with them. My people must be tried in all things, that they may be prepared to receive the glory that I have for them, even the glory of Zion; and he that will not bear chastisement is not worthy of my kingdom.

Let him that is ignorant learn wisdom by humbling himself and calling upon the Lord his God, that his eyes may be opened that he may see, and his ears opened that he may hear; for my Spirit is sent forth into the world to enlighten the humble and contrite, and to the condemnation of the ungodly. Thy brethren have rejected you and your testimony, even the nation that has driven you out; [35] And now cometh the day of their calamity, even the days of sorrow, like a woman that is taken in travail; and their sorrow shall be great unless they speedily repent, yea, very speedily. For they killed the prophets, and them that were sent unto them; and they have shed innocent blood, which crieth from the ground against them. Therefore, marvel not at these things, for ye are not yet pure; ye can not yet bear my glory; but ye shall behold it if ye are faithful in keeping all my words that I have given you, from the days of Adam to Abraham, from Abraham to Moses, from Moses to Jesus and his apostles, and from Jesus and his apostles to Joseph Smith, whom I did call upon by mine angels, my ministering servants, and by mine own voice out of the heavens, to bring forth my work; which foundation he did lay, and was faithful; and I took him to myself. Many have marveled because of his death; but it was needful that he should seal his testimony with his blood, that he might be honored and the wicked might be condemned.

[40] Have I not delivered you from your enemies, only in that I have left a witness of my name? Now, therefore, hearken, O ye people of my church; and ye elders listen together; you have received my kingdom. Be diligent in keeping all my commandments, lest judgments come upon you, and your faith fail you, and your enemies triumph over you. So no more at present. Amen and Amen.

The Essence of Latter-day Saint Teaching*

This short statement, written and signed by Joseph Smith, shows in its main points how Latter-day Saint teaching both agrees with, and departs from, mainstream Christian teaching. Note how point 11 asserts the right to practice the faith as its believers see fit, but point 12 asserts the duty to be obedient to the nation.

1. We believe in God, the Eternal Father, and in His Son, Jesus Christ, and in the Holy Ghost.

---

* *Pearl of Great Price,* "Articles of Faith" 1–13

2. We believe that men will be punished for their own sins, and not for Adam's transgression.

3. We believe that through the Atonement of Christ, all mankind may be saved, by obedience to the laws and ordinances of the Gospel.

4. We believe that the first principles and ordinances of the Gospel are: first, Faith in the Lord Jesus Christ; second, Repentance; third, Baptism by immersion for the remission of sins; fourth, Laying on of hands for the gift of the Holy Ghost.

5. We believe that a man must be called of God, by prophecy, and by the laying on of hands by those who are in authority, to preach the Gospel and administer in the ordinances thereof.

6. We believe in the same organization that existed in the Primitive Church, namely, apostles, prophets, pastors, teachers, evangelists, and so forth.

7. We believe in the gift of tongues, prophecy, revelation, visions, healing, interpretation of tongues, and so forth.

8. We believe the Bible to be the word of God as far as it is translated correctly; we also believe the Book of Mormon to be the word of God.

9. We believe all that God has revealed, all that He does now reveal, and we believe that He will yet reveal many great and important things pertaining to the Kingdom of God.

10. We believe in the literal gathering of Israel and in the restoration of the Ten Tribes; that Zion (the New Jerusalem) will be built upon the American continent; that Christ will reign personally upon the earth; and, that the earth will be renewed and receive its paradisiacal glory.

11. We claim the privilege of worshiping Almighty God according to the dictates of our own conscience, and allow all men the same privilege, let them worship how, where, or what they may.

12. We believe in being subject to kings, presidents, rulers, and magistrates, in obeying, honoring, and sustaining the law.

13. We believe in being honest, true, chaste, benevolent, virtuous, and in doing good to all men. . . . If there is anything virtuous, lovely, or of good report or praiseworthy, we seek after these things.

Church Pronouncements on Polygamy and Admission of Men of African Descent to the Priesthood*

In the earlier history of the Latter-day Saint church, one of the most controversial practices was polygamy, a practice that still continues among some splinter groups in Utah. In the middle of the twentieth century, especially as the church grew in the developing world, its prohibition on admitting Africans and men of African descent to the priesthood became controversial. The first "official declaration" of 1890, which reasserts the church's official disavowal of polygamy even as it admits that it is still occurring to some degree, is accompanied by an anguished letter on this change by the church's president, Wilford Woodruff. The second official declaration, a 1978 open letter to the church from Spencer Kimball, N. Eldon Tanner, and Marion G. Romney, opens the priesthood to Africans and men of African descent. These revisions of the teaching of the church are based on revelations to the church presidents of the time.

[OFFICIAL DECLARATION 1, 1890] Press dispatches having been sent for political purposes, from Salt Lake City, which have been widely published, to the effect that the Utah Commission, in their recent report to the Secretary of the Interior, allege that plural marriages

---

* *Doctrine and Covenants,* "Official Declarations" 1, 2

are still being solemnized and that forty or more such marriages have been contracted in Utah since last June or during the past year, also that in public discourses the leaders of the Church have taught, encouraged and urged the continuance of the practice of polygamy—

I, therefore, as President of the Church of Jesus Christ of Latter-day Saints, do hereby, in the most solemn manner, declare that these charges are false. We are not teaching polygamy or plural marriage, nor permitting any person to enter into its practice, and I deny that either forty or any other number of plural marriages have during that period been solemnized in our Temples or in any other place in the Territory. One case has been reported, in which the parties allege that the marriage was performed in the Endowment House, in Salt Lake City, in the Spring of 1889, but I have not been able to learn who performed the ceremony; whatever was done in this matter was without my knowledge. In consequence of this alleged occurrence the Endowment House was, by my instructions, taken down without delay.

Inasmuch as laws have been enacted by Congress forbidding plural marriages, which laws have been pronounced constitutional by the court of last resort, I hereby declare my intention to submit to those laws, and to use my influence with the members of the Church over which I preside to have them do likewise.

There is nothing in my teachings to the Church or in those of my associates, during the time specified, which can be reasonably construed to inculcate or encourage polygamy; and when any Elder of the Church has used language which appeared to convey any such teaching, he has been promptly reproved. And I now publicly declare that my advice to the Latter-day Saints is to refrain from contracting any marriage forbidden by the law of the land.

WILFORD WOODRUFF
President of the Church of Jesus Christ of Latter-day Saints

[Excerpts from three addresses by President Wilford Woodruff Regarding the Manifesto]

The question is this: Which is the wisest course for the Latter-day Saints to pursue—to continue to attempt to practice plural marriage, with the laws of the nation against it and the opposition of sixty millions of people, and at the cost of the confiscation and loss of all the Temples, and the stopping of all the ordinances therein, both for the living and the dead, and the imprisonment of the First Presidency and Twelve and the heads of families in the Church, and the confiscation of personal property of the people (all of which of themselves would stop the practice); or, after doing and suffering what we have through our adherence to this principle to cease the practice and submit to the law, and through doing so leave the Prophets, Apostles and fathers at home, so that they can instruct the people and attend to the duties of the Church, and also leave the Temples in the hands of the Saints, so that they can attend to the ordinances of the Gospel, both for the living and the dead?

The Lord showed me by vision and revelation exactly what would take place if we did not stop this practice. If we had not stopped it . . . all ordinances would be stopped throughout the land of Zion.[7] Confusion would reign throughout Israel, and many men would be made prisoners. This trouble would have come upon the whole Church, and we should have been compelled to stop the practice. Now, the question is, whether it should be stopped in this manner, or in the way the Lord has manifested to us, and leave our Prophets and Apostles and fathers free men, and the temples in the hands of the people, so that the dead may be redeemed. A large number has already been delivered from the prison house in the spirit world by this people,[8] and shall the work go on or stop? . . . I say to you that that is exactly the condition we as a people would have been in had we not taken the course we have. . . . .

---

[7] *Land of Zion . . . Israel:* Latter-day Saint territory in Utah, and Latter-day Saints, respectively.
[8] *A large number . . . people:* a reference to baptism for the dead, allowing them entrance into heaven.

I saw exactly what would come to pass if there was not something done. I have had this spirit upon me for a long time. But I want to say this: I should have let all the temples go out of our hands; I should have gone to prison myself, and let every other man go there, had not the God of heaven commanded me to do what I did do; and when the hour came that I was commanded to do that, it was all clear to me. I went before the Lord, and I wrote what the Lord told me to write. . . . I leave this with you, for you to contemplate and consider. The Lord is at work with us.

[Official Declaration 2; June 8, 1978] To all general and local priesthood officers of The Church of Jesus Christ of Latter-day Saints throughout the world:

As we have witnessed the expansion of the work of the Lord over the earth, we have been grateful that people of many nations have responded to the message of the restored gospel, and have joined the Church in ever-increasing numbers. This, in turn, has inspired us with a desire to extend to every worthy member of the Church all of the privileges and blessings which the gospel affords.

Aware of the promises made by the prophets and presidents of the Church who have preceded us that at some time, in God's eternal plan, all of our brethren who are worthy may receive the priesthood, and witnessing the faithfulness of those from whom the priesthood has been withheld, we have pleaded long and earnestly in behalf of these, our faithful brethren, spending many hours in the Upper Room of the Temple supplicating the Lord for divine guidance.

He has heard our prayers, and by revelation has confirmed that the long-promised day has come when every faithful, worthy man in the Church may receive the holy priesthood, with power to exercise its divine authority, and enjoy with his loved ones every blessing that flows therefrom, including the blessings of the temple. Accordingly, all worthy male members of the Church may be ordained to the priesthood without regard for race or color. Priesthood leaders are instructed to follow the policy of carefully interviewing all candidates for ordination to either the Aaronic or the Melchizedek Priesthood to insure that they meet the established standards for worthiness.

We declare with soberness that the Lord has now made known his will for the blessing of all his children throughout the earth who will hearken to the voice of his authorized servants, and prepare themselves to receive every blessing of the gospel.

THE SCRIPTURE OF CHRISTIAN SCIENCE

Introduction to Christian Science Scripture and to the Work of Mary Baker Eddy*

This selection is Mary Baker Eddy's own autobiographical introduction to her main book. It also details the origin and development of this book,[9] which shows a common feature of scripture in the new religious movements: their writing usually accompanies its founding.

To those leaning on the sustaining infinite, today is big with blessings. . . . The time for thinkers has come. Truth, independent of doctrines and time-honored systems, knocks at the portal of humanity. . . .

Since the author's discovery of the might of Truth in the treatment of disease as well as of

---

Science and Health with Key to the Scriptures, Preface
[9]All excerpts from *Science and Health with Key to the Scriptures* are taken from its 1917 edition (Boston: A. V. Stewart), which has the same wording and pagination as the current edition.

sin, her system has been fully tested and has not been found wanting; but to reach the heights of Christian Science, man must live in obedience to its divine Principle. To develop the full might of this Science, the discords of corporeal sense must yield to the harmony of spiritual sense, even as the science of music corrects false tones and gives sweet concord to sound. Theology and physics teach that both Spirit and matter are real and good, whereas the fact is that Spirit is good and real, and matter is Spirit's opposite. The question, What is Truth, is answered by demonstration, by healing both disease and sin; and this demonstration shows that Christian healing confers the most health and makes the best men. On this basis Christian Science will have a fair fight. Sickness has been combated for centuries by doctors using material remedies; but the question arises, Is there less sickness because of these practitioners? A vigorous "No" is the response. . . .

As early as 1862 [the author] began to write down and give to friends the results of her Scriptural study, for the Bible was her sole teacher; but these compositions were crude, the first steps of a child in the newly discovered world of Spirit. She also began to jot down her thoughts on the main subject, but these jottings were only infantile lispings of Truth. A child drinks in the outward world through the eyes and rejoices in the draught. He is as sure of the world's existence as he is of his own; yet he cannot describe the world. He finds a few words, and with these he stammeringly attempts to convey his feeling. Later, the tongue voices the more definite thought, though still imperfectly. So was it with the author. . . . Today, though rejoicing in some progress, she still finds herself a willing disciple at the heavenly gate, waiting for the Mind of Christ. . . .

Before writing this work, *Science and Health,* she made copious notes of Scriptural exposition, which have never been published. This was during the years 1867 and 1868. These efforts show her comparative ignorance of the stupendous life-problem up to that time, and the degrees by which she came at length to its solu-

tion. She values them as a parent may treasure the memorials of a child's growth, and she would not have them changed. The first edition of *Science and Health* was published in 1875. . . .

The divine Principle of healing is proved in the personal experience of any sincere seeker of Truth. Its purpose is good, and its practice is safer and more potent than that of any other sanitary method. The unbiased Christian thought is soonest touched by Truth, and convinced of it. . . . Many imagine that the phenomena of physical healing in Christian Science present only a phase of the action of the human mind, which action in some unexplained way results in the cure of disease. On the contrary, Christian Science rationally explains that all other pathological methods are the fruits of human faith in matter, faith in the workings, not of Spirit, but of the fleshly mind which must yield to Science. The physical healing of Christian Science results now, as in Jesus' time, from the operation of divine Principle, before which sin and disease lose their reality in human consciousness and disappear as naturally and as necessarily as darkness gives place to light and sin to reformation. Now, as then, these mighty works are not supernatural, but supremely natural. They are the sign of Immanuel, or "God with us," a divine influence ever present in human consciousness. . . .

When God called the author to proclaim His Gospel to this age, there came also the charge to plant and water His vineyard. The first school of Christian Science Mind-healing was started by the author with only one student in Lynn, Massachusetts, about the year 1867. In 1881, she opened the Massachusetts Metaphysical College in Boston, under the seal of the Commonwealth, a law relative to colleges having been passed, which enabled her to get this institution chartered for medical purposes. . . . During seven years over four thousand students were taught by the author in this College. Meanwhile she was pastor of the first established Church of Christ, Scientist; President of the first Christian Scientist Association, convening monthly; publisher of her own works; and (for a portion of this time) sole editor and publisher of the *Christian Science Journal,* the first periodical issued by Christian Scientists. She closed her College, October 29, 1889, in the height of its prosperity with a deep-lying conviction that the next two years of her life should be given to the preparation of the revision of *Science and Health,* which was published in 1891. She retained her charter and, as its President,

reopened the College in 1899 as auxiliary to her church. Until June 10, 1907, she had never read this book throughout consecutively in order to elucidate her idealism.

In the spirit of Christ's charity, as one who "hopeth all things, endureth all things," and is joyful to bear consolation to the sorrowing and healing to the sick, she commits these pages to honest seekers for Truth.

The Essence of Christian Science Teaching*

The "Recapitulation" (ending summary) of Sci-ence and Health gives the main points of Chris-tian Science teaching in very brief form. Note how the main doctrines of mainstream Protestant Christianity at the end of the nineteenth century are recast in Christian Science.

The following is a brief exposition of the important points, or religious tenets, of Chris-tian Science:

1. As adherents of Truth, we take the inspired Word of the Bible as our sufficient guide to eternal Life.

2. We acknowledge and adore one supreme and infinite God. We acknowledge His Son, one Christ; the Holy Ghost or divine Com-forter; and man in God's image and likeness.

3. We acknowledge God's forgiveness of sin in the destruction of sin and the spiritual

understanding that casts out evil as unreal. But the belief in sin is punished so long as the belief lasts.

4. We acknowledge Jesus' atonement as the evidence of divine, efficacious Love, unfolding man's unity with God through Christ Jesus the Way-shower; and we acknowledge that man is saved through Christ, through Truth, Life, and Love as demonstrated by the Galilean Prophet in healing the sick and overcoming sin and death.

5. We acknowledge that the crucifixion of Jesus and his resurrection served to uplift faith to understand eternal Life, even the allness of Soul, Spirit, and the nothingness of matter.

6. And we solemnly promise to watch, and pray for that Mind to be in us which was also in Christ Jesus; to do unto others as we would have them do unto us; and to be merciful, just, and pure.

*Science and Health with Key to the Scriptures, "Recapitula-tion"

Prayer and Its Role**

Prayer and meditation are the chief religious activity in Christian Science, and its main method of healing sickness of body and mind. Here Mary Baker Eddy gives her interpretation of the

Lord's Prayer ("Our Father") in accordance with Christian Science teachings.

Our Master taught his disciples one brief prayer, which we name after him the Lord's Prayer. Our Master said, "After this manner therefore pray ye," and then he gave that prayer which covers

**Science and Health with Key to the Scriptures, "Prayer"

all human needs. There is indeed some doubt among Bible scholars, whether the last line is not an addition to the prayer by a later copyist; but this does not affect the meaning of the prayer itself. In the phrase, "Deliver us from evil," the original properly reads, "Deliver us from the evil one." This reading strengthens our scientific apprehension of the petition, for Christian Science teaches us that "the evil one," or one evil, is but another name for the first lie and all liars. Only as we rise above all material sensuousness and sin, can we reach the heaven-born aspiration and spiritual consciousness, which is indicated in the Lord's Prayer and which instantaneously heals the sick. Here let me give what I understand to be the spiritual sense of the Lord's Prayer.

Our Father which art in heaven, *Our Father-Mother God, all-harmonious,* Hallowed be Thy name. *Adorable One.* Thy kingdom come. *Thy kingdom is come; Thou art ever-present.* Thy will be done in earth, as it is in heaven. *Enable us to know,—as in heaven, so on earth,—God is omnipotent, supreme.* Give us this day our daily bread; *Give us grace for to-day; feed the famished affections;* And forgive us our debts, as we forgive our debtors. *And Love is reflected in love;* And lead us not into temptation, but deliver us from evil; *And God leadeth us not into temptation, but delivereth us from sin, disease, and death.* For Thine is the kingdom, and the power, and the glory, forever. *For God is infinite, all power, all Life, Truth, Love, over all, and All.*

Healing Practices*

The healing practices of the church are based on prayer and meditation that recognize that only the spiritual is good, and the material is evil and illusory. Such prayer and meditation lead to fulness of spiritual insight and goodness. The topics that open each paragraph are in the original.

Bodily presence: If we are sensibly with the body and regard omnipotence as a corporeal, material person, whose ear we would gain, we are not "absent from the body" and "present with the Lord" in the demonstration of Spirit. We cannot "serve two masters." To be present with the Lord is to have, not mere emotional ecstasy or faith, but the actual demonstration and understanding of Life as revealed in Christian Science. To be "with the Lord" is to be in obedience to the law of God, to be absolutely governed by divine Love—by Spirit, not by matter.

Spiritualized consciousness: Become conscious for a single moment that Life and intelligence are purely spiritual,—neither in nor of matter,—and the body will then utter no complaints. If suffering from a belief in sickness, you will find yourself suddenly well. Sorrow is turned into joy when the body is controlled by spiritual Life, Truth, and Love. . . . The Lord's Prayer is the prayer of Soul, not of material sense. Entirely separate from the belief and dream of material living, is the Life divine, revealing spiritual understanding and the consciousness of man's dominion over the whole earth. . . .

Spiritual sanctuary: The Father in secret is unseen to the physical senses, but He knows all things and rewards according to motives, not according to speech. To enter into the heart of prayer, the door of the erring senses must be closed. Lips must be mute and materialism silent, that man may have audience with Spirit, the divine Principle, Love, which destroys all error.

Science and Health with Key to the Scriptures, "Christian Science Practice"

Effectual invocation: In order to pray aright, we must enter into the closet and shut the door. We must close the lips and silence the material senses. In the quiet sanctuary of earnest longings, we must deny sin and plead God's allness. We must resolve to take up the cross, and go forth with honest hearts to work and watch for wisdom, Truth, and Love. We must "pray without ceasing." Such prayer is answered, in so far as we put our desires into practice. The Master's injunction is, that we pray in secret and let our lives attest our sincerity.

Trustworthy beneficence: Christians rejoice in secret beauty and bounty, hidden from the world, but known to God. Self-forgetfulness, purity, and affection are constant prayers. Practice not profession, understanding not belief, gain the ear and right hand of omnipotence and they assuredly call down infinite blessings. Trustworthiness is the foundation of enlightened faith. Without a fitness for holiness, we cannot receive holiness.

Loftiest adoration: A great sacrifice of material things must precede this advanced spiritual understanding. The highest prayer is not one of faith merely; it is demonstration. Such prayer heals sickness, and must destroy sin and death.

Interpretation of Genesis 1*

Here Mary Baker Eddy teaches the ultimate unreality of matter, belief in which is the main cause of suffering. Gender is a mental construct, not a reality. Note how she stresses the feminine aspects of God, most unusual for her time.

Genesis 1:1. In the beginning God created the heaven and the earth.

Ideas and identities: The infinite has no beginning. This word "beginning" is employed to signify "the only"—that is, the eternal verity and unity of God and man, including the universe. The creative Principle—Life, Truth, and Love—is God. The universe reflects God. There is but one creator and one creation. This creation consists of the unfolding of spiritual ideas and their identities, which are embraced in the infinite Mind and forever reflected. These ideas range from the infinitesimal to infinity, and the highest ideas are the sons and daughters of God.

Genesis i. 27. So God created man in His own image, in the image of God created He him; male and female created He them.

Ideal man and woman: To emphasize this momentous thought, it is repeated that God made man in His own image, to reflect the divine Spirit. It follows that man is a generic term. Masculine, feminine, and neuter genders are human concepts. In one of the ancient languages the word for "man" is used also as the synonym of "mind." This definition has been weakened by anthropomorphism, or a humanization of Deity. The word "anthropomorphic," in such a phrase as "an anthropomorphic God," is derived from two Greek words, signifying "man" and "form," and may be defined as a mortally mental attempt to reduce Deity to corporeality. The life-giving quality of Mind is Spirit, not matter. The ideal man corresponds to creation, to intelligence, and to Truth. The ideal woman corresponds to Life and to Love. In divine Science, we have not as much authority for considering God masculine, as we have for considering Him feminine, for Love imparts the clearest idea of Deity.

Divine personality: The world believes in many persons; but if God is personal, there is but one person, because there is but one God. His personality can only be reflected, not trans-

---

* *Science and Health with Key to the Scriptures,* "Genesis"

mitted. God has countless ideas, and they all have one Principle and parentage. The only proper symbol of God as person is Mind's infinite ideal. What is this ideal? Who shall behold it? This ideal is God's own image, spiritual and infinite. Even eternity can never reveal the whole of God, since there is no limit to infinitude or to its reflections.

Two Testimonials to Healing*

Testimonies to spiritual healing have been commonplace in Christian Science from the very beginning. These two testimonials, as all the others, relate healing directly to the reading and use of Eddy's Science and Health. *As the first paragraph implies, this section was added to the first editions of* Science and Health *to create the fuller book.*

Thousands of letters could be presented in testimony of the healing efficacy of Christian Science and particularly concerning the vast number of people who have been reformed and healed through the perusal or study of this book. For the assurance and encouragement of the reader, a few of these letters are here republished from *The Christian Science Journal* and *Christian Science Sentinel.* The originals are in the possession of the Editor, who can authenticate the testimonials which follow. . . .

Cancer and Consumption[10] Healed: I was a great sufferer for many years from internal cancer and consumption. I was treated by the best of physicians in New York, Minneapolis, and Duluth, and was finally given up as incurable, when I heard of Christian Science. A neighbor who had been healed of consumption, kindly loaned me *Science and Health* by Mrs. Eddy, which I read and became interested in. In three months' time, I was healed, the truth conveyed to me by this book being the healer, and not only of these diseases, but I was made whole mentally as well. I have not been in bed one day since, or rather in eleven years. I have had many good demonstrations during this time, have passed through many a "fiery trial," but this blessed truth has caused me to stand, at times seemingly alone, and God was with me.

I will mention a demonstration of painless childbirth which I have had since coming to Idaho. Perhaps it may help some sister who is looking through the *Journal* for a demonstration of this kind, as I was before my baby came. Good help being scarce here, I did my housework up to the time I was confined, and was in perfect health. I awoke my husband one morning at five o'clock, and at half past five baby was born, no one being present but my husband and myself. It was quite a surprise to the rest of the family to see me sitting by the fire with a new baby on my lap. My son got the breakfast, of which I ate heartily; at noon I joined the family in the dining-room. I was out on the porch the second day, around the yard the third day, and have been perfectly well ever since, which has been now over three years. To one who had previously passed through agony untold, with a physician in attendance, this seemed wonderful. I hope this will interest some one who is seeking the truth, and I wish to express my sincere love for our beloved Leader, who has given us the *Key to the Scriptures.*—E. C. C., Lewiston, Idaho.

Saved from Insanity and Suicide: A few years ago, while under a sense of darkness and despair caused by ill health and an unhappy home, *Science and Health* was loaned me with a request that I should read it. At that time my daughter was given up by [physicians] to die of lingering consumption, supposed to have been inherited.

Science and Health with Key to the Scriptures, "Fruitage"
[10]*Consumption:* tuberculosis.

My own condition seemed even more alarming, as insanity was being manifested, and rather than go to an insane asylum, it seemed to me the only thing to do was to commit suicide. Heart trouble, kidney complaint, and continual headaches caused from female trouble were some of the many ailments I had to contend with. My doctor tried to persuade me to undergo an operation as a means of relief, but I had submitted to a severe operation ten years previous, and found only additional suffering as a result, so I would not consent.

When I began with *Science and Health*, I read the chapter on "Prayer" first, and at that time did not suppose it possible for me to remember anything I read, but felt a sweet sense of God's protection and power, and a hope that

I should at last find Him to be what I so much needed, a present help in time of trouble. Before that chapter on "Prayer" was finished, my daughter was downstairs eating three meals a day, and daily growing stronger. Before I had finished reading the textbook she was well, but never having heard that the reading of *Science and Health* healed any one, it was several months before I gave God the glory. One by one my many ailments left me, all but the headaches; they were less frequent, until at the end of three years the fear of them was entirely overcome. Neither myself nor my daughter have ever received treatments, but the study of the Bible and *Science and Health*, the Christian Science textbook by Mrs. Eddy, has healed us and keeps us well.—E. J. B., Superior, Wisconsin

THE SCRIPTURE OF THE UNIFICATION CHURCH

Dual Characteristics of the Universe and of Human Beings*

The beginning of Sun Myung Moon's Divine Principle *relates the principles of creation. Dual characteristics are built into everything in the world, reflecting the nature of God. The yin-yang explanation (see earlier, p. 160) shows Moon's concern to combine Christianity and Asian thought, especially in their Korean forms.*[11]

Let us begin by pointing out the common elements which are found universally throughout the natural world. Every entity possesses dual characteristics of *yang* (masculinity) and *yin* (femininity) and comes into existence only when these characteristics have formed reciprocal relationships, both within the entity and between it and other entities. For example, subatomic particles, the basic building blocks of all matter,

possess either a positive charge, a negative charge or a neutral charge formed by the neutralization of positive and negative constituents. When particles join with each other through the reciprocal relationships of their dual characteristics, they form an atom. Atoms, in turn, display either a positive or a negative valence. When the dual characteristics within one atom enter into reciprocal relationships with those in another atom, they form a molecule. Molecules formed in this manner engage in further reciprocal relationships between their dual characteristics to eventually become nourishment fit for consumption by plants and animals.

Plants propagate by means of stamen and pistil. Animals multiply and maintain their species through the relationship between males and females. According to the Bible, after God created Adam, He saw that it was not good for the man to live alone. Only after God created Eve as Adam's female counterpart did He declare that His creations were "very good." Let us take human beings as an example. A human being is composed of an outer form, the body, and an

---

Divine Principle 1.1.1.1

[11] All excerpts from *Divine Principle* are taken from its third edition (New York: HSA-UWC Press, 1996). Copyright © 1996 by the Holy Spirit Association for the Unification of World Christianity. Used by permission.

inner quality, the mind. The body is a visible reflection of the invisible mind. Because the mind possesses a certain structure, the body which reflects it also takes on a particular appearance. This is the idea behind a person's character and destiny being perceived through examining his outward appearance by such methods as physiognomy[12] or palm reading.

---

[12]*Physiognomy:* the study of external physical characteristics to determine the character and/or destiny of an individual.

Here, mind is the internal nature and body is the external form. Mind and body are two correlative aspects of a human being; hence, the body may be understood as a second mind. Together, they constitute the dual characteristics of a human being. Similarly, all beings exist through the reciprocal relationships between their dual characteristics of internal nature and external form.

The Purpose of the Creation of the Universe*

Why did God create the world—or as one modern philosopher has asked in a nonreligious mode, why is there something rather than nothing? Sun Myung Moon states here that God created the universe for God's own enjoyment.

It is recorded in the Bible that after God completed each day of creation, He saw that it was good. This suggests that God wanted His creations to be object partners embodying goodness that He might take delight in them. How can the creation give God the greatest joy?

God created human beings as the final step in creating the universe. He created them in His image, in the likeness of His internal nature and external form, and gave them sensibility to all feelings and emotions because it was His intention to share joy with them. After their creation, God blessed Adam and Eve: Be fruitful and multiply, and fill the earth and subdue it; and have dominion over the fish of the sea and over the birds of the air and over every living thing that moves upon the earth (*Gen.* 1:28). These are the *three great blessings:* to be fruitful (mature and ready to bear fruit), multiply and have dominion over the creation. Had Adam and Eve obeyed this divine mandate and built the Kingdom of Heaven, there is no doubt that

God would have felt the greatest joy as His sons and daughters rejoiced in the world of His ideal.

How can God's three great blessings be fulfilled? They can be realized only when the four position foundation, which is the fundamental foundation of creation, has been established. The three great blessings are fulfilled when the whole creation, including human beings, completes the . . . foundation with God as the center. This is the Kingdom of Heaven, where ultimate goodness is realized and God feels the greatest joy. This is, in fact, the very purpose for which God created the universe.

The ultimate purpose of the universe, with human beings at its center, is to return joy to God. All entities have dual purposes. As was explained earlier, every entity has dual centers of movement, one of internal nature and another of external form. These centers pursue corresponding purposes—for the sake of the whole and for the sake of the individual—whose relationship is the same as that between internal nature and external form. These dual purposes relate to each other as cause and result, internal and external, subject partner and object partner. In God's ideal, there cannot be any individual purpose which does not support the whole purpose, nor can there be any whole purpose that does not guarantee the interests of the individual. The infinite variety of beings in the universe form one vast organic body interwoven by these dual purposes.

Divine Principle 1.1.3.1

The Spiritual Fall and the Physical Fall of Adam and Eve*

Duality of being and action leads to a duality in the human fall. Moon's emphasis on the key role of sexual intercourse in the fall itself (largely unknown in Jewish, Christian, and Islamic traditions) ties into his prescription for the salvation of the world by the propagating of a true, heavenly family on earth.

God created human beings with two components: the spirit self and the physical self. The human Fall likewise took place in two dimensions: the spiritual and the physical. The fall which took place through the sexual relationship between the angel and Eve was the *spiritual fall,* while the fall which occurred through the sexual relationship between Eve and Adam was the *physical fall.* . . .

(The Spiritual Fall:) God created the angelic world and assigned Lucifer (Isaiah 14:12) to the position of archangel. Lucifer was the channel of God's love to the angelic world, just as Abraham was the channel of God's blessing to the Israelites. In this position he virtually monopolized the love of God. However, after God created human beings as His children, He loved them many times more than He had ever loved Lucifer, whom He had created as His servant. In truth, God's love toward Lucifer did not change; it was the same before and after the creation of human beings. . . . Lucifer, feeling as though he were receiving less love than he deserved, wanted to grasp the same central position in human society as he enjoyed in the angelic world, as the channel of God's love. This was why he seduced Eve, and this was the motivation of the spiritual fall.

Everything in the universe is created to be governed by God through love. Thus, love is the source of life, the key to happiness, and the essence of the ideal to which all beings aspire. The more one receives love, the more beautiful one appears to others. When the angel, created as God's servant, beheld Eve, the daughter of God, it was only natural that she looked beautiful in his eyes. Moreover, when Lucifer saw that Eve was responding to his temptation, the angel felt the stimulation of her love to be deliciously enticing. At this point, Lucifer was seducing Eve with the mind to have her, regardless of the consequences. Lucifer, who left his proper position due to his excessive desire, and Eve, who wanted to open her eyes and become like God (*Genesis* 3:5–6) before the time was ripe, formed a common base and began give and take action. The power of the unprincipled love generated by their give and take led them to consummate an illicit sexual relationship on the spiritual plane.

All beings are created based on the principle that when they become one in love, they exchange elements with each other. Accordingly, when Eve became one with Lucifer through love, she received certain elements from him. First, she received feelings of dread arising from the pangs of a guilty conscience, stemming from her violation of the purpose of creation. Second, she received from Lucifer the wisdom which enabled her to discern that her originally intended spouse was to be Adam, not the angel. Eve was in the position to receive wisdom from the Archangel because she was immature and her wisdom was not as seasoned as that of the Archangel, who was already in a state of angelic maturity.

(The Physical Fall:) Perfect Adam and Eve were supposed to have become an eternal husband and wife in God's love. But Eve, who in her immaturity had engaged in the illicit relationship with the Archangel, joined with Adam as husband and wife. Thus, Adam fell when he, too, was still immature. This untimely conjugal relationship in satanic love between Adam and Eve constituted the physical fall. . . . Eve then seduced Adam with the hope that by uniting with him, her intended spouse, she could rid

Divine Principle 1.2.2.1–2

herself of the dread and once again stand before God. This was Eve's motivation which led to the physical fall.

Once Eve had united with the Archangel through their illicit sexual relationship, she stood in the position of the Archangel with respect to Adam. Thus, Adam, who was still receiving God's love, appeared very attractive to her. Seeing Adam as her only hope of returning to God, Eve turned to Adam and tempted him, playing the same role as the Archangel had played when he had tempted her. Adam

responded and formed a common base with Eve, and they began give and take action with each other. The power of the unprincipled love generated in their relationship induced Adam to abandon his original position and brought them together in an illicit physical relationship of sexual love. When Adam united in oneness with Eve, he inherited all the elements Eve had received from the Archangel. These elements in turn have been passed down to all subsequent generations without interruption.

The Restoration of Humanity*

Fallen humans cannot restore the creation to achieve its purpose. Only with a new group of humans, a new human family sprung from True Parents, can the Kingdom of Heaven come about. Note the emphasis on moral perfectionism, often a hallmark of new religious movements.

We dwell in ignorance of history, uncertain about its origin, the direction in which it is heading, and its final destination. Concerning eschatology, or the doctrine of the "Last Days," many Christians believe literally what is written in the Bible. . . . One pertinent question for Christians is whether these events will take place literally or whether the verses are symbolic, as are many parts of the Bible. To address this issue, we should first understand such fundamental matters as the purpose of God's creation, the meaning of the human Fall, and the goal of the providence of restoration.

[1.1] We have discussed how God's purpose in creating human beings was to rejoice with them. Thus, our purpose of existence is to bring joy to God. What must we do to bring joy to God and fully manifest our original value? Created beings other than humans are endowed

with the innate nature to grow to maturity naturally and become object partners which bring God joy. Human beings, on the other hand, can become true and authentic object partners who bring joy to God only through their free will and free actions. . . .

The relationship between God and a person who has attained individual perfection can be compared to that between the mind and the body. The body is the dwelling place of the mind and moves according to the mind's direction. Likewise, God abides within the mind of a fully mature person. Such a person becomes a temple of God and leads his life in harmony with His Will. . . . Living in oneness with God, he acquires a divine nature. Thus, it is impossible for him to commit sin or to fall. A person who has perfected his individual character embodies total goodness and fulfills the purpose of creation. If a person embodying total goodness could fall, this would lead to the illogical conclusion that goodness contains the seed of its own destruction. Moreover, if human beings, who were created by the omnipotent[13] God, could fall even after becoming perfect, we would have reason to doubt the omnipotence of

---

Divine Principle 1.3. Introduction

[13] *Omnipotent:* all-powerful.

God. God is the absolute and eternal Subject. To give Him true joy, His object partner must necessarily also be eternal and absolute. For these reasons, a person who has perfected his individual character can never fall. Had Adam and Eve reached perfection, being thereafter unsusceptible to sin, they would have borne good children and founded a sinless family and society in complete concordance with God's blessings. They would have founded the Kingdom of Heaven, which consists of one great family with the same parents. . . .

Regardless of the purity of the people of this society, if they were living in primitive circumstances like cavemen, this could not be consid-

ered the Kingdom of Heaven which both God and human beings desire. God gave us the mandate to have dominion over all things. Hence, to realize the ideal of creation, people of perfected character should advance science, harness the natural world, and create an extremely pleasant social and living environment. This will be the Kingdom of Heaven on earth. Once people have attained full maturity and enjoyed life in God's earthly Kingdom, then when they shed their physical bodies and pass into the spirit world, they will form the Kingdom of Heaven in heaven. Accordingly, God's primary purpose of creation is to build the Kingdom of Heaven on earth.

Salvation through the Second Messiah, the True Parent*

This short reading presents the essence of the Unification teaching of salvation—through the Second Messiah, the True Parent who will begin a new, perfect human family that will bring in the Kingdom of Heaven.

The *providence of restoration* refers to God's work to restore human beings to our original, unfallen state so that we may fulfill the purpose of creation. As discussed in Part I, human beings fell from the top of the growth stage and have been held under Satan's dominion ever since. To restore human beings, God works to cut off Satan's influence. Yet, as was explained in

Christology, we must have the original sin removed before we can sever Satan's bonds and be restored to the state before the Fall. This is possible only when we are born anew through the Messiah, the True Parent. To explain further: we first need to go through a course to separate Satan from ourselves. We do this in order to restore ourselves in form to the spiritual level which Adam and Eve had reached before the Fall—the top of the growth stage. On this foundation, we are to receive the Messiah and be reborn, and thereby be fully restored to the original state of human beings before the Fall. Finally, by following the Messiah, we should continue our growth to maturity where we can fulfill the purpose of creation.

Divine Principle 2, Introduction

The Advent of the Second Messiah as a Korean**

In Unification thought, which now explicitly identifies Sun Myung Moon as the Second Messiah, this Messiah "returns" by being born as a human. He finishes the work that Jesus began and founds the

Kingdom of Heaven on earth by means of propagating a "True Family." The first part of this reading defends Moon's knowledge of the end times against traditional Christian teaching that it is hidden from human knowledge; the second part advances the idea that when the Second Messiah comes, he will come from Korea.

**Divine Principle* 2.6, Introduction; 2.6.3.2–3

Jesus clearly foretold his return. Yet he added that no one knew of the day and hour of his return, not the angels, not even himself (*Matthew* 24:36). Hence, it has been commonly thought unwise to speculate about the date, place and manner of the Second Advent. Nevertheless, we can deduce from the words of Jesus, "But of that day and hour no one knows . . . but the Father only," and the verse, "Surely the Lord God does nothing, without revealing his secret to his servants the prophets" (*Amos* 3:7) that God, who knows the day and hour, will surely reveal all secrets about the Second Advent to His prophets before He carries out His work. . . .

[2.6.3.2-3] As Jesus explained through the parable of the vineyard, when the Jewish people, like the tenants in the parable who killed the son of their master, led Jesus to the cross, they lost their providential mission. Which nation, then, will inherit the work of God and bear its fruits? The Bible suggests that this nation is in the East.

The Book of Revelation describes the opening of a scroll sealed with seven seals . . . (*Revelation* 5:1–5). The Lion of the tribe of Judah signifies Christ; it is he who will open the seven seals in the Last Days. "After six of the seals are opened: Then I saw another angel ascend from the rising of the sun, with the seal of the living God, and he called with a loud voice . . . saying, 'Do not harm the earth or the sea or the trees, till we have sealed the servants of our God upon their foreheads.' And I heard the number of the sealed, a hundred and forty-four thousand" (*Revelation* 7:2–4). This indicates that the seal of the living God will be placed on the foreheads of the 144,000 in the East, where the sun rises. These chosen ones will accompany the Lamb at his return. We can thus infer that the nation which will inherit the work of God and bear its fruit for the sake of the Second Advent is in the East. There Christ will be born and received by the 144,000 elect of God. Which among the nations of the East is chosen to receive the Lord?

[3.3] Since ancient times, the nations in the East have traditionally been considered to be the three nations of Korea, Japan and China. Among them, Japan throughout its history has worshipped the sun goddess Amaterasu-omikami. Japan entered the period of the Second Advent as a fascist nation and severely persecuted Korean Christians. China at the time of the Second Advent was a hotbed of communism and would become a communist nation. Thus, both nations belonged to Satan's side. Korea, then, is the nation in the East where Christ will return.

THE SCRIPTURE OF THE CHURCH OF SCIENTOLOGY

The Life and Work of L. Ron Hubbard*

This reading outlines the adventurous life of L. Ron Hubbard, the founder of Scientology. It also provides a brief introduction to the early history and thought of the Church of Scientology, including the genesis of its key scriptures. Note how Scientology is based on both Dianetics and further, more religious developments in Hubbard's thought. This passage is attributed to the Church of Scientology International.[14]

Early Years: Son of United States Naval commander Harry Ross and Ledora May Hubbard,

---

* *Scientology: Theology and Practice of a Contemporary Religion*, 7 pp. 87–93

L. Ron Hubbard was born March 13, 1911, in Tilden, Nebraska. Frequent travel was the rule rather than the exception for the military family, and shortly thereafter, the Hubbards settled in Helena, Montana. While there, Mr. Hubbard became friendly with the indigenous Blackfeet, and particularly a tribal medicine man, who was ultimately to honor the young Hubbard with the unique status of blood brother.

With his father's posting to the U.S. naval station on the island of Guam in 1927, L. Ron Hubbard began a period of travel that would consume the next several years. Included were extended voyages throughout the South Pacific and South China Sea and treks across China to western hills. He was later to write of his intense curiosity and this examination of Asian culture, that "my basic interest was the field of religion. Buddhism, Taoism were fascinating to me." As a circumstance of that interest, he was puzzled by the human suffering he found rife amongst those who claimed to practice these Eastern faiths. He soon concluded that his searches would need to go further, and deeper.

He returned to the United States and subsequently enrolled at George Washington University where he studied engineering. As a natural result of the interest that was kindled in Asia, he soon embarked on a search for what he then termed "the Life essence." To that end, he enrolled in one of the nation's first nuclear physics classes where he examined the possibility that life might be explained in terms of small energy particles. "Is it possible," he asked, "that with this new branch of physics we might be able to locate the energy of life?" It opened a small crack in the door, but it was methodology such as this that led him to take a wholly scientific approach to inherently spiritual questions.

Following his stint at George Washington University, he embarked on an international ethnological expedition to the Caribbean and then to Puerto Rico. Returning to the United States in 1933, Mr. Hubbard launched his literary career. His work spanned all genres, and between 1934 and 1950, he was to author

more than 200 novels, stories and screenplays. Mr. Hubbard's literary career was his means to continue his research into what he now spoke of in terms of the "common denominator of life." In the late 1930s, he conducted experiments concerning cellular memory retention and memory transmission to later generations, concluding that some unknown factor was capable of recording and transmitting the memory of a single event from one cellular generation to the next.

Milestones: In 1938, the first summary of these and other findings appeared in his unpublished manuscript, *Excalibur*. The work proposed that the dynamic thrust of all life is the urge to survive. The scope of *Excalibur* was immense and proposed not only the means of placing all life into a definitive framework of survival, but a method of resolving any problems related to existence. Mr. Hubbard chose not to publish it, however, as it did not also offer a workable therapy. . . .

With the outbreak of the Second World War, Mr. Hubbard was commissioned a lieutenant (junior grade) in the United States Navy, and saw service in the Pacific and Atlantic. By early 1945, he was adjudged partially blind from injured optic nerves and lame from hip and back injuries, and admitted to Oak Knoll Naval Hospital in Oakland, California, for treatment. While at Oak Knoll, Mr. Hubbard began his first concerted test of therapeutic techniques he had developed during the course of his research. His subjects were drawn from former prisoners of Japanese internment camps, and particularly those with an inexplicable inability to assimilate protein in spite of hormone treatments. Utilizing an early version of Dianetics, Mr. Hubbard proceeded to determine if there were not some sort of "mental block" inhibiting normal recovery. What he found was that thought did indeed regulate endocrine function and not, as then commonly held, the reverse. Utilizing these same techniques, Mr. Hubbard was eventually able to restore his own health. At war's end Mr. Hubbard embarked upon an intensive testing program and continually refined Dianetics techniques. In essence, those techniques addressed what he defined as the sole source of all psychosomatic ills and mental aberration, or what he termed the reactive mind.

Dianetics Goes Public: The first summary of Mr. Hubbard's finding was informally presented to friends and colleagues in a manuscript entitled *Dianetics: The Original Thesis*. Response was immediate and considerable and eventually Mr. Hubbard was persuaded to write a full-length handbook, showing how Dianetics could be employed. This was published on May 9, 1950, under the title *Dianetics: The Modern Science of Mental Health*. It was an overnight success, and L. Ron Hubbard found himself the subject of immense public demand for personal instruction in Dianetics techniques. Soon, six Dianetics Research Foundations were formed throughout the United States.

Concurrent with his extensive instruction and lecturing, Mr. Hubbard continued his research, and by 1951 he authored his second book on *Dianetics: Science of Survival*. In this book he described in detail the precise nature of the relationship between the fundamental life force—the spirit—and the physical universe. *Science of Survival* also explained how this relationship can lead to unwanted encumbrances of the spirit as well as the means for overcoming these barriers to spiritual freedom.

The Spiritual Essence of Man: As Mr. Hubbard's research continued, he encouraged increasing evidence of man as a wholly spiritual entity with experiences extending well beyond the current lifetime. His research also suggested potential states of existence far beyond those previously envisaged. What followed was the foundation of all that is addressed by Scientology—his definition of that seemingly immortal life-source he eventually termed the **thetan**,[15] a potentially omnipotent and limitless being that was, in fact, the source of life.

Given the inherently religious nature of these discoveries, it was not surprising that those studying Scientology came to see themselves as members of a new religion. Consequently, in 1954, Scientologists established the first Church of Scientology in Los Angeles. With the founding of Scientology, the impact of Mr. Hubbard's work increased internationally, as did his movement. By the mid-1950s, he was regularly traveling between lectures in Europe and instruction at the Founding Church of Washington, D.C. As Executive Director, he also saw to the worldwide administration of Scientology through these years, and drafted the organizational policies that still form the basis of Church Administration.

In 1959, Mr. Hubbard moved to Saint Hill Manor in East Grinstead, Sussex [England], where he established his home and continued research, instruction and lectures into the spirit. Among the significant developments in the early 1960s were the inauguration of the Saint Hill Special Briefing Course lectures, the delineation of the Scientology Bridge to Total Freedom[16] and the gradual increments of that Bridge to increasingly higher levels of spiritual gain. To accommodate his research into Scientology's highest levels of spiritual attainment, Mr. Hubbard resigned as Executive Director of the worldwide network of Scientology churches, and moved to sea in 1967 to focus on his research in the distraction-free environment. While on board the 3,200-ton *Apollo*, Mr. Hubbard streamlined the lower levels of Scientology and continued his research toward the attainment of higher spiritual levels. He also began to search out solutions to society's more salient problems. . . .

Returning to the United States in 1975, Mr. Hubbard devoted his energies to the founding

---

[15] *Thetan:* the immortal spiritual being which is the essence of the individual human.

[16] *Bridge to Total Freedom:* in general, the way of health and salvation in Scientology; specifically, it denotes the steps of auditing that are completed in order to become fully healthy, an "Operating Thetan."

of the Church of Scientology's Flag Land Base in Clearwater, Florida. To fulfill a pressing need for instructional films on the disciplines of Scientology, he then moved to Southern California, where he wrote and produced numerous such films for the religion. The 1980s culminated in Mr. Hubbard's completion of his research into man's ultimate spiritual potentials. After finalizing that research, and, in fact, all the Scientology Scripture he had spent most of his life developing, Mr. Hubbard departed this life on January 24, 1986.

The Legacy: Today, the Scripture of Scientology comprises tens of millions of words in books and lectures by L. Ron Hubbard. In all, there are more than 120 million copies of L. Ron Hubbard books in circulation. And Mr.

Hubbard's legacy extends beyond Scientology per se. His educational discoveries have been used to help millions of children better read, write and comprehend. Hundreds of thousands of men and women have ended their substance abuse or prevented themselves from falling into the trap of abuse through his discoveries in drug rehabilitation. And literally more than 50 million have been reached through his non-religious moral code. But for Mr. Hubbard, what was important was not acclaim or recognition, but that he achieved his intended aim of helping man "become a better being" by founding the religion of Scientology. [Pursuant to legal agreement to reprint this excerpt, I reiterate that it is attributed solely to the Church of Scientology International.]

The Creed of the Church of Scientology*

The Creed of the Church of Scientology was written shortly after the Church was formed in Los Angeles on February 18, 1954. Its second and fourth sections provide a very brief overview of the basic beliefs of the church, and the longer first and third sections indicate how important matters of civil rights and church-state relations are to Scientologists. Its author is L. Ron Hubbard.[17]

We of the Church believe:

That all men of whatever race, color or creed were created with equal rights;

That all men have inalienable rights to their own religious practices and their performance;

That all men have inalienable rights to their own lives;

That all men have inalienable rights to their sanity;

That all men have inalienable rights to their own defense;

That all men have inalienable right to conceive, choose, assist or support their own organizations, churches or governments;

That all men have inalienable rights to think freely, to talk freely, to write freely their own opinions and to counter or utter or write upon the opinions of others;

That all men have inalienable rights to the creation of their own kind;

That the souls of men have the rights of men;

That the study of the mind and the healing of mentally caused ills should not be alienated from religion or condoned in nonreligious fields.

And that no agency less than God has the power to suspend or set aside these rights, overtly or covertly.

And we of the church believe:

That man is basically good;

That he is seeking to survive;

*From *Scientology: Theology and Practice of a Contemporary Religion*, Introduction pp. 87–93

[17]Copyright © 1954 by L. Ron Hubbard, from *Scientology: The Theology and Practice of a Contemporary Religion*, copyright 1998 by the Church of Scientology International, published in 1998 by Bridge Publications, Inc. All rights reserved, reprinted by permission.

That his survival depends upon himself and upon his fellows and his attainment of brotherhood with the universe.

And we of the Church believe that the laws of God forbid man:

To destroy his own kind;

To destroy the sanity of another;

To destroy or enslave another's soul;

To destroy or reduce the survival of one's companions or one's groups.

And we of the Church believe that the spirit can be saved and that the spirit alone may save or heal the body. [Pursuant to legal agreement to reprint this excerpt, I reiterate that the author of this Creed is L. Ron Hubbard.]

The Scientologist View of Human Nature*

This psychological essay outlines the Scientologist view of individual human nature. Great emphasis is put on the spirit, the separate, guiding "thetan." Next is the mind, which is divided into the active, reactive, and somatic minds. Finally comes the physical body. The author of this essay is L. Ron Hubbard.[18]

The individual man is divisible into three parts: The first of these is the spirit, called in Scientology the *Thetan*. The second of these parts is the *Mind*. The third of these parts is the *Body*.

Probably the greatest discovery of Scientology and its most forceful contribution to the knowledge of mankind has been the isolation, description and handling of the human spirit, accomplished in July 1952, in Phoenix, Arizona. I established along scientific rather than religious or humanitarian lines that that thing which is the person, the personality, is separable from the body and the mind at will and without causing bodily death or mental derangement.

In ages past there has been considerable controversy concerning the human spirit or soul, and various attempts to control man have been effective in view of his almost complete ignorance of his own identity. Latterly spiritualists isolated from the person what they called the astral body, and with this they were able to work for various purposes of their own. In Scientology, the spirit itself was separated from what the spiritualists call the astral body and there should be no confusion between these two things. As you know that you are where you are at this moment, so you would know if you, a spirit, were detached from your mind and body. Man had not discovered this before because, lacking the technologies of Scientology, he had very little reality upon his detachment from his mind and body; therefore, he conceived himself to be at least in part a mind and a body. The entire cult of communism is based upon the fact that one lives only one life, that there is no hereafter and that the individual has no religious significance. Man at large has been close to this state for at least a century. The state is of a very low order, excluding as it does all self-recognition.

The Spirit: The thetan is described in Scientology as having no mass, no wavelength, no energy and no time or location in space except by consideration or postulate. The spirit, then, is not a *thing*. It is the *creator* of things.

The usual residence of the thetan is in the skull or near the body. A thetan can be in one of four conditions. The first would be entirely separate from a body or bodies, or even from this universe. The second would be near a body and knowingly controlling the body. The third would be in the body (the skull) and the fourth

---

*L. Ron Hubbard, *Scientology: The Fundamentals of Thought*, 7, pp. 77–91

[18]Copyright © 1988, 1990, 1997 by L. Ron Hubbard Library from *Scientology: The Fundamentals of Thought*, published in 1997 by Bridge Publications, Inc. All rights reserved, reprinted by permission.

would be an inverted body and cannot approach it. There are degrees of each one of these four states. The most optimum of these conditions, from the standpoint of man, is the second.

The thetan is subject to deterioration. This is at first difficult to understand since the entirety of his activity consists of considering or postulating. He uses, through his postulates, various methods of controlling a body. That he does deteriorate is manifest, but that he can at any moment return to an entirety of his ability is also factual. In that he associates beingness with mass and action, he does not consider himself as having an individual identity or name unless he is connected with one or more of the games of life.

The processes of Scientology can establish this for the individual with greater or lesser rapidity, and one of the many goals of processing in Scientology is to "exteriorize" the individual and place him in the second condition above, since it has been discovered that he is happier and more capable when so situated.

The Mind: The *mind* is a communication and control system between the thetan and his environment. The mind is a network of communications and pictures, energies and masses, which are brought into being by the activities of the thetan versus the physical universe or other thetans. A thetan establishes various systems of control so that he can continue to operate a body and through the body operate things in the physical universe, as well as other bodies. The most obvious portion of the mind is recognizable by anyone not in serious condition. This is the "mental image picture." In Scientology we call this mental image picture a *facsimile* when it is a "photography" of the physical universe sometime in the past. We call this mental image picture a *mock-up* when it is created by the thetan or for the thetan and does not consist of a photography of the physical universe. We call a mental image picture a *hallucination* or, more properly, an *automaticity* when it is created by another and seen by self.

Various phenomena connect themselves with this entity called the mind. Some people closing their eyes see only blackness, some people see pictures. Some people see pictures made by body reactions. Some people see only black screens. Others see golden lines. Others see spaces, but the keynote of the entirety of the system called the mind is postulate and perception. Easily ten thousand new, separate mental phenomena, not hitherto seen by earlier observers, have been classified in Scientology and Dianetics.

The thetan receives, by the communication system called the mind, various impressions, including direct views of the physical universe. In addition to this he receives impressions from past activities and, most important, he himself, being close to a total knowingness, conceives things about the past and future which are independent of immediately present stimuli. The mind is not in its entirety a stimulus-response mechanism as old Marxist psychology, as once taught in universities, would have one believe. The mind has three main divisions. The first of these could be called the *analytical mind*, the second the *reactive mind* and the third the *somatic mind*.

The *analytical mind* combines perceptions of the immediate environment, of the past (via pictures) and estimation of the future into conclusions which are based upon the realities of the situation. The analytical mind combines the potential knowingness of the thetan with the conditions of his surroundings and brings him to independent conclusions. This mind could be said to consist of visual pictures either of the past or of the physical universe, monitored by, and presided over by, the knowingness of a thetan. The keynote of the analytical mind is awareness. One knows what one is concluding and knows what he is doing.

The *reactive mind* is a stimulus-response mechanism, ruggedly built, and operable in trying circumstances. The reactive mind never stops operating. Pictures, of a very low order, are taken by this mind of the environment even in some states of unconsciousness. The reactive mind acts below the level of consciousness. It is the literal, stimulus-response mind. Given a certain stimulus it gives a certain response. The entire subject of Dianetics concerned itself mainly with this one mind.

While it is an order of thinkingness, the ability of the reactive mind to conclude rationally is so poor that we find in the reactive mind those various aberrated impulses which are gazed upon as oddities of personality, eccentricities, neuroses and psychoses. It is this mind which stores up all the bad things that have happened to one and throws them back to him again in moments of emergency or danger so as to dictate his actions along lines which have been considered "safe" before. As there is little thinkingness involved in this, the courses of action dictated by the reactive mind are often not safe, but highly dangerous. . . .

The third portion of the mind is the *somatic mind*. This is an even heavier type of mind than the reactive mind since it contains no thinkingness and contains only actingness. The impulses placed against the body by the thetan through various mental machinery arrive at the voluntary, involuntary and glandular levels. These have set methods of analysis for any given situation and so respond directly to commands given. . . .

In that the thetan is seldom aware of the reactive mind, it is possible, then, for the reactive mind, with its stimulus-response content, to impinge itself directly, and without further recourse or advice, upon the neuron, muscles and glandular system of the body. In that the reactive mind can hold a fixed command in place, causing a derangement in the somatic mind, it is possible, then, for illness to exist, for bizarre pains to be felt, for actural physical twists, and aberration to occur, without any conscious knowledge on the part of the thetan. This we call physical illness caused by the mind. In brief, such illness is caused by perception received in the reactive mind during moments of pain and unconsciousness.

Whether the facsimile in the mind is received while the thetan is awake or unconscious, the resulting mass of the energy picture is energy just as you see energy in an electric light bulb or from the flames of a fire. At one time it was considered that mental energy was different from physical energy. In Scientology it has been discovered that mental energy is simply a finer, higher level physical energy. The test of this is conclusive in that a thetan "mocking up" mental image pictures and thrusting them into the body can increase the body mass and, by casting them away again, can decrease the body mass. This test has actually been made and an increase of as much as thirty pounds, actually measured on scales, has been added to, and subtracted from, a body by creating "mental energy." Energy is energy. It has different wavelengths and different characteristics. The mental image pictures are capable of reacting upon the physical environment, and the physical environment is capable of reacting upon mental image picture. Thus the mind actually consists of spaces, energies and masses of the same order as the physical universe, if lighter and different in size and wavelength. For a much more comprehensive picture of the mind one should read *The Dynamics of Life* and *Dianetics: The Modern Science of Mental Health*. These were written before the discoveries of the upper levels of beingness were made and are a very complete picture of the mind itself, its structures and what can be done to it and with it.

The Body: The third part of man is the physical body. This can best be studied in such books as *Gray's Anatomy* and other anatomical texts. This is the province of the medical doctor and, usually, the old-time psychiatrist or psychologist, who were involved, in the main, in body worship. The body is a purely structural study, and the actions and reactions among its various structures are complex and intensely interesting.

When Scientology established biophysics, it did so because of the various discoveries which had accumulated concerning the mental energy in its reaction against physical energy, and the activities which took place in the body because of these interactions. Biophysics only became feasible when it was discovered in Scientology that a fixed electrical field existed surrounding a body entirely independent of, but influenceable by, the human mind. The body exists in its own space. That space is created by anchor points. The complexity of these anchor points can cause an independent series of electronic flows which can occasion much discomfort to the individual. The balance structure of the body and even its joint action and physical characteristics can be changed by changing this electrical field which exists at a distance from, or within the body.

The electrical field is paramount and monitors the actual physical structure of the body. Thus the body is not only influenced by the three minds, it is influenced as well by its own electrical field. An expert Scientologist can discover for the average person this field, and can bring about its adjustment, although this is very far from the primary purpose of the Scientologist. The use of electrical shocks upon a body for any purpose is therefore very dangerous and is not condoned by sensible men. . . .

A knowledge of the mental and physical structure of the body would be necessary in order to treat the body, and this knowledge has not existed prior to Scientology. The medical doctor achieved many results by working purely with structure and biochemical products, and in the field of emergency surgery and obstetrics and orthopedics, he is indispensable in the society. Medicine, however, did not even contain a definition for *mind* and is not expected to invade the field, which belongs properly to Scientology.

These three parts of man—the thetan, the mind and the body—are each one different studies, but they influence each other markedly and continually. Of the three, the senior entity is the thetan, for without the thetan there would be no mind or animation in the body, while without a body or a mind there is still animation and life in the thetan. The thetan *is* the person. You are *you, in* a body. [Pursuant to legal agreement to reprint this excerpt, I reiterate here that the sole author of this excerpt is L. Ron Hubbard.]

The Axioms of Scientology*

The following excerpt from a much-reproduced essay, originally in Dianetics, *indicates some of the theoretical bases of Scientology. "Axioms" are here, as generally in academic study, self-consistent terms and ideas that form the basis of a system. Reading the axioms is more meaningful when one notes that they proceed in step fashion. The author of this excerpt is L. Ron Hubbard.*[19]

Scientology as a science is composed of many axioms. There are some fifty-eight of these axioms in addition to the two hundred more axioms of Dianetics which preceded the Scientology axioms.

Axiom 1. Life is basically a static. (Definition: a life static has no mass, no motion, no wavelength, no location in space or in time. It has the ability to postulate and to perceive. Definition: In Scientology, the word "postulate" means to cause a thinkingness or consideration. It is a specially applied word and is defined as causative thinkingness.)

Axiom 2. The static is capable of considerations, postulates and opinions.

Axiom 3. Space, energy, objects, form and time are the result of considerations made and/or agreed upon by the static, and are

---

*L. Ron Hubbard, *Scientology: The Fundamentals of Thought*, 8, pp. 101–103
[19]Copyright © 1988, 1990, 1997 by L. Ron Hubbard Library from *Scientology: The Fundamentals of Thought*, published in 1997 by Bridge Publications, Inc. All rights reserved, reprinted by permission.

perceived solely because the static considers that it can perceive them.

Axiom 4. Space is viewpoint of dimension. (Space is caused by looking out from a point. The only actuality of space is the agreed-upon consideration that one perceives through something, and this we call space.)

Axiom 5. Energy consists of postulated particles in space. (One considers that energy exists and that he can perceive energy. One also considers that energy behaves according to certain agreed-upon laws. These assumptions or considerations are the totality of energy.)

Axiom 6. Objects consist of grouped particles.

Axiom 7. Time is basically a postulate that space and particles will persist. (The rate of their persistence is what we measure with clocks and the motion of heavenly bodies.)

Axiom 8. The apparency of time is the change of position of particles in space.

Axiom 9. Change is the primary manifestation of time.

Axiom 10. The highest purpose in the universe is the creation of an effect.

These first ten axioms of Scientology are the most fundamental "truths" (by which we mean commonly held considerations). Here we have thought and life and the physical universe in their relation, one to the other. Regardless of further considerations, ideas, assumptions and conditions, there lies beneath them these first ten truths.

It is as though one had entered into an honorable bargain with fellow beings to hold these things in common. Once this is done, or once such a "contact" or agreement exists, one has the fundamentals of a universe. Specialized considerations based on the above make one or another kind of universe.

The physical universe which we see around us and in which we live was created on these fundamentals without regard to who created it. Its creation was agreed upon. In order to perceive it, one must agree that it exists. [Pursuant to legal agreement to reprint this excerpt, I reiterate here that the sole author of this excerpt is L. Ron Hubbard.]

The Religious Practices of Scientology*

This reading describes the practices of auditing and training to become an auditor, the central practices on the Scientologist "Bridge to Total Freedom." It also relates the process of study in Scientology scripture and teaching. This excerpt is solely attributed to the Church of Scientology International.[20]

* Scientology: Theology and Practice of a Contemporary Religion, 3, pp. 31–41.
[20]Copyright © 1998 by the Church of Scientology International, from Scientology: The Theology and Practice of a Contemporary Religion, published in 1998 by Bridge Publications, Inc. All rights reserved, reprinted by permission.

The Scientology religion embodies a rich tradition of ceremonies, rites and services. Yet the religious practices of auditing and training are by far the most significant. They are the sine qua non of Scientology, for they light the path to higher states of spiritual awareness and ability and, eventually, to spiritual salvation. While Churches of Scientology hold congregational services to celebrate a religious holiday, perform rites of passage and acknowledge other significant dates and events, the essence of Scientology lies in the distinctive methods by which its principles can be applied to the betterment of individual lives.

Auditing: The central religious practice of Scientology is auditing (from Latin audire, "to listen"), which is a precise form of spiritual counseling between a Scientology minister and a parishioner.

It is readily apparent that, in many respects, man's efforts fall short of the ideal of infinite spiritual survival. He has lost sight of the Supreme Being, lost awareness of his own spiritual nature and, in most cases, forgotten that life requires successful participation in all eight dynamics. Rather than playing his part in the conquest of the physical universe, he suffers failures, to a greater or lesser degree, resulting in pain, unconsciousness, and unwillingness to face the challenge of existence.

In the course of an average life as man, the thetan is certain to encounter many experiences that can reduce his level of spiritual awareness. Over the course of many lifetimes, he may entirely lose sight of his true nature, and with that fall from spirituality, the level and quality of his participation in all eight dynamics is diminished.

Auditing reverses this decline. It enables the being to cast off the spiritual chains that grow heavier from lifetime to lifetime—the accumulation of his pains and misfortunes, confusion and his own moral transgressions. Just as these experiences bring about his fall from spiritual awareness, trapping and enmeshing him in the material universe, auditing provides the route to spiritual salvation by restoring the thetan's full awareness of his essential identity and abilities.

The practice of auditing was developed from the understanding of the fundamental laws of life contained in the Scientology Axioms. It is based on the principle that only the truth can set one free, and it enables the person to come to terms with the truth of his own existence—past, present and future. Through auditing, the person regains an understanding of and responsibility for his relationship to all of life and the Supreme Being. With full spiritual awareness and responsibility restored comes complete spiritual freedom—Scientology's spiritual salvation.

During auditing, a person can have many realizations about life. By honestly looking at the factors which have inhibited his spiritual growth, he is able to overcome them and experience a true spiritual resurgence. When auditing is understood as a spiritual practice that incorporates the theta-MEST[21] theory and the concept of the eight dynamics, it is apparent that increased spiritual awareness brings about great responsibility and participation as regards one's family, one's group and all the other dynamics, including the Supreme Being.

In auditing, the minister, or auditor ("one who listens") asks the parishioner a series of specific questions in the area of spiritual travel being addressed in that particular session. Once the auditor locates the area of spiritual trauma, he will ask further specific questions or give directions needed to help the parishioner address and come to grips with that incident, experience or area of life. The minister does not offer any "advice" to the parishioner. One of the essential principles of Scientology is that the individual can advance spiritually only if he is allowed to find his own answers to life's problems. This is accomplished by helping one to examine his own existence and improve his ability to face what he is and where he is—peeling away the layers of experience that have weighed so heavily upon him. [I]n the spiritual realm, auditing leads to personal revelation by posing precise questions based on the Scientology cosmology. In seeking for his answer, the parishioner discovers intrinsic truths about life and the underlying factors of existence which transcend the physical universe.

Yet there is another factor in auditing which is even more important: the role of communication itself. Communication is indeed necessary to all aspects of life; but the understanding of communication in Scientology goes far beyond any ordinary concept of the commonplace exchange of ideas in social intercourse. One of the Axioms of Scientology, Axiom 28, present the fundamental principle of commu-

---

21 *MEST:* an acronymn for Matter, Energy, Space and Time, the physical universe.

nication, and a substantial portion of Scientology Scripture is devoted to its application in auditing. In fact, auditing and spiritual salvation through Scientology practices only become possible through the proper application of communication as defined in Axiom 28. Through communication, the auditor directs the parishioner's attention to confront aspects of his existence to find the answers to auditing questions, erase the harmful mental and spiritual energy in which the thetan is enmeshed, and thus experience relief from spiritual travail.

This precise process of communication, as practiced in auditing, is essential for one to come to a complete understanding of life. . . . [U]nderstanding exists to the degree that one can have affinity for something, can perceive or experience its reality, and can communicate with it or about it. The precision of communication in auditing therefore plays a direct role in raising a person's understanding and spiritual state.

The Electropsychometer—An Aid to Auditing: Most auditors use a special electropsychometer—called an "E-meter"—to assist them in helping parishioners address experiences which lie at the root of spiritual travail. . . .

The religious instrument is vital because the mental image pictures that harbor these experiences also hold very minute amounts of electrical energy that can be detected with the E-meter. As this charge varies or dissipates, the auditor knows the parishioner has successfully addressed—and resolved—the source of that aspect of his spiritual entrapment. Thus, while the E-meter by itself does nothing, it is an invaluable guide for the auditor.

Higher States of Existence: Auditing ranges from very simple and basic to more searching and intensive religious experiences as one participates in further and higher level services. Auditing enables an individual to achieve the spiritual state of Clear. In this state the individual is no longer trapped by the prior traumas recorded on his time track and is capable of living a rational, more spiritual existence. Beyond Clear, one attains higher states of awareness called Operating Thetan. In this spiritual state it is possible for the thetan to possess complete spiritual ability, freedom, independence and serenity, to be freed from the endless cycle of birth and death, and to have full awareness and ability independent of the body.

The Advanced Levels of auditing employ a special auditing procedure which the individual conducts alone; the person acts as his own auditor, alternately posing precise questions and then seeking their answers. These levels deal with the highest truths of existence. The ability to conduct "solo" auditing presupposes a thorough and intimate knowledge of all fundamental Axioms and principles of Scientology. The Advanced Levels therefore appear at the very top of the Bridge to Total Freedom and are open to those who have completed the lower training and auditing levels necessary for full understanding of these advanced procedures. These individuals are not only spiritually prepared but are required to meet high ethical standards.

Scientology Religious Training: As described above, the Bridge to Total Freedom is a spiritual path consisting of the two complementary religious practices of auditing and training. Participation in both is essential for the attainment of a complete understanding of all life—all eight dynamics. While auditing enables the individual to inspect and overcome spiritual encumbrances and rise through a series of ascending levels of spiritual awareness, training consists of the intensive study of the tenets of the religion.

Study of the Axioms and fundamental truths contained in Scientology Scripture leads to a complete understanding of man's spiritual nature . . . and the precise means by which a thetan becomes entrapped in the physical universe. There is no part of life that Scientology training fails to address—from the seemingly mundane to the highest truths of existence. Studying these truths invariably answers many questions the individual has had about himself, his fellows, and the universe in which he finds himself. Training is thus a path of personal revelation and an indispensable part of an individual's personal progress up the Bridge.

But training is also the route by which Scientology ministers acquire the knowledge and skill to conduct auditing. The Scripture studied in training is organized into courses that align with the specific levels of spiritual awareness through which auditing progresses. As the minister completes each level in training, he acquires the knowledge and exact skills required to conduct auditing up to that level. And as Scientologists become more spiritually aware, they translate this awareness into direct action to help others. Training enables the Scientologist to do that in the most valuable way possible—auditing others to help them achieve their own total spiritual freedom.

Training materials contain all of Mr. Hubbard's books and other written materials, tape-recorded lectures and technical training films that are necessary to impact a complete understanding of Scientology theory and technique. Mr. Hubbard stressed that the disciplines of Scientology are just as important as its Scripture, and thus training places great emphasis on mastery of the skills of auditing.

Scientology training allows each individual to progress at his own rate. Each course is organized around the checksheet—a list laying out the books and scriptures to be studied, the practical exercises to be completed, and the sequence in which these steps are to be done. There are no teachers in the Scientology course room. Instead, students make their own progress through their checksheets, assisted by a Course Supervisor. The Supervisor does not lecture, or give his own rendition of Scripture. However unintentional, such interpretations would inevitably include alterations from the original. Instead, the Supervisor assists the student to apply the study principles developed by L. Ron Hubbard, so that he overcomes any misunderstanding and grasps the meaning directly from the Scripture. [Pursuant to legal agreement to reprint this excerpt, I reiterate that it is solely attributed to the Church of Scientology International.]

GLOSSARY

Book of Mormon the leading new writing in the Church of Jesus Christ of Latter-day Saints, relating the story of the coming of ancient Israelites to the Americas and the creation of golden plates of sacred writings.

Dianetics L. Ron Hubbard's system of psychology and psychotherapy, the basis for Scientology thought and practice; as a book, *Dianetics* is the first work in the Scientology scripture.

Divine Principle the main scripture of the Unification Church, written by Sun Myung Moon.

Doctrine and Covenants the second new canonical writing of the Church of Jesus Christ of Latter-day Saints.

Holy Writings the scriptures of Baha'i, written by the Bab, Baha'u'llah, Abdu'l-Baha, and Shogi Effendi.

new religious movement one of the religious groups that arose since the nineteenth century with sufficient size, longevity, and cultural impact to become important for the academic study of religion.

Pearl of Great Price the third new canonical writing of the Church of Jesus Christ of Latter-day Saints, a selection of the translations and story of Joseph Smith.

Science and Health with Key to the Scriptures the new scripture of the Christian Science Church; "Science and Health" explains the principles of healing, and "Key to the Scriptures" explains several biblical passages in terms of Christian Science.

thetan Scientologist term for the spiritual component of humans.

QUESTIONS FOR STUDY AND DISCUSSION

1. How adequate is the term *new religious movement,* in your view? What are its strengths and weaknesses?

2. What are the main similarities and differences between Baha'i scriptures and the *Quran?* In what sense are the Baha'i *Holy Writings* a successor to the *Quran?*

3. Critique this statement: "The *Book of Mormon* is, among all world scriptures, most American."

4. Although it was not a part of the original title of the *Book of Mormon,* the Church of Jesus Christ of Latter-day Saints now has given it an unofficial subtitle: "Another Testament of Jesus Christ." Give your reflections on the church's reason for doing so and what this subtitle may mean in relation to the New Testament.

5. Discuss the origin and growth of the Christian Science scripture from "Science and Health" to its supplement by "Key to the Scriptures" and the testimonial section "Fruitage."

6. Discuss the main teachings of the *Divine Principle.* How is it based on, and how does it depart from, the teachings of mainstream Christianity? Would you say that Unificationism is a Christian church? Why?

7. Explain in your own words Scientology's view of "sin" and "salvation," based on your knowledge of the writings of L. Ron Hubbard.

8. From your knowledge of science and Scientology, evaluate the statement of L. Ron Hubbard that Scientology is "a wholly scientific approach to spiritual questions."

SUGGESTIONS FOR FURTHER READING

Scholarship on scripture in new religious movements is slim. Aside from scholarship on the *Book of Mormon,* academic inquiry into the nature and use of other scriptures has hardly begun. Therefore, the student should concentrate on the scriptures themselves. The book publications of these scriptures are listed in the footnotes in this chapter, and access to most of these scriptures is available on the World Wide Web by way of the website accompanying the present book, which is located at Wadsworth's religion site: http://religion.wadsworth.com.

INFOTRAC COLLEGE EDITION

You can locate InfoTrac College Edition articles about this chapter by accessing the InfoTrac College Edition website (http://www.infotrac.collegeedition.com/wadsworth/). Using subject guide, enter the search terms relevant to this chapter, and then read abstracts for relevant articles.

Index

(Note: boldface entries indicate pages where subjects are defined in a glossary section.)